LEGEND AND LEGACY

LEGEND AND LEGACY

The Story of Boeing and Its People

Robert J. Serling

St. Martin's Press
New York

Editor: Jared Kieling
Copyedited by Barbara Price and Leslie Sharpe
Design by Robert Bull Design

Library of Congress Cataloging-in-Publication Data
Serling, Robert J.
    Legend and legacy : the story of Boeing and its people / Robert J.
Serling.
        p.   cm.
    ISBN 0-312-05890-X
    1. Boeing Company—History.   2. Aircraft industry—United States—
History.   3. Conglomerate corporations—United States—History.
I. Title.
HD9711.U63B637   1991
338.7′629133′0973—dc20   90-27408
                                                            CIP

First Edition

10   9   8   7   6   5   4   3   2   1

This book is dedicated to the men and women of Boeing past, present, and future, and with special gratitude to:

Don Smith for his support, counsel, and patience.

Sandee Baker, who made a difficult task not only easier but fun.

Harold Carr, for editorial assistance that was not only helpful but scrupulously fair.

And the late Gordy Williams, who many years ago introduced me to the Boeing tradition of Pride.

CONTENTS

ACKNOWLEDGMENTS

A journey back in time, which is all history is, can never be a solo flight. Some very special people accompanied me on my trip through Boeing's first 75 years and deserve special recognition for their cooperation, guidance and, above all, the friendships that were formed. So I would like to express my deep gratitude to the following:

The staff of the Boeing Company's 75th Anniversary Committee—Don Smith, Sandee Baker, Ric England, Bob Scarber, Bob Moffatt, and last but not least, Marcie Burkhart, who helped me in a hundred ways.

Marilyn Phipps and the archives staff, especially historian Paul Spitzer; without their unfailingly courteous assistance, it wouldn't have been possible.

Lucy Lark of facilities, who made my temporary little office at corporate headquarters a home away from home.

Kim Brown; for her invaluable aid in transcribing a number of interviews.

Dr. Manuel Cooper, for many favors.

Deane Cruze, for whom I would have liked to work.

Ryan DeMares, who did a lot of incisive interviewing on her own and helped me in several of my interviews.

Dave Olson, my first contact at Boeing when this project was just a dream, who helped me launch it.

Susan Calbeck, Patrick Palmer, and Pat O'Donnell of Boeing public relations in Wichita; Bob Torgerson and JoAnne Carroll in Philadelphia—they all made me realize Boeing is not just Seattle.

Donna Ciero of Boeing's graphics, for help with the jacket.

Mary Kennedy, whose smile helped a lot of interview subjects relax before the ordeal.

Tim Mooney of Air New Zealand, who helped me ascertain the fate of Boeing's first two airplanes.

Also, thanks to Patrick Pranica, Fred Kelley, Leo Hall, Maurin Faure,

Lynn Hess, John Friars, Joyce Price, Starr Tavenner, Jay Cutting, Madelyne Bush, Fred Cerf, Ruth Dumar, Karen Armstrong, Margie Ehmke, Vaughn Blumenthal, Jim Komoll, Norm Smith, Pat Childs, Barbara Chappell, Doris Seeley, JoAnne Seeley, Kathy Martinson, Debbie Rhoton, and Pippa Pratt-Brown. You all aided me in little ways and big ways you didn't even realize.

To the following interviewees, I offer not only my gratitude but my hope that the final product justifies the time they so graciously gave me. They are listed alphabetically:

David Abernathy, Richard Albrecht, Lionel Alford, Mef Allen, Jim Axtell.

Bob Bateman, Douglas Beighle, Marge Blair, Jim Blue, John Borger, Tex Boullioun, Wally Buckley, Marcella Burkhart.

Art Carbary, Harold Carr, Fred Carroll, JoAnne Carroll, Art Carter, Vern Castle, Q. L. Clancy, Carl Cleveland, Forrest Coffey, Ted Collins, Phil Condit, Bill Cook, Dr. Manuel Cooper, Bob Craig, Deane Cruze, E. J. Cutting.

Mary Dawn, John DePolo, Jack Diamond, Bob Dickson, Carl Dillon, Bob Dryden.

Richard England.

Dick Floyd, Carl Foncanno.

Dale Garrison, Andre Gay, Bruce Gissing, Harry Goldie, Abe Goo.

Bob Hager, William T. Hamilton, Hal Haynes, Al Heitman, Art Hitsman, Ken Holtby, General Bob "Dutch" Huyser (ret.).

Gil Jay, Tex Johnston, Bill Jury, Gary Jusela.

George Kau, Jerry King, Norm Kingsmore, Dave Knowlen, Denis Kuhnhausen.

Gene Laughlin, Russ Light, Stan Little, Art Lowell, Sam Lowry, Ken Luplow.

Lisa Magee, Al Mansi, Edith Martin, George Martin, Roy Maus, Larry McKean, Lowell Mickelwait, Byron Miller, C. O. Miller, Mark Miller, Boris Mishel, Jim Morrison, Dick Muffett, Dan Murray.

Floyd Nestegard, George Nible.

Ernie Ochel, Lynn Olason, Dave Olson.

Mike Pavone, Maynard Pennell, Bob Perdue, Jack Pierce, Dan Pinick, Jack Potter, David Provan.

Ed Renouard, Tom Riedinger, Rusty Roetman, Del Rowan.

Don Sachs, George Schairer, Sterling Sessions, Donna Seybert, Frank Shrontz, Clyde Skeen, Don Smith, Otis Smith, L. C. Smyth, Mal Stamper, Jack Steiner, Howard Stuverude, Joe Sutter, John Swihart.

Dick Taylor, Bob Tharrington, Dean Thornton, Harley Thorson, Jerry Tobias, Sof Torget, Guy Townsend, Bob Twiss.

Frank Verginia.

Lew Wallick, Frank Waterworth, Bert Welliver, George Weyerhaeuser, Ben Wheat, Clancy Wilde, T Wilson, Bob Withington, Ron Woodard, Brien Wygle, Bob Wylie.

Fred Zappert.

Marilyn Phipps provided me with the transcripts of many previously recorded interviews, including some conducted so recently that a further interview was not necessary. I found Eve Dumovich's manuscript on the history of Boeing's Washington office of great value.

My thanks to the many Boeing employees who responded to a request in *Boeing News* for anecdotal material. Space limitations prevented my using all the stories they submitted, but I would like to acknowledge their contributions by listing their names:

Robert Bassett, Richard Beall, Roland Belrose, Mitchell Berry, Al Bremer, Russell "R.D." Brown, Isla Carstensen, Dave Carswell, Don Chalmers, Harvey Cox, Paul Fantin, Eddie Fogg, Richard Friend, Art Gerald, Ken Gieshers, Lauri Hillberg, Chet Hodgkins, David Holliday, Marvin Jahnke, Linn Johnson, Warren Joslyn, Lou Kiersky, Louise Hannah Kohr, Duane Landis, Won-Fan Lin, Howard Martin, Michael McClain, Albert McDonald, Jean McGrew, Karl Merz, W. Raymond Motz, Robert Nielsen, Bob Perry, Paul Phipps, Calvin Reuther, Fred Robbins, Paul Roberts, Donald Ross, Donald Schelp, Stuart Schufrieder, Robert A. Smith, R. E. Stevenson, Robert Swiler, Richard Vranjes, Wallace Weber, Maynard Wege, George West, H. C. Woodington, and Jack (last name indecipherable).

For every author there's an editor and I have the best in Jared Kieling. My appreciation to him and also his editorial assistant, Ensley Eikenburg. And a loud ditto to my agent and old friend, Aaron Priest.

I've saved the most inadequate but heartfelt thanks for my wife, Priscilla. She manned the Mac Plus computer and the Hewlett-Packard printer, soothed her husband's fragile ego, contributed her usual sage advice, and proved once more she is grossly underpaid if deeply loved.

—Robert J. Serling
Tucson, Arizona, February 1992

PROLOGUE

Boeing...

The very word, cold in print but rich in association, invokes images as vivid as man's memories and imagination can create.

Images of mighty jetliners, leaving white contrails frozen against the blue sky as they streak across continents and oceans, shrinking a world that now measures distance in hours, not miles.

Images of the great bombers defending the nation.

Images of an American corporation whose name has become synonymous with technical excellence and integrity.

Boeing is the world's most successful aerospace company. In 1990 alone, its jets carried more people than live in the earth's 100 largest cities—675 million, the equivalent of 12 percent of the world's population.

Excluding the former Soviet Union, 60 percent of the jets operated by the world's airlines are Boeing-built, and Boeing commands more than half the entire market for new jets on order, with a backlog of $97.9 *billion* by the end of 1991.

It is a corporate Horatio Alger. Seventy-five years ago, it ended its first six months of existence with $3,287.91 in the bank and unpaid bills and assessments totaling $7,408.64. The value of its buildings, real estate, and machinery/tools amounted to less than $46,000. Today Boeing's land, buildings, machinery, and equipment are valued at more than $9 billion. Its 1916 monthly employee payroll was slightly under $1,400. Boeing's 1990 payroll, including benefits, was more than $6.5 billion.

The first airplane Boeing built, three-quarters of a century ago, weighed 2,800 pounds, with a 52-foot wingspan and a length of 31.2 feet. It carried two people, cruised at 67 mph, and had a top speed of 75 mph with a maximum range of 320 miles—and its price was slightly over $10,000.

The latest version of the 747, the 747-400 series, has a gross weight of 870,000 pounds, a wingspan of 213 feet, an 8,000-mile range, and its 231-foot fuselage carries more than 400 passengers who fly at more than 500 mph. Price: $120 million.

Yet no statistics, however impressive and reflective of progress they may be, can tell the full and real story of a unique company like Boeing. It also is a company of paradoxes, of contradictions and inconsistencies that could have sunk an organization with a lesser sense of purpose.

It stands tall at the top of the aerospace world, yet through most of its 75 years it has skated on precariously thin financial ice; at one point it went through a dark 17 months without selling a single commercial jet to a U.S. carrier and came close to bankruptcy.

It has achieved, in addition to its reputation for building superior products, a certain reputation for arrogance—an attitude that seems to say, "We're Boeing, we know how to do it, so if you want to play ball with us you'll do it our way." Yet it has become in recent years one of the most introspective companies in the United States, with a willingness to admit mistakes, to learn from others (Japan in particular), and never to take its present exalted status for granted.

It is a dominant force among the handful of American firms that have kept the trade deficit from being far worse than it already is; a company whose reputation for product support has been imitated not only by its competitors, but by such prestigious organizations as Mercedes-Benz. Yet the names of top Boeing executives were conspicuously missing from a recent *Business Week* survey of the 20 highest paid CEOs, a list of the 10 highest paid non-CEO officers, and the 10 largest "golden parachute" recipients.

Boeing is both conservative and daring. On four occasions it gambled virtually its whole future on the success or failure of a single airplane. Yet at other times it has waited for competitors to test the waters of new markets with new airplanes, confident that the Boeing name could overcome any lead.

It has achieved the greatest sales of commercial jetliners in history, more than 6,000 in the past 34 years. But before the jet age began, Boeing's record in that field was a collection of failures.

It is supposed to be a company historically dominated by graduate engineering types. Yet two of its three most recent chief executives were lawyers by training. And of the 66 current or retired vice presidents interviewed for this book, 20 started with Boeing as hourly workers on the assembly line or in tooling, with nothing but high school educations.

Boeing may dominate the jetliner market, but in less affluent times it has produced such products as furniture, boats, railcars, mobile asphalt plants, windmills, low-income houses, experimental potatoes, simulated high-speed railroad tracks, and milk. Yes, milk; at one time

Boeing owned a herd of cows. All these were desperate attempts at diversification when airplanes were almost impossible to sell, and one of Boeing's most fascinating inconsistencies is that this much-envied and frequently emulated company flopped almost every time it tried to diversify.

In some ways, Boeing is curiously introverted. In 1991 alone, the company and its employees contributed more than $50 million to various community educational, health, human services, and cultural organizations, but with almost no fanfare and very little publicity. This is in keeping with a traditional "low-profile" policy that has been in place since the company's founding.

It was and remains a company of diverse personalities and Characters—and that last word is capitalized deliberately.

But then, the Boeing story is, above all else, the story of its people.

For *Boeing is people*. It always has been and will be forever. It is not just an inanimate corporate entity, but the living, breathing sum of all human parts that went into it from the day it began.

The inconsistencies and contradictions that have marked Boeing's history inevitably add up to ironies. It is typical of the Boeing saga that its greatest irony was the departure of the man who gave it birth and its very name. He became fed up with the way politics had invaded aviation, and in 1934 walked away from the company he had founded in 1916.

ONE

THE EARLY YEARS

His FULL NAME WAS WILLIAM EDWARD BOEING, SON OF A German father who died when he was only eight, and a Viennese mother who raised him as the German father would have wanted—in a strict fashion.

This kind of parental background belied the kind of independent-minded man he was to become. He had wealth: his father had made a fortune in Minnesota timber and iron ore. Born in Detroit, Michigan, October 1, 1881, Boeing was sent away to private school in Switzerland, attended other private schools in the United States, and wound up at Yale studying engineering.

Little in this affluent educational environment seemed to rub off on him. From all accounts, Bill Boeing was something of a restless loner with no particular roots, either Midwest or East. He quit Yale after his junior year, a decision that may have been partially influenced by his mother's remarriage. Boeing didn't get along with his new stepfather and apparently wanted to get as far away from him as possible.

The Pacific Northwest was a natural choice, beckoning him with its vast timberlands. So in 1903—the same year the Wright brothers made aviation history at Kitty Hawk, North Carolina—Boeing settled in Hoquiam, Washington, and launched a profitable lumber business. He was only 22, a tall, bespectacled, professorial-looking youth with a dapper mustache—rather stern and forbidding in appearance but with friendly, softening eyes and a shy smile.

It was a chance meeting that put Bill Boeing into the aircraft business. At the University Club in Seattle one day, he was introduced to Conrad Westervelt, a young Navy lieutenant commander stationed at a local shipyard. Neither had ever been in an airplane, although both had become interested in flying—Boeing when he saw a Los Angeles air show, and Westervelt when he saw his first real airplane as a spectator at the 1910 air races at Belmont Park, New York.

Idle conversation brought out how much they had in common, starting with their interest in airplanes. The two bachelors shared a love of boating and bridge, and both had studied engineering. This casual relationship gelled into a friendship, and on July 4, 1915, each took his first airplane ride with a barnstorming pilot. Bitten by the aviation bug, they made several other flights with the same flyer in the same airplane. It was Boeing who finally mentioned what had been gnawing at him for a long time: he climbed out of the rickety Curtiss seaplane after one flight and told Westervelt he thought they could build a better one.

And that was how it all began.

It may have been better but it wasn't beautiful. The first Boeing aircraft was a handmade, clumsy seaplane copied from a Martin seaplane Boeing had purchased in 1915 before work began on his plane. He also had taken flying lessons in the Martin, and when Boeing Model 1 was completed—its original name was the *Bluebill*—it was Boeing himself who made the first flight off the waters of Seattle's Lake Union.

Few called it the *Bluebill*, however. It was more commonly known as the B&W, after the first initials of its creators' last names. Actually, it could well have been called the B, W, and M, for the seaplane was mostly the product of three men: Boeing the financier and test pilot, Westervelt the designer, and a young mechanic/pilot named Herb Munter, hired by Boeing to help build it.

Westervelt, however, didn't stay around long enough to enjoy either the fruits of his labor or a chance to share in Boeing's future. The Navy transferred him to the East Coast and his association with Boeing was over. The first of many ironies in Boeing's history was the fate of this dedicated Navy engineer who designed its first airplane; he was gone before Boeing demonstrated the B&W to the Navy, and long before the Navy turned out to be Boeing's first customer.

The product wasn't the B&W, though. The seaplane flunked its Navy trials, which didn't discourage Bill Boeing. He hired as the naval officer's replacement Chinese engineer Tsu Wong, a Massachusetts Institute of Technology graduate, who was given the job of improving on the design. Wong enjoyed one distinct advantage over the man he succeeded—he was salaried, at $80 a month, for Boeing had decided to get serious about building airplanes.

On July 15, 1916, the company's official birthday, Bill Boeing incorporated the Pacific Aero Products Company, listing himself as president, Edgar N. Gott (his cousin) as vice president, and James C. Foley as secretary. Another irony was the location of Pacific Aero's factory, a shipyard on the banks of the Duwamish River that Boeing had purchased six years earlier, where his yacht was built; the B&W's wings and floats had been built at the shipyard while the fuselage was being assembled in a hangar on the shores of Lake Union. There were 16 hourly employees listed on Pacific's books, their pay ranging from 14 to 40 cents an hour. Physical assets included one Pierce Arrow truck with a listed value of $450.

At the time of incorporation, Pacific Aero's inventory consisted of two unsold seaplanes: the original B&W, and an identical twin-float aircraft constructed after Westervelt left. Wong's improved version, called the Model C, was a slightly smaller two-seater also with twin floats, and after some modifications to the prototype Boeing built another five in hopes of winning a Navy contract. America's entry into World War I was the catalyst; the Navy tested two Model Cs and then ordered 50 as trainers, a $575,000 contract that put Boeing into business for good.

Originally called Oxbow and later known as Plant One, the shipyard facility was enlarged in the wake of the Navy order, and at the same time Boeing changed the name of his infant firm to the Boeing Airplane Company. The new name was painted in large white letters the entire width of what constituted a combined headquarters building and factory. It was a wood structure painted a bright red—the famous Red Barn, which can be seen today in perfectly restored condition as part of the Museum of Flight in Seattle.

Boeing himself maintained an office in downtown Seattle, spent a lot of time on business in Washington, D.C., and visited the plant only infrequently during the war. His cousin Ed Gott ran the day-to-day factory operations, supervising about 100 workers and an office staff of fewer than a dozen people. One of these was a teenager more familiarly known by her later married name of Mary Dawn, a combined telephone operator and bookkeeper who made out invoices, paid the bills, and delivered paychecks. She had a small office just inside the Red Barn's entrance; engineers and draftsmen worked on the second floor, while the aircraft were assembled in the main plant behind what passed as the executive offices.

Her immediate boss was Boeing's first chief auditor, Charlie Brink, unforgiving of mathematical mistakes but a good-natured man willing to go to bat for deserving employees. He got Mary a raise after her first three months and another one at the end of her first year. More than seven decades later, she remembered that the second raise boosted her to $100 a month, "which was a pretty good salary for a woman in those days."

Mary went to work for Boeing shortly before the 1918 armistice, and it was a wonder anyone got a pay increase after the war ended. In addition to the contract for the 50 Model Cs, Boeing also had been awarded a contract to build, under license, 50 Curtiss HS-2L flying boats, a large three-seater patrol seaplane. Only 25 had been completed when the war ended and the rest of the contract was cancelled. Boeing reluctantly laid off most of the work force after the 25th Curtiss was built, the only bright spot being the sale of the two B&Ws to what eventually became Air New Zealand—Boeing's first international customer.

The two historic seaplanes, *Bluebill* and *Mallard*, were shipped on the freighter S.S. *Niagara*, arriving in Aukland, New Zealand, December 12, 1919. *Bluebill*, the same plane rejected by the Navy, proceeded to set a New Zealand altitude record of 6,500 feet. It also made the first New Zealand cross-country flight from Aukland to Tairua; flew the first experimental airmail flight from Aukland to Dargaville; and was employed along with *Mallard* over the next two years helping to develop the country's embryonic air service.

Bluebill and *Mallard* were designated aircraft F and G respectively, the latter flown far less frequently because of persistent aileron problems. Both suffered an ignominious fate: in 1924 they were used as artillery targets by the New Zealand army and destroyed, in the case of *Bluebill* an incalculable historical loss. Certainly if Bill Boeing could have foreseen the future of his struggling company, he would have hung on to that first airplane; the B&W on display at the Museum of Flight today is a replica.

As it was, Boeing had other things to worry about besides preserving Model 1 for posterity. During the war he had been forced to loan the company more than $30,000 to meet the payroll, not the first time he did this; to raise additional cash he kept issuing new stock, most of which he had to buy himself. War's end found the nation gripped in a depression and no one was hit harder than the aircraft industry. Nor was it merely the drying up of military orders that decimated America's aircraft manufacturers; they also were plagued by a national indifference to postwar aviation.

In desperation, the Boeing factory began turning out furniture: dressers, dressing tables, nightstands, and beds. Only one airplane was built, a new flying boat called the B-1; on March 3, 1919, Boeing himself and a new pilot he had hired, Eddie Hubbard, flew the seaplane from Victoria, British Columbia, to Seattle, carrying 60 letters—the first international airmail flight in North America and Boeing's first tentative step into commercial aviation.

Of more immediate import that year was an Army Air Service contract to modify 111 de Havilland DH-4 observation planes. British-designed but built in the United States and powered by the famous Liberty engine, DH-4s during the war had acquired such unsavory nicknames as Flying Coffins and Flaming Coffins, both alluding to the plane's nasty habit of catching fire and trapping the pilot, whose seat was directly behind the fuel tank.

Boeing's job was to change the location of the tank, a relatively modest assignment but one that probably kept the company itself from crashing in flames. The only other business that came Boeing's way was a few sales of a new speedboat; like the furniture sideline, it helped keep the work force employed but was not a profit-making enterprise. The company lost $300,000 in 1920, and the future looked bleaker than Puget Sound on a rainy day.

Bill Boeing, however, never let his engineering staff stop dreaming up new or improved aircraft designs. Wong had resigned while Boeing still was building the 50 Model C trainers, and two rookie graduate engineers hired out of the University of Washington took up the slack. The first was Clairmont Egtvedt, known to everyone as Claire, a shy, brilliant Norwegian youngster who signed on as a draftsman and within a year was promoted to chief experimental engineer. The other was Phil Johnson, a personable, unusually mature youth whose real flair was administration. He made superintendent in 1920 and a year later became vice president. Egtvedt and Johnson, hired at $90 a month, were two names that would play prominent roles in Boeing's first three decades.

The Boeing people tried hard, from the youthful designers like Egtvedt and Johnson to the youngest employee of all—a feisty little guy named Mike Pavone whose first job was sweeping woodshavings off the factory floor. An airplane lover, he had shown up every day for two months trying to get hired and each time was told curtly by a secretary, "We're not hiring today." He arrived again one rainy day and this time got yelled at.

"Look," she shouted, "when we *are* hiring I'll let you know!"

What she hadn't realized was that a supervisor had noticed the wiry little youth's persistence and had heard her outburst. He turned to bookkeeper Mary Dawn and snapped, "Mary, hire this guy."

Thus began Mike Pavone's half-century of loyal service to Boeing. Grateful for the supervisor's intercession and vaguely aware that he was going to work for a company apparently ready to go belly-up, he had no way of knowing that the tide was about to turn. It wasn't very apparent at first. Egtvedt and his crew had designed a pretty little sports plane with wheels instead of floats, which made it Boeing's first land plane. It was demonstrated at the San Francisco Aero Show of 1920 but found no takers. The only airplane sale in 1920 was to Eddie Hubbard: the balding pilot bought the B-1 seaplane and operated a scheduled airmail service between Seattle and Victoria, while still working part-time for Boeing as a test pilot.

The work force had dropped to fewer than a hundred, and even these survivors were paid only because Bill Boeing dipped into his wallet to meet the payroll. Fortunately, however, 1920 happened to be the year General Billy Mitchell began clamoring for a separate, independent air force and touting heavy bombers as the ultimate weapon. In those days before he was court-martialed for insubordination, he possessed enough clout to wangle hard-to-get funding for a new type of bomber: Ground Attack Experimental, or GAX.

The Army Air Service (AAS) of that time had two ways of buying new military aircraft: the Army either designed the plane itself and then invited manufacturers to bid for its construction, or it put manufacturers' designs up for bid—meaning that Boeing, for example, could have won a design competition only to have some lower-bidding company build it.

The GAX was Army-designed and Boeing outbid all other manufacturers for the construction contract. Giving the Seattle firm a financial breathing spell was the best thing that could be said about the GAX order for 20 bombers. The phrase *a camel is a horse designed by a committee* was roughly applicable to the GAX, which charitably could have been labeled a flying turkey. It was a triplane powered by two Liberty engines, armed with a 37-millimeter cannon plus eight machine guns, with heavy armor plate for protection against ground fire. The monstrosity added up to a grossly overweight, slow, and clumsy-flying aircraft that nobody liked, including the Army.

As had happened with the wartime Curtiss flying boats, Boeing completed only half of the GA-1s the Army had ordered when the remaining 10 were cancelled. But the AAS still had enough faith in the concept to award Boeing a contract for three GA-2s, redesigned by the Army into a biplane, but still so heavily armored that it flew like an iron girder. The other major flaw was a cockpit enclosed in a steel canopy with small windows, which made pilot visibility the equivalent of trying to see out of a closed phone booth.

However poor the planes' design, the GAX contracts kept the Boeing plant busy. It got even busier when the company won a contract to build 200 Thomas Morse MB-3 pursuit planes, as fighters were called in those days. It was another example of a manufacturer taking advantage of someone else's winning design by outbidding him for the actual production. It was no secret why Boeing could bid low: Bill Boeing owned a lot of timberland, and airplanes were then made largely from spruce, a strong and durable wood.

The airplane business was now good enough for Boeing to get out of the furniture business. Notices to EMPLOYEES OF THE BOEING AIRPLANE COMPANY ONLY were posted around the Red Barn, offering at sizable discounts FINISHED BEDROOM SUITES AND OTHER MATERIAL WHICH ARE TAKING UP THE ROOM NEEDED FOR THE USE OF AIRCRAFT MATERIAL AND OTHER SPACE REQUIRED FOR THE MANUFACTURE OF AIRCRAFT WHICH THIS COMPANY IS CONCENTRATING ON.

Employees were offered dressers in walnut, mahogany, or ivory finish at $22.40, chiffoniers or dressing tables for $20, and beds for only $17.50. Terms were NET CASH WHEN DELIVERED OR PAYROLL DEDUCTION, PROVIDED PAY CHECK COVERS THE VALUE OF THE PURCHASE. Considering the prices, that last little warning gives some idea of what the pay scale was in 1921.

The notices went up in December of that year, but posting them on Valentine's Day might have been more appropriate. At the bottom of the announcement was this friendly nudge from Cupid: "P.S. IF YOU HAVE DELAYED GETTING MARRIED ON ACCOUNT OF THE HIGH PRICE OF FURNITURE, NOW IS THE TIME TO GET A GOOD START."

Discounted furniture wasn't the only bonanza for Boeing's 278 employees at the end of 1921. They also received their first bonus: a $500 paid-up life insurance policy thanks mostly to the profitable $1.4 million MB-3 contract. Yet far more important to their future was the conviction of Boeing and his tiny design staff that they could build a better fighter than the Thomas Morse. Egtvedt began working on a new design called the Model 15. The prototype, designated XPW-9 by the Army, was completed and flight-tested in the spring of 1923. A biplane, of course, but with a steel-welded tube fuselage; Bill Boeing may have been a lumberman, but even then the company seemed to be looking ahead to the time when airplanes would be all metal, facilitating mass production as well as providing more strength and durability. In terms of labor hours expended, planes like the PW-9 were built more by women than by men—women who wielded foot-long needles laboriously to sew linen fabric on the wings and fuselage.

The direct competition for Boeing's new fighter was the Curtiss PW-8. Both planes used the same engine, made by Curtiss, and they were roughly similar in appearance and performance. The PW-9 was slightly faster and the Army liked its armament arrangement better, but the PW-8 was considered more stable and Curtiss won a contract for 25 fighters. Yet the race had been close and the Army thought enough of the Boeing entry to buy the prototype plus the two PW-9s still under construction. All three went through further tests, and the Army wound up ordering a total of 30 more.

Bill Boeing, apparently satisfied that the company was finally going to survive, moved up to board chairman and named Ed Gott as president. Gott lasted less than three years in the job before resigning to join rival Fokker Aircraft as vice president. He was capable and well-liked, but he had a mind of his own and in some ways was more conservative than his cousin, with whom he reportedly had a few arguments. Boeing was a company that resembled a small family, where everyone knew everyone else.

Several office employees used to wait each morning in front of the Hoge Building, where Boeing maintained his downtown office, so Phil Johnson could pick them up in his White Steamer and drive them to work. Other employees would be picked up at the same spot by the company's White truck, which ran a daily scheduled service between the Hoge Building and the factory. The driver for years was Walter Domonoske, who eventually became security guard captain, and his riders learned to be punctual. If you missed the truck, you had to take a streetcar to the end of the line, and then walk almost a mile over a planked road and through mud.

Boeing remained, however, exclusively a supplier of military aircraft.

Its next big order was the Egtvedt-designed NB-1, a trainer that won a Navy contract for 41 of the versatile planes adaptable to either floats or wheels. The Army came through with another DH-4 modification job, this time equipping the antiquated de Havillands with steel tube fuselages. Then the Navy fell in love with the PW-9, ordering 10 of them (in Navy nomenclature, they were FB-1s) and subsequently buying a number of improved versions.

To succeed Gott, Boeing chose Phil Johnson. Only a few years before, he had worked his way through college by driving a laundry truck, and he now found himself president of a fast-growing company at the age of 30. The selection, however, surprised no one. Underneath Johnson's extroverted personality lay a tough executive talent that Boeing had recognized almost from the first day Phil came to work. And the chairman also acknowledged Egtvedt's ability by naming him vice president and chief engineer.

Eddie Hubbard returned to Boeing full-time after losing his airmail contract to a competitor. Along with Herb Munter, he had established the tradition of great Boeing test pilots. Yet that was not his most significant contribution, for Hubbard remained the tenuous link between Bill Boeing and the nearly forgotten but still-beckoning world of commercial aviation.

The importance of that thin link wasn't immediately noticed; Boeing's heavy involvement with military business occupied everyone's attention. Egtvedt and his merry men were busy designing a new Navy fighter and the PB-1, a naval patrol bomber that would be the largest aircraft Boeing had ever built. So big it was called the "Flying Dreadnought," its most unusual feature was a seaplane hull made partially of aluminum—the first major use of this lightweight metal by Egtvedt's team.

The PB-1 required a five-man crew and was truly huge for its day, with a wingspan of nearly 88 feet, a gross weight of nearly 27,000 pounds, and a bomb capacity of one ton. Its projected range was 2,500 miles, sufficient for a non-stop California–Hawaii flight the Navy was planning to make. But after Boeing built the big aircraft, the Navy staged the flight with a seaplane of its own design and the PB-1 remained a one-of-a-kind.

Another disappointment was the XP-9, an experimental fighter that was Boeing's first monoplane. Its failure couldn't be blamed on Boeing's engineers, however, for the XP-9 was an Army design that Egtvedt was forced to follow. The location of its high wing blocked pilot vision and Eddie Hubbard refused to touch it after only one test flight. One writer has called it the worst plane Boeing ever built. But Egtvedt hit the jackpot with his new Navy fighter, the FB-4, one of the most beautiful little airplanes in aviation history and Boeing's first to be powered by an air-cooled radial engine. The FB-4 and subsequent more powerful versions were to serve as the Navy's standard carrier fighters for years.

And on the drawing boards was another kind of airplane, one that was finally to project Boeing into commercial aviation. Early in 1925, the U.S. Post Office announced its interest in the development of a new mail plane. The government's airmail fleet consisted almost entirely of obsolete DH-4s, and while they had shed their wartime "Flaming Coffin" stigma, the lumbering de Havillands were still a deterrent to pilot longevity; of the first 40 pilots hired by the Post Office in 1919, 31 had been killed in crashes by 1925—the majority in DH-4s.

All DH-4s were powered by water-cooled Liberty engines, a design almost as old as the plane itself. The Post Office's requirements for a new mail plane specified that it use the Liberty, presumably because it was more powerful than any available air-cooled engine. The requirement made no sense; Pratt & Whitney and Wright both were producing air-cooled radial engines as muscular as the Liberty and superior in every other respect, especially in weight—they didn't need a radiator, water, and a lot of plumbing.

Nevertheless, Boeing had to follow the specs and in July 1925 rolled out the new Model 40 with the mandated Liberty engine. The Post Office bought it but, as expected, it was overweight and sluggish, and the Post Office didn't buy any more. Egtvedt, however, had learned his lesson; when Pratt & Whitney came up with a new 425-horsepower air-cooled radial Wasp engine, Egtvedt mated it to the Model 40, installed two passenger seats in the fuselage, and Boeing had its first real commercial airplane.

The 40A was a sturdy, reliable aircraft that couldn't have been developed at a more auspicious time. On February 2, 1925, Congress passed the Contract Air Mail Act, more familiarly known as the Kelly Act after the Pennsylvania congressman who introduced the legislation. It was an aviation Magna Carta, for it turned virtually the entire job of flying the mail over to private contractors who would bid for the mail routes.

Thus was the U.S. airline industry born. And the 40A was Boeing's ticket of admission into that fledgling industry.

Figuratively speaking, Bill Boeing almost had to be dragged into it.

It was Eddie Hubbard who first got the idea that Boeing itself should fly the mail. He had cultivated enough contacts among postal officials to be tipped off when the Post Office was ready to put the mail routes up for bids. Hubbard had his eye on one route in particular: San Francisco–Chicago. He thought the 40A was just the right airplane for the job.

Phil Johnson was the first one Hubbard had to convince, but Johnson was in Washington trying to sell more fighters to the Navy. So Hubbard talked to Egtvedt, who was dubious at first and pointed out the hazards of flying over the Rockies, especially at night. Hubbard suggested installing airway lights every 25 miles, and the more he talked, the more Egtvedt's doubts dissolved. He was half-sold anyway; he already had been thinking of recommending that Boeing start a passenger service between Seattle and Vancouver. Hubbard's proposal sounded even more promising—you could make more money carrying the mail than people.

They went to see Boeing at his Hoge office and the reception was lukewarm at best. Bill Boeing, whose willingness to gamble on long-shot ventures may have helped cause the estrangement from the more cautious Gott, was himself being cautious. But that night he told his wife about Hubbard's plan to put Boeing into the airmail business and to his surprise, she liked it. Boeing stayed awake half the night pondering what Hubbard and Egtvedt had told him, and the next morning summoned them back to the Hoge Building.

Green light.

The 40A could carry 1,200 pounds of mail. Hubbard and Egtvedt had it all figured out: Boeing could submit a bid of $1.50 a pound for the first thousand miles plus 15 cents a pound for every additional 100 miles, and still make money. Revenue from the two intrepid passengers would be pure gravy, and an even thicker gravy, thought Egtvedt, if the fuselage was modified to accommodate an additional two.

That was the bid Boeing filed for the San Francisco–Chicago route. The competing bid came from Western Air Express: $2.24 for the first thousand miles and 24 cents for each additional hundred miles. Boeing's offer won, but it was so far under WAE's that postal officials required Boeing to post an $800,000 bond to guarantee operations. Even then, the bid was not accepted officially until U.S. Senator Wesley Jones of Washington assured the Post Office that William E. Boeing was a reliable and financially responsible businessman.

So the Boeing Airplane Company now had a subsidiary: Boeing Air Transport. Eddie Hubbard was named BAT manager, and the new airline's first pilots came from the Post Office's airmail roster—they were quite happy to be on the Boeing payroll and just as happy to be flying brand-new 40As instead of ancient de Havillands.

Service was inaugurated July 1, 1927, after William Boeing had been duly sworn in as an employee of the Post Office. His wife, Bertha, christened the first plane *City of San Francisco* but not until the second day of service did BAT carry its first passenger. Jane Eads of the Chicago *Herald-Examiner* rode in a 40A from Chicago to San Francisco and deserved a medal; the flight took 23 hours.

BAT bought 24 40As from the parent company, the first batch with the two-passenger configuration but equipped later with four seats.

The pilot sat in an open cockpit while the customers rode like sardines inside the center of the fuselage.

The Boeing Airplane Company charged Boeing Air Transport $25,000 per plane; BAT was run as a separate, technically independent organization, yet beholden to the parent company for all its equipment. A cozy arrangement, yes, but in reality an obviously beneficial one. The 40A was far superior to its competitors, the Douglas M-2 and the Curtiss Carrier Pigeon, both powered by the inefficient Liberty and carrying only a single passenger. Even with its low mail rates, derided by much of the infant airline industry, BAT was profitable right from the start, and the 40A was largely responsible.

Someone asked Boeing how he could fly the mail for $1.50 a pound and make money.

"Because we're carrying mail over those mountains instead of radiators and water," he explained blandly, which literally was true. The Wasp-powered 40As carried twice the payload of any other mail plane with no increase in aircraft weight or fuel consumption.

A 40A admirer was Vern Gorst, a colorful entrepreneur who ran Pacific Air Transport (PAT) and had bid successfully for the Seattle–Los Angeles mail route. Gorst wanted to buy some 40As but couldn't arrange the financing; PAT was losing money and his only solid asset was the mail franchise. Disappointed, he was on the verge of selling out to Harris "Pop" Hanshue of Western Air Express, who offered him $250 a share for Gorst's controlling voting stock. Gorst would have gone through with the deal except for some words of caution from a small, dapper, unofficial financial advisor representing the Wells Fargo bank, which held most of PAT's notes.

"If you sell to Hanshue," he warned, "you'll leave hundreds of nonvoting shareholders out in the cold and they won't get a cent for their stock. If you have to sell, sell to Boeing and merge the two airlines."

The advisor worked out the details with Bill Boeing, who offered $200 a share for all PAT stock, as well as agreeing to absorb every PAT employee. He paid more than that for much of the stock because when word spread that Boeing was buying up every share, the price soared. The last two outstanding shares were owned by an Oregon prostitute who demanded and got $1,332 for them. Boeing handed Gorst a $94,000 check for his shares but he immediately spent $20,000 of it on a Boeing flying boat, which he used to start a Seattle–Alaska airline that lasted only five years.

One smiling witness to this transaction in the Hoge Building was the young financial advisor most responsible for it. While the BAT-PAT merger was still being worked out, Phil Johnson had hired him as his executive assistant.

Diminutive in stature but a giant in ambition and brains, he was to become an aviation legend. His name was William A. Patterson, better known as Pat Patterson, and the merger he had recommended and worked to arrange was the first step toward the formation of America's largest transportation conglomerate.

Unfortunately, it also was a conglomerate destined to be involved in a controversy that would tear the entire aviation industry apart and shatter the dreams of one man in particular: William Edward Boeing himself.

TWO

MARRIAGE TO AN OCTOPUS

THE AIRLINES WERE GROWING UP FAST AND CLAIRE Egtvedt's task was to keep pace.

Off the drawing boards at Oxbow came the Model 80, a new three-engine airliner sporting 12 leather-covered seats enclosed in a heated cabin so spacious that a six-foot-four passenger could stand upright and not hit the ceiling. There were individual reading lights over each seat and hot and cold running water. It was a biplane, however, because Egtvedt had insisted on designing a transport plane that could land slowly at the high-altitude airports between San Francisco and Chicago. And the Model 80 landed almost as tamely as the old DH-4.

One of the Model 80's best features was, according to the pilots, its worst. They hated the new-fangled closed cockpit, complaining bitterly about the lack of visibility, although their gripes weren't unanimous. A minority dissenter was a Boeing Air Transport (BAT) captain named Edmund T. Allen who thought his brother airmen were being too conservative.

It figured, because Eddie Allen was a test pilot at heart and, as it turned out, destined to be one of Boeing's greatest. He welcomed innovation, helped develop a two-way radio system on the 40A, and left the line to flight-test the Model 80, which had some early teething troubles. The first four built had a single tail that created stability problems, and Egtvedt put a triple tail on subsequent aircraft. The original Model 80 was underpowered, too; its three 410-horsepower Pratt & Whitney Wasps proved inadequate for an airplane that weighed more than 9,000 pounds empty. It cruised at only 115 mph, slower than the Model 40, and Boeing went to 525-horsepower P&W Hornets that added 23 mph to the cruising speed—aided not a little, it should be mentioned, by enclosing the engines in newly developed stream-lined cowlings; this improved version was designated Model 80A.

Eddie Allen took the new airliner up for its first test flight in August

1928 and narrowly escaped disaster. Mike Pavone, by now assigned to the flight department as a combined mechanic and flight engineer, was riding with Allen and remembered the harrowing incident only too well.

"A bolt on the horizontal stabilizer had been installed without a securing nut," Pavone recalled. "The vibration worked the stabilizer loose and it dropped four inches before it jammed. I had to help Allen with the control yoke so we could land safely."

The same plane had another close call on a later test flight when an engine failed. The device to "feather" a propeller—keep it from wind-milling—hadn't been invented yet, and the runaway prop caused such severe vibration that it began tearing the engine apart. The Model 80, with new engineer Lysle Wood on board as an observer, went into a series of wide figure S's. When the pilot finally managed to land, Wood asked him about the repeated S turns.

"Were you looking for a place to land?" he inquired.

The pilot wiped the sweat from his brow. "Hell, no," he confessed. "We were out of control."

Other than those near-mishaps, however, the Model 80 proved to be a competent if not a sensational performer. Boeing built 12, but only 11 went into airline service. The 11th, the Model 80B, was unusual in that it was the only Model 80 to have an open cockpit, a sop to pilot complaints about poor visibility. It is interesting to note that after a few winter flights, the pilots asked that the cockpit be enclosed again.

Historically speaking, the most interesting piece of equipment installed a bit later on BAT's Model 80s was the thirteenth seat, about a third the size of a regular passenger seat. This was intended for the cabin attendant and was forevermore known as the jump seat. The exact derivation is unknown, but "jump seat," the accommodation for any extra crew member, quickly became part of airline nomenclature, just as airplane lavatories in the pre-jet era always were called "blue rooms" (because they invariably were painted blue).

BAT wasn't the first U.S. airline to employ cabin attendants. Western Air Express put stewards on its Los Angeles–San Francisco route in 1928, and a British airline had employed stewards on cross-channel flights as far back as 1919. But BAT was the first to hire female cabin attendants, all registered nurses, for its San Francisco–Chicago flights. Eight of them, recruited from San Francisco and Chicago hospitals, joined the airline in 1930 but only on a three-month trial basis. Virtually everyone at Boeing was adamantly opposed to the idea, from Bill Boeing right down to the pilots, who considered the presence of a female crew member to be in the same undesirable category as an engine fire.

Certainly no one expected the experiment to last longer than the allotted three months except, perhaps, the women themselves. But the passengers loved them, and the stewardesses or hostesses, as some airlines called them, became a permanent part of aviation. Fortunately, no airline adopted the title originally suggested: courier.

The Model 80 might be termed an artistic success and a financial flop. Advanced though it was in terms of passenger comfort, it could not be classed as a successful airplane, not when only 12 were built, and all but one were purchased by Boeing itself. Its disappointing sales helped convince Boeing that the biplane had outlived its usefulness in commercial aviation. Every crystal ball in the industry recognized planes of the future for what they had to be: all-metal monoplanes, which eliminated the "built-in headwinds" generated by a biplane's forest of wing struts and guy wires.

The Model 80 was not the last biplane transport; that distinction belongs to the twin-engine Curtiss Condor sleeper plane of 1933 vintage. But it was the last one that Boeing ever built. A superbly restored Model 80 on display at the Museum of Flight in Seattle is believed to have been the last operational one. It ended its honorable career in Alaska in 1945 and its remnants, like the bones of an extinct dinosaur, were found in a scrap heap.

Yet a biplane proved to be the best seller Boeing was to have for a long time. Claire Egtvedt designed a new Army Air Corps fighter, the sleek little P-12, and also came up with a slightly different version for the Navy: the F4B-4. Until the late 1930s, they were the most popular fighters either branch of service had ever flown; nearly 600 were sold.

Under full throttle, the P-12 could get airborne at only 65 mph and climb almost 3,000 feet a minute. Leveling off at 5,000 feet, the P-12's airspeed indicator would be nudging 160 mph, which was mighty close to hot-rod performance for its time.

Frank Tallman of movie stunt fame flew a P-12 years after it had become obsolete.

"One thing that all Boeing biplane fighter series had in common," he wrote later, "was that they were all built like a certain brick edifice and the pilots took advantage of the planes' near-indestructibility in flight and outstanding performance to practice maneuvers unknown to the earlier generation of pilots."

This, too, was remarkable because the P-12 and its first cousin, the F4B-4, still had fabric-covered wings with wood spars and ribs. Throughout its entire history, Boeing's proudest tradition has been its reputation for building airplanes that can take incredible punishment, yet it's seldom realized that the reputation was established even before the all-metal age began. It was true of the Model 40 as well as the fighters. Two of the old mail planes actually saw combat in World War II, flying for the New Zealand Air Force during the New Guinea campaign; like the B&Ws before them, they were destroyed by gunfire—this time at enemy hands.

As it turned out, the P-12 and its Navy cousin were Boeing's last fighter biplanes. They also were the last fighters with fabric-clad wings and wood spars, for every new design Egtvedt and his staff were dreaming up now called for metal construction. They had had a chance to study how the pioneer of all-metal aircraft built them; in the summer of 1929, a Soviet ANT-4 seaplane landed at Sand Point in Seattle's Lake Washington after a flight from Siberia.

The ANT-4 was nothing but a German Junkers manufactured in the Soviet Union, and no one knew more about metal airplanes than Hugo Junkers; he had been building them since 1915. The Russian airmen who landed in Seattle were scheduled to make a goodwill flight across the United States, and Boeing was assigned the job of replacing the floats with wheels. Its engineers also were told to check the plane's airworthiness, which was fortunate because they found the control cables badly frayed.

The inspection and repairs, of course, gave them the opportunity to examine the internal structure, but if they learned anything—and Mike Pavone, for one, thinks they did—it was never admitted publicly. Regardless, a certain amount of design copying was a way of life in the early years of aviation, and Boeing was to prove a victim far more often than it was a perpetrator.

For that matter, Claire Egtvedt didn't need to steal anyone's ideas; in aeronautical engineering he had few peers, which he was about to demonstrate. But as Phil Johnson's second-in-command, both he and the Boeing president had more to keep them occupied than just building and selling airplanes. Bill Boeing had become close friends with Fred Rentschler, president of Pratt & Whitney, and the friendship had gone beyond the fact that Boeing airplanes were using the reliable Wasp and even mightier Hornet engines exclusively.

In the fall of 1928, Rentschler had suggested merging Boeing and BAT with Pratt & Whitney. It made sense, he pointed out, to have an airline, an airplane factory, and an engine manufacturer all under the roof of a powerful, well-financed holding company. It would be particularly advantageous to Boeing Air Transport, Rentschler added, because airlines all over the United States were beginning to merge, forming larger carriers that eventually would threaten BAT's dominance. At the time he proposed consolidation, BAT was carrying 30 percent of the nation's mail and passenger traffic.

Boeing was sold on the idea and the wheels began to turn. Rentschler's original merger plan was expanded to take on additional partners. Boeing absorbed Chance Vought's company, a small but capable manufacturer of naval aircraft. Pratt & Whitney bought out two propeller companies, Hamilton and Standard Steel. All these were merged under the banner of the new holding company: United Aircraft & Transport Corporation. United then acquired Stearman Aircraft of Wichita and Northrop Aircraft, which made light biplanes and military trainers, respectively. And to cover the entire spectrum of airplane manufacturing, the holding company purchased Sikorsky, which then specialized in amphibian aircraft. Rentschler had created an aeronautical goliath so diverse that it even owned several airports.

By the time all the wheeling and dealing was over, a number of executives had played musical chairs. Heading the conglomerate as president was Rentschler with Phil Johnson and Chance Vought named vice presidents; Johnson retained the presidency of Boeing. Bill Boeing, content as usual with a backstage role, became United's board chairman. The one officer left out of the reshuffling was the pilot who had talked Boeing into entering the airline business: Eddie Hubbard.

In the winter of 1929, Hubbard suffered a fatal heart attack while shoveling snow in front of his home. Johnson gave the job of running Boeing Air Transport to Pat Patterson as the airline's general manager, but BAT's own existence under that name was to be short-lived. Over the next two years, the holding company gobbled up Varney, Stout Airlines and National Air Transport, and combined all airline operations into a subsidiary called United Air Lines, Inc.

Over the cabin doors of the Model 80s, some now equipped with 18 seats to accommodate the booming passenger traffic, the United designation appeared for the first time. And the corporate expansion continued, gathering momentum like an avalanche. In quick succession the holding company established the Boeing School of Aeronautics in Oakland, California, to guarantee a supply of trained pilots and mechanics; Boeing of Canada, which started out building Model 40B mail planes; and an aircraft export subsidiary.

United Aircraft & Transport's first annual report in 1929 showed an $8.3 million profit and liquid assets totaling more than $27 million. Rentschler and Boeing had constructed a money-making machine that not even the 1929 stock market crash could silence. And in Seattle, Claire Egtvedt took advantage of all this prosperity by shifting Boeing's aircraft design philosophy whole hog into the development of new monoplanes.

The first was a relative failure: the XP-15 and its Navy equivalent, the XF5B-1 (the X stood for experimental), were compromises between a biplane and a monoplane, and both looked like biplanes with the bottom wing removed. They were "parasol" monoplanes, with a framework of struts attaching the fuselage to the single wing above it. Neither went into production, but Egtvedt always learned from mistakes.

His next effort was one of Boeing's most famous and significant airplanes: a low-wing, Hornet-powered all-metal monoplane dubbed the Monomail. The name fit, for it originally was designed to serve only as a mail and cargo plane. A later version carried six passengers and a third model was modified to carry eight. Whatever the configuration, however, the Monomail was truly revolutionary except for one detail: the pilot again sat in an open cockpit, above the narrow cabin.

It was the most aerodynamically streamlined airplane Boeing had ever produced, with a retractable landing gear and an enormously strong cantilever wing structure built along the same principle as bridge girders. The sturdy wing spars were completely internal; gone were the struts and supporting guy wires of the old biplane days.

Monomail test flights, as with all Boeing airplanes, originated down the street from Oxbow at Boeing Field—Seattle's then-only airport had been so called since 1928, although officially it is the King County Airport. The flights were routine until one morning when test pilot Slim Lewis, to the horror of onlookers, put the new airplane into a full loop and then repeated the maneuver twice, testifying to the Monomail's strength.

Like the Model 80 before it, the Monomail was simultaneously a commercial disappointment and a technical triumph. Its chief drawback had nothing to do with the basic design; the culprit was propeller technology of that time. The variable pitch propeller—a kind of aerial gearshift, which allows the blades to be set at a steep angle for takeoff, and then changed in flight to a shallower angle of attack at cruising altitude—hadn't yet been perfected. On the Monomail, the blade angle could be changed only on the ground, and with a full load the pitch had to be set at a takeoff angle to obtain the greatest "bite." But when the plane reached cruising altitude, there was no way to change the pitch and the Monomail's aerodynamic efficiency was wasted; the plane cruised at a leisurely 135 mph, negating its finer qualities.

Yet the Monomail was worth every cent that was spent on its development. It can be likened to a slow racing stallion that somehow sires a stable of champions. In 1931 the Army Air Corps invited bids for a new twin-engine heavy bomber and Boeing's entry, the B-9, was simply an enlarged Monomail with a retractable gear and two beefed-up Hornets that gave it a cruising speed of almost 160 mph, faster than many fighters. The B-9's first flight was in April 1931, and the Army ordered both test prototypes plus an additional five production aircraft.

Martin won the competition for a large production order, however, with its new B-10. The Army's preference was embarrassingly easy to explain: the B-9 simply had too many deficiencies. The fuselage was so narrow that the two pilots couldn't sit side by side; one rode ahead of the other in what amounted to a double open cockpit. The gunners' stations were open, too, and the streamlined fuselage provided an exceptionally small internal bomb bay that required most of the 2,400-pound bomb load to be carried in external wing racks. In contrast, the B-10's cockpit and gunners' stations were enclosed, the bomb bay was entirely internal, and the overall design was good enough to win the 1932 Collier Trophy for outstanding aeronautical achievement.

Once again, however, Egtvedt turned a past mistake into a future success. He took the B-9's basic structural concept and began work on a new airliner that would make aviation history and win a Collier Trophy of its own. It would be called the Boeing 247, and one of the young engineers assigned to the project was a recent Stanford graduate named Edward C. Wells.

Before the 247, however, there was the P-26, the best-performing prewar fighter ever to come out of Oxbow.

The stubby little low-wing monoplane had a top speed of well over 200 mph and won the affection of every Army pilot who flew it, although some complained it landed like a high-speed rock. Like the B-9 before it, the P-26 bore not only the Boeing name but the Boeing willingness to gamble on new airplanes with its own design philosophy and, equally important, its own money. The then-common practice among aircraft manufacturers was to obtain at least partial military funding prior to building a prototype—a share-the-risk policy, as it were.

Not at Boeing. Both the B-9 and P-26 were developed at company expense; the military supplied specifications and general require-ments, period. The gamble had failed with the B-9 but not with the "little pea shooter," as the P-26 was known. The Army eventually bought more than 130 and Boeing sold 12 overseas—11 to China and one to Spain. The P-26 program, however, was never profitable. The original contract set a price of $10,000 per plane; it cost Boeing $13,000 to build one, and even though the price went up in subsequent orders, the increase was offset by numerous design changes. By World War II the fighter was obsolete although a squadron of outgunned P-26s flown by the Philippines Army saw brief action against the Japanese.

If the P-26 was a tough hill to climb, the twin-engine 247 was a mountain. It blazed new aviation trails, hacked out new aeronautical paths and, to paraphrase the creator of *Star Trek*, it went where no airplane had gone before; it was a revolution wearing wings. Yet the 247 also is one of Boeing's greatest ironies: it could have been and should have been better than it was, and it wound up being unwittingly sabotaged by the very men who flew it.

Its pioneering virtues were many. It was the fastest multi-engine transport, with its sleek, low-drag aerodynamics borrowed from the Monomail and B-9. The Wasp engines were equipped with new three-bladed Hamilton Standard variable-pitch propellers that gave the 247 excellent takeoff characteristics and a higher yet economical cruising speed; the airliner actually was as fast as the P-12. The immensely strong cantilever wings were equipped with landing lights and de-icers, and the landing gear—a specialty of new engineer Ed Wells—was retractable.

The prototype had a close call on one winter test flight that was to determine how well the cabin heater worked under severe conditions. It was late afternoon when Eddie Allen, then a free-lance test pilot, took off, flew east, and found his cold weather at an altitude of some

25,000 feet over rugged mountain terrain. The cabin heater worked fine, flight engineer Mike Pavone reported, but just as they were about to return to Seattle, the weather closed in and they ran into ice-laden clouds.

The radio antenna froze and snapped off; now they were flying blind with all radio communications out, a compass that was acting erratically, and low fuel. Superb pilot though he was, Allen became disoriented and they were hopelessly lost. Both men were sickeningly aware that if the plane crashed, no one would ever know the real cause and the 247 probably would be doomed.

Then Pavone suddenly spotted a red streak in the sky.

"Sunset!" he yelled. "That's gotta be west!"

Allen turned the airplane toward the faint glow. When they landed, they had only 40 gallons of fuel left, enough for not more than another 30 minutes of flight.

The airplane that finally metamorphosed from drawing board to prototype to production model, however, was not the one originally conceived by Egtvedt's team. The 247 was supposed to be powered by two Hornets, which would have allowed 14-passenger capacity and a 180-mph cruising speed. But United's pilots, given an advance briefing on the new airliner, objected vociferously. They took one look at its projected 16,000-pound empty weight and claimed the airplane was too heavy to land safely.

"That's why we're using Hornets instead of Wasps," Egtvedt explained patiently.

It was the wrong argument. The inherently conservative airmen loved the reliable Wasp in the same proportion they disliked the more powerful Hornet. Their fervent plea to United's management was for a smaller 247 that would be adequately powered by Wasps. The inevitable compromise, with Egtvedt's reluctant approval, was to scale down the 247 to a 10-passenger plane that weighed less than 13,000 pounds. And it was, eventually, to be a fatal compromise.

A scaled-down 247 notwithstanding, United ordered 60, including one that the airline used as a flying test bed for new communications equipment. With this $4 million commitment, United figured it had the transcontinental market sewn up, throwing its new 160-mph fleet against TWA's slow and noisy Ford trimotors, and American's even slower Curtiss Condor biplanes. American and TWA both wanted to buy the 247; fine, Boeing said in effect, but you'll have to wait at least a year because the United order will tie up the production line for that long.

Stymied by this circumstance, TWA's Jack Frye turned to a small manufacturer in Santa Monica, California, inquiring whether it could build a transport better than the 247. The answer from Donald Douglas was the DC-1, prototype of the 14-passenger DC-2 and forerunner of the famed DC-3. If ever there was a classic case of being hoisted by one's own petard, United and Boeing had provided it. The 247 was obsolete almost before it went into service and besides the 60 United ordered, Boeing sold only 15 more, including two to Lufthansa Airlines of Germany.

At the time, the 247 looked big enough to most people at Boeing, including Egtvedt and his chief engineer, Charles "Monty" Monteith. A former Air Corps lieutenant whose textbook on aerodynamics was required reading at West Point, Monteith watched the 247 take off on its first flight—February 8, 1933—and shook his head admiringly.

"They'll never build 'em any bigger," he's supposed to have commented. According to another account, what Monteith really said was "It'll be a long time before anyone builds a better or faster plane than this," which sounds more likely coming from an aeronautical engineer who knew that aviation is never content with the status quo.

Whatever he actually said, both versions were somewhat off target. Only a year later, the DC-2 was flying and less than 40 years later the Boeing 747 was carrying more flight attendants than the 247 carried passengers.

Yet the 247 was still quite an airplane. A miniature battleship in structural integrity, it set the standard for ruggedness that was to be the trademark of every future Boeing transport, piston or jet. Many years ago a now-legendary incident occurred when a 247 operated by Pennsylvania Central Airlines made a forced landing in open country and skidded between two large trees. The trees went down but the wings stayed intact.

One of the two massive main wing spars, which provided much of that strength, was something of a drawback: it ran annoyingly right through the center of the cabin and had to be covered by a carpet. The bulge was an eyesore useful solely to stewardesses; they'd sit on it while talking to nearby passengers. Those passengers forward of the spar had to step over it to reach or leave their seats, and few if any realized they were traversing a major structural component.

During the early days of World War II, when the Army was commandeering two-thirds of the airline industry's aircraft, an officious young Army lieutenant arrived one day to inspect a Western Airlines 247.

He strode briskly through the cabin en route to the cockpit and tripped over the covered spar.

"The first thing we gotta do," he ordered, "is get rid of that goddamned step!"

The 247 was one of the first airplanes to undergo static testing—deliberately adding stress to key structural components, especially wing spars, until they break. A premature failure meant major redesign. In the old days, a structural test consisted of an engineer kicking his foot against a piece of tubing to see if it would hold. Before aircraft manufacturers designed giant hydraulic jacks to apply more realistic stress loads, such as would be applied in actual flight, the common practice was to load the top of a wing with lead-filled bags until the weight snapped the spars. That was the method used on the 247, in the basement of Oxbow.

The 247 was to win the 1934 Collier Trophy for Boeing and the airplane was a smash hit at the 1933 Chicago World's Fair, where it attracted almost as many viewers as Sally Rand's fan dance. It also became the first Boeing airliner to be featured in a motion picture: Paramount's 1938 *Men with Wings* starring Fred MacMurray and Ray Milland. In a convoluted example of miscasting, the 247 played a revolutionary new bomber, although it obviously was non-military in every respect. The 247's appearance in *Men with Wings* set a precedent: 32 years later, the 707 would be featured in the original *Airport*, a film that one critic called, more in admiration than malice, "a two-hour Boeing commercial."

Once the DC-2 went into service, United couldn't get rid of its 247 fleet fast enough and sold them at bargain-basement prices. Western bought four for $25,000 apiece, and these were airplanes only two years old that had cost United $65,000 brand-new.

The pair of 247s purchased by Lufthansa reportedly saw little airline service. They were appropriated by the military, which dismantled them to study their internal construction. How much of it went into the design of Germany's wartime bombers is anyone's guess, although it wouldn't be surprising if some of the Luftwaffe's warbirds had 247 blood running through their metal veins. One case of copying was to be confirmed during the war; the British had captured a German Heinkel 111 twin-engine bomber intact, and shipped it to Seattle so Boeing engineers could examine it. They found the tail and some of the internal structure identical to that of the 247.

The ascension of the DC-2 was a bitter blow to Egtvedt and Bill Boeing. If anything, it proved that the close relationship between Boeing and United could be more of a liability than an asset. United couldn't be blamed for trying to corner the air travel market with a radically new airliner, and it might be said that the ploy would have worked better except for its overly conservative pilots. But what really killed the 247 was the holding company's inherent "sole source" policy. United was obliged to buy planes from Boeing, and Boeing was obliged to give United first priority in delivery positions: they were each other's captives.

If Bill Boeing ever realized that his company would be better off as an independent manufacturer, he didn't communicate those feelings to anyone. He didn't have to, because matters were about to be taken out of his hands—by the United States government.

Historians have called it the airmail scandal, which is stretching the facts considerably, because no one ever proved that anyone did anything morally wrong or illegal. Nevertheless, this so-called scandal resulted in a legislative and corporate earthquake that crumbled not only powerful United Aircraft & Transport but every similar conglomerate.

Its genesis was a poorly written piece of legislation that replaced the Kelly Act: the McNary-Watres Act of 1930, named after the two Republican lawmakers who introduced the bill. Its real author was Postmaster General Walter Folger Brown, a Harvard-educated lawyer and Ohio politician named to the post by President Hoover. History has cast Brown in the role of a villain, but he was in fact a capable, farseeing if rather stuffy public servant, who took literally the job description outlined in the leather-bound portfolio given to all cabinet officers after being sworn in.

That portfolio listed as one of his tasks the promotion of commercial aviation. Brown did some homework and came to the conclusion that the U.S. air transportation system was a mess; there were 44 airlines trying to survive mainly on mail pay and showing little interest in developing passenger traffic, which happened to be the new postmaster general's favorite subject.

McNary-Watres not only lowered mail rates drastically but laid out some vague restrictions on who was going to carry it. The bill was written so loosely that it gave Brown what amounted to a blank check for interpreting its language. His translation added up to a death sentence for most of the nation's small carriers: he wanted only solidly financed carriers with their bigger planes to fly the mail routes, and this meant well-heeled companies like the Boeing-Pratt-United coalition. The terms Brown laid down—such as not awarding a mail contract to any airline that wasn't already operating night flights over routes of at least 250 miles—effectively eliminated the smaller operators.

McNary-Watres contained one provision that gave the postmaster general authority to extend or consolidate routes "when in his judgment the public interest will be promoted thereby." These 11 words were all Brown needed. Only two weeks after Hoover signed McNary-Watres into law, Brown summoned the top executives of the large airlines to Washington for a meeting that would go down in history as the infamous Spoils Conference. It was by no means a secret meeting, as was later charged; the smaller carriers just weren't invited.

Phil Johnson represented United, and for 12 days he and his fellow executives listened to Brown plead, cajole, and threaten, trying to win approval of his blueprint for a new air transportation system. His main pitch was the establishment of three competing transcontinental routes: the northern one—already operated by United—and central and southern routes. Because the U.S. air route system resembled a plate of spaghetti, Brown knew his plan had to involve some touchy and potentially volatile mergers. The wily postmaster general also knew that this collection of rugged individualists couldn't have agreed on the time of day, and he warned that if they didn't reach agreement he'd make the final decisions himself.

That is exactly what happened. The conferees bickered right up to and through the deadline, and the postmaster general sat back and figuratively licked his chops. He already had made up his mind on the key issue: he wanted to award the southern transcontinental route to American Airways and the central one to Transcontinental Air Transport. The latter wasn't even eligible under the terms of McNary-Watres because TAT didn't fly at night, but Brown solved this problem by suggesting that TAT merge with Western Air Express, which had considerable night flying experience—a shotgun wedding if there ever was one.

Now, having rewritten the airways map of the United States, Brown put all mail routes up for rebidding with a lower ceiling on what any carrier could bid.

Three years later, shortly after Franklin D. Roosevelt took office, an enterprising reporter unearthed evidence that the Post Office's mail awards hadn't always gone to the lowest bidder. The specific case that kicked open the can of worms involved the tiny Ludington Line, which operated passenger flights between New York, Philadelphia, and Washington. The reporter (Fulton Lewis, Jr., who was later to become a controversial radio commentator) found out that Ludington had bid 25 cents a mile to carry the mail but that the award had gone to Eastern, which had bid 89 cents.

Lewis dug further into Post Office files, and he discovered the entire Spoils Conference scenario. It wasn't hard to find because Brown never made any attempt to hide anything, including the fact that the Spoils Conference had taken place. The former postmaster general simply didn't think he had done anything wrong under his interpretation of McNary-Watres. Lewis couldn't get his own bosses to print the story, so he leaked it to Democratic Senator Hugo Black of Alabama.

Subsequent Senate hearings supported Brown's contention that he had acted legally. While the law required mail contracts to go to the lowest bidder, he explained, it also allowed certain exceptions if the postmaster general thought a higher bidder was better qualified. But Black wasn't satisfied, and convinced FDR that the airlines were run by a bunch of crooks who had obtained mail contracts through skullduggery.

Against the advice of new Postmaster General Jim Farley, Roosevelt cancelled all existing contracts and ordered the Army to fly the mail. The result was a debacle. The order went into effect February 9, 1934, in the middle of the worst winter weather the country had experienced for years. Army pilots, untrained in bad-weather flying and forced to operate over unfamiliar terrain, took fighters like the P-12s, old observation planes, and even B-10 bombers into this murderous environment. Some of the aircraft lacked navigational instruments and aids that airline pilots had taken for granted. In the first week alone, five Army pilots were killed and six seriously injured, and eight planes were destroyed. By the end of March, another seven pilots had lost their lives.

Their epitaphs were black headlines denouncing Roosevelt and the innocent Farley. Will Rogers, one of aviation's most stalwart supporters, compared the cancellation to "finding a crooked railroad president and then stopping all trains." Stung by loud criticism from virtually the entire press and such luminaries as Eddie Rickenbacker and Charles Lindbergh, FDR announced he would return the airmail to private operators but under new rules.

These rules were written by Black himself in a bill called the Air Mail Act of 1934 and it lowered the boom. No aircraft or engine manufacturer could be connected in any way to an airline—a provision that shattered the United Aircraft & Transport colossus and every other aviation empire. No airline executive who had attended the Spoils Conference could hold office in any airline that had a mail contract. And finally, no airline that had participated in the conference would be allowed to bid for any mail contract.

It was legislation that literally demolished the entire U.S. air transportation system, and if put into effect the way it was intended as the harshest of punitive measures, it would have come close to seriously damaging companies like Boeing. The civil market would have been populated solely by small carriers who might have found it difficult to finance purchases of large transport aircraft.

Fortunately for all concerned, there was at least one official in Washington who was cannier than Hugo Black, and that was Jim Farley. He privately advised the stunned airlines to take advantage of a loophole in the new law's careless wording and merely incorporate under new names. Thus, for example, American Airways became American Airlines, Eastern Air Transport switched to Eastern Airlines, and United's airline subsidiary was incorporated under United Air Lines Transport.

Among the airline executives hit by the falling boom was Phil Johnson. In 1933 he had succeeded Rentschler as president of United Aircraft & Transport; Rentschler became vice chairman and Patterson was named president of the airline operating division, which included BAT, Varney, Stout, and NAT. Patterson was left untouched by the Black bill but Johnson was forced out of office. Embittered, he moved to Canada and helped start Trans-Canada Airlines for the Canadian government.

Boeing itself came out of the Black vendetta independent once more, but one man was badly scarred by the experience: Bill Boeing. He had been one of the badgered witnesses before the Black committee, fuming at what he considered totally irrelevant questions.

He returned to Seattle and fumed anew when FDR signed the bill that dismantled into fragments the corporate edifice he and Rentschler had built. His own company was in trouble again; 247 orders had dried up completely, the P-26 program still was losing money, the government had mandated minimum-wage increases for hourly workers, and a new fighter design hadn't impressed either the Navy or the Air Corps.

Yet he considered the company to be in capable hands, even with its problems and even without Phil Johnson. He probably would have taken Johnson back to run Boeing, but when Phil had been promoted to the holding company's top spot, Boeing had named Claire Egtvedt to succeed him. Boeing probably realized anyway that Johnson, through no fault of his own, was a pariah in official Washington—a status certain to hurt the company's military business.

William Boeing had made no secret of his desire to retire at age 50. He was now three years past that self-imposed deadline, he was wealthy enough to enjoy the rest of his life without lifting another pen or telephone receiver, and—the most salient factor of all—he was fed up with the industry being used as a political football.

Not even aviation's most prestigious honor could ease his inner turmoil and disillusionment. He was awarded the 1934 Guggenheim Medal "for successful pioneering and achievement in aircraft manufacturing and air transport," the sixth recipient of this treasured accolade from his peers. Six other Boeing men would be honored with the medal in years to come, but to William E. Boeing his own recognition was not only too late, but empty.

He severed virtually all official relations with the Boeing Airplane Company, including the sale of his Boeing stock, and retired to spend most of his remaining years in leisure. Boeing died of a heart attack aboard his yacht on September 28, 1956, just when the company he fathered was on the verge of entering the jet age with a plane as revolutionary as the 247.

His legacy was Tradition, expressed succinctly in a bronze plaque that can be seen today as one enters the Boeing corporate offices about a mile from the Red Barn:

I've tried to make the men around me feel, as I do, that we are embarked as pioneers upon a new science and industry in which our problems are so new and unusual that it behooves no one to dismiss any novel idea with the statement that it "can't be done!" Our job is to keep everlastingly at research and experiment, to adapt our laboratories to production as soon as practicable, to let no new improvement in flying and flying equipment pass us by.

—William E. Boeing

He wrote those words in 1929.
They also could have been his epitaph.

THREE

B IS FOR BIG

OUT OF THE RUBBLE THAT WAS ONCE MIGHTY UNITED AIR-craft & Transport, Boeing salvaged only one subsidiary: Stearman Aircraft of Wichita. It did retain Boeing Aircraft of Canada, which it already owned.

Boeing even lost its aeronautical school in Oakland, which went to United Air Lines, and at the time it looked more promising than Stearman, which had never built anything except presumably now-obsolete biplanes. The school turned out not only pilots and mechanics, but engineers; an engineering diploma from the Boeing School of Aeronautics was considered the equivalent of a bachelor of science degree from conventional universities, although the Oakland learning center was exclusively technical. Even under United's ownership, the school remained one of Boeing's engineering talent sources for some time.

As it turned out, however, Stearman was to prove itself one of Boeing's greatest assets. Its small but dedicated work force had been building light airplanes since 1925, the year Lloyd Stearman founded the company. An architect by profession, Stearman had created a biplane design so good that it remained basically unchanged for years. The Stearman division was to turn out its last biplane in 1944, but as late as 1960 there still were some 2,000 Stearmans registered as operational, airworthy aircraft in the United States, many of them used as crop dusters and in sport flying. A Stearman Model 75—the Kaydet trainer Boeing built during the war—in mint condition is worth about $50,000 today.

Until the war clouds gathered, however, Boeing really didn't know what to do with its Kansas "country cousin"—Seattle had enough worries of its own. Layoffs during 1934 shrank the payroll from more than 1,700 workers to fewer than 700, and the carnage would have been even worse if the employees hadn't come up with a unique "work share" plan. Half the survivors in the shop worked for two weeks while the other 300 went on furlough. Then the second group returned and the first went on a two-week furlough. It says much for their loyalty that a number of laid-off people came in anyway, working without pay during the two weeks they were supposed to be loafing at home.

Economy measures ranged from drastic to petty. Someone in engineering management posted a sign over the paper towel dispenser in the men's washroom reading, WHY USE TWO WHEN ONE WILL DO?

The next day, under that heartrending plea was an engineer's response: WHY USE ONE WHEN THE JOB IS ONLY HALF DONE?

But the engineers, too, felt the cost-cutting pressures. Twenty of a staff of 90, all unmarried, received brief furloughs. Ed Wells survived but one of the temporary casualties was a husky young stress analyst named George Martin, who had come to work for Boeing in 1931. He had been employed as a surveyor for the state highway department after graduating from the University of Washington, and took a pay cut to join Boeing. If you added up the combined monthly income of two engineers like Wells and Martin, the total would barely reach $300, but in those days every aeronautical engineer considered himself lucky to have a job in his field.

Wells and Martin were the brightest young stars in vice president Monty Monteith's engineering stable. John Ball, the lanky engineer in charge of structures, was especially high on Martin, who had helped design the 247's sinews.

The 247's drawbacks were sharper in Claire Egtvedt's mind than its virtues, however. He knew, too late, that he should have stood up to the pilots and built a bigger airplane. And "big" had always fascinated him, anyway. Even long before the 247 went from dream to drawing board, Egtvedt had started thinking about a huge bomber so heavily armed that no fighter could touch it.

He had been aboard the Navy carrier Langley, a converted collier that became America's first aircraft carrier; Mike Pavone, a special favorite of Egtvedt, was with him as they observed carrier takeoffs by Boeing fighters. A rear admiral, their host, made some comment to the effect that battleships made more sense than bombers, because a battleship could defend itself.

"The only logical bomber would be a kind of flying dreadnought," Pavone remembered him saying.

That remark apparently never left Egtvedt's mind. And as Boeing licked its Depression-inflicted wounds, he decided its only hope lay in big airplanes. He needed promising young engineers like Wells and Martin. Huge aircraft were nothing new in aviation but they had been spectacular only in appearance, definitely not in their flying qualities. A good example was the Army's 1920 Barling bomber, a giant six-engine triplane with a 120-foot wingspan. It needed a stiff tailwind to reach 90 mph and ran out of fuel if it flew more than 300 miles. Such aerial goliaths had a terrible track record, and there were those who claimed there was a limit to how big an airplane could be and still fly competently.

Egtvedt didn't buy this, and fortunately for Boeing neither did a handful of far-seeing officers in the Army Air Corps who also didn't buy their more conservative older brethren's argument that all military airplanes, including bombers, were meant solely to support ground forces. The impetus for America's first true heavy bomber came in the form of a modest 1934 Air Corps contract to develop a long-range experimental heavy bomber. Boeing's answer was the XB-15, a monster with a 149-foot wingspan and weighing 37,709 pounds empty.

It had a range of more than 5,000 miles with a four-ton bomb load, but its four new 850 horsepower Twin Wasp engines were inadequate for the size and weight of the airplane. It had a flight deck instead of a cockpit and was the first aircraft that required a separate station for a flight engineer. Because of its tremendous range, the bomber was equipped with a galley and bunks for off-duty crew members on long flights. The XB-15's outstanding feature, however, was its enormous wing area of nearly 2,800 square feet; by contrast, the B-9s and 247s were 932 and 836 square feet, respectively—this was indeed a giant airplane.

The XB-15 was Army-funded simply because it was never intended to be a production prototype. It was strictly a one-of-a-kind flying laboratory, built to determine if a bomber this huge was practical. And what Boeing learned from its design and construction helped lead the way to America's most legendary warplane: the B-17.

The B-17 was born even before the XB-15 made its first test flight late in 1937. While the experimental bomber was still in its preliminary design stage, there arrived in Seattle a blue-jacketed circular labeled "U.S. Army 98-1800 General Specifications for Airplanes . . ."

Those specs called for a "multiengined" bomber that could carry a ton of bombs 2,000 miles at more than 200 mph; the company that could build such a plane, document 98-1800 promised, would receive a production order for at least 20 aircraft, provided that the prototype was ready for flight testing within a year.

With the engineering staff already laboring on the XB-15's design, the Air Corps had thrown Boeing a curve. Its competitors, Douglas and Martin, had only one airplane to design; Boeing had two. Egtvedt, in one of the gutsiest decisions he ever made, interpreted multi-engined to mean that the Air Corps wasn't limiting the bomber to only two engines, something no other manufacturer had seriously considered. He told Monteith to proceed on this risky assumption, which didn't come as any surprise to the engineers. Egtvedt already had them working on some preliminary studies for a four-engine bomber that would be smaller than the XB-15, along with a proposed commercial version. The bomber project was assigned to engineering as Model 299 and the transport plane as Model 300. Those two designations identified them as Boeing's 299th and 300th aircraft designs, respectively, which gives some idea of how many airplanes never leave the drawing board, or don't even get beyond preliminary sketches.

Work had scarcely begun on either project when Air Corps document 98-1800 arrived. Model 300 was almost forgotten in the rush to win a lucrative military contract, and Monteith named E. G. Emery to head the bomber project with Ed Wells as his top assistant.

Edward Curtis Wells never forgot the circumstances under which he was assigned to Model 299. He was married on a Saturday, took Sunday and Monday off, and went back to work Tuesday as the new assistant project engineer. He stayed in that post only four months before replacing an ailing Emery, a significant promotion in a 50-year career that would establish him as one of the world's most respected and honored aeronautical engineers.

Boeing's board of directors had allocated $275,000 in development funds, not a modest sum considering the fact that the company ended 1934 with $266,000 worth of red ink. One of the younger directors voting for the allocation was an attorney for the Seattle law firm that handled Boeing's legal affairs. And William M. Allen was to cast quite a few more important votes over the next three and a half decades.

Model 299's designers borrowed much from the still unborn XB-15, especially its internal structure and its concept of heavy defensive armament; the larger plane carried six machine guns and the 299 five, plus a strength-enhancing feature called "stress skin"; the wing skin was internally braced, making it an integral part of the entire stress-absorbing structure. Until George Martin came up with the idea of applying it to the huge XB-15, all Boeing airplanes had relied solely on wing spars doing the job. The 299 was too far along in construction for Martin to use stress skin on the prototype, but it was to go on every Boeing airplane from then on, including the B-17.

Ahead in design but not in manufacture, the XB-15 didn't make its first flight until two years after Model 299. When it finally did take to the air in October 1937, its deficiencies were only too apparent. "Just a big kite," Martin once aptly described the experimental bomber with the then-incredible wing square footage, and it definitely was underpowered.

Model 299 was another story. Boeing kept the new bomber under wraps but there were plenty of rumors about a great new "mystery ship" taking shape in what was now known as Plant One. When 299 was finally unveiled on a warm day in July 1935, an awed press almost ran out of adjectives trying to describe the gleaming silver giant, so huge that the horizontal stabilizers on the tail were three feet wider than the P-12's entire wingspan.

Reporters tagged it with such nicknames as "aerial battlecruiser," and "flying dreadnought." The name that stuck, however, was the one reportedly uttered by a Seattle newspaperman who took one look at the new bird and for the first time blurted a description that would be etched into aviation annals like words chiseled into granite: "She's a flying fortress!" he proclaimed.

Yet the road from prototype to production was a highway marked by setbacks, tragedy, and bitter disappointment. The first obstacle was higher-than-expected development costs, forcing the board of directors to spray some more red ink on the books by allocating another $150,000 to the Model 299 project. Any new commercial transport was not much more than a vague concept at the time; Boeing was betting the pot on the bomber.

It looked like a good bet at first. Model 299 performed better than expected in early test flights, and the competition wasn't that impressive. The Martin company had an improved version of the B-10 and Douglas also came up with a twin-engine bomber that borrowed heavily from the DC-3. Pitting Model 299 against these two competitors was like matching Notre Dame against a couple of high school teams.

Or so it seemed.

On October 30, 1935, the bomber was at Wright Field in Dayton, Ohio, undergoing a series of military test flights. They had been flown by Boeing test pilot Les Tower, who in eight years of hazardous flying had compiled the enviable record of never scratching any airplane he had tested. Tower was considered Eddie Allen's equal as a pilot, and that was saying a lot. On this day, however, Tower was on 299 merely as an observer. Tragically, one thing he didn't observe was to cost him his life.

The bomber was equipped with a gust lock, a new device that locked the tail section's elevators from the cockpit while the aircraft was parked, to protect it against sudden strong winds. It was a vast improvement over the time-honored method of attaching wooden blocks to the elevators, and then trusting a mechanic to remove them before each flight.

This flight was the first in the final phase of Air Corps evaluation tests, and at this stage 299 was so far ahead of the Martin and Douglas entries that Egtvedt and Wells, who were at Wright Field to witness the competition, would have wagered their life savings on the outcome. Model 299 actually had exceeded document 98-1800's specifications in every major category.

Two Army pilots were in the cockpit when 299 took off, with Tower behind them, watching. The big bomber got airborne but suddenly pitched up into an abnormally steep climb. It stalled, fell off on one wing, smashed into the ground and burst into flames. Three of the four Air Corps men aboard managed to escape the burning wreckage, but Tower and the major who was flying the airplane died later from burns.

It didn't take investigators long to discover why the plane had crashed; the pilot had attempted to take off with the gust lock still engaged. On the 299, an activated gust lock limited the elevators to two positions: neutral and extreme elevation. As they rolled down the runway, the elevators were in neutral but when the major pulled back the yoke, the gust lock automatically dropped into the elevator-up position, which raised the nose so sharply that a stall was inevitable.

The official Air Corps findings declared that the accident could not be attributed to "any faulty structural or aerodynamic design of this airplane, or any undesirable or adverse flying or handling qualities of the airplane."

But that complete vindication didn't help Boeing very much. What might be termed a whispering campaign began, among Army brass and within Congress, to the effect that maybe the 299 itself was to blame. It wasn't a malicious rumor, yet it did reflect the belief of some conservative officials that a four-engine bomber was simply too much airplane, too complex, for any pilot to handle safely. The Air Corps didn't feel that way, not after what the Boeing bomber had demonstrated before the accident. But the Air Corps was then part of the Army and lacked control over equipment funding decisions. The Army's General Staff pointed out that Boeing had to be eliminated from the competition because the destroyed 299 hadn't completed its tests—a grim technicality.

The result was a devastating blow to Boeing. Douglas won a contract for 133 B-18 bombers (later upped to 350), twin-engine planes that not only were woefully slow but had virtually no defensive armament; the B-18 had been completely outclassed by the 299 in competitive flight tests. During the war it was demoted to training flights and anti-submarine patrol because the lumbering bomber was too vulnerable to enemy fighters.

The big bomber concept still had enough believers for the Air Corps to recommend the purchase of at least 65 B-17s—299's military designation. It also recommended against ordering so many B-18s, but the General Staff overruled the airmen. It confirmed the Douglas contract and gave Boeing a consolation prize by approving the purchase of only 13 B-17s, and then later ordered B-17Bs, a slightly improved model. On that thin thread, Boeing's future hung.

Even the order for 13 aircraft was too much for Plant One to accommodate—the factory was simply too small. And if it was inadequate for the B-17, trying to build the even larger XB-15 would be impossible. The latter's wings were so immense that they included small tunnels through which a mechanic could crawl to make emergency repairs on an engine in flight.

Enormous for its day, Plant Two was erected on a 28-acre site across from Boeing Field at a cost of $235,410 for the basic structure, a ridiculously low price by today's standards. For that sum, Boeing got an assembly building 300 feet wide and 200 feet deep, with slightly more than 466,000 square feet of floor space. Its 35-foot height provided what aircraft manufacturers refer to as a "high-bay" facility, so it can accommodate aircraft with tall tails.

That was in 1936, of course. The 747 cockpit is almost as far from the ground as Plant Two's roof, and its tail stands 28 feet higher. Yet in its time, the new factory was one of the largest industrial facilities under one roof in the world, and still is serving Boeing after 56 years.

Plant Two blossomed on land that had cost Boeing one dollar. It was owned by a wealthy truck gardening family named Desimone who became alarmed when word spread that Boeing might move south to California—the Los Angeles area was seriously considered. Even in the late 1930s, this was the heart of the U.S. aircraft industry, the home of such giants as Douglas, Lockheed, and Northrop.

Some of Boeing's directors thought Southern California was preferable to Seattle because of its large supply of skilled aircraft workers. Another pro-California argument was its weather, more favorable to flight testing. The family that owned acres of land along East Marginal Way took due notice of the moving reports and offered the Plant Two site to Boeing—at the one-dollar price—on condition that the company stay in the Seattle area.

Until the new facility was completed, Plant One bore the production burden, as it had since the day it was first built. In its earliest days it was isolated from any urban area, located on flat land between the Duwamish River and a steep, wooded hillside. Employees who could afford cars parked them in the company's small lot. When a circus came to Seattle, it was customary to pitch the tents on vacant land adjacent to the parking lot.

Bill Cook, who was to become a key and much-respected figure in the history of Boeing engineering, arrived for some overtime work one weekend and discovered a circus employee was charging attendees to park in the Boeing lot, including Cook. Cook, whose bluntness could intimidate a commando, proceeded to put matters straight. He gave the man a glare that could have burned through asbestos.

"I park here every day," he growled. "This lot belongs to Boeing."

Circus customers about to pay an illegal parking fee listened with great interest. The circus chiseler beat a strategic retreat.

"Boeing officials don't have to pay, of course," he announced lamely, thereby promoting a $125-a-month rookie engineer into management.

Plant One used to be so far away from any other buildings that squawking crows became an irritating distraction. One Fourth of July, figuring a little extra noise wouldn't be noticed, some engineers brought shotguns out to the plant, hid behind trees, and blasted what seemed to be half the crow population of King County into eternity.

While Plant Two was under construction, the first of the production B-17s rolled out of Plant One, a mirror image of the ill-fated 299 except for its engines; Boeing changed the power plants from Pratt & Whitney to more powerful Wrights. Only a handful of the work force of some 1,400 men and women witnessed the rollout ceremony, later to become a traditional and invariably emotional occasion for the people who design and build airplanes.

Yet most of them had given up Saturdays and even many evenings to keep production on schedule. Boeing pride-in-product goes back to the B&W, but not until the B-17 had any Boeing airplane generated the kind of sentimental affection that was to be bestowed on the Flying Fortress. It was almost as if employees sensed they were making history.

They were.

The first 12 B-17s (the 13th was used for various Air Corps test purposes) were assigned to the Second Bombardment Group based at Langley Field, Virginia, and proceeded to stage a number of spectacular demonstration flights, including a 12,000-mile goodwill mission to Buenos Aires and back by a six-plane squadron. Even more spectacular was an unpublicized incident involving the test B-17. It flew into the heart of a vicious thunderstorm, with turbulence so violent that it flipped the 15-ton bomber on its back, sending it out of control and into a spin.

The pilot managed to recover and land at Langley, badly shaken and admitting the whole crew expected the plane to come apart—bombers are not designed to survive a spin. But although the wings were bent and a few rivets missing, they had stayed on—startling proof of the B-17's brute strength.

Another mission sent three B-17s 700 miles out over the Atlantic. Their assignment was to intercept the Italian liner *Rex* inbound to New York. They not only found her but flew so close to the ship that a lowered landing gear would have hit the funnels. The bombers and the flight commander got all the publicity, so little attention was paid to the lead navigator, a stocky, glowering, cigar-smoking lieutenant who gruffly allowed that Boeing seemed to build good airplanes. Such praise, coming from a lowly shavetail, was quickly forgotten, but not by the young officer himself.

His name was Curtis LeMay.

The intercept stunt was more of a let's-thumb-our-noses-at-the-Navy gesture than anything else, designed to refute the firm conviction of most admirals that only the Navy could defend America's seacoast against an invading fleet. It must be emphasized that before World War II, the B-17 was considered to be primarily a defensive weapon; its future role in *strategic* bombing—the destruction of an enemy's industrial capability—wasn't clearly defined yet. Initially, in fact, the XB-15, not the B-17, represented the belief of a few forward-looking Air Corps officers in strategic aerial warfare, waged by heavy bombers with the ability to defend themselves.

The grinning bomber pilots who had intercepted *Rex* 700 miles out to sea found that, figuratively speaking, they had shot themselves in the foot, for the Navy took a dim view of the whole thing. Such a dim view, in fact, that with Navy prodding, the Army's General Staff issued orders to the Air Corps that future practice missions were not to exceed 100 miles from any U.S. coastline. The Navy shouldn't have worried; the only targets a B-17 couldn't hit with any accuracy during the war were moving ships.

The XB-15 had its moments of glory, too. "Old Grandpappy," as the Army pilots affectionately called the giant plane, set one record by climbing to 8,200 feet with a 31,205-pound load added to the 37,709-pound weight of the airplane—two tons more than the XB-15 was designed to carry in gross weight. It also flew a 3,000-mile mercy mission to Chile, its cavernous fuselage jammed with relief supplies for earthquake victims. Grandpappy made two refueling stops on the southbound flight and flew back non-stop; carrying only fuel, the XB-15 could stay aloft for 24 hours, incredible endurance for an aircraft of that era. If the engines of the mid-thirties had been as advanced as that airplane, the XB-15 might have gone into production.

Old Grandpappy even saw service during World War II, flying troops and cargo in the South Pacific theater. After the war, despite pleas to preserve the big plane for the future Air Force Museum in Dayton, Ohio, the XB-15's career ended at Kelly Field, Texas, where it was broken up for scrap. It was an ignominious fate for a truly historic airplane—a bomber that never dropped a bomb in anger, yet one that added more luster to what was fast becoming a Boeing trademark: big and brawny airplanes.

It also was an image being applied not just to bombers but to commercial airliners as well.

Like many Boeing engineers who followed him, Wellwood Beall was a unique employee: a combination of aeronautical engineer and salesman. He was hired as the latter although he also was a graduate of the Guggenheim School of Aeronautics at New York University, and he had taught engineering at the Boeing school in Oakland after it was taken over by United.

Beall was in China trying to sell fighter planes when he was recalled to Seattle and assigned to engineering. He arrived in the summer of 1934 with his own project: a huge flying boat for transocean passenger service; he had gotten the idea when he heard Pan American Airways was considering operating its flying boats all the way from the West Coast to China, via Hawaii, Midway, Wake Island, Guam, Manila, and Hong Kong. His initial reaction to that report was to scoff at it, but on the way back to the U.S.—by ship, naturally—his wife told him she couldn't understand how anyone who loved airplanes could be so negative about their future. Before they landed in Seattle, Beall already was envisioning a new flying boat that dwarfed anything then flying.

Not a lot was done about it at first, because the engineering staff was stretched too thin to take on a new flying boat design. Bill Cook always insisted that was the real reason Boeing was unable to exploit the 247's early advantage over the DC-2: there weren't enough engineers to do the necessary fast, major redesign job. But a year after Beall returned from China, Pan American invited proposals from seven manufacturers for a long-range flying boat that would achieve new standards of transocean luxury.

Pan Am's Juan Trippe even threw in the added inducement of a $50,000 bonus to the winner. "I believe in tying the bag of oats out front," he remarked—and Boeing was ready with Beall's preliminary rough sketches, made hastily at his dining room table, as the design nucleus. It must be considered a minor miracle that the small engineering staff was willing to take on such a challenging assignment on top of the two bomber projects, but they had done it before; during the 247's gestation period, they simultaneously worked on new fighter and even small racing plane designs. Multiple assignments meant little.

In those days, they were hourly workers, punching in and out on time clocks just like assembly line personnel and everyone else except top management and supervisors; engineers didn't become salaried until the war, when their overtime began costing the company too much money. And they were an unusual breed, too, the aeronautical version of a general practitioner in medicine. Each was a jack-of-all-trades who disdained the word *specialization*—a point of pride with a veteran like Bill Cook, whose own brilliant 36-year career at Boeing spanned three generations of engineers.

When Cook came to work at Boeing in 1938, some specialization already had affected engineering assignments, inevitable as aircraft became increasingly complex. Yet most of Cook's cohorts still were capable of performing in every phase of design. He served Boeing long enough to see hundreds, even thousands, of specialized engineers assigned to a single project, their work made easier by computers, electronic instruments of great accuracy, and precise tooling equipment—design and production aids unheard of in the prewar days. About 100 engineers designed the B-17; more than 3,000 would some day be assigned to the 747.

But Bill Cook also remembered, with understandable nostalgia, what it was like to be a Boeing engineer in the 1930s, when every engineer had to be a draftsman as well as a technical designer, making his own drawings and layouts; sitting on a high wooden stool at a drafting table made of thick plywood and resting on a tall saw horse; providing his own tools of work—slide rule, T-square, triangles, scales, and erasing shield. Pencils and vellum were the only company-furnished items.

Yet an undisciplined, often makeshift atmosphere somehow produced a unity of purpose, a common commitment to achievement based on sheer loyalty—and this in a chaotic, unpredictable environment where layoffs between military and airline contracts were an accepted if unpleasant way of life.

Howard "Bud" Hurst, who came to Boeing as a sheet metal worker in 1927 and eventually rose to the rank of vice president, was typical of many workers both in manufacturing and engineering who sweated out demoralizing furloughs, then came back to Boeing as if nothing had happened. In his first two years, Hurst was laid off four times. Twice he went to Alaska on sheet metal jobs and twice he worked as an Alaskan miner.

The company again tried to be humane, making unmarried men the quickest candidates for layoffs. Boeing recognized its first union in 1936, Local Lodge 751 of the International Association of Machinists, then called Aero Mechanics Union, but not for some time would seniority become a protective factor in layoff decisions. Local 751 had begun with 35 charter members, a second-hand wooden filing cabinet, a typewriter that had seen better days, and a tin strongbox.

That morale could survive and even flourish under roller-coaster economic conditions can only be attributed to the mystique, the intangible but powerful *esprit de corps*, that has always been part of aviation. Which is why the rollout of a new airplane is a lump-in-the-throat experience for everyone from the newest hourly employee to the chief executive officer. That airplane is *everyone's* creation, a product of both pride and hope.

And certainly those were the two qualities that went into Boeing's next two commercial transports: the magnificent Model 314 flying boat and the pioneering, precedent-setting Model 307—the Stratoliner.

FOUR

OF FLYING BOATS, STRATOLINERS, AND HOWARD HUGHES

AMONG THOSE ADVISING PAN AM NOT TO BUY THE NEW Boeing flying boat were two competing manufacturers—Martin and Sikorsky—and Charles Lindbergh.

Opposition came naturally from the first two detractors. Pan Am already was operating Martin M-130 *China Clippers* and Sikorsky S-40 and S-42 seaplanes. Both manufacturers were so angry at Juan Trippe that they refused even to bid. Glenn L. Martin, in fact, expressed his outrage in a letter that should have been typed on fireproof paper. The irascible aviation pioneer—who, it was said, took advice only from his mother—temporarily abandoned the flying boat business and to his dying day swore that Trippe had ruined him. He had sold Pan Am its three M-130s at a loss, expecting to recoup either from reorders or a contract for larger seaplanes.

No one else entered the competition, so Boeing won by default. Pan Am signed for six Model 314s, plus an option for an additional six. The price was $512,000 per aircraft, not including spares—the most any U.S. airline had ever paid for a commercial transport. A new DC-3 at the time was selling for $100,000.

For its $4.8 million order including spares, however, Pan Am got the most luxurious airplane in the world, a literal flying ocean liner. Its spacious lower deck could seat 82 passengers by day and accommodate 40 in sleeping compartments at night, although the configuration was changed later to 74 day and 50 night. The 314 required a 10-man crew, 6 of them on the big flight deck: 3 pilots, navigator, flight engineer (the first on a U.S. commercial transport), and radio operator. Behind the upper-level flight deck were crew sleeping quarters and a huge baggage area. On transatlantic flights, however, passenger capacity was only 35 and cut to 30 for West Coast–Hawaii operations; the 74-passenger configuration applied to trips of not more than 1,500 miles.

The lower deck included a dining salon, cocktail lounge, and separate lavatory/dressing room facilities for men and women. The *pièce de résistance* was a bridal suite, another one of Wellwood Beall's ideas. Beall, a portly little dynamo with a thin dapper mustache, had a flair for such swankiness—he happened to be a lover of good food and wine, and his girth showed it. He was as much salesman as engineer; as much interior designer as aerodynamicist, although at this point Egtvedt had named him head of engineering and Ed Wells' superior.

Marge Blair, who started at Boeing as a timekeeper and retired 37 years later as administrative assistant to the chairman of the board, worked for Beall a number of years.

"His eyes were always twinkling," she remembered, "and he looked like Santa Claus without a beard. He even rolled when he walked."

It was Beall's notion to install a spiral stairway between the upper and lower decks. Pan Am's own engineers objected, on the grounds that it constituted a safety hazard.

"A passenger could fall off and get hurt," one of them pointed out.

"Hell, that's easy to fix," Beall jauntily replied. "We'll put a railing on the staircase."

The most significant aspect of the Beall-inspired interior was the impression it made on Juan Trippe. The Pan Am contract specified that first deliveries of the 314 would begin only 17 months after signing; failure to meet that timetable would result in heavy penalties. Boeing ran into one delay after another, but Trippe never exercised the penalty clause—he was that enamored of the passenger comforts the giant flying boat provided.

To Pan Am's technical people, however, the 314's flying qualities were vastly more important than bridal suites and spiral staircases. One of them was John Borger, an assistant engineer who, starting with the 314, was heavily involved in every Boeing airplane Pan Am bought—especially the 707 and 747. Borger had heard Lindbergh was cautioning Trippe against the 314 order; at the time, Lindy was living in England, the result of a self-imposed exile after the kidnap/murder of his infant son, but he still kept in touch with Pan Am as a technical consultant.

"He was unhappy with the 314 because he thought Boeing didn't have much of a track record in commercial transport design," Borger said. "It had a great reputation for building military airplanes, period."

Borger had his doubts, too, and the pessimism at first seemed justified when the 314 finally made its initial test flight June 8, 1938; Boeing already was way behind on the prototype's test phase and wouldn't make the first delivery until March 1939—13 months past the original deadline. Even before the June 8 flight, the 314 had flunked its early taxiing tests. To provide on-water stability, the flying boat was equipped with miniature wings attached to the belly; on the M-130 they were called "sea wings," but Boeing's nomenclature was "hydro-stabilizers" because Martin had copyrighted *sea wings*. On the

314, their dihedral—the angle at which they were attached to the fuselage—initially was too sharply tilted upward. When Eddie Allen tried to taxi in a stiff crosswind, the wing dipped so badly that the outboard prop bit into the water. Borger, who witnessed all the testing, recalled, "There were times when water actually entered the cabin."

Flattening the dihedral cured some of the problem, although the 314 always was temperamental while taxiing in anything except perfectly calm water. A far more serious problem was uncovered on the first test flight. Allen was at the controls with Earl Ferguson as his copilot and Bill Lundquist, project engineer for the new Wright GR-2600 Cyclones that powered the four-engine 314, acting as flight engineer. According to Borger, it was the first time anyone had put an engine that had no prior military experience on a commercial transport and this, too, proved to be a drawback; the early 314s were underpowered and the Cyclones had to be beefed up.

Also aboard that 38-minute flight was Wellwood Beall, who wasn't his usual effervescent self after it was over. Allen informed a disappointed Egtvedt that it was back to the drawing board—they had almost crashed. The rudder was too small, so inadequate that Allen could make turns only by using asymmetrical power on the engines plus some aileron input.

These were the Model 80 troubles all over again, and the solution was the same, too. Boeing installed a triple tail; the outboards provided the necessary lateral control and a rudderless center tail gave additional stability. The new tail arrangement was designed by Ed Wells and John Sanders, an assistant engineer, in one weekend—that was how fast Wells could work under pressure.

Once the bugs were eradicated, the 314 proved to be a superb airplane. Boeing had borrowed the XB-15's wing design for the flying boat, giving it a 3,500-mile range. With the improved Cyclones, it cruised at 183 mph and had a top speed of just under 200 mph, remarkable for a bulky seaplane that grossed 82,500 pounds. It was the huge wing that not only gave the 314 its tremendous range, but also the capability of making minor in-flight repairs on the engines: like the XB-15, there was a passageway inside each wing through which a crew member could crawl.

One less-publicized feature was the first flushable toilets ever put on a transport aircraft. Beall was prouder of these than his bridal suite gimmick, because he was largely responsible for their design. Unfortunately, aviation's first flushable toilets nearly caused a rift between Boeing and Andre Priester, the fiery-tempered Dutchman who ran Pan Am's engineering department. He was a brilliant technician whose brusque orders were hard to understand, being delivered in such a thick accent that they almost needed an interpreter.

Beall was invited on the 314's inaugural flight to Hawaii. He was sound asleep in his berth when a furious Priester shook him awake to report that neither of the two toilets was working. The bleary-eyed Beall finally got them to flush again, but the same thing happened on the return flight, and this time Beall couldn't fix them. Priester, a perfectionist whose Dutch profanity didn't need translating, was even angrier. As soon as Beall got back to Seattle, he turned the problem of the non-flushing flushable toilets over to Boeing's engineers. They expressed mystification; the flushing mechanism had gone through almost a year of testing and worked perfectly every time.

The solution, however, was so simple that even Priester had to laugh—along with admitting it was Pan Am's fault to begin with. The ingenious flushing system consisted of a rotating drum with a bucket inside. When a passenger put the toilet lid down, the drum turned the bucket upside down and the contents were dumped out of a large vent into the ocean. The bucket righted itself when the lid was raised. The culprit turned out to be the toilet paper Pan Am was using: it was ruffled and somewhat thicker than the paper Boeing had used in its tests, just thick enough to clog the drum and keep it from turning.

The flushing crisis notwithstanding, Pan Am was pleased enough with the 314 to exercise its options on the six tentatively ordered, although it didn't operate all of them. Three were diverted to British Overseas Airways (BOAC), a switch Borger believed was the result of a personal plea from President Roosevelt to Trippe, presumably as a means of aiding Britain.

The 314s were built at Plant One, the hulls constructed inside the factory and the rest of the aircraft assembled on two huge outside docks, each 100 feet long. Once completed, the Clippers (Pan Am's traditional designation) were flown to Astoria, Oregon, where they were delivered officially to Pan Am.

The Boeing Clippers served Pan Am and BOAC well during their relatively short careers, carrying valuable cargo to various war theaters and such famous passengers as FDR and Winston Churchill. But the advent of faster four-engine land planes, which traded Clipper luxury for speed and greater operating economy, doomed the giant flying boats. Not a single 314 exists today; six were scrapped within five years after the war ended, two were lost in accidents, one sank near Baltimore during a storm, and two more were sunk in collisions with rescue ships after forced landings due to engine trouble. The scrap heap was the fate of the last Clipper.

The demise of the flying boat, however, was preordained even before World War II broke out—the same Boeing engineering capability responsible for the magnificent Clippers made their extinction inevitable. For even as the 314 was being developed, so was another prewar airliner of far more revolutionary stature.

One of aviation history's minor disputes involves the origin of Boeing's Model 307 Stratoliner, the first pressurized airliner capable of flying above the weather.

Boeing didn't invent the idea of compressing the thinner air of the upper atmosphere into heavier, breathable air inside an aircraft cabin; it had been done before, albeit experimentally. But Boeing was the first manufacturer to incorporate pressurization into a production airliner, although it's not clear whether its engineering team instigated this pioneering step.

Some accounts credit TWA, not Boeing, for introducing the concept of pressurization to commercial aviation, claiming that a TWA test pilot first suggested it to the airline's then-president, husky, curly-haired Jack Frye, who was an ex-pilot himself. Frye, so the story goes, knew Boeing was putting superchargers on the new B-17 so the bomber could climb to higher altitudes, and asked Wellwood Beall to investigate whether an airliner could be designed utilizing a combination of four supercharged engines and a pressurized cabin.

It may have happened that way, but there is equal evidence that Boeing began considering a plane like the Stratoliner before Frye even approached Beall or anyone else in Seattle, and that the 307 already was on the drawing board when Frye actually contacted Beall.

Which version is correct is immaterial. The important fact is that the Stratoliner *was* conceived, built, and put into scheduled airline service not only by TWA but also Pan Am—the latter largely because of Andre Priester and Charles Lindbergh, both of whom were gung-ho about the prospect of flying over bad weather. And it was a Boeing-designed airplane that, like so many airliners of the propeller era, borrowed heavily from military aircraft.

The Stratoliner was the offspring of a marriage between the B-17 and a brand-new circular fuselage shaped like a dirigible; the symmetrical cross-section distributed the stresses of pressurized air equally throughout the cabin structure. The 307's wings, tail, nacelles, and engines came off the B-17, in effect another commercial/military hybrid, but a very effective one.

Frye ordered six Stratoliners for TWA, and Pan Am signed for four; the only other potential "launch" customer was the Netherlands' KLM, which expressed enough serious interest to send a technical delegation to Seattle for evaluation. Lindbergh, too, arrived at Boeing as a technical consultant for Pan Am, and secretarial hearts fluttered enough to generate a strong breeze. As was his custom, he went through the charade of using a fictitious name, a transparent device because he was easier to recognize than any movie star; at Boeing he was known either as "Mr. Charles" or "Mr. Morrow."

He showed up ahead of schedule for a meeting one day, found Marge Blair rearranging some chairs, and offered to help. While they were lifting a chair together, his hand accidentally brushed hers. Lindbergh's face turned beet red, he mumbled an apology, and fled the room.

"Talk about being bashful and shy." Marge laughed. "You would have thought he had tried to assault me. Most of the time he looked like a young farmer lost in the big city."

Frye had some grandiose plans for TWA's Stratoliners. He hired Raymond Loewy to design the interiors, envisioning an airliner that approached the Boeing Clippers in sheer luxury, with indirect cabin lighting and separate dressing rooms and lavatories for men and women. TWA's configuration called for a 33-passenger daytime configuration. The sleeper version would have 16 berths plus an additional nine chaise lounges for those not wishing to pay a berth surcharge. Frye actually signed a contract with Marshall Field in Chicago for a number of chaise lounges that were never delivered; financial problems forced Frye to go for a more conventional interior. Those problems, in fact, led directly to new ownership of TWA by a man who had once worked as a copilot for American Airlines under an assumed name just to learn the airline business: the brilliant but eccentric Howard Hughes. The Stratoliner was the catalyst that brought him into contact with Boeing for the first time. It would not be the last.

TWA's contract for six airplanes, scheduled for delivery in the summer of 1938, represented a $1.6 million commitment. Before any could be delivered, however, TWA had defaulted on the required "progress payments"—money down on signing, plus additional installments during construction—and Boeing cancelled the contract.

The instigator of this confrontation was not Frye, but TWA's majority stockholder, John Hertz, founder of the car rental firm, who thought Frye was a wild-eyed spendthrift driving TWA into bankruptcy. Aggressive, staccato-voiced, and a hard-headed conservative who knew little about aviation, Hertz dominated the airline's board of directors and had personally blocked the progress payments.

Frye didn't even know about the cancellation until TWA's factory representative in Seattle went out to the assembly line one day and discovered that the airline's red insignia had been stripped from two of the four TWA planes under construction. He demanded an explanation and was told TWA didn't own the airplanes anymore.

Hertz ordered TWA to sue Boeing for failure to deliver the airplanes on schedule; Boeing counter-sued on the grounds of contractual violation. Desperately seeking a way out of the Hertz-Boeing legal morass, Frye spilled his troubles to Hughes.

He couldn't have found a more willing listener. Hughes was intrigued by any new aviation innovation, and the Stratoliner was enough to convince him to bail out Frye, which he proceeded to do by buying up enough TWA stock to unseat Hertz as majority shareholder. The Stratoliners reverted to the airline.

A few eyebrows had been raised when Boeing cancelled the contract because it had failed to generate much airline interest toward the 307. American considered buying the Stratoliner and its technical chief, Bill Littlewood, spent several weeks in Seattle conferring with Wells,

Beall, and other Boeing engineers. His initial impression was negative; he considered the 42,000-pound plane underpowered and he recommended a number of modifications, mostly involving engines and propellers. He also was turned off by the cabin mockup Boeing was showing to prospective buyers; for some unknown reason, seats had been installed three abreast on one side of the aisle, and a single row on the other.

But at that stage, Boeing itself couldn't afford major design changes. Engineering hadn't even been able to get funds approved for a full-size pressure chamber to test the Boeing-developed regulator that kept cabin pressure constant in every phase of flight; they had wound up using an improvised 55-gallon oil drum. The pressurization system, being totally new to everyone, presented problems that required some crude solutions. Bob Dickson, who retired in 1981 after a 34-year Boeing career, could testify on that score. He was assigned to the 307 line shortly after he was hired.

"The biggest headache with the Stratoliner was sealing the pressurization system," he said. "All the skin joints were covered by what we called 'paw' tape. You fit the skin, then you trimmed it, put the paw tape on, and covered it with kerosene to soften the tape. Then you drove the rivets through, which supposedly sealed it. To check for leaks, which generally occurred when you got a bum rivet, you covered the joints with Ivory soap suds. If you saw a bubble come up, you had to rerivet the area."

Littlewood finally recommended that American reject the 307, despite his admiration for the pressurization feature. There was a time, however, when both TWA and Pan Am wondered if they shouldn't have emulated American's rejection, for the Stratoliner received a black eye even before entering airline service. On March 18, 1938, a bright Saturday afternoon, Boeing test pilot Ralph Ferguson, two KLM representatives, several Boeing technicians, and TWA chief pilot Harlan Hull took off in a Stratoliner on what was supposed to be a routine test flight. Mike Pavone was scheduled to be on the plane but at the last minute received another assignment, a switch that saved his life.

The aircraft, earmarked for eventual delivery to Pan Am, was the second 307 to come off the Plant Two assembly line. Somewhere in the vicinity of Mt. Rainier, the plane was seen disintegrating at an altitude estimated by eyewitnesses to range between 3,000 and 5,000 feet. There were no survivors, and shocked Boeing engineers went to work trying to find out what had happened.

One of them was a new Boeing employee, George Schairer, recruited away from Consolidated Aircraft by Eddie Allen, who knew his reputation as one of the most promising young aerodynamicists in the aircraft industry. He had helped design the B-24's wing at Consolidated, and in Schairer Boeing had acquired a man who some day would be instrumental in taking it into the jet age.

The flight was meant primarily to determine how the Stratoliner would behave in the event of an outboard engine failing while the aircraft was flying at a relatively low speed. The two men flying the airplane were Boeing test pilot Julius Barr and a KLM pilot who was in the copilot's seat. Barr was an exceptionally colorful character; he had been Chiang Kai-shek's personal pilot in the early thirties when Boeing was selling P-12s to China.

It was obvious from the available evidence that the accident occurred while the two pilots were testing the 307's low-speed stability with an outboard engine shut down. The aircraft stalled, rolled over, and went into a spin; both wings failed when they tried to pull out.

The problem was not so much aircraft strength as aircraft stability, and that sent shock waves through the engineering department. They remembered the B-17 that had gone into a spin, but that was in thunderstorm turbulence capable of sending even the heaviest airplane out of control. The 307's engine shutdown had been deliberate, and no stall should have occurred, unless . . .

The *unless* meant only one thing: regardless of cost and admission of engineering error, the Stratoliner needed major design changes. By the same token, however, no one in engineering was really surprised that the 307's design had some unanswered questions. Schairer, for example, once pointed out that the Stratoliner was one of the very first four-engine transport planes, and its flight tests were taking it into some uncharted skies. It could not be compared with the B-17 in every respect; the latter was built for different purposes, missions, and flight regimes.

Schairer emphasized that the wind tunnels available to Boeing when the 307 was being designed were too primitive to simulate every emergency condition a new airliner might encounter.

"Sure, it would have been better to see the characteristics of an airplane in a wind tunnel before you go out and risk your neck fussing with the thing," he explained. "But in those days, we had no way of anticipating what trouble an airplane could get into. We had no way to compute it, no way to simulate trouble in a wind tunnel. So all you could do was build the airplane, then go out and fly it. That's what they did that day, and it got out of hand."

The plane had gotten "out of hand" for several reasons that were determined quickly. The ailerons were too small, almost useless in spin recovery. So was the rudder, which provided inadequate stability in an abnormal maneuver. Veterans in engineering must have had a sense of *déjà vu*; the same ailment had afflicted the first Model 80 and 314. Pan Am's Borger, a Boeing critic at times but also a fervent Boeing supporter, never could explain why this flaw persisted until World War II.

"Boeing just had a habit of not putting enough tail on its early transports," Borger said. "It was true of the first B-17, too. But Boeing wasn't the only offender. The DC-2 had the same problem and that's why the DC-3 came out with a dorsal fin that became part of the tail structure."

The addition of a dorsal fin helped solve the Stratoliner's stability problems, too, and was applied to later models of the B-17. Boeing, however, didn't stop with the 307's fin. The rudder was enlarged, and a slotted leading edge was installed on the wings to improve stall characteristics. The irony was that engineers had decided the Stratoliner needed a dorsal fin *before* the fatal test flight.

"The large dorsal had been tested in a wind tunnel before I came to Boeing," Schairer said. "It hadn't been put on the 307 yet but they were ready to."

George Martin's memories of the March 18 tragedy are grim ones; like Mike Pavone, he almost went on the flight.

"We had a meeting the night before, at the Olympic Hotel," Martin recounted. "There were about eleven of us, including an aerodynamicist from KLM. I was there because I had done the stress analysis work on the pressurized fuselage, which had gone along quite well. The KLM engineer was very interested in how an airplane would react with an outboard engine out as the plane slows down. We talked about the plans for the flight the next day; of all the people at the meeting, I was the only one who didn't go along on the ride.

"We recovered a data sheet from the wreckage that had recorded the aircraft's speed. They were at 10,000 feet, which was assumed to be a safe altitude for recovery if anything went wrong. The data sheet showed they kept reducing speed, and that's when it happened. We figured they shut down an outboard, then the plane stalled and the vertical tail let go, followed by a rollover and a spin. The wings failed when they pulled out. I always thought the KLM guy, who was a powerful man and was in the copilot seat, may have tried to help pull the yoke back and yanked too hard."

There is one indisputable conclusion that can be drawn from the accident: it gave the Stratoliner a bad reputation that wrecked its chances to become a dominant force in air transportation.

Its only competition at the time was the larger Douglas DC-4, which was unpressurized and had a poor reputation of its own; the prototype was badly overweight and flew like a truck. U.S. entry into World War II was another major factor in the Stratoliner's competitive failure, but the plane probably was licked even before the war began, and in the postwar era it was too small.

A scary forced landing shortly before TWA put the 307 into service darkened the Stratoliner's black eye. The aircraft was on a proving flight and ran into a violent thunderstorm at 20,000 feet over southeastern Colorado. It was hit by everything in nature's arsenal: ice, sleet, snow, and hail. All four carburetors iced up and the engines quit. TWA

Captain Otis Bryan found himself with more than 21 tons of dead-weight fighting the inexorable law of gravity.

The Stratoliner came out of the overcast at 500 feet, and Bryan headed for the only level terrain in sight: a small plateau with a menacing deep canyon at one end. The aircraft hit the ground with the wheels still down; the impact drove the landing gear back into its well but also jarred loose the doors of the belly baggage compartment, a freak development that saved all 14 occupants, most of them TWA hostesses who had been practicing making up berths. The doors acted as plows, slowing down the skidding plane until it came to a stop only 200 feet short of the canyon rim.

A few days later, Bryan flew the plane off the plateau and it went back to Seattle for repairs. A combined team of Boeing and TWA mechanics had propped up the fuselage with pieces of angle iron, so the wheels could be lowered. Boeing developed a better means of preventing carburetor icing but the incident didn't help the 307's image, even though there was surprisingly little publicity—one Colorado paper ran this headline: HUGE AIRLINER MAKES PRECAUTIONARY LANDING. Offsetting the dearth of general publicity—the plane came down so far from civilization that Bryan took off before any reporter or photographers could reach the site—was the airlines' rumor mill, as effective as a prison grapevine.

The consensus was that the 307's best feature, its ability to fly above the weather, hadn't done much good in this instance. One TWA pilot commented wryly, "All it proved was that with the Stratoliner, we could get high enough to get into the middle of the roughest part of the storm."

Such criticism was unfair; the 307's service ceiling was slightly over 26,000 feet, adequate to escape *most* bad weather, not *every* storm. Thunderheads can be present at much higher altitudes, and not until the jet age were airplanes, aided by radar, truly able to cruise above the weather. Given its limited technology, the 307 did better than any other airliner of its day.

Strangely enough, Howard Hughes asked Boeing to deliver its six Stratoliners without their pressurization systems. No one knew why, unless he was merely trying to save money; Hughes seldom explained his whims. Boeing understandably refused; the Stratoliner already was a lost cause financially and it would have cost too much to remove the pressurization equipment from a completed airplane. It took a threatened lawsuit for Hughes to back off, yet there was no doubt he liked the 307. He even appropriated one of the six TWA had ordered, converting it into his personal airplane with a plushy interior that included divans, well-upholstered armchairs, and a complete kitchen.

Ray Motz, chief clerk in Plant One's hammer shop, was bent over his desk one day and looked up at the sound of someone clearing his throat. In front of Motz stood a slender young man in slacks, a sport shirt, a baseball cap, and sneakers.

Motz figured he might be a new employee, until the visitor inquired how the 307 work was coming along. Motz thought, *God, another damned customer expediter trying to bug me!*

"Keep your shirt on," he grumbled. "I've got a couple of hot B-17 jobs to worry about first."

The young man sat on the edge of Motz's desk for almost a half-hour while Ray went off to handle his priorities. When he returned, he gave the "expediter" a rundown of how the 307 program was progressing.

"Thank you." He smiled and left.

Supervisor Max Estep had watched the little exchange. He walked over to Motz. "Ray, do you know who that was?"

"Yeah. Just another nosy expediter."

Estep laughed. "That, my chief shop clerk, was Howard Hughes!"

The next day, Hughes came through the plant, escorted by Egtvedt. As they passed the clerk's station, Hughes caught Ray's eye, laughed, and waved.

Hughes used his 307 sporadically until after the war, when he sold it to Houston millionaire Glenn McCarthy. Then he bought it back, only to sell it again—this time to a Florida real-estate developer who removed the wings and engines, and turned the fuselage into a powered houseboat.

For a brief 18 months, TWA's five Stratoliners ruled the nation's domestic airways, bettering the DC-3's best transcontinental time by at least two hours. The margin would have been even greater if TWA had operated them at the altitudes at which they were designed to fly: up to slightly above 26,000 feet. The airline generally kept them at only 14,000 feet, a conservative choice that still avoided most bad weather. TWA inaugurated service July 8, 1940, with a LaGuardia–Burbank flight that made intermediate stops at Chicago, Kansas City, and Albuquerque, yet was fast enough to cross the continent in 14 hours and nine minutes. Pan Am based its three Stratoliners in Miami and used them for Latin American service; significantly, Pan Am declined to replace the lost 307 that would have been among the four it ordered.

Pearl Harbor put TWA's five Stratoliners into olive drab and gave them the names of five native American tribes: *Navajo, Apache, Comanche, Cherokee,* and *Zuni.* The Army gutted their interiors, including the pressurization systems, and converted them into combined passenger/cargo planes. Under the banner of the Air Transport Command, they were the first land transports to operate transatlantic service between the United States and the European theater.

All eight Stratoliners resumed brief airline careers after the war. Neither airline restored the pressurization systems, but Boeing installed new B-17G wings, nacelles, and tail surfaces on the TWA planes, and they were operated in this modernized condition until 1951, when all five were sold to a French cargo airline. Pan Am peddled Clippers *Rainbow* and *Comet* to an airline training school, and *Flying Cloud* to a charter air carrier.

The quintet of ex-TWA Stratoliners spent their remaining years flying cargo in some of the world's most remote locations, literally becoming aviation's version of the tramp freighter. Two were seen in Saigon as late as 1966, another in Nigeria, and a fourth in Cambodia, also in the mid-sixties. A former TWA employee spotted a 307 in Kenya, Africa, while he was waiting for a flight from Mombasa to Zanzibar. Curious, he walked over to the battered old plane, still being operated by the French cargo line, and because he spoke French he couldn't help eavesdropping on a conversation between the captain and the copilot. The Stratoliner was having hydraulic problems and the copilot didn't want to take off. The captain just shrugged.

"*C'est la vie!*" he proclaimed, and climbed aboard.

That incident occurred in the mid-sixties, too, and presumably there are no more operational Stratoliners left. The only one known to exist in the United States is Pan Am's former Clipper *Flying Cloud*. It went on display at the Pima Air Museum in Tucson, Arizona, where it rested under the desert sun, a weather-beaten monument to aviation's most underrated airliner.

Johnny Guy, a retired TWA mechanic and aircraft inspector and a lifelong admirer of the 307, summed it up best: "In many ways, it wasn't just an airplane," he philosophized. "It was an epic."

It also was the last commercial transport Boeing was to build for a long time—for onto the stage of history marched the two bombers that would help win World War II.

FIVE

THE WAR YEARS—
TRAGEDY AND TRIUMPH

VOLUMES HAVE BEEN WRITTEN ON THE EXPLOITS OF THE B-17 and B-29 during World War II. This being a corporate, not a military, history, it is not disparaging to either of these two winged legends if those exploits are summed up in one significant paragraph:

According to official records, although B-17s and B-29s comprised only 17 percent of all U.S. bombers during the war, they dropped 46 percent of the bombs that destroyed German war production, and 99 percent of those that wreaked havoc on Japan. In the European theater alone, 67 percent of enemy fighters shot down were the victims of Flying Fortress guns.

The larger, longer-legged B-29 never won the affection and respect accorded the B-17 by the men who flew and fought in these planes. Yet Curtis LeMay himself, who commanded the 20th Air Force in the Pacific theater, always wished the B-29 could have been used in Europe.

"Had the B-29s been available three years earlier and earmarked for use against Germany," he once wrote, "the job could have been accomplished much more quickly. We wouldn't have needed all the range capability of the B-29 and so we could have flown on missions with heavier bomb loads."

The price paid by the B-17s and their crews was heavy. A third of the Forts that flew into combat were either shot down, ditched, or damaged beyond repair; the casualty rate of B-17 crews was exceeded only by that of the U.S. submarine service. Still, the B-17 could absorb unbelievable punishment: one came home with more than a thousand bullet holes in its hide, and another landed safely with the entire tail section hanging by a few thin strips of metal. Such stories of survival were to be repeated countless times, and even today—almost a half-century after the shooting stopped—the surest way to start an argument is to have some former B-24 pilot tell an old B-17 jockey that the Liberator was a better airplane than the Flying Fortress.

The B-24 had its vociferous defenders, who pointed out that the Liberator was faster and carried a heavier bomb load. The rebuttal to that argument came from Don Sachs, an ex–B-17 copilot, who after the war spent many years as an engineering supervisor in various Boeing military airplane programs.

"Those who flew B-24s loved the airplane," he said. "Those who flew the B-17 loved *that* airplane. But ask a pilot who had flown both airplanes, and the Boeing was the overwhelming choice."

When Boeing celebrated the B-17's 50th anniversary in 1985, Sachs was in charge of the celebration. He was hoping for around 2,000 attendees, most of them former Fort crews and their wives. An estimated 12,000 people showed up and there may have been as many as 14,000—eventually, they stopped counting heads. Three still-flyable B-17s were the feature attraction, and chances were drawn for rides. But an ex-aircraft commander approached Sachs for a favor.

"I'd appreciate it if you'd arrange for my old flight engineer to go on one of the flights," he said.

"Sure—and you can go with him," Sachs promised.

After the flight, the former pilot told Sachs, "Don, you don't know what that meant to him. He's dying of cancer."

Curtis LeMay was watching when the three Forts did a flyby over Boeing Field. Tears in his eyes, he turned to Sachs and murmured, "Don, this is one of the most exciting things that ever happened to me."

And Sachs, although in love with the B-17 himself, was surprised at the intense emotion displayed throughout the festivities.

"A lot of them hadn't seen each other since the war. Boeing did the whole affair with class. The company had artists paint a series of B-17 oils depicting the plane's historical highlights, and the originals were on display in a big tent. One guy kept staring at a painting and finally turned away, his eyes streaming with tears. It depicted his own crew on their last mission. And when I talk about class, it wasn't just those paintings. We had five Medal of Honor winners there as the company's guests—they had earned the award on B-17 missions. There was a hangar dance on the last night of the show and Tex Behneke's band with singer Kay Starr supplied the music. When they played the Air Corps song, there wasn't a dry eye in the place."

There are nine B-17s still flying today, but it is much harder to find a flyable B-29; the only known one is owned by the Confederate Air Force in Texas, which uses the restored Superfortress in its air shows.

It must be admitted, however, that most of the sentimental and nostalgic affection heaped on the B-17 was directed toward the later, vastly improved models. The B-17 was Ed Wells' baby, and one of his outstanding qualities was a total lack of engineering ego; he was not one to insist he knew more than the men flying the airplane. Wells studied every report from combat crews, especially the critical ones, and by the time the war ended the final B-17G series was a far better warplane than any preceding Fort.

The first B-17s that flew into combat were armed with 30-caliber guns, "not much more lethal than Daisy's best rifle," went one harsh critique. By the time the B-17E went into production, it carried 50-calibers. Twin power-driven turrets were installed on the top fuselage and under the belly. A Schairer-designed dorsal fin was added, the fuselage was stretched six feet, and the horizontal tail surfaces were enlarged. The superior G model had strategically placed armor and a chin turret just under the nose, to counter the German tactic of striking head-on.

It is interesting to note that when the Soviet Union was offered North American B-25s and Martin B-26 medium bombers, the Russians declined and said the only American bomber they were interested in was the B-17. They were turned down, but they did get their hands on a B-29 that had been forced down in Soviet territory; the crew was interned for the rest of the war and the airplane confiscated. Several years later, a postwar Soviet Air Force bomber was virtually a carbon copy of the Superfort.

The B-17 was the airplane that wrote the book on strategic bombing, always daytime missions—the British considered the concept suicidal—because they pinpointed specific targets and bombed more accurately than the Royal Air Force's devastating nighttime area attacks. Historians credit the B-17 for proving that strategic bombing was a potent, even decisive weapon against a heavily industrialized enemy—which simply makes another historical fact incredible: Boeing was almost forced to abandon the entire B-17 program a year before Nazi Germany marched into Poland.

It was the last major crisis Claire Egtvedt was to face as Boeing's president, and it stemmed from the price tag Boeing had placed on the original B-17 contract. The company had confidently expected to win the bomber competition, which would have meant an order for more than 200 planes. Boeing accordingly had set the price at $205,000 per aircraft, a profitable figure only if the B-17 was bought in large quantity; Boeing stood to lose its corporate shirt on a disappointing order for only 52 airplanes.

Despite a strong preference for the B-17 within the Air Corps, there were some high-ranking officers who insisted $205,000 was too much to pay for a military airplane—after all, the Air Corps could buy a couple of twin-engine bombers or four fighters for that amount, and the economy-minded War Department agreed.

Late in the fall of 1939, Jim Murray, head of Boeing's Washington office, was informed that a tentative contract for 38 B-17Cs on order would have to be renegotiated if it was to meet Army funding under the 1939–1940 budget. The timing couldn't have been worse; this shocker came on the heels of other bad news: Air Corps chief of staff General Oscar Westover, a strong B-17 advocate, had been killed in a plane crash. His replacement was another heavy bomber supporter, General H. H. "Hap" Arnold, but Arnold had been handed an assistant, General George H. Brett, who was determined to cut the B-17's price.

There was a change in command in Seattle, too. Claire Egtvedt moved up to board chairman and Phil Johnson returned from Canada to replace him as president. The now-balding Johnson had hardly warmed up the presidential seat when Murray handed him the renegotiation problem. Murray had met with Brett, who told him bluntly that the Air Corps wouldn't pay more than $198,000 for a B-17, either for the planes already on order or any future ones. When Murray pointed out that Boeing was already losing money on the $205,000 price, Brett ordered him out of his office.

Murray called Johnson. "Stick to the two hundred and five thousand," the new president said firmly. Johnson had no other choice but to play hardball; in the first nine months of 1939, Boeing had lost $2.6 million. The only orders on its books were for the 38 unfinished B-17s, six remaining flying boats for Pan Am, and 255 Kaydet primary trainers being built at the Stearman plant in Wichita.

Murray got sympathy but not much help from Hap Arnold. The best Arnold could do was take him in to see Assistant Secretary of War Louis Johnson, who offered to up the $198,000 ceiling by a thousand dollars.

"That's not good enough," Murray protested. "We can't afford to stay in business if we sell an airplane for less than it costs to build."

Johnson's shouted answer was directed at the unhappy Arnold. "Take this man out of here and don't bring him back until he can talk our language!"

In truth, neither Johnson nor the Air Corps was entirely responsible for what came close to being a dangerously shortsighted decision. Even though President Roosevelt had just declared a national emergency, the congressional view of what constituted a national emergency differed radically from that of the White House. The $199,000 maximum price was all the Army thought it could afford for an airplane that so many isolationist lawmakers regarded as an "aggressive" weapon, and Congress controlled the military purse strings.

The impasse continued well into the spring of 1940, a period in which the Army tentatively exercised an option for a few more bombers, this time B-17Ds; based on unfavorable combat reports on the performance of the B-17s that had been turned over to the Royal Air Force, Ed Wells was still incorporating design changes. But even for this improved model, the War Department held fast to its $199,000 limit. And at this stage, Johnson was ready to scrub the whole B-17 program as an unacceptable drain on the company's already-strained finances.

There was an easy way out, but Johnson refused to take it. Some aircraft manufacturers had accepted money-losing contracts, then made them profitable by charging extra for any design changes. When Murray mentioned this tactic as a possible solution, Johnson flatly refused.

"We won't do anything that won't stand the light of investigation," he declared, "and we don't want to take business at a loss." He had been away from Boeing for five years, yet he had never forgotten the standard of integrity that William Boeing had imposed on the company bearing his name—nothing was worth soiling that name. Murray wasn't surprised at Johnson's decision, either; years later he revealed that Boeing had a chance to sell three Model 314s to Japan and cancelled the deal at FDR's request, even though the company needed every sale it could make.

Four developments were to save Boeing and the heavy bombardment program itself. The first was an unexpected helping hand from rival Douglas. France was negotiating with the Santa Monica firm for 240 twin-engine attack bombers, plus another 140 for the Air Corps, an order too large for Douglas to handle alone considering the urgent need for the plane. At first Donald Douglas wanted to invite both Boeing and Consolidated to share in the contract, then decided he wanted only Boeing. Boeing's share of the order totaled 250 planes and when France fell, Britain assumed the French contractual obligation. It was enough to give Boeing some margin with which to haggle further with the War Department. Additional margin was provided by a $5.5 million loan Johnson obtained from the Reconstruction Finance Corporation and the sale of newly issued stock.

And the fourth development was just some old-fashioned bazaar-type bargaining. It occurred at a meeting Murray and Wellwood Beall had with Air Corps contract officials, including General Carl "Tooey" Spaatz who considered the B-17 essential. He warned the Boeing representatives that the future of heavy bombardment was at stake, and asked if there was any possible way to get the price down to that mandatory $199,000.

Beall at first said $205,000 was the rock-bottom figure and had been kept at that level only because of the Douglas contract. Then Spaatz had an idea.

"What can you take off the B-17 that would lower the price?" he asked.

Beall left the meeting to call Seattle—it is not recorded exactly to whom he talked, but it probably was Ed Wells—and came back with a proposition: if the Air Corps would accept the B-17D without electrically controlled cowling flaps, external bomb racks, and a few minor features, Boeing could knock the price down to $202,500. Spaatz raced down the hall to Arnold's office and returned with the chief of staff's approval. With that $2,500 price cut, the heavy bombardment program had been saved.

It was a victory whose significance was lost on one of America's future enemies. When FDR announced that the United States was gearing up to build 50,000 warplanes, Hermann Göring laughed and told Hitler it was empty propaganda—after all, even Lindbergh had called the figure "hysterical chatter."

It turned out that everyone was wrong about 50,000 airplanes. As of the day Japan surrendered, the U.S. aircraft industry had produced more than 137,000 combat aircraft, a figure that did not include thousands of trainers and hundreds of experimental planes, some of which planted the seeds for future American military aviation. Boeing alone built 7,000 B-17s (Douglas and Lockheed contributed another 5,000), and more than 2,700 B-29s. To that total were added 380 Douglas attack bombers, 8,428 Wichita-made Kaydet trainers, and 750 troop-carrying gliders; out of Boeing of Canada's plant came 362 patrol flying boats and 17 Blackburn torpedo bombers.

At the peak of production, Boeing was rolling out as many as 363 B-17s a month—averaging between 14 and 16 Forts a day, the most incredible production rate for large aircraft in aviation history. Yet this was a complex, difficult airplane to build, and the B-29 even more so. The latter, in fact, went from an Air Corps "data request" (general specifications for the design) to a fully operational bomber in only four years, a pace unequaled for any four-engine aircraft, military or civil, during the war and since.

A whole platoon of future vice presidents and key managers came to work for Boeing in the immediate prewar years; most of them started out as junior engineers and accountants, in tooling or on the assembly line. Names like Maynard Pennell, Tex Boullioun, Wally Buckley, Frank Verginia, Don Whitford, Jack Steiner, Howard Stuverude, George Nible, Bob Withington, Ben Wheat, Clyde Skeen, Bayne Lamb, Ken Luplow, Bob Dickson, Sof Torget, Dick Nelson, Russell Light, Sterling Sessions, and Bob Tharrington.

The most experienced engineer among them was Pennell, who had done stress analysis work on the DC-3 and was hired away from Douglas in 1940. It was something of a culture shock for the tall, soft-spoken newcomer; Douglas, although it built military airplanes, was known far better for commercial planes; its only large bomber, the B-18, was a DC-3 derivative. Boeing, Pennell found, reversed the process: its transports were derived principally from military aircraft, especially in the critical area of wing design.

"It wasn't the best idea because you didn't get the optimum commercial design out of the practice," Pennell said, "but it made it possible for Boeing to rise."

Eventually, Pennell would come close to Ed Wells' stature in the aeronautical engineering world. But in 1940 he was just another promising young engineer. The man contemporaries credit for Boeing's amazing wartime output was not an engineer, but a manufacturing specialist named H. Oliver West. Half-crippled with arthritis, he could hardly negotiate even the smallest flight of stairs and got around the sprawling factories in a tiny Fiat car; workers had to clear the aisles for him when he showed up to inspect a plant. He had started with Boeing in the days of the Model 40, and it was said that until aircraft became more complicated, West could recite by heart the numbers of every part that went into an airplane.

He was especially close to Phil Johnson, whom West had worked for at United Air Lines. West headed maintenance at United, and Johnson brought him back to Seattle as his special assistant in charge of production, for the art of creating efficient assembly lines was West's true love. They formed an unusual team; Johnson, an engineer by training, respected his own profession yet always recognized that the best-designed airplane in the world isn't worth much unless it's built right. Football provides the best analogy: the engineers are the glamorous backs; the production men are in the pits, creating the holes through which the backs run.

West was equally adept at spotting production talent—line and tooling workers and supervisors like Bud Hurst, Frank Canney, Harry Salvage, Charlie Williams, and Leo Castle. Castle was West's alter ego; if West suggested, "There should be a better and faster way to attach wings," Castle usually was the one who thought up the better and faster way. And Hurst, in turn, often became the man who put the new method into operation.

In a relatively short time, Boeing went from a company in which building 35 airplanes was a year's work to one that could turn out the same number in less than three days. One of Boeing's smartest moves was to raid the automobile industry for people who could design tools for the bigger presses and stamping machines needed for mass production of large aircraft. As vice president of operations (Boeing's term for manufacturing), West ordered a drastic shift from limited to high-production tooling, and that meant reducing the amount of hammer forming, welding, and lathe spinning that had gone into the manufacturing of a tool. The old ways invited human carelessness and mistakes, and the answer was to recruit men from General Motors, Ford, and Detroit technical schools who had been weaned on tooling for mass production.

Another improvement was a gradual shift from steel tools to aluminum, the logic being that it made sense to form aluminum parts with the same metal, thus assuring uniformity. Better utilization of labor was another major achievement. Hurst recalled that at one time 6,000 people were working on the B-17 wing line when the word came down that production was going up to eight planes a day. "And," West told him, "not only are you going to do eight a day, you're going to do it with three thousand fewer people."

"That was a shocker," Hurst admitted. "So I hid a bunch of them. I sent some upstairs to the offices and I put some in other shops. I also had what I called 'the cabbage patch'—if I needed extra people, I could draw them right out of the cabbage patch."

Hurst never did feel he circumvented West's orders just to protect his people; as he was to prove later, he was a superb production man and he merely juggled his manpower around until improved manufacturing methods enabled his crew to do more with fewer hands. The bigger jigs and presses were one aid. Bob Dickson, one of Hurst's smarter young men, worked out a system by which the B-17's navigator's floor and the adjoining bombardier's floor were assembled in one piece, so the whole structure could be lifted into the airplane. Rookie engineer Sof Torget invented a sling for lifting B-17 wings into position for fuselage joining, and wound up designing slings, dollies, and stands for other large components.

In the end, the wing shop alone was cut from 6,000 workers down to about 300 per shift, and the overall production rate at one stage was sending a completed B-17 out of the plant every 49 minutes!

Boeing secured a number of presidential deferments for key engineers and supervisors during the war, including unmarried men considered essential for airplane production. The deferments were renewed every six months and seldom was a deferment request turned down.

The accepted policy for draft-eligible employees was to wait until the draft notice arrived before committing to military service. It made sense, for a skilled aircraft worker was valuable to the war effort. Boeing supervisors were as patriotic as anyone else, but they hated to lose experienced men and they frowned on voluntary enlistments.

George Nible, destined to become one of Boeing's most colorful characters, was on Hurst's wing line installing fuel tanks in the early days of the war. His best friend was Dale Cross, a riveter, who came in one day carrying his draft notice.

"No infantry for me," he announced. "George, we're joining the Navy."

Nible was seized with a terminal case of patriotism and informed supervisor Roger Spur, "Roger, I'm quitting to take my Navy physical."

"You can't quit," Spur told him. "Wait till you're drafted, stupid!"

Nible disagreed, a little too vehemently.

"Okay, Nible," Spur finally snapped. "But your dismissal papers are gonna be marked 'not eligible for rehiring'—you'll never work for Boeing again."

Nible and Cross took their physicals together; Nible finished first and, having passed, waited for Cross to emerge. When Dale showed up, Nible said proudly, "Well, Dale, we're in the Navy."

"*You* may be," Cross sighed, "but I flunked."

As hundreds of men began leaving for the armed forces, "Rosie the Riveter" became part of America's wartime legends. By 1944 almost half of Boeing's total work force was female, a percentage that applied to production personnel as well as clerical. The only men in the wire bundle shops in Plant Two, for example, were supervisors. Women worked as expediters, inspectors, and even security guards; despite the catchy phrase, not all Rosies were riveters.

These women forged some unforgettable memories, many of them poignant. One thrice-married woman lost all three husbands in the war; with each receipt of the dreaded The-War-Department-regrets-to-inform-you telegram, she insisted on coming back to work the next day, quietly acknowledged expressions of sympathy from fellow workers, and wielded her rivet gun as if it were an avenging weapon.

Sterling Sessions, another future vice president who started at the bottom of the ladder—his first job was running a vacuum cleaner over Plant One floors—always remembered one Rosie in particular. "She was my helper on B-17 spars in Plant One," he said. "I got some debris in my eyes, and I was in agony. She was a big woman, built like a linebacker, while I weighed about a hundred and ten pounds soaking wet. She picked me up in her arms and carried me to the infirmary."

A handful of Rosies turned out to be prostitutes from an Alaskan red-light district. When the Army closed down the brothels, the women migrated to Seattle for presumably more honorable employment. Unfortunately, old habits die hard; the air raid shelters at Plant Two became their second work place during the night shifts, and they had a lucrative moonlighting business going until someone blew the whistle and fired them.

Yet it was difficult to keep nature from taking its course. Couples always managed to find privacy; company parking lots were an obvious if sometimes risky choice, and so were the Plant Two tunnels in the wee hours of the third shift. Occasionally, the search for privacy bordered on the ingenious. The B-29's bomb bay was unpressurized, so the crew had to crawl through a long tube to reach the plane's aft section. During production, the tubes were piled in a 10-high stack until it was time to install them in the fuselage. The triangular stack was held together by a wooden wedge.

One night during the third shift, an amorous couple crawled into one of the stacked tubes. Things were progressing nicely until someone—whether deliberately or innocently—removed the wedge. Down tumbled the entire stack. Eyewitnesses said the tryst tube rolled at least 75 feet before the couple was able to crawl out.

Removing that wedge would have been just the kind of mischief expected from Bud Hurst, who was something of a practical joker. He wasn't responsible for the tube incident, but he admitted culpability for quite a few others.

A big mountain beaver wandered into Plant Two and Hurst killed it before the animal could cause any damage. Instead of disposing of it, however, he sneaked the carcass into supervisor Bill Collins' office. Hurst placed the dead beaver into a box Collins kept under his desk; it held important paperwork and Hurst knew Collins used it frequently.

He put a toothpick into the beaver's mouth, propping the jaw open so it showed teeth that would have done justice to a saber-toothed tiger. Hurst then alerted the rest of the shift to await future developments.

They didn't have long to wait. Collins returned to his office and shot out of it a few second later, screaming like Fay Wray the first time she saw King Kong.

Admittedly, the wartime work force didn't have to face bullets and shells, but life on the home front wasn't exactly normal. On-the-job injuries were not infrequent; the drop hammer shop in Plant Two was an especially hazardous place in which to work. Paul Phipps, a 42-year Boeing veteran, spent only a year there and still carried scars after he retired: one on his chin, a second on his head, and a smashed big toe that never healed.

"The hammer shop," he said, "was an accident waiting for you. The vibrations were so bad that they kept moving the jigs in final assembly—they had to move the hammers to another location."

The peacetime security force before 1939 included janitor Johnny Zipp who stood in front of the Plant One entrance each morning and checked the arrivals. No one had ID badges with photos then, and Zipp knew practically every face. After Pearl Harbor, Army troops supplemented Boeing's own security guards, and badges became a way of life.

West Coast aircraft factories were considered prime targets for air raids. They never materialized but the precautions taken were impressive; the most unusual was the ingenious camouflage installed over Plant Two. Designed by Army engineers, an entire neighborhood was erected over the plant rooftops, complete with streets, houses, trees, and automobiles. The homes were made of canvas, trees and shrubbery were fashioned out of chicken wire covered with painted feathers and spun glass, and the streets were nothing but canvas under oil and dirt. Two homes, however, were real—they housed hidden anti-aircraft guns.

The illusion was impressive; from the air, an enemy pilot would have seen a typical small town incapable of producing anything larger than children, and the fact that no enemy pilot ever showed up didn't detract from the amazing deception. Nevertheless, there were a number of false alarms that sent air-raid sirens screaming and all workers into the bomb shelters Boeing had built in the parking lots.

Bayne Lamb, who spent his entire career in facilities, helped build the shelters, along with guard and sentry gates; East Marginal Way (the street on which corporate headquarters still is located) was blocked off at both ends. The headlights on employee cars had to be taped over for night driving, the only illumination coming from slits cut into the tape.

Lamb hired a number of new people from Midwest farms, not realizing the extent of their unsophistication. The first time an air-raid alert sounded, they dutifully evacuated the premises and headed for the bomb shelters as instructed. When the all-clear sounded, half of them went home.

Boeing's wartime recruiters occasionally resorted to desperation measures—such as straying slightly from the truth. Engineering schools were a favorite hunting ground, and it didn't make much difference whether the youngster being courted had graduated yet. A Boeing interviewer zeroed in on a young engineering student at the University of Washington named Frank Verginia, who was offered part-time employment in his junior year.

"What would I be doing?" Verginia inquired innocently. "I'm majoring in structural engineering."

"And that's exactly what you'll be doing," the interviewer assured him. "We've got a great job for you in structural testing."

Convinced, Verginia signed up. His "structural testing" position turned out to be in a department called Receiving Inspection. Two days after reporting to work, he was trying unsuccessfully to clean kerosene and iron filings from his hands and fingernails, the result of inspecting drag links on B-17 landing gears.

His almost daily requests for transfer to engineering were rejected, so he finally took matters into his own hands. He carried samples of his college work over to the administration building and was hired as an engineer, but he neglected to officially inform the boys in Receiving Inspection where they could deposit his old job. For a month, Verginia achieved the dubious honor of being the only Boeing employee listed on the payrolls of two separate departments; the status ended when his former boss sent someone around to his house, inquiring why he hadn't shown up for work the past 30 days.

No matter in which department one worked during the war, the hours were long. B-17 and B-29 production required three shifts a day, seven days a week; neither Thanksgiving nor Christmas was observed as a time-off holiday, and most employees put in at least a 10-hour day. Hourly pay started at 62.5 cents an hour, lower than local shipyard wages and what many defense workers in the Midwestern and Eastern war plants were receiving—a source of labor-management friction at Boeing throughout the war. The new IAM local didn't have much bargaining power; wartime strikes got about as much public sympathy and support as a flu epidemic.

Puget Sound's social event of the war was a Boeing-written, Boeing-produced musical review: "Flying High." It played to full audiences for a week at Seattle's Metropolitan Theater, proceeds going to the Air Force Aid Society. The cast was composed primarily of Boeing employees who rehearsed on their own time; the production featured 30 original songs. Many of the professionals associated with the show were Boeing employees, too; typical was dance director Judd McCoy, who had been either a performer or stage director since he was 11 years old—he worked as an electrician on the B-17s and B-29s.

The home front needed such diversions; there wasn't much else to do except build airplanes, and build them they did. It became obvious in the early days of the war that Boeing's Seattle facilities were going to be inadequate, even with Plant Two's expansion. A major addition already had been acquired in neighboring Renton, where new high bays were constructed in a Navy-owned factory that eventually became available for B-29 production. The Navy originally had built it to handle the construction of 57 new Boeing PBB-1 Sea Ranger patrol bombers.

The Renton factory was erected on a 95-acre site on the south shore of Lake Washington—a facility created out of swampland and river channels drained of silt and water. But only one Sea Ranger was built— naturally, it was nicknamed "Lone Ranger"—for the Navy cancelled the contract for the remaining 56. The PBB-1 was a large twin-engine plane incorporating many of the 314's better design features. It was an excellent airplane and met the Navy's specifications for a long-range patrol bomber that was supposed to replace the reliable but smaller and shorter-ranged Consolidated PBY Catalina.

After cancellation, the Navy willingly turned over the Renton plant to the Air Corps, and following the war Boeing bought it outright. It became an ideal facility for production of the bomber that, like Model 299 before it, personified both triumph and tragedy.

Curtis LeMay, the man who made the B-29 famous, always felt that the man most responsible for the bomber was General Hap Arnold. It is hard to argue with that conclusion; the B-29 probably would have been built eventually even without Arnold's input, but Henry Harley Arnold hastened its creation with a faith that bordered on fanatical conviction—that to achieve the full capability of strategic bombardment, an airplane bigger, faster, and longer-ranged than the B-17 was needed.

As far back as 1939, Arnold had appointed a special staff to draw up specifications for such a bomber; coincidentally, this was about the same time Boeing engineers were doing a similar study—it was one of Claire Egtvedt's last orders before Phil Johnson took command. After Germany marched into Poland, Ed Wells and his staff were ready with a new bomber design even as Arnold won War Department authorization for issuing Air Corps Data Request R-40B, a document requisition proposal for a giant bomber with a range of more than 5,000 miles.

The key element in the design of the plane that would become the Superfortress was its wing, which combined a new Schairer-created airfoil with enormous strength; the wing that eventually went on the B-29 could support nearly twice the weight per square foot of wing area as the B-17. In its final configuration, Schairer's wing was only nine times greater in area than that of a Piper Cub, but could carry 90 times more weight. R-40B's specifications, as far as Wells was concerned, could have been written by Boeing itself.

With Arnold's prodding, the Air Corps ordered two XB-29 prototypes, a contract signed just as the Luftwaffe began blitzing England. Models of the new bomber were tested in Boeing's new wind tunnel, designed mainly by crusty little Bill Cook and Bob Withington, an assistant Cook had hired out of MIT. Arnold came out to Seattle, inspected a mockup of the bomber, looked at the wind tunnel performance data, and proceeded to take the biggest gamble of his illustrious career: he ordered that full production begin on a minimum of 250 B-29s—*a year and four months before the first prototype even flew!*

Arnold wasn't the only airman to be a B-29 believer. General Oliver Echols, red-haired chief of the Material Command and the Air Corps' top procurement officer, was a key figure in the decision and subsequent program, and so was Colonel Don Putt, who had been one of the survivors of the 299 crash, muttering as they took him out of the wreckage, "Don't blame the airplane." He was to become the B-29's project engineering officer. But the man with the most clout was Arnold—people like Echols and Putt took their marching orders as well as their enthusiasm from Hap.

Never in the history of U.S. military aviation had a combat aircraft been ordered in such large quantity without competitive flight tests— or *any* tests, for that matter. The contract was signed May 17, 1941, and Eddie Allen made the first XB-29 flight September 21, 1942, a time span that is testimony to Hap Arnold's faith in the airplane, the largest aircraft to see combat in World War II.

When the B-29 went into production, it incorporated a feature Boeing's engineers picked up from that Heinkel 111 bomber referred to previously. They got a look at its interior construction and found that Heinkel had reduced the number of rivets needed, by spot welding the ribs and skin; the only rivets used were at the skin joints. Boeing adopted this method for the Superfort, saving considerable weight and facilitating assembly. "It all went together like a Tinker Toy," Bob Dickson said.

The pressure to build the B-29 was so great that often there wasn't time to fix drawings after an engineering change was needed. "I saw engineers make sketches on the cuffs of their shirt sleeves," Dickson recounted, "and then they'd give the shirt to someone else to copy."

Changes, of course, were anathema to the manufacturing side, where patience was not only a virtue but a necessity. Not a few production supervisors and foremen envied a quality control inspector named Bill Hedberg, whose deafness required a hearing aid. When he talked to anyone—subordinate or superior made no difference—he'd turn up the hearing aid. But if the person talked back, Hedberg would turn off the device and the man would be talking to the wall.

The dimensions of the pressurized crawl tube that went from the cockpit to the tail were determined in an unusual fashion. Ed Wells asked the portly Wellwood Beall to crawl through mockups of varying sizes.

"If Beall can get through, anybody can," Wells is said to have commented, and the smallest tube through which Beall could navigate without getting stuck actually ended up as the final width and height.

Figuring out the size of that tube was a minor problem compared with some of the other technical headaches encountered. First and foremost was the powerful but untried Wright R-3350 engine, which had enough bugs to satisfy a convention of entomologists, and they were to plague B-29 crews throughout the war—there simply wasn't enough time to cure all the engine's ailments. Wells used to say that the ideal way to design an airplane was to find a good engine first, then build the airplane around it, but he also would admit rather wistfully that it was seldom if ever done that way.

Aircraft engine technology often has lagged behind airframe technology almost since the Wright brothers; the B-29 and its original Wrights were just one more example. Bob Robbins, a Boeing test pilot of that era, remembered that one of the two XB-29 prototypes had 16 engine changes and 22 carburetor changes in only 27 hours of test flight. Eddie Allen liked the plane's flying qualities but the engines gave everyone fits.

Allen began complaining that the epidemic of various malfunctions prevented him from compiling sufficient test data and had put the entire B-29 program behind schedule. In the first five months of the test phase, the prototypes completed a total of less than 35 logged hours in the air; at that stage the plane should have flown at least 200 hours.

On February 17, 1943, Allen landed after one more test flight had been cut short by engine failure. As he stepped from the plane, fuming and worried, he remarked to flight engineer Don Whitworth, "I don't know if we should continue flying or not." Robbins said Allen was a razor's edge away from recommending to Wells that the prototypes be grounded until the engine problems were cured; he needed those 200 hours of test flight data before he could honestly pronounce the B-29 ready for full production.

Apparently he had second thoughts that night. There were some 1,600 B-29s on order at that point, and enough parts were on hand to start production on nearly half of them. Four planes actually had started down the assembly line. He must have reasoned that despite his very real concerns, the B-29 still was a potentially fine airplane badly needed in the Pacific.

The next day, a Thursday, he went ahead with another scheduled test flight.

It was to be his last.

Edmund Turney Allen was an unusual test pilot—and an even more unusual man.

Not by any stretch of the imagination did he meet Hollywood's image of a dashing, romantic airman; Central Casting more likely would have handed him the role of a rather mousy accountant or bookkeeper. Allen was short, well on his way to total baldness, and wore a mustache that would have looked more at home on someone like Clark Gable.

In those times, Eddie was considered a bit flaky. He was a vegetarian, practiced yoga, studied Egyptology, and his favorite reading matter was poetry. But as a test pilot, his peers could be counted on the fingers of one hand. Honesty was an inbred trait; if something was wrong with an airplane, Allen wasn't afraid to bruise the ego of any thin-skinned engineer—Ed Wells more than anyone else appreciated the fact that Allen was as much scientist as pilot.

Bob Robbins was one of Allen's test flight "students." He went up with Eddie one day in a B-17C to check rudder hinge movements under various gear angles and power conditions.

"He taught me the techniques of slowly working up into more and more potentially severe flight conditions," Robbins said, "taking everything small step by small step, so you wouldn't get into serious trouble. What impressed me the most was his modesty. He never really talked about himself or blew his own horn."

Allen's reputation was such that when he was a free-lance test pilot, before joining Boeing permanently, insurance companies actually gave lower premiums to a manufacturer when Eddie was testing. He could be brutally frank. He summed up the first flight of the XB-29 with what may have been intended sarcasm. "It flies," he said laconically, although those who heard the remark apparently thought he was praising the airplane. What he really meant is open to speculation, but sarcasm is just as likely as praise.

Like all test pilots, he might skirt the truth slightly for public consumption, with something like, "For a new airplane, it has excellent flying qualities." To the engineers, however, the translation would be, "Your bird flies like a damned penguin." Honest test pilots are an enormous asset and necessity to an airplane manufacturer, and Eddie

Allen established that tradition for all the Boeing test pilots who followed him.

On the last day of his life, he saved someone else's. Mike Pavone was supposed to board the second XB-29 prototype as a flight engineer. When Mike arrived on the flight line, Allen shook his head.

"Sorry, Mike," he said, "but we're short one parachute. I'm afraid you can't go."

Pavone offered to find an extra chute but Allen was a stickler for keeping to a schedule. Disappointed, Mike watched the great silver bomber take off shortly before eleven A.M. Approximately 20 minutes later, Allen radioed Boeing Field they had an engine fire, but that he had it under control and was returning to the field. At 12:21, however, Allen reported the number one engine was still on fire, and asked that crash equipment stand by.

Yet he also assured the tower, "Trouble not serious."

Three tense minutes went by. Wellwood Beall, Ed Wells, and Oliver West were in the boardroom for their regular meeting on B-17 production when Wells answered the ringing of a telephone in an adjoining room. He returned, his face sheet-white, and told the others what was happening. All three rushed to Boeing Field.

The XB-29 was over Lake Washington at 1,500 feet when the control tower heard someone in the cockpit shout, "Allen, better get this thing down in a hurry—the wing spar's burning badly!" From the calmness in Allen's response, he might have just heard a weather report. He informed the tower, in his last communication, "Have fire equipment ready. Am coming in with a wing on fire."

Two of the 11 Boeing technicians aboard jumped, but by this time the flaming aircraft was too low. Neither chute opened; one man fell into a major power line and knocked out all power in south Seattle. The XB-29, with flames already having consumed most of the left wing and by now biting into the fuselage, fell onto the roof of the Frye meat-packing plant on Seattle's south side and set the building ablaze. The plane's occupants and 19 Frye employees were killed along with five firemen; the toll would have been far worse if most of the plant's work force hadn't been on their lunch hour.

Sabotage, with no evidence to support it, was an immediate theory and the FBI entered the investigation. All the Seattle papers could report was that an experimental plane had crashed; the B-29's existence still was top secret. A bus driver had snapped pictures of the plane as it swept toward the packing plant and innocently submitted them to the City Transit Weekly, the bus company's employee newspaper. The FBI confiscated all copies before they could be distributed.

The entire company was devastated; grief affected every department. Every victim on the plane had many friends, which made the tragedy even more personalized. Young Sterling Sessions, for example, was told not to come back to work for three days—one of the men who had bailed out had once been his roommate. Even years later, Sessions could not forget the crash. "I still think if Allen could have brought that plane in from the south instead of the north," he insisted, "they would have made it."

The most demoralized group was Boeing's flight test department. Al Reed was supposed to succeed Allen, but when he insisted that like Allen he run the aerodynamics department as well as flight test, Wellwood Beall refused and appointed George Schairer as chief aerodynamicist. Reed resigned, which for a brief time left Boeing with no one to fly the remaining XB-29; Allen and Reed were the only pilots who had ever flown the prototypes. N. D. Showalter was named chief of flight test and quiet and capable though he was, no one envied him for the size of the shoes he was trying to fill.

Bob Robbins, who had worshipped Allen, was so unhappy that he considered quitting. "I can remember thinking that maybe I should get out of this organization before it falls apart," he said. "Then I got to thinking that no, Boeing's a pretty big company so I'll hang around and watch how a big company falls apart."

It didn't fall apart. Numerous changes went into the B-29, including better firewall protection and a major redesign of the engine superchargers. Most engine fires had been traced to their overheating, although a fire in the number-one XB-29 prototype a year later indicated that a more likely culprit was the carburetor induction system, a flaw that wasn't corrected until Wright switched to fuel injection toward the end of the war. All this was too late for Eddie Allen and the people who had died with him, but the basic faith he had in the airplane was to be vindicated.

The wartime log books of Boeing flight test engineer Bob Swiler show that of the 750 B-29s that his crew tested before delivering them to the Air Corps—each for two and a half hours including three takeoffs and landings—less than five percent required a delivery delay of more than two days. Considering the peak B-29 production pace of four aircraft a day, such assembly line quality was a remarkable achievement and so was the elimination of most B-29 flaws.

Allen received two posthumous honors. The first was the 1943 Guggenheim Medal; the award, presented to his widow by Phil Johnson, cited in particular his contributions to "the development of scientific and systematic methods in the flight testing of aircraft for basic design and performance data."

Johnson also announced the second honor: Boeing's new wind tunnel and flight laboratory facility would carry Allen's name. A third honor was unspoken, unwritten, and unpublicized: the B-29 program went on, which is the way Eddie would have wanted it.

Even with the new Renton plant, Boeing's facilities in the Seattle area were inadequate to meet total production goals for both the B-17 and

B-29. At the insistence of General Echols, numerous subcontractors joined the production parade, and coordination with Seattle was a constant challenge. B-29 engineering changes alone ran into the thousands as the program matured. Additional changes resulted from actual combat experience.

The B-29's bomb bay provided an outstanding example. Crews reported that Japanese fighter pilots could tell when a B-29 was lined up for a bombing run, a bomber's most vulnerable moment. The bomb bay doors were electrically operated, and the actuators were ponderously slow. To a Zero fighter pilot, this was a dead giveaway that the B-29 was getting ready to drop its load and wouldn't try any evasive maneuvers—exactly the right time to attack.

The Air Corps wanted a bomb bay door that would open faster, eliminating all advance warning of a bomb run. Howard Stuverude remembered working around the clock with other engineers to develop a pneumatic actuator that could open bay doors in a fifth of a second.

A good chunk of B-29 production was transferred to Wichita, along with flight testing. This was mostly the Air Corps' idea, not Seattle's; General K. B. Wolfe, the hard-nosed chief of the B-29 program during the war, hated Seattle weather and insisted that testing could move ahead faster in the skies over Kansas. But Renton remained a mecca for official dignitaries wanting to see the big bombers assembled, and Plant Two also had its share of visiting VIPs. Hap Arnold was there several times, always accompanied by his personal friend Oliver West, who seemed to have more military contacts than a camp follower.

Eleanor Roosevelt showed up at Plant Two one day and FDR himself inspected the B-17 line in Seattle, an occasion marked by an unusual number of soldiers assigned to guard the area. The most unexpected visitor, however, was neither a general nor a president. William Boeing began attending occasional engineering meetings during the war, an interested listener rather than a participant in the discussions. Listening came hard to him; he had become quite deaf, and George Schairer recalled that when Boeing was present, microphones and amplifiers had to be planted around the conference table so the company's founder could hear what was being said.

It would have been interesting to know his thoughts as he listened to them talk about planes like the B-17 and B-29, spewing out of huge factories by the hundreds and even thousands, remembering perhaps the flimsy B&W . . . the glory days of Boeing Air Transport and the Model 80 . . . the pride of achievement that had gone into the 247. But shy and private as ever, he was not the one to confide his thoughts on the business he had fathered in the old Red Barn, not even to Phil Johnson.

Boeing's president in September 1944 decided to inspect the company's booming facilities in Wichita, where B-29s and Kaydets were rolling off assembly lines, and he intended to talk to the people working on those lines. It was a rare day in Seattle that Johnson didn't find the time to visit the factory floors and chat with the hourly workers.

Johnson had stopped off in Wichita on his way back from an aircraft industry conference in Washington. He had intended to visit the plant that day but phoned to say he wasn't feeling well and would rest in his hotel room. The next day he never showed up; on September 14, 1944, he suffered a fatal cerebral hemorrhage.

Boeing sent a company-owned B-17 to Wichita and flew Johnson's body to Seattle for burial; Clyde Skeen, then a young accountant in the Wichita division's finance department, was one of the men who loaded the coffin into the B-17's bomb bay for Johnson's final flight.

The sudden, unexpected loss of a charismatic leader and a truly brilliant administrator sent Boeing's board into an emergency session, but the only immediate decision was to ask Claire Egtvedt to take over the presidency temporarily, while the directors searched for a permanent replacement.

Egtvedt already had his own choice in mind: Bill Allen, who had been the company's lawyer for the past 20 years and a director during 14 of those years. But when he sounded out Allen, the lawyer just laughed and said he wasn't qualified. He did, however, offer to help find Johnson's successor. There were plenty of able executives in the aircraft industry under consideration who would have jumped at the chance to run Boeing, but their desires might as well have been transmitted to Samoa. Except for hiring occasional engineers from other companies, Boeing was traditionally inbred when it came to executive talent; it usually promoted from within.

There were two such candidates available: Wellwood Beall and Oliver West, both serving with Egtvedt as the "inside" directors on the board. Beall badly wanted to be president according to Bill Cook, who said Wellwood told him the story years later, but felt there was too much friction between engineering and manufacturing; he suggested Allen as the best compromise—a man with no ties to either faction.

Thus the selection pendulum swung back in the direction of a reluctant candidate who by his own admission knew little about airplanes. On March 23, 1945, less than two months before Germany's surrender, William McPherson Allen accepted the board's offer to serve as Boeing's fifth president.

The directors had picked a pragmatic lawyer who was neither airman, engineer, manufacturing specialist, nor financier. They also had chosen a basically conservative man who was to guide Boeing's fortunes for the next quarter of a century, taking some of the biggest gambles in the history of American industry.

SIX

CHANGING OF THE GUARD

NO ONE KNEW WHAT TO EXPECT OF THE NEW PRESIDENT.

Bill Allen didn't know, either; as Boeing's new leader, at first he was as much an enigma to himself as to everyone else. A widower trying to raise two little daughters, he was to confide in the woman he married three years after taking over the company that he had doubts whether he could be an effective president.

"I'm a lawyer, I've always been a lawyer, and now I'm running a company that's always been heavily oriented toward engineers," he told her.

A lesser man might have been intimidated by the likes of Ed Wells, Wellwood Beall, George Schairer, and George Martin, but in fact the opposite happened: the engineers quickly learned that although Allen respected their views and relied to an enormous extent on their input and advice, he remained his own man. He wasn't dictatorial or arbitrary, but when the chips went on the table, William McPherson Allen could be very decisive.

He had to be, for the postwar years were traumatic throughout the aircraft industry. The euphoria of peace brought overnight cancellation of multi-million-dollar military contracts and even the deliberate destruction of airplanes already built. Bob Tharrington, then a young Boeing accountant in Wichita, remembered seeing bulldozers chew up scores of just-completed B-29s, as if they were nothing but aluminum eyesores on the landscape of peace. No one could have witnessed such a scene and not think of a B-29 that had come off the assembly line only a few months before V-J Day; Boeing engineers had been told to modify its bomb bay and doors to accommodate a coffin of specific dimensions. Not until much later did they learn that the "coffin" was an atomic bomb. The airplane was the *Enola Gay*, the B-29 that bombed Hiroshima.

The man picked to lead Boeing out of the thicket of forthcoming cancelled contracts didn't look the part. Thin, of medium height, rather benign in appearance with a rather shy and infrequent smile, he was a lot tougher than he seemed at first glance. He was 45 years old when he took the job, still grieving over the loss of his first wife, Dorothy, who had died of cancer in 1942, shortly after their second daughter was born.

They lived in the affluent Highlands section of Seattle, and one of their neighbors and best friends was Margaret Ellen Field, a divorcee whom everyone called Mef, after her three initials. Allen married her in 1948.

Allen loved to entertain, and their home became known for the fun parties he threw. The biggest regular event was the annual summer party for Boeing supervisors; up to 300 would attend. Allen usually retired around midnight and would never say a word about the few hardy souls who kept things going until six A.M.

Their houseguests could have been a list of Who's Who in Aviation. C. R. Smith of American Airlines was a favorite visitor; his is the only picture of an airline president still hanging on a wall in the Allen home, for C. R. probably was closer to Allen than any other airline executive—a friendship that was to pay off when Boeing entered the jet age. The cantankerous Eddie Rickenbacker came to a party one night and surprised everyone by playing a banjo. Mef Allen's fondest memory, however, was the time Bob Six of Continental arrived with his then-wife Ethel Merman, the Broadway musical star.

"Vernon Crudge, Boeing's United Kingdom consultant, was in town," Mef said, "and he and Ethel sang the entire score from *Kiss Me Kate*. It was one of the most exciting nights I ever spent, and I even got the children out of bed to listen to them."

The guests often included some of Boeing's bitterest competitors, like Bob Gross of Lockheed and Donald Douglas. The Aircraft Industries Association (AIA later became Aerospace Industries Association) would meet in Seattle for three days, the grand finale being a party at the Allens' home. He loved to throw "theme" parties; one year was Mardi Gras, another was baseball, with guests wearing mandatory baseball caps, and Mef recalled one with a Gay Nineties theme at which the dignified Donald Douglas wore an old-fashioned striped bathing suit.

Allen needed these moments of relaxation among his peers and friends. He worked hard—dinner was always late because of the long hours he kept at Boeing—and he soon succeeded at dispelling his own fears that there might be resentment toward a lawyer running the show. Instead of resentment, there was almost instant respect for a man who wasn't adverse to seeking engineering advice, yet could make up his own mind once he had a few answers. George Schairer described Allen's *modus operandi* quite vividly:

"Anytime there was a big decision to be made, he'd call all of the interested parties in and he'd go around the table asking for opinions. He'd just sit there writing in a notebook he always carried into a meeting. As each spoke, Allen wouldn't say anything himself except to ask a question now and then. He refused to make any decision, or provide any leadership, until he had gone completely around the table listening to everyone have his say. Sometimes he'd say, 'well, we'll figure out a decision later,' but sometimes he'd decide right there on the spot. We used to tease him about the notes he kept—we'd ask him where he hid all those notebooks so we could get a peek at what he had written. But we never found out."

Besides occasional entertaining and playing gin rummy, Allen's other favorite form of relaxation was golf; he loved the game but the game didn't always love him—he was pretty good but erratic. He used to practice chip shots on the terrace lawn in back of his Highlands home; the glass doors leading to the terrace patio still carry two small indentations, like bullet marks, the result of his hooking or slicing practice balls. The Highlands was a refuge, his sanctuary away from Boeing's problems, and he never brought those problems home.

For a while he smoked a pipe as a tension-relieving device, then quit cold turkey. "If you want to smoke, do it out of my sight," he told Mef sternly. Allen never did anything halfway.

He was an articulate, forceful speaker, and at his best when it was off the cuff. Boeing had no better spokesman at congressional hearings than Bill Allen—the intimidating atmosphere never daunted him; in fact, it was the other way around: "Allen of Boeing" seemed to command instinctive respect, a kind of immediate admission that any scandal-seeking congressman was going to get his fingers burned if he tried tangling with this symbol of industrial integrity.

Integrity.

He had it in spades, not only preserving the tradition that William Boeing had established but enhancing it, so that in more modern times it became an integral part of the Boeing mystique—a corporate image of such solidness that only a few American companies are mentioned in the same breath as Boeing. Veteran Boeing employee Dave Olson, who in his later years became a kind of unofficial company historian, said Allen "had a reputation throughout the entire aviation industry as the most honest, up-front CEO in the business. When he said he was going to do something, he did it."

Allen established something else at Boeing: its low profile in the Seattle area. He didn't want the city to become known as a company town, so he insisted that Boeing's contributions to the community be kept in the background, with as little publicity as possible. He was always being pressured, both from inside the company and from without, to move corporate headquarters to downtown Seattle or even away from Puget Sound and the Pacific Northwest.

The most frequent suggestion was that Boeing buy or construct a

"Boeing Building" in the downtown area to house its main administrative offices. Some directors—and a few officers, too—felt that keeping corporate headquarters in the south end of Seattle was somewhat undignified, and detracted from the image of an important aircraft manufacturer. It would not be surprising if there were a few who feel the same way today—a visiting writer once described Boeing's starkly functional administration building as a "place of bureaucratic neutrality." It has been extensively remodeled to accommodate the company's growth in the more than 50 years it has served as corporate headquarters, but even the remodeling was on the practical side. It was Allen's firm belief, carried out faithfully by his successors, that a company's public image is best served by its reputation, not by fancy offices in a downtown skyscraper.

Boeing's immediate postwar image, however, was that of a company in deep trouble. The day Allen took office, the Air Force cancelled a previous B-29 contract. He had to bite the bullet; layoffs reduced the payroll in Seattle from 35,000 to 6,000, while Wichita went from 16,000 down to only 1,500.

Years later, when a Boeing officer was trying in vain to convince Allen to staff a contract proposal team in a certain way, he finally said, "Look, Mr. Allen, I know it's hard for you to understand this because you started at the top, not the bottom."

Allen smiled. "I'll have you know, my friend, that when I started it was *all* bottom."

The layoff shocks were eased somewhat by the large percentage of voluntary resignations, many of them women shifting to careers as housewives. Not all returning Boeing veterans demanded their old jobs back; hundreds took advantage of the GI Bill of Rights to continue their educations. A number of the previously deferred younger engineers were drafted, but significantly Boeing managed to keep its engineering cadre relatively intact, and this wasn't true of several other aircraft manufacturers hit by the cancellation crunch.

The airlines were the only inviting sales target for the aircraft industry, for the war had exposed thousands of young Americans to flying for the first time in their lives, not merely as crew members but as passengers riding in military transport planes. And Bill Allen knew Boeing could no longer rely almost solely on military business.

Engineering already had developed the C-97, designed mostly as a tanker for aerial refueling of B-29s and B-50s—the latter a larger, improved cousin of the Superfort. But the C-97 originally was intended as both a military transport and tanker, and Boeing's preliminary design department had started sketching plans as far back as 1942.

The C-97 was a typical Boeing hybrid: it used the B-29's tail, wings, and lower fuselage; a second larger fuselage was grafted onto the bottom section. In effect, it was a double-deck airplane with tremendous commercial potential, offering not only unprecedented interior space for passengers but generous room for cargo. The civil version was designated Model 377; its more popular name was the Stratocruiser.

Some future greats and near-greats in Boeing's history began to establish their reputations in the immediate postwar years. First and foremost was an engineer named Thornton Wilson. Everyone called him T. He was a tall, thin youngster from Missouri and Iowa State, with a commanding presence and an air of self-assurance and authority belying his age.

T started out as a junior engineer on the C-97 program, just another face in Ed Wells' army of technicians. And T, who was someone Allen would end up watching carefully, never bought the claim by some that Boeing's president was too easy on the engineers.

"He was easy on them," T held, "but he damned well managed them. Beall didn't push him around and neither did Wells. The engineers revered Wells but they revered Allen, too."

Another unknown face among the newcomers was Joe Sutter's, whose first assignment was on the Stratocruiser working under Jack Steiner, chief aerodynamicist in the program. Both were to play major roles in the jet age; Sutter's sharpest memory of Steiner was that even then, "he could see the jets coming and was always looking to the future."

Then there was a quality control inspector who didn't like his given first name. Shortly after he came to Boeing, he acquired a new name by the simple process of betting on a college football game involving Oregon and Texas. He took Texas and gave an Oregon fan 60 points. The Ducks scored first but the Longhorns won 72–6—and from that day he was known as Tex Boullioun, marked by future events to become, by all standards of measurement, the world's greatest airplane salesman.

Boullioun became known around Boeing as a man who would bet that the sun would rise in the west tomorrow if you gave him good enough odds. This worried him as he rose through the ranks; he started wondering if his nickname might be a handicap. He confided his concern to Stan Little, a good friend who, like T Wilson, was an Iowa State graduate.

"Stan," Boullioun began, "you know how I got this damned nickname. It's followed me around and it isn't dignified enough. You hear the name 'Tex,' and everyone gets an image of this high roller, this gambler, this guy who'd bet on anything. I'd like to get rid of it and have people call me by my real name. I figure that maybe if you kind of got it started, it would catch on."

"Sure," Little agreed affably. "What *is* your real first name?"

"Ernest."

Little's eyebrows soared to full staff.

"Ernest?"

"See, you're making fun of me already," Boullioun protested.

"Now wait a minute, Tex—I mean, Ernest—if you want me to start calling you Ernest, I will—and I'll do it in front of everybody."

"I'll give you eight to five you won't!" Boullioun blurted.

The company's more colorful characters weren't limited to future vice presidents. No one who ever worked for Mike Welch could forget this old-time supervisor of the delivery and flight test center, who had a vocabulary that would make a longshoreman blush. John DePolo, who would some day run the same center, was a nervous young applicant back in the Stratocruiser days and was being interviewed by a personnel man. It went quite well until the interviewer decided that if DePolo wanted to work on the flight line, maybe he also should be interviewed by Welch.

He put a call through to Mike, talked briefly, then hung up, pale and not a little shaken. Clayton Ritchie, the personnel supervisor, asked him if anything was wrong.

"I don't think I should tell you."

"You'd better—I'm your supervisor."

"Well, I told Mr. Welch I had this young man here for an interview and would he please send someone over to escort him to his office. And Mr. Welch said, and I quote, 'If he can't find the [censored] building I don't want him!' "

DePolo heard all this. "I'll find it," he sighed. "Just give me the directions."

The delivery and flight-test center wasn't exactly filled with hordes of Stratocruisers waiting to be flown away by airline customers. The sad truth was that the 377 was another Boeing airplane victimized by its engines. The Stratocruiser was equipped with the same Wasp Majors that had powered the B-50; Pratt & Whitney combined them with General Electric turbo-superchargers and Hamilton Standard hollow-steel propellers. The latter, whose main advantage was lighter weight and reduced noise and vibration, were to prove as much of a headache as the engine itself.

The R-4360 Wasp Major was enormously powerful, necessary for an airplane whose gross weight topped 142,000 pounds—more than 10 tons heavier than the B-29—but it also was enormously complex, with 28 cylinders that gave it the unflattering nickname of "corncob engine."

Pan Am, the Stratocruiser's launch customer, had accepted the Wasp Major for the airplane when it ordered 20 377s and simultaneously cancelled a previous contract for a civil version of the Douglas C-74, a huge military transport. It was the best thing that could have happened to Douglas, for the Pan Am defection pushed the Santa Monica company into concentrating on the DC-6, pressurized successor to the

DC-4. The Stratocruiser's other competitor was Lockheed's Constellation, and the total sales for these three postwar four-engine airliners tell the story: the airlines bought nearly 600 Douglas piston transports and more than 200 Connies; Boeing sold only 55 Stratocruisers and if it hadn't been for the C-97 tanker version, the program would have been a complete disaster. Most industry observers felt it was mostly the temperamental Wasp Major that caused carriers to shy away from the 377, actually superior in many respects to the DC-6 and Constellation.

For the new Boeing airliner was truly a passenger's idea of air travel heaven: spacious, comfortable, and a lot faster than its deceptively bulky appearance would indicate. The Stratocruiser was 25 mph faster than the DC-6 and a whopping 100 mph swifter than the early Constellation models. Its interior was the first of a long line of Boeing cabin interiors designed by Walter Dorwin Teague Associates, launching a relationship that still exists today. Wellwood Beall chose Teague over Raymond Loewy and Henry Dreyfuss, the other two leading industrial designers, primarily because Loewy was too closely associated with Lockheed, while Dreyfuss was working with Douglas and American Airlines on the DC-6.

Teague sent one of his top assistants, Frank Del Guidice, to Seattle on the Stratocruiser assignment. One of the first people he met was a Pan Am representative introduced to him as "Mr. Augustus"—it was Lindbergh, of course, using another of his transparent pseudonyms; he had a different one every time he visited a Boeing plant. Del Guidice worked out the 377's attractive color scheme, avoiding the common decor of the DC-3 era when all aircraft interiors usually were a nondescript gray or mauve lacquer applied to stretched fabric on cabin walls and ceiling.

The Stratocruiser's outstanding feature, however—still remembered fondly by everyone who ever flew in it—was the lower bar and cocktail lounge, and the spiral staircase that led to it from the upper main cabin. The lounge was Beall's idea, a throwback to the one he had created for the old Model 314 flying boat, and it set the Stratocruiser apart from every other airliner of its time. So popular did the lounge become on long transocean flights that the passengers' only complaint was that it couldn't hold everyone who wanted to use it. The lounge accommodated 14 people who sat on a curved divan that was more like a well-upholstered half-circular bench, but this advertised capacity was somewhat theoretical—squeezing 14 six-footers into that lounge was asking too much of its limited dimensions.

The exceptionally roomy main cabin could hold slightly more than 100 passengers, although the usual airline configuration was 75. Beall spent $250,000 designing a luxurious reclining seat, and created a honeymoon suite located in the aft section. All in all, when it came to sheer luxury the Stratocruiser surpassed anything flying in the postwar years, and the price tag showed it: $1.75 million per aircraft. By contrast, the DC-6 and Constellation sold for about a million apiece, another reason why the airlines didn't beat a path to Boeing's door.

In addition to Pan Am, Stratocruiser customers were United, British Overseas Airways (BOAC), American Overseas, and Northwest; SAS signed a contract but cancelled it later, turning over its three planes to BOAC. There was one unusual aspect to the orders: Pan Am, AOA, and BOAC Stratocruisers had round windows; those on United's and Northwest's were square. For the only time in commercial aviation history, window shape on a new airliner was a customer option. Boeing chose round windows to save weight, but Northwest and United thought they smacked too much of ship portholes, and didn't provide as much view for passengers. (If one wonders why window shape was so important that airlines were willing to accept a weight penalty, it might be recalled that Capital Airlines once painted square lines around the circular windows of its DC-4s, so passengers would think they were flying on the more modern DC-6.)

The windows' shape was a decidedly minor item in the 377's career, for the airplane turned out to be a passenger's dream and a maintenance nightmare. The three airlines operating the Stratocruiser across the Atlantic—Pan Am, AOA, and BOAC—suffered so many engine failures that a running gag went, "It's the best three-engine airplane flying the Atlantic." It took about two years before Pratt & Whitney cured most of the R-4360's various ailments, the majority of which were blamed on a design that had traded off reliability in favor of power.

The engine was turbo-supercharged, a means of boosting horsepower by pushing compressed hot air into the intakes; the problem was that an air-cooled radial engine prefers cold air to hot, and this led to cylinder overheating—a flaw compounded, according to Pan Am's John Borger, by Boeing's cowling design. "Boeing did a lousy job with those cowlings," Borger said, "and we had a hell of a problem with the engines always running hot."

In the vital area of safety, however, the propellers actually presented a far more serious problem. They had a hollow core; the blade tips were filled with a hardened plastic foam for balance, a substance that had a tendency to work loose under excessive heat. Once that occurred, the prop would begin vibrating so badly that the violent oscillations could tear an engine apart. Two fatal Stratocruiser crashes, one in the Pacific and the second over the Amazon jungle, were blamed on this propeller imbalance. The eventual solution was a switch to solid aluminum props.

There were distinct advantages to the original hollow-steel design. The airplane's weight required exceptionally large props, and a solid steel prop of the size the 377 needed would have been too heavy. That size allowed for relatively low RPMs, reducing vibration by a considerable amount—the Stratocruiser was one of the quietest piston transports ever built, a decided asset on long overwater flights when vibration and noise increased passenger fatigue.

Its engine and propeller difficulties notwithstanding, the 377 also was as much a pilot's airplane as a passenger's. The flight crews loved its ruggedness. A Northwest captain once said, "I'd rather fly a Stratocruiser through a thunderstorm than any other airplane ever built." Cockpit visibility was the best of that era. Inadequate visibility was the most common beef among DC-6 and Constellation pilots; compared with those two planes, the Stratocruiser's cockpit was a flying greenhouse.

There was something else unique about the Stratocruiser. It was the first airliner that incorporated the input of engineers whose sole task was to eliminate any design feature that might lead to pilot error; cockpit layout and placement of instruments and controls were a traditional source of pilot mistakes. Boeing had established such a group during the war for its B-17s and B-29s, a nine-man safety committee headed by Amos L. Wood, a graduate engineer out of Purdue who had joined Boeing in 1937.

Wood had invented the "squat switch" that prevented inadvertent retraction of the B-17 landing gear on the ground, typical of the accident-preventing devices his group developed. He had under him post-accident analysts, and a design project liaison engineer. They worked with field engineers reporting from the war theaters on accidents involving crew error. A classic case concerned a series of incidents in which B-29 pilots were inadvertently feathering props and turning off ignition switches. Wood's group found that on long flights, the crews had the habit of stretching their legs by putting their feet on the supporting structure above the rudder pedals—not realizing that their shoes might brush against prop and ignition toggles.

Postwar cutbacks reduced the nine-man committee to four people, but the accident prevention goal remained the same and was applied to the Stratocruiser's cockpit design and to all subsequent Boeing airplanes, military and civil. In later years, the concept was extended beyond cockpit design.

The Stratocruiser blazed an important trail in this regard, not only in the initial design phase but in the policy of not taking for granted so-called pilot error—a tacit admission that when a pilot makes a mistake, a manufacturer should find out if anything on the airplane caused him to make that mistake. More than anything else, Boeing's policy of looking for the reasons behind accidents and trying to prevent them reflected Ed Wells' and Bill Allen's philosophy. Allen was known to say at engineering staff meetings, "It sounds good, gentlemen, but would it involve any safety risk?"

Boeing did make mistakes in the 377 program, but it was a better and safer airplane than history has painted it. The Stratocruiser's disappointing sales record tagged it as a failure far more than its technical troubles did. The proof of its basically excellent airframe design lies in the performance of the Air Force's C-97 fleet. These airplanes in their refueling role were to be a vital part of the Strategic Air Command during the early years of the Cold War, forming an integral link in America's deterrent power.

The Stratocruiser period marked the first time Boeing actually had a sales department, although at the time it was staffed almost entirely by engineers—which figured, because although Beall technically was vice president of engineering, he dominated the company's sales efforts and thought technical products should be sold by technical people. Ken Luplow, slated to be a high-ranking figure in sales, was one of the engineers assigned to the new department.

"Our first offices were in the administration building where the executive dining room is today," he recounted. "Before we moved in, it was an employee cafeteria and we had to get rid of all the pots and pans to make room for a few desks."

In truth, Beall shared sales responsibilities with Allen and Wells. Allen tried hard to sell the 377 to American but not even his friendship with C. R. did any good; Smith went for the DC-6. Allen probably never would have gotten involved in sales, but he worried about Beall's enthusiastic methods.

"Bill always felt that Wellwood would give away the plant to sell an airplane," according to Maynard Pennell. "But Beall figured that if we sold enough airplanes, the sheer volume would produce a satisfactory profit."

There seems to have been some friction between the ebullient, hard-living Beall and the far more conservative Allen—their life-styles were as far apart as the two poles. Boeing's president enjoyed an occasional party, but usually at his own home where he had some control over a social event; Wellwood could party every night and often did. Theirs was an uneasy relationship that kept festering like an untreated boil.

Slow Stratocruiser sales led Boeing, known for its ability to build big airplanes, into hazardous territory: the twin-engine transport market, which was more crowded than a popular bar at happy hour. Douglas had gone nowhere with its prewar DC-5, and after the war made a half-hearted attempt with the Super DC-3. Lockheed was offering the Saturn, Convair the 240, and Martin the 202. Boeing's twin-engine entry may have been the most forgotten plane it ever designed: the Model 417.

It was a high-wing transport with a tricycle landing gear, carrying 17 to 20 passengers in its proposed conventional configuration, offering airlines the option of converting part or all of the space to cargo. The cockpit was right off the Stratocruiser, though scaled down somewhat, and actually gave the plane the appearance of a miniature 377. The airplane might have been a winner but the timing was poor, starting with the fact that the market was not only overcrowded but a lot smaller than the industry had anticipated.

The 417, which would have been built in Wichita, didn't even get to the prototype stage. Bill Allen was unwilling to continue a program that spelled red ink almost from the very start, and Jack Steiner, who was assigned to the Model 417 project briefly, remembered the day Allen passed the word, "I'd like a meeting with everyone associated with this project."

At that point, there had been some preliminary design work done on a larger version of Model 417 to compete directly with the 240 and the 202, instead of aiming solely at the feeder market. But Allen told his assembled engineers that both Convair and Martin were too far ahead of Boeing in overall design, and added the airplane's death sentence. "We cannot take the financial risk that this involves," he declared. "We can't compete if the terms of competition are a known loss."

In the piston era, Boeing had not yet found the key to compete successfully in the civil market. The answer was not the Stratocruiser even though initial hopes were high. There were many "what ifs" about the big airplane—what if, for example, it had used the Wright R-3350 engine, which Boeing originally had intended to put on the 377? The Wright-powered XC-97 prototype had flown from Seattle to New York non-stop in a little over six hours, but Boeing apparently had become disenchanted with Wright because of the B-29's engine problems. Or what if Boeing hadn't already acquired a reputation of trailing Douglas and Lockheed in civil transport technology? Justified or not, that reputation stemmed from the 247 and Stratoliner experiences, and there is no doubt anti-Boeing prejudice existed among the airlines, both in the United States and abroad—a kind of they-build-great-bombers-period attitude. There even was a feeling that Boeing didn't give its commercial customers the same kind of support its military customers received, which also may have been true at the time; if Boeing learned anything from the Stratocruiser disappointment, it was in this crucial area.

Like the Stratoliner before it, the 377 was underrated and unappreciated. Pan Am's Borger always wondered why United didn't operate its Stratocruisers non-stop transcontinentally, on its New York–Los Angeles and New York–San Francisco routes, instead of solely to and from Honolulu.

"They would have driven American and TWA nuts," Borger said. "The Stratocruiser was the only airplane that could operate non-stop coast to coast then—Pan Am and United were flying them between the West Coast and Hawaii, which was about the same distance as New York–California. It took another four years before any airline went non-stop transcontinentally, with the DC-7."

Bill Allen always looked back with pride on one Stratocruiser delivery in particular. The occasion was the dedication of the new Sea-Tac International Airport in July 1949, and the highlight was Northwest's acceptance of its first 377. The airline brought in a stewardess from every country or area in which it operated: Alaska, Hawaii, Japan, Korea, Nationalist China, Hong Kong, and the Philippines. All were dressed in their native costumes and the airplane was christened with a bottle containing water from each of the seven seas or oceans bordering the lands Northwest served.

Mef Allen swung the bottle, having practiced her christening speech around the house for at least two weeks.

"I knew it backwards and forwards," Allen chuckled later, "and I was ready to see it buried in the archives."

One interested spectator was Clarence "Clancy" Wilde, Northwest's tall, lanky factory representative, who had been in Boeing's hair since the start of construction on his airline's Stratocruisers.

"I was probably the most disliked plant representative on the premises," Clancy admitted. "I was always griping and complaining about the airplane, although its major problems were things Boeing didn't have anything to do with."

Four years later, Wellwood Beall talked Wilde into returning to Seattle as one of his engineering salesmen, the first steppingstone in a long career at Boeing that saw him rise to the top of the sales organization and achieve the status of one of the company's most beloved figures. That Beall could hire a man who had been driving Boeing's engineers bonkers was typical of Wellwood; like Wells, he had a sixth sense about talent, even when the talent consisted of a harshly critical young engineer.

Wilde had a perfect right to be critical. The first Stratocruiser built was so overweight that lightening holes had to be drilled throughout the internal structure. The 377's wiring was the most complex Boeing had ever installed in an airplane, but in those days there was no wire coding, so that if a wiring change or modification was needed, it was almost impossible to locate the wire section causing the problem. Bud Hurst suggested to Oliver West that they use codes and got turned down because it was too expensive. Today, every five or six inches of aircraft wiring carries a coded number, so each wire can be followed anywhere.

Stratocruiser deliveries fell way behind schedule. West had bet Andre Priester a case of scotch that Boeing would deliver Pan Am's first Stratocruiser on time; it was two years late and Priester collected on a bet he would have preferred to lose. Part of the delay could be blamed on the shift from military to civil production—an assembly-line learning process was inevitable. But the principal reason for the demolished delivery timetable was a union contract provision that caused Boeing's first strike.

Like most strikes, it was acrimonious, damaging to both sides, and left a residue of mutual bitterness that took years to dissipate. It lasted 140 days and ended with the union seriously weakened and the company seriously wounded, its Stratocruiser schedule in shambles.

The chief issue was a seniority-rights clause that Bill Allen was determined to abolish. Under a contract negotiated during the war, a floor sweeper could dislodge a skilled mechanic out of his job if the former had greater seniority. Only if the sweeper showed that he couldn't handle more responsible work could the man he bumped get his old job back.

The seniority rule raised chaos after the war ended, especially in Plant Two where the bulk of the hourly employees worked. Bumping reached epidemic proportions when contracts were cancelled overnight and the layoffs began. As unskilled veterans replaced skilled junior workers, productivity fell through the cellar on existing contracts like the Stratocruiser, C-97, and B-50.

Neither side would budge during more than a year of negotiating and District Lodge 751 of the Aero Mechanics union struck on April 22, 1948. They didn't return to work until the following September 13.

A couple of future Boeing vice presidents were among the strikers. Al Heitman had started working as a rivet bucker a couple of weeks before the strike. He was still living at home and when a walkout appeared imminent, his father—a strong union member himself—asked him what he was going to do if the union went out.

"I haven't made up my mind yet," Heitman said.

His father just looked at him. "Let me help you decide, son. If you go on strike, you have a place to live and food to eat. If you don't, move."

Heitman went out. So did Jack Potter, who would one day run Wichita manufacturing. Potter had joined Boeing during the war at age 17, spent 19 months in the Navy, and was hired back only because he was a veteran. He was known as an uninhibited free soul who was always warring with foremen and supervisors. Bud Hurst was the only one he seemed to respect, even to the extent of calling him "Mr. Hurst." Potter's particular *bête noire* was a tough old supervisor named Nick Carter, who raised pheasants as a hobby and had a tongue like barbed wire.

"A superintendent in those days was God," Potter reminisced. "If you waved your arm the wrong way he might fire you. I had one boss like that, Ed Gibson, who everyone called Gibby. He chewed Copenhagen tobacco and we needed spittoons all over the place to keep the floor clean. But Nick Carter was the toughest of them all."

It would not have been surprising if some workers struck just to get away from Carter's temper for a while. Sometime after the strike ended, they gained a small measure of revenge. Nick loved the two-wheel motorized plant scooters and developed a technique of starting them by compression, running alongside the bike and then hopping aboard when the engine caught. A worker named Bill Durant surreptitiously tied a 40-foot rope onto Carter's scooter. A curtain of charity must be drawn over what happened the next time Carter tried to use the scooter.

"Durant was a prime suspect," Potter reflected. "But everybody was out to get Carter one way or another, so there were just too many suspects for Nick to find out who did it."

The inexperienced local union leaders made some crucial mistakes in calling a strike, which cost them dearly. They walked out without the sanction of the international IAM, and they failed to give sufficient notice as required under the new Taft-Hartley Act. Once they struck, Allen refused to bargain further with anyone except the IAM's national leadership on the grounds that the strike was illegal.

Complicating the dispute was a jurisdictional war between the IAM and Dave Beck's Teamsters' union; the Teamsters represented a small number of Boeing workers and Beck wanted to displace Local 751 as sole bargaining agent throughout all Boeing plants. There was little doubt Allen preferred the Teamsters and this was a source of bitterness, too; the IAM accused Beck of helping Boeing hire scabs during the strike, an allegation that may have been true.

Lowell Mickelwait, a longtime Boeing director and Allen's former law partner, represented the company during the strike and confirmed that Allen deliberately played hardball throughout the long battle.

"Bill was stubborn in wanting to get rid of a contract that had been built up during the war," Mickelwait said. "He felt that for the company's very future, he had to start over with a brand-new agreement and that the only way to do it was to survive the strike. He was not anti-union, but he hated that seniority provision which allowed an hourly worker in Renton to bump a more experienced man in Plant Two. There was a continuing shift of people from one plant to another and it created unbelievable inefficiency."

Local 751 did win a major victory after the strike ended, when it defeated the Teamsters in a bargaining representation election. But the strikers went back to work on company terms, without a contract, and it was to take years before the union regained its strength and the acrimony faded. Boeing for a long time enjoyed what amounted to an open shop, the seniority system replaced by "performance analysis," which promoted employees on the basis of supervisory reports. This led to resentment, too, because there were cases of abuse in which supervisors played favorites.

It was during this period of labor turmoil that Boeing's engineers formed their own collective bargaining unit—with engineering management's approval. Under the Wagner Act, it was possible for a union to sign up employees in jobs outside its normal bargaining scope.

Ed Wells encouraged the engineers to organize, simply to keep them from falling into the willing arms of a national union like the IAM or

Teamsters. So a number of them created the Seattle Professional Engineering Employees Association, drew up a proposed contract, and presented it to Archie Logan, then Boeing's director of industrial relations. Logan went to Wells with a complaint.

"These damn engineers," he told Wells. "I can't understand their language. I'm used to dealing with guys like the IAM and Teamsters."

Most of the bitterness during the IAM strike and for a long time afterwards was directed at Allen. While this was natural, it was something of a bum rap; he actually was a compassionate, though reserved man who to some came across as rather cold and unfeeling. He didn't have Phil Johnson's charisma with the rank and file, but to his dying day he resented the anti-union tag that had been hung on him.

The strike might have lasted even longer than it did if the Air Force, increasingly concerned over delayed B-50 and C-97 deliveries, hadn't quietly put pressure on Boeing to end the mess. And with the Cold War turning ominously chillier, the Air Force also had become involved in another Boeing project with far-reaching implications.

It had begun with a letter George Schairer had mailed from Germany after the Nazi surrender . . .

A letter whose import was to shape not merely Boeing's future destiny, but that of all aviation.

SEVEN

WINGS OF THE FUTURE

IT WAS A SEVEN-PAGE LETTER WRITTEN IN LONGHAND, dated May 10, 1945, but postmarked May 20, and addressed to Ben Cohn, an aerodynamicist in Boeing's engineering division. May 10 was the day Germany surrendered.

"Dear Ben," it began. "It is hard to believe that I am in Germany within a few miles of the front line. Everything is very quiet and I am living very normally in the middle of a forest. We have excellent quarters including lights, hot water, heat, electric razors, etc."

A prosaic, tourist-like opening to a missive that launched an aviation revolution. The second paragraph that George Schairer scribbled on his personal stationery began, "We are seeing much of German aerodynamics. They are ahead of us in a few items which I will mention . . ."

The remaining six pages were devoted to a brief description of those "few items"; the "forest" to which he referred was the site of the Reichsmarshal Hermann Göring Aeronautical Research Institute outside of Braunschweig, and what Schairer and other members of an American scientific team had stumbled onto were files of German research into sweptwing aircraft.

The team, led by Hungarian-American physicist and aeronautical engineer Theodore von Karman, included two other Boeing engineers: George Martin and Bert Kineman. They found little of interest in the research library, but discovered several suitcases packed with wind tunnel test reports on wing sweepback and its effects on airplane speed. Schairer in particular was amazed; the wind tunnel data showed the Germans had investigated wing sweepback earlier than anyone had known—earlier, in fact, than the United States, which supposedly had pioneered the concept at Langley Field, Virginia, the research center operated by the National Advisory Committee on Aeronautics (NACA was the predecessor of NASA). More important, the German data showed that to be truly effective, sweepback had to be mated to the jet engine; no piston engine could drive an airplane fast enough to take advantage of sweepback. And German wind tunnel experiments, which showed sweepback involved certain high-speed stability problems, also provided data on the aerodynamic effects of various degrees of sweep.

Schairer's letter sent sparks flying in Seattle, and it couldn't have come at a more opportune time. Boeing and four other manufacturers had received study contracts aimed at the development of a medium-weight jet bomber; the Air Force held out the possibility that the most promising designs would lead to funding for two prototypes from each company. All five designs on the drawing boards offered conventional straight-wing aircraft.

Boeing's thinking, thanks to Schairer, changed overnight. The data the team uncovered were quickly made available to all U.S. airplane manufacturers; almost unbelievably, only Boeing applied it full-scale to the new jet bomber program.

The assigned model number was 450. The Air Force designation was B-47.

Ed Wells was no stranger to jet power; in 1943, he had taken Dan Hage, Dick Taylor, and Bob Judd from his engineering staff to an Air Corps conference on jet engines at what eventually became Edwards Air Force Base. The discussion mostly concerned information the British had sent on the turbine power plant invented by Britain's Frank Whittle, and the far-seeing Wells, although he was impressed, also recognized the chief disadvantage to such an engine: it gulped fuel voraciously, a whopping 65 percent faster than a piston engine, and this severely restricted range.

In the early stages of B-47 development, pessimism over range limitations predominated; among the doubters was Curtis LeMay, head of the Strategic Air Command, who happened to love the B-50 and questioned whether a jet bomber was even feasible within the foreseeable future. Bill Allen shared those doubts, but he also listened to his engineers and believed what Ed Wells was fond of expounding whenever anyone asked him whether it was better to be innovative or conservative.

"You have to strike a balance between the two," Wells would say in his dry, quiet voice. "If you're too innovative, you may find yourself out on a limb that's going to be sawed off. But if you're too conservative, you may die on the vine."

Pessimism was a dirty word around Boeing—and still is. And if the company was going against the grain with the B-47, it possessed a weapon no other manufacturer had: its own high-speed wind tunnel, named after Eddie Allen. Built at a cost of $750,000 mostly out of profits from the B-29 program, it was chiefly the bailiwick of Bill Cook and his main disciple, Bob Withington. It featured an 18,000-horse-power motor driving a huge 16-blade fan with a 24-foot diameter, capable of simulating aircraft speeds up to 0.975 Mach—more than nine-tenths the speed of sound, or 626 mph. Other companies shared time in university-owned and -operated high-speed wind tunnels like Cal Tech's excellent facility, but Boeing could run its own show and it paid off with the B-47, the first Boeing airplane whose design was determined completely by wind tunnel data.

It says much for Boeing's postwar financial shape that to save money, the wind tunnel was used mostly at night when other buildings weren't using electricity. One major tool was the penknife Wells, Cook, Vic Granger, Martin, Schairer, and Withington used to carve different-shaped models out of clay. They were obsessed with reducing drag, trying to achieve the most aerodynamically clean airplane ever created.

T Wilson, one of the aerodynamicists assigned to the program, said, "Martin and Cook had an unwritten pact that nothing was to be external on the B-47—no one was allowed to add any appendage that would incur drag, unless it had both their consents."

T took this sermon at face value. A few months later, when the first XB-47 prototype was being built, Art Hitsman was on the assembly line and was told to install a piece of electronics equipment that required cutting a hole in the fuselage for a cooling scoop.

"But you'd better check with aerodynamics first," Hitsman's supervisor warned.

The aerodynamicist Hitsman consulted was Wilson, who reacted to this heresy as if he had just been asked to stab his mother.

"Hitsman," T protested, "you can't go around cutting holes in this airplane. It's an aerodynamically perfect piece of machinery."

Hitsman assured him the scoop hole had been approved at the highest level of engineering. They argued for several minutes before Wilson grumpily agreed to find someone to help Hitsman. But T added, "This is gonna be the safest airplane in the whole damned United States Air Force."

"Why?" Hitsman asked.

"Because it's so full of holes, nobody can shoot it down."

Schairer suggested a 35-degree sweepback angle on the wings, although the maximum angle in the German data was 29 degrees. The wind tunnel tests showed that the sharper sweepback would make the bomber faster than any existing fighter, and this was the final configuration. But the rest of the airplane's shape went through several versions without pleasing anyone. One problem was the early assumption that the engines, like those of jet fighters, had to go inside the fuselage. The first mockup displayed an unattractive, fat-bellied body with the traditional tricycle landing gear; Air Force officers who saw that mockup sniffed disdainfully. One of them, Colonel Ed Nabell, remarked, "A good airplane is always a good-looking airplane and that isn't."

Wells and company couldn't agree more. An alternative was to put the engines in or on top of the wings. But Wells and Bob Jewett came up with the idea of installing the engines in pods, suspended *under* the wings, and insisted that if the pods were properly placed, the wings still would be aerodynamically clean.

This radical arrangement had to be tested in the wind tunnel, and more than 50 different pod placements were tested before they arrived at the best location. No more important decision was ever made; the pod concept was to be incorporated into most four-engine jetliner designs and a number of jet transports with two or three engines, copied not only by American airplane manufacturers but by those in other countries.

Boeing did some copying of its own with the B-47. Instead of a more conventional tricycle landing gear, Boeing adopted the new bicycle landing gear Martin had put on its competing XB-48—it was called a bicycle gear because of the tandem arrangement of the wheels. It took some soul-searching for Boeing to adopt anything of a competitor's; traditionally and historically it has been known for its "NIH" attitude, meaning "not invented here."

Angle of sweepback, pods, and bicycle gear didn't solve all of the new bomber's development problems, which was to be expected with such a revolutionary design. No company had ever built a large swept-wing airplane before, or any large jet for that matter; all previous jets had been fighters or light bombers.

The first obstacle the B-47 project had to overcome was Air Force prejudice against the whole idea of a sweptwing bomber. The opposition surfaced when Boeing requested a one-year delay in the program so it would have more time to work on the design, arguing that the concept would render every straight-winged military plane in the world obsolete the first time the B-47 flew.

Ken Holtby, who became one of the engineers in the B-47 program, remembered a meeting at Wright Field during which almost every Air Force officer in the room bluntly informed the Boeing representatives that putting a swept wing on a bomber was a lousy idea and that George Schairer had to be some kind of eccentric.

Among the number of colonels present, only one supported Boeing: Pete Warden. He told Holtby, "You'd better get Ed Wells on the phone and have him come out and talk to this group."

Holtby did. Wells and Bob Jewett flew to Dayton and convinced this collection of doubting Thomases that adding a year to the sweptwing program would result in leapfrogging straight-wing technology. The Air Force decision to continue the research was a reluctant reprieve, but it saved the program.

The pod idea hadn't been born yet; both Boeing and the Air Force were still operating on the assumption that the best place to put the engines was inside the fuselage. Then Wells and Jewett flew out a second time to witness a dramatic test at Wright's own wind tunnel: engineers punctured a P-80 jet fighter fuselage with holes that simulated 50-caliber bullet penetrations. When the engine was started, Holtby recounted, "We got an eighteen-inch blowtorch that melted the aluminum fuselage in about two seconds. Ed started drawing pictures of pod engines on the way home."

Gradually, Boeing and a handful of supportive airmen wore down Air Force resistance to the extent of awarding a contract to build two prototypes. The pro-Boeing officers included Warden, Ed Nabell, and Ken Holtby, who was a lowly lieutenant at the time and actually negotiated the $19 million contract for the two prototypes.

A later supporter was Air Force test pilot Guy Townsend, an unabashed Boeing fan, who didn't mind defending the B-47 against all comers, including generals. He had flown both the B-17 and B-29 during the war and was enthusiastic about a bomber so fast that it didn't need much defensive armament against fighters. At one SAC briefing after the B-47 went into service, a three-star general was criticizing the bomber for some early problems and added sarcastically, "The B-36 [a piston plane] doesn't have these problems and can still do two hundred and eighty knots."

From the back of the room came Townsend's southern drawl. "Hell, General, that's no faster than the speed of smell."

The wings and fuselages of the two prototypes were built at Plant One, then transported by tug-towed barges to Plant Two for final assembly. They were the last major airplanes turned out at the site of the old Red Barn, and Bud Hurst watched over their construction like a worried obstetrician. No one was allowed to step on any section of the plane unless he was in his stocking feet. Hurst had been told that a shoe scuff on a wing or fuselage surface could cut speed by several miles an hour, and that warning was all he needed to enforce his edict.

Hurst was a rather short, handsome man who dressed simply but immaculately. He could walk into any Boeing shop and call everyone by his first name. Boeing veteran Don Smith, a Hurst admirer, noted that "every guy on the assembly line would lay down and die for him."

T Wilson once called Hurst the best pitchman Boeing ever had, and Smith agreed. "At Air Force meetings, Bud would make all kinds of grammatical errors but the generals and colonels would nod and whisper, 'This guy knows what he's talking about—he's been there.' He was far more effective than a real egghead giving a pitch to a bunch of officers who'd mutter that he probably didn't know how to drive a rivet."

A number of the newer, younger engineers assigned to the B-47 program received their first exposure to the vastly different personalities of the two Georges—Martin and Schairer—and Bill Cook. The phrase *absent-minded* had to have been invented for Martin. Ben Cosgrove, another of many future vice presidents, was working at a drafting board during the B-47 program, next to 6'5" Ellis Roscoe, who had been at Boeing long enough to know Martin's idiosyncrasies. Their drafting tables were close to an aisle and both looked up as a figure shot by at full speed.

"Ellis, who the hell was that?" the startled Cosgrove inquired.

"That's George Martin."

"Our chief project engineer? Why's he running like that?"

"I guess he forgot to go to the bathroom again," Roscoe explained.

The absent-mindedness stemmed from Martin's intensity; whatever project he was working on shut out every other subject from his mind. Once he got interested in something, a major earthquake couldn't distract him. He would walk through Plant Two head down, immersed in deep thought, oblivious to anyone who said hello—the entire work force might as well have been invisible. One of his most devoted students, Jack Steiner, had the same intense concentration: half the time Steiner would forget where he parked his car, and Martin was even worse. He probably set a record for replacing damaged front grilles because, buried in thought, he constantly was rear-ending other drivers.

Clyde Skeen described Martin as "the most dedicated, hardest-working man I ever saw—a hands-on engineer if there ever was one."

Martin was scheduled to meet in Wichita one night to discuss a B-47 problem with Jack "Shifty" Shaffer, project officer for the plane's production program—the same Shaffer who would one day head the Federal Aviation Administration. He was a major then, and Clyde Skeen picked him up at the airport. Weather had delayed Shaffer's flight and it was past three A.M. when he finally arrived.

"George is asleep by now," Skeen said. "We'll set something up for later this morning."

Shaffer had another idea. "Let's wake old George up with a bucket of ice water," he suggested.

They gave a bellboy five dollars for a pitcher of ice water and the key to Martin's hotel room. Skeen opened the door, Shaffer behind him with the pitcher poised. Both stopped dead in their tracks.

"Martin was still up," Skeen said, "and he had blueprints all over the damned room—on his bed, nightstands, coffee table, and floor. We felt like a couple of idiots but George didn't even know what time it was."

Cook was the biggest maverick of all the engineers of that time—stubbornly independent, a true perfectionist and an inspiring teacher. Ken Holtby called him "the complete engineer, one of the few guys around who was really original. He was the one who basically fixed every problem associated with the XB-47."

Cook had one problem of his own, and that was his jaundiced view toward management. If Cook came into his office and found please-call-back messages from four vice presidents and one assembly line worker, he'd call the worker and throw the rest away. He definitely was not the corporate type.

T Wilson was assigned to Cook during the B-47 program, and as T remembered it, this was mostly because Schairer took a dim view of Cook's managerial style: Bill simply hated paperwork and would have flunked out of any conventional business school in a week. The first day Wilson reported, he looked at Cook's in-basket; it was piled with about 18 inches of accumulated mail and assorted memos.

"Bill," Wilson said, "I understand I'm over here, among other things, to take care of your mail. Just hand me that in-basket and I'll go through it."

T discarded all but four pieces and handed them to Cook. "I think something should be done about these four."

Cook agreed, although it turned out he already had handled three of them. Then he leaned back in his chair. "I think you might as well know my system. I always keep a pile of mail eighteen inches thick in my basket. I never look at it, because ninety-five percent of it's no good anyway. If anything's really important, somebody will call me and the only reason I keep those eighteen inches is so I'll know where to reach if someone does call."

"Sounds like a good system," T ventured.

Cook said nothing, but a few minutes later he turned back to Wilson. "Incidentally, once in a while you'll get something that's more than eighteen inches ago, so I keep more mail in the left side of my desk. You might check through it."

"He opened all the drawers on the left side," Wilson related. "It was all in there chronologically and God, some of it was old. I'm not an idiot so I threw it all away and Bill liked that. He was one of the great people at Boeing, outstanding technically and one of the best supervisors I ever had."

Every order Cook issued was prefaced with, "If you're gonna last in this company . . ."

That advice was his opening remark to Wilson the first time T reported to him. "If you're gonna last in this company," Cook began, "you gotta do something technical."

T always had a soft spot in his heart for the unconventional Cooks in Boeing's world—*squirrels* was the term he used for the company's mavericks, with which Boeing always seemed well populated. Schairer was one, too, but in a totally different manner. Like Cook, he was very demanding and in his own way an excellent teacher. Russ Light, who worked for him at one time, said, "He made you mad but he made you think."

Light remarked to Schairer one day, "George, if I hear you correctly, you're telling us to stop doing everything we're doing."

Schairer shook his head. "No, that's not what I'm telling you. I'm telling you to start *thinking*."

Bob Withington felt the same way about Schairer and even regarded himself as something of an interpreter, telling the other engineers after a Schairer meeting what their mentor really was after.

"His communication technique was interesting, to say the least," Withington allowed. "He didn't always say what he meant and I learned over the years never to underestimate what he said. It may have defied translation but it was there if you thought about it. Schairer was pretty close to being a genius, and Wells really was one. Funny thing about Ed—the only way you could tell he was upset was when he'd have two martinis instead of one. But he never raised his voice."

Schairer's thinking process occasionally wandered off in 10 different directions. Wells was the ideal man to handle him; Schairer would pepper him with ideas and Ed would accept some immediately, while quietly discarding those on the wild side. Maynard Pennell in his earlier years was much like Schairer, and Wells handled him the same way. Wells had enough clout to give his mavericks creative leeway, especially after Allen named him to the board of directors. He played no favorites among the engineers, but there is no doubt he was especially close to Cook, Martin, and Schairer, who were more his contemporaries.

Schairer could be something of a hairshirt at times, but always for a reason. William "Bill" Hamilton was one of his subordinates—there were two William Hamiltons at Boeing then, and this one was known as Wind Tunnel while the other was called Water Line. Wind Tunnel admitted, "There were people who resented Schairer because he'd trample all over them. But he wanted engineers who were smart and willing to work hard. There were a lot of times when he made me do things I didn't want to do, and I'd wind up doing them just to prove he was wrong—which was what he intended all along."

That was engineer Bob Bateman's opinion, too. "Schairer could drive people nuts, challenging them by telling them they didn't know what they were talking about. The engineers would kill themselves trying to prove he was wrong, and that's when he'd turn around and join you."

Even among engineering mavericks, Wells became almost a father figure—the man to whom they looked for support and guidance in the internecine battles that are an inevitable part of the corporate world.

"When something goes wrong with an airplane," Schairer reflected, "what should a company do? Send out public relations? The lawyers? Or the engineers? It's easy for the bean counters to call out the lawyers—and the lawyers will say, 'There was nothing wrong with our airplane—it was pilot error.' A manufacturer can go on for years this way. Wells wouldn't put up with that. He'd say, 'Well, if it's wrong, fix it!' He'd tell us how to fix it and he'd go to the board of directors if it was a fixed price contract, or a commercial contract, and he'd get the money to fix it. Or he'd go to the Air Force and get the money. That was his strength, his philosophy—let's find out what our problems are and do something about them."

Wells had a quietly effective way of throwing cold water on some engineering proposal he considered too radical or unwise. Schairer and the other engineers got to calling it his let's-draw-a-horse routine. He compared ideas to breeding a race horse, and he'd say, "Now this horse will win lots of races," or conversely, "I'm afraid we've got a nag here." On the notepad he always brought into a meeting, he would sketch a horse and note its good points or flaws. Schairer remembered one session at which Wells finished his drawing and announced, "Well, this horse has thirteen fatal defects, any one of which would kill it."

If it's wrong, fix it!

It was a motto with muscle, and if any airplane needed a strong philosophy behind the design and development process, it was the B-47.

From the very start, the bomber was intended to be a delivery vehicle for the atomic bomb; this mission dictated the relatively narrow fuselage and facilitated its almost perfect aerodynamic streamlining. But it also resulted in a cockpit configuration unusual for an airplane that grossed more than 100 tons.

The narrow width put the two pilots in tandem, the aircraft commander in front and the copilot behind him in what amounted to a second cockpit. In a conventional side-by-side cockpit, the two pilots can monitor each other; in the B-47's tandem cockpit, the command pilot had all the fuel gauges, the copilot had the entire electrical panel, and no cross-monitoring was possible.

The sole purpose of the tandem design was its contribution to drag reduction. Speed was the essence of the B-47, both offensively and defensively. Its only defensive armament was two radar-guided 20-millimeter cannons mounted in the tail. During the flight tests, the only U.S. fighter fast enough to be used as the chase plane was the brand-new F-86 Sabrejet.

Bayne Lamb remembered with wry amusement the day the wings and fuselage of the first prototype were loaded on a barge for the short trip up the Duwamish River to Plant Two. They were covered with canvas and cheesecloth to hide their outlines, for the bomber still was top secret.

"We kept waiting for the tugboat to arrive," Lamb said, "and when it finally showed up more than an hour late, the skipper was absolutely smashed and the crew wasn't in much better shape. There was no way we were going to let him move the barge, so we had to wait at least two more hours for another tugboat with a fresh crew."

The frayed nerves on that occasion were nothing compared with the tension evident at the XB-47's maiden flight: December 17, 1947, the 44th anniversary of the Wright brothers' first flight at Kitty Hawk. Bob Robbins and Scott Osler were the assigned test pilots and one of the spectators, standing next to N. D. Showalter, was Robbins' wife, Anne. She was squeezing his hand so tightly that he finally murmured, "Don't worry—it's going to be all right." But he was nervously squeezing her hand, too.

Bob Withington watched from the roof of the wind tunnel building across the street from Boeing Field. He said later, "I wasn't sure it would fly."

A false fire warning aborted the first takeoff. But on the second, the world's first sweptwing bomber lifted off at 2:02 P.M., screamed skyward, and headed for Moses Lake in eastern Washington where the initial testing would take place. There was an enormous amount of work still ahead, and although the flight tests disclosed deficiencies— as flight tests are supposed to do—they also confirmed the value of that wind tunnel. Its tests had correctly predicted the most efficient placement of the engine pods, telling the engineers that if the nacelles were moved forward of the wing's leading edges, there was no interference with the wing airfoil and the amount of pod-produced drag was acceptable. Even the shape of the nacelles, a vital aerodynamic factor, was derived from the wind tunnel and substantiated by the flight tests.

No one assigned to Moses Lake will ever forget its primitive living conditions before it was converted into a modern, full-fledged test facility.

"It was an old Air Force base," Ken Holtby said, "and we lived in what used to be the barracks. Bill Cook and I went up there with Guy Townsend for the B-47's initial tests. All we had for heat was one of those GI space heaters. It was fourteen degrees outside and almost as cold inside. If you wanted to keep warm, you had to wait until that heater turned cherry-red. After a test flight, we'd come in and make hot buttered rum on the space heater."

The B-47 was supposed to be a four-engine bomber, but ended up with six: two under the outboard sections of each wing and a pair of double-podded engines placed close to the fuselage. Boeing went to six because the early General Electric J-35 jet engine developed less than 4,000 pounds of thrust, and 16,000 pounds of thrust for four engines wasn't enough to get the B-47 off the ground. Even with six, the bomber needed JATO (jet-assisted takeoff) bottles—actually 18 tiny rockets protruding from the aft fuselage. Fired for 12 seconds toward the end of the takeoff roll, they blasted 18,000 additional pounds of thrust into the air. JATO subsequently was increased to 33 bottles installed on a horse-collar rack under the airplane. The later J-47's 5,000-pound thrust made it more powerful than the biggest piston engine, but compared with today's jet engines it was an outboard motor. Just one engine of a 747 is rated at more than 60,000 pounds of thrust.

The early jet engines like the J-47 were notoriously slow to spool up—that is, to accelerate from low to full thrust. They presented serious safety problems in the B-47; as test pilot Bob Robbins pointed out. "If we had to make a go-round it took between thirty and forty seconds to go from low to full thrust, which is an eternity."

So hazardous were the test flights in the early phases of the program that Boeing paid a bonus to those who flew them; some pilots were really afraid of this radically different airplane. They earned every penny, inasmuch as landings in particular were of the crossed-fingers variety. The XB-47 touched down at nearly 140 mph, and such devices as thrust reversers and anti-skid brakes hadn't been developed yet. Brakes couldn't be applied above 95 mph, which meant the bomber used up 6,000 feet of runway before stopping—and that was on a dry pavement.

The Air Force had learned to use drag chutes on jet fighters, which also had high landing speeds, but no one thought of installing them on a 200,000-pound bomber until Colonel Pete Warden asked Boeing to find some kind of solution before his superiors decided the B-47 was simply too hot to land safely.

Pilot-engineer Dick Taylor was present when Warden voiced his concern.

"Pete," Taylor said, "we once had to figure out a way to stop the B-17 if it ever landed on an ice cap—all we did was throw some open parachutes out the waist gun windows and it worked real good."

Drag chutes deployed after touchdown were installed on the B-47, but the bomber also was used to test a German-developed approach chute activated in flight to lower the approach speed without affecting thrust. The B-47's low drag permitted low thrust on approach, yet because of the interminably slow spool-up time, the airplane couldn't be flown at minimum thrust if a pilot wanted to abort an approach. Approach chutes achieved the purpose of increasing drag during the crucial approach phase; the test pilots deployed the chute out of the tail on the downwind leg at an altitude of about 1,000 feet. The chutes were never used on production B-47s but they became standard on the B-52.

The Air Force general who Boeing had to sell on the B-47 was not so much LeMay as K. B. Wolfe, procurement director for the Air Material Command. Like LeMay, he was skeptical toward the entire concept of large sweptwing bombers until Bill Allen finally convinced him to visit Moses Lake and see how the B-47 performed. Wolfe agreed, but with all the alacrity of a man following a suggestion to visit a dentist.

Pete Warden was at Moses Lake when Wolfe arrived and somehow convinced the general that seeing the airplane wasn't enough—he had to take a ride. Wolfe had never been in a jet airplane before and sensing that the admittedly apprehensive general might feel more at ease with an Air Force pilot at the controls, Warden asked Guy Townsend to fly the XB-47. Townsend did more than demonstrate the bomber's speed; he let Wolfe fly it from the rear cockpit for a few minutes, and it was like introducing a truck owner to a sports car.

Wolfe had asthma and his heavy breathing was plainly audible to those listening to radio communications. After watching him try some maneuvers with the bomber, Townsend drawled, "Now that didn't take much wheeze, did it, General?"

The next day, July 20, 1948, Wolfe ordered the B-47 into production—with a condition that put Bill Allen into shallow orbit.

Wolfe insisted that all testing as well as production be shifted to Wichita, on the grounds that Russian bombers could reach Seattle or Moses Lake a lot easier than Kansas. If Allen had one blind spot, it was his low opinion of the Wichita area—he couldn't see why anyone would want to live in the middle of a prairie, let alone work there. On one of his rare visits to Wichita, he was volubly expressing his dislike of Kansas to division vice president Earl Schaefer and one of his manufacturing assistants, Otis Smith. Schaefer was a short and strict West Point graduate—a tool left where it wasn't supposed to be drove him up the wall.

"You haven't got anything out here to look at," Allen complained. "Hardly any trees. The damned wind's always blowing. In the summer it's a hundred and ten degrees. Now in Seattle, we have great scenery, like Mount Rainier."

"Mr. Allen," Schaefer said gently, "if we had Mount Rainier we could at least see it."

His feelings about Kansas scenery aside, Allen honestly felt that Wichita lacked the production talent necessary to build a $3 million airplane—the price Wolfe agreed to pay, which made the B-47 the most expensive aircraft Boeing had ever built.

The general's meetings with Allen became confrontational; Wolfe would show him a map displaying the shortest air distances between Russia and the various U.S. aircraft factories, Seattle in particular, pointing out that Wichita was the safest place in the nation in which to build the B-47.

Allen would counter with the claim that the bomber could be built cheaper in Seattle because its work force was more experienced. He also wanted Wichita to become more of a technical center, developing its own new military business such as an experimental fighter—a category Boeing had almost abandoned except for a Navy fighter with counter-rotating props called the XF8B-1, which doubled as a one-man torpedo bomber; developed toward the end of the war, it was dropped because piston fighters obviously were obsolete.

The B-47 was the first Boeing airplane whose cost was derived from the total man-hours spent on each pound of airframe. Wichita estimated this at 15 man-hours per pound. Bud Hurst thought it was too high but he lacked the data to prove it, and even if he had, Allen would have lost the battle—Wolfe threatened to cancel the contract unless production went to Wichita, and Allen surrendered.

The initial contract was negotiated in Seattle on the usual cost-plus-fixed-fee basis, but as Wichita gained production experience on the bomber, subsequent contracts were set at a fixed price—far riskier but potentially more profitable if no snags developed. Wichita handled the latter deals under its chief controller, Clyde Skeen, and he had some high-powered young talent under him: Bob Tharrington, Carl Dillon, and a brash newcomer named Ben Wheat. All four would rise to vice presidencies.

Wheat reported directly to Marvin Swim, chief of estimating, which was a newly created post, and the two of them had to work out new methods of determining exactly what it cost to build an airplane because the fixed price no longer guaranteed a profit—not if the cost went beyond the estimates. Swim and Wheat must have done something right, because Boeing eventually made reasonable profits on the overall B-47 program and some of their estimating techniques, supplemented by computers, still are in use today.

Schairer's famous letter had warned that any sweptwing aircraft, with wings shaped primarily for speed, was going to have inherent stability problems—and the larger the airplane, the greater the problems. The XB-47, because it was the first of its breed, had them in spades, although it was surprisingly easy to fly. Bill Cook always claimed the best way to sell an airplane was to build light aileron forces into it. And the B-47 had them. "It was a fun airplane to fly," Bob Robbins said. "An easy airplane to handle."

There was excellent camaraderie between Boeing's test pilots and their Air Force counterparts who participated in the XB-47 test flight program. Most prominent among the latter was Guy Townsend, who was flying the prototype the day one of its most troublesome flaws was uncovered: aileron reversal, a condition not unknown to straight-wing aircraft. He was turning to buzz the Moses Lake field at high speed when he discovered he had lost aileron control.

Ailerons are used to bank an airplane; a raised aileron on the wing causes the airplane to roll, because the airflow over the wing has been deflected. But airplane wings are flexible, especially flexible on sweptwing jets, and the B-47's wings were so flexible that on the ground they actually drooped, giving the bomber the appearance of a squatting ruffled grouse. Aileron reversal occurs when the rolling motion produced by bending and twisting the wings equals or exceeds the rolling movement produced by the ailerons.

On the B-47, the critical speed for aileron reversal was above 470 mph, a speed at which the rolling motion due to wing twist overcame the rolling motion from aileron deflection. "If you turned the wheel to the left," Robbins explained, "you'd normally expect the left wing to dip, but the opposite happened above four-seventy—the airplane acted as if the controls were reversed."

By determining the effects of flexibility on airflow, Ken Holtby and his tech staff eventually developed spoilers, small deflective flaps on the upper side of the wings that reduced wing flexing and bending during roll maneuvers.

Another ailment common to sweptwing jets, which arose during the B-47's flight tests, was the tendency of the aircraft's nose to pitch up at a high Mach number—so sharply that loss of control was possible, even to the extent of falling into an unrecoverable spin. One of the newer Boeing test pilots, Alvin "Tex" Johnston, encountered the phenomenon, as did other pilots, and beefed long and loud about it. A Tex Johnston complaint by its very decibels seemed to make a greater than normal impression on engineering: he was a big, likable but forceful mustached individual who always wore cowboy boots when he flew. He acquired his nickname from this habit, although he actually was from Kansas.

Johnston came to Boeing from Bell Aircraft. The Air Force had recommended him to Boeing because of previous jet experience at Bell and the fact that he had flown virtually every airplane in the Air Force's inventory. Tex was a pilot's pilot, enormously skilled in his profession; it was said that Johnston could fly a bathtub if you put wings and an engine on it. He also fit in well at Boeing, being something of an independent-minded maverick who didn't think test pilots were required to genuflect before either engineering or management.

Tex flew the XB-47 one day and came back to report he was getting severe vibrations at high Mach numbers, so bad it amounted to a stall warning. T Wilson looked at the in-flight recorder data and shook his head. "I don't see anything that shows me it's a high Mach stall."

"Goddammit, I felt it," Johnston argued.

"You felt it? Where?"

"Wilson, right in my ass."

T decided to call him on that claim. He took out the pilot's seat cushion, installed a data recorder where the cushion had been, and told Johnston to try another flight.

"After he landed," Wilson said, "I looked at the fresh data. It showed the exact same frequency, the exact same amplitude, as a high Mach stall. Talk about seat-of-the-pants flying—the guy had a great intuitive feel for an airplane."

The high Mach instability problem was turned over to Bill Cook, who once said half-jokingly, "I'm only needed when aerodynamics has screwed up." Cook's own knowledge of aerodynamic history was encyclopedic; he was famous for turning away problem-solving compliments by remarking that neither the problem nor the solution was exactly new. It was true in this case, too; NACA documents derived from flight tests on experimental jets had pinpointed the cause of pitch-up on a swept wing: as the wing approached high Mach, the shock wave generated by the speed disturbed the airflow and destroyed the lift over the wing's outboard section.

NACA's suggestion for overcoming such instability: "vortex generators," tiny vertical tabs on the wing's upper surface, which maintained the airflow against the shock-wave effect. No one had ever used vortex generators on such a large airplane, but that didn't stop Cook from trying it. It meant drilling holes in the XB-47's wing to install the little tabs, and Bob Brown came up with the best location for tab placement on the first try—Jim Osborne's subsequent wind tunnel tests using various other locations showed they weren't as efficient.

Cook at first was dubious about the value of vortex generators, feeling that too much already had been stuck on the B-47's wing. In fact, the first time Brown and Vaughn Blumenthal suggested the device, Cook threw them out of his office. Not until after the flight tests did he relent.

The XB-47 with the new vortex generators was turned over to Tex Johnston and Dick Taylor, but Cook deliberately didn't tell them exactly what had been done to the airplane. They were just told to try high Mach speed at maximum altitude.

"I'll do it," Tex agreed, "but it isn't gonna work."

He and Taylor took the XB-47 up to its assigned altitude of 40,000 feet, at which point they were instructed to achieve the highest speed possible by putting the big bomber into a dive. This was the best way to test whether the vortex generators would prevent the nose from pitching up in the classic preamble to dangerous instability.

On the ground, the engineers could hear Johnston's metallic voice over the radio.

"At forty thousand. Here we go."

Pause.

"At thirty-five."

Another long, excruciating pause. No one knew if anything had happened, good or bad.

"I'm gonna go back up and try that again," Johnston said to Taylor.

The ensuing radio transmissions were a carbon copy of the previous ones, and the engineers still didn't know what, if anything, had happened.

Johnston and Taylor landed a few minutes later, and Tex marched right over to Bob Brown.

"Brown," he announced, "I don't know what the hell you did but it worked."

Next on the headache horizon was the sweptwing idiosyncrasy known as "Dutch roll"—in simplest terms, the scary tendency of such airplanes to go into unchecked yawing from side to side, like riding a swing that can't be stopped, until the increasing oscillations send the aircraft over on its back and out of control. Turbulence can cause yawing and so can overcontrolling a jet while banking, and the greater the degree of sweepback, the greater the susceptibility to Dutch roll—a condition in which rudder forces become useless.

The phrase's origin is uncertain, although Bob Jewett, who used to skate on Minnesota's frozen lakes, told Cook once that Dutch roll was derived from an ice-skating maneuver in Holland—the Dutch would skate down frozen canals and do S turns, rolling from the inside to the outside edge of the skate. Cook thought this a logical explanation, but not necessarily valid. He found the term *Dutch roll* in an old aerodynamics paper, and also remembered that Anthony Fokker—a Dutchman himself—years ago built an experimental airplane so unstable that the phrase may have stemmed from that ill-advised effort.

Whatever the origin, it became Boeing's problem when Bob Robbins and Scott Osler inadvertently let the XB-47 go into a Dutch roll while Robbins was concentrating on cockpit paperwork during a test flight. He stopped the roll with rudder application before the yawing became uncontrollable, but the experience was frightening enough to warrant a discussion with Bill Cook.

He agreed that some kind of yaw dampening device was needed. With Ed Pfaffman, who was something of a mechanical genius, Cook figured out the general requirements for a yaw damper prototype and Pfaffman fashioned one out of old B-29 rudder parts he found in an East Marginal Way junkyard. This improvised component was good enough to earn them a patent, although under the terms of the B-47's military contract, they had to give the patent to the Air Force.

Like vortex generators, yaw dampers would be applied to future jet transports, and Dutch roll in the B-47 was the last major problem to be addressed—the bomber could head into full production.

A tragedy occurred before the Wichita assembly line began hatching its B-47 eggs. Scott Osler was killed on a test flight when the canopy came loose and struck him in the head. His copilot on the flight, Jim Frazer, landed the airplane but was so shaken that he quit flying.

When full B-47 production did begin, the assembly line supervisor was a hard-boiled veteran from the Stearman days: Charles "Chick" Pitts. Anyone who ever worked for him, over him, or with him testified that it was a memorable experience. He was Bud Hurst's Wichita counterpart, and they were alike in some respects: both started at the bottom of the ladder with limited formal educations, they were tough, and they knew how to build airplanes. Where they differed the most was in their handling of subordinates. Hurst was stern and demanding but well-liked; Pitts was respected but mostly feared.

Three men who knew Chick well were Fred Carroll, Ernie Ochel, and Otis Smith, all Wichita veterans; Ochel and Smith eventually headed the Kansas facility at different times. Each worked for Pitts at various stages of his career, and both offered the same appraisal of this colorful character.

"Pitts knew a lot about manufacturing," Smith said, "and he knew how to make parts. But he was a tyrant and the only way you could get along with him was to stand up to him."

Ochel and Carroll agreed with that assessment. "Pitts was one of the best production men around," Carroll said, "but he was hell to work for. He'd yell and curse at people and he could scare you to death. Yet the funny thing was that he had an aversion to firing anybody."

Pitts was known as a master of the malaprop, which is a polite way of saying that he treated the English language like he did his underlings. Ochel actually got into the habit of writing down what he called "Pittsisms." His favorite was, "Don't get so flusterated that you'll end up hanging down from a preface by your fingernails." A fiscal year to Chick was a "physical year," and he referred to congressional hearings as "congregational hearings." He was equally renowned for his temper, which to put it conservatively was lost frequently. The expected profanity often was accompanied by Pitts throwing his old felt hat on the floor and stomping it into the shape of a pancake.

Yet a lot of people had a kind of grudging admiration for Pitts, and it came right from the top. Bill Allen liked him and thought there must be a diamond buried under all that hardened coal. Some years later it was decided that all Chick needed was a few lessons in how to get along with people, and he was ordered to take a course in human relations—a kind of industrial charm school.

A new Chick Pitts emerged from this contact with higher education. Or so everyone thought until Ernie Ochel, Chick's right-hand man for years, inadvertently punctured the facade. They were observing some assembly line operations and Pitts suggested politely, "Ernie, I think it would be a good idea if we moved that stamping machine over there."

Ochel shook his head. "Chick, it's not necessary."

"Ernie, I really think it would be better to move it."

"Too much trouble," Ochel argued.

The thin thread that stretched from charm school to Chick's temper snapped. He threw his hat on the floor and down came both feet.

"Dammit, Ochel! Do it! Just do it!"

"I knew Pitts when he was thirty-two years old," Fred Carroll observed. "I still knew him when he retired, and he wasn't any different."

Yet while the irascible Pitts wouldn't have won any popularity contests, it must be said that no one had many complaints about Wichita's B-47 production. The factory had troubles not entirely of its own making at first; numerous engineering changes, stemming from the continuing flight test program and actual Air Force experience with the new bomber, put the program behind schedule briefly. The

31st airplane built was supposed to be the first combat-ready B-47; this status wasn't achieved until the 54th airplane came off the line.

In the end, however, Wichita was to turn out some 1,400 B-47s. The airplane was dubbed the Stratojet, although this was one designation for a Boeing bomber that never really caught on, as had "Fortress" and "Superfort." The B-47 never dropped a bomb in anger, yet its existence helped keep the Cold War from exploding into real combat. NATO commander General Alfred Gruenther called it "the best airplane in the world" and noted that "alone it gives Western forces the balance of power over the Communists."

Boeing produced the B-47 on schedule for 49 consecutive months, and the Air Force's opinion of the bomber can best be measured by the fact that Boeing was asked to let Lockheed and Douglas assume some of the production. It was not the easiest decision for Bill Allen to make. It meant more than merely turning the design over to these two capable competitors: Boeing also had to provide technical assistance including the training of assembly line workers. In return, Boeing was granted an increase in its allowable profit margin: one half of one percent.

Lockheed and Douglas, however, probably received more benefits from this production sharing than Boeing. The B-47 was truly the forerunner of the commercial jets, and it was as if General Motors had handed over the design of a radically new automobile to Ford and Chrysler. Obviously Lockheed and Douglas, which together manufactured about 700 B-47s, were to prove perfectly capable of creating their own jetliners eventually, but they must have learned much from the B-47 that they utilized later—not the least of which was production efficiency. By the end of 1954, the man-hours required for each pound of B-47 airframe had been reduced to only seven percent of what was needed to build the first production airplane.

The B-47 did develop structural problems later, traced mostly to a new aluminum alloy that wasn't as fatigue-resistant as expected. In 1958, the Air Force lost two B-47s from structural failure on the same day, a double disaster from which Boeing learned a great deal about the implications of metal fatigue and the punishment a high-speed bomber had to absorb in service life.

Overall, however, the Stratojet was a popular airplane that earned its place in aviation history—a larger niche than it is sometimes given. It was the first jet to fly over the North Pole and it set two transatlantic speed records, averaging just over 617 mph on one flight and more than 650 mph on the second. In 1954, a B-47 flew 21,000 miles non-stop with the aid of mid-air refueling—it was at Wichita, incidentally, where modern refueling techniques using the so-called flying boom were perfected, giving the Air Force long-range striking power of devastating proportions, applicable to fighters as well as bombers.

Aerial refueling had made it possible for a B-50, the *Lucky Lady*, to fly around the world non-stop (24,452 miles) in 1949.

There was an attempt to modify the B-47 into a turboprop; Boeing didn't want to build it but the Air Force insisted, on the grounds that a propjet bomber would burn less fuel and achieve greater range. Schairer and Withington attended a Pentagon meeting at which they were reminded that other manufacturers were submitting various turboprop medium-bomber designs to Wright Field. Schairer murmured to Withington, "I think we could hang a couple of propjet engines on the B-47 and leave the outboard jet pods where they are."

He drew some sketches on the back of an envelope, and in due course Boeing won a contract to build a prototype: the XB-47D. The *D* might as well have stood for *dud*; the test flights showed that the combined propjet-turbojet configuration actually was dangerous, and the concept was scrapped.

If there was anything that stamped the B-47 as one of the most significant airplanes ever created—and a harbinger of Boeing's future— it was a remark made by a British visitor to Plant Two shortly after the prototype was completed.

The visitor knew airplanes; he was British aviation great Sir George Edwards, head of Vickers, an aircraft company with its own distinguished history. Wells, Schairer, and Steiner escorted him through the factory and he gazed as if mesmerized at the gleaming bomber, its giant wings flexed downward like a great bird at rest. Then he said quietly:

"No one except Boeing would have had the courage to build an airplane like that."

He was right—but Boeing was going to build an even bigger and better one.

EIGHT

METHUSELAH WITH WINGS

From the day it was first proposed to the day it reigned as the most potent weapon in America's aerial arsenal, the B-47 was never the favorite airplane of a man whose opinion counted the most.

And that was General Curtis LeMay, the barnacled boss of the Strategic Air Command of whom it was once said, "When he walked into a room full of officers, you could hear the spines stiffen."

LeMay was strictly a heavy bomber advocate, and the B-47 was classed as a medium bomber even though its SAC role was the same as that played by the B-17, B-29, and B-50. It was an arm of strategic warfare, but one LeMay considered too limited; the B-47 could carry only a single atomic bomb. Even while the Stratojet was being developed, the SAC chief wanted something bigger, longer-legged, and reasonably fast.

In 1946, a year before the XB-47 first flew, the Air Force invited several manufacturers to submit proposals for a bomber more to LeMay's liking. And because range had a higher priority than speed, the specifications called for a turboprop airplane. At that time, with jet engine technology still in rompers if not in diapers, no one considered it possible to build a long-range, pure jet bomber; Boeing was still cutting metal on the untried XB-47, and even Ed Wells and his associates may themselves have questioned whether the state of the art in 1946 was capable of combining jet speed with the kind of range and payload the Air Force was seeking—a 10,000-pound bomb load over 10,000 statute miles. The actual operational combat requirement was to carry the same load to a target 3,300 nautical miles away and return. This roughly matched the performance of the huge but relatively slow Consolidated B-36, a bomber with pusher-type propellers.

Boeing had already won a contract to build the B-55, a four-engine jet bomber slightly larger than the B-47; it had started out as a propjet design and was later changed into a pure jet. It still was a paper airplane when LeMay began pressing for a bigger bomber, presumably a huge turboprop.

On Thursday morning, October 21, 1948, a three-man team headed by George Schairer walked into a conference room at Wright Field armed with plans for a straight-wing, propjet bomber with counter-rotating props. Accompanying him were Art Carlsen (representing production), and Vaughn Blumenthal, an easygoing aerodynamicist popular even among the hard-nosed types like Cook and T Wilson—T once referred to him as "just a sweetheart of a guy."

The delegation from Seattle might as well have brought plans for a biplane bomber. Colonel Pete Warden was there and what the Boeing people didn't know was that Warden had been talking with Dr. Walde-mar Voight, a German scientist who was an advisor to the USAF Bombardment Branch; Voight had recommended that Boeing should go the route it already was taking with the B-47 and B-55: design a bigger sweptwing pure jet bomber.

Warden merely glanced at the turboprop proposal. "The first thing you've got to do is get rid of those propellers," he announced. "If you stick to that design, I'm going back to the Pentagon and recommend that the Air Force reject it."

Schairer called Ed Wells, who arrived in Dayton that same night and was joined by Bob Withington and Maynard Pennell—both were in the city on B-55 business.

Boeing's contingent met at the Van Cleve Hotel in Dayton for a weekend of work—and what they accomplished became one of Boeing's great legends. Schairer went to a local hobby store and returned to Wells' room with a sharp knife and a supply of balsa wood and glue. Over the weekend, they designed a new sweptwing bomber with eight engines; Schairer fashioned a model of the plane, Wells carving the nacelles, following drawings that Wells himself produced with a ruler and pencil. While they worked, Blumenthal, Withington, and Carlsen compiled weight and performance data. By Monday morning, they had a new proposal ready for Warden's approval—and approval they got. Warden told Carlsen to forget the B-55 and left that afternoon for the Pentagon.

The amazing thing is that the drawings and the model were almost identical to the B-52 Boeing subsequently built. Schairer, for one, wasn't surprised. "You have to remember that Wells was a very good artist in his later years," Schairer pointed out, "and he did a lot of oils and watercolors. Drawing an airplane was easy for him."

The only competition was Convair's YB-60 and Boeing won a con-tract to build two prototypes, the YB-52 and XB-52, both constructed under strictest secrecy at Plant Two. The XB-52 came out of the factory first, on a rainy night in November 1951, its 185-foot wingspan and 153-foot-long fuselage completely covered by enough canvas to double for a circus tent. Troops from Fort Lewis blocked off both ends of East Marginal Way to keep curious visitors away. So security-conscious was the Air Force that Boeing also was asked to build a revetment on Boeing Field to hide the bomber during the day, and conduct the first test flight at night—two requests that were turned down.

Even the canvas was a travesty of security. It was like trying to hide the shape of an elephant under Saran Wrap—the sweptback wings and fuselage were plainly apparent, and if any Soviet spy had somehow wandered onto the scene, he would have had to be an idiot not to recognize what was under the canvas. But this was the Cold War climate of that era, and if one is tempted to laugh at the Air Force's almost paranoiac sensitivity, in a way it was a compliment to the airplane; the B-52 was a very real balance-of-power weapon, something no other nation—including the Soviet Union—possessed, and the Air Force knew it from the moment Ed Wells' contingent showed up with the drawings, the balsa model, and a 33-page binder filled with performance data. The significance of what Boeing eventually achieved with the airplane lies in this fact: *40 years after the prototype's first flight, the B-52 was still serving the nation's defenses as a fully operational aircraft of the Strategic Air Command, a record of longevity unmatched by any other airplane in the history of military aviation!*

Yet this incredible airplane, flown in combat during the 1991 Persian Gulf War by pilots younger than their bombers, actually got off to an unhappy start when it incurred the wrath of the general so instrumental in its birth. Curtis LeMay's initial reaction on seeing the new bomber was disappointment, disbelief, and dismay.

Both the YB-52 and the XB-52 had the tandem cockpit that LeMay had hated in the B-47, and he let Boeing know the arrangement was unacceptable. It was too late to retool the prototypes, but all production models were built with the conventional side-by-side seating for the aircraft commander and the copilot. It was not, however, a conventional airplane by any means but rather the most complex Boeing had ever created—so sophisticated that it could be flown by a five-man crew (two pilots, a bombardier, a radar operator, and a tail gunner), whereas the Air Force's other heavy bomber, the B-36, required 22 men. The price tag reflected the bomber's size and complexity: $6 million, twice that of the B-47.

There was virtually no commonality between the B-47 and B-52, so the tooling for the new bomber had to be completely new. Harvey Buffum, a tool design liaison engineer in the experimental tooling unit, supervised the creation of the necessary dies and jigs. Boeing's switch to a sweptwing airplane after Buffum already had begun designing tools for a straight-wing complicated his task. Not only was the wing shape changed; so was its location on the fuselage, and the jigs

Buffum had constructed for the original wing were 100 inches too long.

This wasn't the only problem. On the straight-wing bomber, the entire vertical fin would have been movable; the new design called for a stiff fin with a rudder attached. Then the Air Force threw Buffum a curve by insisting that all major wing joints and landing gear components had to be forged, and forging dies took longer to manufacture. This meant that most of the airplane would be built before the wing joints and landing gear were ready.

The B-52's staying power over four decades can be attributed to two factors: the basic design was good to begin with, and Boeing kept improving on it. Eight different series were produced, starting with the B-52A and continuing through the B-52H—a total of 744 aircraft including the prototypes, of which 272 were built in Seattle and the rest in Wichita. The Wichita-built G series was the most widely used; the Air Force operated nearly 200 of this model and more than 100 of the Hs. The B-52s still in service today are mostly retrofitted with the latest electronics gear.

Two men began their climb up the corporate ladder during the B-52's development period, although neither had much to do with the bomber. One was John Yeasting, a tall, dignified-looking accountant who had earned Bill Allen's trust and eventually became one of Boeing's top officers. The second was George Stoner, a brilliant aeronautical engineer vastly intrigued with a subject to which Boeing had begun to pay some interest: unmanned missiles.

Bob Jewett thought the world of Stoner, and Jewett as much as anyone else at Boeing had become fascinated with the military potential of guided missiles. He was in an engineering unit called Preliminary Design (PD), a small, rather elite group that included Maynard Pennell and Dick Nelson. The unit's main job was to think ahead to future airplane designs, but as far back as the Stratocruiser and C-97 programs this group had dipped the company's toes into the missile waters—a modest beginning that was to have enormous implications.

At that time, however, the bomber programs overshadowed everything else, absorbing most of the engineering and production talent as well as the company's resources. The Air Force, in fact, paid less attention to guided missiles at first than either the Army or Navy, and Jewett himself believed this initial slow reaction probably was due to the airmen's reluctance to accept any vehicle that didn't have a human pilot. Ironically, the B-52s still in service in 1991 were not only bombers, but launching platforms for cruise missiles.

No one in the B-52 program could envision such a future role for the Stratofortress, the ultimate in striking power. Its eventual gross takeoff weight was 480,000 pounds, more than double that of the B-47, yet the B-52 was just as fast and its service ceiling of 50,000 feet was nearly 10,000 feet higher than the Stratojet's.

Teething problems were inevitable in an airplane this huge and complicated, but nowhere near the sometimes hairy moments of the XB-47's test program. One thing that emerged from the B-52 testing phase was the superb work Vaughn Blumenthal did in compiling estimated performance data before either plane flew. Test pilot Guy Townsend paid this quiet, unassuming engineer the ultimate compliment.

"It was the most fantastic job I ever saw," Townsend commented. "We used to plot the data from the test flights against what Blumenthal had predicted, and the airplane did exactly what he said it would do."

Another unsung engineering hero in the B-52 program was a Blumenthal assistant, Paul Higgins; Paul was an expert on stability and control. "One of his prime responsibilities," Blumenthal once remarked, "was to keep me honest."

Just as it had with the B-29, the Air Force committed Boeing to production even before a prototype flew, ordering 13 B-52As sight unseen in February 1951; Tex Johnston and Guy Townsend didn't make the first flight in the YB-52 until April 15. Actually, the test flight program went off surprisingly well, thanks to the experience gained with the B-47; in basic aerodynamics, the Stratofortress was merely a larger version of the Stratojet and was aided immeasurably by the availability of more powerful engines.

The engines originally were Pratt & Whitney J-57s that developed nearly 9,000 pounds of thrust each, and power was steadily upgraded in subsequent series—the fanjet engines on the B-52H were rated at 17,000 pounds. Even the earlier engines provided enough muscle to give the bomber 600-mph speed, so fast that the F-86 chase plane couldn't keep up with the prototypes at high altitudes.

To make room for the production airplanes at Plant Two, the B-50 and C-97 production lines were shifted to Renton. Fred Laudan, a quiet, religious, old-time manufacturing hand who was then vice president of operations, gave the job of planning the move to young Sof Torget, who never had a tougher task in the 40 years he spent at Boeing.

"We had to move those lines without missing a beat," he said. "We had to figure out how to move the whole damn thing one piece at a time and not miss scheduling. It took about a year, and for that whole year I never got home until nine at night. We'd have a meeting every morning and decide exactly what the day's move would be. For example, we'd select a certain body section, establish the specific hour and on what shift we'd move that section off the assembly line, so when the last body part had been completed, the tooling group would move in to tear down the jigs. Trucks would be standing by to load the jigs, take them over to Renton, and tooling would reassemble them for the Renton line."

The Air Force had an immediate love affair with the B-52 when it began joining SAC squadrons. It was heavier on the controls than the

B-47, but an airplane that was easy to fly once a pilot got used to its bulk. A fictitious description in the fine novel *The Wild Blue Yonder* accurately summed up the bomber's characteristics: "The B-52 was a truck on the ground and a family sedan in the air."

It was not so much the way it flew but how it did its job that impressed the Air Force. The Stratofort could carry 54,000 pounds of conventional bombs or four nuclear bombs; the conventional bomb load was 26,000 pounds more than the B-50's. In range, it met or exceeded all prescribed specifications and with aerial refueling, its range was limited only by the endurance of its engines. In 1957, three Stratoforts flew non-stop around the world in less than 46 hours—a spectacular 24,325-mile journey during which the bombers were refueled by C-97 tankers four times.

To increase the range, Boeing installed outboard drop tanks on the wings that could be jettisoned when they ran dry. It was not a Boeing-manufactured item, however; the drop tanks were subcontracted out to Fairchild and an immediate problem surfaced: the Fairchild tanks didn't fit on the wings. George Nible was general foreman at the preflight and delivery center, where the tanks were supposed to be attached to completed airplanes. He complained to engineering that the field was getting filled with B-52s lacking drop tanks, and what was he supposed to do about it?

Engineering's suggested solution was to remove the wings and send them to Fairchild for proper fit.

"Hell," Nible argued, "if we do that we'll never get a B-52 into service."

"Then go take up your problem with the chief project engineer," he was told. "But when you go into his office, don't put your feet up on his desk or he'll throw you out."

So Nible put on a tie that matched his pants and jacket and marched into the office. There was dapper little Art Carlsen, B-52 project chief, and there, along with other engineers, was tech staff engineer T Wilson in shirt sleeves with *his* feet on the desk.

"I understand you have a problem," Carlsen said.

"Yeah," Nible said, and delivered his tale of the wrong-size drop tanks. "It's a waste of time to take off the wings and ship 'em to the East Coast," he concluded. "I can fix those fittings myself—you guys are always over-designing everything."

There was a momentary silence before Carlsen said in a friendly tone, "Well, I think we understand your problem, George. We'll adjourn now and meet again at one o'clock next Monday for further discussion."

Nible thought, *Crap—here we go again*, but he was wrong. Next came Wilson's deep voice.

"Wait a minute—nobody's going anywhere. This guy has a problem we haven't solved, and we're not leaving this room until we do."

The next morning, Nible got a call from T. "George, there'll be a tooling coordination chief in your office at ten-thirty. Figure out how to grind those fittings so you can hang the tanks."

And that was Nible's introduction to the *modus operandi* of one T Wilson. Later that evening, Nible bet someone $20 that he had just met Boeing's future president. Wilson even then was solidifying his reputation as a get-it-done leader who hated the procrastination of lengthy debates. It had made no difference that Carlsen was his nominal superior, or that T had great affection and admiration for him. Frank Verginia, who worked for both men in the B-52 program, observed, "If T had any mentor, it was Carlsen—I heard T say many times that he wished people who compared him with Art really meant it."

Carlsen was one of those rare people who apparently went through life without making a single enemy; like Wells, he was something of a father figure to the younger engineers such as Verginia himself, whose own experience with Art demonstrated why. Verginia was in the middle of a plan to spend two years on the tech staff gaining background in electronics when Carlsen called him.

"Frank, we've got an opening for a guy in the electronic countermeasures going into the B-52."

Verginia said he wasn't very interested because he was getting valuable research experience in the tech staff assignment. "I've only been here a year and I want to spend another year here," he explained.

"That's a very good idea," Carlsen agreed. "After your two years are up, you should have two years in transportation, two years in materiel, two years in procurement, two years in contract administration, and so forth. By this time, you'll have had about thirty years of experience but the problem will be that Boeing will be looking for a guy who's only twenty-eight years old. So get off your ass and go to work for me—when opportunity knocks, Verginia, open the door and go through it."

Verginia took his advice and admitted later, "If I hadn't followed it, I don't think I ever would have made vice president." He also learned why Art had requested him in the first place: the B-52's countermeasures electronics were awesome and beyond Carlsen's own expertise.

After the first 32 Stratoforts went into service with no complaints about the intricate gear, Carlsen put Verginia in charge of new electronic programs for the bomber, including improved fire control, bombing, navigation, and communication systems. The G and H series incorporated all of them, and when Boeing encountered some Air Force resistance to buying the new B-52G, T Wilson was dispatched on a selling mission. By that time the B-52 was old hat and the Air Force had found a new and younger love: the lightning-fast B-58 Hustler.

T had just replaced Carlsen, who had suffered a heart attack, and he had never been able to rid himself of his aerodynamicist's prejudice against any piece of equipment that protruded from the fuselage and caused unwanted drag or additional weight. This applied to Verginia's electronics, and prior to a scheduled procurement meeting at the Pentagon, Wilson announced there would be limitations on any electronics presentation.

"We've got only so much time so everyone gets to show just so many charts," Wilson decreed. "Verginia, you get two charts—maybe three at the most."

"That's not enough," Verginia protested. "Electronics are too important to limit my pitch to only three charts."

"Three is all you get."

"Okay," Verginia said, "but I'm gonna bring a full portfolio just in case anyone wants more information."

"That's fine with me," T warned, "but if you let 'em know you've got all these charts without their asking first, you're dead."

The presentation went well, much of it involving a new engine Boeing was planning to put on the B-52G that would reduce fuel consumption and allow the bomber to hit any target in the world from bases in the continental United States. T was armed with a number of slides depicting the G's improved performance. The last slide showed a B-52 with a huge sling suspended under the fuselage. In it was a B-58.

"What the hell's that supposed to represent?" a general inquired.

"Gentlemen," Wilson replied, "I don't know how you want to spend your money, but the B-52 will carry a B-58 farther than that whole damned plane can fly."

Everyone laughed, but another general commented, "It seems like a good airplane, but I'm still concerned about electronics. All we've been told is that it'll have improved gear and I'd like more information."

T didn't bat an eyelash. "I'm glad you asked, General. It so happens we do have a complete oral and visual presentation that addresses the entire subject." He stole a glance at Verginia. "Charts and everything," he added.

So Verginia got to make his whole pitch including every chart in his briefcase. Outside the conference room, T grabbed Verginia's arm. "You know, it was a damned good thing you brought all those charts. Come on—I'm gonna buy you a drink."

As it did with all military airplane programs, the Air Force assigned inspectors to the B-52 assembly and pre-flight delivery lines, and they were treated like visiting royalty. One of them, however, deserved combat pay.

It seems there was an old-timer named Bud Chase who every morning at nine sharp would head for the men's room and take a nap while sitting on the john. Someone decided to break him of the habit and the next time he saw Chase dozing off on the commode, he placed a cherry bomb in the stall and lit the fuse.

Unfortunately, Bud awoke in time to see the fuse still burning. Frantically, he kicked the bomb about 10 feet away and it landed in a stall occupied by an Air Force inspector.

"There was hell to pay for three days," Al Heitman remembered. "The Air Force launched an official investigation but never did find out who did it. I've always suspected George Nible."

There was some logic behind this suspicion, for Bud Chase was the bane of Nible's existence. One day Nible was boasting to another supervisor how hard his people were working and how faithful they were, when they happened to glance outside Nible's office. There was Chase, legs crossed and arms folded, sound asleep on the wing of an airplane.

Nible and Heitman became close friends as they rose through management's ranks, but in the B-52 period they were on opposite sides of the fence: Nible as a foreman and Heitman as a brand-new shop steward who was just waiting for management to pull something detrimental to his members. His opportunity came when it was decided that the rolled toilet paper in the lavatories should be replaced by leaf toilet paper. Several workers complained to Heitman, who told Nible the leaf paper had to go. About a week later, the rolls were back and Heitman was still congratulating himself on this major victory when Nible hit him with a complaint of his own.

"You made a federal case out of that toilet paper," he told Heitman. "Well, I was making the rounds this morning and I found five of your guys sitting in the tail section of a B-52 and they were using an Air Force hot plate to make tea! Now if they had been putting bourbon in their cups I could understand it, but why the hell would anyone make tea at eight o'clock in the morning?"

While the B-52 program was getting under way, a young man fresh out of the Navy applied for a job and wound up being interviewed for an hour and a half by Mike Welch, whose interviews usually lasted about the length of time it took to smoke a cigarette. There must have been something about the youngster that impressed the hard-as-nails Welch—maybe the applicant's humble background. He had been raised in the Xenia, Ohio, Sailors' and Soldiers' Orphanage, and worked full time while in high school. In the Navy he had had been trained as an electronics specialist.

"When can you go to work?" Welch finally asked.

"Right now."

He was assigned to bench work on the B-52, and that was how Deane Cruze began his career at Boeing; 37 years later, he was corporate senior vice president of operations—a success story that has been repeated many times in this gigantic melting pot of a company.

Wichita got into the B-52 act when the Air Force insisted on dual production sources, and it had become apparent that Plant Two couldn't handle the demand. So the "Battle of Kansas" erupted anew, as Seattle sent key engineering and manufacturing personnel to Wichita. Chick Pitts welcomed the latter group as if it were an army of occupation bent on pillage and destruction.

Sof Torget was part of the incoming delegation from the production side and collided immediately with Pitts. It was necessary for Wichita to absorb all the production engineering and planning, tool design, and tooling itself, literally building its own B-52 tooling from Seattle's designs. Torget's specific task was to advise Wichita how to streamline its methods of incorporating engineering changes into the production line.

At the first morning meeting to discuss the general production problems that Wichita would be facing, the atmosphere was thick with acrimony. At the afternoon session, when Torget was to make his presentation on fitting design changes into the assembly line, Pitts got up just as he started and left the room. He returned when Torget was about halfway through but he didn't sit down. He stood in the doorway and barked, "Now dammit, Torget, you're not gonna come in here and tell us how to run our business!"

"I'm not trying to tell anyone how to run your business," Torget retorted. "Your people asked me to make this presentation which is what I'm doing. So if you'll just shut up and sit down, I'll continue."

Which is exactly what Pitts did and he never gave Torget any trouble after this incident. For both the B-47 and B-52 programs, Pitts was in charge of tooling; the manufacturing supervisor was another Stearman alumnus named Al Schupp, who wore a flattop haircut and never smiled—which was an asset in dealing with Chick. Two dour dispositions added up to an atmosphere made for feuding, and feud they did.

Otis Smith never defended Chick's abrasiveness, but he did defend Wichita's work force. Most of the rank and file, he pointed out, came from Midwest farming backgrounds and were natives of Kansas, "used to working with their hands," as Otis put it. Quite a few were veterans of the Stearman days and the majority were hired during the war.

"They wanted to put out a day's work for a day's pay," he added, "and I'd match Wichita's output then against Seattle's any time."

People like Otis Smith considered Wichita's production superior to Seattle's. People like Bud Hurst thought Wichita was Disasterville when it came to meeting schedules and cost estimates. The bitterness between the two facilities was so pronounced in those days, any real objectivity was impossible. One of George Martin's hardest assignments was serving as engineering liaison man between corporate headquarters and the Wichita factory, and it took someone like him, universally respected and scrupulously fair, to reduce the friction.

The truth was that meeting B-52 production schedules wasn't the worst problem either city had. The airplane itself went through a traumatic period after it had been in service several years, when structural failure was blamed for a series of B-52 crashes. The Air Force had begun practicing low-level missions as a means of avoiding enemy radar, and "low-level" meant that pilots were flying this 244-ton giant, built for high-altitude bombing, at full speed only 300 to 500 feet off the ground, exposing it to stresses for which it wasn't designed.

The very technique for dropping a nuclear weapon from a low altitude was tortuous on the airframe. It involved an acrobatic maneuver known as the Cuban Eight: a half-loop followed by a half-roll into a dive that changed direction 180 degrees. Boeing's Dick Taylor actually developed the technique for the B-47; it was designed to avoid radar and deliver a nuclear bomb from low altitude, while still protecting the plane from the blast effects. The aerial about-face was necessary because when the bomb was released at high speed, it was hurled forward and the aircraft had to head in the opposite direction as fast as possible.

B-47s had encountered structural problems using the violent maneuver, but no one expected the B-52 to be flown this way. The switch from high to low penetration for the Stratofort was ordered after the Soviet Union began producing guided missiles that reportedly could reach a B-52 bombing from at least 40,000 feet; such missiles were useless against a fast-flying bomber coming in under a radar screen at some 600 mph.

It was mostly during the B-52 program that T Wilson began drawing upper management's attention as the kind of guy who demolished red tape and, figuratively speaking, would knock down his grandmother if she got in the way of an important task. One of the key incidents that stamped Wilson as a fearless troubleshooter involved a Stratofort explosion attributed to a fuel leak. As the new head of the technical staff, T ended up with the problem, and it was quite a problem—all B-52s had been grounded until further notice.

Wilson asked one of his engineers to list every component in the airplane that might deteriorate or melt when exposed to temperatures of less than 425 degrees—the temperature at which fuel would explode. The answer: the rubber ducts used in the aircraft's pneumatic system; the rubber began deteriorating at around 275 degrees.

"What's the highest temp they're exposed to?" Wilson asked.

"Well, when you start the engines, as high as seven hundred and fifty degrees."

T went to Boeing's experimental process unit, knowing they had a small rubber-making facility, and was told a duct made out of silicone rubber could withstand almost any temperature.

"Can you make some?"

"I don't see why not."

"How many can you make?"

"Maybe one and a half ship-sets a week, if we work around the clock. Three and a half a week if we work Saturdays and Sundays."

"Start making 'em," Wilson ordered.

Three weeks later, T received a call from an angry Mike Lewis of experimental manufacturing. "Wilson, are you the guy who's making these silicone rubber ducts?"

"Yeah."

"What the hell for?"

"We're gonna put them on B-52s," T replied.

"Look, there's a company rule against making any production part in the experimental shop. So you can stop right now."

Wilson exploded. "Mike, I am *not* gonna quit making them and if you try to stop me, both of us are going to wind up in George Martin's office and I'll have your ass."

That was the last T heard from Lewis, but he wasn't out of the woods yet. Engineer Charlie Brewster of flight test came into his office and asked if the ducts he had just seen were the silicone jobs he had heard about. Wilson nodded.

Brewster left T's office with three sets to be used on test airplanes. By this time, the process shop already had turned out 19 ship-sets, not counting the three Brewster had appropriated. A few days later, Charlie Williams of manufacturing phoned T.

"Wilson, are you the SOB who's sitting on all those silicone ducts?"

"That's right."

"I need 'em. We're having a meeting so get your butt over here."

Wilson arrived at the meeting to be confronted by a platoon of B-52 project engineers and Williams, who obviously had been talking to Brewster.

"This is the guy who has nineteen sets of those ducts," Williams announced. "We can start shipping them to Castle [a major Air Force base] right away."

An engineer spoke up. "You can't do that."

"Why not?"

"Because they haven't been qualified yet."

T said, "Well, they're going to be qualified by ten o'clock tomorrow morning."

"You still can't use them," the engineer protested. "Boeing's not an authorized supplier."

Wilson thought that was the silliest objection he had ever heard, but he didn't have to voice that opinion because at that moment in walked Charlie Brewster, who informed the group that the ducts were in the test airplanes, and as far as he was concerned, they were qualified.

Boeing started shipping the new ducts the same day until every B-52 was so equipped and the grounding order lifted. It is anyone's guess how much longer it would have taken to get America's premier bomber back into the air if T hadn't broken a few company rules. He didn't have much to do with the B-52's basic design, but he had a great deal to do with the Stratofort's continuing improvements in the eight months he spent on that program.

The first day he took over from Carlsen as B-52 project engineer, he called in Clarence Anderson, who had been Art's administrative assistant.

"Clarence," T began, "I've written down the ten items that have been driving George Martin nuts. Things like the bomb racks, integrating the Hound Dog missiles, and the bomb nav system. If I went to work on this list, do you think Chuck Davies can run the project?"

Anderson said he thought it would work out fine and Wilson tackled the priority trouble items, those requiring fast decisions. T's decisiveness—a cross between a surgeon's scalpel and a meat cleaver—was his hallmark.

T always had a soft spot in his heart for Charlie Brewster. "One of the funniest men I ever met," Wilson reminisced. "He never did anything in moderation, whether it was liquor, hunting, gambling, training bird dogs, or growing roses and rhododendrons."

Brewster was insatiably curious. One day he wanted to know what happened to an engineering drawing when it was released, so he put a drawing number on his wrist and released himself.

"He just went everywhere a drawing would go," T recalled. "Nobody else had ever done that and frankly, I doubt whether anybody at Boeing knows even today what happens when you release a drawing."

Brewster was a Swede with a pale complexion. T trusted him implicitly as a problem-solver. His greatest non-engineering feat was staged at a poker game with Tex Boullioun, who played poker like Heifetz played the violin. This event took place at Bill Allen's house; the participants had been playing poker in Allen's basement recreation room for some time when Brewster showed up.

He didn't just stumble down the staircase leading to the rec room— he fell down them, glassy-eyed, and invited himself into the game.

They were playing five-card stud and Boullioun had three of a kind. There were modest table stakes in effect and everyone dropped out quickly except for Boullioun and Brewster, who was blearily examining his cards as if trying to focus on the pattern painted over a spinning top. The table stakes were forgotten as the betting heated up.

Boullioun finally raised Charlie $40, figuring he couldn't possibly have that much money on him. Brewster took a wad of large-denomination bills out of a bulging wallet, and raised him $200. Tex covered the bet and raised again. Brewster matched that and raised once more. Boullioun thought, *Well, any drunken idiot can get lucky,* so he folded.

Charlie, his eyes mysteriously and suddenly clear, picked up the pot. One of the players said later that Brewster didn't even have a pair.

The only man who ever really put down Brewster was Ed Wells. Charlie became fascinated with something called "value engineering"—which seems to have been a way of describing every engineering job in its simplest form, such as with a single noun and verb that established its goals. For weeks he would talk about nothing except value engineering. One day he sat down to lunch with Wells and began spouting examples of simplified engineering vocabulary.

Finally Wells said, "I've got one for you, Charlie."

Brewster beamed—at last he had a disciple. "Fine, what is it?"

"Horse crap."

Both Boullioun and Brewster belonged in that special category T assigned to Boeing's "squirrels"—those unique characters whose sheer abilities caused everyone to ignore, tolerate, or forgive their idiosyncrasies. Such a man was Wesley M. Maulden, perhaps the greatest squirrel of them all, who joined the company as an unknown industrial engineer and economist in 1951, just as the B-52 program was getting under way. In the 36 years he spent at Boeing, Maulden established a love-hate relationship with almost every person whose life he touched, fellow officers and underlings alike. Yet respect for his brilliance was almost universal. Ask most anyone who ever worked for or with Wes Maulden what he was like, and the answer was unanimous: "He was the smartest man I ever knew."

A minority opinion, usually held by intimidated secretaries and some executives he outranked, went: "He was the worst SOB I ever knew." Those who espoused that view, however, didn't know Wes as well as they thought—he had a marshmallow heart hidden under layers of gruffness, temper, and some of the weirdest work habits in American industry.

Maulden kept his office virtually dark, all blinds drawn, and illuminated only by a single lamp with a low-watt bulb. He seldom used his desk; he would spread papers on a large, low-slung coffee table and read them from an overstuffed chair next to the table. He seemed to think best with his eyes closed, a disconcerting habit at executive meetings; at first everyone assumed he had dozed off, bored with the proceedings, but toward the end of the session someone would ask, "Wes, what do you think?" Maulden would open his eyes and deliver his succinct appraisal of everything that had been said.

He was a holy terror on secretaries, firing so many for what he considered incompetence that he had to borrow temporary replacements from other officers out of town or on vacation. The trouble was neither their supposed incompetence nor Maulden's perceived tyranny—you had to understand Wes to work for him. Among a few who did were Donna Seybert and Sandee Baker. They dreaded taking dictation from him because the room was so dark they had trouble seeing their note pads. They also learned to fear the rare occasion when they'd find him sitting at his desk instead of next to the coffee table. "That meant he was going to raise hell about something," Donna said.

Maulden was a creature of habit. He insisted that when a secretary brought him his morning coffee, the cup had to be placed so that the handle was at an exact right angle to where his right hand was resting— a half-inch to either side would cause an eruption. But both Donna and

Sandee discovered that he was about as hard-hearted as Santa Claus. Sandee, who succeeded Donna, confided, "No one at Boeing except his secretaries knew how much money he gave to various charities—he was the biggest soft touch in the company."

Once he got to trust a secretary, he became almost totally dependent on her. He sent one out to buy him a new car and she phoned from the dealer.

"I picked one out," she informed him.

"What color did I buy?"

"Blue."

"That's fine," Maulden said, and hung up.

He liked to sleep late and not even Bill Allen or T could get him to show up at the usual executive starting time of eight A.M.; arriving as early as 10 was in the minor miracle department. Often he'd be heading home as early as two-thirty or three P.M., yet as Frank Verginia once observed, "Wes could get more work done in less than five hours than any other three officers combined."

Maulden was an exceptionally skilled writer and every time there was a farewell party for some retiring executive, Wes would compose a poem for the occasion—always appropriate, funny, and gently needling the retiree. When Maulden retired, Deane Cruze became Boeing's "poet laureate."

Maulden's office would have resembled a teenager's untidy bedroom if his secretaries hadn't kept it neater than he did. Maulden would read the documents and reports piled on the coffee table and throw them over his shoulder when he finished, littering the carpet.

Marcie Burkhart was borrowed by Maulden during one of his secretaryless periods. She walked into his office one day and for a half-hour listened to him soliloquize about how he had kept a certain vice president from getting promoted—the man he was talking about happened to be her regular boss.

He was capable of kind gestures that he did his best to hide. He was a gourmet chef who liked to cook for his friends; cooking and a love of anything Asian were his two greatest affinities. Divorced, he lived alone during much of his later career at Boeing, where he achieved the rank of senior vice president.

That title, however, didn't do justice to the impact he had on the company. Under T, Maulden was more like an assistant president whose word carried almost as much authority as Wilson's. Wes probably was closer to a fellow officer named Wally Buckley of manufacturing than to anyone else, although they had a kind of "Odd Couple" friendship. Maulden was well-educated, with a degree in economics and a master's degree in industrial management. Buckley, who also rose to a vice presidency, had nothing but a high school education and started out in the sheet metal shop pushing carts around—he had hitchhiked his way from Minnesota to Seattle to find a job.

Yet the bond between these two men of such vastly different back-grounds was that of two brothers. What they had in common was the same blunt decisiveness that fueled T, and an abiding devotion to Boeing. Stick either one of them and he'd bleed Boeing blue.

The influence they would wield on the company's fortunes lay in the future—they were not really a part of the B-52 story. But Maulden joined the company and Buckley started climbing the management mountain in that era, both on their way to becoming legends within the Boeing legend. They are mentioned somewhat out of chronological context because the B-52 helped establish Wilson's management rep-utation, and they were to become part of the executive team T would forge for his own regime.

There were a few others, like Bob Bateman—an engineer who went to work for Withington and Blumenthal. His first assignment was numbering the pages on some B-52 performance documents. There were 53 pages in all but Bateman numbered them wrong and came out with 54. Just when the memory of that gaffe had faded, Bateman emptied still-burning pipe ashes into Withington's wastebasket and it caught fire.

"Bateman," Withington roared, "you're a damned knothead!" With-ington still was calling him Knothead even after the inadvertent arsonist became a vice president himself.

Withington was no squirrel, but he had one particular idiosyn-crasy—he never came to work in other than gray slacks and a blue jacket or blazer. That was one trademark. The other was a limited tolerance for mistakes.

"You always knew where you stood with him," Bateman remarked. "You could screw up twice on the same subject but never a third time. Now Schairer had a different rule. As long as you were right, you could get away with anything. But if you were wrong, God help you."

The B-52 deserved the plaudits it received; from its very inception, it was a very special airplane. The September 1951 issue of *Fortune*, speaking of the new bomber, editorialized, "In terms of urgency of current production and work in progress, no manufacturer in America, in a sense not even Oak Ridge or its satellites, is more important to the free world than Boeing."

Yet among many of the engineers and production people who cre-ated and built both the B-47 and B-52, the Stratojet is considered by far a more significant airplane.

"The B-47 was the spectacular, breakthrough airplane," Wilson commented.

Production totals for the B-47 were three times higher than the B-52's—about 2,100 Stratojets were built compared with some 700 Stratoforts. But what mattered more than the numbers was the sweptwing technology the B-47 had proved to be feasible. This was the major factor in weaning Boeing away from almost total reliance on military business, for the next logical step was to apply this technology to commercial aviation.

The Air Force itself gave Boeing a slight shove in that direction. The C-97 tankers were deemed too slow for efficient refueling of fast jet bombers, and there was some military interest expressed in the development of a jet tanker after a turboprop version of the C-97 aroused little interest. This wasn't the main reason for Boeing venturing down the commercial jet road, however.

Even during the hectic years of jet bomber development, Allen and Beall had insisted on keeping up airline contacts by maintaining a small commercial sales force, although with the Stratocruiser line shut down there were no airplanes to sell. Ken Luplow was one of the engineers assigned to the group.

"There were four, maybe five of us in that group," he said. "Joe Sutter was with us and there were two or three non-engineering types. We made the rounds of airlines both in the U.S. and Europe—I took several trips to Europe with Allen and Beall, talking kind of big about the fact that we were developing new airplanes and not to lose sight of Boeing."

The tiny sales force went around talking vaguely about an airplane that existed only on paper. What they were peddling was a four-engine jetliner with a scaled-down B-52 wing, and carrying the model number 473-60C, but airline interest both in the United States and Europe was nil.

In 1950, accompanied by Maynard Pennell, Allen flew to England where Ken Luplow joined them for the Farnborough Air Show, Britain's aviation showcase held every two years. The star attraction was the new de Havilland Comet, the world's first operational jet transport, which had made its maiden flight a year before and was scheduled to go into airline service in the spring of 1952.

It put on an impressive show at Farnborough, screaming over the airfield at almost rooftop level and then knifing its way into the sky, a silver streak symbolizing the future of air travel. For a long time, a belief has existed at Boeing that Allen made up his mind to go for broke with a jet transport that day at Farnborough when he saw the Comet. That is not the way it happened, however, according to the two men who were with him on the occasion.

They had dinner that night in a London restaurant and discussed what they had just witnessed. Pennell mentioned that Ed Wells had seen the Comet a year before and came back convinced that jet transportation was not only aviation's future, but Boeing's as well. As Luplow remembered the conversation, Allen expressed not only serious doubts but threw cold water on the idea.

"He sort of dug in his heels on the subject," Luplow said. "He didn't seem too interested in getting involved with another risky project. He mentioned that the company had lost a lot of money on the Stratocruiser and he really considered the commercial business a losing proposition. He also pointed out that we were doing very well militarily with the bomber contracts and that maybe we just ought to stay with government business. But we kept jabbing away at him and while we didn't perceive we had made much progress, in retrospect I think we got him thinking about the possibility of a jet transport."

Allen did ask Pennell, "Do you think we could build a better plane than the Comet?"

"Much better," Pennell assured him.

And Pennell, as head of preliminary design, wasn't just talking through his hat. When Wells returned from England in 1949, he told the engineering staff, "Anyone interested in the commercial transport business had better get into jet design as quickly as possible, or time will pass him by."

Wells had briefed Pennell, who proceeded to make a number of sketches, drawings, and clay models—work Allen may not have been aware of. It would not have been unusual for the president of the company not to know what Pennell was doing.

"Preliminary design had always been a kind of cloak and dagger operation," Luplow explained. "But Maynard knew what he was talking about, what Boeing could do, and what the engineers already were thinking about."

It would, indeed, be a better plane than the Comet, and it would be called the Dash-80—the forerunner of the 707.

NINE

A LITTLE MATTER OF FOUR INCHES

WITH THE POSSIBLE EXCEPTION OF A CITY TELEPHONE DIREC-
tory, nothing makes for duller reading than the minutes of a corporate
board meeting. They seldom if ever reflect the drama, the nuances, the
personalities involved, or the significance of what was discussed at
even the most controversial sessions.

All this applied to the April 22, 1952, meeting of Boeing's board of
directors. The minutes cover 12 pages; not until the 10th page of this
chronological account of the proceedings is it recorded that the directors finally discussed and then voted on the biggest gamble the company had ever taken in its 36 years. The first nine pages are devoted to
reelection of officers, the election of a new vice president of administration—Jim Prince, who was a partner in Bill Allen's old law firm—
fixing of annual salaries, issuance of new stock, and 12 other agenda
items including an authorized $5.6 million expenditure for a new
hangar at Boeing Field, and a resolution declaring "that it is the
considered opinion of the Board of Directors that all those having a
part in the successful design, development and manufacture of the XB-
52 and YB-52 be commended."

At that point, the minutes noted, "Mr. [Dietrich] Schmitz, Mr.
[Darrah] Corbet and Mr. [William] Reed excused themselves from the
meeting."

In view of the next item on the agenda, the departure of these three
"outside" directors might have seemed strange. No Boeing officer or
director who was present at the meeting after the trio left the boardroom is still alive; whether the three had pressing business elsewhere
or did not want to take part in the momentous discussion that followed
was never made clear. John Yeasting, Wellwood Beall, and Ed Wells were
there as the three "inside" directors.

Allen presided, although Claire Egtvedt was still chairman and
would be until he retired in 1966. Allen began by announcing that the

designation Model 707 had been assigned to a jetliner project and emphasized that the proposed airplane also had military possibilities. This was not only a selling point but happened to be the truth—the Air Force had been complaining that KC-97 tankers were forcing B-47s to fly at near-stall speeds during refueling.

Allen then called in Maynard Pennell as head of preliminary design, technical staff chief George Schairer, and chief engineer Lysle Wood to brief the directors on the transport's design. Assistant sales manager Ralph Bell talked about possible competition and how the 707 might fit into military and airline requirements.

Yeasting, as vice president and company controller, gave the board his assessment: a jet prototype would cost between $13.5 and $15 million to develop and test. That was the bad news. The good news, Yeasting said, was that he believed the Treasury Department would allow Boeing to write off the cost. Such a request already had been made, he added, but he also warned that even if approval was granted, it wouldn't be for several months and Boeing couldn't waste any time waiting for a ruling.

Beall rose to disclose he had talked with engine manufacturers who said they'd furnish free engines for the prototype. The rest of the board meeting was summed up in the typically understated language of corporate minutes: "Considerable discussion ensued," which was like describing the Custer massacre as a mild native American protest meeting. The discussion must have been not only considerable but heated, because the final action taken was a rather tentative resolution that "management proceed with the program for the design and construction of a Model 707 jet transport with authorization to spend up to $500,000 until a Treasury Ruling is received, and if such Ruling is favorable then to proceed with the entire program."

Favorable ruling notwithstanding, Allen still was taking a mighty big gamble. Yeasting's $15 million maximum cost estimate was too low; some accounts put the actual cost of the 707's development as high as $20 million, although the generally accepted figure is around $16 million.

Allen walked into that board meeting with the unanimous support and endorsement of all his officers. About a month before facing the directors, he had called in about 25 or 30 key officials from engineering, manufacturing, and finance, and armed with his ubiquitous notebook he went around the room starting with Beall.

"Wellwood, why don't you contact Pratt and Whitney and see if they'd be willing to give us the engines for a prototype, or at least loan them if we decide to build it?"

Then he proceeded to question each man in turn. How much manpower would be needed? Did engineering have enough people to do the job? Where would the money come from? What were the sales prospects? Every person was asked to gather certain information and data. Allen concluded, "We'll meet again a month from now and see what we've accomplished."

A few days before the scheduled directors' meeting, Allen held the second staff conference and listened to the various reports he had requested. Every man voiced the opinion that Boeing should proceed with the project, but one officer confessed he didn't have the data Allen wanted.

"It's going to take about six more weeks' work," he added.

Allen said gently but in a tone coated with steel slivers, "Don't you think you can get me these answers by next Monday? Because that's when I'm going to go before the board."

The officer, a little red-faced, agreed. Allen finished his polling, leaned back in his chair, and said calmly, "Well, that's it."

As Allen had announced at the board meeting, the prototype was supposed to have the same numerical ID as the jetliner that would go into production: 707. But after getting the directors' green light, Allen had second thoughts and changed it to 367-80—apparently to throw off would-be competitors as to Boeing's real plans. Model 367 happened to be the number assigned to the KC-97, so presumably he thought the rest of the industry would assume the airplane was going to be a derivative of that series. It is doubtful whether he fooled anyone; keeping a secret in the aircraft industry is like trying to hide pregnancy in the eighth month.

To date, all Boeing jetliners have been assigned numbers in the seven hundred series. Technically the 707 should have been called the 700 but 707 somehow sounded better—maybe luckier—and Allen reportedly went along with Carl Cleveland's public relations department on this. Wellwood Beall wanted to call the airplane "Boeing 707 Jet Stratoliner," but Cleveland argued that such a lengthy name wouldn't fit any headline or story lead, and Boeing's advertising agency agreed with him. There never were any airplanes in the 500–600 series; those numbers were assigned to missiles, pilotless aircraft, and other non-airplane products.

The prototype adopted the same 35-degree sweepback as the B-47, and also the engine pod concept. But Pennell discarded one of the earlier designs, which would have had adjoining pods—two clusters under each wing—and opted for four widely separated pods.

From almost the very start, Boeing went for a big airplane with at least 100 passengers, in contrast to the Comet's original 36. Yet Pennell admitted there was some opposition to building a 100-passenger jet.

"It was a question of policy," he said, "as to whether you should expose one hundred people to the hazards of commercial aviation, and whether Boeing could survive the headlines of a hundred people being killed in a single crash. This was the only reason we at first considered building a smaller jet that wouldn't have been much larger than the Comet—say about the size of the DC-6 or Constellation."

The *B*-is-for-big policy that was Boeing's trademark effectively elim-inated all competition from overseas when it started selling jets to the world's airlines. The Comet's chances were to be wrecked by tragic events early in its career; the British jetliner subsequently went through major structural changes including a cabin enlargement that accommodated additional passengers, but it was a case of too little, too late.

The only other jet transport already flying while the 707 prototype was being assembled was the Soviets' TU-104, derived directly from the twin-engine Badger Bomber. And that's all it was—a bomber, overweight and plagued by engine and pressurization problems.

At this point in time, Boeing was miles ahead of any current or even potential competition. Neither Lockheed nor Convair had anything definite on the drawing boards and Douglas, although it had jetliner studies under way, seemed content with its successful long-range DC-7 piston series. The failure of these three major U.S. airframe manufacturers to recognize the shape of the future was to prove Boeing's greatest asset. At best, the competition had paper airplanes; Boeing had been working on jetliner designs since 1948 when Dan Hage was assigned to such a project, and now it was cutting metal on a real flying machine.

Prototype gestation was occasionally painful. Wells and Pennell were among the few in engineering who worried about a subject that didn't seem to concern anyone else then: noise.

"All I had to do was listen to the B-47 or B-52," Pennell said, "and I knew people who lived around a commercial airport weren't going to stand for jet noise."

This led to the development of the first primitive noise suppressors on the prototype's engines, along with new methods of stopping the 95-ton beast that landed faster than the old Model 80 flew. Bomber-type drag chutes obviously were impractical on a commercial jet, and the answer was reverse thrust capability and the use of "clamshell" devices that folded to redirect the engine exhaust after touchdown. The government's certification rules involved only the use of brakes, but Schairer recognized that a jet needed something to take the place of reversible propellers.

Ben Cosgrove was among a group of Boeing engineers sent out to the Civil Aeronautics Authority (the FAA's predecessor) test facility in Indianapolis for a "bird-proofing" demonstration. "We never had a transport plane that could hit a bird doing five hundred miles an hour," he explained, "and we had to show that the 707's cockpit windshield could withstand the impact."

The sample windshields they brought to Indianapolis consisted of a thin shield of vinyl between two glass layers, the outer glass almost an inch thick and the inner pane about a quarter of an inch. The vinyl was coated with a substance that would expand into a small bag when heated. If a bird-strike broke the outer glass, the carcass would become emeshed in the bag and couldn't puncture the inner glass layer. "The trick," Cosgrove said, "was to use the highest heat setting for the demonstration—there were only two settings, low and high."

With some 200 spectators watching, Ben mistakenly punched the low setting. A dead chicken was fired out of an improvised cannon and took out the entire windshield. On the next try, using the correct setting, the windshield held.

Then the Society for the Prevention of Cruelty to Animals protested the way Boeing was killing its test chickens—by decapitation—and ordered that they be electrocuted instead. The engineers complied, but as Cosgrove noted sadly, "You don't know how bad an odor can be until you've sniffed an electrocuted chicken."

Flush riveting was essential to cut drag, but the prototype took to the air with a few roundhead rivets installed toward the rear of the fuselage. This was the doing of Bob Bateman, who in his early engineering days was Boeing's self-admitted klutz. He made the mistake of listening to the advice of fellow engineer Don Finley.

Both Jack Steiner and Joe Sutter, the project's top aerodynamicists, had issued strict orders about mandatory flush riveting. But Finley had another idea.

"Hey, Bateman," he said, "if we put roundhead rivets on the back of the airplane, we could save a lot of time and money. Do you really think there's any drag back there?"

"I don't know," Bateman admitted, "but I'll find out."

He ran some tests and thought the drag would be minimal, so on went the roundheads. Steiner came through the factory one day, spotted the rivets, and hit the ceiling. The offense was referred to Sutter, who determined quickly the identity of the culprit. An immediate confession was obtained.

"Bateman, you're stupid!" Sutter roared. "You don't ever allow anyone to put a roundhead rivet on an airplane—and I don't care if it's in the toilet!"

But Bateman later swore the offending rivets were never removed. "As far as I know, that airplane still has half-roundhead and half-flush rivets in the back end," he claimed.

During the early phases of the 707 program, second-shift maintenance supervisor Dale Garrison noticed that some floor areas mopped by the previous shift were slippery. He decided to put up a few warning signs and summoned the redoubtable Nick Carter.

"Nick, I need about a dozen A-frames for signs that say 'floor is wet' or something like that."

The next night, Carter marched up to Garrison. "I got those signs for you."

"Great," Garrison said. "Where are they?"

"Over there."

Garrison looked. Every sign read OR SOMETHING LIKE THAT.

Producing Model 367-80 required new tooling designs, new methods of bonding in areas where bonding was preferable to riveting, and the limited use of titanium. Harvey Buffum, the project's chief tool design engineer, remembered asking for and getting $10,000 to start development work on what was then considered an exotic metal. It was a modest expenditure but one that was to pay dividends in the future.

The prototype already was taking shape on the Renton assembly line when an event occurring thousands of miles from Seattle sent shock waves throughout the aviation world. On January 10, 1954, a BOAC Comet exploded in mid-air at an estimated altitude of 27,000 feet over the Mediterranean. The Royal Navy, in a miraculous job of salvage, recovered much of the wreckage from the bottom of the ocean. It was still being examined when a second Comet en route from Rome to Cairo disappeared.

All Comets were withdrawn from service and stayed grounded after British investigators discovered the cause of the first accident. They immediately attributed the second disaster to the same cause: explosive decompression of the fuselage, traced to a tiny metal fatigue crack that propagated so fast that the effect was like a bomb exploding in the cabin. The crack originated in the frame of a small escape hatch at the top of the fuselage, and it had developed because of the repeated strains of pressurization and depressurization cycles, the equivalent of bending a piece of metal back and forth until it breaks. The initial fracture was only a few inches long, but once it began there was nothing to stop it from progressing—the entire fuselage simply split open. The devastating consequences were compounded by the fact that de Havilland, to save precious weight, had used a relatively thin gauge of skin on the pioneering jet.

Boeing and Douglas did learn a lot from the Comet, but they had learned on their own how to prevent explosive decompression. The first Comet tragedy occurred when Boeing's jet prototype was virtually completed, and the second tragedy happened only a little more than a month before Model 367-80 rolled out of the Renton plant; Maynard Pennell and his staff already had designed fatigue crack propagation out of the airplane even before the destruction of the first Comet.

Few among the spectators at the May 15, 1954, rollout ceremony had any idea of the ingenious preventive measures built into the gleaming yellow and copper-brown Model 367-80. William Bocing was present, at 72 showing both his age and his deep emotions: there were tears in his eyes when the giant jet emerged from behind the rising plant doors. Bill Allen had not only graciously invited Boeing's founder to attend, but asked his wife, Bertha, to christen the plane.

She broke a bottle of champagne over the nose, proclaiming, "I christen thee, the airplane of tomorrow, the Boeing Jet Stratoliner and Stratotanker." Carl Cleveland must have winced but it didn't make much difference; employees referred to the prototype as "Dash-80" and this was the name it still was bearing when it retired years later.

Impressive though the rollout ceremony was, even more impressive was something shown to Boeing's potential customers that was never seen by the public: a movie appropriately titled *Operation Guillotine.* Boeing engineers filmed it for two purposes: to show the vicious destructive force of explosive decompression, and what they had done to keep it from happening.

The movie opened with a conventional pressurized airliner fuselage, as the Comet's was, placed under a platform. Suspended from the platform were two huge steel blades—it was easy to see where Boeing got the title. In slow motion, the blades dropped, piercing the fuselage like sharp knives cutting through cheese. At the two points of penetration, the metal began curling outward, the fracture spreading until the cabin split open and disintegrated.

Seats, dummy bodies, overhead racks, and even the cabin floor were spit out in a terrifying sequence of destruction that lasted several seconds on the screen, but in actuality took only a fraction of a second. "My God," was the whispered reaction of an airline president when he saw the film.

The second scene showed a pressurized 707 fuselage, complete with triple-strength windows rounded at the corners to distribute the pressurization stress equally over the window area; the Comet's original windows were square. The fuselage, covered with a thicker-gauge skin than the Comet's, was braced in a manner that went back to the technique of reinforcing wooden barrels with iron staves. And running the length of the fuselage were small straps or "stoppers," strategically placed so that no matter where a fatigue crack might occur, the fracture would quickly encounter a stopper that blocked its path. It was the structural design philosophy known as "fail-safe" and no manufacturer applied it more religiously than Boeing.

Before filming this part of *Operation Guillotine,* the engineers had deliberately loaded the dice by weakening the fuselage with saw cuts up to 22 inches long, some of them deep enough to gouge through the outer skin into the bracing ribs. Then not two but five blades dropped into the already-scarred fuselage and pierced the structure.

Nothing happened. Small puffs of air escaped the five penetration points but the cabin remained intact—there was no explosion, no instantaneous disintegration, and in a real flight oxygen masks would have dropped from overhead receptacles so passengers could breathe safely during an emergency descent.

"I'm convinced—you've got it licked," the chief engineer of one airline remarked to Maynard Pennell when he saw the film.

Yet the Comet did teach Boeing an invaluable lesson, and that was the absolute necessity of flying these unforgiving aircraft by the numbers and by the book—a lesson reinforced when Dash-80 launched its flight tests two months after the rollout. Prior to the Mediterranean accidents, there had been two Comet crashes on takeoff under identical circumstances: both aircraft, trying to take off in hot, humid weather, had failed to get airborne and in one case the accident was fatal to all aboard.

Pilot error was blamed but the accidents were excellent examples of pilot error not being the whole story. Sweptwing jets may need more runway length than piston aircraft, especially in hot weather or at high-altitude airports where the air is thinner; temperature and air density affect lift, and in the two Comet takeoff accidents the pilots, afraid they were going to run out of concrete, rotated (lifted the nose) too soon. There was insufficient lift at that speed, the drag increased when the nose came up, and they were still on the ground at the end of the runway. "They got on the back side of a power curve," was the way Tex Johnston laconically phrased it.

Dash-80 ran into trouble before it ever flew. Johnston and Dix Loesch were running the final high-speed taxi test and were moving slowly toward the flight test center when the main left landing gear collapsed.

"We've got a slight problem," Tex informed the Renton Field tower in a masterpiece of understatement. George Martin rushed to the scene and figured out how to jack up the plane without inflicting further damage. That night, engineering went to work redesigning the landing gear struts.

Johnston and Loesch were the test pilots who took Dash-80 skyward for the first time, July 15, 1954. Bill Allen was there to watch the takeoff and Tex noticed how nervous he was. Allen was walking around with his head down and slightly stooped over, as if the weight of that $16 million investment had been attached to his shoulder like an iron parachute. Johnston walked over to him and patted him on the back.

"Bill, this airplane is perfect. It's in good shape. We've done everything we can on the ground. Now it's time to fly and all indications are that it's going to be great."

After they landed, Tex recalled, "I think he was an inch taller."

The first flight was uneventful, which is more than can be said for subsequent ones. Despite Tex's use of the word *perfect*, the prototype fell short of that description. The braking system, a constant source of early troubles, failed during a landing and the nose wheel collapsed when Tex ground-looped to keep the plane from going into a ditch and hit an obstruction. George Martin, who had witnessed the crash, advised Johnston and Loesch to phone their wives before any wild rumors got started.

"I'll take care of the airplane," he added.

It was three A.M. before the Dash-80 finally was put into a hangar. Martin knew the Aircraft Industries Association was holding a meeting in Seattle and that Wellwood Beall had promised to show the prototype to members later that day. He called Beall and told him what had happened.

"Nothing to it," Beall assured him. "Just cover up the damage somehow."

They managed to prop up the nose and threw a canvas over the smashed nose gear. The AIA members showed up on schedule and didn't suspect a thing. In fact, Hall Hibbard, Ed Wells' counterpart at Lockheed, looked admiringly at Dash-80 and remarked to Martin, "It's beautiful but there's only one thing wrong with it."

Martin, thinking he had spotted the damaged nose gear, gulped, but Hibbard continued, "It's got Boeing's name on it instead of Lockheed's."

That incident was nothing compared to one that occurred later when the same AIA group and representatives of the International Air Transport Association held joint meetings in Seattle. The Gold Cup hydroplane races were being held at the same time, and Allen invited the industry dignitaries to watch the events from three yachts Boeing had chartered for the occasion. As a special treat he also told Tex Johnston to stage a flyby in the Dash-80 on the day of the races so everyone could see the airplane of the future.

Tex never did anything halfway. PR director Carl Cleveland had told him to come over Lake Washington, where the boat races were being held, at a prearranged time. When that moment arrived, the Dash-80 was in the middle of a routine test flight over the Olympic Peninsula and Johnston said to copilot Jim Gannett, "I'm gonna roll this bird over the Gold Cup course."

"They're liable to fire you," Gannett warned.

"Maybe, but I don't think so."

The Dash-80 was doing 450 mph when Tex brought it over Lake Washington at only 300 feet, put the jet into a 35-degree climb and proceeded to do a complete 360-degree barrel roll. Then he reversed course, came back over the lake and repeated the maneuver—again in full view of 300,000 awed spectators, some vastly impressed industry officials, and a very unhappy William McPherson Allen.

After the second roll, Allen turned to Larry Bell of Bell Aircraft, one of his guests. "Larry, give me about ten of those heart pills you've been taking. I need them worse than you do."

Bell laughed. "Bill, I think he just sold your airplane."

Allen ignored him and said to Carl Cleveland, "I don't think we should have anything in the newspapers about this."

Poor Carl pointed out it was going to be a little difficult to keep something out of the papers that 300,000 people had just witnessed. Allen didn't pursue that matter further, but at eight o'clock Monday morning, Johnston appeared in his office where not only Allen but Wells, Beall, Schairer, and Martin were waiting.

Allen's first question was directed not at Tex but at Schairer.

"Did you tell him to do it?"

Schairer never had a chance to reply, for Johnston immediately said, "No, he didn't."

Allen turned to Tex. "What made you do it?"

"I was selling the airplane," the test pilot answered. He went on to explain that the Dash-80 was never in any danger, that an airplane doesn't recognize altitude if the forces imposed on its structure do not exceed one g (the force of gravity).

Allen, still openly upset, was silent for a moment. "You know that," he finally said, "and now we know that. But the public doesn't know it. Don't ever do it again."

Tex promised to behave. What he didn't tell Allen, however, was that he had rolled the prototype near Mt. Rainier on a previous flight and his fellow test pilots agreed with him that the maneuver, while spectacular, never endangered the airplane because the roll was slow and carefully controlled. They heard later of one incident in which an Air Force pilot actually did a *full loop* with a KC-135, the 707's military designation, and got away with it, although both outboard pods were torn off.

Maynard Pennell didn't get mad at Tex, either. "It was an unnecessary sales job," Pennell commented, "but it really was a spectacular way to demonstrate the airplane. With a skilled pilot, the risk was minimal."

Johnston believed Allen had forgiven him. In fact, he was invited to Allen's home for dinner the same day of the on-the-carpet session, and the first person to greet him was Eastern's crusty Eddie Rickenbacker.

He grabbed Tex's Stetson hat, pulled it down over the pilot's ears, and chortled, "You slow-rolling son of a bitch—why didn't you let me know you were gonna pull that? I would have been riding the jump seat!" Allen overheard this and smiled when Rickenbacker added, "Damn, Bill, *that's* the way to get attention with a new airplane."

Mef Allen said the roll was the talk of that evening, most of it expressions of approval and admiration that a huge commercial jet could be rolled safely. But while Tex left the house convinced he had been exonerated, there is considerable evidence that it took a long time before Allen really forgave him.

Many months went by and Johnston was attending the annual management lawn party at the Allen home. He poked Allen in the chest with a finger and asked, "Bill, are you finally willing to admit that slow-rolling the Dash-80 was the greatest thing that ever happened to that program?"

Allen gave him a look that would have frozen boiling water.

"No," he said icily.

In a 1977 speech to the Washington State Historical Society, Allen said he thought at first the rolls might have been unintentional and that he summoned Johnston to his office merely to ask if something had gone wrong with the controls. He didn't get angry, he insisted, until the test pilot admitted he rolled the $16 million prototype deliberately.

"It has taken nearly twenty-two years for me to reach the point where I can discuss the event with a modicum of humor," he told the audience.

Ironically, the same test pilot who so confidently stunted Dash-80 was never quite satisfied with the plane's stability. The prototype had a yaw damper to prevent Dutch roll, but Tex considered it inadequate. When the airlines began training pilots for jet operations, two carriers lost new 707s while practicing Dutch roll recovery, and after the second accident Johnston called Beall.

"Wellwood, I need to have a meeting."

"What about?"

"The 707's stability."

"Okay," Beall said, "I'll get some people together in a couple of days and . . ."

Tex interrupted. "I want that meeting *now*, Wellwood."

"Who do you want to be there?"

"You, Wells, and Schairer."

"How about in five minutes?" Beall asked.

"Perfect."

Those three were present when Johnston walked into Beall's office, and so was Bill Cook. Wells said in his usual calm tone, "Tex has something he wants to tell us."

Tex wasted no time. "If I'm going to represent the Boeing Company as a test pilot," he began, "the tail of this airplane has to be fixed. It has directional stability problems." He went on to recommend installation of an irreversible rudder power boost with a maximum pressure of 40 pounds, and an increased high-aspect ratio vertical tail. In lay terms, what he was suggesting was a more powerful yaw damper on the rudder and a larger vertical tail. The latter recommendation brought back memories of John Borger's old complaint that in its earlier days Boeing had a habit of putting undersized tails on new airplanes.

Johnston went on to discuss the Comet takeoff accidents, each involving premature and excessive rotation. "I think we should put a ventral fin under the rear fuselage and stress it so that if pilots try to over-rotate, they can't because the fin will be dragging on the runway. It would also stiffen up the airplane and help solve our directional stability problems."

Wells asked Cook to draw some graphs depicting directional stability curves for the current 707 and corresponding curves for a 707 with the larger tail and ventral fin.

Wells looked at Schairer. "Well, how about that, George? Will it help?"

Schairer didn't hesitate. "Yes, it would."

"Does that satisfy you, Tex?" Beall asked.

"That's what I wanted," the test pilot said, "but when?"

Wells smiled. "Now."

Someone remarked, "That's fine, but who's going to pay for all this?"

"Boeing will," Wells snapped.

That episode furnishes an illuminating insight into the healthy relationship between Boeing's engineers and its test pilots. Yet it wouldn't be stretching credibility to speculate that Wells, Schairer, and Pennell, too, would have fixed the 707's early stability problems without Johnston's pressure—they were not blind to the jet's initial faults. One problem had been that the government certificated the first 707 model with no prior experience with large jet transports.

It would be difficult to find anyone associated with the Dash-80 and 707 program who didn't regret the early mistakes. Pennell, long after he retired, summed it up best: "If I could live it all over again," he mused, "I would have avoided the Dutch roll problem. We should have paid more attention to its qualities, but we depended on Tex and the other test pilots to prove that this was something you could train around, or whether we should do something about it. They assured us Dutch roll could be trained around."

As it was, Douglas was to make an issue out of stability when it came time to start selling the world's airlines in a battle that pitted the 707 against the DC-8.

The Dash-80 was not so much a technological innovation as it was a marketing tool—a demonstration vehicle used to sell not only the commercial 707 but the military KC-135 tanker/transport version. An experimental prototype, yes, but its genes were those inherited from the B-47 and B-52, and as a commercial sales weapon it was superb, giving Boeing a tremendous early advantage over Douglas. The Dash-80 was setting speed records and taking airline executives on impressive demonstration rides while Douglas salesmen were extolling the virtues of a jetliner that existed only on paper.

Offsetting that advantage, however, was Boeing's poor commercial track record and Douglas' solid one; in effect, the Douglas pitch went, "Wait a little longer and you can buy a better airplane." It wasn't all hyperbole, either. The DC-8 on the drawing boards was larger and longer-ranged than the production 707; the latter's only real technical advantage was speed, and its major sales advantage was earlier delivery.

Those were the publicly voiced arguments; privately Douglas salesmen were claiming the DC-8, with only a 30-degree sweep, would be

easier and even safer to fly—more stable and forgiving, and less suscep-
tible to Dutch roll than the admittedly faster 707. It would be more
comfortable for passengers, too—wider, with larger windows for better
vision. Added to the Douglas reputation as the world's leading transport aircraft maker, it was a pretty effective argument.

The Dash-80's very existence kept Boeing in the race, and Seattle
became a mecca for airline executives and technical representatives
wanting to experience jet flight; the test pilots were alternating between technical missions and demonstration rides. Pan Am, naturally,
was the first potential customer—Juan Trippe had made a career out of
his airline's being the first to introduce new equipment. In fact, he
originally had ordered three Comets but cancelled the contract when
the British jet was grounded.

Trippe's desire to be always the first with a new airplane was a booby
trap for Boeing. So confident were Allen and everyone else that Pan
Am would choose the 707 over the DC-8, they ignored some critical
warning signs. Trippe still relied heavily on Andre Priester and John
Borger in any aircraft acquisition, and when negotiations began, Borger
bluntly told the Pan Am president and Boeing officials alike that the
707 was deficient in one key respect absolutely vital to an international carrier: range.

At first, Trippe wouldn't even consider the DC-8—it was too far
down the line. But Borger wasn't pleased with Boeing's selection of the
Pratt & Whitney JT-3 engine, rated at less than 13,000 pounds of
thrust. With that engine and the Dash-80's wing, Borger predicted, the
707 wouldn't even have non-stop transcontinental range, let alone
transatlantic.

Borger had heard rumors that P&W was going to modify a military
engine for commercial use, developing 15,000 pounds of thrust. Even
with water injection for takeoffs (the reason the early 707s were dubbed
"water wagons"), the JT-3's maximum thrust was less than 14,000
pounds.

"We tried to convince Boeing to put the JT-4 on the 707," Borger
said, "and we also tried to convince Douglas it should use that engine
on the DC-8. We got nowhere with Boeing and at first didn't do much
better with Douglas, although at least they were listening. Schairer
was absolutely convinced the JT-3 had non-stop transatlantic capability, but the problem wasn't just the engine—the 707's wing was too
small."

To help sell the 707, Boeing retained the services of Walter Dorwin
Teague Associates as the interior designer, and this task was assigned
to the Stratocruiser's cabin creator, Frank Del Guidice. Boeing built a
mockup that reproduced the 707's fuselage dimensions but was just an
empty shell awaiting Del Guidice's ideas. The designer laid down one
hard and fast rule: no one from Boeing was allowed to see the mockup

until Del Guidice and his crew had finished the interior, except for two engineers who could make periodic inspections.

"This was to keep Boeing engineers from kibitzing, criticizing, and suggesting changes that would have delayed completion indefinitely," Del Guidice related. "For that reason, we insisted that the mockup work be done in New York instead of Seattle. Fortunately, Beall agreed we had to use this approach."

Boeing leased space in a huge manufacturing building on New York's west side between 23rd Street and 11th Avenue; it was so big that a semi-trailer could take an elevator to the 11th floor. The completed mockup, constructed so it could be taken apart and shipped easily, cost slightly under $400,000, a figure that didn't include what Boeing paid for the building lease.

The price was a bargain considering what Del Guidice accomplished. One of his first challenges was to overcome the confining tube effect of the 130-foot-long cabin, a length that invited claustrophobia.

"This was accomplished primarily by breaking up the seat rows in blocks of different colors, and providing additional accents with headrest covers," Del Guidice said. "And there were other visual interruptions that eliminated the tube atmosphere—the life raft receptacles in the ceiling, for example, and the overhead passenger service unit containing the oxygen mask, lights, call button, vents, and seatbelt/no smoking signs." What he was unable to do anything about were the overhead racks above the seats. "We tried to fill them in with doors, but the airlines wouldn't have it and neither would Boeing, because of the extra weight. In those days, passengers didn't bring so much carry-on luggage and when that began to happen, Boeing shifted to overhead bins with doors."

The first priority in cabin furnishings, aside from attractiveness, was maintenance—everything had to be durable and easy to clean. For the largest single item, the cabin sidewalls, Del Guidice picked a new material, vinyl-clad aluminum. Over this material went silk-screen graphics of various designs from which the airlines could choose.

Del Guidice organized his people into teams of specialists. One group designed the galleys, another the lavatories, a third the seats, and so on. Laminated fabrics were used on the galley and washroom walls, and the shatterproof bulkhead dividers were made of laminated glass between two vinyl sheets.

The only Boeing engineers allowed to see the mockup interior under construction were Jim Yates and Milt Heineman, who flew to New York about once a month to check on progress. The mockup took five months to complete, and before the unveiling Walter Dorwin Teague held a luncheon at the Waldorf Astoria for about 60 or 70 airline brass, plus Boeing officials who already had seen it at a private showing.

After the luncheon, the guests were transported to the mockup building to see what Teague described as "Flight into the Future." Del

Guidice stood outside the mockup room like a playwright listening for applause and laughs. He finally couldn't stand the suspense and went inside.

"Beall was writing on the sidewalls with lipstick and crayons, then wiping off the smears to show how easy the material was to clean." Del Guidice laughed. "And everyone was hanging up his jacket in the washroom and turning around to see if the lavatory was adequately sized."

Beall joked that the washrooms "were built around Del because if he could hang up his jacket and turn around, anyone could." It was a case of the pot calling the kettle black—if anything, Beall was more rotund.

The unveiling included a nice touch of showmanship. When all guests were in the mockup, the lights dimmed and a rosy dawn illuminated the cabin windows. A simulated captain's voice came over the cabin PA system: "In the length of time it took to make this presentation, we have flown from New York to Washington."

But some 700 miles from the New York display was another mockup that had a far greater impact on the 707's future. United's own engineers had built it at the airline's headquarters so UAL officials could compare what the two competing manufacturers were offering.

It actually was a hybrid mockup: one section had the 707's interior dimensions and the other the DC-8's; the latter was only three inches wider, but those three inches might as well have been three miles because they provided sufficient width for six-abreast seating, three on each side. The 707's cabin was configured for five-abreast seating, three on one side and two on the other.

Pat Patterson looked carefully and often at the double mockup and eventually chose the DC-8 mostly on the basis of its greater seating capacity. This was handwriting on the wall that Wellwood Beall couldn't erase. The airlines traditionally have played follow-the-leader in equipment selection, and United—very much an industry leader—had made a choice that also made an impression.

It was a gamble for Patterson; if American or TWA picked the 707, United would be pitting its 300-mph DC-7s against 600-mph 707s on the lucrative transcontinental routes for about a year. Yet the general feeling throughout the airline industry, both here and abroad, was that if United was willing to wait for the DC-8, maybe it really was a superior airplane.

While Patterson was still consulting with his engineering staff, Boeing was working hard to sell Pan Am. At that stage, the only jets either manufacturer had sold were an initial order of 29 KC-135s to the Air Force, a victory that had its drawbacks: it convinced some at Boeing that the company's real future lay in military business, an opinion that Bill Allen had shared for some time. It was a measure of the man, however, that he could change his mind, and his negotiations with Juan Trippe proved the point.

Clyde Skeen and Beall accompanied Allen on a trip to New York for one of the early negotiating sessions. Trippe, in his soft, mellifluous voice, said, "Now, Bill, what about the price? No one has ever sold an American jet before so tell me about the price and how you arrived at it."

Allen nodded at Skeen, who launched into a lengthy explanation of Boeing's experience in pricing its bombers—labor, overhead, tooling amortization, the man-hours-cost-per-pound formula, and a few other details.

"How many 707s do you think you'll sell?" Trippe inquired. Skeen knew what the Pan Am president was getting at—the wily Trippe was aware that much of the cost involved in building a new airplane has to be amortized over a given number of planes sold. Trippe didn't want to pay a lot of money up front. He couldn't care less what it actually cost Boeing to build the 707, knowing that cost wasn't as important as the number of jets sold.

"We figure the break-even point will be about a hundred and fifty airplanes," Skeen answered.

"And the price?"

"Four-point-two-eight million, including engines but no spares."

Trippe turned back to Allen. "Well, Bill, down the hall in another room I have Donald Douglas senior and junior, and Art Raymond [Douglas' chief engineer]. And their price for the DC-8 is three-point nine million."

Allen knew that figure was right off the west wall—it was impossible to price a paper airplane accurately. But he didn't hesitate one second. "I believe Mr. Skeen was wrong," he said smoothly. "Our price is three-point nine million."

Skeen's 150-aircraft break-even figure was to be way off, but he had no way then of anticipating the changes that would have to be made in the 707 program. So was Boeing's final price quote—it came closer to $5 million and would have been higher for Trippe if Pan Am hadn't been the launch customer.

Matching the DC-8's imaginary price did Boeing little good. On October 13, 1955, Pan Am announced it was buying 20 707s and 25 DC-8s, putting Boeing five orders behind a jetliner that hadn't been built. To Seattle, the announcement was an earthquake that confirmed John Borger's warning: the 707 was underpowered, under-ranged, and undersized. Trippe himself told a stunned Allen he considered the 707 merely an interim airplane, and emphasized that Douglas was putting the JT-4 on its jet.

Allen knew the only way to salvage the 707 program from disaster was American Airlines and his friendship with C. R. Smith. Delta was a lost cause—C. E. Woolman's relationship with Donald Douglas was such that the Delta president had been known to order Douglas transports with a phone call. The most unwelcome man in the world at Delta's Atlanta headquarters was a Boeing salesman.

TWA, run by Howard Hughes, who was having financial troubles, was an iffy prospect. Eastern picked the DC-8; despite the impression the barrel roll had made on Rickenbacker, Captain Eddie took the advice of his chief engineer, Charlie Froesch, who hated the JT-3 engine and always opted for power. When Douglas agreed to equip the DC-8 with JT-4s, that tipped the scales.

Northwest fell to the DC-8, too, over the objections of Harley Thorson, an NWA engineer in charge of evaluating aircraft designs. Thorson recommended the 707 but Northwest president Donald Nyrop balked—the conservative Nyrop was suspicious of jets anyway and preferred to wait for others to operate them before he committed his airline.

When Thorson recommended the 707, Nyrop shook his head. "Harley, Douglas has been in the transport business for a long time, while Boeing's in this just trying to reap as much out of the KC-135 program as possible. Are they in the commercial business to stay?"

Thorson said he honestly didn't know. But he respected Boeing—he had loved the Stratocruiser—and after Nyrop overruled him, Thorson decided there wasn't much of a future for an engineer under Nyrop and joined Boeing, working first for Jack Steiner, then shifting later to sales under Clancy Wilde, another Northwest alumnus.

The lack of engineering influence at Northwest at the time wasn't true of other airlines. Chief engineers like Pan Am's John Borger, Bill Mentzer of United, Froesch at Eastern, Bob Rummel of TWA, and Frank Kolk at American, all served under presidents who relied tremendously on their advice; Nyrop always was his own man. It was Kolk, in fact, who was instrumental in swaying C. R. Smith toward the 707. Kolk admired Ed Wells, he liked Boeing's reputation for building strong airplanes, and his most persuasive argument was the 707's 20-mph speed advantage over the projected DC-8. Yes, the Boeing jet was underpowered, but engines could always be improved.

In fact, Kolk had been studying the potential of the fanjet engine, a major breakthrough in engine technology. The fanjet, still in the development stage in the mid-fifties, involved the separation of the air being drawn into the engine, funnelling part of it into a huge fan located ahead of the turbine section. By utilizing this otherwise excess air, not only were thrust and range increased, but fuel consumption and noise were decreased—the fan literally added power without using fuel. And Kolk correctly regarded the JT-3 as a stopgap that would be replaced as soon as fanjets were available.

The biggest stumbling block to an American order was the fuselage width. It had been the stumbling block at United, too; Patterson actually might have bought the 707, but when he asked Boeing to widen the 707's, he was turned down. Boeing, he was told, had committed its production tooling to fuselage commonality between the 707 and KC-135, and to change the tooling for the commercial jet would be too expensive. As a compromise, Boeing offered to lengthen the fuselage to add more seats, but Patterson rejected this. Theoretically, the 707's diameter would have accommodated six-abreast seating, but only by narrowing the aisle, which would have made in-flight service unreasonably difficult.

Kolk informed Ed Wells that American wouldn't order the 707 unless Boeing widened the fuselage, and Wells passed this news on to George Martin, in charge of structures in the 707 project.

"You'd better tell Bill Allen we're in trouble," Wells warned him.

Martin did, but Allen immediately ran into opposition from two key men, Bob Regan of manufacturing and Don Finley of engineering, who were adamantly opposed on the grounds of cost, not to mention the headaches involved in changing jigs and dies already established for a joint KC-135/707 line. Wells and Martin fought for the larger body diameter and Allen was caught between the two conflicting sides.

He talked to C. R., who hit the roof.

"Bill," Smith declared, "I'll buy the 707 but, by God, Boeing is going to do it my way, and not what's right for the KC-135! We've bought all the warmed-over military airplanes from Boeing we're ever gonna buy." (He was referring to the Stratocruiser order American assumed after it acquired American Overseas Airlines as a subsidiary during the war.)

Allen's mind was made up. He told George Martin to figure out the best way to widen the 707 fuselage to at least the dimensions of the DC-8's. Martin, Wells, and Pennell went him one better: the final additional width was four inches, making the 707 one inch wider than the DC-8. Shortly after American was notified of this decision, the airline announced it was ordering 32 707s at a cost of $5.5 million each, not including the engines, which the airline was going to lease from Pratt & Whitney.

The next item on the agenda was to repair the damage at Pan Am, and this involved a marathon session in New York that ended with a major Boeing victory made possible by what Borger called "the smartest move Boeing ever made."

Beall was in Paris trying to sell the 707 to Air France when the Pan Am meeting began; he already had informed Allen that European carriers were unenthusiastic about the 707 for the same reasons as Pan Am—not enough range or power. This came as no surprise to Boeing's president, because Ed Wells had been telling him the same thing. After Pan Am announced the split order that had stunned Boeing, Wells refused to get pessimistic.

"There's no point in just licking our wounds," he declared at an executive staff meeting. "The message is loud and clear—we have to build a bigger airplane with a bigger wing and better engines."

The Boeing delegation that came to New York was led by Bruce Connelly, head of sales and contract administration, a likable man and a favorite of Allen's. Also present were Wells, Steiner, Pennell, and Clancy Wilde. Trippe knew they were in town but claimed he was too busy to see them. He finally agreed to send his technical people over to the Ritz Tower where the Seattle contingent was putting the finishing touches on a new design proposal.

Disappointed but determined, Connelly made his pitch to Priester, Borger, and Pan Am vice president Frank Gledhill, a tough negotiator known as Trippe's hatchet man. "Juan always wanted to come off as the nice guy," Wilde said, "and Gledhill did his dirty work for him."

The Boeing proposal brought smiles to Borger's face. Mostly over the weekend, Pennell, Wells, and Steiner had redesigned the 707-120, the official designation of the original production model Pan Am and American had ordered. The new series would be called the 707-320 Intercontinental, Connelly said, and the name fit. With a bigger wing and JT-4 engines, it had the non-stop transatlantic range Pan Am wanted and also the wider diameter that had garnered American.

Priester was as happy as Borger, but Gledhill wouldn't commit one way or another without Trippe's approval, and that approval turned out to be harder to obtain than a ham sandwich in Tel Aviv. For five days, Trippe kept Connelly and the others cooling their heels in the hotel before Bruce finally got fed up. He had called the president's office every morning, only to be told, "Mr. Trippe will get back to you as soon as he's available." The sixth time he heard this, he snapped, "Tell Mr. Trippe we're on our way over and we'll see him in his office."

They waited outside that office for another 45 minutes. The secretary finally admitted them and Connelly didn't bother with pleasantries.

"Mr. Trippe, we've got an airplane your people liked and we're holding early deliveries for Pan Am. We've got other airlines interested [which was mostly bluff] and we can't give you first delivery position much longer."

"Well, we're interested," Trippe allowed, "but you have to realize we've already got forty-five jets on order and we don't need any more at the present time."

Connelly said quickly, "Boeing is willing to change some of the twenty you've ordered from us to the newer model."

That did it. Negotiations in the Pan Am conference room began that same day and went on non-stop for almost another two days. "I remember seeing two dawns come up," Borger sighed. Wells went back to Seattle after the first session and Steiner followed him the next day, leaving Connelly, Pennell, and Wilde to fight the negotiation war.

Borger insisted that Boeing put specific range guarantees into the contract, such as New York–Rome non-stop. Boeing had always been and still is conservative about performance guarantees. Borger finally won the argument but then clashed with Trippe himself. Trippe had been talking to C. R. and knew Frank Kolk was pushing Boeing to extend the 707-120 fuselage 120 inches to accommodate additional seats. The Intercontinental's design already had a fuselage 40 inches longer than the 120 and Trippe wanted it stretched another 80 inches to match American's extension.

Borger knew those 80 inches meant more weight, and unsuccessfully tried to talk Trippe out of the stretch. Both Trippe and Smith had decided there should be as much commonality between Pan Am's and American's jets as possible, and Borger finally gave in. He later admitted the stretch was a better deal for his airline than for American.

"American got into a little trouble with that longer one-twenty," he said, "and had to put fanjets on it to handle the extra weight. But those eighty inches added to the Intercontinental made it one beautiful airplane that met the guarantees right across the board. If Boeing had stuck with the original one-twenty design, they wouldn't have sold more than eighty airplanes."

Wilde, who lasted through all the negotiating, said that in all the years he sold Boeing airplanes he never experienced anything like that endurance contest at Pan Am's headquarters in the Chrysler Building.

"Frank Gledhill smoked cigars and everybody else smoked cigarettes. Add that odor to the stale leftover food and the conference room got so bad, the secretaries should have worn surgical masks when they came in to clean up every morning. Gledhill was the only one who left occasionally to shower and shave—the rest of us looked like bums. I could have bought a new car with Beall's phone bill; he kept calling from Paris every hour to see how things were going."

It wasn't any wonder Beall was so anxious. He had headed the European sales effort from the start of the 707 program, with Ken Luplow as his right-hand man and Joe Sutter pitching in with his own engineering expertise. They concentrated on Air France, Sabena, Lufthansa, Swissair, and SAS, five carriers operating either Lockheed or Douglas transports and very much satisfied with those two manufacturers. Only the Dash-80's exciting performance and the lure of deliveries a year ahead of the DC-8 allowed Boeing's salesmen even to get their foot in most doors.

Of all the foreign carriers they approached, Lufthansa seemed the most receptive, but for a rather ironic reason. Luplow and Sutter were making a presentation to Lufthansa in an old German university town that had been hit hard by air raids; even the airline's headquarters building they were in was badly damaged, with only a few rooms still intact. Luplow was talking about Boeing's great experience in designing and building large, reliable airplanes when a Lufthansa official interrupted.

"Look outside, Herr Luplow," he said quietly.

Luplow did, at a scene of nothing but rubble and skeletonized ruins.

"We know all about Boeing airplanes and their reliability," the German continued. "The B-17, for example."

Boeing's technique was to station a man at every airline prospect and ride herd on the carrier until it made its jet decision—Sutter, for example, parked on Sabena's doorstep for months. He and the Douglas salesman assigned to the Belgian carrier became casual friends. They were staying at the same hotel and were having dinner together one night.

"Joe, I'm having an awful time with my home office," the Douglas rep confided. "Sabena's insisting on more range for their routes to the Belgian Congo but that means increasing the DC-8's gross weight and the company just refuses to change the design."

Sutter expressed dutiful sympathy but when he got back to his room he phoned Seattle and asked if it was possible to increase the 707's gross weight above that of the Douglas jet and extend the range. He knew nothing of the Pan Am meeting and was overjoyed when he heard the plans for the Intercontinental. Before the next week ended, he had Sabena's order.

What Pan Am did was always an important factor. It was recognized then as the world's leading international airline, and Luplow believed Trippe's choice of the 707-320 may have influenced Air France (the first European carrier to pick the 707), and to some extent Sabena and Lufthansa. SAS and Swissair stayed loyal to Douglas and so did KLM. But BOAC, which wasn't even considered a prospect at first because of its Comet fleet, was courted successfully later. Considering the foothold Douglas had maintained in Europe for so many years, four out of seven was an encouraging start for the 707—a better early showing than what Boeing at first experienced in the United States.

After the Pan Am Intercontinental order, Bill Hamilton put the new prospective wing shapes into the wind tunnel. The final configuration showed a 2.5 percent improvement in aerodynamics, but Hamilton didn't tell anyone except Ken Holtby about those encouraging results.

"If they knew how good that new wing is," he told Holtby, "they'd probably order heavier johns and a lot of other stuff."

The sales force kept hammering away, its chances vastly improved after Boeing decided on the wider fuselage and the new Intercontinental model. In other instances Boeing tailored its product to a customer's special needs: Qantas, which had been operating Douglas airplanes since the DC-3, bought the 707 after Boeing agreed to produce a special model with the fuselage shortened by 10 feet. The lighter weight gave Qantas the extra range needed for its transpacific routes. The shorter-bodied jet was called the 707-138, and prompted an industry gag that Boeing possessed a secret Great Fuselage Machine. GFM, it was said, turned out an endless fuselage from which Boeing cut off pieces to match the length an airline wanted.

A sale to Braniff was another example of Boeing's adaptability. The airline favored the DC-8 solely because the jet had JT-4 engines, and Braniff needed more power for the high-altitude airports it served in South America. Boeing offered to put the JT-4s on the standard 707, and Braniff became the only airline to operate a model designated the 707-220.

Victories were mixed with defeats as the international sales race heated up. Japan Air Lines and Trans-Canada, the airline Phil Johnson had started, picked the DC-8. Air India went for the 707. Inevitably, the competing salesmen were drawn together by mutual interests even as they fought for customers. They usually stayed in the same hotel while they were courting an airline and often became at least social friends. But they were not above trying to get a jump on the opposition, sometimes resorting to a little espionage.

Luplow was trying to sell the 707 to a certain foreign airline and lost out to a Douglas salesman, somewhat to Ken's surprise because he figured Boeing had offered the airline an excellent deal. Months later, the victor invited Luplow to dinner in honor of Ken's birthday. By four in the morning neither was feeling any pain, and that stage often creates an urge to confess past sins.

"Ken," the Douglas rival said, "remember when you blew that sale to such-and-such airline?"

"How could I forget? We had the damn thing clinched."

"Ever wonder *why* you lost it?"

"Hell, I guess you gave 'em a better deal, although how I'll never understand."

The Douglas man grinned. "Well, no harm in telling you now. We had access to all your telexes back and forth between here and Seattle. We bribed the gals in the hotel telex room to show us your messages before you sent them and Seattle's before they were delivered to you. We knew the details of Boeing's whole package, and all we had to do was sweeten ours a little."

There were some Boeing salesmen who matched such dirty-pool tactics, but they would have died before admitting it to Bill Allen. He was integrity personified, a man whose reputation awed even the hostile participants in that modern version of the Spanish Inquisition known as a congressional investigative hearing.

In February 1956 a subcommittee of the House Armed Services Committee opened hearings on charges that U.S. aircraft manufacturers were guilty of gouging excessive profits out of the government in their military contracts. Boeing representatives, led by controller Clyde Skeen, testified on the fourth day. Allen was present but at first let Skeen and one other Boeing official do all the talking. Skeen's main thrust was to show the tremendous investment inherent in the development of bombers like the B-47 and B-52, and the length of time it takes between the initial design phase and when the company actually begins to make any reasonable profit.

When Skeen finished his presentation, the subcommittee chairman asked Allen if he wished to add any comments to Skeen's testimony. Allen did.

Speaking entirely off the cuff and without a single note, Boeing's president talked for more than 20 minutes in a masterful performance. He talked about the myth of excess profits—in 1944, when Boeing grossed more than $600 million, it netted only $6 million, a profit of less than one percent. He talked about the millions Boeing had risked in the development of new bombers that turned out to be the linchpins of America's defenses.

"I submit to the committee," he declared passionately, "not only think about whether we are making too much money, but ask yourselves whether we are making enough in light of our responsibilities. Not money to pass to stockholders. Our record speaks for itself on that."

He emphasized that Boeing was putting 70 percent of its earnings back into research and new product development; the U.S. industry average was only 45 percent, and Boeing still was being accused of making too much. He reminded the committee that a law already on the books, the Vinson-Trammell Act, had set 12 percent as a reasonable profit margin in government contracts. "To my knowledge," Allen said, "we have never even approached that."

When he finished, the committee gave him a standing ovation. One member told him, "Mr. Allen, that was a magnificent statement. I think you were performing a tremendous service to not only the United States but for the entire free world, because if it was not for Boeing today, perhaps, there would be no free world."

It *was* a magnificent statement—even in the impersonal official transcript, Allen's words come alive with the emotion he felt. And their timing may have been more significant than at first it seemed. The hearings were held only two months before the Boeing board meeting that launched the 707 project, and Allen's frustrations with bureaucratic policies and political sniping may well have influenced his decision to support the jetliner program.

Now it was well under way and Walter Dorwin Teague's slogan for the mockup unveiling could have applied to that program: Boeing was indeed embarked on a flight into the future.

TEN

COMES THE REVOLUTION

IN ONE RESPECT, DOUGLAS TOOK AN EVEN BIGGER JETLINER gamble than Boeing: there was no DC-8 prototype; the first one built was a production model targeted for United, and much of the test program was accomplished with this airplane.

It was the only way to play catch-up, and it must be conceded that Douglas did an excellent design job on the DC-8 to sell as many as it did. "It was a remarkable job," Jack Steiner once remarked, "considering that unlike Boeing they didn't have B-47 and B-52 experience. To build a satisfactory jet transport from a standing start was a real accomplishment."

True, Douglas benefited from what Boeing had learned from the Dash-80's flights, just as Boeing benefited from the unfortunate Comet. And the Dash-80's role as a demonstration vehicle cannot be overestimated—there was no doubt it sold airplanes.

Among the customers it impressed was Howard Hughes, although there were times Bill Allen must have wished Hughes had taken TWA's business to Douglas. While Hughes still was trying to arrange financing for jet equipment, he phoned Allen and requested that Boeing send the Dash-80 down to Los Angeles so he could fly the plane himself.

"The damned banks are crowding me," he told Allen, "and this would convince them it's good business to buy the 707."

Brien Wygle was the pilot chosen for the mission, accompanied by Harley Beard, who served as flight engineer. The first demonstration flight was at night, and waiting for them at Los Angeles International was Lee Flanagin, a veteran TWA captain. Wygle was curious about his presence, but learned later that Hughes always tried to have Flanagin around before every flight.

With Flanagin waiting on the ground, they flew around Los Angeles for about an hour. Hughes insisted that he try a landing and Wygle ran him through the approach and pre-landing checklist, emphasizing above all that the airspeed had to be kept down on final approach. The Dash-80 had strict speed limits for every flap setting, especially with full flaps (40 degrees) because excessive speed could damage a fully extended flap.

Hughes ignored those instructions. "He kept flying it too fast," Wygle related. "I reduced from forty to thirty when he exceeded the full flap speed restriction, but it was too late."

A flap section failed, and the severed part—about eight feet long and 18 inches wide—fell on top of a parked automobile. Unless Hughes had dropped the piece on the control tower itself, he couldn't have picked a more inappropriate target: the car belonged to a Federal Aviation Agency employee. Wygle landed the Dash-80 safely, but there were FAA inspectors waiting for them when they taxied the crippled jet to the TWA maintenance hangar.

Flanagin's first look at the plane told him what had happened. As it rolled to a stop, Flanagin steered the FAA inspectors over to the rear of the wing where they could see the damage. While they were thus occupied, Hughes slipped away unseen in a car that had been stationed at the hangar. Wygle, as the aircraft's commander, took all the blame and paid a nominal fine, but he always felt the experience of working with Hughes was worth it. His recollections offer a fascinating insight into the mind of this troubled, lonely man, to whom a cockpit seemed a place of blessed refuge, and where a relatively strange pilot could become a rare friend in whom he could confide:

After we repaired the plane, we flew it five or six more times. He always said he was going to fly in the morning, but we never went up until late afternoon or evening. We'd go over to the Mojave airport and do touch-and-go landings until we were almost out of fuel.

I was staying in a cottage at the Beverly Hills Hotel. Harley and a Boeing ground crew were in another hotel. If Hughes was going to be late, his office would call me and they'd have everything worked out to the second. They'd say, "Brien, the car will pick you up at your cottage at eight-fifteen, so leave your room at eight-eleven because you need four minutes to get from the cottage to the curb."

Hughes kept a close rein on me. His driver warned me never to leave my hotel in case Hughes wanted to reach me. One day he cancelled the flight so I went over to the other hotel to have a few drinks with Harley and the ground crew. I hadn't been in Beard's room for fifteen minutes when the front desk called and said I was wanted in the lobby. I went down and there was a very upset driver. "Mr. Hughes is very distressed that you left your hotel," he told me.

I'll never forget the way Hughes looked. Very thin, even gaunt. He wore shoes with holes for laces but there were no laces, and he never wore socks. Sometimes he'd take off his shoes in the cockpit and fly in his bare feet. His trousers looked new and were well-pressed. He had a belt but he didn't put it through the loops—he tied the belt around his waist with a square knot.

He didn't fly badly except that he had no discipline whatsoever. He was very stubborn and didn't like to be told anything. The tower would give us headings and he'd refuse to fly them. I had to make up reasons for the non-compliance. In some ways he flew very well, but he was out of his element in a jet. He was a seat-of-the-pants pilot and things like checklists and clearances meant nothing to him.

He loved to talk to me just because I was a fellow pilot. One time he told me stories for four hours before he let me start the engines. Stories about airplane designs, about his dealings with Kelly Johnson [chief designer of the Constellation] and how he'd argue with Kelly about everything. About the time he flew a Connie solo from New York to Los Angeles. He had stopped in Wichita to refuel, took off again, climbed to what seemed like a good altitude, set the autopilot, took out a briefcase and started working on some papers. Two hours went by and he saw something flash by the cockpit window. "Brien," he says, "I suddenly realized these things going by me were trees—I was in the middle of a mountain range."

Those few days with him were quite an experience. He made me nervous flying because it was difficult to control him, but I did enjoy the conversations and the camaraderie. He was always very polite and friendly, and I got the feeling it was because I *was* a pilot.

Bill Allen thought Hughes was the most unreasonable customer Boeing ever had. Hughes called him one night around nine and kept him on the phone until past one. There was no telling how long Wygle and Beard would have stayed in Los Angeles if Allen hadn't finally ordered them to bring the Dash-80 back. Hughes protested, then asked if he could have it one more day. When Allen refused, pointing out that the Dash-80 was needed in the flight test program, Hughes swore he would never buy a Boeing airplane—an empty threat because TWA became a valued customer even when Hughes was running the airline.

Bob Six of Continental could be difficult, too, but for different reasons; he was a maverick, not an eccentric—a brash, flamboyant showman with a flair for marketing that kept his then-tiny airline competitive with the giants. Only a Bob Six could have attacked United, American, and TWA over the hotly contested Chicago–Los Angeles route; he actually ran TWA out of the market.

But he was a demanding terror to deal with. He ordered only four 707s but insisted they be different from anyone else's—including tails painted gold because he wanted to introduce them as "Continental's Golden Jets." At the time, the airline's headquarters were in Denver and Frank Del Guidice flew there to discuss Six's preferences for the planes' interiors. With him was Sid Weiner of Boeing's customer engineering, but when they arrived on time for their scheduled meeting, they were told that Six had just returned from a hunting trip and would be a little late.

There was a twin-engine French-built Caravelle outside, and Six's secretary suggested, "Why don't you go out and take a look at it?" They did and when they returned, they heard Six bellowing, "Where the hell are those guys? I broke my ass getting back and they're late!"

Six always paid as much attention to the inside of an airplane as he did its technical details. He loved bright colors, and those he chose for Continental's 707s may have been a bit loud for some tastes, but they were attractive and cheerful. He was inordinately proud of the interior, too. A reporter once asked him what he thought of Pan Am's 707 cabin decor.

"It must have been designed by a Seattle casket company," Six growled.

Even Boeing had doubts that Six could operate jet service over half the United States with only four airplanes. He asked Boeing what the highest possible safe daily utilization of a 707 was, and he was told they could be flown 16 hours a day, seven days a week, provided they received eight-hour maintenance checks every 24 hours. And that was exactly how Continental operated its tiny fleet: the four jets flew the airline's routes for 16 hours and were scheduled in such a way that each was back in Los Angeles every night for eight hours of maintenance. The 16-hour utilization rate was then double the industry's average.

One of Continental's 707s, however, acquired the reputation of an almost haunted airplane. It was the second of the four CAL had ordered and almost from the day it was delivered, the plane seemed to invite trouble. On one of its first flights, a mechanic in Chicago noticed a crack in the nose wheel's oleo strut. They jacked up the plane, changed the wheel, and a week later the same mechanic discovered a small crack in a main landing gear oleo strut. It was not only something that never happened before, but it had happened twice on the same airplane.

Incident number three: a main gear door fell off in flight.

Incident number four: the plane was hijacked in San Antonio by a father and son who eventually were captured, but to prevent the jet from taking off, FBI agents shot up the tires and put some 500 bullet holes in the fuselage.

Incident number five: after the 707 was flown back to Los Angeles for repairs, it was going through a taxi test before being returned to service and hit a rabbit. The carcass went into the electronic access door and ruined the sensitive equipment.

Incident number six: more repairs, then the 707 was flown to Denver, where it picked up a load of passengers for a scheduled flight to Chicago. En route, a bomb placed in the rear lavatory exploded, severing the tail section. There were no survivors.

Al Heitman, who was on the team that repaired the original hijacking damage, remarked, "You hear about lemon cars but I never heard of a lemon Boeing airplane—that 707 was just jinxed."

Another early 707 was involved in an incident that might be termed the Great Boeing Air Raid. This was Pan Am's second airplane off the line, being flown by Boeing's Lew Wallick and Walter Haldeman, an FAA check pilot. They were doing some tests around the Los Angeles area and just before heading back to Edwards Air Force Base for refueling, Wallick remembered that the DC-8 was to make its first flight that day.

They were about 20 miles from Long Beach where the maiden flight was scheduled to take place later that morning, and Wallick asked the Long Beach control tower for permission to fly over the airport. He requested a modest 5,000 feet but the tower turned out to be more cooperative than he expected.

"What is your identification number?"

"Seven-oh-seven Peter Alpha."

"Are you a Boeing 707?"

"Affirmative."

"Well, you're cleared to cross the airport at one thousand."

About one mile out the tower controller, apparently a Boeing fan, changed his mind.

"You're cleared to cross the airport as low as you want," he decreed.

At this particular moment, the airport coffee shop was jammed with media people having breakfast before covering the long-anticipated first flight of the DC-8. Wallick came screaming over the field at 500 feet, rattling the coffee shop windows. Everyone rushed outside in time to see a four-engine jetliner clawing skyward, four black plumes streaming in its wake. Reporters did the natural thing; they phoned their offices to report that the DC-8 had just taken off on its maiden flight.

Once that news was broadcast, Douglas employees planning to attend the first-flight ceremonies stayed away by the droves. Donald Douglas was livid; Wallick heard later that he called Bill Allen, raised hell, and when he found out that Wallick's copilot was an FAA employee, tried to get Haldeman fired.

Lew himself claimed he just wanted to get a look at the new Douglas jet, pointing out that he never expected the tower to let him make a low-altitude flyby. Not for another 32 years, however, did he confess there was a sequel to that "raid" on the Long Beach airport on the same day—and this one was deliberate.

Wallick had friends at Edwards who tipped him off that two Air Force pilots were going to fly a pair of chase planes carrying cameramen assigned to photograph the DC-8 after it took off.

"If you'll let me know approximately where you are with the DC-8," Wallick told the pilots, "I'd like to come by and take a look."

Boeing, Lockheed, Douglas, and Convair all used the same radio frequency during test flights in the Los Angeles area, so it was easy to follow the progress of the first flight.

"I had the radio turned to that frequency," Wallick said, "and heard them report their position. That's where I headed and saw the photographers taking pictures from the chase planes. I sneaked up alongside the DC-8, about three wing lengths away, and flew alongside for at least a minute. The unbelievable thing was that the cameramen never even noticed us and missed the shot of their lives—a 707 escorting the DC-8 on its maiden flight!"

Boeing's test pilots played additional roles in the forthcoming air travel revolution; they also were salesmen on the Dash-80 demonstration rides, and teachers when Boeing established a school for the transition of airline pilots into jets.

Another spectacular Dash-80 show was Tex Johnston's record-breaking transcontinental flight from Seattle to Baltimore March 11, 1957. The prototype covered the 2,350-mile route in 3 hours and 48 minutes; average speed was 612 miles an hour.

Aboard were 42 guests, including several media representatives, airline officials, and a number of senior airline captains. Among the latter was American's Sam Saint, who called the flight "the most exciting moment of my twenty-eight years as a pilot."

When it came to training the airline veterans, however, such enthusiasm was by no means universal. Men with thousands of hours logged in piston aircraft approached jet transition with decided misgivings—in some cases, even fear. They had heard too many horror stories about these unforgiving sweptwing beasts, and their chief concern stemmed from what they had heard about the B-47.

The rumor among airline pilots was that a jet flying at too high a Mach number would hit uncontrollable buffeting, and if you tried to slow down, you'd stall. It was true that the B-47 could get an unwary pilot into some trouble flying fast at high altitudes; in fact, the speed at which buffeting would occur acquired the frightening name of "coffin corner." The trouble was that many airline pilots believed coffin corner applied to all jets.

"On the B-47," Wygle said, "there wasn't much of a margin between buffet and stall if you were at high altitudes, and the rumor spread that if you got into a buffet situation, you were trapped. These guys also got the idea that all jets had too many bad habits, coffin corner being just one of them. When we started training them, our first job was to debunk all the scare stories."

Jim Gannett and Tom Layne set up the training program; Wygle, Wallick, Jack Waddell, Sandy McMurray, and a few others were assigned to the "faculty." Every one of them had lived with the 707 program since its inception, and most of them had jet experience dating back to the B-47. The idea initially was to train just chief pilots and check captains who, in turn, would help the line pilots make the transition. It didn't work out that way, because as the airlines began taking deliveries, they also sent line pilots to Seattle for training in increasing numbers. There were no sophisticated 707 simulators available until 1959, so most of the work had to be done in real airplanes.

"What we didn't realize," Wygle said, "was the difficulty in teaching a pilot who had been flying pistons for fifteen or twenty years how to fly an unforgiving jet."

Wallick agreed. "We didn't perceive the 707 as difficult to fly—we had been living with sweptwing aircraft for ten years. But now we were teaching senior captains, most of them in their fifties, who had spent a lifetime in propeller airplanes, and we were a little stunned when they didn't do very well at first. They were totally out of their element."

One major problem was "keeping up with the airplane." Wygle said most of them tended to be about two minutes behind the 707, because it flew faster than they had ever flown before and everything happened faster. Learning the necessity of flying by the book was another difficult experience. There were exceptions, like American's Sam Saint and Pan Am's Bill Moss, who made the transition as if they had been born in a jet. The worst ones were in the most senior category, the 58–60 age bracket. "They were always leery of jets anyway," Wygle said, "and their habits were too ingrained."

Foreign carriers, too, sent their pilots to Boeing for jet training, many of them veterans of World War II whose numbers included former enemy airmen. There were none from Japan at first, but several years later an All-Nippon captain drew Wallick as his instructor and Lew asked him what he had flown during the war.

"A Zero floatplane."

"Oh? I flew Corsairs [a Navy fighter]."

"Don't like Corsairs," the ANA pilot commented.

"Why not?"

"They shot me down."

Boeing also trained FAA check pilots, the ones who would be riding herd on airline crews, although in those days everyone was feeling their way with the unfamiliar jets. The 707 certification process itself was rather hit and miss; the rules, originally based on piston aircraft performance, were modified as more jet operation experience was acquired. In fact, the test pilots helped write the certification requirements when they discovered some of the earlier ones were irrational.

The initials *VMU* and *RTO* became familiar to the test crews, for they were applied for the first time to the 707 and subsequently to all jets. VMU stood for velocity minimum unstick—to pass this certification test, the airplane had to be rotated on takeoff until the bottom of the tail was almost dragging, and then take off without stalling. It stemmed from the Comet's takeoff accidents and was not the safest maneuver to try.

Even worse from the standpoint of inflicting real damage to the aircraft was RTO: refused takeoff. In the 707's earlier days, an RTO test could ruin brakes and tires and the Dash-80 itself once caught fire during an emergency braking test. The procedure is no longer considered dangerous, thanks to improved brake and tire design, but during the 707's certification ordeals RTO was considered downright risky.

The 707-120 inherited the sweptwing tendency to "tuck-under," a kind of first cousin to the pitch-up problem at high speed because the latter could follow the former. At high Mach speed, if the nose pitched up and the pilot trimmed to compensate, the airplane wanted to go nose down and stay there. This was a dangerous characteristic because unchecked tuck-under retained the high Mach speed—the jet could keep diving and build up more speed. Tuck-under was worse on the B-52 and both the early 707 and KC-135, but even the DC-8 with its lesser sweepback wasn't immune.

To eliminate tuck-under, Boeing developed a Mach trim device that was automatically activated if the 707 got into an unwanted dive and picked up too much speed; the trim brought the nose up before the dive became excessively fast. Then one cold winter night late in 1958, only two months after the first 707s went into airline service, an incident occurred over the Atlantic that could have set back the jet age at least five years or perhaps longer.

A Pan Am 707-120 was flying from Paris to New York at 35,000 feet. Captain Waldo Lynch, a Pan Am veteran, left the cockpit to chat with passengers—in those days it was not only legal but an encouraged practice for captains to perform this public relations gesture. He was still in the cabin when copilot Sam Peters and the flight engineer began to feel buffeting and a sensation of speed buildup. At this point the Mach trim device should have kicked in. It had been disengaged before takeoff from Paris, as required, but apparently the crew had forgotten to reset it when they reached cruise altitude.

The instrument panel lights in front of Peters suddenly went out. The copilot glanced at the captain's panel, still lit, and saw to his horror that the artificial horizon indicator had tumbled. Outside, the stars were moving counter-clockwise like a huge pinwheel. The jet had been on autopilot and Peters suspected it had somehow either malfunctioned or become disengaged.

He pushed the autopilot release button and attempted to stop the roll by applying rudder and left aileron. But by this time, the 707 was diving g toward the ocean at nearly the speed of sound and the g forces were building up, gripping Peters' arms and legs like a giant vise. The Mach warning bell clanged, indicating they were close to breaking the sound barrier, and to the crew it was the sound of doom.

Lynch returned to the cockpit by crawling on his hands and knees, and climbed into the left seat with the navigator's help. The altimeter was spinning so fast he could hardly read the dial, but he made them out to be at 17,000 and going down fast.

"I have command!" he shouted to Peters.

The jet plunged into a thick overcast and the whirling stars disappeared. Lynch's feet seemed pinned to the floor and his arms felt as if there were two iron blocks hanging from the sleeves, but with a superhuman effort he managed to roll the wings level. With the roll halted, the g forces lessened and the flight engineer finally was able to move. But the jet was still in a steep dive.

The altimeter read 8,000 feet. Lynch slowly pulled back on the yoke. 7,000. 6,000.

The plane shook with violent buffeting but it lasted only a few seconds and the nose came up with agonizing reluctance.

7,000. 8,000.

The captain eased off slightly but kept the yoke back. All instruments now were normal. The navigator took a fast position check and Lynch climbed back to 31,000 after advising air traffic control the flight had experienced "some difficulty." They landed at Gander, Newfoundland, where the 117 passengers were taken off to await the arrival of a substitute 707. An examination of the plane revealed damage to the horizontal tail stabilizers, wing panels, and ailerons, yet after some emergency repairs the jet was sound enough to be ferried to Seattle for major repairs.

It was estimated that in the length of time it took to dive from 35,000 feet to 6,000, the plane had been subjected to loads of at least 4.5 times the force of gravity. Al Larson, a Boeing structures engineer, told Pan Am's Borger the loads probably hit 5 gs. The 707's supposed design limit was 3.75 gs. Boeing engineers figured the jet had reached Mach .95 before Lynch pulled it out of the dive—a classic example of what could happen in an unnoticed tuck-under situation. When Lynch climbed out of the plane at Gander, he had two black eyes from the g loads.

The damage went beyond the stabilizers, ailerons, and wing panels. The repaired 707 went back into service with two inches of permanent bend in the wings, and Pan Am pilots who flew it swore it was faster than any other 707 in the fleet.

Lynch paid a $1,500 fine for being out of the cockpit, a questionable penalty inasmuch as there was no rule against it at the time. Actually, he saved the lives of 117 passengers and he probably saved more than that.

"He saved the jet age itself," Borger remarked. "If that plane had gone in, it would have been a mysterious disappearance that no one could explain, and jets would have been suspect for at least another five years."

Yet the near-tragedy demonstrated what not even Boeing's own engineers had realized: the enormous strength that had been built into the 707. It was to be proved again on more than one occasion.

June 28, 1965: a Pan Am 707 had just taken off from San Francisco International bound for Honolulu when the outboard engine on the right wing caught fire and exploded, taking 25 feet of the wing with it as the entire pod severed. The captain landed the stricken jet safely.

Even Boeing had considered it aerodynamically impossible to keep a 707 in the air with one-third of a wing gone. "We run just about every kind of structural test imaginable," an engineer marveled, "but you never imagine a plane in this kind of situation remaining flyable. That cockpit was full of real pros."

Freak? Pure luck?

December 4, 1965: a TWA 707 collided with an Eastern Constellation at 11,000 feet shortly after the jet had taken off from New York's Kennedy International Airport. The impact tore off 35 feet of the 707's left wing. Nineteen minutes later, the jet landed safely at JFK with even worse damage than the Pan Am 707 had suffered.

After these two incidents, someone sent a tongue-in-cheek message over TWA's Teletype system:

AMENDMENT TO INOPERATIVE EQUIPMENT LIST—EFFECTIVE IMMEDIATELY ALL BOEING 707S MAY BE DISPATCHED WITH RIGHT OR LEFT WING MISSING.

The last scene in the movie *Airport* shows the mechanic played by George Kennedy looking at a 707 that survived a bomb blast and landed with the tail section almost in shreds, but still intact. Kennedy murmurs, "Thanks, sweetheart." And a pilot remarks, "Remind me to send a note to Mr. Boeing."

It was more fact than fiction.

At a time when air transportation has become mass transportation, it is easy to forget what the brave new world of the jetliners was like more than three decades ago. It was a world filled with glowing expectations and promises of what jet travel would mean to the average passenger. A full-page Boeing advertisement in a 1958 issue of *Time* said it all.

It depicted a mother flying with her son. She is wearing a fresh corsage and is balancing a coin on the tray table in front of her. The boy, about eight, is listening to his wristwatch. The caption under the picture reads, *"The coin, the watch and the flower . . ."*

The copy goes on:

Within a few weeks you'll be able to board a luxurious Boeing 707. Your first flight in this jetliner will be one of the travel highlights of your life. You'll cruise serenely through high, weatherless skies, so completely free from vibration you'll be able to stand a half-dollar on edge. The 707 cabin, the most spacious aloft, will be so quiet you'll be able to hear the ticking of a watch. The flowers you brought when you left will be fresh when you arrive, for the 600-mile-an-hour Boeing jet will carry you across a continent or an ocean in half the time needed by a conventional airliner. Flight in the 707, even veteran airline travelers will find, is new and exciting—and secure. This superb luxury liner is by Boeing, the most experienced builder of multi-jet aircraft in the world.

There was a modicum of hyperbole in the ad, such as the fact that "the most experienced builder of multi-jet aircraft in the world" had produced, in its first 707 model, an underpowered jet that lacked true non-stop transcontinental range, let alone transatlantic. When American began operating its 707-120s, the airline found that many westbound flights, when they encountered strong headwinds, had to refuel in Phoenix. And hot weather takeoffs with the JT-3s, even with water-injection assist, ate up almost every foot of runway.

Knowing that the new and powerful fanjet engines were on the way, the airlines didn't really complain about the water wagons and their marginal takeoffs and range deficiencies. From the very start of service, the jets were money-making machines. They did guzzle fuel—a 707 taking off on a transcontinental flight burned more fuel in the first three minutes than Lindbergh's *Spirit of St. Louis* consumed in the 33 hours it took to cross the Atlantic. But jet fuel in 1958 cost only 10 cents a gallon, and a $5 million 707 could gross $8 million in just one year. One of the least-remembered facts about early jet operations was the $10 surcharge on each ticket; it was dropped eventually after the airlines discovered that the new jetliners were cheaper to fly than the pistons, were more profitable than early forecasts predicted, and had far more reliable engines than anyone anticipated. In 1958 the FAA required that turbine engines be overhauled at least once every thousand hours. Ten years later, the TBO (time between overhaul) was up to 8,000 hours.

An amazing number of passengers flew first class, and the usual 707 configuration in the first years of the jet age would raise eyebrows today—American and TWA, for example, divided the 112 seats in the 707-120 equally between first class and coach. As late as 1965, both carriers offered 44 seats in first class; by the early seventies, the total was down to 12.

For a number of years, many 707s also featured a lounge area just ahead of the first class section—a large, curved settee and artificial flowers in a vase resting on an attractive coffee table; it brought back memories of the Stratocruiser's most popular feature. The lounge, however, was a non–revenue-producing gimmick and fell victim to the increasing demand for seats.

American's 707s, and later TWA's, clobbered United's DC-7s in the transcontinental market. So overwhelming was the public's preference for jets that Pat Patterson suspended DC-7 non-stop transcontinental service until his DC-8s were delivered.

Yet not everyone loved the jet age. As Wells and Pennell had predicted, noise was an immediate problem that was to grow steadily worse, even though only a handful of U.S. airports were being served by jets. The first unofficial noise protest appeared on the roof of a Fort Worth apartment house a few days after American inaugurated 707 service to the Dallas area—a sign reading, JETS GO HOME.

Flight attendants were subjected to the same jets-are-unsafe rumors as the pilots, and the word spread that dire things would happen to women bidding jet trips. It was claimed that women working these flights regularly would wind up with severe menstrual problems, varicose veins, and sterility. "That last one," a stewardess supervisor commented wryly, "apparently was started by pilots."

The unfamiliarity of jet travel and the knowledge that the new planes would be flying higher and faster than any previous transports spawned public fears, too—aided and abetted by occasional newspaper stories quoting self-styled experts to the effect that the accident rate was going to soar with the introduction of jets. One of them predicted 10,000 crash fatalities a year by the turn of the century. He based that grim forecast on what the accident rate was at the start of the jet age, assuming that if traffic continued to increase and the rate remained constant, the carnage would be horrifying.

The opposite happened: even during the learning curve years of jet operations, the accident rate began declining in direct proportion to the increase in jet flights. In the first full two years of jets, there was one fatal accident for every 150,000 flights; by 1975, the rate was a fatal crash for every million flights, and as the nineties began, the rate was one for every 2.5 million flights.

No in-print airline or manufacturer advertising could match word-of-mouth praise; rare was the passenger who took a first jet flight and didn't rave about it to anyone who'd listen. The experience of vibrationless flights at speeds that shrank distance in half more than made up for the strange sensations and noises associated with this new way to fly. For a long time, the airlines felt it necessary for cabin attendants to announce before every takeoff or landing, "For those making their first jet flight, the unfamiliar sounds you may hear are caused by the landing gear being raised (or lowered) and are perfectly normal."

The magic word at Boeing from the day the Dash-80 went on the drawing boards was *redundancy*—a design philosophy that insisted there had to be as many as three backup systems in case a primary system failed. That, plus the Boeing design trademark of brute strength, were two major factors in the Air Force's selection of the 707 as the first presidential jetliner. Another factor was Curtis LeMay's satisfaction with the KC-135; LeMay actually pushed for the 707 over the DC-8, although he lost a battle to have only SAC's KC-135 tanker pilots assigned to Air Force One. All previous presidential aircraft were flown by airmen from the Military Air Transport Command's Special Air Missions squadron (SAM), and Air Force chief of staff Thomas White overruled LeMay.

Selection of the 707 was a decided honor for Boeing. FDR's flying

White House had been a Douglas DC-4, Truman used a DC-6, and Eisenhower chose the Constellation although it was Ike's secretary of state, John Foster Dulles, who first suggested it was undignified for the president of the United States to attend foreign conferences via a propeller-driven airplane. Dulles reached this conclusion when he saw Soviet premier Khrushchev arrive at such meetings in a brand-new TU-104 jetliner. To Dulles it was a matter of national pride and prestige, and he convinced Eisenhower to request funding for a jet transport.

The 707-320 that became Air Force One was delivered May 12, 1959, and its first commander was Colonel Ralph Albertazzi, a veteran MATS pilot who had gone through Jim Gannett's 707 school as the top candidate. The blue-and-white exterior color scheme with the eye-catching block-lettered words *United States of America* was the work of Raymond Loewy, but Walter Dorwin Teague's firm did the plush interior.

Air Force One may have been the most prestigious sale Boeing ever made, but in bread-and-butter terms far more important were the victories won on the airline sales front. By the fall of 1957 Boeing finally had forged ahead of Douglas with 145 jet transport orders against 124 DC-8s; it was a lead the company was never to relinquish.

Success came hard and sometimes didn't come at all, especially when long-standing hostility toward Boeing was encountered. Nowhere was this more prevalent than at KLM. After KLM announced it was going to buy the DC-8, Vernon Crudge, Boeing's European sales consultant at the time, insisted that KLM could be talked into changing its mind. Ken Luplow, knowing how hard the Dutch carrier had taken that 1938 Stratoliner crash, thought it was a terrible idea but finally agreed to try after Wellwood Beall sided with Crudge.

"We chartered a helicopter from Sabena," he recounted, "and flew from Brussels to the Hague where KLM's board chairman, Dr. Albert Plesman, had agreed to see us. His greeting was on the icy side, but that didn't stop Vernon. Crudge proceeded to tell him he had made the wrong choice and that he would regret not buying the 707. Dr. Plesman never said a word.

"When Crudge finished, the chairman said coldly, 'Well, are you gentlemen through?' Crudge said yes. Plesman got up and walked out of his office and that was the end of the meeting. We never went back to them on the 707, but we did try to sell KLM later jets: they finally bought the 747 as their first Boeing airplane and are a valued customer, but it took a long time.

"Sometimes we couldn't even get our foot in the door of a carrier loyal to Douglas. When we tried to sell the 707 to SAS, its president met us at the Stockholm airport instead of his office, told us they had decided to buy the DC-8, and hoped we'd have a pleasant trip back."

At least one airline did have second thoughts about its DC-8 decision: Northwest. Douglas had promised to add more fuel capacity and increase the gross weight so NWA could fly the DC-8 non-stop between Seattle and Tokyo. After Nyrop signed the contract, however, Douglas withdrew the offer; its engineers discovered that installing a center fuel tank created serious climb problems. Nyrop had to take delivery and he was equally angry about another Douglas promise: they had agreed to build a completely new jet about a third smaller than the DC-8, then decided the development costs would be too high.

Nyrop's door suddenly was open to Boeing salesmen and Clancy Wilde, accompanied by Harley Thorson, accepted the invitation. They were dealing from strength, for Boeing early in 1957 already had committed itself to a 707 variant with a shorter fuselage: the 720A. They suggested this airplane, equipped with new fanjet engines, to Nyrop, who thought the 720A didn't have enough range. Wilde offered to increase fuel capacity by adding more weight, a modification that would meet Northwest's three main range requirements: non-stop transcontinental, one stop to the Orient via Seattle, and two 3,500-mile stages between New York and Tokyo.

Nyrop was suspicious. "You know, I made two mistakes buying the DC-8 and Electra [Lockheed's four-engine propjet]. I don't dare make another one. Are you guys sure this airplane is going to do what you say it will?"

Wilde was senior member of the sales team, so Thorson turned to him, expecting an answer. Clancy hesitated—"God, it was the longest hesitation of my life," Thorson remembered—and finally said, "Yes."

The beefed-up 720 fanjet that Northwest ordered became the 720B. Northwest's load factors on its Orient routes turned out to be so heavy, however, that the 720B wasn't large enough and the airline bought a number of 707 Intercontinentals.

This was a good example of an engineer knowing the airplane he was trying to sell. While the 720 still was in the design stage, engineering went to work on the job of adapting the plane to fanjets. It meant beefing up the wing to take the heavier engines, and changing the size of the tail on the shorter fuselage, but the finished product was the fastest of the entire 707 series.

"It was a flying hot rod with tremendous thrust," Thorson reminisced. "Pilots said it flew like it had a burning tail between its legs."

Nyrop tried to get Wilde to take his DC-8s in trade for the 720Bs, but Bruce Connelly refused unless Boeing could find a customer for the unwanted jets. He sent Thorson over to Swissair, a DC-8 operator, but Harley struck out and Connelly dug in his heels. Not for some time would Boeing seriously consider trade-ins.

Unlike Northwest, United was happy with the DC-8. But United, too, was after Douglas to build a smaller jet transport and when Douglas declined, another door opened for Boeing—not only the genesis of the 720 program, but the real start of Boeing's domination over

the commercial airplane market. United wasn't the only airline pressing manufacturers to build a medium-to-long-range jetliner for routes
that didn't require planes the size of the 707 or DC-8. Western's
president Terry Drinkwater was interested, and Drinkwater originally
had rebuffed any large jet with the comment, "Would you buy the
Queen Mary to sail across Lake Tahoe?"

The Convair division of General Dynamics was trying to nudge its
way into jet transport competition with the sleek 880, which promised
the kind of range and performance being sought. The design looked
promising enough to alert Boeing to the possibility of a potentially
lucrative market among airlines that didn't need large, long-range jets.
And it was a chance to capitalize on what engineers like Wells and
Steiner, not to mention the salesmen, had been dreaming of—the jet
family concept: different-size airplanes for different-size routes.

United was turned off by the 880's comparatively narrow fuselage
and its five-abreast seating, and Pat Patterson wanted no part of propjets
like the Lockheed Electra. But Patterson and his technical staff were
extremely interested in the 720 design. UAL's 1957 decision to buy 28
720As prompted Boeing to establish its first fleet-planning department, a group of route-analysis specialists who could tell an airline
how specific jet models could fit into its route system.

Such data finally brought Eastern into Boeing's camp. Clancy Wilde
led the sales force pitching the 720A and ran into immediate opposition from Rickenbacker's technical guru, Charlie Froesch.

"We don't need any more jets," Froesch said sourly.

Wilde hauled out the fleet plan Boeing had prepared for Eastern.
"Okay, Charlie, here's what we figure is the best route utilization for
your DC-8s. The Electras are fine for some of the routes they're
serving, but on others they'll be competing against pure jets. The
DC-8 is too big for those routes and that's where the 720 comes
in . . ."

Froesch wasn't convinced but Rickenbacker was, and Eastern became the second launch customer the 720 program needed. Western
liked the 720A's size but not its engines and bought 720Bs, eventually
operating them not only domestically but over the Pacific when the
airline won Los Angeles–Honolulu authority. Western later bought
some Intercontinentals, but the 720B was always the favorite among
its pilots. The airline also acquired three 720As when it merged with
Pacific Northern Airlines. One of them, according to its crews, always
flew slightly sideways and Boeing engineers spent weeks trying to
figure out the reason without success. They finally concluded the
plane had to be afflicted with the same mysterious peculiarity as the
repaired Pan Am 707 that somehow flew faster.

Technically, the 720 was nothing more than a smaller, lighter 707,
but its importance was far greater than that of a mere derivative. It told

the airline industry that Boeing was adaptable and versatile, willing to produce not just a single model but a whole stable of jets.

As the company headed into the first full decade of the jet age, the 707 single-handedly had ended the Douglas domination of the world's commercial airplane market. Despite its early technical problems, Boeing's first jetliner represented an aeronautical engineering triumph whose scope can be judged by this single fact: 37 years after the Dash-80's first flight, the last 707 was produced as an AWACS (Airborne Warning and Control System) military aircraft. Basically, it was still the same 707, one of the more than 1,000 built since the first production model came off the Renton assembly line in 1958—the longest continuous production of any airplane in aviation history, and one that didn't end until May 1991, with more than 400 still in service.

Not even its creators could foresee that kind of achievement, nor could they come close to imagining that 36 years after the Dash-80's maiden flight, this historic aircraft would take to the air again on the most sentimental voyage of its illustrious career. Most of that career was spent as a flying test bed for new systems, engines, flaps, and other components that Dash-80 tried out before they were deemed good enough to install on production airplanes.

For a long time, the jetliner Dash-80 spawned looked like just another Boeing artistic success and financial flop; it took almost eight years before 707 sales amortized all development, tooling, and modification costs—the switch to a wider fuselage and the changes made to improve stability helped keep the program in red ink. Yet those very changes were solidifying Boeing's reputation for engineering and product integrity.

John Yeasting had an unshakable belief that Boeing would be better off concentrating on commercial airplanes; from all accounts, Boeing's chief financial officer didn't like doing business with the government and sincerely believed that if everyone paid more attention to the bottom line of controlling cost, the company wouldn't need government contracts. He convinced a few other officers of this, too, among them Bob Regan of manufacturing. But while Yeasting had great influence with Bill Allen, it didn't apply to this subject.

Ben Wheat, who worked for Yeasting in finance, mentioned his superior's anti-government feeling one day to Allen.

"My boy," Allen remarked, "the only thing worse than government business is no government business."

And it was a military project, somewhat less glamorous than building jetliners, that helped keep Boeing afloat while it was struggling to establish a place in the commercial transport market.

The program was called Minuteman, an intercontinental ballistic missile system that was to join the B-52 as a major deterrent weapon. It was more than that, however. Minuteman was to be Boeing's most successful non-aeronautical venture, and one that gave the company its next generation of leaders.

ELEVEN

MISSILE MUSCLE

THE GENIUS OF EDWARD WELLS IS BEST UNDERSCORED BY the fact that it was not confined to designing airplanes.

Long before World War II ended, the preliminary design (PD) unit he established within Boeing's engineering department was studying projects that had nothing to do with bombers or transport aircraft. During the early years of the war, they involved mostly esoteric military products that never got off a drawing board.

Bob Jewett, who was the second chief of PD replacing Don Euler toward the end of the war, said many suggestions came from outside the company. One in particular was a proposal that Boeing build rockets that could be launched against Germany from a hiding place in the dry canyons of eastern Washington state. Such a weapon was patently beyond the state of the art in both range and accuracy, but Jewett never forgot it because it was so close to what Minuteman eventually would become.

Wells never discouraged PD from considering even the wildest ideas and going ahead with those that weren't so wild. Among them was the development of a small gas turbine engine with a number of possible applications, from powering small ships and ground vehicles to auxiliary propulsion on rockets.

Dan Hage headed the group assigned to design a gas turbine engine. The project was modestly successful; the engines were purchased by the Navy as auxiliary units for ships and by the airlines as starters for the main engines. The engineers did, however, stray pretty far afield at times, especially in the immediate postwar period when Wells convinced Allen to exempt as many engineers as possible from the mass layoffs, keeping the engineering talent intact. Said talent went to work on a number of civilian products they designed in "the Cave"—a loft in an uptown office building where the PD people were told to keep busy, even if a project was light-years away from airplanes.

The projects included a prefabricated kitchen-bathroom unit that could be taken through the door of a house and assembled inside, an eggbeater with a pistol grip adjustable for southpaws, a refrigerator with uniquely arranged storage areas, an improved automobile spark-plug, a shaft-driven bicycle, a low-slung railroad coach for high-speed travel, and—perhaps the most intriguing—an automobile that could have been designed in the 1980s.

The mockup built in the loft had the inside room of a Cadillac or Lincoln, with the exterior wheelbase and length of today's mid-compacts. The bumpers were extended completely around the body for collision protection, and an aisle ran between front and back seats so a passenger could move around without leaving the car.

It was a rear-engine design, but the mockup lacked an engine; no one got serious enough about the automobile to design or adapt an existing power plant, although Wells was fascinated with cars and at one time almost went to work for Chrysler.

Even engineless, the car was a better idea than the unusual mouse-trap the engineers built. It threw a dead mouse across the room, then reset itself for the next victim. From the standpoint of viability, the portable kitchen-bathroom unit was mildly successful; Boeing obtained patents for this design and sold them to a company that installed the units in Alaskan housing projects.

By far the best, however, was an electronic analog computer, essentially a box the size of a large filing cabinet filled with vacuum tubes capable of solving math problems in analog form. Lockheed bought a number of units and they proved so popular that Ken Luplow, who didn't have any airplanes to sell, wound up peddling the computers. A small brochure describing the device was mailed to major companies throughout the United States, and except for a single appearance at a trade show, all the sales were from mail orders. When airplane business picked up, the analog computer died a natural death—no one could foresee the day when Boeing would have its own computer services division.

While Wells was content to let PD imaginations run wild—mostly to keep the boys busy—he had his eye on an area far more challenging than mousetraps, eggbeaters, and far-out automobiles. Boeing's involvement in non-airplane activities, it should be emphasized, had the wholehearted support of Wellwood Beall, who in contrast to Bill Allen was diversification-minded. Allen's attitude was ambivalent; he was dubious about any diversification, yet he didn't forbid it. His respect for Wells was too great, and when Wells and Beall pushed the company into missile projects, Boeing's president—who could never get really enthused about missile involvement—gave them his blessing.

About a year before the war ended, Wells hired Dr. Cecil Stedman, a professor of electrical engineering, to work on autopilot and flight test instrumentation projects. But with military interest growing in missiles, he had Stedman set up Boeing's first scientific research department: the physical research unit. With that uncanny crystal ball ability of his, Wells could grasp the future importance of missiles to the military and at the same time recognize Boeing's lack of talent and experience in the highly technical areas of rocket propulsion, gyro guidance systems, servo-control systems, and radar.

In a relatively short time, Stedman recruited a small cadre of specialists for the new unit. Early Air Force indifference to any flying weapon that didn't have a human being at the controls evaporated as both the Army and Navy began developing missile systems—the Army would have its Nike and the Navy the Bumblebee. Boeing, still tied to the Air Force's apron strings, finally got its chance in the form of an invitation to Wright Field to discuss the company's possible role in developing an Air Force missile.

Beall, Wells, Stedman, and Jewett were the Boeing attendees at this meeting, out of which came their unanimous choice of a project: GAPA, for ground-to-air pilotless aircraft. The goal was to develop an unmanned interceptor against enemy planes, and Wells assigned a group of about 35 engineers to the program.

They worked in a small building at the south end of the Plant Two area, called Annex D. The project engineer was Dick Nelson, a key figure in Boeing's aerospace history. One of the younger engineers was newly hired Harry Goldie, another of the company's legendary characters. A major contributor, however, wasn't even a Boeing employee: Dr. Rudolph Hermann, a German scientist brought to the United States after the war and considered one of the world's leading experts on supersonic aerodynamics.

No one at Boeing knew much about this phase of aerodynamics, which was essential to the development of missiles fast enough to intercept and destroy enemy jets. Nelson won Hermann's assistance, albeit briefly, after some recruiting that would have done justice to a college football coach trying to sign a halfback with 4.5 speed.

He flew to Wright Field where Hermann was temporarily working as an Air Force advisor. They had dinner at the Van Cleve Hotel, a pleasant but inconclusive meeting at which the only progress made was Hermann's agreement to visit Seattle. Upon his arrival and introduction to Boeing's top engineers, Dr. Hermann developed a sudden case of reticence to talk about much of anything except Seattle weather.

"We couldn't get Hermann to open his mouth," Nelson related. "He had decided he wasn't going to tell us anything. But in general conversation, we found out he liked to ski. So I got a group of aerodynamic types who could ski, including Bill Cook. I furnished Hermann with some boots, skis, and skier's clothing and we took him up to Stevens Pass.

"He had a wonderful time—it was the first time he had been skiing since before the war. On the way back, he suddenly opened up and started to tell us all about supersonic aerodynamics and some of the idiosyncrasies and problems we'd encounter. I couldn't drive slow enough—everyone was sopping up all this very valuable information. We didn't have any inkling of the depth to which the Germans had already been working in this area. And that was how we got into supersonic aerodynamics."

GAPA, powered both by rockets and a ramjet engine, was too far along in the design stage to utilize fully much of what Hermann imparted to the engineers, but his expertise was applied directly to the shape of the wings on Boeing's second guided missile. Flying at supersonic speeds, GAPA could reach altitudes of 60,000 feet or more and was guided to a target with a radar locking beam.

It was first tested at a range near Wendover, Utah, and over the next 18 months more than 50 were launched—the last four, aimed at remote-controlled planes, intercepted and destroyed all four targets.

This launch pad and observers' blockhouse are still standing at the Utah site, marked by a plaque on the wall of the blockhouse stating that the first supersonic flight in the United States had taken place there. Boeing leased an Air Force C-46, the pot-bellied wartime Commando, to haul the missiles from Seattle to Wendover; one of the pilots was future vice president Dick Taylor, then in the flight test department.

The final tests were moved to the White Sands Proving Grounds in New Mexico, but these were the end of the line for GAPA. Economy-minded Secretary of Defense Louis A. Johnson decided the three branches of service were overlapping in their missile programs. He ruled that any missile with a range of less than 35 miles belonged in the category of anti-aircraft artillery, and therefore must be considered an Army weapon. This not only eliminated GAPA from the Air Force arsenal but axed the program altogether, because the Army already had Nike and didn't want or need the Boeing missile.

Dick Nelson felt strongly that GAPA was superior to Nike but his arguments fell on deaf ears. So the PD team went to work on a longer-range missile, Nelson likening the task to a duck-hunting club that wanted to bag every bird at the perimeter of a big pond.

"To do that," he explained, "we have to space the hunters' blinds around the pond just far enough apart so that if one blind doesn't stop an incoming bird, then the second blind can because we have complete coverage. But then someone does a cost analysis and discovers that if we could increase the range of the shotguns, we could have fewer blinds, and the more we increase the range, the less it will cost to bag all the ducks.

"And that's exactly what happened. As we increased the missile's range, we reduced the number of firing points and the cost of the defense system went down. But there was a bucket at the bottom of the cost curve which started going up if the range increased too much.

So we determined the ideal range was about three hundred and fifty miles—if we could develop a missile that would shoot down an enemy bomber at that range, we'd achieve the most cost-effective defense system."

The second missile Boeing developed was called Bomarc.

Bomarc was an acronym—*Bo* for Boeing and *marc* for the Michigan Aeronautical Research Center, the University of Michigan facility that helped Boeing create the missile. By the late 1950s, Bomarc was the key element in an air-defense system protecting the vital northeastern area, including Washington, D.C., New England, and part of Canada. The Michigan scientists developed the aircraft warning system that was linked to Bomarc bases.

A new missile is not like a new airplane, which is almost guaranteed to fly on its first takeoff. In the 1950s, a missile that achieved success on its first flight was a rarity, and Bomarc was no exception. On August 1, 1954, it became the first American missile to be fired at Florida's Cape Canaveral and Nelson's summation said it all: "It was a very unhappy day."

The Bomarc blasted off, did a couple of loops, and crashed ignominiously behind the blockhouse where Nelson, Keith McDaniel, and the rest of the Boeing team were watching with dismay. Vibration had caused one of the fragile electronic components to fail, sending a false signal to the rocket motor and resulting in a hard-over swerve that severed one wing. Electronic gear fragility was always a problem in those days, and it was an area in which Boeing admittedly lacked experience. Harry Goldie, who majored in electronics at college, once remarked that "everybody said I was nuts to come to work for Boeing with an electronics degree."

But the learning curve applied to missiles as well as airplanes, although the Bomarc first-launch debacle cost Nelson his job. He had to explain personally to Secretary of Defense Charles Wilson, as Nelson put it, "how we blew up a million bucks on that one shot, and it wasn't easy."

Vice president Lysle Wood headed the pilotless aircraft division that had been established with the original GAPA contract. Under Pentagon pressure, he removed Nelson as project engineer and replaced him with Jewett; Nelson was transferred to manufacturing. He took the rap but he took it well, for in the end he was to contribute much to Boeing as an engineer who understood the problems of the people who turned designs into products.

The truth was that Boeing had troubles building a missile as complex as Bomarc, which required circuitry far more complicated than GAPA. GAPA was an anti-aircraft missile; Bomarc was designed to intercept other missiles as well as airplanes. GAPA basically was a pilotless aircraft with a jet engine; Bomarc used either a solid or liquid propellant fuel for launch and automatically switched to two ramjet engines for Mach 2 cruise—in other words, it was a hybrid: part rocket, part pilotless airplane.

Nelson found himself looking at Bomarc through different eyes when he moved over to the production side: those of the men who had to build what others designed.

"What became immediately evident was that engineering wasn't paying any attention to the manufacturing people," he said. "The engineers lived up on the fourth and fifth floors of Plant Two, the manufacturing guys lived down on the first and second floors, and quite literally the engineers were throwing their drawings down a chute to those guys below and saying, 'Here, make this.'

"And the production people would open it up and say, 'Look at what those jerks have done now. But if that's the way they want it, that's the way we'll build it, no matter how much it costs.' Every time they'd open their mouths and say, 'Look, if you could change this just a little bit, we could make it for half the price,' nobody in engineering would listen.

"It became obvious to me that we had to increase the stature of the manufacturing people. We had some engineers in tool design, but Bomarc was a new kind of product different from any airplane. Building a missile is like building a mechanical man, and that presents two problems—first, getting orders to him, which is a communications job, then getting him to obey those orders. You don't want him to move left when you tell him to turn right.

"At Boeing in the fifties, the manufacturing side was managed by a lot of guys who came up from being sheet metal snippers and riveters. They weren't technical people, and technical people didn't want to work for them. It was a case of feeling you were smarter than the boss. So what I perceived as necessary was to bring up the level of technical people in the manufacturing process."

Nelson did just that. He hired about 40 engineers "who didn't mind getting their fingers in the grease buckets of the manufacturing side," as he phrased it. "We had guys who were as smart as the ones upstairs, and it changed the relationship between engineering and manufacturing starting with the Bomarc program."

This new interrelationship on Boeing's second missile project was carried over into subsequent programs, where it worked as well as it had with Bomarc. The new fraternalism between engineering and production, however, was just one factor in Bomarc's success. Even engineers who had resented Nelson being the fall guy in the first-launch disaster found Jewett to be a quietly effective leader. Jewett, who went from preliminary design over to Bomarc full time, could point with pride to Bomarc's national defense role. Boeing not only built the missiles but installed them in 12 bases across the U.S. northern tier, with two of the sites located in Canada.

The Air Force put the Bomarc team in something of a dilemma when it decided to develop SAGE, an interconnected radar and computer warning system. It was intended originally to alert fighters of the Air Defense Command, but linked to Bomarc plus the fighter squadrons, SAGE eliminated the Michigan Aeronautical Research Center from the project. Boeing had to do some fast reshuffling to fit in Bomarc with the new warning system contractor, Lincoln Laboratory.

The Air Force ordered Bomarc into full production after a series of successful and even spectacular test firings at targets SAGE detected up to 400 miles away. A Bomarc launched toward a Regulus II drone flying at 80,000 feet hit dead-center on the supersonic missile; another target destroyed was a radio-controlled, crewless B-47. The learning curve had completed its course.

Bomarc bases were closed in the early 1970s when they were made obsolete by newer missile technology. Nearly 600 of them were produced for a system that protected 500,000 square miles of U.S. and Canadian soil; of the total built, slightly more than half used solid rocket fuel, which almost doubled the range of the previous liquid-fueled missiles. Yet relatively successful though Bomarc was, its achievements were overshadowed by Minuteman, a weapon second only to the B-52 in longevity.

In 1958 Wells established a systems management office (SMO), which Stedman headed, but it was as much George Stoner's bailiwick as anyone's. SMO's value was realized with the challenge of Minuteman—it was not just another missile, but an entirely new weapons *system*, and it led to Boeing's heavy involvement in the space program.

T Wilson was working for George Martin when T was named to head the Minuteman program in 1958, after Boeing received an RFP (request for proposal). By his own admission, T didn't know a ballistic missile from a non-ballistic one. But Allen and Wells had seen how T operated when he was trouble-shooting the B-52's problems.

Almost coincidental with Minuteman, Boeing had won a contract to build a manned spacecraft called Dyna-Soar, and Stoner was supposed to head both programs. But he told Wells he couldn't do justice to two projects simultaneously and suggested "someone like T Wilson" for the missile assignment.

Martin would have preferred to keep Wilson on the B-52, but he thought that Minuteman was a good opportunity for the hard-driving young engineer and that it would be good for the company, too.

T was receptive. "George," he said, "you're giving me an opportunity to work with people like Wells, Clyde Skeen, and George Stoner, aren't you?"

"That's right."

"Then I guess I'll take it."

A simple but typically quick and decisive response, although neither man could know what it would mean to Wilson's future at Boeing. The job itself was mountain-size. In football terminology, GAPA was playing at the high school level, Bomarc was college, and Minuteman was National Football League. Minuteman was originally conceived by Air Force Colonel Ed Hall, and would be operated under the Strategic Air Command.

The victory didn't come easily; no fewer than 11 major firms bid on Minuteman, and they included most of America's technology giants.

The proposal Boeing submitted, as an associate contractor responsible for assembly and testing, followed the Air Force specifications, which called for an intercontinental ballistic missile fueled by solid propellant instead of liquid rocket fuel. Liquid fuel has a high specific impulse, meaning that it produces an extremely high thrust after ignition, and can lift large payloads. Solid fuel has a rubber base that solidifies when mixed with other materials; Howard Stuverude, one of the engineers assigned to Minuteman, described it as "a texture that looks like a rubber eraser when it's put through a curing process and put into a rocket motor."

Although solid fuel doesn't have the powerful initial punch of liquid, its chief advantage is that it can be stored for a long time inside a fuel cell. This was important to Minuteman, for the initial $270 million contract Boeing signed with the Air Force after two years of research included not only production of the missiles themselves, but building and maintaining the silos to house them. Solid propellant added up to low maintenance, readiness to fire, high reliability, and greater safety, plus elimination of the intricate plumbing liquid fuel required. The technical risks were especially challenging; Minuteman installations would be unattended, and no missile had ever been fired out of a fixed silo.

It was as though Boeing had been asked to build a new airliner, construct its hangars, train its crews, and periodically maintain, overhaul and modernize it for as long as it remained in service.

The project took Boeing into some unfamiliar technical areas, such as the problem of preventing a missile that traveled 20 times the speed of sound from burning up during the ascent and descent phases. Bud Hebeler and a little group within SMO came up with the idea of using cork as an insulation material on the transition sections between the engine stages. Outside experts they consulted said they were crazy, insisting they needed a more exotic material that wouldn't ablate (melt or vaporize). But Hebeler, who would one day head Boeing's aerospace division, insisted on trying it and cork, one of the most common materials known, worked perfectly.

In a rough sense, Minuteman was a much larger and more complex

Bomarc. For both projects, Boeing had to develop and test the missile itself, including its electronics hardware and propulsion, then select and construct the sites where they would be deployed. The company's final responsibility was to coordinate the deployment task with rural communities that might be near the missile sites, an especially sensitive subject with Minuteman: this was an ICBM carrying a nuclear warhead. The deployment contract required Boeing to deliver each Minuteman on a "turn-key" status: complete with silos and fully operational.

Wells gave T pretty much a blank check in forming a team. The one he commanded included Stuverude, Hebeler, Doug Graves, Ben Plymale, George Hage, Wally Buckley, Jim Blue, Bud Hurst, Tex Boullioun, Art Hitsman, George Nible, Art Carter, Mark Miller, Lionel Alford, Jerry King, Deane Cruze, Abe Goo, and Ollie Boileau. Some, like Boileau and King, were fairly new engineers who had been enlisted for their specialized knowledge applicable to a missile program; Boileau, for example, knew electronics. King had been a technical assistant at the White Sands test facility. Goo got his start working on B-52 and KC-135 electrical systems.

Others were production men, led by the redoubtable Bud Hurst, who had always ranked high on Wilson's very selective list of people whose ability he admired. Nible went to Washington with Hurst early in the program and listened to him brief a room full of three- and four-star Air Force generals on how Boeing was going to blanket the United States with Minuteman silos. He had flip charts showing the proposed sites in such states as Colorado, Montana, and Nebraska. The longer he talked, the more enthusiastic he got, until he finally concluded before an audience that was speechless.

One general finally found his voice. "Bud, are you sure you can build these silos?"

"Hell, I'll punch holes in the White House lawn if you tell me to," Hurst assured them.

Tex Boullioun, Wilson's second-in-command, brought Nible into the program and assigned him to Hurst. At the time, Boeing was run like a quasi-military organization. "You didn't go over your boss's head," Nible said, "because if you did you were fired. But that wasn't true in Minuteman where T and Tex didn't run things that way."

The first day Nible reported, Wilson told him, "I don't want you to bother me unless you need something, and I won't bother you unless I need something. Otherwise, just do your damned job."

A pair of Air Force generals arrived one day to attend the monthly program review. T took them to lunch, accompanied by Hurst and Nible. The waitress asked if anyone wanted a cocktail.

"Yeah, I'll have a martini," one general said.

"Me, too," the other one announced. "Vodka on the rocks."

Hurst snapped, "I don't drink at lunch." He frowned at Nible. "And neither does anyone who works for me."

Now it was Nible's turn. "I'll have a vodka on the rocks, too," he chirped.

On the way out of the restaurant, T whispered to Nible, "You're a gutsy son of a bitch."

Hurst was one of Allen's favorites, too, and owed his first sizable raise to Allen. At that time, Allen reviewed all salary recommendations involving people who made $10,000 or more. Fred Laudan had brought Allen a list of plant superintendents and supervisors who were up for raises, but Hurst's name was missing.

"What's wrong with Hurst?" Allen asked.

"Nothing. He's a good man."

"If he's a good man, why doesn't he get a good raise?"

Laudan hesitated. "Well, he has a personality problem. It's the way he handles people."

Allen wanted an example and Laudan supplied it. Hurst had told one of his machinists the way he was drilling holes was unsafe. For several days Bud kept watching him and noticed he still was drilling the same way. Hurst went to the worker's foreman. "Straighten that guy out," he ordered.

That didn't accomplish anything, either. Hurst brought the matter up at a production staff meeting and was told, "The man's one of our best workers, he wouldn't hurt himself, and besides, you can't tell him anything."

The next day Hurst approached the errant machinist.

"You gonna do that drilling the right way?" he asked.

The worker gave him the well-known freeway salute, and Hurst decked him with one punch.

That was the story Laudan gave Allen, who laughed. "If that's his personality problem," he remarked, "it sounds like an excellent reason to give him a raise."

Under T, Minuteman was a no-frills, almost Spartan operation with scant executive privileges. The only status symbol in any Minuteman office was a rug, and the rug total was exactly three: T, Boullioun, and Hurst each had one. Nible, as head of field operations, made the mistake of dropping hints that he deserved a rug, too. George went out of town one weekend and returned to find a "rug" in his office—the entire floor was covered with a painter's dropcloth. There was a picture of Hurst, illuminated by two burning candles, and a fake organizational chart that showed Nible demoted to a proposed Minuteman installation at Gila Bend, Arizona.

"He never asked for a rug after that," T said.

Wilson reported to Lysle Wood, head of the aerospace division, but they didn't see eye to eye on many things, and T remained his own man. Their feuding was no secret around Boeing, and the fact that

Wood was a vice president and Wilson just a project manager made no difference to T. He told everyone in the Minuteman program, "If you don't think a rule makes sense, come to me and if you're right, we'll get it changed."

When Hurst and Nible began installing the silo sites, it became apparent that Boeing needed some small airplanes to carry essential parts from one silo to another. Each Minuteman base consisted of a cluster of silos spaced about 10 miles apart, with a launch control center for every 10 silos. The planes also were used to fly key technicians to the various bases, which were off the regular commercial airline routes.

The company leased a pressurized Cessna 320 and chartered several other small planes when needed. Once a month, base managers would meet near or at a base; Hurst and Nible usually traveled together. One day they picked up a couple of Air Force colonels who wanted a site tour, and en route to the Great Falls, Montana, base the Cessna's pressurization system failed. Severe thunderstorms had been reported over the Rockies, so they landed in Las Vegas to repair the system, stayed there three hours, then completed the trip to Great Falls.

Neither thought anything about the unscheduled stop until the next month's meeting in Kansas City. Stan Leith, head of company security, was the featured attraction with a lecture on the importance of security. He was a former Navy diver with a face that could have been carved out of solid granite, a rasping voice, and the unsubtle demeanor of an old-time Irish beat policeman. Carl Cleveland once said if you put 10,000 people into a stadium and asked someone to pick out the one person who was a cop, Leith would have been the first one chosen.

After the meeting, Leith discovered that Continental Airlines was on strike and he had to get to Denver, where he planned to make connections to Seattle.

"How am I gonna get to Denver?" he complained to Hurst and Nible.

"We've got the Cessna, Stan," Nible told him. "We'll drop you off in Denver and go on to Rapid City."

Leith looked embarrassed, which for him was about as incongruous as hearing a nun curse. "I can't go with you guys," he said. "I'm investigating you."

"What the hell are we being investigated for?" Hurst demanded.

"For that stop you made in Las Vegas last month," Leith explained. "Somebody reported you to Lysle Wood."

The investigation wasn't the only thing Wood had instituted. He also issued a written order that "no more airplanes will be leased for work at Minuteman sites without the approval of T Wilson or myself."

A few weeks later, with work on Minuteman Wing One completed and Wing Two next on the agenda, Hurst and Nible needed an airplane. Nible took the requisition in to T for approval.

"What the hell is this?" Wilson wanted to know.

"Well, Lysle Wood put out this letter and I need your okay to get an airplane."

"I didn't put out any letter," T growled. "Take that requisition to Wood and tell *him* to sign it."

Nible went to Wood. "Lysle, we're opening up Wing Two and I need an airplane."

Wood looked at the requisition. "T hasn't signed it."

Nible, not wanting to get Wilson into trouble, resorted to a slight fib. "I couldn't find T," he explained.

Wood wouldn't accept that. "I'll not sign the authorization unless Wilson signs as well."

Nible went back to T with this firm edict. Wilson picked up the phone and called Wood.

"Lysle, I'm not going to sign any letter of authorization for airplanes we need on the missile sites. And if you don't sign it, you're going to be responsible for the damned system not going in on time!"

Three days later, Wood cancelled the authorization rule.

T's engineering staff assistant was Flip Jendrik, and every time a program review meeting was called, Jendrik and Nible would get into an argument. One day Nible got a call from T's secretary.

"Mr. Wilson wants you to come to his office at five minutes to five. He also says you are to leave exactly at five."

Mystified, Nible arrived on time at 4:55. There was Jendrik, with an empty chair next to him in front of T's desk. Nible sat down.

"I don't want either of you to open your mouth," Wilson began, "and when I finish, both of you leave. Now, I love both you bastards. I think each of you has a lot of talent. But you two have interrupted my staff meetings for the last time. And if either of you do it once more you're fired!"

Nible looked at his watch. It was five P.M., so without saying a word, he got up and started walking out. From behind him came T's voice.

"Well, Nible, at least you pay attention to instructions."

If anyone hated procrastination and red tape as much as T—who considered unnecessary delays the equivalent of spitting on the flag and insulting motherhood—it was Wally Buckley. When the first Minuteman test firing was scheduled at Cape Canaveral, technicians in Seattle were still working on a sequence-monitoring device essential for the test. Deane Cruze was assistant general foreman at the plant and informed Buckley of the delay.

"Find out who's working on it," Buckley ordered. "Get their names and addresses from personnel so we can send someone out to their homes and pick up their suitcases. Tell the technicians to get their equipment together—we'll fly them to the Cape this afternoon and they can finish their work there."

There was a C-130 transport at Boeing Field waiting for the hastily summoned group, but Buckley ran into a protocol snag. The manager in charge of shipping informed Wally, "You can't ship that stuff."

"The hell I can't," Buckley retorted. He turned to the C-130's captain, an interested spectator. "I want this equipment on the airplane, Captain."

The shipping manager turned red. "You can't accept it!" he yelled at the pilot. "Not without proper authorization."

"Yes you can!" Buckley roared back. "I'll sign your manifest if you'll accept my signature as authorization."

The captain looked at Buckley's ID badge; in those days, the badges carried job titles and Wally's read MINUTEMAN MANUFACTURING MANAGER.

"Sounds like a big enough title to me," he decided. "Here's the manifest—just sign."

"I guess you don't need me," the shipping manager huffed.

Buckley glared at him. "I told you that when you first stuck your damned nose into this."

Cruze respected Buckley. "A lot of people thought Buck was a real hard-ass, which he was around a factory. But I knew from personal experience through many years that underneath he was the softest-hearted guy you could find. He did a lot of things for his people that no one knew about, except the ones he helped."

The first firing test for which Buckley had expedited the monitoring equipment went off well, although some of the pre-launch preparations were on the better-push-the-panic-button side. Doug Graves, a tough taskmaster, was running the show as the first Cape manager, and a few days before the launch the engineers were trying to trouble-shoot circuit problems in the connections to the guidance control system. They had the wiring spread all over the floor of the pad tower when Graves walked in and surveyed the mess.

"Okay," he announced, "who do I fire?"

T would admit later he didn't get his biggest thrill out of the successful launch itself. "I got it when we were checking out the electronics and went through the countdown," he reminisced. "The real thrill was seeing it all come together, all the stuff that had to work before anyone pushes the firing button."

Wilson was so pleased he threw a big party, then put the bill (between $2,000 and $3,000, he remembered) on a general expense account that was supposed to go to George Martin. Martin never saw it; Doug Graves, apparently afraid Lysle Wood might hear that T had spent all that money, signed it off himself.

The next two firings were successful, too, but the fourth Minuteman blew up, victim of malfunctions in the guidance control unit. This was the first missile to be launched from a silo; the electronic components weren't anchored securely and were disrupted by vibration inside the silo.

Wilson and General Sam Phillips, the Air Force's top representative in the Minuteman project for whom T had enormous respect, were watching from the blockhouse when the fourth missile exploded. So was Jerry King, then an electronics specialist in his early 20s, who got his first glimpse of Wilson at a moment of dire crisis.

"I'd have to say his reaction was one of considered calm," King remembered. "All he said was, 'Well, let's find out what happened,' and I knew right then and there this was one special guy."

It took about a month to determine the exact source of failure, but King wasn't surprised at the final verdict. "In this modern world," he philosophized, "there are three ways to go broke. Gambling is the quickest, women the most fun, and software the surest."

The fourth launch at the Cape wasn't the only Minuteman setback. T himself admitted that in the program's early stages, Boeing was faltering and fumbling with disturbing overruns due partially to over-staffing in some areas, which is typical for a new program.

"We were luckier than hell to win the proposal in the first place," Wilson said. "We spent about five million on the proposal and we probably did a lousy job in the early part of the program—we had too many people. Whenever you have a surplus, say a couple of thousand people, it takes another two thousand people to fix what the first two thousand are screwing up."

At one point, the Air Force was concerned enough about rising cost to ask all contractors associated with Minuteman to come up with some ideas on cost savings. Tom Riedinger in corporate public relations sent a one-page memo to Wilson, suggesting that Boeing rent the University of Washington football stadium and invite the world's most famous cheapskate—Jack Benny, of course—to make a speech about saving money. Riedinger figured the stadium could easily hold the total number of Boeing employees assigned to Minuteman.

It didn't take long for T to reply to this suggestion. He sent the memo back to Riedinger with only one comment scrawled on the page: "You are sick."

The response shouldn't have surprised Tom, who already had soured Wilson on almost anyone from corporate public relations. After T's appointment to Minuteman, he called a meeting to outline how he was going to run the program. The packed room lacked air-conditioning and while waiting for T to arrive, Riedinger dozed off. Wilson finally marched to the dais and saw Riedinger.

"When the representative from corporate public relations wakes up," T announced, "we can start the meeting."

Riedinger opened his eyes. "When the program manager for Minuteman says something important, I'll wake up."

Minuteman's later public relations man was Bill Jury, who was assigned the job of selling the program to the communities throughout the western states that would be affected by the system's deployment.

In some respects the silos posed bigger problems than the missile development, and getting people to accept them was just one of the challenges.

Because the missiles were to be left unattended in the underground silos, there were all kinds of security problems at first. Rabbits, birds, coyotes, and curious school kids penetrating security would set off alarms.

Art Carter worked primarily on the silo installations. Certain criteria had to be met: the silos had to be a safe distance away from habitable buildings and roads, and sometimes the site selection was marginal. Carter mentioned one in Missouri that was just on the edge of meeting the distance criteria—it was near a junior high school and the kids would run to the site during recess to watch installation activities.

"Parents became concerned that someone was going to get hurt, especially if there was an accidental blast," Carter said, "so I was on a task force that would prove the silos were safe. After all the analysis we did on a bunch of suggested tests, we decided to fill up the hole and move to another site."

Carter talked frankly about what it was like being a young black engineer in his profession. "There were at least thirty blacks in Minuteman," he said, "and yes, there was some prejudice at first— Boeing was a microcosm of our outside society, and there were times when you'd run into individuals or processes you would deem as racist or bigoted, but no more than you'd get anywhere else."

Carter, a graduate of the Illinois Institute of Technology with a degree in electrical engineering, joined Minuteman as a systems engineer. He spent most of the program at Vandenberg Air Force Base, where Minuteman was first tested as an entire system.

His most vivid memory of Minuteman dated back to the 1962 Cuban missile crisis. It occurred when there were still only a few non-operational silos installed in Montana; the test sites at Vandenberg were the only ones capable of firing ICBMs at Cuba if war broke out.

"We were told to structure the Vandenberg missile sites toward Cuba," Carter said, "which was kind of awkward because all the test facilities there were positioned to fire toward the west, an uninhabited area around Kwajalein. There was frantic rejiggering of equipment and recalibrating the system. I suspect if we had actually fired the missiles, we probably would have wiped out New Orleans."

Carter had his tongue-in-cheek, of course, but it was true no one at Vandenberg knew what would happen if a missile had to be fired in anger. The very first one launched at this base had blown up, self-destructing for no apparent reason, and nothing had been fired since that failure. Mark Miller, Vandenberg base manager, remembered the turmoil of the crisis only too well.

"Missile control hadn't been handed over to SAC yet," he said. "Even if it had, it wouldn't have helped. SAC's technicians had very little knowledge of the system at that point. In fact, the only group capable of running it was Boeing's own people, and when the crisis broke, SAC asked Boeing to take over control. We actually were under contract to the Systems Command, but they weren't prepared, either. So when SAC told us to put everything in a war configuration, we did."

For the next few days, Boeing personnel poured concrete, moved cables and instrumentation, and switched from test to war footing. Miller went to a SAC colonel.

"We'll be ready tomorrow," he advised the officer. "All we need is targets."

"I'll tell Omaha [SAC headquarters]."

The next day, the colonel called Miller to his office, opened the second drawer of his desk, and handed him the target coordinates.

"We were doing all this without Seattle's participation," Miller recounted, "and they were getting a little nervous. T called and wanted to know what the hell we were doing. God, we were nervous, too. For one thing, we weren't certain about the missile itself."

With good reason. After three weeks, they began putting everything back into test configuration and early in 1963, they fired their second test missile—the one that would have been aimed at Cuba. It self-destructed in 31 seconds, and at first no one could figure out why. Minuteman had been fired previously at the Cape 27 consecutive times without mishap. A team led by Jim Axtell found that a thermal block designed into the Vandenberg rocket engines had built up an electric charge. At about 70,000 feet, the charge sent a 29,000-volt spark into the guidance system, causing the missile to self-destruct. The fix, including removal of the thermal block, was made immediately and before the year ended Vandenberg had chalked up eight flawless firings.

Minuteman was test-fired from Vandenberg over the Pacific missile range, and even though it was an Air Force missile, the range was Navy-run. Jerry King was given the job of briefing a Navy captain on the program. He explained what was involved, and kept emphasizing how well everything had gone at Cape Canaveral. The captain listened politely, then pointed to a sign on the wall in back of King, which he hadn't noticed before. It read: WE DON'T GIVE A SHIT HOW YOU DID IT AT THE CAPE.

Everyone who was associated with Minuteman still mentions the youth of its personnel. Many engineers, like Carter and King, were in their 20s, and maybe the occasional setbacks required both the resilience of youth and what was absolutely essential to survive at Boeing: a sense of humor. Even the most serious-minded, strictest supervisors and managers were not immune from the irreverence that is so much a part of Boeing.

There was Mark Miller, for example, who was an absolute terror when it came to spelling. He actually got angry at anyone who would misspell a word. One day he was reviewing a Minuteman progress presentation being delivered on a chart by Bob Edelman of engineering. The word *relieve* appeared on the chart, but it was spelled *relieve*.

"Dammit, Edelman," Miller scolded, "*i* always goes before *e*."

"You're absolutely right," Edelman agreed. He took out a grease pencil and at the bottom of the chart, he changed *Boeing* to *Boieng*.

Came the time for Wilson to leave Minuteman, and everyone agreed T should have a munificent gift. Flip Jendrik was in charge of the selection process and announced he had picked out a fancy leather-upholstered chair with a plaque attached to the back.

"That's not T's style," Nible protested. "What the hell is he going to do with it?"

"He'll put it in his den," Flip predicted. "Anyway, I want twenty-five bucks from each of you."

He collected, then got into a poker game and lost it all. He wound up paying for the chair himself.

Minuteman's eventual success more than made up for the stumbles along the way. The program originally called for three wings, but these were later expanded to six as Boeing instituted continuing improvement and modernization of both the missiles and their underground nests. The entire program was completed ahead of schedule, at budget, and included upgraded Minuteman II and III. Some 1,000 missiles were produced, each capable of carrying a nuclear warhead 6,000 miles at a speed of 15,000 miles an hour—a sword of Damocles poised over the Soviet Union during the most frigid years of the Cold War.

T always insisted he was prouder of his work with the B-52 than with Minuteman, but few agreed with him—what he accomplished in the missile program stamped him indelibly throughout the company's upper echelons as a consummate leader. Until Wilson took over Minuteman, only once had he spent more than a year in any job; he ran the missile program for five years, and suffered a mild heart attack right in the middle of it. Lysle Wood wrote him a letter suggesting that he give up Minuteman and go to work for him as his administrative assistant.

"That almost caused me to have another heart attack," T remarked. "I thought it was an offensive letter and I never answered it." Wilson's idea of restful recuperation consisted of not going to work full time for a month.

Allen once tried to pull him off Minuteman, too, offering him an executive post in corporate headquarters. T politely turned him down, saying, "I'd rather stay with Minuteman and clean up some of my own messes."

"I thought he'd forget to ask me again," T said later, "but he finally did. Anyway, I did have a chance to follow a program through from a proposal until it became operational, and that was a very good experience."

It was a good experience for quite a few others as well; just as T's performance enhanced his stature at corporate headquarters, so did their performance enhance their stature in Wilson's eyes—he marked them for future advancement. Inevitably, there would be some whispered complaints to the effect that to get ahead at Boeing, it helped to have been a member of T's Minuteman team.

True in the sense that men like Boullioun, Boileau, Nible, Buckley, and at least a dozen others did rise high in the company in tandem with Wilson. But the other side of the coin was that to succeed in Minuteman under Wilson, you *had* to be good—T did not suffer fools gladly.

He was proud of the program, of his own role and that of everyone who worked on Minuteman. But he gave most credit for its success to the three Air Force officers most closely associated with the system: Ed Hall, who conceived the basic design, General Benny Schriever, and Colonel (later General) Sam Phillips.

"People tend to forget Minuteman was an Air Force concept, not a Boeing system," T said. "Our job was important, but there were a lot of other associated contractors."

Equally important, of course, were the program's long-range effects on Boeing's involvement in future high-tech, non-aeronautical projects. Minuteman was the ultimate test of Boeing's ability to compete in this area. Because of Minuteman's success, Boeing became a true aerospace company, capable of taking on any task as people began to look at the heavens in a new way. It was no coincidence that because of Minuteman, Boeing established a separate aerospace division, and that its massive efforts in the space program would bring out the unique brilliance of George Stoner.

Aerospace itself implies a kind of schizophrenic corporation in which airplanes may have to compete with even more exotic technological ventures for engineering and administrative attention. At Boeing, it is a split-personality environment that at times seems to have put its two principal sources of income into an adversarial position: of commercial or government business, which deserved the greater priority, and which was best for Boeing?

Historically, however, these conflicting areas have tended to compensate, rather than divide. In periods when military and other government projects were hemorrhaging red ink, commercial airplanes were dyeing the ledgers black. The reverse often occurred when airplanes weren't selling. Bomarc, Minuteman, and later Saturn/Apollo were welcome financial transfusions at a time when Boeing was struggling to get expensive airplane programs into gear.

T Wilson himself, more of an airplane than a missile man, put it most succinctly when a Boeing director once asked him, "What percentage of military business would you like to have?"

"All I can get," T replied. Like Allen, he recognized the main requisite for prosperity in an industry where prosperity is cyclical and terribly vulnerable to adverse factors beyond the control of the most skilled executive talent. Boeing needed military *and* commercial.

And even as the Minuteman silos were being dug and the test missiles were thundering skyward, the transport division was conceiving a devastating commercial weapon of its own.

It was the next member of Boeing's jetliner family, born amid swirling controversy, yet destined to become one of its most stunning successes.

TWELVE

"YOU DON'T LOWER THE FLAPS—YOU DISASSEMBLE THE WHOLE DAMN WING"

CONTENTIOUS COULD HAVE BEEN JACK STEINER'S MIDDLE name. He was one of Boeing's bigger-than-life characters: big in stature, ambition, ability, and what some saw as ego, others as self-confidence.

He had both defenders and detractors, but nobody ever knocked him for an unquenchable enthusiasm that made so many contributions to the company—among them an airplane that smashed every existing sales record. His ebullience could be infectious, amusing, or grating, but colleagues had to accept it as something that came with a cyclonic personality—Steiner wore enthusiasm as though it were part of his wardrobe.

He kept working hours that made slavery look easy. He was the only Boeing officer who needed two full-time secretaries, one during regular daytime hours and the other for when he worked evenings, which was virtually all the time. He probably would have used a third if Allen had let him get away with it, because it was not uncommon for Steiner to be at his desk at two or three in the morning. That he had a happy marriage despite his workaholic life-style was due more to his patient wife; if anyone was married to Boeing, it was Dorothy Steiner.

"She was the one who raised our three kids," Steiner admitted. "I never even made out an income tax return in my life—she did everything."

The only thing she didn't do was complain, an incredible achievement for anyone married to a man who had absolutely no sense of time. "That included the time of day," an associate observed. "He'd call from London when it was three o'clock in the morning in Seattle."

It might even be wondered if Jack knew what day of the week it was. He was notorious for being late to meetings, including the ones he had called himself. He would amble in with his pixie grin and long, rather awkward gait, oblivious to everything except whatever project was uppermost in his mind—George Martin had nothing on him when it came to absent-mindedness. He even walked like Martin, head down in deep concentration. His staff dreaded any new idea he might come up with; Steiner would call an immediate meeting, even if the idea had occurred to him in the middle of the night.

Dave Olson worked for Steiner at one time and was heading for Germany to confer with Ernst Simon, Lufthansa's chief engineer, on a new Boeing jet. Simon had lost an eye during the war, and Steiner decided to brief Olson on possible sensitivity regarding the wound.

"Now when you talk to him," Jack cautioned, "you want to make sure you look directly at his good eye. It's the left one. Make sure you look at the left eye." He paused, brow furrowed. "Or is it the right eye?"

"I went over there," Olson sighed, "not knowing which eye I was supposed to look into."

Steiner prided himself on his considerable knowledge of subjects not associated with aviation. Unfortunately for members of the news media, this included journalism. Bob Twiss, retired aviation editor of the *Seattle Times* who covered Boeing for years, considered Jack "one of the world's great characters, even though he could drive me nuts."

No matter what Twiss wrote, Steiner would call him—sometimes even months after a story appeared—and voice mild criticism. "Now, Bob," he'd say gravely, "that seventh paragraph was too low in the story and should have been placed much higher, while the third paragraph contained a minor inaccuracy . . ."

Like Wellwood Beall, Steiner was as much salesman as engineer—perhaps more so, for Jack even sold on social occasions. Fishing is one of the great attractions in the Pacific Northwest and Boeing liked to take visiting airline officials on fishing trips. Dave Peterson was in charge of customer relations for many years and used to shake his head in mixed dismay and admiration when Steiner showed up for a fishing trip.

"Here were all the guys trying to fish," Peterson said, "and there would be Jack with his flip charts—engine performance graphs, aircraft economics, and operating statistics. You couldn't stop him."

Veteran Boeing salesman Bob Perdue took Steiner to Atlanta once as part of a contingent trying to sell Delta some airplanes. Tex Boullioun and Clancy Wilde were along, too, and every man had brought his wife.

"This was September," Perdue related, "Atlanta was hotter than hell, and Dorothy Steiner had a panic attack—she forgot to pack Jack's flannel pajamas and he can't sleep in anything else. So all the wives start going from store to store, trying to find flannel pajamas in the middle of a heat wave. I think they finally located a pair in about the twentieth store. He was a real character."

Steiner wasn't the easiest man to work for, given his propensity for ignoring all clocks, but it was hard to stay mad at a man whose enthusiasm also was an ingrained habit. Some even took advantage of it. A young engineer was driving past the plant late one Sunday night and he noticed the lights were on in Steiner's office. He parked the car, went up to Jack's office, and poked his head in.

"Jack, it's past one A.M., so I think I'll call it a day and go home."

Steiner looked up from the papers and blueprints stacked on his desk, and flashed that ingratiating little smile of his. "Thanks for working so late—I really appreciate it."

His most influential supporter at Boeing was none other than Bill Allen, who felt Steiner's loyalty, contagious exuberance, and vision more than offset his eccentricities. Allen not only liked Jack but respected him, and this was John E. Steiner's greatest asset when, against considerable opposition and equally daunting odds, he proposed the jetliner that will always be associated with his name: the 727.

Its genesis dated back to early 1956, when Boeing began design studies on a short-to-medium-range jet transport to supplement the 707. Ed Wells had named Steiner assistant chief of preliminary design and put him in charge of the embryonic project. The thick file he handed Jack contained 38 proposed designs aimed basically at developing a jetliner that could operate at airports too small for the 707. By the time the advance studies had evolved into a more specific proposal, however, the attitude around Boeing toward a smaller jet ranged somewhere between ice-cold and lukewarm. The company was struggling in the late fifties and early sixties. The 707 was selling, but the program's break-even point was a long way off, and Boeing lost out on three promising military contracts: two supersonic bomber proposals and later an advanced tactical fighter called the TFX.

Convair's B-58 Hustler was selected over Boeing's equally fast (Mach 2) Model 701, designated the XB-59 by the Air Force, and this defeat was followed by another setback when the Defense Department rejected Boeing's B-110, a huge Mach 3 bomber, in favor of North American's B-70. The only consolation was a subcontracting arrangement in which Boeing was supposed to build the B-70's wing and actually had tooled up for it, when North American decided to do it in-house.

If the loss of the two bomber programs was disappointing, what happened with the TFX in 1962 was even worse. The concept called for a fighter-bomber versatile enough to serve both the Air Force and Navy; this, of course, required commonality between the versions produced for each service. Six manufacturers submitted TFX proposals to the Pentagon, which then narrowed the choice to Boeing and General Dynamics. Although technical evaluations favored Boeing's design, Defense Secretary Robert McNamara picked General Dynamics.

Added to the military frustrations was the cost of acquiring a brand-new member of the family: in 1960, Boeing had purchased Vertol, a helicopter company with potential but also risk. Bomarc was winding down, Minuteman hadn't gotten rolling yet, and it was against this background that Steiner waged his fight for the 727 program.

The arguments against the project were threefold: the potential market for a smaller jet was overcrowded; the 727 would compete against Boeing's own 720; and the company couldn't afford the gamble.

The first argument was impressive. France was offering the Caravelle, the first jet transport with aft engines, one on each side of the rear fuselage. Its chief drawback was size: the Caravelle couldn't carry more than 80 passengers. Britain was developing the three-engine Trident, with two aft engines mounted like the Caravelle's and the third inside the rear fuselage, drawing its air via an *S*-shaped duct whose inlet was located just ahead of the tail section. Larger than the French jet, the Trident was a de Havilland design but became a Hawker Siddeley airplane when the two companies merged.

In the United States, Convair's 880 fit airline requirements for a medium-range jetliner, but it was not designed for short-haul operations. Douglas, at United's urging, had designed a drastically scaled-down DC-8 with four engines to meet the airline's interest in a jet transport that could serve smaller airports but also operate safely at high-altitude Denver. It was called the DC-9, the same designation given the twin-engine jet Douglas would produce later. The propjet Electra was in the race, too; it didn't have pure jet speed but its versatility was impressive.

This was the competition the 727 faced; of the lot, the Trident initially seemed the most formidable because in many respects the British jet was a slightly smaller 727—to the eye, they were almost identical. They were so similar, in fact, that in 1959, by which time the 727's design was well along, Boeing was invited to combine the 727 and Trident programs.

The suggestion came from Lord Douglas, chairman of British European Airways for which the Trident had been specifically created. Acting on Lord Douglas' proposal, the two companies exchanged technical visits. Hawker Siddeley sent a delegation to Seattle while Boeing engineers looked over the Trident. What the British thought of the 727 was never recorded, but their American counterparts recognized the Trident for what it was: a well-designed airplane victimized by over-conservatism in size, range, and power. A joint program never got to any serious discussion stage and both jets were on their own.

Steiner had traveled a rocky road before Boeing's board of directors in 1958 tentatively approved the 727 program—a green light that was more of a yellow caution signal. The board conditioned its approval on Boeing's obtaining at least two launch customers out of the so-called Big Four airlines: United, American, TWA, and Eastern. It wasn't a case of having to bat .500, either—United and Eastern were the only legitimate prospects. American, having ordered a sizable fleet of Electras, wasn't interested in the 727. TWA still was having financial problems; Howard Hughes already had difficulties raising funding for his 707s, let alone the 727.

The road after board approval was equally bumpy, for United and Eastern were miles apart on the kind of airplane they wanted. United wouldn't have even considered the 727 if Douglas hadn't aborted its four-engine DC-9 program when it found no one other than UAL interested in a small four-engine jet; Douglas, too, had needed a second launch customer. Eastern *was* intrigued by the 727 but only if it had two engines.

Eastern's Charlie Froesch imposed the stiffest requirements: the 727 would have to be capable of taking off fully loaded and landing safely on runway 4-22 at New York's LaGuardia Airport—the sole LaGuardia runway then equipped with an instrument landing system (ILS) and only 4,860 feet long. Furthermore, Froesch said the 727 would have to meet those specifications and still be able to fly non-stop to Miami.

In one sense, Froesch's stern demands effectively eliminated the argument with which Steiner was grappling inside Boeing—that the 727 would compete against the 720. No way. When United's Bill Mentzer informed Boeing he liked Eastern's performance requirements (except for two-engine insistence), that meant the team had to design an entirely new, even revolutionary jetliner—the most versatile ever created. An airplane with the speed of the 707, the short-field capability of a propeller-driven transport, and the range of the Convair 880 with just as many passengers.

Preliminary design had toyed with a number of engine configurations, most of them either two or four. Three became an obvious necessity as a compromise between United and Eastern, and virtually dictated the decision to build an aft-engine airplane; the Trident showed where to put the third engine, fed by an S-shaped duct, and the Caravelle had demonstrated the feasibility of the aft-engine design. Maynard Pennell laid out the basic final configuration and turned it over to Steiner for execution.

Bill Cook hated the idea of rear engines and never really liked the 727 for that reason, although ironically he did as much as anyone to make it a success.

"It's a bum way to design an airplane," Cook expounded. "In a good, balanced airplane, the center of gravity should be the same when it's empty as when it's fully loaded. That's impossible with aft engines."

One configuration the engineers considered would have put an engine under each wing, locating the third engine in the aft fuselage like the Trident's. Steiner held out for putting all three power plants in the rear, citing such advantages as reduced forward cabin noise, better coordination of engine systems, less drag if they were clustered relatively close together, and cheaper to build. If Boeing had gone with the underwing/aft engine combination, the 727 would have resembled a couple of future airliners that hadn't been designed yet: the Douglas DC-10 and Lockheed L-1011.

There were others who opposed putting any three-engine configuration on the 727. Three still amounted to a compromise, they argued, and seldom did any compromise result in an optimum design. Throughout the design process, Steiner was getting input from airline technical staffs, and if he had followed all their advice the airplane never would have been built.

"Each time Jack would hear from the airlines," Clancy Wilde recalled, "we'd have a big staff meeting and go through mountains of presentations on what design alternatives we had."

Given the Boeing directors' dictate, however, there weren't any real alternatives. United and Eastern were the only prospects, and a compromise airplane was inevitable. The logjam between those two carriers was broken when they agreed on three engines, satisfying Froesch's objections to four as uneconomical, and Mentzer's objections to two as insufficient power for Denver.

Then came an impasse over the choice of engines. Boeing originally wanted to equip the 727 with a Rolls-Royce Spey derivative that would be built under license in the United States by Allison, a proven power plant with a good reliability record. But Eddie Rickenbacker refused to accept the Spey. Boeing turned to Pratt & Whitney and convinced it to modify an existing military turbine for commercial use. It became the famed JT-8D, one of the most successful engines ever built.

The biggest challenge in the 727 program was meeting Eastern's criteria: a short-field capability combined with New York–Miami nonstop range. This may have been Bill Cook's finest hour, although characteristically he refused to accept credit for climbing this mountainous obstacle. Cook developed an ingenious flap system for low-speed approaches to short runways: in effect, it stretched a 5,000-foot runway to a 7,000- or 8,000-foot length, providing high-lift qualities to the wings that were unprecedented for a sweptwing aircraft. And Steiner's insistence on giving the 727 almost the same 35-degree sweep as the 707 (32 degrees) made Cook's contribution even more essential, because it became a best-of-both-worlds airplane: a high cruise speed combined with excellent approach and landing characteristics.

What Cook devised came close to a Rube Goldberg contraption. It consisted of large, triple-slotted flaps on the trailing edges of the wing with smaller flaps extending the entire length of the leading edge. Fully deployed, they increased the wing area by 25 percent. Retracted, they folded back to create a thin, aerodynamically clean wing. The track mechanism over which the flaps moved was equally inventive, although lowering the flaps gave the visual impression of a wing being taken completely apart, and raising them was like seeing Humpty Dumpty being put back together.

"On this bird," an airline pilot commented in awe, "you don't lower the flaps—you disassemble the whole damn wing!"

Steiner was to take many bows for the 727's success, but he was the first to admit that without Bill Cook's flaps, the airplane would have failed. Yet just as important was a decision Steiner made: he decreed that the 727 share the 707's cabin width, allowing six-abreast coach seating and an all-coach passenger capacity of 131, greater than the 880's. The goal was not only to save on tooling costs through commonality, but to improve the plane's viability to airlines.

The general design was fairly well established by February 1960, when Jack Steiner walked into the Boeing boardroom to plead his case for continuing with a program that few thought the company could afford. At that point development costs were as well established as the design: approximately $130 million for full design and production tooling. That didn't include building a prototype, because Bill Allen decided that if the program went ahead , there would be no prototype—the first few production airplanes would be used for testing.

Steiner didn't make his evangelistic pitch to a hostile audience, but it definitely was a dubious one. And like the airplane he so vigorously espoused, the best he could win was a tough compromise. Allen, with the directors in full agreement, said Steiner could proceed with the 727 only if Boeing received 100 orders by December first of that year. Engineer Steiner went back to work on the airplane, while salesman Steiner preached its virtues to the Boeing sales force and airline prospects alike.

The airplane they were selling looked better and better as its design evolved. Ed Wells wanted the 727 to handle as easily as the Electra, a pilot's dream with a fighter plane's responsiveness. The Electra's all-hydraulic controls had been designed by a Lockheed engineer named Bob Richolt, who retired after designing a system regarded as the best ever put into a transport-type aircraft. Steiner talked him into coming out of retirement long enough to help Boeing with the 727, working with Ed Pfaffman.

Thanks in large part to Richolt, the 727 became the first Boeing airplane to have all hydraulically boosted controls. The engineers also came up with a mechanical computer that sensed the aircraft's center of gravity (CG), and automatically adjusted the stick force to compensate for any change in the CG as fuel burned off. The flight controls that eventually went into the "three-holer," as airline pilots would dub the plane, literally made the 727 an airplane that could be flown with one hand. The system was a combination of what Richolt had designed for the Electra and what Boeing had previously created for the B-47. Comparing the 727's stick forces to those of the 707 was like comparing a car with power steering to a truck with no power assist.

Center of gravity balance was one of the toughest problems that Pennell and Steiner faced. "It was hard to design the plane so that the CG was under control," Pennell said. "The rear engine configuration put a lot of weight aft of the CG, and we had to take care of it with the passenger load forward of the CG, designing with sufficient and very powerful longitudinal control to keep the CG well in hand."

And that's where the CG sensor came in. "It was a very important element," Steiner explained, "because the CG on an aft-engine airplane encounters wide variations during a flight."

Joe Sutter and Ray Pierson were the engineers who worked most closely with Cook on the high-lift devices, which Bill—as he so often did—insisted were old hat to anyone who read aviation history. And, as usual, he was right.

Cook's files showed that the idea of a slotted wing to increase lift was first mentioned in a textbook used at MIT in 1927. A few years later, Britain's Handley-Page installed such a device on a real airplane, one developed by a German World War I fighter pilot named G. B. Lachmann. Then in the United States, Curtiss built an experimental airplane, the Tanager, which had slotted flaps and won a Guggenheim Award for a significant aeronautical advance. According to Cook, the man largely responsible for applying the theory to the 727 was Ray Pierson, an engineer who had served as an executive officer on a submarine during the war.

"He was a design genius," Cook declared. "I remember after he retired from Boeing, he developed an artificial limb joint for amputees."

While engineering labored to create a jet transport worthy of the $4.2 million price tag it would carry, Boeing's salesmen concentrated on the two crucial launch customers: United and Eastern. Other carriers weren't ignored; the ubiquitous Steiner made sure they were kept abreast of the program. Harley Thorson, then assigned to Delta, drew a blank. One official, mindful of C. E. Woolman's feelings toward Douglas, admitted to Thorson, "Hell, Harley, you might as well face facts—if your airplane carried the Douglas name, we'd be interested."

Harley went back to Northwest on an early 727 sales mission and made his pitch to Frank Judd, vice president of engineering and maintenance. He might as well have been talking to Woolman. This was before anyone had seen the Trident or the 727's similar configuration, and what Thorson was showing him were various three-engine designs Boeing was considering at the time. The most bizarre was a 727 that had two engines under one wing, and a single engine under the other. Another sketch showed a jet with two aft engines, and the third one parked on top of a wing.

"You guys are just drawing cartoons out there," Judd scoffed.

Not even John Yeasting could budge Northwest, and Yeasting had the same close relationship with Don Nyrop as Bill Allen had with C. R. Smith at American. The people Nyrop trusted could be counted on the fingers of one hand, with a couple of fingers left over, but he concluded airplane deals with Yeasting on the strength of a handshake. Not the 727, however; among the things Northwest's leader didn't trust were airplanes that didn't have four engines.

Allen tried hard to sell the 727 to American, but C. R. was happy with his new Electra fleet. He even told Allen he would never buy the 727—a promise that would be shattered when two fatal Electra crashes disclosed serious structural problems. But during the initial 727 sales efforts, there wasn't the remotest chance of landing American. TWA's chief engineer, Bob Rummel, liked the three-engine concept but Rummel wasn't calling the equipment shots at an airline run by the financially strained Howard Hughes.

Tough Stan Shatto, Frank Judd's counterpart at Western, laughed when he was shown a 727 presentation.

"A three-engine airplane will never make it," he declared. "You've got a dead horse unless it has four engines. The 727's going to be nothing but an albatross."

George Sanborn, Boeing's director of sales who reported to Bruce Connelly, was anxious to stir up interest overseas, but it was too soon; this time Boeing was the manufacturer selling a paper airplane. Of all the European carriers Ken Luplow sounded out, only Lufthansa seemed like a possible prospect, albeit a very cautious one. Yet despite the generally cool reception the 727 was getting from the airlines, there was a growing sense of excitement at Boeing, a feeling that this paper airplane was going to become one hell of a *real* airplane.

Dash-80 served as an ersatz 727 for flight-testing Cook's new flap system and the aft engine arrangement. The latter was tried out simply by hanging a JT-8D on one side of the Dash-80's rear fuselage. The wind tunnel data looked promising and actually turned out to be too conservative, thanks to something Bill Cook did without telling anyone until much later.

Cook was concerned that the triple-slotted flaps would leak—in other words, produce too much drag even when fully retracted. So without even informing Steiner or Pennell, he put in a deliberately conservative drag factor estimate for the final configuration. It turned out that the 727 had 10 percent less drag than Cook had predicted.

"It was like a hidden insurance policy, coupled with what was a good design to begin with," Steiner said.

As Allen's December deadline approached, Eastern came through with an order for 40 727s. United followed with another 40-plane contract, and took options on an additional 20. But on November 30, Boeing still was 20 aircraft short of the mandatory 100 firm orders needed for board approval of the production go-ahead. And it was Bill Allen, munching meditatively on the Triscuits that were his favorite snack, who came to one of his most crucial and gutsiest decisions.

"We should regard United's twenty options as contributing to the criteria we set," he told the directors. "Added to the eighty firm orders, they give us our one hundred airplanes."

This time, there was no yellow tinge to the green light.

It was decided to build the 727 at Renton, producing the new jet jointly with the 707. The 727 passed a critical test before the first complete plane rolled off the Renton line. Ben Cosgrove was chief of design for wing structure, and his most vivid memory of the entire program involved the day they static-tested a 727 wing to destruction. It was a tense moment of truth for Cosgrove.

"Your name's on the line," he said. "This is what you said the wing would do. The worst thing that could happen was to have it break before reaching one hundred percent of design strength. The second worst thing was to have it go too far over—that said you were too conservative and had put too much weight into the airplane."

Cosgrove watched the wing bend upward, inch by inch. The big dial recording stress loads edged past the 100 percent mark, and Ben's heart began pounding.

Someone called out, "She's at one hundred and ten," and Cosgrove thought, *My God, we can't go much farther than this.*

"She's leveling at one-twelve . . . almost to one-thirteen . . . the wing tips are lagging . . ."

Then came an ear-splitting roar as the wing broke. The entire room seemed to explode, but to Cosgrove it was sweet music.

"Thank God," he remembered murmuring.

Rollout day was November 27, 1962—the first public glimpse of another Boeing bet on the future. The E-1 (the *E* was for Eastern) wore the same copper-and-yellow markings as the Dash-80; a color that wasn't visible but very present in Bill Allen's mind was the red ink the airplane carried: $150 million had been spent on design and tooling, $20 million above the original estimate. Yet Allen had no quarrel with the major reason for the overrun. At the insistence of Ed Wells and George Schairer, three non-flying airframes had been built: the first was the one Ben Cosgrove had sweated out to destruction; the second had been subjected to unprecedented metal fatigue tests; and the third was used to measure every conceivable flight load that might be encountered.

On February 9, 1963, a beautiful, sunny Saturday morning, E-1 took off from Renton Field on its first flight; Lew Wallick was in the left seat, and Dix Loesch was copilot with M. K. "Shuly" Shulenberger serving as flight engineer. Only a handful of people watched the takeoff; most Boeing engineers and officials, including Allen, were at Everett's Paine Field where the plane was scheduled to land after the initial two-hour test flight.

The few who witnessed the takeoff heard a loud popping sound as the 727 started its climb. In the cockpit, the crew knew immediately what had happened. The center engine had surged—twice, in fact—in a compressor stall, because the airflow pouring into the S-shaped duct was uneven. Wallick eased back on the center throttle and the surging stopped.

"It really got my attention," Wallick recalled years later. "I thought my hair had turned white."

The rest of the flight was uneventful, except for another unexpected development. The test crew was unable to retract the leading edge flaps, because the air loads on the devices were heavier than the hydraulic system could handle. The scheduled speed test had to be scrubbed, but Wallick and Loesch put the 727 through required stall and buffeting tests, which the aircraft handled well. They landed at Paine, a runway paint job that brought cheers from the waiting crowd. Bill Allen was so excited, he was jumping up and down with one foot in a mud puddle.

Wallick commented to the press and public, "The control systems are better than expected. I think they are well advanced over previous airplanes. It feels good. I think airline pilots are going to like this one."

Loesch chimed in, "The entire period of flying was very smooth."

But in private the pilots informed Steiner of the center engine surging problem and the retractable leading edge flaps that wouldn't retract. The fixes were quick and relatively easy: vortex generators were installed inside the center engine duct to smooth out the airflow, and the hydraulic flap actuators were beefed up.

Every pilot associated with the 727's test phase had nothing but praise for Steiner.

"When we had a problem," Wallick said, "Jack was always right there, completely involved, and he didn't hesitate one second to get his engineers working on any item we reported. He'd tell them, 'Don't worry about the cost—fix it and get it right.' "

Brien Wygle agreed. "Steiner was never defensive about the 727. If the slightest thing was wrong, he'd want it corrected and quickly. He has come in for his share of criticism, but in the early days of the 727, when Lew was flying the airplane and right through the certification tests, it was Jack's finest hour. He knew the airplane thoroughly, his judgment was good, and his decisions in manufacturing, engineering, and flight testing were superb."

Men like Wallick, Loesch, and Wygle sensed almost immediately that the 727 was something special—a pilot's airplane, the highest accolade an airman can bestow on an aircraft. They really appreciated this "one-handed" bird and the effort the engineers had made to achieve easy, smooth controls with harmonizing rudder and aileron forces.

"We used the 727 as the standard for the airplanes that followed," Wallick said. "When it went into service, airline operators would tell

Douglas and Lockheed that their next airplanes had to fly like the 727."

Wygle remembered one demonstration flight in particular. He had four pilots representing an Air Line Pilots Association evaluation team aboard, each from a different carrier that had ordered the three-holer. One of them was flying the airplane and Wygle was explaining that the 727 had two hydraulic control systems, a primary and a backup.

"What happens if both fail?" the pilot asked.

"Then there's a manual backup, which is, mind you, a last-ditch device to get you home safely. It's really a miserable way to fly the airplane, because the stick forces are very heavy. But I'll let you try it."

He turned off the primary system, then the backup. The pilot flew on manual for a few minutes, then grinned.

"Just like a DC-6," he commented.

The test flights confirmed Cook's "hidden insurance" gambit. Not only did the 727 produce 10 percent less drag than predicted, it also proved to be 15 knots faster, consumed three percent less fuel, and could carry 10 percent more payload.

An item of early concern was the T-tail design, which put the horizontal stabilizers at the top of the rudder section instead of the usual location at the bottom of the rudder. The engineers knew that a T-tail airplane can be especially vulnerable to the "deep stall," a problem that arrived with the introduction of sweptwing aircraft.

Any airplane stalls when the airflow over the wings diminishes to the point where lift cannot be maintained. On a straight-wing airplane, however, loss of airflow stalls the entire wing, and recovery is relatively simple. But on a sweptwing aircraft, loss of airflow stalls the wing tips first, causing the nose to pitch up sharply and accelerating loss of airflow to the leading edges of the wings. Forward speed deteriorates rapidly, and descent speed picks up.

This is the deep stall, and the final stage in this chain is the tendency of the elevators, caught in the turbulence of the stalled wing, to become almost totally ineffective. If recovery is even possible, it requires a tremendous, instantaneous forward push on the control yoke before all control is lost.

Not on the 727, however. Boeing engineered the deep stall hazard out of the airplane before it ever flew, first with wind tunnel tests that provided the best way to shape the leading edges of the wings and horizontal stabilizers, so both would retain at least some airflow if the nose pitched up. To this was added an extremely efficient stall warning system. The final cure was rigging the leading edge flaps to extend with the first movement of the flap handle, facilitating recovery if a pilot did get trapped into the start of a deep stall.

The three-holer did have some quirks of its own, the landing gear being a prime offender. The airplane started out with a projected gross weight of less than 150,000 pounds, but adding weight as the design progresses is almost inevitable. Because the 727 would make more takeoffs and landings than the bigger jets, the gear had to be stiff even with the original 150,000-pound goal. But as weight increased, the gear was stiffened further.

"Anyone who's flown the 727," Wallick said, "knows that it's like trying to land on stilts."

The stiff gear was an ego-buster to many pilots who prided themselves on "paint-job" landings that wouldn't break an egg tied to a main wheel. "We used to say," Wygle mused, "that no matter how clever you were in landing an airplane, the 727 would get you sooner or later."

Dix Loesch remembered that at one time, the engineers installed a softer metering pin on the struts. But this resulted in airport complaints; 727s equipped with the softer gear were breaking up thinly paved taxiways and runways.

The 727 was its own best salesman, and this was proved not only on demonstration flights for U.S. airline officials and pilots, but spectacularly so on a world tour Boeing staged in late 1963. With Bill Allen aboard, the fourth production airplane made a whirlwind tour of 44 cities in 26 countries: it covered Europe, South Africa, the Middle East, India, Japan, and Australia. The 727 was the first jet transport to carry its own APU (auxiliary power unit), an immense aid when landing at airports that had never seen a jet before and lacked the proper ground service equipment.

The aircraft covered 95,000 miles without a single mechanical delay. Dave Peterson of customer relations, who took many a demonstration tour, said, "I can't remember a single one I was on, including the 727's, where we missed our schedule by more than five minutes."

On one demonstration landing in Australia, the three-holer came to a dead stop after using up only 1,500 feet of a rain-slick runway, bringing spontaneous applause from the cabin occupants. Almost every takeoff, here and abroad, prompted gasps from the passengers; the plane often was rotated at 18 degrees instead of the normal 15 and climbed like a scalded eagle; more than one reporter wrote that it was like being in a fighter. The short-field landing capability wowed the novice and experienced flyer alike.

"I must stress," a British pilot declared, "the visible, palpable effect of that slow approach speed. It gives the pilot time when he needs it the most—when the chips are down, in low ceilings and poor visibility."

In Nome, Alaska, to demonstrate the 727's anti-skid and braking prowess, the plane landed easily on a runway covered by two inches of snow over solid ice, without using thrust reversers.

The world trip, and a U.S. tour with the same airplane, brought more than rave reviews; the orders began coming in to Seattle. Australia's Ansett and Trans-Australia, Japan's All Nippon, Sabena, Lufthansa, Air France, National, TWA—even recalcitrant American and Northwest—fell into line. Boeing's original projected market for the plane was 300; by the time it went out of production in 1984, a total of 1,831 had been sold and delivered.

Boeing's customer relations department came of age with this truly brilliant airplane; even more than the 707, it established the company as the world's commercial transport leader, Seattle as an airline mecca, and Bill Allen as an industry giant. With this stature, however, came the need for more customer entertaining—and this was an area in which Boeing was comparatively inexperienced and certainly not as savvy as Douglas and Lockheed, which had the advantage of California weather. Many airline executives, particularly the Europeans, preferred to visit Seattle during the week, and spend weekends in Los Angeles. Entertaining became a learning experience for the company, including the ultra-conservative Allen, who laid down stringent customer relations rules that basically still are in effect.

He forbade any Boeing employee to accept a gift from a vendor, a free ride from an airline customer, or even a free meal, unless the employee could prove he reciprocated. The most stringent no-no was lining up women for customers. Dave Peterson first went to work for customer relations under George Sanborn, who was made director of commercial sales when Boeing split military and commercial sales into two separate departments. On one of his first days on the job, Allen called him in.

"I just want you to know something, Dave," he said. "If I ever catch you pimping for some customer, don't bother coming to work the next morning because you're fired."

It was during the 727 era that Boeing acquired its first and only limousine—a stretched Cadillac everyone called the Green Hornet. It was used solely for greeting VIPs, like airline presidents and visiting royalty; most visitors were met by station wagons, and Boeing today uses mostly vans. It took some fast talking to convince Allen the company needed the flashy big Cadillac, and what finally sold him was the realization that most European VIPs *expected* such treatment.

The only other displays of corporate entertaining ostentatiousness stemmed from the main attraction Seattle had to offer: the magnificent waters of the Puget Sound area. This led first to leasing temporarily a yacht owned by movie star John Wayne, the *Wild Goose*.

Peterson flew down to Balboa to work out the lease, but it was quickly apparent that Wayne's idea of accommodating guests didn't quite fit Boeing's needs. He had only one huge stateroom, and the yacht's two heads (toilets) belonged on a tramp steamer. Boeing remodeled the interior into four staterooms, and also modernized the toilets with new basins and linoleum. Wayne didn't object to the revised staterooms, but he told Peterson, "Dammit, if those heads were good enough for me, they're good for you guys."

The fact that the *Wild Goose* belonged to a star of Wayne's magnitude made more of an impression on guests than if Boeing had leased the battleship *Missouri*. The wife of an airline executive boarded the yacht one day and was escorted to the largest stateroom by the steward assigned to the boat. She looked around in awe and gushed, "Just think, John Wayne slept here! I imagine it must be quite a thrill for you to work here."

"I wouldn't know, ma'am," he said. "I never slept with him."

The *Goose* was one of Boeing's four hospitality centers. The Allen and Beall homes were two others, Wellwood usually entertaining important out-of-town guests on Friday evenings and Allen hosting them Saturdays. The fourth was a suite Boeing maintained at the old Olympic Hotel (now the Four Seasons Olympic), which in its day was *the* Seattle hostelry. Prior to the suite, Allen used a private club at the hotel for wining and dining visitors, but members complained Boeing was using their facilities too frequently and Peterson suggested to Allen that the company rent a permanent suite.

"All right," Allen agreed, "provided there's no bedroom. I don't want directors fighting over who gets the suite."

So the suite Peterson rented had just a sitting room and a small dining room, used for lunches and dinners. It was an oasis for visitors like Lindbergh and C. R. Smith, who hated to go out in public. "I remember Lindy sitting there, philosophizing with Ed Wells," Dave reminisced. "I used to tend bar there a lot because they didn't want any strangers in the room."

Such privacy precautions never deterred Bob Twiss of the *Seattle Times*. He must have had a spy network at the Olympic that would have had the CIA saluting in admiration; somehow Twiss always managed to find out what airline executives were staying at the hotel, and he'd reveal airplane deals even before Boeing's public relations department could announce them. C. R. always claimed Twiss had to be on Boeing's payroll. Either that or he figured Twiss had someone in Boeing on *his* payroll.

"Nobody could find out what he does without having a mole inside Boeing," Smith complained to Peterson.

For a short time, Ken Luplow was one of Bob's best sources until Ken decided he might be talking too much and changed tactics. Twiss would call him for an interview, and Luplow would deliberately pick a day when he was leaving town.

"How about Tuesday?" Luplow would suggest.

"Great."

So Twiss would arrive on schedule, and five minutes into the interview Luplow would look at his watch. "Bob, I'm sorry, but I gotta catch a plane."

Boeing's unofficial goodwill ambassadors were the company drivers who provided transportation for visiting VIPs. They were and still are a breed apart, loyal to Boeing and never reluctant to talk about the company and its products. Even visiting royalty didn't faze them.

Prince Philip of England once arrived in Seattle on an unofficial visit, accompanied by a single security guard and a State Department representative. The DOS man asked Dave Peterson, "Does your driver talk?"

"No, he'll just take you where you want to go," Peterson assured him.

The driver, however, turned out to be a frustrated tour guide, and insisted on pointing out various Seattle highlights. "You gotta see this," he'd proclaim. "Can't see much just driving by—you should take the time to really see it."

Peterson thought he'd never stop talking, but the prince was fascinated and finally suggested, "Why don't you pick us up a little earlier tomorrow morning so we can do all you recommend?"

This impressed Dave, too, until the security guard insisted they make a dry run over the next day's sightseeing route—at three A.M.

Recently, a *Wall Street Journal* reporter was doing a story on Boeing and when she finished the assignment, Dean Thornton, president of the commercial airplane division, asked her what had impressed her the most about the company.

He expected her to pick out something like the awesome size of the 747 factory at Everett, or something incongruous like the simplicity of corporate headquarters, which had reminded one previous writer of "a prosperous YMCA." Thornton was wrong.

"The van drivers," she replied. "They're so proud of what they're doing, so proud of their company, and they refer to officers like yourself by their first names."

"That's right."

"But they don't do that to your face, do they?"

"They sure do," Thornton admitted.

They also referred to some customers that way. Bob Six was especially fond of a Boeing driver named Ollie Flohr, and it was mutual. Anytime Six arrived at Sea-Tac, he would walk right past all the Boeing brass there to greet him and head straight for Ollie.

"Ollie, you old goat—how the hell are you?"

"Pretty good, Bob. How the hell are you?"

Then all the way to whatever Boeing facility Six was visiting, they'd discuss the stock market, airplanes, Continental's load factors, and Colorado's football team—one of Six's favorite topics.

Thornton, who came to Boeing from the accounting firm of Touche Ross, was one of two future top executives joining the company in minor roles during the 727's gestation period. The other was Frank Shrontz, a soft-spoken yet quietly decisive lawyer who began his career at Boeing negotiating contracts for the old transport division. Along with Dick Welch and Hal Haynes, who labored under John Yeasting in finance, they were typical of the more conservative executive talent Boeing had always needed to maintain an effective balance with the exuberant Boulliouns and Steiners. Welch, who preceded Shrontz and Thornton by several years, was a self-admitted "bean counter" who also happened to be immensely popular among employees and respected by customers; above all else, he shared Allen's commitment to integrity, and he inspired more than a few future officers in that respect.

Hal Haynes, like Wes Maulden, was someone you had to know well to understand and appreciate—Egypt's Sphinx was more garrulous. But no company ever had a more brilliant and dedicated financial officer. He came to Boeing in 1954 from the same accounting firm as Thornton, serving first as controller Clyde Skeen's assistant. His taciturnity became legendary at Boeing. Deane Cruze once sat down to breakfast with him in the executive dining room, and Haynes didn't say one word throughout the entire meal. Cruze finished eating, rose, and shook his head.

"Hal," he said, "I want to thank you for one of the most stimulating thirty-minute conversations I've ever had."

Although it was Skeen who hired Haynes, Clyde left the company in 1960 for several years and Yeasting was more Hal's mentor. They could have been mistaken for brothers; both were tall, good-looking, and very dignified.

Dignity and decorum were not the specialties of a fast-rising Bud Hurst protégé, Wally Buckley. Fresh from Minuteman, Buckley was assigned new responsibilities in 727 production, and to Wally meeting production schedules was like fulfilling wedding vows. Any vendor delay ruined his whole day, and at one stage he became incensed when 727 galleys manufactured by Norskog were arriving late. Boeing not only sent a team to California to help president Bob Norskog straighten things out, but also loaned him money. The galleys began arriving on time, but that didn't placate Buckley, who occasionally could carry a grudge as a camel carries water.

Art Carbary and Deane Cruze figured it was time to mend fences—Norskog was one of Boeing's most reliable and oldest suppliers. They presented their case to Buck.

"Bob's paid back all the money Boeing loaned him," Carbary pointed out, "and deliveries are getting back on schedule. He's in town and we want you to sit down with him, tell him how glad you are that everything's better for him, and how much you appreciate the loan repayment."

Buckley went into a window-rattling tirade. "He's caused us enough trouble without my having to thank him for one damned thing! He screwed up the 727 program royally and cost us a fortune even if he did pay us back. And I don't care if I never see him again!"

They finally convinced Wally he should at least talk to Norskog, although both held their breath when the vendor came into Buckley's office.

Wally jumped to his feet with a smile the width of a tiger's yawn, and shook hands warmly. "Bob, you old son of a gun—how are you? Come sit down. I want to tell you what a great job you're doing! I'm so proud of you I don't know what to say. Want some coffee?"

Cruze looked at Carbary. Carbary looked at Cruze. They both shrugged.

Buckley was picked to help develop the new Auburn fabrication facility in 1965, as tough a construction and planning job as Boeing ever undertook until the 747 plant at Everett. The Auburn site, a little more than 20 miles south of Seattle, was chosen to avoid the increased traffic congestion that would have resulted from a new major facility located in or too near Seattle. Auburn became a jack-of-all-trades plant, handling metal bonding, tooling, welding, plastics, ducts, sheet metal, and virtually every industrial material known to man.

When Auburn was in operation Buckley thought it was an opportune time to end the practice of having each airplane division manufacture its own blankets—blankets being the cabin insulating material installed next to an aircraft's inner skin. He summoned Bob Gamrath, Deane Cruze, Bill Shineman, and Sterling Sessions, his key production aides.

"What I want to do," he announced, "is establish one blanket shop in Auburn that will serve all divisions. What do you guys think?"

Unanimously they called it a lousy idea.

"Well, I don't give a damn what you think," Wally snapped. "Go to the divisions and coordinate the consolidation, so we can get Auburn rolling."

A few days later, all four reported back that the divisions had about 500 arguments against the plan. Cruze spoke for the quartet. "The problem, Wally, is that we've got too many personalities involved and we can't come to any consolidation agreement."

Buckley looked at him coldly. "Are you telling me you can't do the job I gave you?"

"That's right, we can't."

Buckley said nothing but proceeded to set up a meeting with everyone associated with the various blanket shops. It lasted approximately 30 seconds.

"All right," he proclaimed, "we're gonna have one blanket shop and Gamrath's gonna run it. Now you guys go figure out how to do it. That's the end of the meeting."

"Six or seven months later," Cruze said, "we had all the shops combined at Auburn, and we've been making money on this arrangement ever since."

Buckley's softer side was never more poignantly revealed than when Boeing, as an experiment, hired five totally deaf riveters. It was a program aimed at easing the problem of riveting noise on the 727/707 assembly line at Renton, and the idea was to train and develop such people while shifting workers with normal hearing to less noisy tasks. The five trainees arrived for their first day's work, and Buckley came out of his office to make a speech.

Yes, a speech. He addressed them in perfect sign language, welcoming them and expressing the hope that they'd be the first of many hearing-impaired people to find good careers at Boeing. The five newcomers weren't any less surprised than Buckley's colleagues; no one had the slightest idea he knew sign language. Not until later did they learn that Wally had a hearing-impaired brother and had been taught sign language long ago.

Unfortunately, the experiment didn't have the happy ending Buckley's gesture deserved. Although everyone rallied around the five trainees, it was discovered that riveting vibrations disturbed the deaf as much as noise bothered the regular workers.

Don Whitford and Joe Miles were a couple of other much-admired men from the manufacturing side. Whitford was to rise to vice president and general manager of the Renton division before retiring. A tall, powerfully built man, he was a lot like Buckley: gruff and hard-boiled but fiercely protective of any worker who did his job well. Cruze called him "one of the best developers of managerial talent the company ever had."

"He could be tough," Cruze said, "but he'd allow you to have your head, to make mistakes, and sit down with you and go over those mistakes. Then he'd always ask, 'Did you learn anything from this?' "

If Whitford had any favorite, it was Miles, a chubby, good-natured materiel veteran who in his later years looked like everyone's grandfather should look. Miles is often remembered for the time he got the best of sharp-tongued Ben Wheat—and to blunt Wheat's wicked needle took some doing. They were at a manufacturing meeting and Ben said to Miles, "Joe, why don't you take a minute, get up there, and tell us everything you know."

Joe smiled. "Ben, I'll tell you what I'll do. I'll tell 'em everything we *both* know and it won't take any longer."

Sterling Sessions was another tough but fair boss who felt that the assembly line work force was undisciplined at times, but that management could be at fault, too. When 727 production was going full steam, Sessions was assigned to Renton as plant superintendent and immediately began raising Cain: the plant was dirty, and too many people weren't producing.

"We had a bar chart," Sessions related, "a simple graph showing work progress status. Each man had to color the work he'd completed toward what industrial engineering had established as the standard for getting so much accomplished in an eight-hour shift. It could be a three-day chart, a five-day, or whatever. You've scheduled a complete assembly in an allotted time, and if you haven't got an airplane finished, it's easy to find out whose bar chart is holding up the works."

Sessions zeroed in on one tardy area: section 46, the 727's aft fuselage. One man's bar chart was the main bottleneck. Sessions told his immediate supervisor, "Give this guy a poor-work slip."

Three of those slips meant dismissal. But the worker's chart continued to lag and Sessions summoned him.

"You've had three slips," Sessions said. "I'm sorry, but unless you've got one hell of an excuse, you're fired."

"I could get my job done if you guys would do yours," the worker retorted. "Just go out there and look at the rivet gun I'm using. It's no good."

Sessions did some investigating. He found that some drill motors employed on section 46 were producing only 30 percent power and were burning out prematurely. This particular worker's drill motor wasn't getting enough compressed air; the compressor he was using was located near Sessions' office, which was about as far away from section 46 as anyone could get, and a further check showed that the compressor lines were too small to be efficient at that distance.

"We ended up tearing out all the pipes in the building," Sessions said. "The drill motors were supposed to be lubricated automatically with a drop of oil from a valve, but when we tore out the pipes we found that no hole for the oil drip had ever been drilled, and it was no wonder all the motors were burning out.

"We increased production in that one section by an incredible amount, just because one guy had the guts to tell us he could do his job if we'd do ours."

Boeing built more than 80 percent of the 727 at Renton, and what was farmed out was the lowest percentage of subcontracted work of any jet transport the company produced.

The most popular managers and supervisors, however, couldn't compensate for the long-festering resentment against the performance analysis system—the policy of promoting hourly production workers solely on the basis of supervisory reports, with no consideration given to seniority. Instituted after the 1948 strike, it still was in existence in 1965, and the resentment boiled over into an IAM strike that shut down 707 and 727 production for 19 days.

Three years earlier, Allen had made Lowell Mickelwait, who had been the company's legal counsel, a vice president in charge of both industrial relations and public relations. The logic behind combining these two widely divergent assignments was unclear, but as a skilled lawyer Mickelwait was more at ease with the labor relations aspects of his job. They were old friends, but Mickelwait undoubtedly was more objective than Allen when it came to dealing with the unhappy machinists' union.

His chief aide was Stan Little, who had joined Boeing in 1944 as an engineer but drifted into the administrative side of engineering and possessed three qualities essential for a labor negotiator: fairness, patience, and a sense of humor. Mickelwait represented the company in the negotiations but when talks reached an impasse, he decided to let things cool off for a couple of days and took his wife to San Francisco to play some golf. Little and another lawyer from Allen's old firm, DeForest Perkins, were left behind to hold down the management fort at the hotel where the warring parties were staying during the negotiations.

Perkins took a dim view of their chief's absence. "That damned Mickelwait's out playing golf and we're working our tails off," he complained to Little.

"Dee, do you know what today is? April first. So a little practical joke's in order."

They obtained a supply of hotel phone message blanks and composed a series of notes which they left in Mickelwait's box.

8:30 A.M. Please call Bill Allen.
9:15 A.M. Call Bill Allen, urgent.
10:20 A.M. Call Mr. Allen immediately.

And so on, until the final message, which they timed at 7:45 P.M.:

Mick: We were unable to reach you, so we took the liberty of issuing the following press release in your absence:
    Lowell Mickelwait, when contacted on the 16th tee at the Burlingame Country Club, said, "I was as surprised as anyone to learn that the union had gone on strike. We hope it will be a short strike because we have many things of mutual interest."

Mickelwait took the real strike with slightly more equanimity than he did those phony notes. The strike was settled amicably when Boeing agreed to replace performance analysis with a seniority system, but the settlement provided that in case of layoffs, the company could retain a certain percentage of less senior employees whose job performance had proved superior. Preceding the settlement, Mickelwait had set up a committee, consisting of Stan Little, Wes Maulden, and Tex Boullioun, plus a couple of outside experts, to determine whether performance analysis was really impartial in its promotion process.

"What they found," Little recalled, "was that despite all the union horror stories, the guys with the highest job performance grades were actually winning promotions, and also were more senior. The cases of supervisory favoritism and nepotism were rare, but they did occur, and the final settlement that established a job performance system basically is the same one that exists today with some modifications."

The 1965 strike was less traumatic for Boeing than a series of fatal 727 accidents, which prompted congressional demands for grounding the new jet that had entered airline service in February 1964. Within a space of less than six months, between August 16, 1965, and February 6, 1966, four 727s crashed on final approach to four different airports: three in the U.S. and the fourth in Japan. The common denominator in each crash was excessive rate of descent, so rapid that in two cases the airplanes were flown into the water, a third hit high terrain near the airport, and the fourth landed so hard that the gear rammed into the belly, rupturing fuel lines.

Several congressmen charged to the attack, claiming the 727 was inherently dangerous because of "an abnormally high sink rate." This was malarkey; the four accident investigations established that each had been caused by the pilots exceeding established limits on descent rate, and the real culprit was a jet transport that handled like a fighter but still had to be flown strictly by the book.

The FAA asked a special NASA committee to study the 727's flying qualities and determine whether its design was inherently dangerous. The unanimous verdict cleared the plane completely. Airline 727 operators began putting more emphasis on training to handle high sink rate, and the plane's black eye faded away.

Boeing has never tried to sweep under the rug accidents involving its planes. In fact, its interest in safety has resulted in a number of Boeing-financed research projects applicable to all aircraft. A good example was a project instituted after the spate of 727 accidents. Night visibility was a common factor in three of the crashes: two final approaches were over water, and a third was over unlighted and sloping terrain between the airplane and its assigned runway.

Boeing engineers built a make-believe city on a tabletop placed in front of a cockpit simulator, and put 12 experienced company pilots through identical approaches to the miniature city's airport. All 12 were told they were making a routine approach on a clear night to "Nighterton Field," well-lighted and just south of the city, located on a three-degree slope. Bisecting Nighterton was a river. The city lights were bright, but there were no lights between the beginning of the approach path and the runway—a typical approach over water or unlighted sloping terrain.

None of the pilots had altimeters for reference. They were told to concentrate on flying the best approach path possible, reporting their *estimated* altitude every two miles starting at a point 18 miles from the airport. Their only active instruments were an airspeed indicator and a vertical velocity gauge.

Eleven of the 12 crashed while making the approach. The closest any of these 11 got to the runway before pranging into the imaginary ground was five miles. One crashed a full eight miles away. They had been instructed to fly at an estimated 5,000-foot altitude while 10 miles out, and at 1,240 feet, four and a half miles out. Except for a single pilot, all gave visual estimates of their altitudes up to 2,500 feet higher than they actually were. Nighterton had reproduced the hazards present at hundreds of airports—lack of lights between the aircraft and the runway, and the treacherous, misleading slope of terrain over the approach path. The project's message was clear: potential hazards have to be engineered out of airports as well as airplanes.

One key figure wasn't around to witness the 727's trials and triumphs. Wellwood Beall was gone, forced to resign in 1964 by Bill Allen, who had lost patience with Beall's free-swinging life-style in general and with his reported fondness for the grape in particular. Beall promptly went to work for the "enemy"—he became a vice president at Douglas, and some of his contemporaries felt Allen had made a mistake letting any competitor acquire a man of Wellwood's talent. Others defended Allen, pointing out that Beall had been warned more than once to straighten up his act.

There is no doubt Allen was fed up. He came home one night, apparently after hearing about some incident involving Beall, and told Mef, "If this kind of thing doesn't stop, out he goes!" Whether it was some specific incident that precipitated the drastic action or a culmination of supposed transgressions, no one but Allen knew. Whatever the cause, Wellwood's departure was a stunner around corporate headquarters. A man prominent in Boeing's financial history, Carl Dillon, thought Beall's firing may not have hurt Boeing to any great extent, but that it certainly helped Douglas.

"It was a bad mistake," Dillon said. "No matter how badly you get along with a guy of Wellwood's ability, keep him as a consultant if nothing else. Within a few months after he went to Douglas, they announced the stretched DC-8 and that's the only thing that kept them in the commercial transport business. They were broke, but they sold enough stretched Eights to keep their production line going and draw in some cash flow. I don't know for a fact whether Beall was instrumental in that decision, but I don't think it was a coincidence."

Two definitive histories of the Douglas Aircraft Company don't even mention Beall's name, but he always will be remembered at Boeing. He had been part of the company for more than 30 years, his engineering and/or sales input stamped on virtually every airplane Boeing built during those 30 years.

Every corporate annual report has a page listing the names of all directors and top officers. The name of Wellwood Beall was missing from that page in Boeing's 1965 annual report, of course, but a number of names had been added that told stories of their own.

T Wilson, vice president of operations and planning. Tex Boullioun, vice president and assistant general manager of the commercial airplane division under John Yeasting, whom Hal Haynes had replaced as vice president of finance. A newcomer from the AC Sparkplug division of General Motors, Malcolm Stamper, was listed as vice president and general manager of the gas turbine division. Bob Jewett was now vice president and general manager of missile and information systems, a combination reflecting Boeing's growing participation in computer technology. (The job titles also reflected a far more diversified company; in 1961 the directors had voted to change the corporate name from *Boeing Airplane Company* to *The Boeing Company.*)

Jack Steiner's reward for the 727 program was the title of vice president of product development for the commercial airplane division. Ben Wheat, who had once worked the third shift at Stearman as a parts dispatcher because it paid 10 cents more an hour than the first and second shifts, had become vice president and general manager of the Wichita division. In the commercial airplane division were four more vice presidents: Bob Regan (operations), Dick Rouzie (engineering), Carl Dillon (finance and service), and Don Euler (planning).

The name of board chairman Claire Egtvedt appeared for the last time on this 1965 executive roster; inactive for almost two decades, he was one year away from official retirement and 10 years away from his death. Two of the strongest directors who ever served Boeing were listed and bear mention: Crawford Greenewalt, Du Pont's board chairman, who wasn't afraid to oppose Allen; and George H. Weyerhaeuser, whose father had been a Boeing director—the Weyerhaeuser name had won respect throughout the Pacific Northwest, and the son was carrying on the tradition within his own company and at Boeing as well.

Names that told stories . . .

The familiar names of men who had roots to the past, yet kept their eyes to the future . . .

Ed Wells, of course. In 1965, he was on the board along with John Yeasting and serving as vice president of product development. George Schairer had the post of vice president, research and development, while George Martin remained very active as vice president of engineering. Manufacturing's top executive was vice president C. B. Gracey. But if names really tell stories, look hard at three others.

At Maynard Pennell, listed as vice president and director of the supersonic transport program.

At George Stoner, vice president and general manager of the space division.

And at Bob Tharrington, a feisty little accountant who went to work for Boeing in 1940 as a clerk in the Wichita accounting department; he now was vice president and general manager of the Vertol division in Philadelphia.

Supersonic transports. Space. Helicopters.

These, too, were part of Boeing's future.

THIRTEEN

PHILADELPHIA STORY

PHILADELPHIA IS 2,388 AIR MILES FROM SEATTLE.

But when Boeing bought the Vertol Aircraft Corporation in 1960, the distance might as well have been 2.4 million miles. The purchase price was $3.6 million plus an exchange of stock—three Boeing shares for every two Vertol shares. For that sum, Boeing acquired a tradition-rich company that had been building helicopters for 17 years, a relatively small plant ill-equipped for large-scale production, and a work force that regarded the new owners with the same enthusiasm the post–Civil War South displayed toward carpetbaggers.

Seventeen years was not much time in which to build tradition, nevertheless it was true of Vertol. The company was founded in 1943 by Frank Piasecki, son of a Polish immigrant tailor. Piasecki was still in his teens when he went to work for Kellett Aircraft, an autogiro manufacturer. He became fascinated with helicopters, a concept that dated back to a 15th-century drawing in one of Leonardo da Vinci's notebooks. In 1940, after earning a degree from New York University in aeronautical engineering, Piasecki enlisted the aid of a few friends and by 1943 was building a small helicopter in a rented garage in the Roxborough section of Philadelphia. They operated under a rather unique name: the P-V Engineering Forum (the "V" was for one of Piasecki's partners, Harold Venzi).

Piasecki, a handsome, husky youngster with a thin mustache, would have felt right at home with any of Boeing's "squirrels." He once landed his first helicopter in front of a gas station, climbed out and told the startled attendant, "Fill 'er up—and don't forget to clean the windshield."

He also had the same kind of "build 'em big" creed that had made Boeing famous, envisioning the helicopter as a military and commercial workhorse capable of lifting large payloads in and out of places an airplane couldn't reach. With that in mind, he designed the first successful tandem rotor helicopter, the PV-3 (Navy XHRP-X Dogships), with rotor blades mounted at each end of a large fuselage to distribute the lifting load equally. The rear fuselage curved upward so one rotor blade wouldn't interfere with the other, giving the unusual-looking aircraft the shape of a banana—which is precisely the nickname its production offspring quickly acquired: "the Flying Banana."

The XHRP-X's first flight was March 7, 1945, and its performance was impressive enough to attract the venture capital interest of Laurence Rockefeller and Felix DuPont, who bought into the fledgling company that a year later became Piasecki Helicopter Corporation. Under that name, the company sold 20 10-passenger XHRP helicopters to the Navy, and over the next 10 years established itself as a small but innovative helicopter manufacturer struggling to compete with Sikorsky and Bell. In 1956, founder Piasecki lost a bitter internal war with the Rockefeller and DuPont interests when the latter brought in someone else to run the company. Piasecki then resigned as board chairman and Piasecki Helicopter became Vertol Aircraft Corporation (vertical takeoff and landing), the name under which it was operating when Boeing took over.

The helicopter grew up during the Korean War, proving its airlift versatility in countless ways. It grew up even more during the same period when engineers began applying turbine engine technology to rotorcraft; the shift from reciprocating engines to jet power was as big a revolution in helicopters as in airplanes, bringing new smoothness and efficiency to an aircraft that literally must lift itself up by its own bootstraps.

Kaman Aircraft is credited with building the first turbine-powered helicopter—using a Boeing gas turbine, incidentally—but Vertol didn't lag in that respect. One of Frank Piasecki's last efforts before leaving the company was the giant twin-turbine YH-16A (YH for experimental helicopter), and after this came two variants of the ubiquitous H-21 that Piasecki had built for the Air Force, Army, and several foreign countries.

In 1958, Vertol brought out a company-funded prototype of a modern turbine-powered helicopter designated Model 107, which led to its two most successful product lines—the H-46 Sea Knight and the CH-47 Chinook. The prototype went into production as the Vertol Model 107-II, a 25-passenger commercial helicopter purchased first by New York Airways. The Army bought two subsequent military versions of Model 107, a basic design that gradually evolved first into the H-46, a Navy and Marine Corps chopper, and then the CH-47 Chinook, one of the most successful helicopters ever built.

The Army had begun naming its helicopters after native American tribes, and the CH-47 was named for a tribe in Oregon that derived its own cognomen from the word *chinook*, describing a wind common to the area where Chinook tribal settlements were established.

When Boeing acquired Vertol, the Chinook was well along in the design process. The CH-47 prototype's rollout on April 26, 1961, was five months behind schedule, and at least part of the delay stemmed from the trauma of the acquisition—morale was low, tempers ran high, and there was instant animosity between the new management and the Vertol work force, much of it consisting of men who had started out with the company in the early days of Piasecki.

The Wichita–Seattle relationship was a skirmish compared to the Philadelphia-vs-Wichita/Seattle adversarial situation. Boeing eventually populated Vertol's management ranks with a sizable contingent from Kansas, and as far as Philadelphia was concerned, Wichita's shoe was on the other foot—this time Wichita people were the target of resentment toward outsiders coming in to tell Vertol veterans how to produce helicopters, and any newcomers from Seattle were held in the same jaundiced view.

At the time Boeing took over, Vertol's president and general manager was Don Berlin, whom Rockefeller and DuPont had brought in to run the company before Piasecki left. Berlin was well-liked and respected throughout the helicopter industry as a good engineer who also understood manufacturing. Yet not even a competent leader like Berlin had been able to solve all of Vertol's production problems; he had been grappling with the same kind of resentment that greeted Boeing, resentment largely born of the fierce loyalty so many in Vertol still felt toward Piasecki.

They remembered, perhaps with a fondness that affected their objectivity, the man who had started the company at age 23 and worked incredibly long hours. Jack Diamond, who became vice president of helicopter engineering, looked back on the Piasecki days with understandable nostalgia.

"I went to work for Piasecki in 1948," Diamond reminisced, "when no one in the place was over thirty years old and everyone worked his tail off. It was typical to work six or seven days a week for months on end. Once we were competing with Sikorsky for some government contract and the word spread that Frank's birthday was coming up, so we had to get a prototype ready in time for him to celebrate both the rollout and the birthday. Crazy, very personal stuff like that motivated us. To meet that birthday target, I worked for twenty-eight straight days. Piasecki himself set the example. He was single, had a bed and shower in his office, and practically lived at the factory."

Diamond, an MIT graduate at 19, was project engineer on the Model 107 program that led to the brilliant Chinook and Sea Knight (the CH-46 series produced for the Navy and Marine Corps). Diamond was not one of those who greeted Berlin like a fresh arrival from a leper colony. "He shaped up the H-21 production line," Diamond remembered, "and he saved the company when it was about to go under. But there was friction between Berlin and Piasecki, which was why Frank left."

According to Diamond, Berlin rescued the entire H-21 program, which the Pentagon was about to cancel. The H-21 was a money winner and provided the cash flow necessary to fund the Model 107's development. In 1960, however, Berlin was on the verge of retirement at age 65 and didn't stay around long enough to really help the transition to Boeing; he was a lame duck and lame ducks seldom are very effective.

Boeing's interest in Vertol dated back to the late 1950s and was generated mostly by Wellwood Beall, Ed Wells, and George Schairer. All three recognized the impact turbine power would have on the helicopter. From an engineering standpoint, they were being far-sighted, but in terms of understanding the East Coast industrial environment, Boeing walked into the Vertol acquisition blindfolded. For nowhere was that environment more volatile and hostile than in the Philadelphia area.

Factionalism was rife at Vertol even before Boeing came in, as a young worker named Al Mansi discovered when he was hired in 1960. He was fresh out of the Marines and came in for an interview that wasn't going too well until an elderly man poked his head into the interviewer's office. He looked at the nervous Mansi, and nodded approvingly.

"Hire this kid," he ordered. "Anyone who comes in here with his shoes shined and his shirt pressed should be working for us."

Mansi found out later the old man was Russ Marshall, a former Navy chief petty officer, who was assistant to factory manager Rudy Koch. Mansi was hired as an office clerk but was immediately put to work in the plant. Within two months, he realized the divisive problems that existed.

"There were a number of people from the old Piasecki days, and there were some from Vertol," Mansi said. "They were two different factions and I felt like a man without a country because I wasn't either Piasecki or Vertol. Then in came Boeing."

It would be hard to find a more qualified and objective observer of that time period than Mansi. He came from South Philly, a tough blue-collar neighborhood, and for the next 30 years he viewed the Vertol scene first as an hourly worker and later as part of management—at this writing he is director of labor relations for the helicopter division.

"It was a case of three different cultures colliding—Seattle, Wichita, and Philadelphia," he recalled. "A large influx of Wichita people started coming in around 1962 and made up about ninety percent of management in manufacturing. From that time until 1974, it was World War Three around here.

"Labor-management relations were a disaster. There were fistfights and wildcat strikes. The work force was from a heavily ethnic area with a large black population at a time when black leaders were battling to get more of their people hired. Each faction was a clique, and the one thing the Piasecki and Vertol factions agreed on was that Wichita didn't understand the East Coast labor market."

That last observation undoubtedly was true. The powerful, well-organized United Auto Workers (UAW) held bargaining rights at Vertol and Boeing had never dealt with this union before, nor with the strongly militant "us-against-them" attitude of the UAW's Vertol members toward management. In fact, the Wichita managers who came into Philadelphia were less prepared to deal with this than managers from Seattle. The average IAM worker in Kansas was not the average UAW worker in Philadelphia. And Mansi described what happened from the vantage point of someone who could sympathize with management, yet understand labor:

"All we did was make the union stronger and stronger because of what management did. We made a mistake a minute, and if ever there was a chapter written on what not to do when you purchase a company, Boeing wrote it on what was then Vertol. In those days, Vertol had about four thousand hourly employees and we were getting up to three hundred grievances a week. Seattle, with fifty-six thousand hourly workers, didn't get that many in a year. We were going into arbitration two or three times a week.

"Vertol used to give out turkeys to hourly people at Christmas. Then someone decided to end the tradition on the theory that if every employee didn't get a turkey, nobody should. You would have thought the world was coming to an end. There was so much howling and screaming that the union took Boeing to court, arguing that the turkeys were a fringe benefit. It took two years of litigation before we got a court ruling that the Christmas turkeys weren't a legal contractual requirement. I think Boeing's legal fees probably would have paid for free turkeys over the next ten years."

Yet the labor unrest that marked the first years of Boeing's control was not the whole story. The new managers may have made serious mistakes in dealing with that problem, but they also made a number of important contributions that turned a stumbling, generally inefficient company around—far better equipped to deal with the future.

Bob Tharrington was the second Boeing officer handed the somewhat thankless task of assimilating the fractious Philadelphia plant into the Boeing family. He had acquired a reputation as a troubleshooter, the kind of person adept at recognizing a problem, figuring out how to solve it, after which he'd be moved to some other similar assignment. His one gaffe was the time he suggested moving corporate headquarters to San Francisco or Washington, D.C., and when he got no immediate response he reiterated the proposal.

"The next day," Tharrington said dryly, "I was told that as long as

Bill Allen was running the company, its headquarters would remain in Seattle."

Tharrington, who was one of those recommending the Vertol purchase in the late 1950s, later described it as "a pretty bad mistake," but not because of the labor situation.

"Boeing didn't really examine Vertol's capabilities. They had been building twenty helicopters a month in the fifties, but those contracts had run out, and they had lost their capability to build in any quantity. Vertol had excellent conceptual and engineering ability, but after building and selling a great prototype, they couldn't meet production schedules."

Shortly after buying Vertol, Boeing sent Ken Brown to Philadelphia as Don Berlin's assistant. What had sold Allen on the acquisition in the first place was a $65 million military contract with the Army, Air Force, and Marines for the new Chinook. By early 1962, however, Chinook production was far behind schedule. Brown had fired the previous Vertol manufacturing chief and brought in a new head from Boeing, but production still floundered. The new management couldn't seem to organize production programs of such a relatively small quantity that Vertol almost seemed like a job shop operation.

Even while Brown was trying to straighten the place out, Vertol won an Air Force contract to produce Model 107-IIs, a long-range rescue mission helicopter. But when the Air Force sent in a facilities survey team, it found the manufacturing process so confused that the contract was cancelled and the job turned over to Sikorsky, which proceeded to build the HH-3—otherwise known as the Jolly Green Giant. That unhappy loss of military and commercial market opportunities got Bill Allen's attention.

Obviously the Brown–Berlin combination hadn't worked out, so Allen decided to put Tharrington in charge. He was offered the job on Monday, accepted on Tuesday, and was on his way to Philadelphia on Wednesday. His wife had asked him what would happen if he said no. "We're never going to find out," Tharrington replied.

When he first arrived in October of 1962, he tried not to make waves. "I gave everyone what I thought was a fair chance," he said. "I didn't have much time, but I was willing to see if they could do the job."

When production kept slipping, Tharrington asked Allen for permission to transfer Chick Pitts from Wichita and take over as head of manufacturing at Vertol. Allen agreed, but Pitts said he wouldn't come unless he could bring along all his top people. Tharrington met that demand with the exception of one person, and eventually some 300 managers from Wichita and Seattle were exported to Philadelphia. Within three months, Pitts informed Tharrington that parts control was a disaster and he had to have Otis Smith from Wichita. Otis, whose roots were in Kansas, at first flatly refused but finally gave in.

*B*oeing's top leaders over the company's first seventy-five years. (TOP) William E. Boeing and Philip G. Johnson. (CENTER) Claire L. Egtvedt and William Allen. (BOTTOM) T. A. Wilson and Frank Shrontz.

*M*ore than half a century separated these two pictures.
(TOP) The B & W, Boeing's first airplane.
(BOTTOM) Rollout of the 747 prototype at Everett, Washington, in 1968.

The famous Red Barn as it appeared in 1917, a year after Boeing's founding.
Bottom picture shows the reconstructed factory as it looks today at the
Museum of Flight in Seattle.

*T*he way it was.
Upper photo shows draftsmen on the second floor of the Red Barn;
in the lower shot, a worker is assembling a biplane fuselage.

*W*ould this fool an enemy plane?
Plant Two's remarkable camouflage seen from the air during World War II.
Bottom picture is a close-up of the roof camouflage,
showing the fake houses and shrubbery.

*B*oeing's experimental automobile (TOP) parked in front of the Administration Building after World War II. The car probably was superimposed into the photo—there is no record of it having left the engineering loft where it was created. (BOTTOM) Model 417, one of Boeing's airliner designs that never flew. It was supposed to be the DC-3's successor in the feeder airline industry.

*L*aunching a Bomarc missile. Designed to intercept enemy aircraft, the Bomarc system defended a large area of the eastern seaboard during the early days of the Cold War.

A Minuteman test firing at Vandenberg Air Force Base in California.
This was the program that was instrumental in T Wilson's climb
to the top of Boeing's management.

*C*onsiderably more successful than Bocing's experimental car,
this Lunar Rover Vehicle played a major role
in the Apollo program's exploration of the moon's surface.
(BOTTOM) The Dyna-Soar mockup. Although it never flew, Dyna-Soar was the
forerunner of today's NASA space shuttles.

*T*he giant Everett plant in 1970. Most of the parked 747s lack engines; this was the period in which engine problems plagued the world's first "jumbo jet" and deliveries had to be delayed. (BOTTOM) The revised version of the Boeing SST that would have cruised at 1,900 mph. Notice the "droop snoot" nose, designed to give pilots better visibility during landings and takeoffs.

*T*he famed Dash-80 on one of its numerous test flights. No, it wasn't a five-engine airplane—it's trying out the engine that went on the 727.
(BOTTOM) A commercial version of Boeing's hydrofoil boat.
The six hydrofoils operated by the U.S. Navy were the fastest ships in the fleet.

*T*he YC-14, a military transport that never went into production. Two prototypes were built and are still mothballed in Arizona.
(BOTTOM) The unique V-22 Osprey, pride of Boeing's Philadelphia helicopter facilities. This shot shows the engines tilted for either takeoff or landing.

*T*wo models of a proposed 747 trimotor
that would have challenged the McDonnell DC–10 and
Lockheed L–1011. Neither configuration was adopted.

The nose section of a 707 blown up by terrorists at the Damascus Airport in Syria. Lower photo shows a Boeing "Aircraft on the Ground" (AOG) crew ready to graft a new nose onto the fuselage. The repaired plane was flown back to the U.S. and returned to service.

*A*irliner in evolution. Boeing's new 777 was designated the 767X in the early planning stages, and these are three of the configurations considered. The middle design comes closest to the final version. (BOTTOM) The 777 as it might appear at major airports. Folding wingtips would enable the wide-winged plane to use existing gates without sacrificing its tremendous range.

*A*n artist's rendition of the living quarters module
on NASA's space station program.
Designing and building it represent the company's
commitment to the continued conquest of space.

The Vietnam War had created an increasing demand for helicopters, but turning Vertol around was laborious and it wasn't helped by the labor-management friction. The Army asked Boeing to increase Chinook production to 15 a month, and the Navy made the same request for its CH-46. At that point, the Pentagon threatened to turn the Chinook design over to Sikorsky if Vertol's production didn't improve, and Tharrington assured them it would—a promise he wasn't sure could be kept. He wasn't happy with Vertol's facilities anyway, and he had been looking at an abandoned steel plant in the area. A Philadelphia realtor was urging Tharrington to buy it, and when he finally dropped the price to $1 million, Tharrington flew to Seattle with Pitts and met with Allen and several other Boeing officials.

He argued that Vertol badly needed more space to meet production demands, and that the steel plant was a bargain at $1 million. Allen polled the others and drew negative responses from all but George Martin.

"I know Bob will need more additional factory space," Martin said. "He's also going to want new laboratories and a wind tunnel, so I think this looks like something in which we're getting a lot for a little."

Allen turned to Pitts. "Chick, what do you think?"

Pitts, who had inspected the old steel plant and privately thought renovating the entire South Bronx an easier task, just grunted. "That damned Tharrington's brainwashed me—I'd buy it," he allowed.

Allen promised Tharrington he'd let him know his decision. He called him in Philadelphia a few days later, doubt in his voice. "Except for Martin, all my top people are telling me we should do something else, such as building an entirely new factory."

"This is something we have to do because it's the fastest way," Tharrington insisted.

"Okay," Allen said, "but you'd better make sure it turns out right."

Tharrington set an almost impossible deadline: he wanted Vertol to move into a completely renovated plant in not more than four months. He asked Neil McCormick, then director of facilities, to inspect the dilapidated factory and McCormick suggested that he hire the Austin Company, which had done good work for Boeing in the past. "They're your only chance at doing it right and on time," he advised.

Everyone else was telling Tharrington the project would take at least a year. Vertol moved in on schedule, and by the end of 1965 Chinook production also was on schedule. Improved production was achieved in spite of the ever-present labor-management tension; not even Tharrington could solve that problem, relying mostly as he did on the Wichita managerial importees. Yet his high regard for an abrasive personality like Pitts wasn't surprising—Chick was considered a crack production man who had performed especially well in Wichita's difficult transition from B-29 production to the B-47—creating a new assembly line for an entirely different kind of airplane, and one far more complicated to build, was no mean achievement. But Pitts, to put it mildly, was not exactly pro-union. Even in Wichita, where management and labor got along pretty well, Chick tended to place the IAM in the same category as migraine headaches and flat tires on rainy nights. His opinion of the UAW could be judged accordingly.

Pitts had been operations director at Vertol for some time when the local UAW launched a campaign for a union shop. Boeing was dead set against it, and the National Labor Relations Board ordered an election to determine whether the majority of UAW members themselves wanted a union shop. Weeks before the election, small sticker posters reading OVER THE TOP WITH A UNION SHOP began appearing all over the plant. They were plastered everywhere, and to say Pitts was unhappy would be the understatement of the century.

The election was only a few days away when Pitts phoned Mansi, then assistant to labor relations director John Nau.

"Dammit, Mansi, there's a goose running around the shop with one of those stickers on it!"

Mansi felt sick. "I kept thinking," he remembered, "that the guys had really done it this time—bringing in a live goose, plastering it with a sticker, and turning it loose."

He toured the plant, asking everyone in sight if they had seen a goose running around.

One worker told him, "One thing I know about geese, Al, is that they crap a lot. All you gotta do is find goose manure and you'll find the goose."

It was excellent ornithological advice but it didn't help Mansi. After another hour of fruitless searching, he reported his failure to Nau, who had returned from lunch.

"We have to find it," Mansi worried. "They'd put an OVER THE TOP WITH A UNION SHOP sticker on an elephant if they could get one into the plant."

Just then in charged an even angrier Pitts. "I just came up from the cafeteria and there's a blankety-blank goose outside the caf with a sticker on it! I want it off my property!"

Mansi resumed his frantic search. Not for another two hours did he find out that in Wichita, a forklift truck is called a goose.

"Funny as it was," he reflected, "the incident typified the gulf that existed between Wichita and Philly—there was a language difference along with everything else."

Mansi wasn't the only one who could examine those differences with an impartial attitude. George Kau, at this writing vice president of operations in the helicopter division, didn't come to Vertol until 1974, but he had started his Boeing career in 1948 as a beginner mechanic and spent the next 24 years building fixed-wing aircraft—B-52s, C-97s, 707s, 727s and 747s. Kau believed an underlying problem at Vertol was a very simple fact of life. "The helicopter," Kau pointed out, "is a very different breed of cat to build.

"Also, the helicopter is probably thirty years behind the fixed-wing airplane in development, so we're still learning. It has so many very critical parts. Its dynamics are such that if any single thing fails, you'll have a catastrophic situation, unlike the fail-safe and redundant qualities of the fixed-wing. Redundancy is impossible with dynamic components like the transmission and rotors on a helicopter. The production rate is slower because a helicopter is harder to build and more expensive in terms of man-hours per pound of aircraft. Remember, a helicopter doesn't fly—it just beats the air into submission."

It wasn't that Boeing didn't try. The remodeled steel plant, the new wind tunnel (the only VSTOL tunnel operated on-site at a U.S. helicopter manufacturer), and a new flight test center in Wilmington, Delaware, all testified to Boeing's willingness to pour millions into improving the helicopter division's facilities. But these were physical improvements that didn't entirely address the unhappy human equation—a don't-give-a-damn atmosphere for which both sides were to blame.

In 1972, Boeing sent several heavy hitters to Philadelphia to interview Vertol people about the labor problem. The team included Wally Buckley, Don Whitford, and Wes Maulden; as usual Maulden, who loved creature comforts, never left his hotel room and did his interviewing there. Mansi, as assistant director of labor relations, was among those interviewed mostly on the subject of seniority and job assignments—the union's two key issues. They asked him why employees were so hostile. The burly, blunt-talking Mansi told them.

"Look, I've lived through more organizational changes, more flip-flopping directions from management, than I care to think about. You want to know what to do? Go down to a hardware store, buy the biggest padlock in the place, put it on the plant door, and go home, because the union isn't gonna buckle. The only consistent thing we have around here is the union. I recognize that. The employees recognize that. The only people who don't recognize it is management."

Mansi never knew how much of that advice was taken back to Seattle, but it didn't make much difference anyway. The end of the Vietnam War in 1975 was devastating to Vertol. It had been building 29 Chinooks a month, but as the war wound down, production even by 1971 already had dropped drastically. Vertol's payroll was slashed from 13,000 to less than 4,000, causing more bitterness and frustration that culminated in the second-longest strike in Boeing's history.

The UAW struck Vertol in November 1974, and a settlement wasn't reached until the following February, a period of almost 100 days that turned out to be a cathartic for both sides.

"A strike," Mansi explained, "kind of gives everybody an opportunity to sit back and think about what happened and why, what was really accomplished, and what each side lost."

In Mansi's opinion, the employees themselves believed Boeing ended up the winner. "They realized when they came back after three months that they really didn't get what they wanted. Seniority was the main issue but the company won some concessions on seniority and also job assignments."

But the union had won something, too—an awareness on the part of Boeing's management that a strike often is symptomatic of problems deeper than the issues on the bargaining table. When it was all over and the discouraged, still disgruntled employees had gone back to work, John Nau and Al Mansi sat down for a talk.

"What do you think we should do?" Nau asked.

"I think it's time we started talking to these people," Mansi said.

George Nible had come to Philadelphia as Vertol's executive vice president and helped Nau and Mansi put together a program called "Pride in Excellence" (PIE), bringing recognition for jobs well done, and aimed at ending the constant arguing and fighting that were getting management and labor alike nowhere. Its message was simple: Boeing is here to provide jobs so you can make a living and support a family. And regardless of what level you're at, that's what you're here for. The very essence of that goal is that the company must be successful in order to do all these other things.

Nible admittedly had his doubts at first whether PIE would work; he saw a few examples of union militancy that infuriated him—and not by any stretch of the imagination was George Nible anti-labor.

"If a supervisor chewed out guys for coming back late from lunch, he'd find all four tires on his car slashed when he got off work," Nible related. "We didn't see things like that in Seattle. We had a supervisor fire two guys for drinking a bottle of whiskey on the premises during their lunch hour. It went to arbitration, and the arbitrator told us, 'Well, the supervisor didn't actually see them drinking' and they got their jobs back, along with back pay. We found another worker who was smuggling out some of the most expensive cutting tools in the plant and selling them to shops around Philadelphia."

In April 1975, with the PIE program ready to be implemented, Nau was transferred to corporate and Mansi became director of labor relations. He needed help from management as well as labor if he was ever to achieve his goal of getting the union to at least sit down and talk to management regularly, and he found the right man in Al Smith, Vertol's director of operations who had succeeded Pitts.

"He was the kind of manager I had been looking for," Mansi recounted. "He was going down on the floor every day, talking to people and listening to them."

As PIE took hold, Smith and Mansi realized its very success had the potential of alienating union leaders who felt their power base was eroding. They started a quarterly update meeting with the union leadership—what Vertol was doing, where it was, the economic outlook for helicopters, and so on. By the third or fourth meeting, both sides were beginning to talk about specific problems.

Deane Cruze had become director of operations for the Renton Division in 1976, and began working with Al Smith to bring some commercial airplane business to Philadelphia. Yet Cruze, like other executives in Seattle, wasn't immune from the lingering belief that despite all the improvements, Philadelphia's labor problems were permanent and terminal. It was a source of worry for Smith, who came into Mansi's office one day.

"Al, Deane Cruze is going to be in Philly to look over the plant and see if he can get some work in here. Can you get Joe Wood [president of the UAW local] to pass the word—pull everyone together and end all doubts about the labor situation here?"

Mansi agreed. When Cruze arrived and was walking around the plant, Mansi took Wood into the assembly area.

"That's Cruze, Joe. Just go over and talk to him."

The next day, Smith charged back into Mansi's office. "What the hell did you tell Joe Wood? He went over to Cruze and told him Philly workers could out-produce Seattle any day of the week, and if they didn't he'd personally kick their butts. Did you write his speech?"

"Hell, no," Mansi said. "He wrote it himself."

Mansi, an emotional, intense man, had a lump in his throat. Only a few short years before, he couldn't have gotten Wood or any other union officer to even say hello to a Boeing executive. It was another break in the crumbling logjam of ill-will.

Eventually, the Vertol division was to become Boeing Helicopters, the very change in name a symbolic gesture that brought Philadelphia a lot closer to Seattle than 2,388 air miles. This is out of chronological context, of course. Before it truly became part of the Boeing family instead of just a far-flung outpost with a work force that to Seattle seemed like a collection of aliens, the helicopter division went through some rough times.

Its biggest disappointment was the YUH-61A, an assault/transport helicopter designed as a larger replacement for the Army's aging fleet of Hueys. The competition was tough, Vertol pitting its entry against Sikorsky and Bell for what was known technically as Utility Tactical Transport Aircraft System, or UTTAS. Bell was favored because it had built the Huey, workhorse of the Vietnam War, but Bell was eliminated in the first round of the evaluation.

The choice was now the YUH-61A against Sikorsky's YUH-60A. Jack Diamond and his engineering team thought they had a winner, although they started the project under a handicap—Vertol had never built a single rotor helicopter before, and flight tests had disclosed vibration problems.

"We knew we had them the first day we flew it," Diamond recalled, "but Sikorsky had the same problems. We struggled with it and made it better, but Sikorsky did something we didn't do until it was too late—they decided early on to raise the rotor higher above the fuselage, and apparently it made a significant difference in vibration characteristics."

It apparently did. The Army pilots who tested both prototypes at a Fort Bragg fly-off picked the YUH-60A because of less vibration, and Sikorsky won the competition late in 1976, leading eventually to the voluminous production of YUH-60s now known as the Blackhawk. Later, Sikorsky also beat Vertol in a Navy competition, known as LAMPS (Light Airborne Multi-Purpose System) with a variant of the UH-60 that utilized the Blackhawk's dynamic components.

Nevertheless, the YUH-61A was an excellent design whose most unusual feature was its rotor system. It was hingeless, with a weight-saving titanium hub and four huge fiberglass blades. Boeing built a commercial version but that never got beyond the prototype stage, either. The third major helicopter program—HLH (for Heavy Lift Helicopter)—was cancelled even as Vertol was readying the prototype to fly. The engineers had been developing it since 1971 when Boeing beat out Sikorsky and Hughes in a preliminary design competition, but congressional defense-funding cuts killed the program only a few months before what would have been the first flight of the free world's largest helicopter.

What helped keep Vertol in business was continual improvements of the Chinook's various models, a constant program of upgrading that gave the helicopter an enviable reputation for reliability and performance. Its exploits in Vietnam were legendary, and the growls of its turbines became familiar sounds in at least 17 other countries that either bought Chinooks or ones built under license.

The Chinook (CH-47) had vibration problems at first, too, so serious that for a time the Marines refused to accept delivery on the Sea Knight (H-46) version; Vertol was building airframes that piled up outside the factory awaiting solution to the excessive vibration. The engineers' fix was ingenious—they put a vibrating device under the cockpit seats, a mass of springs that moved up and down at the same vibration frequency as the rotors. This creation of an equal and opposite force to the rotor's oscillations had the desired damping effect, and the Marines began accepting Sea Knight deliveries.

The Chinook had started out with conventional metal rotor blades, but Vertol pioneered the development of fiberglass blades after trying out a number of combination materials, from carbon fibers to boron, in an effort to cure the chief weakness of all helicopters: metal fatigue that caused a high rate of blade failures. High-strength fiberglass along with carbon fibers proved to be the best composite, so good that Vertol retrofitted earlier Chinooks with the composite blades and saved the military millions of dollars in maintenance costs. Firing a 20 mm shell through a fiberglass blade wouldn't affect its performance.

Howard Stuverude, who was sent to Philadelphia as a Chinook project engineer, replaced Tharrington as Vertol's president when the latter left in 1970 to establish Boeing Computer Services (BCS). Stuverude couldn't have taken over at a worse time—the payroll cuts already had begun under Tharrington, and Stuverude, with Chinook production down to a trickle, couldn't stop the hemorrhaging.

He inherited the labor situation along with all the other problems and he tried manfully to turn things around—he even learned how to fly a helicopter so he could understand the test pilot reports. He also got plenty of advice from Boeing's senior engineers like Wells, Martin, and Schairer—sometimes more than he wanted. Bill Allen paid several visits to Philadelphia and one morning Tharrington hosted a breakfast meeting that Stuverude attended.

"Howard," Allen inquired, "are you going to need any more help from Schairer?"

"I'm getting more help than I can stand!" Stuverude blurted, and Allen burst out laughing.

Stuverude, like everyone else who worked with Schairer, had difficulty understanding exactly what point he was trying to get across. "George always talked in parables," Stuverude said, "and you had to keep asking yourself what it was he really wanted you to do."

It was Allen's consistent support, even through Vertol's hard times, that Stuverude really appreciated. When Boeing bought Vertol, Allen pointedly made it clear that the company's reputation for integrity would apply to helicopters as well as airplanes. That was Wells' position too. "He reviewed every change we put into a helicopter to make sure it had the technical integrity that was behind the Boeing name," Stuverude said.

Allen even went along with a joint venture involving a German aircraft manufacturer, Messerschmitt-Boelkow-Blohm, which was planning to build a small commercial helicopter called the BO-105. In 1964, Boeing had bought a small share of MBB and five years later Stuverude suggested that Vertol market the five-place, twin-engine German helicopter in the United States. The proposal drew some opposition—never before had Boeing taken someone else's product and tried to sell it, the objections apparently being a case of the "it wasn't invented here" syndrome.

The BO-105 was not a great commercial success, but it was far from a flop. A competing helicopter, Bell's popular single-turbine Jet Ranger, outsold it by a wide margin, largely because it was more economical to operate; the BO-105's two turbines, which gave it greater speed and range, also carried the penalty of higher operating costs. It compiled an excellent safety record and still is being used for patrolling long distances—over the Gulf of Mexico, for example, and Alaska.

Vertol, like every other helicopter manufacturer, always found the commercial market fairly limited because of the vehicle's inherently poor economy. To the military this was less of a concern, but commercial operators did care and preferred the airplane except for jobs only a 'copter could handle. Carrying passengers over short distances was the most uneconomical assignment of them all, which was largely the reason Vertol's attempt to sell the commercial version of the Chinook was another disappointment.

The two major customers for the Chinook Model 234 were British Airways, which bought them to support North Sea oil exploration and drilling, and Helicopter Service A/S of Norway, which employed its Chinooks in similar operations. Model 234 carried 44 passengers in an airliner-like interior that included the 727's overhead luggage bins, and for a helicopter its 600-mile range and 150-mph cruising speed were impressive.

Even with a dearth of new helicopter orders, Vertol's continuous upgrading program meant a healthy cash flow to the parent company; military choppers take a worse beating than military airplanes, and parts replacement is not only a constant source of income but something that fits in with Boeing's tradition of customer support. That's why Vertol helicopters built 30 years ago still are flying, and that also is why the Chinook—whose basic design is more than three decades old—in 1992 remained a major unit in the Armed Forces' helicopter armada. And after nearly 30 years, Chinook production was still continuing with a healthy program of modifying older Chinooks into more modern CH-47D standards and the building of entirely new CH-47Ds. In 1989 Boeing unveiled still another Chinook version, the MH-47E, for use by the Army's special operations forces.

"There has never really been a helicopter to replace it," noted Stuverude, who left Vertol in 1979, and he undoubtedly was right. An upgraded Chinook provided the same new technology that would have been applied to a brand-new design: Vertol's modernization kits have included new systems for hydraulics, rotors, electronics, transmissions, avionics, and cockpits.

Otis Smith replaced Stuverude but stayed only a year. To succeed him, Boeing went back to Vertol's own family—Joe Mallen, an MIT graduate who had joined the helicopter company in 1949 and had been involved in most of its technical programs since then. He ably headed Vertol for the next seven years, a period in which some of its most important projects were launched and its facilities greatly expanded. The latter included a modern new wind tunnel and 1 million square feet of new office space—translated into vertical footage, that amounted to a 100-story skyscraper.

It was during Mallen's tenure as president that Vertol undertook the massive modernization program that involved nearly 1,000 CH-46s and CH-47s. But perhaps his greatest contribution was to recognize the uncertainty of the high-risk military marketplace and lead Boeing into joint ventures with its helicopter competitors.

In 1983, Boeing and Bell Helicopter Textron of Arlington, Texas, joined forces to win a preliminary design contract for a tiltrotor aircraft, literally a hybrid aircraft whose two gas turbine engines could tilt completely up, providing the vertical takeoff and landing capability of a helicopter, then tilt down to horizontal, achieving the faster speed of an airplane.

Both Boeing and Bell had been working on the concept since the 1950s. Vertol had flown an advanced tilt-wing prototype for the Army called the VZ-2 and continued development of tiltrotor systems under company and NASA-funded research. Bell, meanwhile, also had been working on the concept since the 1950s. It flew an experimental tiltrotor, the XV-3, in 1958, and 15 years later flight-tested a pair of larger prototypes, the XV-15. These two tiltrotors, which were still flying in 1991, achieved a speed of over 300 knots in level flight and an altitude of 25,000 feet.

The XV-15 was exhibited at the 1981 Paris Air Show where it upstaged every other aircraft on the premises, although it had its share of bugs and was purely experimental. But it raised enough eyebrows in the Pentagon to lead to the preliminary design contract two years later. What mostly attracted Bell to an alliance with Boeing was Philadelphia's modern wind tunnel and its unequaled experience with composite materials. And thus was born one of the most exciting, challenging programs in aviation history—the V-22 Osprey.

The seven-year, $2.5 billion contract called for six V-22 prototypes—Boeing building the fuselage, Bell the wings, Allison responsible for the engines, and Grumman as a subcontractor for the tail. Test flights over the next four years unearthed some problems but none serious enough to challenge the belief that the tiltrotor Osprey represented an entirely new era for aviation—an aircraft that combines all the virtues of both the helicopter and the airplane, while eliminating their limitations. The Osprey is simply an airplane that doesn't need a runway; it can do everything a helicopter can do, but with the greater speed and superior operating economy of a fixed-wing aircraft. It is good enough, in fact, to have won the 1990 coveted Collier Trophy for outstanding aeronautical achievement.

The complex tilt mechanism that turns the huge propellers—driven by a pair of Allison turbine engines—into rotor blades, then back to propellers for level flight, provided the biggest technical difficulties the engineers had to overcome. But the enthusiasm for the V-22 on the part of the 6,500 people in Boeing Helicopters actually could be felt throughout the entire company—the same kind of tangible pride and faith that had affected every major Boeing airplane program from the B-17 on.

Defense budgetary problems began jeopardizing the V-22 early in

1989. Yet no one could walk into any Boeing Helicopter facility, from the bustling shop areas to the Flight Test Center in nearby Wilmington, without sensing the universal hope that existed for this aircraft of the future, regardless of what was happening in the immediate present. Visitors couldn't walk 10 feet without seeing an Osprey poster.

"The V-22," predicted George Kau, "will revolutionize the helicopter industry. It requires some refinements and improvements, but the need for vertical lift and descent is better satisfied with rotorcraft technology than anything else flying."

Composites, from the fiberglass rotor blades Vertol pioneered to the graphite epoxy components now going into major aircraft structures, also are the wave of aviation's future. The Osprey, with an airframe almost 80 percent composite, weighs 20 percent less than it would if built out of conventional materials, but weight reduction is only one benefit. Composites are impervious to corrosion and are far less vulnerable to fatigue.

The second major joint venture begun during Mallen's regime led Boeing to combine with arch-rival Sikorsky against another team of old rivals—Bell and McDonnell Douglas—to design a new U.S. Army light helicopter now known as the RAH-66 Comanche. The Boeing/Sikorsky team won the competition in April 1991, and eventually the Comanche will replace between 1,300 and 1,700 aging and virtually obsolete choppers.

In the waning months of 1991, with the V-22 still facing an unsettled future, Philadelphia remained the second-largest Boeing facility outside of the Puget Sound area. That in itself is an accomplishment, considering Vertol's turbulent history, and a distance from Seattle that for so many years was measured not in miles, but by the width of the cultural and personality differences. It was never an easy place to run, as any of the six men who served as the division's presidents between 1962 and 1991 could testify; for a long time, in fact, Philadelphia was considered a managerial obstacle course for even the ablest executive.

Don Chesnut succeeded Mallen in 1987, and Ed Renouard took over from Chesnut two years later just after Vertol became the helicopter division of Boeing's Defense & Space Group. Renouard, personable and people-oriented, came out of Gonzaga University in Spokane as a mechanical engineer in 1959 and was hired by Boeing as a developmental support engineer in the Bomarc program—part of Dick Nelson's plan to get young engineers to work in the shop and support the factory in assembling the missiles.

"We could redline a drawing and make changes right on the floor if there was a problem," Renouard said. "I think it was an idea ahead of its time, because now the big goal at Boeing is to get engineering and manufacturing working together. Some engineers have an easier time with manufacturing—the good ones will go out and talk to the blue-collar people. Others have a tendency to be prima donnas who don't worry about the poor guy who has to build the damned thing."

Renouard came to Philadelphia from aerospace, where he had learned that lesson well. Renouard's management philosophy could be summed up in two words: worker motivation.

"Most people have a great desire to be part of a team, part of a moving force, and it's fundamental. People are the same everywhere—they want to be appreciated and the majority want to do a good job. The problem of management is its relation to the employee and that's the same everywhere. The person who knows most about the job is the guy doing it, the guy on the floor. The tendency in the past, for some people, has been to shoot the messenger—so the guy who has a problem keeps it to himself.

"One of the biggest challenges I've had in all my assignments over the last ten years was getting people to tell me the truth. It cuts across all levels of management. It comes down to people trusting you, and believing that by telling you the truth they won't get killed or fired. Because from the manager's side, the only way he's going to fix something is to know it's broken."

When Renouard was assigned to the Boeing facility in Huntsville, Alabama, before taking the helicopter post, he found certain programs plagued by overruns because Boeing, as so many companies do when they go after a government contract, had "bid aggressively"—a euphemism for bidding too low. And no level of management wanted to pass on to the next higher level the bad news that the program was losing money.

"The same thing happened to some extent in Philadelphia on the V-22 program," Renouard said. "We had overruns at first. We had to build up a trust with employees so they weren't afraid to tell us the bad news along with the good, and we could take corrective action without worrying about who shot John."

Renouard, like Mallen and Chesnut who preceded him, was grateful for inheriting the vastly improved labor relations climate. All ranks closed behind the V-22 effort, and that included the United Auto Workers. Renouard singled out one event indicative of a different atmosphere.

"When the IAM struck Boeing in 1989 and shut down Seattle and Wichita production," Renouard said, "our UAW guys stayed on the job—a lot of things have changed."

A lot have, including the trend toward partnership among the four helicopter manufacturers: Boeing, Bell, Sikorsky, and McDonnell Douglas. "Critical alliances," Frank Shrontz once called them, and they became almost imperative in high technology projects, where the sheer enormity of the required technical talent and money investment makes it impossible for any single company to handle them alone.

That Boeing could join forces with Bell to design a tiltrotor, then turn around and unite with Sikorsky on the RAH-66, made technical and economic sense.

It made more sense, in fact, than what Vertol had tried in the early 1970s when it began building railcars for urban ground transportation. It was one of Boeing's several attempts to diversify at a time when neither airplanes nor helicopters were selling, most of the attempts at diversification failing—and rather incongruously, coming as they did after one of Boeing's greatest technological triumphs. . . .

Helping man reach the moon.

FOURTEEN

BOEING IN SPACE—AND A FEW OTHER PLACES

GEORGE STONER WAS THE ED WELLS OF BOEING'S SPACE PRO-grams.

They had much in common—intellect, integrity, and vision being among the attributes they shared; "genius" is the one word invariably associated with both their names. Among the hundreds of engineers who worked closely with them, they are mentioned most frequently as the two men who had the most lasting influence on individual careers—by the examples they set more than anything else.

Stoner, armed with a degree in chemical engineering, began his Boeing career in Wichita in 1941, where he earned promotion to assistant superintendent of B-29 functional testing before he was transferred to Seattle, where his career took off like one of the rockets he loved.

Stoner and Wells were far from twins in personality. Wells was a solid rock, a man who led with a quiet firmness. Stoner was more extroverted, almost a busybody who couldn't resist getting involved in everything—including telling people how they should live. Typically, he was one of those who gave great advice to others but never applied it to himself. He was a chain smoker and cigarettes finally killed him.

Mark Miller, who admired Stoner tremendously, remembered the time when Boeing was trying to find office space in Washington, D.C., and Stoner had his heart set on the L'Enfant Plaza building owned by the family of former Air Force general Pete Quesada. Negotiating with the hard-boiled Quesada was like trying to mine coal with a nail file—Quesada was the first FAA administrator and was known around the nation's capital as "the smiling executioner."

"He met his match in Stoner," Miller related. "But when we moved in, George drove us bananas. He was telling us where to put the telephones and how to arrange the furniture."

Stoner was a big man, well over 200 pounds, with a huge, bristling mustache that would have looked very much at home on a Buckingham Palace guard. He could be very witty, but he wore steel-rimmed glasses that made him appear sternly unhumorous. He had a disciplined, well-organized mind, and also a deceptive habit of seemingly falling asleep at important meetings.

Stoner did this at one of Bill Allen's regular Wednesday executive staff sessions, a few weeks after the 1967 pad fire at Cape Kennedy that killed three astronauts. One could set his watch by Allen's arrival at those scheduled 10 A.M. meetings—he came in at 10 sharp, not 9:59 or 10:01. As usual, he had two pairs of glasses with him, which he kept switching, and he began going around the table asking questions of each officer. Dean Thornton was present and described what happened.

"Old George sat there like a Buddha, with his eyes almost closed. Finally Allen came to him and asked, 'George, what was the problem that killed those fine young men?'

"Stoner didn't say a word for several minutes, and I was thinking, *Jesus, the guy's asleep.* Then George opened his eyes. 'Well, Bill,' he says—and he proceeds to deliver, in non-technical terms, a perfectly organized, completely understandable explanation of what had happened at the Cape. He had used those few moments of silence to organize his thoughts, and he was very articulate, always speaking in complete sentences and paragraphs as if he were reading from a prepared text. He'd have some proposal outlined in his mind, then he'd dictate it for three hours. His secretaries worked in relays. One would take dictation for thirty minutes, and go out to type while another girl would come in and take dictation for the next half-hour."

Allen's own interest in space exploration was as much a matter of patriotism as anything else. As Thornton put it, "He believed your country, your family, and your company were all tied for first."

It was Wells who pushed Boeing's president toward committing the company to full-scale participation in the nation's space program, and he had sown some early seeds.

"We're falling behind in some of the most critical technology, missiles, and spacecraft," he had warned as far back as Bomarc, and before Boeing won the Minuteman contract.

That was when Allen put him in charge of the Systems Management Organization, which became the nucleus of the company's own space program. But it was a program Allen admitted he never really understood. He once attended a NASA meeting, under duress, and said later everything he heard was complete Greek.

"It was one of the most mysterious and frustrating meetings I was ever at," he related. "I discovered there was a new language abroad in the land, one I didn't understand either in words or concepts. Occasionally I'd catch an adjective or verb I recognized, so I knew everyone must be speaking English."

What they were discussing was sending a man to the moon and the various ways to achieve it. "I sat there being sure none of them would work and I wondered if I was the only sane man in the room," he added.

But one of Bill Allen's greatest strengths was the willingness of this inherently cautious man to take risks, to gamble, to accept projects that were beyond his ken and, as far as he knew, even beyond the company's talent and resources. He had done it with Bomarc and with Minuteman, and he also had done it with Boeing's first real venture into the manned conquest of space.

It was called Dyna-Soar, and Stoner was program manager.

Dyna-Soar was an Air Force project, its name a contraction of the words "dynamic" and "soaring," for it was supposed to be a winged space vehicle that would be launched into orbit by a booster rocket and then soar around the earth with its wings allowing it to be maneuvered and landed like a conventional airplane. If that sounds like today's NASA shuttles, it should; Dyna-Soar was nothing but a one-man version of the shuttle and 20 years ahead of its time.

Boeing won the competition to build such a vehicle, and Stoner drew on a cadre of engineers who had worked on ROBO, a little-known unmanned hypersonic bomber project that was strictly a paper design. The idea of ROBO was to launch the bomber into the stratosphere at hypersonic speed, then have it "skip-glide" toward a target—skip-glide meaning it would skip in and out of Earth's upper atmosphere as it lost speed, gradually cooling off from the atmospheric friction.

But the engineers who designed Dyna-Soar abandoned the skip-glide conception in favor of direct re-entry. Bud Hebeler's group, which had come up with the idea of using cork to insulate Minuteman, applied the same heat shield material to Dyna-Soar, which would have allowed the spacecraft to withstand the 4,000-degree Fahrenheit temperatures generated by hypersonic speed through the atmosphere. Hebeler, in fact, later developed and patented an even better thermal protection system composed of lithium.

Dyna-Soar, which the Air Force called the X-20, never got beyond the mockup stage, although a number of astronauts who saw that mockup were impressed with its potential—especially the fact that it would permit a pilot-controlled landing, in contrast to NASA's Mercury and Gemini spacecraft, which had to be fished out of the water after each orbiting mission.

Another visitor to the mockup was England's Prince Philip. His escort was Harry Goldie, Stoner's deputy on Dyna-Soar, and Harry was delivering a lecture on the spacecraft's safety features.

"You'll see that it has a triple-redundant hydraulic control system," Goldie bragged.

The prince consort looked puzzled. "Young man, if they're redundant, why don't you get rid of them?"

Goldie wasn't going to argue with the husband of Britain's queen, but made a point of looking up "redundant" in a dictionary. "He was absolutely right," Goldie confessed. "Redundant means unneeded."

The Dyna-Soar program lasted six years and cost some $410 million before Defense Secretary McNamara cancelled it two weeks before Christmas 1963. Goldie flew to Washington with McNamara on Air Force One the same day the secretary pulled the plug, and spent the entire flight trying to talk him out of the decision. Goldie, along with everyone else in the program, suspected it was a lost cause anyway; McNamara had been progressively cutting funding for Dyna-Soar until it had been emasculated to the status of a minor research program. The day he cancelled it, the jigs for a flying prototype had been built and were ready for production.

There has always been some controversy as to why McNamara killed Dyna-Soar after a half-billion dollars had been spent on it. Frank Borman, the astronaut who flew the Gemini 7 and Apollo 8 missions and was intrigued by the Dyna-Soar concept, believed the cancellation was a signal that NASA, and not the Air Force, was going to run the nation's space program. The Air Force contributed 90 percent of Dyna-Soar's funding and NASA the rest, but that was one of the program's major problems.

"NASA stuck its finger in at every point wanting to make Dyna-Soar purely a research project," Goldie said. "The Air Force wanted it developed as a weapon. That was the trouble—it was never decided what mission Dyna-Soar was supposed to have. That was the main reason McNamara, who was as hard-headed as they come, finally cancelled it altogether. He couldn't think of a damned use for it."

The aborted project also happened to be Tex Johnston's first non-flying assignment at Boeing—and one of his last. He had been flying every conceivable type of aircraft from biplanes to helicopters and jets for some two decades (he was a barnstorming pilot before World War II), and he had begun wondering whether it might be a good time to quit.

Stoner offered Johnston the job of Dyna-Soar's program manager, and it was Tex who integrated seven astronauts into Dyna-Soar simulated flight training. When the project was terminated, Johnston was assigned to the Saturn program as one of its managers, working both in New Orleans and on the Cape. He finally decided to retire from Boeing and went to work for a company that built the Guppy—a C-97 with an enormous cargo compartment grafted onto the top of the fuselage. It looked like a pregnant whale. "It wasn't the greatest flying machine in the world," Tex said, "but it did its job."

So had Alvin M. "Tex" Johnston. Around Boeing, he probably will be remembered mostly as "the guy who rolled the Dash-80," but that would be an unfair epitaph to his Boeing career. He did a lot of the test work on the B-47—it was no secret that some of the test pilots were afraid to fly the bomber—and his input into the B-52 and 707 made them better and safer airplanes.

Not many people knew—and Allen probably was one who didn't—that Tex also rolled the XB-47 without permission. Engineer Warren Joslyn was in the flight test radio room when Johnston was flying the bomber and heard Tex ask the duty engineer, "Could this thing roll?"

"I don't know," the duty engineer replied. "I'd better ask George Schairer."

A few minutes later, the engineer relayed Schairer's answer: "Schairer says probably, Tex, but don't try it until we make a few calculations."

Back came Johnston's answer. "Too late."

Five months after Dyna-Soar was cancelled, Boeing took on a unique task.

A company used to building 125-ton jetliners and 240-ton bombers signed a contract to design and construct an 850-pound space vehicle whose only payload would be a camera.

Quite a vehicle, however, and quite a camera. The former would circle the moon while the latter was photographing its surface. It was right up George Stoner's spacious alley; the day he first heard John F. Kennedy's 1961 speech to the Air Force Academy pledging that America would land men on the moon within the next decade, Stoner wanted Boeing to be part of that step toward the stars.

Project Mercury, the first stage of NASA's carefully orchestrated moon program, had been completed and the second stage—Gemini—was just getting underway when the space agency invited bids on a Lunar Orbiter Vehicle (LOV). It would be a small unmanned spacecraft carrying a camera that would take pictures of the moon's surface—producing a kind of aerial map that hopefully would determine the best spot for Project Apollo's lunar landings.

In 1964, no one knew for sure whether a moon landing was even feasible, because no one knew for sure what the moon's surface was like. Some scientists claimed it was the equivalent of quicksand and that even the lightest object, including a human being, would sink right into it. Others said the lunar landscape was so bumpy and rocky that no ground exploration vehicle could move over it. A third theory held that the moon's surface was like a powdery dust, as difficult to traverse as trying to move through deep, dry sand.

NASA sent an unmanned probe that landed on the moon but this effort answered only one question: the texture of the surface where it came down. And it was a Japanese-American Boeing engineer, Tommy

Yamauchi, who had come up with the idea of a camera-carrying lunar orbiter—a proposal that convinced NASA to invite bids.

Yamauchi actually suggested a lunar orbiter *after* the space agency announced it was seeking proposals for a lunar exploratory vehicle in which astronauts could move over the moon's surface. It was one of those occasional bureaucratic decisions that defied logic—NASA had absolutely no idea of what the surface was like, yet was asking manufacturers to design a vehicle for exploring that surface.

There were nine companies bidding on the initial NASA Orbiter RFP (Request for Proposal), and Stoner's team on the scene included former Bomarc program manager Bob Helberg, Harlowe Longfelder, chief engineer George Hage (one of the three Hage brothers who worked for Boeing), and Yamauchi himself. Also there was a new engineer assigned to Boeing's space program—Bob Wylie, a 32-year-old Air Force veteran who had answered a "help wanted" ad in the *Wall Street Journal*. On the plane en route to Seattle, he struck up a conversation with the man in the adjoining seat and mentioned he was going to work for Boeing.

"Oh? What part of Boeing?"

"Aerospace."

"That's good. Stay away from the airplane company—they're going under."

It was an unusual contract that Boeing finally won, an incentive arrangement with virtually all the incentive resting on the quality of the pictures Lunar Orbiter would transmit. Stoner put Bob Helberg in charge of the project, with Tommy Yamauchi taking responsibility for the photography. He worked directly with Eastman Kodak on the camera technology, for Kodak was then developing its own instant film-processing system to compete with Polaroid.

The camera Kodak provided weighed 50 pounds. It developed the pictures, then scanned them electronically and sent pulses back to Earth where the pulses were "rebuilt" into the original photographs. Yamauchi, with a slide rule, figured out the correct angles and the right times for triggering the camera. Most of the competing bidders proposed using television systems, but Yamauchi insisted right from the start that still pictures would be far sharper.

Boeing built five Lunar Orbiters, and all five completed their missions successfully, the first being launched August 10, 1966, aboard an Atlas Agena rocket.

It took a day or two for the transmitted pulses to be transformed into actual photographs. Boeing had built an image reconstruction facility in Pasadena, and when initial pictures began emerging from the reconstruction process, the laboratory looked like the rejoicing locker room of a winning football team. Bill Allen, Stoner, Bob Jewett, Helberg, and Lysle Wood were all present, plus a covey of jubilant NASA officials. Tommy Yamauchi was the happiest man there, wearing a big sign on his chest that read: "WE ALSO BUILD AIRPLANES." Helberg was passing out cigars like a proud new father—20 years later Bill Jury, who became public relations director of the aerospace division, still had the one Helberg gave him; he had kept it as a souvenir.

Bill Allen presented the team with a case of scotch, keeping a promise he had made when he reluctantly agreed to a high-risk contract that provided full payment only if the Lunar Orbiter worked perfectly.

"I think it's folly and a rip-off," he told Stoner and Helberg, "but it won't break us if we don't make it. And if it goes like you say it will, I'll buy you a case of scotch."

It was a day of triumph for the gentlemanly, hard-working Helberg. He had developed a heart condition whose seriousness he unsuccessfully tried to hide from his cohorts. Wylie remembered that during the LO's development he saw Helberg surreptitiously popping nitroglycerin pills into his mouth with increasing frequency.

"In my book," Wylie said, "he should have retired right then and there, and started to take life easy. But he just kept on traveling and working almost to the day he died."

With its four solar panels deployed, the Orbiter looked something like a four-leaf clover. It was controlled by radio signals transmitted from Earth, but one of the problems the team had to solve was severance of all contact when the LOV passed around to the dark side of the moon. So the engineers designed and built onboard flight computers programmed to take over the controls automatically when the Orbiter reached the moon's dark side. All five Orbiters, incidentally, were deliberately crashed on the lunar surface after their missions were completed.

The five Orbiters shot nearly 2,000 photographs, but the most famous one was a shot not of the moon but of the earth—a spectacular picture that showed the moon's horizon in the foreground and our planet as a small sphere in the distance; it was the first ever made of an earthrise in its entirety, and it was taken during the first mission in direct violation of Helberg's established procedures.

The LOV team was divided into three shifts working around the clock seven days a week. Helberg's strict orders were not to deviate from the command signals being transmitted to the LOV, but he unwittingly left a loophole in those orders. Each of the first two shifts had a supervisor in charge, but Helberg, figuring nothing important was going to happen on the third shift, left it in the hands of a lead engineer. It was during this shift that it happened. An engineer named Dale Shellhorn suggested that they could get a great shot of Earth by inducing a 170-degree roll and 20-degree pitch in the LOV, coinciding with the exact moment the camera was set to snap a picture.

It worked, but Helberg heard rumors of this unscheduled maneuver and spent several days trying to nail down the culprit. No one snitched and Helberg still hadn't found out who did it by the time Stoner and a contingent of NASA officials arrived in Pasadena to view photographs. That one shot of Earth upstaged all the ones taken of the moon's surface. Stoner congratulated Helberg on a brilliant achievement, and NASA happily released the picture to the media.

Amid all this acclaim, Shellhorn finally confessed to Helberg, who found himself on the proverbial horns of a dilemma. He solved it by announcing that henceforth a supervisor would be in charge of the third shift as well as the other two. Then he made Shellhorn a supervisor, although it's doubtful whether he really forgave him. Shellhorn went on to become Boeing's program manager in the B-2 bomber project.

The Lunar Orbiter was Boeing's first major achievement in America's space program, but it was to be dwarfed by the next one. LOV had established where man could land on the moon; the aerospace division already was building part of the mammoth rocket that would take him there.

Saturn S-1C was the first and most powerful stage of the three-stage rocket that launched all Apollo spacecraft.

Boeing built it in what had been the most unlikely facility in the world: a rat-infested, decaying New Orleans factory whose wartime products had included Higgins PT boats, C-46 cargo planes, and engines for army tanks. It was known as the Michoud Ordnance plant, and if the place had been haunted no one from Boeing's Saturn team would have been surprised—it was in even worse shape than the old steel plant Vertol had to renovate.

Stoner put Dick Nelson in charge of the S-1C program, and just getting Michoud cleaned up deserved a 13th spot on the mythical 12 labors of Hercules, right ahead of his job on the Augean stables. The rats, cobwebs, dust, dirt, cracked floors, rusting rafters, and corroded overhead cranes were bad enough; the cleanup crews also were greeted with the residue of a recent flood that had left high-water marks eight feet off the floor. Boeing moved late in 1961 into a plant that hadn't been occupied since 1945, when Chrysler stopped building tank engines there. Boeing actually occupied only two-thirds of Michoud; Chrysler moved back in with an assignment to build the Saturn S-4B, a smaller booster rocket.

Nelson's insistence that engineering and manufacturing work closely together—something he had developed in Bomarc—paid off with the Saturn V manufacturing process. In simplest terms, it meant stationing a developmental support engineer alongside the design engineer, coordinating design with manufacturing so that the "flow time" between the design of a part and putting it into production was reduced sharply.

This coordination was applied to every team Nelson and Stoner established for the S-1C's design and production. Separate groups worked on the oxidizer tank, fuel tank, inter-tank structure, engine thrust structure, and so on. "We had all the various kinds of people necessary to make key components grouped together," Nelson said. "The engineers, tool people, manufacturing people, all worked together in closely knit groups."

The miracle that emerged from the spotless, antiseptically clean floors of this cavernous, once-decrepit factory was a 138-foot-long cylinder whose five engines could produce 7.5 million pounds of thrust—enough to lift its own fueled weight of 5 million pounds off a launch pad, plus the combined weight of two other giant rockets and the Apollo spacecraft itself, attaining a speed of 6,000 miles an hour up to an altitude of 38 miles; at that point, the S-1C separated from Saturn V; the other two stages, built by North American Rockwell and McDonnell Douglas respectively, took over. One of the key factors in Boeing winning the first-stage contract was the fact that Wichita had machines capable of milling cylinders with a 33-foot diameter.

Boeing's other major space facilities were at NASA's Marshall Space Flight Center in Huntsville, Alabama; the Manned Space Flight Center in Houston (later renamed Johnson Space Center); and the Cape itself. Counting the Minuteman project, by 1962 Boeing's aerospace division personnel numbered some 55,000 men and women, with Huntsville the center of attention during Saturn V's initial planning stages.

Boeing built 15 S-1Cs at Michoud, the 12 used on actual Apollo missions performing flawlessly. Construction was under a sequence of "Zero Defects" campaigns, one of which developed a defect of its own. To keep "Zero Defects" firmly fixed in everyone's mind, Boeing gave each Saturn V employee a calendar with ZERO DEFECTS printed in large letters across the top. The calendar had to be reprinted when someone pointed out that it had two October 29ths.

This was one minor glitch. Another occurred at the Cape while Boeing engineers were pumping more than 300,000 pounds of liquid oxygen from a storage tank that was nothing more than a huge thermos bottle sealing the LOX, a liquid so cold that its boiling point is 280 degrees below zero Fahrenheit. The tank was about a half-mile from the launch pad, and the LOX was being pumped through a vacuum-jacketed pipeline that ran along a small pond. It was a warm, sunny afternoon, and adding to the idyllic scene was a flock of ducks swimming in the pond.

The pipeline suddenly burst—right at a spot adjacent to the pond. Engineer Karl Metz was an eyewitness.

"Hundreds of thousands of gallons of LOX poured into the pond, which was about five feet deep and a hundred and fifty feet in diameter. Everything froze immediately, including the poor ducks. In seconds we had an ice skating pond with the outside temperature in the nineties."

Boeing had as many as 5,000 people assigned to the Cape during Apollo, and the technical staff was working seven days a week on at least two and usually three shifts. Francis Coenen, who replaced Tex Johnston as the director of the Boeing Atlantic Test Center when Tex left the company, remembered launch day in particular.

"We worked all night to get ready for a six A.M. launch," Coenen said, "and if things went well we'd manage to get out of there by noon. Once an Apollo was in orbit, Houston took over. I was there through Apollo 13, lived right on a golf course, and didn't get to play once."

Boeing's first job at the Cape was to install about 3,000 modifications to the 17 ground systems that were part of the launch complex. An unexpected problem arose after the first launch of a test Saturn V—the rocket exhaust, generating more heat than any previous booster, burned up much of the tower, including crucial cables. The engineers put in long hours between the first and second launch, beefing up and hardening the tower structures for all subsequent launches.

The Cape activities at least didn't have the overruns that plagued the S-1C program at first—$176 million against a base contract of $440 million. Boeing sent an audit team to New Orleans and Huntsville, an audit team being Boeing's equivalent of a police internal affairs investigation. George Snyder headed the group, which also included Mark Miller.

"I don't think the word 'overrun' was in Boeing's vocabulary until we got into missiles," Miller reflected. "Someone asked me what the hell was an overrun, and I said it's when we spend more than we have to.

"The audit concluded that we easily could have spent that one hundred and seventy-six million, but that we probably didn't have to," Miller added. He himself ended up as chief engineer on the S-1C. And overruns notwithstanding, there was nothing wrong with the Boeing-made product that launched a dozen Apollo spacecraft to spectacular triumphs.

Watching a Saturn V launch was one of the most exciting sights in the world, a thundering, fiery spectacle that awed even the most blasé observer. Boeing invited an important airline customer to see one of the Apollo moon shots, with Dean Thornton and Jack Steiner among the hosts. After it was all over, Thornton was shaking his head in disbelief.

"We were in a bunker," he reported, "about to witness one of the great moments in the history of mankind. And here's Steiner, trying to show the guy a 727 brochure."

Maybe Steiner should have been forgiven; back in the decade of the sixties, Boeing's role in the space program wasn't that widely publicized—as far as the public was concerned, it still was a company that built airplanes. Which may explain what happened to Boeing employee

Lauri Hillberg, who rented a car while on a vacation trip to Canada. The rental clerk asked where Hillberg worked.

"Boeing Aerospace Company," Hillberg replied.

Later, Hillberg happened to glance at the completed form. In the line for *place of employment* was written:

"The Bow and Arrow Space Company."

The S-1C program was staffed with a large nucleus from Bomarc; when Dick Nelson took over, he transferred about 1,500 people from Seattle to New Orleans—most of them under duress.

"Not many wanted to go," Nelson related later, "but strangely enough, after they had been living down there and it came time to close down the Saturn program, none of them wanted to come home."

Stoner at first established his headquarters in New Orleans, with Nelson wearing the title of assistant general manager of the booster branch. Stoner stayed in New Orleans only two years, Nelson replacing him as general manager, and Michoud became almost strictly an assembly facility, with Huntsville more of an engineering center.

Boeing initially had been reluctant to assign black engineers to these Southern sites, being only too well aware of the prejudice they might encounter. But while the concern was justified during the 1960s, Boeing's people handled it their own way. Wallace Weber, a white engineer who worked in Huntsville, was very cognizant of the situation existing then.

"The aerospace companies that provided a majority of the jobs in the city were equal opportunity employers," Weber related, "but the official county and city buildings had segregated drinking fountains and restroom facilities. Us Yankees, imported by our employers to work in this alien environment, used to refer to the city as 'Huntspatch.' We made mistakes quite often, but the local residents were pretty tolerant of us when we sat in the wrong seats on a bus, drank from the wrong fountains, or went to a movie theater for blacks. On the job there was no problem mingling with our black co-workers."

The first real problem surfaced when Boeing announced that a company picnic would be held in the city park. One of the black draftsmen told his supervisor, "I can't go—the park's segregated."

The word spread quickly, with much speculation of how management was going to juggle this hot potato, and the answer was soon forthcoming. A few nights before the scheduled picnic, a light rain fell—"actually, it was more of a heavy dew," Weber remembered.

The next day, Boeing issued a memo to all Huntsville employees:

"The company picnic has been cancelled out of concern that the waterlogged park would be damaged by company use so soon after the recent downpour."

White employees took even more direct action when it came to standing up for their black cohorts. Arne Bruskland was one of the white engineers transferred from Seattle to Huntsville. Came the time when Arne was transferred back to Seattle, and a going-away party was arranged at one of the better Huntsville restaurants.

Included among the guests was a black engineer, one of Bruskland's friends. The restaurant manager informed Arne that the black man couldn't be seated.

"Unless *all* of us are seated," Bruskland told him, "nobody will be seated. And furthermore, no one from Boeing will likely be seated in this restaurant for the duration of this century."

The manager took one look at Bruskland's set jaw, and decided that an exception would be made in this case.

There was a touchy incident at the Cape during the Apollo launches that another Boeing engineer, Karl Merz, handled with similar firmness. Preceding each launch, NASA conducted a Flight Readiness Test (FRT) on the Saturn V rocket and the spacecraft. The space agency had issued a strict rule that once the FRT was completed, no one was to be left alone at the launch pad at any time; it was a precaution against sabotage and carelessness, and it meant that even if a task required only a single worker, he had to have someone with him.

To implement the rule, NASA required that a Boeing engineer accompanied by a co-worker walk down the Launch Umbilical Tower (LUT) every four hours, inspecting all tower areas, systems, and gauges on the way down. Merz drew this assignment one day and with him was a 220-pound, muscle-bulging mechanic from West Virginia named Scotty. They had gone more than halfway down the LUT when they saw a man peering over the edge—alone, in violation of the rule.

"Grab him, Scotty," Merz whispered.

The mechanic did, so hard that the man screamed in agony. The more he cursed and yelled, the harder Scotty squeezed.

"I'm an astronaut!" he finally screeched. "I'll have you fired for this!"

They hauled him down to Security where it was quickly determined that he was, indeed, an astronaut scheduled to fly an Apollo mission that same day. And he did try—unsuccessfully—to have Merz and Scotty fired.

It was a far more serious incident at the Cape, however, which plunged Boeing into a project Bill Allen didn't want and the company didn't need; yet one that played an unheralded but vital role in Apollo's eventual success.

On January 27, 1967, astronauts Gus Grissom, Ed White, and Roger Chafee perished when fire destroyed their Apollo spacecraft during a routine pre-launch countdown test procedure. It was a disaster that shook NASA to its very core; no one would have been surprised if a tragedy had occurred during a space flight, but to have three astronauts die in a spacecraft parked inertly on a launch pad was almost unbelievable. And it led NASA Administrator James Webb to the unhappy conclusion that there was something wrong within his own agency, namely insufficient coordination among the various Apollo contractors and NASA itself.

Webb, universally regarded as one of the ablest men ever to serve in government, had the courage to admit the agency needed help. He sent letters to all major NASA contractors requesting suggestions for reorganizing management of the space program—in effect, he was asking them what was wrong with the space agency. Bill Allen showed Webb's letter to Stoner and asked him to compose a reply, which Stoner, Wilson, and Allen personally delivered to the NASA chief on a Friday, before flying back to Seattle.

Its gist was that NASA had ineffectual control over a program that was spread too wide, with Cape Kennedy, Houston, Huntsville, and Washington each calling its own shots, and Washington headquarters in particular not really knowing what was going on at the various major centers. It said there was no coordination between contractors because there was no system for managing such a huge endeavor. Allen signed the Boeing letter, which ended with this key statement:

"This is what you need to do, but we do not covet this work."

Allen meant it—he knew, and so did Stoner, that any company willing to assume the massive job of integrating all the technical aspects of the Apollo program would have to take key manpower away from its own space projects. And the Boeing trio went beyond the written suggestions—Wilson recommended that General Sam Phillips, who had done such a superb job in Minuteman, run Apollo with the same degree of authority Phillips had in the missile program. (Webb's subsequent decision to give Phillips more say in the Apollo program was hailed by every astronaut.)

Monday morning, Webb phoned Allen. "Bill, I'm going before the Senate subcommittee investigating the pad fire later today, and I want you to listen to a statement I'm reading to the subcommittee."

"Go ahead," Allen said.

" 'I have just hired the Boeing Company to perform an Apollo technical integration and evaluation program.' "

Webb waited a few seconds for Allen to digest that announcement, then added, "Bill, you've got to do this for us."

Allen didn't hesitate. "I told you we don't covet this, but if it's in the national interest we'll do it."

The program carried the name Webb had used at the Senate hearing: Apollo Technical Integration and Evaluation—the acronym TIE was a natural, for what Stoner and the rest of the Boeing team created was a system for tying together the many facets of the space program: contractors, agency centers, astronauts, and everything else.

Stoner wasn't one to spin his wheels, either. He assigned more than 2,000 people to TIE centers in Houston, New Orleans, Huntsville, Cape Kennedy and Washington, and put one of his own deputies—Bob Brock, chief of technology in the space division—in charge. Reorganization of communications was Stoner's first priority, and for that he enlisted the aid of IBM and Bell Telephone.

Into Huntsville went IBM's new 360 system, a vast improvement over the IBM 705 vacuum tube mainframe computer Boeing had acquired in the late 1950s, mostly for accounting purposes. (It was installed in a building on the west side of Boeing Field, and was constantly out of service either from tube overheating or interference from a radar unit on the roof.) The 360 linked all NASA facilities, achieving Stoner's goal of coordinating the various project schedules so NASA would know immediately the status of each project. IBM sent observers to Huntsville to see how the new system was being utilized— they knew it had tremendous data capacity but they had never seen the 360 employed on such a large scale.

Stoner was fascinated by computer technology. Brock remembered Stoner telling him once, "Bob, computers are going to become much, much smaller and far faster—you won't recognize the revolutionary changes." This was when a vacuum tube computer filled a large room.

Stoner, at the very beginning of TIE, said something else to Brock. "You guys flying back and forth between the Cape, Huntsville, Houston, and Washington won't be able to do this job," he declared. "If we're going to get everyone playing a tune together, we have to find some way to network them."

Which is exactly what he created, with Bell Telephone's assistance. It was called the Blue Network, a voice hookup involving Seattle, New Orleans, Huntsville, Washington, the Cape, and Houston. It was available on a 24-hour basis, but was used most frequently for a regular Monday morning conference call with these six points participating— a joint telephone session that usually lasted at least an hour.

"It was all prepared ahead of time," Bob Wylie recalled. "If there was a presentation from New Orleans, the other centers would get Michoud's flip charts in advance and we'd flip them as New Orleans talked."

The Blue Network was operated out of Huntsville. Each center had a network room, carpeted to cut down on noise—this was at Stoner's insistence; as he had done outfitting Boeing's quarters in the L'Enfant Plaza, Stoner laid out the conference call facilities.

"At the beginning," Brock said, "half the people were complaining about having to pay for the network because they didn't think they were going to use it, that they didn't need anything like this. Stoner also enhanced the telephone and computer setup with a high-speed data fax system that could move a sheet of paper between the centers in thirty or forty seconds. And no matter where you were, you couldn't get away from the Blue Network. George must have had a spy system that wouldn't quit."

Brock was taking a swim one night around nine o'clock and his youngest son came running out of the house. "Dad, there's a telephone call for you."

"I'm not taking any calls," Brock grumbled. "Who is it?"

"Some guy by the name of Blue Network."

Stoner had something in common with Jack Steiner—he seemed oblivious to clocks. Like Steiner, he usually worked late, so he would hold network staff meetings on West Coast time when it was close to midnight in the east.

"We'd have guys dozing off during the meetings," Brock admitted.

When Saturn began to pick up steam, Boeing was adding 100 people to the project daily, which meant several hundred new telephones were needed every week. Stoner insisted that the Cape, New Orleans, and Huntsville get updated telephone books to keep up with the phone installations.

"You don't want to put out new phone books more than once a month," the directory publisher told him.

"I want a new phone book every other day," Stoner declared, "because people must know how to reach other people to get their jobs done."

He set up a system by which each new hire was assigned a location and handed a phone number on an identification card. A fresh phone directory, actually a stapled list, was published three times a week until the employment list stabilized.

"A lot of people thought Stoner was nuts," Dick Nelson once remarked. "He wasn't. He was just ahead of everyone else."

Some of the finest talent in Boeing's space division went into Apollo TIE, men like Miller, Clint Wilkenson, Don Jacobs, Lionel Alford, and Hal McClellan. All TIE personnel, from Stoner and Brock on down, encountered resentment from NASA officials and Apollo contractors alike—the general reaction to TIE at first was a replay of Seattle-vs-Wichita, and Seattle/Wichita-vs-Philadelphia. In other words, "Here come the big shots from Boeing telling us how to run Apollo and build rockets."

Typical was Brock's first TIE meeting at Cape Kennedy. He brought two other Boeing men with him and they were facing NASA's chief engineer at the Cape and about 16 other NASA officials. After some cursory introductions, the chief engineer's opening remarks set the tone of the chilly reception.

"I hope none of your people are going to buy homes down here," he announced, "because you're not going to be here very long. We didn't ask for you, we don't want you, we don't even know what you're going to do here, and we're not going to let you do anything anyway."

Brock was neither surprised nor angry. He knew how they felt—here was a big corporation coming in with a big battery of people, supposedly telling them how to run their operation, and Boeing's very presence was an implication that they were doing a poor job.

"But over a period of time," Brock said, "we won the respect of the NASA guys. Eventually we had seven hundred and fifty people at the

Cape alone involved in TIE, but we didn't come in and try to run their programs. We simply did what TIE was all about—technical integration and evaluation. We were able to tie things together among the centers in purely a technical sense, because they simply didn't have the manpower to do this. And it worked out fine. We got to be very good friends with all of them, but it was a pretty tough sell at first."

The bottom line on what TIE achieved was the overall Apollo program itself—a series of brilliant successes that overcame the Soviet Union's early lead in space. Apollo was the apogee of America's own space program and represented a complete turnaround from the pad fire disaster that had led to TIE's creation. But how much harm TIE did to Boeing's other programs was another matter. Brock admitted as much.

"For a period of time," he said, "TIE did drain us terribly in terms of senior staff manpower. We had to go in and acquire people from other major programs and it worked hardships on them. In many cases, lower management simply wouldn't let them go, because they couldn't meet their own commitments, and we'd have to go all the way to the top when we asked for a certain percentage of these people."

Mark Miller, after his TIE tour of duty ended, summed up the program in these words:

"It was an unrewarding job in some respects. It took some of the best engineering people we had for over a year and a half to two years, and that hurt us competitively in other programs."

One of these programs, in fact, was NASA's major post-Apollo space effort: the shuttle, on which Boeing bid but lost. There was some feeling in the space division that Boeing didn't bid very aggressively, yet some veterans from the Apollo era believed the loss of George Stoner was the major factor in the company's virtual abandonment of serious space involvement for a long time. Stoner had great rapport with Wernher von Braun, the legendary German rocket scientist who played such a major role in America's space program.

Stoner died in 1971, and Dick Nelson was one of those who thought his death, more than anything else, took Boeing out of the space program temporarily. In Nelson's view, if it hadn't been for Stoner, the company probably wouldn't have been involved to begin with, and that Stoner was the only Boeing officer who could have talked Allen into getting involved.

"Allen never understood the rocket and missile business at all," Nelson said. "He wasn't interested. Stoner was Boeing's space program, absolutely."

Francis Coenen agreed. "A lot of the impetus was lost when George died. At the top level of the company, Stoner *was* the only one who really believed in space. We didn't bid on some jobs subsequently, or when we did bid, it was something less than our best effort."

Stoner was cast in the same visionary mold as Wells. He had his staff doing studies on various space projects that included meteorology, global communications, and navigation, and even one on land mapping from space to give farmers better agricultural data. And this was before the widespread use of satellites.

He was constantly looking ahead to new uses for space technology based on his belief that satellite communications would be one of the most beneficial fallouts from the space program. Bill Jury remembered a Stoner prediction that one day we could put into orbit a satellite containing all of man's knowledge, gleaned from the world's libraries.

"George said we all might wear a little computer like a wristwatch, and when we needed an answer to a question, we'd just dial it up on our wristwatch and we'd get the answer from the orbiting library. It didn't make any difference where we were—we could be in the middle of the Mohave Desert—and he was telling us this back in the late nineteen-sixties."

"I worked very closely with him," Brock reminisced, "and each night I'd go home and ask myself if this guy was for real, or someone out of science fiction. George was very much a futurist, but he blended this beautifully with the practical aspects of getting things done in the near-term, in order to get to the long-term goals."

Boeing's last major effort in Apollo was the design and construction of a lunar surface vehicle for extended exploration of the moon. Boeing, with General Motors as a partner, signed a contract to develop a Lunar Roving Vehicle (LRV) in October 1969, and delivered the first one less than 18 months later, an amazing feat considering that the engineers came up with 11 different versions before settling on the final design.

Boeing beat out Bendix, the other finalist, for the LRV contract and built three production models. The "moon buggy's" original name was Lunar Rover Vehicle, but the second word was changed to "Roving" when British Leland, which made the Land Rover truck, objected, figuring that if the LRV flopped the bad publicity might wash off on their truck. Later, when the LRV was seen by some 400 million television viewers successfully bouncing over the moon's surface, Leland stopped objecting and probably would have been delighted if Boeing had changed the name back to Lunar Rover Vehicle.

It resembled a dune buggy, but no dune buggy ever went through the design problems Boeing encountered with the LRV, not the least of which was the fact that it had to be collapsible, in order to fit inside the relatively tiny Lunar Exploration Module (LEM) that landed on the moon. Reducing weight was top priority for LRV chief engineer Eugene Cowart, whose team finally came up with a vehicle tipping the scales at 482 pounds empty. Powered by two silver zinc batteries, it could travel up to nine miles an hour for almost 60 miles before the batteries gave out.

The LRV team was willing to accept any idea to fight weight, and someone came up with a plan to offer savings bonds for usable suggestions. As a consolation prize, those submitting rejected ideas were given a ballpoint pen. It sounded great, except that the engineers received a long list of suggestions from Ollie Boileau, the new vice president of the aerospace group.

This presented Cowart with a worse problem than weight reduction: would said vice president regard a consolation ballpoint pen an insult to his intelligence, ability, and scientific knowledge? There was considerable debate over this protocol problem before Cowart decided to bite the bullet and send Boileau a pen, like the rest of the losers.

At the start of the project, no one had much of an idea of how efficiently the LRV would move over the lunar surface, because at that point the consistency of moon soil was an unknown. The soil experts Boeing consulted weren't much help; they couldn't agree on any one theory. General Motors' Delco division finally designed wheels made of zinc-coated, woven piano wire, which turned out to be a better idea than what was originally proposed: tank treads.

The LRVs were assembled in the Huntsville Industrial Council building, once a cotton mill, which Boeing had taken over. Dr. Eberhard Rees, the German rocket scientist who was Wernher von Braun's deputy at NASA's Saturn V program in Huntsville, arrived at the HIC building one day to see a demonstration of the vehicle's unfolding mechanism.

"At the last minute," Cowart recounted, "someone thought we should make it as realistic as possible and sprinkle what would pass as moon dust over the vehicle. It folded up like a big pup tent and was supposed to come out of the LEM and open up when an astronaut pulled a D-ring. So we went downtown for a whole bunch of talcum powder to double for the moon dust, and covered the LRV with the stuff."

Rees stood close to the LRV rig, watching with great interest when an engineer yanked the D-ring. The vehicle emerged only halfway, and there was a loud noise as it tried to unfold. A bolt gave way and talcum powder was sprayed over everyone in sight—Rees included.

"I didn't think it would work like that," he remonstrated in a thick German accent.

GM was proud of those woven piano wire wheels and a Delco official once asked Cowart if the General Motors name would appear on the Lunar Roving Vehicle.

"Yeah," Cowart assured him. "Under the belly."

Deployment and driving over the moon's surface went off with no serious hitches in the three times the LRV was used. Astronaut Scott Carpenter spun out once, and Boeing sent his copilot—Jim Irwin—a pair of dark sunglasses with the explanation that if he wore them, he wouldn't have to see Carpenter driving again.

The greatest compliment the LRV team received came from Dick Smith, NASA's Saturn V program manager. He told Cowart after the final Apollo mission that the Lunar Roving Vehicle "was one of the best technical programs Marshall ever had."

"Financially," Cowart remarked later, "it probably was one of our worst."

But profit was not Boeing's motive throughout Apollo, which in itself was remarkable because the company was going through a serious financial crisis long before Apollo wound down. The aerospace division took its lumps, too, with manpower reductions occurring after the last S-1C had been delivered and more following the final Apollo moon mission. At Cape Kennedy alone, where Boeing once had some 5,000 people, employment dropped to about 30. (One of the few survivors was Jim Owen, engineering and flight test manager, who by 1990 had spent his entire 30-year Boeing career at the Cape.) Similar cuts in New Orleans and Huntsville could be likened to an army reducing a division to platoon strength. Huntsville, for example, also went from 5,000 employees down to exactly 35 people, who began calling themselves "the thirty-five cockroaches"—a reference to the insect that has avoided extinction since the days of the dinosaurs.

The Saturn V and post-Apollo layoffs might have been less drastic if NASA had bought one of Boeing's most ingenious proposals: a flyback booster rocket. The engineers designed a booster with wings and landing gear, so that after separation it could be flown back to Earth via remote control and used again for another launch. Guy Townsend, who worked on the flyback booster program, said it would have been an extremely cost-effective vehicle but that NASA just lacked the funds to buy it.

"When Apollo ended," Townsend observed sadly, "NASA went from a chateaubriand taste to a hamburger budget."

So, in effect, did Boeing's space program.

T Wilson had become Boeing's new president in the spring of 1968, and a year later airplane orders had begun drying up even as the company was pouring millions into new aircraft development. With Boeing's various space programs running out of gas along with military and commercial aircraft business, he asked Stoner to look into diversification possibilities.

Stoner set up a blue ribbon committee that investigated a number of potential diversification markets, but while they appealed to Stoner's more esoteric, visionary side, virtually all of Boeing's efforts in this area during the 1970s were financial flops even when they were technical triumphs. "Competing against established companies," Ed Renouard remarked, "Boeing was a babe in the woods."

A typical example of venturing into the jungles of unfamiliar markets, where understanding customers was crucial to success—or conversely, staying out of them altogether—was Vertol's railcar program.

From a technical standpoint, the railcars (actually modern streetcars) Vertol designed and built were excellent products, but the limited market consisted of municipally owned urban transportation companies and dealing with them was a frustrating experience.

Boeing won contracts to supply a total of 175 electrically powered Light Rail Vehicles to the Massachusetts Bay Transportation Authority (MBTA) and the San Francisco Municipal Railway (MUNI).

The cars were quiet, economical to operate, and popular with passengers who liked riding in air-conditioned comfort. But in 1978, when Otis Smith arrived in Philadelphia to serve under Howard Stuverude as Vertol's executive vice president, he stepped into a pile of municipal manure. Wes Maulden was there under instructions from Wilson to get Vertol out of the railcar business.

Getting out was harder than getting in. MBTA was refusing to accept delivery of some 80 cars remaining under the contract, claiming the cars they already were operating were constantly breaking down. The complaints, naturally, were accompanied by hints of a lawsuit if Vertol insisted on delivering the rest of the cars. It didn't take Smith long to find out the real cause of the breakdowns: poor maintenance.

"They were trying to maintain sophisticated equipment with people whose ideas on streetcars dated back to 1930," Smith said.

Otis went as high as Governor Dukakis trying to settle the dispute. In his second meeting with Dukakis, the governor told him, "Now, Mr. Smith, the Boeing Company builds great airplanes, but this stuff you're delivering to us is a bunch of junk!"

Smith, who knew all about MBTA's maintenance practices, replied, "Governor, I'll tell you what we'll do. Let us bring our own people in here, we'll maintain those cars for three months, and I'm sure they'll meet all your requirements."

Dukakis turned down the offer, and litigation dragged on for some time, before Boeing finally settled for around $40 million (MBTA had demanded about $100 million). The remaining undelivered MBTA cars were sold to MUNI at a considerable loss.

One of the most interesting diversification efforts was a government-funded project begun at the University of West Virginia, known as the Morgantown People Mover system. It consisted of 70 driverless, computer-controlled vehicles moving around the widespread campus over 3.6 miles of guideways—"like a horizontal elevator," someone described it.

Boeing's aerospace division won the bid to create the system, which, although it was an experimental prototype, still is in operation carrying some 17,000 passengers daily. The day it opened in 1975 was a big media event, with Tricia Nixon the first passenger. The Morgantown project stemmed from a belief among some Boeing officials that could be expressed in these terms: "Look, we're a transportation company, so why not get involved in ground transportation?" But it was the only one Boeing built.

The saddest aspect of all these diversification sorties was that their viability couldn't match the technical competence that went into them. This was true of virtually every such project Boeing touched; lack of funding and/or marketing judgment was their downfall, not technology. And it was typical of another case of successful failure: hydrofoil boats.

Bob Bateman was in charge of this one, taking over a division within aerospace called Boeing Marine Systems that had been established in 1958 under Noble Bryan and for several years dabbled with experimental craft; it was work that would have been close to the heart of Bill Boeing, whose fascination with boats often equaled his interest in airplanes. Bateman was a natural to head BMS—although he was a graduate aeronautical engineer from Purdue, he had been a Navy officer and it was the Navy that got the company deeply involved in a new boat project.

Anti-submarine warfare was one of the Navy's top concerns and priorities. In 1960, it awarded Boeing a $2.08 million contract to develop a hydrofoil subchaser using a waterjet propulsion system; a hydrofoil skims over the water instead of plowing through it.

Bateman submitted a budget request for a small experimental prototype and encountered more resistance from George Schairer than the boat would have met battling a hurricane. The budget required Schairer's approval and he informed Bateman, "You don't need a real boat—you can use models."

So the resourceful Bateman resubmitted his request. He asked for a separate hull program, a control system program, and an engine from the gas turbine division. The overall design came from a team headed by Airo Gonnella, a former engineer in the B-29 program.

"George approved all three items," Bateman chuckled, "without realizing that when you put a hull, a control system, and an engine all together, you have a boat."

BMS christened the hydrofoil "Little Squirt." When Schairer found out they had built a real boat, he went steaming over to Renton where "Little Squirt" had been assembled.

"You've disobeyed my orders!" he yelled at Bateman.

Bateman calmed him down long enough to suggest a compromise. "George, let me have just one day in court. I'll take you out on Lake Washington in this boat. I'll put a glass of water on top of the windshield right in front of you. We'll run through waves at least three feet high, and if we spill one drop I'll cancel the whole damn program."

They went out and ran into waves a yard high. Not a drop spilled, and BMS went on to complete a full-size prototype patrol hydrofoil, the PCH-1 *High Point*, followed by the USS *Tucumcari*, a hydrofoil gunboat that saw active service off the Vietnam coast. She was decommissioned in 1972 but Boeing built six bigger hydrofoils—the PHM series—for the Navy that in 1990 were still in service: *Pegasus, Taurus, Aquila, Aeries, Gemini,* and *Hercules.*

The propulsion system gave the hydrofoil a cruising speed of up to 45 knots, making it the Navy's fastest ship. Admiral John Buckeley—the same Buckeley who as a lieutenant had carried General Douglas MacArthur out of the Philippines to safety in a tiny PT boat—awarded the PHM the service's coveted three brooms for superior performance and told Bateman, "As far as I'm concerned, it's the finest ship in the Navy."

Within a year, BMS had jetfoil customers either in hand or seriously interested throughout the world—South and Central America, Europe, and the Far East. In the end, BMS sold a total of 42 military and commercial hydrofoils. The biggest customer was Far East Hydrofoils, a Hong Kong company that bought its first Boeing jetfoil in 1975, and in 1989 alone netted a $25 million profit operating its 14-ship hydrofoil fleet. In the early eighties, however, Boeing's jetfoil market had dwindled to a maximum of four orders a year. In 1985, it was decided to suspend commercial sales.

The hydrofoil went down the same dead-end road as another major and earlier diversification project: the gas turbine division, which had contributed "Little Squirt's" engine plus a lot of headaches to every manager who had run it since George Schairer established the unit in the mid-1940s. It had produced some excellent small engines, including an exceptionally good one for trucks, but its annual profits were totally invisible. The division always seemed to have great potential, if anyone could figure out how to tap it.

In 1962, Boeing hired an erudite, ex-Georgia Tech football guard and graduate electrical engineer who had spent 14 years at General Motors—the last few in charge of the AC Spark Plug Division's program to develop the inertial navigational system for the Navy's Polaris missile.

His name was Malcolm T. Stamper, an intellectual with a wry, self-deprecating sense of humor and a smorgasbord of outside interests and hobbies. Among other things, he was a voracious reader, a mountain climber, an accomplished artist, and—after a few hectic years at Boeing—the company's most devout, if reformed, health addict.

Stamper liked Boeing even though it had been something of a culture shock after working for General Motors. "I found the company very unstructured," Stamper recalled, "with a distinct difference in emphasis. At GM, they were very precise, down to the last mill in accounting for everything. At Boeing, they just counted heads—how many people do we have or need on this program? And it impressed me that they were constantly changing the product in dramatic ways; in the automobile business, for example, they hadn't changed the crankshaft in twenty years."

(Bob Dryden, who in early 1990 was running the Wichita division, had somewhat the same culture shock coming to Boeing from IBM. Someone asked him how the two companies compared. "Well," Dryden replied, "at IBM there were three hundred and fifty thousand employees when I left. If you told them that the next morning they were all to come to work wearing blue ties, all three hundred and fifty thousand would show up the next day with blue ties. But at Boeing, you could tell a hundred and fifty thousand people that something had to be changed, and the next day they'd be going in a hundred and fifty thousand different directions.")

Stamper had been working in electronics for nearly three years when Bill Allen, to counter an offer Stamper had received from another company, offered him his choice of a half-dozen jobs, a raise, stock options, and a vice presidency.

"I took the turbine division," Stamper laughed, "which shows you I'm not too bright."

Actually, he picked it because while it had a terrible track record— 17 consecutive unprofitable years and a reputation as a graveyard for a procession of managers—it was doing $25 million worth of national and international business with both military and commercial customers, and Stamper regarded it as a challenge. When he accepted, Allen told him: "Make it the best in the world or let's get rid of it."

In the end, Boeing chose to get rid of it, although its gas turbine engines had acquired a competent reputation throughout industry. The cart-mounted Boeing 502 turbine, used widely by airlines to pneumatically start their aircraft, was the nucleus of a varied product line. The engineers had even designed an outboard motor, but as Bob Dickson said, "The only way to market it would have been to buy out Evinrude and Johnson Motors."

Stamper tried every game plan in the books to turn the division's red ink into black, and admitted he was having fun doing it. One of his underlings was a young lawyer named Dan Pinick, who had started out with a law firm in Wichita, then got a job with Boeing in contracts under what was jokingly referred to as the "Wichita Mafia"—Bob Tharrington, Ben Wheat, Ernie Ochel, and Carl Dillon, all people who rose high in Boeing's hierarchy.

Eventually, Pinick wound up in the gas turbine division after a brief stint at Wright Field. He always seemed to be changing jobs, so often that T once told him, "Pinick, you've never held a job long enough to decide what you're good at—maybe all you're good at is changing jobs."

When he reported to Stamper, Mal enthusiastically assured him that "working in this division is better than going to Harvard Business School."

Pinick was impressed with Stamper. "When I first observed him," Pinick recalled, "he was running this moribund division that would start to do something, only to have someone say 'No, let's not take a chance.' Up and down was its history, but Mal was determined to make it the best small turbine manufacturer in the world or nothing. He told me no Boeing company was going to be a backwater outfit; he wanted it to become the General Motors of small turbine companies. Boeing had dabbled in this field for years, but had never made a full commitment."

Allen had given Stamper that commitment, but when Stamper told him after the first year that the division needed a $74 million transfusion for a complete turnaround, Allen pronounced its death sentence. "We don't have the money," he said. "We're going to build the largest airplane in the world [the 747] and we need all our resources for that program. Sell it."

The phase-out group included Wilson, Stamper, and Maulden, and Pinick was ordered to assess all turbine contracts to determine whether they should be cancelled or completed.

Pinick, conscious of his lowly status on the executive totem pole, asked, "Where do you want me to do all this?"

"We'll give you an office," Maulden said.

What they gave him was Claire Egtvedt's old quarters, so plush that it even included a bath and shower. Pinick went to work on all existing contracts, then with Stamper visited every gas turbine customer, explaining why Boeing was closing down the division, but promising to support the products they already had bought. It was Pinick's first exposure to the need for making the right decisions no matter how tough, and he was to become known as a man who wasn't afraid to make such decisions.

The turbine division eventually was sold to the Caterpillar Tractor Co. But gas turbines weren't the only diversification casualty; there were others, all noble efforts until it came to profitability. Most eventually were lumped under a division called Boeing Engineering and Construction Co., organized in 1974 to consolidate the various diversification projects that hadn't been phased out yet.

Harry Goldie had a thankless job that he described as "curing them or killing them." An asphalt plant was a going concern briefly; it was based on a Boeing engineer's design and the process was developed in a facility occupying two unused bays in Plant Two.

A Boeing engineer promoted the idea of desalination plants based on a new process. The company funded a model, but later spun the program off to a subsidiary. Ultimately the program was sold to another company.

During the start-up of the Saturn V program, the company leased 100,000 acres for 99 years in a remote, arid area near Boardman, Oregon, where it could test the huge S-1C engines, which were not only potentially dangerous but capable of producing ear-rupturing noise. It was used only sparingly for engine-testing purposes and sat idle for several years.

Much of it was desert wasteland, so as an irrigation experiment engineers pumped in water from the Columbia River and turned more than 8,000 acres into farmland that for a while had the company growing and selling potatoes; it even formed the Boeing Agri-Industrial Co., which sub-leased the irrigated acreage to qualified farmers. It was far preferable to another suggested use: a landfill for garbage.

Yet the notion of a "Boeing Garbage Disposal Co." wasn't that farfetched. When Bruce Gissing took over the division, he became interested in waste energy plants—facilities that could take in garbage, sort it out mechanically, remove all metal, and burn the rest in a way that produced steam and electricity. Boeing actually built a model waste energy plant in New England and Gissing thought the idea had great potential on a nationwide scale.

Gissing came to Boeing in 1966 from Martin Marietta, where he had been a program manager in its Denver office. He saw a Boeing newspaper ad seeking program managers, applied, and was hired by Stamper for the 747 project. By the time his assignment there ended, Bob Tharrington had become a senior vice president and asked Gissing to run a project in which Boeing Engineering had gotten involved: huge windmills that generated electric power.

At that point in time, the division's diversification projects had lost about $65 million while generating sales of $250 million, but Tharrington believed windmills might have a lucrative future.

They were huge contraptions, with 300-foot blades sitting on a tower 200 feet high; on the top of each tower was a generator and reduction gear originally designed for large ships. The unit produced quality power, but the major problem was that the windmill had to run largely unattended for 10 to 15 years, and the technology wasn't there to make the structure last that long. Each windmill cost about $4 million to build.

Boeing had constructed three of the immense 2.5-megawatt units in eastern Washington, plus a fourth near Oakland, California, and had just been approached by an entrepreneur who wanted to build 50 of them, with large tax credits as his main incentive.

"You don't have to get involved with the engineering division except for this one deal," Tharrington assured Gissing.

The buyer was willing to pay Boeing $12 million per windmill, reselling each for $10 million and taking a $2 million energy tax credit on every unit. But his financing looked shaky and Gissing backed away. Shortly after the deal fell apart, Gissing was talked into running the division with its hodgepodge of different high-tech projects—among them making centrifuges for the Atomic Energy Commission, a solar energy plant in New Mexico, manufacturing bumpers for the Alaskan pipeline, a consulting subsidiary that designed offshore oil rigs, another branch that designed, constructed, and integrated management of atomic energy plants, and an automated baggage-handling system developed under Mel Sharp's direction that Boeing finally sold to another company—it's still in use at several major airports.

Tharrington actually had another diversification project in mind that was turned down faster than his old suggestion for moving corporate headquarters out of Seattle. When he was running Boeing Computer Services, he came up with the idea of making totalizers for pari-mutuel betting at race tracks. Mal Stamper remembered this when Gissing consulted him about really getting into waste energy plants. The pilot program was doing well in New England and Gissing had some grandiose ideas on expanding.

"No," Stamper said flatly.

"Why not? If we built three of those plants a year, it would be like an annuity. Boeing would get tax credits for all the energy they'd produce."

"There are too many problems. There are city politics to deal with, and safety issues."

Gissing said he already had looked into safety precautions—some garbage contains gases that explode if mishandled. "And don't worry about city politics," he said confidently. "We won't be the front man—we'll be working through other people. So I've answered all your questions."

"Bruce, we just don't want to be in garbage, period."

"What's wrong with garbage? We can make money out of garbage."

"We could make money out of prostitution, too," Stamper said meaningfully, and proceeded to relate the story of Tharrington and his pari-mutuel totalizer. "I threw him out on his ear, too," Stamper added.

With that comment, Gissing gave up and a short time later put the Boeing Engineering & Construction Co. officially out of business.

Tharrington, however, more than made up for that totalizer gaffe with his formation of the Boeing Computer Services division. It could not legitimately be called a diversification effort, because when Tharrington launched it in 1970, BCS was mostly an internal organization; before it was born, every division of the company had its own computer organization, and Tharrington began a major consolidation of all computer operations in the Puget Sound area.

After several years in New Jersey as a subsidiary, BCS headquarters were established in Bellevue, Washington, and by 1990, the division was doing more than $1.5 billion worth of annual business with some 13,000 employees working out of six major data centers in Bellevue, Kent, Wichita, Philadelphia, Huntsville, and Vienna, Virginia.

As previously recorded in this tale, board of directors' minutes are not exactly great literature. But this wasn't true of a board meeting at which Tharrington had announced the removal of certain BCS managers. No one had to read between the lines of *these* minutes:

"Mr. Wilson inquired as to the reasons for the changes in top management in a subsidiary corporation, since with regard to ability and potential of some of these managers, Mr. Tharrington had previously expressed high confidence. Mr. Tharrington responded that he had never claimed to be perfect, whereupon Mr. Wilson expressed surprise and elation at this unexpected revelation from Mr. Tharrington, and directed Mr. Hardy to be sure to include it in the minutes."

There were almost as many reasons for diversification failures as there were diversification projects. Harry Goldie, closely associated with so many of them, had one answer:

"Boeing never had a strategy to diversify in any intelligent way. It gets into these things on an ad hoc basis. Somebody promotes an idea and if he's reasonably capable it'll work, but if the guy's an idiot and doesn't do any market research, it'll be a disaster."

Historically, Boeing has had trouble absorbing smaller firms that can't handle the culture shock of a huge corporation applying its own rules and procedures. This certainly was true with Vertol, and proved true in the 1980s when Boeing acquired de Havilland of Canada.

Bruce Gissing believed this was another reason diversification seldom worked.

"It was like a grizzly bear trying to raise a toy poodle," Gissing remarked.

While there is much logic behind these appraisals, equally logical is the fact that many of the diversification projects were desperation measures taken under enormous financial stresses, brought on by the tremendous stretching of company resources in the late 1960s.

Even while the 707 program was at its peak during the late 1960s and the 727 program was establishing itself, Boeing had plunged into the bitter and controversial competition to build a giant military transport called the C-5, started designing a supersonic transport, and launched both the 737 and 747. The company was heavily involved in the space program, and Minuteman was still very active. Few if any corporations in the world had ever juggled so many technical and marketing balls in the air at the same time; all these projects overlapped each other in the turbulent 1961–1969 period.

The C-5 and SST were stillborn. And the 737 and 747 almost wrecked the company before they wrote the greatest success stories in aviation history.

FIFTEEN

BABY BOEING

BOEING'S BABY JETLINER, THE 737, BEGAN LIFE ON ITS OWN one-yard line, facing a field that tilted upward, and against a stiff wind.

Bill Allen's initial enthusiasm for the program was minimal. The day Boeing's board of directors authorized the 737, Douglas already had sold more than 200 DC-9s. Britain's short-range small jet, the BAC-111, had nearly a hundred orders on hand, and its customers included three U.S. carriers: American, Braniff, and Mohawk.

The 737 was not only launched two years behind the competition, it had to compete against four other major Boeing airplane development programs during its early years: the C-5 proposal, the supersonic transport, the 747, and—Jack Steiner's new project—a stretched 727, all of them spreading the company's engineering talent thin. The "baby Boeing" was a stepchild, generally unwanted and unloved. It was considered by some company officials to be more of a loss leader than anything else, an airplane that no one expected would be profitable, but one that might convince small airline customers to buy bigger Boeing jets if their traffic grew; in a way, the 737 was Boeing's "entry level" vehicle for those not yet quite able to buy larger and more expensive models.

There was even a donnybrook of a battle within Boeing over where to build the 737—Seattle or Wichita—and a less acrimonious but equally intense dispute between Bill Allen and an influential director on whether to build the plane at all. In brief, when the board gave the program a go-ahead in February 1965, the 737's future looked questionable; at that point in time, Boeing had only one airline order for the plane.

Twenty-six years later, at the end of 1991, total announced 737 orders were nearing the 3,000 mark, a figure representing almost half the number of *all* Boeing jetliners delivered to the world's airlines since Pan Am bought the first 707. By the end of the 1980s, the 737 had outsold even the 727—Boeing's baby was, indeed, the ugly duckling that became one beautiful swan.

One thing the 737 had in its favor was the large potential market for a jetliner smaller than the 727. Yet in the early sixties, even that market was still undefined and relatively uncertain. The regional or local service airlines were an obvious target, but when one of them—Bonanza—tried to become the first regional carrier to operate pure jets by ordering the BAC-111, the Civil Aeronautics Board blocked the deal on the grounds that local service airline traffic didn't justify jets, even small ones, and in those days the subsidized regionals needed CAB approval of their equipment purchases.

Unlike the 727, which was always regarded as mostly Steiner's offspring, the 737 had no single "father," no one name with which it would be forever associated, no lone engineering champion who would not only oversee its creation but fight to keep the program alive, as Steiner did with the 727. If anyone belonged in the last category, in fact, it was a man who was neither a Boeing executive nor a Boeing engineer—he was a director named Crawford Greenewalt, board chairman of E. I. duPont de Nemours & Co., of Wilmington, Delaware, along with George Weyerhaeuser, he packed the most clout among the outside directors, and he wasn't afraid to butt heads with Allen.

And butt heads they did—over the 737. Greenewalt was strongly in favor of a small jet program as Boeing's entry into a vast, untapped market. Allen was opposed to a go-ahead. He confided to Mef one night that he hatcd to fight Greenewalt over the issue, but he thought the DC-9 and the BAC-111 were too far ahead for the 737 to ever succeed. Furthermore, as he also pointed out to Greenewalt and the other directors, Boeing was heavily involved with missiles and Apollo/Saturn in this time frame, programs that already had drained engineering and manufacturing manpower away from the airplane division. Allen doubted whether the company could take on another major airplane project.

Mef Allen's recollection of her husband's gut-wrenching dispute with Greenewalt, one of his best friends among the directors, was identical to Weyerhaeuser's.

"That stands out for those of us who were on the board then," he said. "I distinctly recall one afternoon session, followed by an evening session, which went on forever and ever. It was the outside directors who were supportive of the 737, and this was the only time I remember having the feeling that Bill Allen was being pushed against his will."

He was being pushed by someone who believed fervently in the 737. "Crawford Greenewalt," Weyerhaeuser said, "for years had been a strong advocate of Boeing getting into smaller airplanes. He even wanted planes smaller than the 737, and I remember Crawford originating many discussions on that subject."

But Weyerhaeuser also admitted there were many times when all the directors, outside as well as inside, wondered if they had made the right decision. The 737 was a rather sickly infant, plagued not only by a rash of technical problems often common with a new airplane, but by its uncertain sales prospects. Boeing's board had given the program a tentative go-ahead in November 1964, but this was contingent on some launch customer orders. On February 1, 1965, when the directors met in New Orleans to determine whether the program should continue, there still were no launch customers lined up.

A few prospects, yes: Lufthansa really wanted the airplane but was hesitating to make a firm commitment without assurance that Boeing was really going to build it. Eastern seemed to be the hottest domestic prospect, and Lufthansa officials informed Allen that if Eastern bought the 737, so would the German airline. Western took about the same position—Terry Drinkwater never wanted Western to be the first in line for any new airplane and he, too, was waiting for Eastern to make up its mind. Delta, with its strong ties to Douglas, already had ordered the DC-9. American had committed to the BAC-111 because the British were promising even earlier deliveries than the DC-9. TWA wasn't interested in a short-range jet right then, and Northwest's Nyrop wouldn't look at any twin-engine airplane whether it was built by Boeing, Douglas, or Black Forest elves.

That left United, which was still recovering from a bad case of corporate indigestion brought on by its merging with Capital in mid-1961. In addition to the headaches of combining the route systems, integrating pilot and flight attendant seniority lists, and other typical merger problems, UAL had acquired Capital's entire fleet of Viscounts, more than 50 of these short-range propjets. Pat Patterson didn't plan to keep them forever and he was looking at both the DC-9 and 737, but he also was playing it cagey, letting both Boeing and Douglas court him.

This was the unsettled situation that faced Boeing's directors when they convened in New Orleans. Even Lufthansa, the most solid prospect, was wavering; Douglas had promised Gerhard Hoeltje, Lufthansa's CEO, excellent delivery positions if he bought the DC-9. Any commitment delay on the part of Boeing would swing Lufthansa over to Douglas, and the consequences of delay was the chief topic of discussion at this board meeting.

John Yeasting, who had gone on the board at the same time as Ed Wells, reviewed the customer prospect lineup, emphasizing the proximity of two dates: Lufthansa would make its 737-vs-DC-9 decision February 16, but Eastern wouldn't announce its choice until at least February 24. Inasmuch as Lufthansa demanded a firm commitment from Boeing, this meant the directors would have to give the 737 program a go-ahead without waiting for a second launch airline. Yeasting told the board Western would buy the plane but not as a launch customer, and that United was leaning toward the 737 but wouldn't decide until March or April.

Yeasting warned that with Lufthansa's deadline only two weeks away, Boeing's board must make up its own mind quickly; he reminded the directors that Boeing already had promised the German carrier to start 737 deliveries by the spring of 1968 if they signed, and that even now this schedule was probably slipping. Allen had brought his conservatism to New Orleans along with his usual supply of Triscuits and two sets of eyeglasses. He said he would recommend proceeding if Eastern would commit to the 737 along with Lufthansa.

"It should be recognized that United's decision is uncertain, and an adverse decision by United would make it difficult for this program to succeed," he added. But he admitted Boeing was between a rock and a hard place with Lufthansa—asking the Germans to delay their decision until Eastern announced its choice might well alienate Boeing's most loyal European customer.

At this point, according to the minutes, "extensive discussion followed." Reading between the lines of this cold print, and judging by the final action taken, that "extensive discussion" must have been the verbal equivalent of World War III. Crawford Greenewalt and two other outside directors—William Reed and D. E. Skinner, both Seattle businessmen—argued that Boeing should launch the 737 program for Lufthansa without waiting for Eastern's decision, and that if Boeing took this step, Western, too, probably would buy the 737 whether Eastern did or not. The latter was a risky assumption that turned out to be wrong; Western didn't commit until after a second U.S. launch customer signed.

It was Ed Wells who probably tipped the scales. He said Boeing couldn't meet its promised delivery schedules unless it committed to the 737 immediately. "In my opinion," he declared, "a decision to proceed at this time would increase the likelihood that Eastern and United will pick the 737."

"I agree," Yeasting said.

Allen had just lost the support of two inside directors, both men he trusted and respected. Yet even then, the board continued its debate after Yeasting was asked how much the company stood to lose if the go-ahead was issued immediately, on the basis of a single launch customer, and the program then turned out to be a failure. Yeasting said the maximum loss would be incurred after 50 airplanes had been produced—a pre-tax loss of about $150 million, he judged.

By today's standards, a $150 million bath would be a drop in the bucket, but not in 1965. This sobering estimate led to more discussion, most of it involving the conviction of people like Greenewalt and Wells that the 737, even if it started out behind a financial eight-ball, still had a great long-range future. More than once, the need for the company to have a full range of airplane products was mentioned as an argument for proceeding immediately.

The board adjourned in mid-afternoon to tour the Michoud plant, and reconvened at 5:30 P.M. when the discussion shifted to a plan for stretching the 707 into two larger models—the 707-620 and 707-820— to meet Douglas' plans to build a stretched DC-8. Yeasting said Boeing was merely exploring the possibility (the longer 707 versions were never built) and the directors turned back to the 737.

Allen settled the matter. He said he had come to the conclusion that Wells and Yeasting were right—if Boeing went ahead with the 737 with Lufthansa the only firm customer, Eastern and United were more likely to pick the baby Boeing. But he hedged this approval by insisting that Boeing's management be allowed to reverse course if "it appeared advisable"—meaning that he reserved the right to cancel the 737 program if the worst happened and both Eastern and United picked the DC-9.

(Years later, T Wilson voiced the opinion that Allen wasn't as opposed to the 737 program as he let on. "I think he was just playing a very cautious game," T said, "letting everyone weigh the pros and cons before committing.")

The board then unanimously passed the following resolution:

". . . that the management be authorized to go ahead with the 737 program upon obtaining a satisfactory agreement with Lufthansa, if in management's judgment it was deemed advisable."

This was passing a very large buck, and the buck assumed alarming proportions shortly after the New Orleans meeting ended. Boeing learned that Eastern already had agreed to buy the DC-9 while it was still talking to Boeing salesmen about the 737. Pat Patterson of United was fence-sitting, and in Cologne, Germany, sat a worried Ken Luplow, wondering himself whether Boeing was really serious about bringing its unborn baby into the world.

Allen had returned from New Orleans in an unhappy mood, and the loss of Eastern didn't improve it. Someone told him Jack Steiner had lobbied some of the outside directors in favor of the 737; furious, he summoned Steiner to his office.

"Are you aware of what happened in New Orleans?" he asked sternly.

"Sure," Steiner replied.

Allen pointed an accusing finger at him. "Jack, how many outside directors did you talk to before that meeting?"

Three, Steiner confessed, including one who was a neighbor.

Out came the finger again, like the point of a threatening sword.

"Jack, never do that again," Allen said in a tone that could have frozen water.

Luplow was in Cologne the day Lufthansa's board met to vote on the 737-vs-DC-9, and Gerhard Hoeltje shared his anxiety.

"We're really concerned about Boeing going ahead with this airplane," he told Luplow. "I have to allay the fears of our directors and this is your biggest problem."

"I know the company will go ahead," Ken assured him, although Luplow wasn't really that sure. Hoeltje, who always admired Boeing because its reputation for integrity reflected his own, still wasn't convinced.

Luplow said, "I'll tell you what we can do. We'll call Bruce Connelly—I know you can't take my word on this, but you can take the word of the man who heads our commercial transport division."

They got Connelly out of bed at three A.M. Seattle time, and Hoeltje received his personal assurance that Boeing would build the 737. Which happened to be the same desperate, unsupported assurance Luplow had voiced—Connelly didn't know for sure, either. "We had to do something," Ken recalled, "so we made the commitment."

Hoeltje and Luplow went to the board meeting armed with elaborate charts and graphs depicting the 737's promised performance, and how the airplane was ideal for Lufthansa's short-haul European routes. But they arrived late because they had been delayed due to unusual circumstances.

"In typical Boeing fashion," Luplow said, "the charts had been shipped in the damnedest container you ever saw. You would have thought it was rare crystal being sent from Seattle to Cologne. Here was this huge hardwood box, with a mass of hinges and an enormous Yale lock, delivered to Hoeltje's office."

"Well," the Lufthansa chief executive said, "let's get the charts out—my board is waiting for us."

"Sure," Luplow said. "But where's the key?"

There wasn't any key—Seattle had forgotten to include one. They sent for a hammer and screwdriver and finally pried the lid off the box. While they were working, Luplow remembered, people kept popping their heads out of the board room to remind them the directors were getting impatient. Ken and other Boeing representatives made the presentation, then waited in the anteroom for the decision.

Eventually, out came Hoeltje, his face grim. "Come down to my office," he ordered. They followed him, certain that Lufthansa had gone for the DC-9.

Hoeltje told his secretary, "Get us a bottle of cognac," and Luplow thought, *Well, it's all over—Gerhard figures we need a drink to cushion the blow.* The glasses were filled and they drank two rounds before Hoeltje broke the news.

"Well, gentlemen, we have a problem. The board prefers your airplane over the DC-9, but the directors are not convinced that we should accept the risk of Boeing cancelling."

Luplow suddenly felt five years older.

"However," Hoeltje continued, "I told them that if I could get a ten million dollar penalty payment from Boeing, in the event you do not go ahead with the 737, that would cover our losses. They agreed that if I could do this, we could proceed with the purchase."

Luplow now felt 10 years older. What Hoeltje had proposed was known as liquidated damages. And Ken knew that Bill Allen hated liquidated damages with a passion, so much so that Boeing had a policy never to agree to such a contract provision. Luplow might as well have picked up the phone and asked Allen to give Lufthansa the airplane. But he also understood the airline's dilemma—by choosing the 737, those DC-9 delivery positions were down the drain.

In the room, however, was Fran Holman, representing Boeing's law firm. He leaned back in his chair and said to Hoeltje, "You know, you're making a big mistake."

"How so?"

"Well, you're overlooking the fact that if you went ahead with this purchase and somewhere down the line we opted not to build the 737, you could sue Boeing for loss of the use of the airplanes during that period, and for a sum far in excess of ten million dollars. Now that's the way you should go."

Hoeltje, elated, poured himself another glass of cognac. "That is great," he said, beaming, and Luplow regained the years he had lost.

Lufthansa signed for 22 aircraft, the 737-100 model, designed according to the airline's request for a 100-passenger plane—15 more seats than Boeing originally had planned. On April 5, 1965, United took itself off the fence and also got Boeing off the hook by ordering 40 737-200s, a slightly larger airplane. Western quickly followed as promised, contracting for an initial 20.

The crucial United sale was a cliff-hanger. Harley Thorson, who was dealing with UAL, got a frantic call from sales chief George Sanborn after it was learned Eastern had bought the DC-9.

"We've got to sell the 737 to United," he almost pleaded. "You can have any help you need from any department."

"What I'll need, George, is a full-scale mockup and a big model. Put them on a truck and ship it all to Chicago."

Thorson set up the display at a Chicago area country club, complete with dramatic backdrop lighting and large charts with performance data. He staged the show for United's engineering and marketing officials, but Patterson wasn't there. The UAL chief executive heard about the display and phoned Thorson.

"I'd like to see it," he allowed, "but I can't get away. Can you bring it over to our headquarters?"

By the time the mockup, model, and charts had been repacked and trucked to the airline's general offices, Bill Allen had arrived to add his support. Patterson had ordered every UAL vice president in Chicago to attend, and before he walked in, they had spent most of their time telling the Boeing people what was wrong with the airplane. The presentation took 30 minutes. Patterson said quietly, "Let's go to my office and talk business."

Allen looked embarrassed. "Gosh Pat, Mef and I have to catch a flight to New York. I don't have much time."

Thorson admitted later he could have throttled the Boeing president, but Allen stayed anyway, helping to negotiate a tough deal that was clinched when Boeing agreed to lease United 25 new 727s at a bargain rate, with an option to buy. United paid only about $15,000 a month for each 727, but the airline later turned the options into outright sales. What Allen and Thorson didn't know was how close Patterson had come to buying the DC-9.

"I found out a few weeks later, when Douglas officials showed up to sign a contract for stretched DC-8s," Harley said. "United was supposed to sign for the DC-9 at the same time."

But in the early going, there were more defeats than victories. Boeing came close to selling the 737 to North Central but lost, partially for a reason no one could have anticipated. North Central liked the airplane but said its tail, 37 feet high, was too tall for the airline's hangar doors. Thorson offered to pay for raising the hangar entrance height by three feet to accommodate the plane, but North Central then decided it didn't want to wait two years for delivery and bought the DC-9.

Another disappointment was Air West, a new carrier created out of a three-way merger involving Bonanza, Pacific, and West Coast Airlines.

"We were sure we had 'em locked up," Thorson recalled unhappily. He was playing gin rummy with John Yeasting at the Airport Hilton in San Francisco, waiting for the Air West directors who were meeting elsewhere in the hotel to finalize the deal. Nick Bez, president of West Coast, phoned and asked to speak to Yeasting. "You gotta improve your offer, John, it's just not good enough."

"Nick, we've gone as far as Boeing can go," Yeasting told him.

Two hours later, the directors came to the room and informed them Boeing had lost. "We can get the DC-9 earlier, and Douglas gave us a good deal," Bez explained.

The DC-9 head start was a killer for Boeing's sales force, yet it wasn't the only handicap Boeing's new baby faced in its adolescence. A deep hole was dug by the men who would fly the plane, and unwittingly it was Delta's pilots who handed their brethren the shovel that almost buried the 737. When Delta bought the DC-9, it won an agreement from its pilots that the cockpit be designed for a two-man crew, eliminating the flight engineer. This was permissible under an FAA regulation that allowed any jet transport weighing less than 80,000 pounds to be flown by two pilots. Both the original DC-9 and BAC-111 met the so-called "80,000-pound rule," heresy and anathema to the Air Line Pilots Association (ALPA). It could do nothing about the precedent Delta's pilots had set for the DC-9, but the union began pressuring the FAA to change the regulation for the 737, and at the same time warned U.S. airlines planning to buy the Boeing jet that future pilot contracts would specify a three-man crew for the 737.

ALPA argued that with no flight engineer to help them, the pilots' increased workload made it difficult to watch out for other traffic, thus enhancing the chances for mid-air collisions, and also created more danger during bad-weather landings. The union's case might have sounded logical until one began wondering why a two-man crew was safe for the DC-9 and BAC-111, and not for the 737. Nevertheless, the FAA changed its regulations to the extent of requiring Boeing to prove that the 737 could be operated safely with two pilots. The irony was that once having been certificated for a two-man crew, three subsequent larger DC-9 models weighing far more than 80,000 pounds also were automatically certificated for two pilots, but not the 737.

Thus the baby Boeing's late start was saddled with a further sales handicap—many airlines considering the 737 bought the DC-9 instead, unwilling to add the expense of a third cockpit crew member who literally was nothing but an extra set of eyeballs. United and Western, after arbitration, agreed to a three-man crew, although that third man was a classic case of feather-bedding—or "feather-birding," as then-FAA administrator Najeeb Halaby expressed it.

Western's pilots referred to the extra crew member as GIBs, for "Guy in Back," but abandoned this nomenclature hastily when a pilot ran across the word *gib* in a dictionary and discovered it meant castrated tomcat.

Lew Wallick once asked a Piedmont captain what the third crew member did, riding in a jump seat just behind the pilots, unable to reach any controls.

"He doesn't do much," the captain admitted. "He sits back there and spills coffee in my brainbag [nickname for the briefcase holding airway maps and aircraft manuals]. But come next summer, he's gonna mow my lawn."

Brien Wygle was in charge of the 737's flight test program, and worked with engineering to design a cockpit whose workload would put the least possible stress on two pilots.

"We went to a lot of trouble proving this out," Wygle said. "We didn't have much computer input—they weren't as sophisticated then—but we designed a very simple cockpit management system because the FAA told us that when we came up for certification, they were going to be very tough. They were under great pressure from ALPA, which wanted the FAA to say that the 737 needed a flight engineer or any third crew member."

Tough they were.

"The FAA made us jump through a lot of hoops," Wygle recalled. "There was an unprecedented amount of testing, all kinds of simulated engine and systems failures, low-visibility approaches and landings, and even test flights through high-density traffic on the eastern seaboard. And to the FAA's credit, they ruled that the 737 was completely safe to fly with a two-man crew."

The ruling, however, couldn't recoup the sales Boeing had already lost because of the ALPA campaign; the union itself eventually came around to admitting that a sophisticated, well-designed cockpit didn't need a flight engineer. And in one sense, ALPA did the 737 a favor. It forced Boeing to improve the plane to the point where it would be so good, it didn't matter how many men were in the cockpit.

Jack Steiner's major contribution was identical to the vital decision he had made with the 727: he insisted that the 737 have the same fuselage cross-section width as the three-holer and the 707, providing not only some tooling commonality but the payload advantage of the same six-abreast seating as the larger Boeings; both the DC-9 and the BAC-111, with narrower cabins, offered five-abreast.

The decision to go to the 727-707 cabin diameter in a shorter fuselage created Boeing's first "square" airplane—the 737's length and wingspan were almost identical, giving it a stubby appearance that led to a couple of affectionate if unflattering nicknames. The 737 was "Fluf" to some pilots, for Fat Little Ugly Fella, while Western's pilots always called it "Fat Albert" after Bill Cosby's character.

Wygle was concerned more with the way it flew than the way it looked. With Wallick as his copilot, Wygle flew the 737 for the first time April 9, 1967, and both liked the airplane. "We were used to the 727," Wygle said, "and this was very much like it, which is what we hoped for."

But the early test flights also uncovered an unhappy fact: the thrust reversers were virtually useless.

"All they do is make a lot of noise and smoke, but they don't slow the airplane down," Wygle told Dick Taylor, then engineering director for the 737 program.

Assuming the 727's thrust reversers would work on the 737—a reasonable assumption inasmuch as both airplanes used the same engine at first—turned out to be a $24 million mistake. That's what it cost to redesign the reversers and retrofit them to 737s already built.

Wygle remembered being called in by Ben Wheat, who had been transferred from Wichita to run the 737 program.

"Brien, are you sure we really need the new reversers?" Wheat asked. "It's gonna cost us a bundle."

"I know it's a big chunk to swallow," Wygle replied, "but if this airplane's going to be around for a while, it has to be competitive in reversing capability and I really think we should do it."

"If that's what you think," Wheat said, "then that's what we'll do."

But it wasn't Wheat's final decision to make and he sent Dick Taylor before the corporate executive council to explain about the thrust reversers and the expensive fix.

"It was a long and very detailed presentation," Taylor recalled, "and all the time I was making it Allen was writing in that notebook he always carried into meetings. I figured I was going down the tube but I kept on, stressing the point that United had bought the plane to operate at places like Monterey, Santa Barbara, and other small airports."

When Taylor finished, Allen glanced at his notes. "Several questions came to mind as you were briefing us, Mr. Taylor, but as you proceeded you answered all of them. Perhaps others may have some questions."

No one did, and the $24 million redesign and retrofit was approved. It also was a strong endorsement of Taylor, who in his 40 years at Boeing earned a reputation for integrity in three fields—he was a test pilot, engineer, and executive. There were a few other early headaches—the nacelles were too short, the oleo struts on the landing gear needed modifications, and the initial wing, which failed at 95 percent of maximum load, had to be strengthened.

Joe Sutter's crucial input on where to put the engines turned out to be a key factor in the plane's excellent aerodynamics. It hadn't been an easy decision, either, for in the early going the 737 was conceived as a scaled-down 727 with two aft engines. As Sutter, who had just been promoted to chief of the technology staff, recalled that gestation period:

"The airplane was being put together in Steiner's group and it was looking much like the BAC-111 and DC-9. One day I was sitting in my office and thinking, there's got to be a better way of designing this mousetrap. It was going to fly slower in the configuration we had, because putting engines so close to the fuselage creates drag. With these little airplanes, I felt if you put the nacelle barrels right underneath the wings, and worked the air inlet and exhaust exit properly, you wouldn't have this adverse drag effect. I went down to Jack's office with a rough sketch and told him the airplane would be lighter this way, because you didn't have those heavy aft engines putting a load on the rear fuselage, and you'd get some weight relief on the wings. [This is because the main load on the wings is upward during flight, the dead weight of the engines tending to relieve that load.]

"Jack and I agreed to really compare the two configurations. We had two teams, a red team studying how the plane would perform with two aft engines, and a blue team working on the underwing design. When the results came in, they showed that putting the engines under the wings would provide the same range as the aft design while carrying six more passengers, which amounted to a six percent operating cost advantage. And it allowed us to eliminate the T-tail with its aft engines, which made the 737 an easier airplane to balance."

Another factor in the 737's eventual success was the revised shape of its engine nacelles in later models. To laymen, all nacelles look about the same, but there can be subtle differences crucial to an airplane's aerodynamic characteristics—as important as the shape of the wings and fuselage. The 737-100 and 200 had nacelles very similar to the 727's, but when Boeing introduced the improved and bigger 737-300 in 1984, a far more successful model, it had nacelles with unusual flat-shaped bottoms.

"The 300 was a perfect example of how to shape a nacelle," Sutter explained. "It looked awful with that flat bottom, even weird, but the combined shape of the nacelle and the strut reduced drag markedly. That was really the first time computers were used at Boeing to develop an aerodynamic shape."

There was some opposition within engineering to the underwing engine placement, on the grounds that the airplane was just too small for that configuration. There also was opposition to the flat-bottomed nacelle suggested later for the 737-300, until Bill Hamilton put it through his beloved wind tunnel. His own engineers came charging back to his office with the data and announced, "Those damned flat-bottom nacelles are better than the round ones!"

Where to build the original 737 caused as much controversy as how to build it. Renton was pretty well occupied with 707s and 727s, and while Plant Two was available, it was not the modern manufacturing facility some officials considered essential for production of a new airliner. Wichita wanted the 737 badly and it was a tough call for Allen. He was getting conflicting advice from people he respected, starting with T Wilson, who at the time was vice president of operations and planning. At Boeing, titles didn't always reflect an officer's stature and influence; Jim Prince had such great clout with Allen that he was really an assistant president without any such title. He later served T in a similar manner, and so did Wes Maulden.

Both Wilson and Maulden had recommended to Allen that the 737 be built in Wichita, predicting it would save the company $75 million. Wichita had plenty of skilled manpower, they argued, in contrast to a Seattle work force already diluted by the demands of other airplane programs.

So Allen asked John Yeasting to study the recommendation. Yeasting, supported by Carl Dillon and Bob Regan, came back with a different figure—building the plane in Wichita, he reported, would cost $75 million more than giving the job to Seattle. It was an unhappy Allen who summoned Yeasting.

"John, I'm disappointed," he said. "I've got two men—you and Wilson—whom I respect very much, and they're giving me two conflicting answers."

Yeasting assured him all cost figures had been studied carefully, and that Wilson and Maulden were being too pessimistic about what Seattle could do. He also pointed out that Wichita had almost no experience producing commercial airplanes. Since the 737 program was Yeasting's responsibility, Allen decided against Wichita.

Because Plant Two was judged unsatisfactory for full 737 production and Renton was too busy, Boeing purchased a few acres on East Marginal Way South for a new factory. The site, right across the street from Boeing Field, was owned by Charlie Thompson, a general foreman in the sheet metal department who had had the foresight to buy the land years before. He sold it to Boeing at a nice profit, a deal Bud Hurst resented with bitterness that approached paranoia—he thought Thompson had taken advantage of the company.

The 737 plant was known officially as Building 14-01, but everyone referred to it as the Thompson Site—except in Hurst's presence; just the name Thompson put him into orbit.

Hurst was in his office one day and an underling mentioned that he was going over to the Thompson tract.

Bud turned purple. "You're going *where?*"

"Building 14-01," the offender revised hurriedly.

While the sales force beat the bushes around the world for additional customers, Wygle and his fellow test pilots flew hundreds of hours demonstrating the plane to prospects. South America was a fertile ground for harvesting sales, and Peter Morton, a 737 engineer, went on several trips there because he spoke Spanish with reasonable fluency. He remembered a Boeing salesman named Jim Robinson who had perfected a standard anti-DC-9 spiel known around Boeing as the "Death in the Andes" pitch. He'd suggest that a twin-engine plane wasn't the safest thing to fly in the rugged Andes.

"It's a good thing Boeing has the 727 available to buy instead of the DC-9," he'd tell the customers.

Naturally, the "Death in the Andes" sales approach was frowned upon when Boeing introduced the 737. Yet while the salesmen working South America had reformed, Morton found some of them "predisposed," as he diplomatically phrased it, to convince the airlines they'd be better off with a three-engine transport.

"If they could talk a customer into buying a three-engine airplane instead of a twin," Morton said, "there was no question whose airplane they'd buy—it was the 727. But if they wanted a twin, the salesmen were faced with competing against the DC-9 and all the concessions they might have to make to sell the 737."

The 737's engineering staff took a dim view of what amounted to putting the airplane into a loss leader category—a kind of foot-in-the-door method of ostensibly coming in to sell the 737, and then pitching the 727 instead. Morton recalled one South American sales/demonstration trip when Dick Taylor and Jim Copenhaver of engineering spent a lot of time in the galley going hot and heavy with the accompanying sales representatives who hadn't quite rid themselves of the "Death in the Andes" sales technique. It was supposed to be a private discussion but Morton could hear them arguing from the rear of the plane.

Until Boeing changed the 737's thrust reversers, the plane was not easy to sell—in South America or anywhere else. Its short-field landing capability wasn't any better than the DC-9-30's, a stretched version of the original DC-9-10 series and the baby Boeing's chief competition. In fact, many airlines at first preferred the 727 to its smaller sister as a short-field airplane. But all this changed when Boeing retrofitted with the new reversers, and the engineers already were planning future improvements that would go on later production aircraft—a so-called "advanced package" that widened the pylon struts and added a more powerful version of the Pratt & Whitney JT8D turbofan.

To make the 737 attractive to airlines serving remote areas where airport runways might not even be paved, Boeing developed a kit to protect the engines from gravel, dirt, or sand ingestion. It consisted of a deflector mounted on the nose wheel that stopped stones from ricocheting from the nose wheel tires into the engines.

The nose wheel deflector actually was first designed for the 727 at the request of Alaska Airlines. When the carrier told Boeing it wanted to land its 727s on gravel runways, Morton said almost everyone in engineering laughed at the idea except Mark Gregoire, chief aerodynamicist on the 727-100. He flew to Alaska, inspected some of the primitive runways the airline was using, came back to Seattle and put a team to work on the problem.

It was the deflector feature, in fact, that had helped sell the 727 to Icelandair, a carrier that had never bought a Boeing airplane before, and the man most responsible was Lynn Olason, another of the many engineers who labored generally unsung but were very much appreciated by their peers. Olason had started his 38-year career with Boeing working on the Stratocruiser and was one of Steiner's top assistants in the 727 program; he was in Europe serving as an engineering representative on a 737 sales trip, when he received a telegram ordering him to Iceland for a meeting with Icelandair officials.

The carrier was considering the 727 for its Iceland–Europe routes, but had questioned the safety of a three-engine airplane. Olason assured them the 727 had been certificated for overwater operations, and had adequate fuel reserves if a flight had to divert. The question of Iceland's frequent fogs was raised; suppose, Olason was asked, the two main airports at the south end of the island were fogged in, and planes had to divert to the third airport on the north end, which had only gravel runways.

"No problem," Olason said, and he explained the nose deflector device. "The 727 uses gravel runways in Alaska," he added.

His audience began conversing in Icelandic, obviously not intended for Olason's ears because they were, in effect, agreeing that the visitor from Boeing was full of bull because everyone knew gravel would tear the innards out of a jet engine. What they didn't know was that Olason had understood every word they were saying—his parents were Icelandic and Olason himself hadn't learned to speak English until he was five years old.

He listened to all the disparaging remarks concerning his veracity and blurted, in perfect Icelandic, "You're absolutely wrong—I guarantee you the 727 can use gravel runways!"

That did it; he was invited to be interviewed on radio that night, and the airline bought the 727.

A sales/test pilot team took a 737 to Africa, and a few days after the plane arrived a telegram was sent to Seattle:

"Need soonest coefficient of friction of crushed centipedes on runway."

It seems the airport runway they were using was covered with centipedes up to seven inches long. But the insect carpet wasn't as tricky as some of the other demonstration demands made on the airplane. Morton remembered showing the 737 to the chief pilot of a Spanish airline that had never bought a Boeing airplane before. The pilot told Shirley Holmgreen, the aerodynamicist assigned to the sales team, "I want you to demonstrate a refused takeoff [RTO] tomorrow at an airport, without using thrust reversers, on a runway five thousand feet long and no overruns at either end."

The test called for a takeoff at maximum gross weight, and test pilot Tom Edmonds asked Shirley, "Is this safe?"

"I don't know," she admitted. "I'll have to look at the margins."

Morton was worried. "I had never seen us demonstrate an actual RTO on such a limited runway under those conditions. Shirley was up half the night figuring out the V_1." (V_1 is the minimum speed at which the aircraft can take off safely, or the maximum speed at which the takeoff can be aborted. Precise V_1 speed is determined by aircraft weight, runway length and surface condition, airport altitude above sea level, and outside temperature and humidity.)

The next morning, she gave Edmonds her calculations, assuring him he had sufficient margins to work with.

They drove out to the airport and found it was raining hard. "That won't help," Morton noted glumly.

"I calculated for a wet runway," Holmgreen said.

Just before takeoff, Edmonds turned to the chief pilot. "It's your airplane, Captain. V_1 is one hundred and five knots."

They went thundering down the runway up to 105 knots, chopped the power, and slammed on the brakes. When the 737 stopped, it still had more than 2,000 feet of runway ahead of it. Yet if that shoebox of a field was tough, Wygle and Wallick had to demonstrate the airplane at an even hairier one in Peru. The airport was 10,000 feet above sea level with a 10,000-foot runway, half of which ran uphill and the other half downhill. Sometimes it was the reaction of an airline's pilots that sold the airplane. Thorson was trying to land Eastern Provincial Airlines of Canada and took several of their pilots for a demo ride. Without Boeing knowing it, the EPA airmen had a ringer in their group—an employee who had never flown anything but small planes. With a Boeing test pilot handling the throttles, the neophyte made an excellent landing.

"The airline guys couldn't believe it," Thorson said.

There was one feature in the 737 that raised a few eyebrows—it was the only jet transport built without main landing gear doors. The nose gear had them, but the main wheels merely folded into two cubicles under the fuselage. Almost every airline official who saw the arrangement questioned its aerodynamic efficiency, arguing that it had to create unnecessary drag. But Bill Hamilton's wind tunnel tests proved otherwise, and the absence of the landing gear doors did save precious weight.

The baby was born overweight, typical of most new airliners, and Jim Copenhaver came up with the idea of asking employees for weight-saving suggestions. Boeing received 3,500 suggestions in the first two days, and a number won cash awards.

Lufthansa's Gerhard Hoeltje had a suggestion of his own. Before the first 737 was delivered to Germany, he proposed that Boeing send a worthy employee over with each Lufthansa airplane as representative of the people who actually built the airplane.

"Have each man bring his wife," Hoeltje offered. "We will host them, show them a good time, and let them see our facilities."

Ben Wheat loved the idea, and called in Bill Clark, who was handling public relations for the 737. "Put together a program for selecting the employee who'll go over," Wheat ordered.

"This was really the harbinger of the Employee of the Month Award," Clark recounted. "It was great for motivation, although we didn't send one over on every delivery—it got to be every other flight, and then every third one. But I'll never forget the kid who was the first one chosen. Unfortunately, we picked a guy whose wife was not only pregnant but almost due. She couldn't go and was fit to be tied."

Employee motivation wasn't the major problem in the 737 program; it was employee inexperience. With so many new airplane programs under way, the 737 had the lowest manpower priority among them, and virtually all new employees were funneled into its assembly lines.

Yet this collection of assembly line rookies did contribute to setting a couple of records for a new airliner—the 737 won FAA certification only eight months after its first flight, and six months after certification the production rate hit 14 planes a month. But there were quality control problems with the greenest work force in Boeing, and this added to the program's disturbing overruns.

Considering its late start, 737 sales were better than anyone really expected. While only three major airlines were among the first customers, and Douglas was gobbling up the majority of larger carriers with the DC-9, Boeing built a market base made up of many smaller airlines both in the U.S. and overseas. It wasn't averse to selling only two or three planes to one of these comparative midgets, and by doing so laid the groundwork for future business when the so-called "midgets" grew with increased air traffic. The small orders accumulated to the point where the 737 overall was outselling both the DC-9 and BAC-111 at least two to one, a margin that mushroomed in the 1980s when newer 737 models—the 300, 400, and 500 series—dominated the short-range jet market.

One initial sales gimmick was known unofficially as the "Dirty Pool Mockup," actually three mockups with the first two representing the BAC-111 and the DC-9 cabins, and the third the 737's. They were built at Renton and were arranged so that visiting airline officials had to walk through the DC-9 and BAC-111 first before entering the 737 cabin. It was an effective contrast that demonstrated the latter's wider cabin and greater seating capacity.

As far as being a profitable program, however, success didn't start happening to the 737 until the late 1970s. Production hit a peak in 1968, then everything began bottoming out; only 14 planes were ordered in 1972, and when orders the following year totaled a disappointing 42, serious consideration was given to shutting down the production line.

"It was a dog everyone in the company would have preferred not to have had around," Bill Clark said.

For a time, the 737's only customer was the U.S. Air Force, which bought a few as navigational trainers. "When production based on sales slumped to about one a month," Tex Boullioun remarked, "it looked as if it didn't make much sense to continue the line. With that kind of production rate, you can lose your shirt building the airplane. Each one becomes that much more expensive to manufacture."

T, with some misgivings, made the final decision not to kill the program. Boullioun always believed that Hal Haynes, who was senior vice president of finance in '73, probably did more than anyone else to convince Wilson the airplane had a future. Wes Maulden was for putting "the dog" to sleep, and he wasn't the only officer who thought that way. Some, like Dick Taylor and Ben Wheat, remembered the 737 more for the headaches it caused than the huge success it became.

Taylor summed up his feelings succinctly: "This plane went through a lot of ups and downs, but there were times when it seemed like there were more downs than ups.

"We had production jigs at the start but no experienced people, so we fell behind schedule. We got into every imaginable production problem you could want on an airplane program."

For Wheat, the 737 experience was even more traumatic; in the end, it cost him his job running the program, the only black mark in his long and honorable Boeing career, and one that left him with some bitterness. He was one of the most interesting characters the company ever had—he was almost two people. He was ebullient, warm-hearted, and very funny. At times he also could be somewhat dictatorial and abrasive. His ability was never in question—Wheat's track record at Wichita was what got him the difficult and demanding 737 assignment.

He certainly didn't fit the stereotyped image of a humorless bean counter. Wheat claimed no Boeing security guard ever looked closely at an ID badge. To prove this point, he started coming to work wearing fake badges—he kept a collection of them in his briefcase. One day he'd be Superman, the next day Batman, and he once went past the guard gate unchallenged wearing a badge that identified him as serial killer "Ted Bundy."

Wheat's chief patron at Boeing was C. B. Gracey, the dignified vice president of manufacturing, who seems to have considered Wheat his star pupil. It was Gracey who recommended to Allen that Wheat be promoted to vice president in charge of the Wichita division.

A fellow officer once asked Gracey his opinion of a certain Boeing manager up for promotion. Gracey shook his head. "He doesn't have the verve of Mr. Wheat," he declared.

Someone told Wheat what Gracey had said. "It was a high-order compliment," Ben remarked later, "although I had to look up *verve* in a dictionary."

His contemporaries gave Wheat mixed reviews on his 737 program performance. Some said flatly, "Ben just screwed it up." Others said Wheat was handed an almost impossible task given the circumstances—untrained workers, too many early engineering mistakes, and a production schedule geared to catching up with the DC-9. Wheat's own verdict may come the closest to what really happened:

"Costs were out of control and production schedules messed up. I didn't pay enough attention to costs because I was trying to meet schedules. So I got pretty bloodied up and never recovered."

But Wheat refused to waver from a belief that the 737 should have been built in Wichita, which in his opinion had higher productivity than Seattle and wouldn't have had to contend with an inexperienced work force. In Wichita, he argued, the 737 would have been given a priority status it lacked in Seattle, where it was treated more like a stepchild who wasn't fed until the bigger, more glamorous sisters finished eating.

The 737-200, the model originally delivered to United and put into service April 28, 1968, stayed in production until June 1988—four years after the 300 series was introduced. Only about 30 of the 100 series were built, and it was the 200 that waged most of the uphill battle against the DC-9. It succeeded because it *had* to be better than its able competitors.

Before Wheat left the 737 program late in 1969, T sent Bud Hurst over to help straighten out production problems. Hurst admitted, however, that Wheat himself was operating under handicaps not of his own making. Bud blamed Yeasting and Regan, among others, for selling Allen the wrong bill of goods when they claimed the 737 could be built more efficiently in Seattle. "They sent the darnedest bunch of junk that ever was over to Plant Two to build that airplane," he declared. "I guess they figured it would be built by itself."

One basic mistake right from the start was assuming that the 737 fuselage, being identical to the 727 in cross-section width, could utilize identical jigs. It couldn't: because the short-range 737 would make more landings and takeoffs, and the pressurization cycles would be more frequent, the 737 required a slightly thicker skin, and the 727 jigs didn't quite fit. In that sense, commonality didn't really add up to lower costs.

"Steiner didn't tell us how uncommon the two planes really were," Carl Dillon complained. "By the time we realized this, it was too late."

Hurst actually was in the third wave of production managers sent in to rescue the 737 from its problems.

"The thing that really dug us out was Wichita," Hurst said. "They sent me about six hundred mechanics who helped tremendously. Until all this was done, we just had too many inexperienced people."

At one time, the faltering 737 program was considered a managerial nightmare to be avoided at all costs by anyone who didn't want his Boeing career jeopardized—it went too long without a real leader, Wilson believed.

"There were a lot of guys in lower management levels who were asked to go down there and refused because they honestly believed it was a kiss of death," Bob Dickson related. "It had to be someone with a thick skin and a hard nose like Bud Hurst who could straighten everything out."

Difficult though the program was, the smallest of Boeing's jetliner family stands as a huge monument to the company's resilience and perseverance, its ability to overcome mistakes as well as adversity, its insistence on product improvement and product support rather than product abandonment, even in the blackest days. And there were plenty of those, both at the start and later when sales had dried up. Some officers honestly thought it was time to give up on Boeing's ugly duckling.

It survived for several reasons, first and foremost being the reputation it earned for itself as a reliable, efficient, economical transport fully capable of doing the job for which it was designed. Second, because enough people at Boeing had faith in the little bird. And third, because two of the programs with which the 737 competed for engineering talent never got past the mockup stage.

One would have been the world's fastest commercial transport; the other the world's largest military transport.

SIXTEEN

THE DREAM AND
THE SHAFT

THE SUPERSONIC TRANSPORT WAS A CASE OF BOEING WIN-
ning a battle but losing the war.

Its engineers had begun dreaming about a supersonic airliner as far
back as 1957, when the company established a small SST design team.
Three years earlier, Boeing had started building its own supersonic
wind tunnel, a project pushed by George Schairer. T Wilson was in
preliminary design at the time, working on a supersonic bomber, and
Schairer told him he could make a greater contribution by taking over
the design and construction of the wind tunnel.

It was in operation by the time the SST team went to work—already
three years behind the British who had launched a supersonic transport
study project in 1954, the same year Boeing authorized its wind tunnel.

Across the English Channel, the French were thinking supersonic,
too; at the 1960 Paris Air Show, Sud Aviation unveiled a scale model of
the Super Caravelle, a medium-range SST. Both England and France,
however, quickly realized that developing a supersonic transport was
too costly for either country to undertake alone; on November 29,
1962, they signed the Anglo-French Supersonic Aircraft Agreement, a
pact that led to the creation of the famed Concorde—still the world's
only operational SST.

To save some time and also reduce the enormous development costs,
the Concorde's designers settled jointly on an aluminum airplane, a
decision that dictated a Mach 2.2 aircraft because the heat generated
by supersonic speed would weaken aluminum above that speed—1,450
mph. The Russians, anxious to beat everyone to a flyable SST, reached
the same conclusion; their TU-144 also would be primarily an aluminum bullet.

The U.S. was proceeding at a much slower and more modest pace,
and wouldn't have been moving at much of any pace except for
President John F. Kennedy's almost obsessive desire not to have Amer-

ica fall behind in any phase of aerospace technology. Into his very receptive ears fell the advice of Najeeb Halaby, JFK's choice as FAA administrator, who early in 1961 recommended that the government fund preliminary design studies for an American SST—a Mach 2.5 steel-titanium airliner with non-stop transatlantic and transcontinental range, carrying up to 175 passengers.

Halaby's proposal collided almost immediately with Air Force opposition, mostly from chief of staff Curtis LeMay who feared that any money spent on an SST would dilute funding for the B-70 supersonic bomber, a project that had been cancelled by former President Eisenhower but revived under the new Kennedy administration. LeMay saw no military use for a supersonic transport and neither did his boss, Defense Secretary Robert McNamara.

The FAA administrator continued to press his case with the White House, and also sounded out the airlines and aerospace companies on the feasibility of an American-made SST. The carriers expressed support for the idea in general, but with no specific commitment; they reminded Halaby they were still paying for the transition to subsonic jets. The airframe and engine manufacturers were more enthusiastic but with one huge reservation: they unanimously agreed that development costs would be so astronomically high, private financing was out of the question—no single company or even a combination of firms could afford the technical and financial risks.

No one was more adamant on this subject than Boeing's Bill Allen, and no one's opinion impressed Washington more. The FAA chief proceeded accordingly, forming a special government-industry task force that eventually urged JFK to ask Congress for authorization to proceed with a federally financed SST program that would cost between $1 billion and $1.5 billion. That sum, it was estimated, would pay for the design, construction, and flight testing of two prototypes.

The task force further recommended that the design, including such factors as speed, range, payload, and type of material used in construction, be determined by a competition among the airframe and engine manufacturers. The minimum goal was an SST with a 4,000-mile range, carrying at least 150 passengers.

Vice President Lyndon Johnson was named head of a special committee to implement the task force's recommendations, which weren't really set in motion until LBJ himself became president. Gordon Bain, a former Northwest Airlines official, was the first director of the FAA's supersonic transport program. When Halaby left the government to become president of Pan Am, his successor—William "Bozo" McKee—named Air Force General Jewell Maxwell as the new SST chief. But the key government official in the post during the final and most controversial months of the supersonic transport program was a crew-cut former Air Force officer and Lockheed test pilot named William Magruder.

From the very beginning, the competing companies were wedded to the idea of an SST built largely of titanium, and so was the FAA. In fact, before the British agreed to a joint SST project with France, they had approached Washington with a similar proposal and were turned down because no U.S. aviation official was interested in an aluminum supersonic transport; aluminum construction, they felt, would limit the plane's speed, payload, and growth to an unacceptable degree.

Under the original authorization bill put before Congress in 1963, the government would underwrite 75 percent of the prototypes' development costs and the two winning manufacturers (airframe and engines) the rest, but to make the project more palatable to American taxpayers, the legislation also called for the federal funding to be repaid through royalties on every SST sold. The 75–25 ratio was revised to 90–10 before the bill cleared Congress, and the battle was on.

When Boeing first established a supersonic transport organization, program headquarters were above a drugstore in Bellevue, a Seattle suburb, a location reflecting the group's low-priority status. Later, as the program grew in scope, the SST was transferred to the Developmental Center on East Marginal Way, just down the street from where the 737 was being assembled.

"We were kind of second cousins at first," recalled Don Smith, who was head of facilities in the SST program. "We'd ask for a thousand feet of office space and we'd be lucky to get eight hundred. But what this status created was a real esprit de corps—we were going to make this program work, come hell or high water."

Maynard Pennell and Bill Cook originally spearheaded the SST program, starting out with a small staff of fewer than 60 that mushroomed when the government got serious about building an American supersonic transport. Almost from the beginning, the Boeing team concentrated on a design concept that looked beautiful in theory but proved extremely difficult to execute. They envisioned an all-titanium SST with the range of a 707 Intercontinental, Mach 2.7 speed, and a 250-passenger capacity, plus the ability to take off and land using no more runway length than the largest 707 while producing acceptable noise levels both on approach and takeoff.

That was a pretty tall order to fill, especially the last two requisites. To achieve noise reduction to the level of a conventional jet, the Boeing SST would need a 707's approach speed; Pennell and Cook at first were in agreement that this could be accomplished only by designing a variable-sweep wing, or "swing wing" as it came to be called—a wing with virtually no sweep during the takeoff or approach/landing phases, which then folded back into an arrow-shaped "delta" wing for supersonic flight.

But Pennell and Cook gradually came to loggerheads over the swing

wing concept; Cook thought more research was needed before Boeing committed itself to this radical design, while Pennell believed there was no other way to go. Eventually, project delays reached Allen's ears and he borrowed T Wilson to audit the SST program. T had assumed the main problem was the overruns associated with a new high-tech airplane, but he was surprised to discover that the Pennell–Cook dispute was the chief source of trouble.

On T's recommendation, Allen pulled Bob Withington off the C-5 program and assigned him to the SST. By that time, however, the designers had gone so far down the swing wing road, Boeing already was committed; Pennell's role became advisory, and Cook went along reluctantly, still believing in the concept but convinced its development needed more time. But there wasn't more time—the swing wing was Boeing's major selling point in the SST competition, the one feature no one else had.

It was no secret that Boeing's two major SST competitors, Lockheed and North American (Douglas backed out of the race early in the game), preferred the simpler delta wing, convinced that the pivots required for moving a variable-sweep wing back and forth involved too much weight; both were willing to accept greater noise instead of weight penalty. Boeing, on the other hand, firmly believed the swing wing was the only way an SST would be welcome at major U.S. airports. Withington and the rest of his team were confident they could lick the weight problem inherent in the massive, 40,000-pound pivots that moved the wings, although they recognized this was the greatest hurdle to be overcome.

The Mach 2.7 (more than 1,900 mph) goal was determined from supersonic wind tunnel data showing this to be the maximum attainable speed consistent with the use of titanium. Giving the Boeing SST a 250-passenger configuration was aimed at producing a viable aircraft for the airlines; there was unanimous agreement that the Concorde's projected payload of fewer than 150 seats was too small. And the TU-144 prototype, so closely resembling the delta-wing Concorde that the British and French press referred to it as the "Concordski," had a passenger capacity of 121. The Boeing SST (and Lockheed's as well) not only would have far greater range, but all-titanium construction provided a growth potential impossible to achieve with an aluminum airplane.

The Soviet SST was the first to fly—December 31, 1968—and was followed two months later by a French-built Concorde prototype. At that point in time, all Boeing had was a magnificent plywood mockup constructed at the Developmental Center. But the Russians had won a Pyrrhic victory; in 1973, while demonstrating the TU-144 at the Paris Air Show, the Soviet SST stalled during a steep climb and crashed. The Soviet Union never made the cause of the accident public, nor did it ever explain why the TU-144, after only 10 months of regular passenger flights, was suddenly withdrawn permanently from service.

North American and the Curtiss Wright engine were eliminated from U.S. SST preliminary design competition, leaving Boeing and Lockheed the remaining airframe combatants and General Electric battling Pratt & Whitney for the engine award. Down the stretch came these aerospace giants, with Lockheed favored by most aviation experts because of well-founded rumors that Boeing was having fits with the swing wing's weight. Yet Boeing had more support than Lockheed among the airlines, which were paying the FAA $100,000 for each guaranteed delivery position, refundable if the plane didn't go into production. The pro-Boeing sentiment was largely based on their belief that if anyone was going to build a safe, viable, environmentally acceptable supersonic transport, Boeing was the best one to do it. The airlines apparently were as sold on the sweep wing as Boeing's engineers, feeling it would be less noisy and easier to fly than a delta wing SST. The weight penalty, of course, was Boeing's problem, not theirs.

Boeing's SST team was closely knit and high-spirited. Symbolic of its "we're gonna win" attitude was a huge plywood cutout of the SST hung on the side of the Development Center. It could easily be seen by passing traffic on East Marginal Way, and it stood out like the Statue of Liberty in New York Harbor.

It stood out even more when one night an unknown employee mounted a six-foot replica of Snoopy on the top of the fuselage. Withington saw it the next morning when he arrived at the Center and hit the ceiling. Furious, he called Don Smith.

"Find out who did it and fire the son of a bitch!" he ordered.

Smith couldn't have located the culprit with the combined help of the FBI, CIA, the entire Seattle police force, and Perry Mason. But he didn't have to, because Withington got a call from T Wilson that same morning.

"You see that Snoopy riding the SST?" T asked. Before Withington could reply, Wilson enthused, "Greatest idea anyone ever had—I hear it's going to be on network television!"

"You're right, T," Withington gulped. "Great idea."

"To this day," Smith said, "no one knows who did it."

On September 29, 1966, Boeing unveiled the $11 million SST mockup to the media, airline officials, and other VIPs—a spectacular show. The visitors were gathered on a balcony in the Developmental Center; a bridge connected the balcony to the mockup, which was bathed in darkness until the moment of unveiling. A series of spotlights came on one by one, illuminating the immense needle-nose blue and white plane in sections. The last spotlight threw its beam at the large "USA" on the tail, as a voice intoned over a loudspeaker:

"This . . . is the Boeing supersonic transport!"

The onlookers applauded spontaneously, and applauded more when the mockup's nose bobbed up and down. Like the Concorde, the Boeing SST had a "droop snoot"—for takeoffs and landings, the nose could be lowered to provide normal cockpit visibility, and raised during supersonic flight to create perfect aerodynamic streamlining.

"Welcome to the Boeing SST," the loudspeaker announced, and the guests were ushered across the bridge into the mockup's interior—as spectacular as the exterior. Walter Dorwin Teague Associates had designed the cabin layout, the seats alternating among deep reds and purples, blended with splashes of orange. The carpeting was an attractive shade of blue. Each seatback contained an individual television screen and there was a "phone-vision" system for passengers to call their offices or home when cruising at more than 1,900 mph. The windows were only five and a half inches in diameter, giving visitors the feeling they were in a windowless plane.

Brochures were distributed describing the technical details of the 2707, the Boeing SST's official designation. What the brochure did not mention, of course, were the headaches that swing wing was giving the engineers, the largest migraine after the weight problem being where to hang the engines. They finally decided to mount them under the horizontal tailplane to give the wings more room to sweep, an arrangement that displeased crusty Bill Cook; he not only disliked any aft-engine configuration, but thought Boeing was trying to rush things in an area of aerodynamics that needed more research. And that was Cook's frankly professed goal: to keep Boeing from rushing everything.

He was head of the transport division's technical staff when he was assigned to the SST. "I had in mind a research effort restricted to the high-tech side," he was to write in a memoir after he retired. "There were others who enthusiastically wanted to gear up for manufacturing and even facility planning."

Cook was convinced that further research was all John Yeasting really had in mind when Bill went over to the program—and Yeasting was one of the few executives this incurable iconoclast genuinely respected. Cook didn't like the delta wing, admitting it was easier to design "but presumably an aerodynamic compromise," as he put it, and he never stopped believing that no one could design and build a practical supersonic transport airframe without an equally practical engine. This was the same conclusion Withington himself eventually would reach.

Lockheed had decided on a delta wing—actually a "double-delta" design—and it was a delta wing SST mockup Lockheed had displayed in a similar "Hollywood premiere" atmosphere three months before the Boeing show. The Boeing-vs-Lockheed SST war boiled down to the swing-vs-delta-wing debate that supposedly was settled December 31, 1966, when the FAA announced the winning airframe and engine companies.

The agency had not relied solely on its own technical people; it enlisted the advice of more than 200 experts including a number of top airline engineers. No one envied them their task, particularly choosing between Boeing and Lockheed and their diametrically opposed wing designs. The far less complicated delta wing, it was noted, had only 16 moving control surfaces; the swing wing required 59, including triple-slotted flaps and retractable canards (miniature wings on each side of the forward fuselage to enhance stability). Offsetting this admitted complexity was the undeniable fact that the variable-sweep provided more flexibility: an airplane that took off and landed like a conventional jet, yet still could cover almost three miles every five seconds.

Most of the betting was on Lockheed, but the FAA picked Boeing and General Electric as the respective manufacturers.

There is little doubt that environmental issues influenced the experts' decision; Boeing's design seemed more ecologically compatible. But having hitched its wagon to the swing wing, Boeing now had to face up to really making it work. Wisely, Withington kept a small group busy on a delta design just in case, emphasizing that whatever they produced, it had to be better than Lockheed's.

He had some good people on his team, including a pair of relative newcomers who cut their Boeing career teeth on the SST. One was John Swihart, like Mal Stamper a Georgia Tech graduate, who was running wind tunnels at NASA's Langley Field and got to know a number of Boeing wind tunnel devotees, among them Schairer, Withington, and "Wind Tunnel" Hamilton himself, who actually hired him.

The other engineer of future prominence was Phil Condit, who joined Boeing three years after Swihart as a brand-new graduate engineer out of Princeton. He was sent to Langley where the Dash-80 was being used to simulate supersonic flight. The controls had been separated so that the left side of the cockpit was a conventional 707 layout, while the right side was an SST simulator flown by computer. Condit was a stability control engineer, and his job was to compare the handling characteristics of different SST configurations.

In the mid-1960s, both Swihart and Condit were just part of the SST team trying to justify a design concept that simply was beyond the state of the art. Boeing's growing doubts on the swing wing were confirmed by General Maxwell, who bluntly informed T Wilson that Boeing was doing a "lousy job" with the SST. Wes Maulden was assigned to the project along with Ken Holtby to help with the engineering. Forrest "Bud" Coffey, who had started with Boeing in Wichita in 1948 as a proposal planner, was with the SST group then as Pennell's administrative assistant, and recalled that the main problem was not in the project's administration or engineering.

"There were some good people in the program," Coffey said, "but they were mostly from the commercial side because it was supposed to be a commercial venture. Well, the customer in this case was the government, which was paying for ninety percent of the program, and it was one hell of a problem for guys used to making their own decisions in dealing with a customer."

Withington didn't need the FAA looking over his shoulder before he bowed to the inevitable, even though the inevitable meant eating crow in front of Lockheed's engineers and everyone else who said the variable-swing wing wouldn't work. Boeing went with a modified delta wing that had an unusual amount of inboard sweep for high-Mach cruise, and less outboard sweep for low-speed stability. To this new aerodynamic wing the engineers added leading and trailing edge devices, balanced out with a horizontal tail. The wind tunnel confirmed that this combination would give the SST a slightly higher approach and landing speed than a 707, but far less than either the Lockheed plane or the Concorde—an engineering achievement that did the team proud.

To Withington fell the task of making a world tour to advise airlines who had signed for delivery positions that Boeing had switched to a delta wing.

"A certain amount of eating crow was involved," he admitted, "but it wasn't as bad as I feared. I honestly don't think Boeing won the competition because of variable sweep. In fact, I believe the airlines actually preferred Lockheed's design but told the FAA they'd rather have Boeing build the airplane."

The new wing design wasn't the only feature of this plane-that-never-was. In the final configuration, the engines were located on the trailing edge of the wings. The air inlets were positioned in such a way as to shield them behind the shock waves of supersonic flight, so the engines actually experienced a lower Mach number than the airplane was flying. The Boeing SST would have had completely electronic controls—the "fly-by-wire" system used on some of today's jets—with four separate systems for redundancy.

The SST's noise suppression engineering was equally impressive. The 2707, unlike the Concorde, would have needed after-burners for takeoff, and after-burners make hard rock sound like a violin concerto. Boeing's noise suppression system consisted of numerous little retractable tubes; unretracted, they would catch the exhaust stream and block the noise, then retract out of the stream as the aircraft's after-burners kicked in and accelerated to Mach 1 and beyond. In Swihart's opinion, the SST wouldn't have been any noisier than a late model 707 or DC-8.

But that wasn't good enough for Withington, who thought the mighty GE engine, capable of producing 60,000 pounds of thrust (the Concorde's Rolls Olympus developed 38,000), was too loud for any noise suppression system to overcome. His unhappiness with the engine led to a dispute with Bill Magruder, who by then was running the government's SST program.

"It was a long time in coming," Withington related, "and it involved the problem of airport noise. This went from no problem to a major problem. The engine that was being built was absolutely unacceptable for airports, even though GE had spent millions on it. I wanted to make sure Bill knew that the engine couldn't survive in a commercial environment, so I had a long talk with him.

"I told him I wasn't going to kid him—that we had to have a new engine. Magruder wouldn't accept this. He called Bill Allen and told him I was screwing up the whole program by telling him the engine's no damned good. Hell, I was just trying to make sure the government knew what was happening and I didn't want them to come back and claim we never warned them."

Events were to render the engine feud moot, and those events consisted of a massive anti-SST campaign involving several influential congressmen, the media, and the privately financed Citizens' League Against the Sonic Boom organized by Harvard scientist William Shurcliff, who as much as anyone else became the SST's *bête noire*.

Shurcliff's role in swinging public, congressional, and press attitudes against the supersonic transport cannot be underestimated. He personally began generating enough scare stories to convince the public that the SST was the worst thing to afflict the world since the bubonic plague. Admittedly, some of those caveats belonged in science fiction, such as one scientist's warning that traveling on a supersonic transport would shorten life expectancy because you'd literally be living your life too fast. But Shurcliff did find plenty of experts to join him in claiming that the sonic boom menace alone would create incalculable environmental harm.

The Concorde itself was to refute most of the scare stories; British Airways and Air France by the end of 1991 had completed nearly 16 years of accident-free, scheduled SST service with not one of all the dire predictions coming true. But the Concorde didn't enter service until 1976, five years after the SST controversy in the U.S. reached its climax. To the doubts Shurcliff and other SST opponents had created, many of them unfounded, were added some very legitimate concerns. Most of them centered around the enormous cost of developing a supersonic transport that the airlines would buy more in self-defense than anything else.

With the Kennedy, Johnson, and later Nixon administrations all supporting the U.S. supersonic transport, one that would be bigger and faster than the Concorde, airline interest in the latter dwindled and left the field wide open for Boeing. But it was a reluctant field; while 13 foreign carriers and seven U.S. airlines, plus one aircraft leasing company, had reserved 91 delivery positions for the American SST, Boeing itself diluted some of the enthusiasm when it began offering delivery positions for the giant 747. The supersonic transport became an airplane that an airline was afraid *not* to buy, just in case a competitor did.

It also became an airplane with just too many enemies. The media itself was overwhelmingly anti-SST, which didn't help, such influential newspapers as the *New York Times, Wall Street Journal,* and *Washington Post* running almost incessant critical editorials and unflattering cartoons portraying the SST as everything from a flying white elephant to a plaything for billionaires. With syndicated columnists adding their own disparaging comments, the public was being fed an almost daily dose of attacks on the project. It was no wonder that congressional constituent mail was largely anti-SST.

Boeing's SST team knew what the score was—the unending propaganda war against the airplane, hostile congressional hearings, a constant avalanche of opposing editorials across the nation, a steady erosion of support among lawmakers who were reading their mail from home, and the yo-yo aspects of government funding. The whole program was on a constant roller-coaster road, full of high peaks and deep valleys, and it was a minor miracle that morale stayed so consistently high.

The SST's fate was decided in Washington, D.C., shortly after midnight May 20, 1971, when the Senate refused to vote further funding for development. By that time, more than $1 billion had been spent on the design itself and Boeing had just started cutting metal for the first plane. The latest estimate for actually finishing the two SST prototypes had soared to some $4 billion and even the Nixon administration had lost heart to continue the fight. The president had asked his Scientific Advisory Council to monitor the project, expecting it to recommend its continuation if only on the basis of national prestige. Instead, the group submitted a blistering report urging cancellation on both environmental and economic grounds.

Almost to the last, the SST team held out hope the program could somehow be saved, even though the odds against it were insurmountable. On May 19, when the Senate was nearing a vote, people kept coming into Maynard Pennell's office to hear the latest reports from Washington. The overflow crowded into Bud Hurst's office—Hurst was in charge of SST production.

In retrospect, the Boeing supersonic transport was the right plane at the wrong time—a dream shattered for the wrong reasons. It was defeated largely because it was regarded as an unjustifiably expensive environmental menace, and the coalition that opposed it was too formidable to be overcome by an aircraft that hadn't even been built yet and never got a chance to prove environmental soundness. From a purely practical standpoint, however, it probably was just as well the program died in 1971. No one could have foreseen the price of jet fuel going from 10 cents a gallon to a dollar, which would have made this particular SST an economic disaster just when it was ready to enter service.

The only real argument in favor of continuing the program was technical. Having already spent some $1 billion on development, it might have made sense to go ahead with the construction of a single SST prototype as a test aircraft, one that might have laid to rest all the ecological and safety fears.

Boeing engineers spent 8.5 million man-hours on the design, and three days after the program was cancelled, Boeing received a $250 million shipment of stressed titanium skin. There were 1,500 people assigned to the SST; many had to be laid off. The 288-foot-long SST mockup was put up for sale, but most of the early bids were from companies who wanted Boeing to pay them for hauling it away.

The winning bid of only $31,000 was submitted by an entrepreneur who trucked it in sections to Kissimmee in central Florida, between Cape Kennedy and Walt Disney World. There it became part of an aerospace museum. The museum, located in an old hangar, folded a few years later and a church group purchased the hangar with the SST mockup thrown in. For a number of years, church services were held in the shadow of the giant plane, but in the summer of 1990, the church decided the building needed renovation and put the mockup up for sale again.

Art Lowell, who was director of finance on the SST project, kept a piece of the mockup's blue carpeting in his home; when the program was cancelled, Withington had sections of the rug cut into small squares that were given away as mementoes.

"Part of the great esprit de corps on the project was because we were all alone," Lowell said. "We weren't really part of commercial and we weren't part of the military division. We were part of only ourselves.

"Toward the end, everyone knew it was going to be cancelled. From an economics view, it didn't make sense just like the Concorde doesn't make sense. But from a technological point of view, we could have learned a great deal by flying a prototype; for example, acquiring some real understanding of how to work titanium.

"I think everyone associated with the program found it a great experience. That Snoopy gag represented how we all felt. One of the prime suspects, incidentally, was Bud Hurst. I always thought that if Bud didn't do it, somebody had to have talked to him before doing it."

The SST program was an unhappy experience for Bill Cook in the final years of his Boeing career, a maverick right to the day he retired in 1974. Someone asked him what he thought Boeing should do to secure its future.

"Burn down everything north of the wind tunnel," Cook growled.

That would have included the administration building, of course. Yet most of the executives he used to blister, battle, and berate never lost their own respect for this curmudgeon. His fierce independence, irascibility, and uncompromising honesty were all accepted as part of Cook's personality; like T Wilson, one of the few officers Bill *did* respect, he never tried to win any popularity contests.

Above all else, he was a perfectionist. To Bert Welliver, a young engineer hired away from Curtiss Wright as a specialist in jet engines and assigned to the SST program, Cook was "the biggest walking encyclopedia in terms of accuracy I've ever known."

Years after Bill retired, Welliver accompanied Cook, Wally Buckley, George Schairer, George Martin, and Dick Rouzie to Washington where the five veterans were Boeing's guests on a special occasion: Joe Sutter's induction as a fellow of the American Institute of Aeronautics and Astronautics. In addition to the black tie dinner honoring Sutter, the quintet of old war horses visited the Smithsonian's Silver Hill, Maryland, facility, where the museum restored and kept in storage vintage aircraft for future display. A special guide took the Boeing group on a tour.

All went well until they came to a long-range Japanese bomber, designed to attack the Panama Canal, and the guide proudly explained how much effort the museum was making to achieve an absolutely authentic restoration. Right in the middle of his discourse, Cook interrupted.

"You've got your running lights on backward," he observed sourly.

"No, they're not," the guide insisted. "They're installed perfectly."

Cook shook his head. "The hell they are. During the war, the Japanese had the lights on the other way and the only reason you've got the lights this way is because they were taking it to the United States and thought they had to switch 'em over to where we put our running lights."

"We finally came to the *Enola Gay*," Welliver related, "and sure enough, Cook straightened him out on the B-29, too. I had to feel sorry for that poor guide—by the time the tour ended, he was a basket case. He didn't realize he was up against three generations of Boeing engineers."

After he retired, Cook kept in contact with a number of younger engineers, among them Welliver who said Bill treated him "as if I still worked for him and like I'm doing everything wrong."

Veterans like Cook had witnessed defeats as well as victories in their careers, and the one that rankled as much as any was the setback suffered even while Boeing was fighting the SST war.

The supreme irony of the C-5, or C-5A as it is more commonly known, is that Boeing thought up the concept of a giant military transport and ended up on the sidelines watching another company build it.

Since the mid-1950s, the workhorse of the Air Force's airlift fleet had been the superb Lockheed C-130 Hercules, a four-engine propjet whose only drawbacks were payload and speed—in reliability and the ability to take off and land at fields that would have daunted a bulldozer, it had no equal and had won over competing designs from Boeing, Douglas, Martin, and Convair.

Its supposed successor was another Lockheed product, the C-141 Starlifter, an all-jet transport but one with disappointing cargo capacity; it carried less load than a KC-135, and it was Boeing which first proposed to the Air Force that it consider a much larger airlift plane. The timing couldn't have been better; the Pentagon, which had drawn up the Starlifter's specifications, had discovered much to its embarrassment that one-third of an army division's current equipment couldn't fit into a C-141.

Airlift mobility, including fast loading and unloading capability, was the magic word in modern warfare. The 1948 Berlin Airlift had required a fleet of more than 200 planes; the same missions flown by the kind of plane Boeing had in mind would have needed only a dozen aircraft.

So in 1964, the Pentagon had informal meetings with leading manufacturers on proposed designs, then narrowed the field down to three prospective bidders: Boeing, Lockheed, and Douglas. Bob Withington remembered that Boeing's 747 specifications submitted later to the airlines were an inch and a half thick, plus a one-page summary of projected performance. "The C-5A proposal," Withington said, "required Boeing to lease a DC-6 cargo plane to carry all the paperwork to Wright Field for evaluation."

The competitive juices flowed copiously. Don Sachs was on Boeing's proposal team; Lockheed's group included an able lawyer, Dave Renfrue. Colonel Tex Rankin, the Air Force's C-5A project officer (he was later succeeded by Guy Townsend) went into a round of introductions and came to Renfrue.

"This is Dave Renfrue of Lockheed," he announced.

"How do you spell that?" Sachs inquired politely.

"R-e-n . . ." Rankin began.

"No," Sachs interrupted. "How do you spell Lockheed?"

There were two judging categories: technical and price. Lockheed, with a $1.9 billion bid for 115 airplanes, was the lowest. Douglas bid $2 billion and Boeing was the highest at $2.3 billion. The 350-man Air Force evaluation team tore Lockheed's design apart and virtually eliminated Douglas.

An Air Force officer told Withington, who was on the C-5A program in its initial phase, that Boeing's bid was too high.

"How much is too high?"

"I can't tell you that."

"You told Lockheed and Douglas what was wrong with their airplanes," Withington pointed out. "In definite terms, how bad off are we?"

The officer still refused to cite a specific figure, but after Douglas was eliminated, Boeing lowered its bid by $100 million, while Lockheed was allowed to submit a one-page letter stating that they would meet performance requirements.

Ken Holtby couldn't believe that kind of leeway. "It was nothing but a paper promise to improve an airplane the Air Force's own evaluation team had found deficient," Holtby said. "Lockheed didn't have to say how they were going to improve their performance, what specific changes would be required, or how much they would cost."

It wasn't enough for Boeing simply to submit a $100 million lower bid; it had to justify how it was going to make that kind of cut. T Wilson, Ed Wells, Bob Withington, and Howard Neffner—then vice president of government contracts and an amiable man the Air Force trusted implicitly—met in Dayton with Allen to discuss the situation. There was a quick and relatively easy engineering solution: a simpler, cheaper, and yet superior landing gear would provide justification for most of the lower bid.

But when they informed the Air Force of the revised and improved landing gear, they realized the fight was not only far from won but almost hopeless.

"Your problem isn't with us," an Air Force evaluation officer told them. "It's with our contracts people. Boeing's bid is still too high."

This news got back to Allen, who refused to go any lower and was said to have remarked, "Well, if we have to reduce our price to match Lockheed, there must be some better way to use our resources."

The company's C-5A presentation included the usual viewfoils for overhead projection and glitzy brochures; Maynard Wege, who was in the hard-working graphics department that produced such materials, recalled the unofficial brochure slogan under which everyone operated: "Spare no expense to make it look cheap."

The business of producing the visual presentations was equally hectic. One illustrator remarked to Wege, "Our charts should show how busy we'd be if we weren't so busy making charts."

Viewfoils and flip charts had become the company's lifeblood. When Bob Nielsen first went to work for the graphics department, a veteran explained to him why Boeing made so many viewfoils.

"You gotta realize, Nielsen, that the entire Boeing company consists of buildings with long halls. Off these halls are hundreds of little rooms. If you look into any of these rooms, you'll see two guys. All day long each guy takes turns showing the other one his viewfoils."

But in the C-5A competition, Boeing's most dramatic promotion gimmick had nothing to do with flip charts or viewfoils. It was a movie that involved Sam Lowry of finance, who had been asked to help put the presentation together. T Wilson was head honcho of the RFP team, but Lowry didn't bother to consult with T when he decided to become the Cecil B. De Mille of Boeing.

A full-scale C-5A mockup had been built at the Army's Fort Lewis near Tacoma, Washington.

"Our scenario was fashioned around that mockup," Lowry related. "We put a cockpit mockup on top of a truck, thirty-eight feet high, and drove the truck down a runway with a camera shooting from inside that cockpit so it looked as if they were filming the start of an actual takeoff.

"Then Jack Waddell [Boeing test pilot] took a 727 down the same runway, also with a nose camera, rotated the aircraft, and took off. By superimposing the 727 footage on the shots from the truck-mounted cockpit, we created the illusion of a C-5A taking off. We used the same technique for simulating a landing."

The next stage was to film what the cavernous Boeing C-5A could carry. Out of the fuselage mockup rolled troops, jeeps, artillery pieces, and a tank. Then a voice-over-camera announced, "Here comes a secret weapon that will shorten any war."

A bugle sounded the cavalry charge.

And from the mockup thundered a troop of real cavalry—horses ridden by troopers in authentic 19th-century uniforms waving sabers. "It could have been filmed by John Ford," Lowry chortled happily. "Those soldiers looked like Custer's Seventh Cavalry regiment at the battle of Little Big Horn. As a matter of fact, the modern Seventh Cavalry was stationed at Fort Lewis and Waddell had arranged for the vintage Indian War uniforms, the rented horses, and everything else."

The C-5A team thought it was the greatest stunt since De Mille parted the Red Sea for Paramount, but at the higher levels there were two exceptions: both Ed Wells and T considered the horse cavalry charge too undignified, and called in Boeing's De Mille to register their objections.

"Look," Lowry argued, "we want to be different and not take ourselves too seriously. This is going to be a great presentation because it'll convey the message that we have a great airplane capable of doing anything the Air Force and Army want it to do."

T and Wells relented to the extent of letting Lowry show the film to Bill Allen who much to their surprise approved it. The brief movie brought down the house when it was shown at Wright Field, but unfortunately the final script was written in Washington, D.C., and it didn't have a typical Hollywood happy ending for Boeing.

Lockheed won the contract and right to the day he retired, T Wilson boiled every time someone mentioned the C-5A.

"We won the program technically," T declared, "though Lockheed did underbid us by a considerable amount. But then Lockheed screwed it up because they didn't have the technical base for a successful program, and the C-5A went over its budget by two billion dollars. Our airplane had more range and carried more payload, so the government wound up paying about one and a half billion dollars more than what it would have spent if it had picked Boeing."

Admittedly, other reasons were involved in Lockheed's victory. The Pentagon obviously was aware that Lockheed, with virtually no commercial airplane business since its disastrous Electra program, badly needed the C-5A contract—more so than Boeing, it undoubtedly reasoned. This is a factor that has plagued Boeing on more than one occasion—the attitude that because of its success in commercial airplane sales, it doesn't need military business as badly as other aerospace firms, even though it may have a superior design.

Boeing deserved to lose on some of its military bids, the B-1 bomber being an outstanding example—the company made the mistake of telling the Air Force what Boeing thought was needed, rather than offering the kind of airplane the Air Force said it wanted.

But this apparently wasn't the case with the TFX fighter and the C-5A. No one at Boeing who ever worked on those programs will ever stop believing their designs got the well-known shaft for various reasons, none of which involved the designs themselves. The C-5A was a special disappointment because of Boeing's "we can build big airplanes" tradition.

But that tradition was about to be upheld—with the 747.

SEVENTEEN

BIG BIRD

ONE OF AVIATION'S MOST PERSISTENT MYTHS IS THAT BOEING took its defeated C-5A design and converted it into the 747.

Myth is the right word. About the only thing the two planes had in common was size; when the C-5A decision was announced late in 1965, the 747 already was on the drawing board and it was an entirely different kind of giant—only the nose resembled its military cousin, which was a high-wing airplane. In fact, Boeing's C-5 looked more like a fat-bellied B-52 than anything else.

Numerous stories have been told and written on the 747's origin, its supposed C-5A genes being the one most often repeated. But the actual moment of the 747's conception probably came in the spring of 1965 at a meeting in New York, and two participants agreed on what transpired—John Borger of Pan Am and Clancy Wilde of Boeing's sales force. Accompanying Wilde was his boss, Bruce Connelly.

The subject under discussion was whether Boeing could stretch the 707 Intercontinental into a 250-passenger airplane, and it was not a very pleasant topic for either Connelly or Wilde to discuss. Both knew the engineers were dubious about their ability to design the longer landing gear that a stretched 707 would require.

The problem, Wilde realized, was that Douglas had just announced it would build a stretched DC-8, the Super Sixty series, starting with the DC-8-61—up to 259 passengers and a range of nearly 4,000 miles. And he also knew Pan Am's Juan Trippe was interested in an airplane larger than either the 707 Intercontinental or the standard DC-8. In fact, Lindbergh had told Trippe that with a new engine being developed as part of the C-5A competition, "We should talk to someone about building an airplane around that engine."

Wilde and Connelly were aware that Pan Am's technical people, Borger included, knew Boeing was having problems stretching the 707. Connelly was loath to admit this was one engineering hurdle even

Boeing couldn't clear, so he deliberately steered the conversation away from any stretched versions—DC-8 or 707—and into a new area.

"Well, we're talking about the future here," Connelly said. "Of course, we could do like our competition and stretch our airplane, but we're also thinking about making a big step—maybe a wide-body airplane. You've already seen our brochure on some prospective designs."

Trippe nodded. "Do you fellows really want to do something bold?"

"We're ready to look at anything," Connelly acknowledged. "How many passengers are you talking about?"

"Four hundred."

The discussion continued along general lines but mostly on the size of the projected airplane. A few days later, Allen called Trippe and asked bluntly, "You really want to buy an airplane that big, or are you just dreaming or window shopping?"

"I'm serious," Trippe assured him.

And that was how Boeing accepted one of the greatest challenges ever presented to an airplane manufacturer. Jack Steiner, as vice president of product development, headed the 747 program during its early design stages, from the fall of 1965 to early 1966, when it became a full-fledged new airplane program with its own general manager. Allen picked Mal Stamper for that post, and Joe Sutter was named chief engineer, with both men reporting to Steiner until the program was taken out of product development and given greater autonomy.

Stamper, whose sense of humor escaped Allen at times, remembered the day Allen offered him the job.

"How would you like to build an airplane?" Allen asked him. "In fact, the biggest airplane in the world."

"Mr. Allen," Stamper replied, "the only airplane I ever built had rubber bands on it."

Allen didn't think that was funny. "Do you or do you not?" he snapped.

"I'd welcome the challenge," Stamper said.

He thereby was handed a real-life Mission Impossible; not just the world's biggest airliner but the world's biggest plant had to be created from scratch, both under a timetable that defied the imagination. Stamper officially took over the program in May 1966 and the unofficial target date for the 747's first flight was December 17, 1968, which would be the 65th anniversary of the Wright brothers' historic feat in a 605-pound airplane whose first flight covered only 120 feet—111 feet less than the length of the 747's fuselage.

Considering the fact that Boeing didn't even have a factory big enough in which to build the huge plane, this was a risk that might have given even a gambler like Tex Boullioun pause. Boeing's own board had its doubts, and they were expressed at a directors' meeting after Allen asked the board to approve a go-ahead based on a letter of intent Pan Am had signed in December 1965.

Crawford Greenewalt, the same director who had fought so hard for the 737, wasn't interested in the stunning pictures of the projected plane Stamper showed to the board. He wanted to know what kind of return on investment Boeing should expect from the enormously expensive program. Greenewalt, in fact, had expressed doubts about the 747 even before the board met. At a cocktail party prior to the meeting, the director remarked to Allen, "You know, Bill, it took Du Pont several years to decide whether to go into nylon and when we did, it cost us only twenty million dollars. Now we're talking about at least two hundred million for this airplane."

John Yeasting, Stamper recalled, hedged on giving Greenewalt a specific answer to his question on return of investment—"He said they had run some studies," Stamper added, "but couldn't recall the results. Greenewalt just put his head down on the table and muttered, 'My God, these guys don't even know what the return on investment will be in this thing.'"

Just before the board voted on a program go-ahead, Greenewalt voiced the opinion that "if it looks like this isn't panning out, we can always back out."

Allen stiffened. "Back out? If the Boeing Company says we will build this airplane, we will build it even if it takes the resources of the entire company!"

The go-ahead vote followed that pronouncement. "You talk about directors making decisions," Stamper noted, "but in my book this was clearly one man's decision."

That it was—which may explain why, to his dying day, Bill Allen always regarded the 747 as his favorite airplane; not even the 707, for which he also was almost solely responsible in terms of financial risk, matched the big bird in his pride and affection. Yet there must have been times when he might have wondered if the decision had been wise, for the headaches the 747 gave Boeing were commensurate with the size of the airplane itself. And they began when Allen sat down to negotiate specifics with Trippe.

They met at New York's Hotel Pierre with Tex Boullioun joining Allen for the initial talks. Negotiating with Trippe on how to split a dinner check was difficult enough; negotiating for a $22 million airplane was something else. Trippe was playing hardball and finally got on Allen's nerves.

"If I have to deal with that man another five minutes, I'll throw up," he told Boullioun. "Tex, I'm going to catch the next flight back to Seattle—it's all yours."

"And damned if he didn't," Boullioun marveled.

The original letter of intent Pan Am had signed called for a 400-passenger airliner with a range of slightly over 5,000 miles, the ability to take off on a hot day fully loaded in not more than 8,000 feet, and cruise at 35,000 feet—2,000 feet higher than what the 707 Intercontinental could reach after fuel burn-off reduced gross takeoff weight. Pan Am added an unexpected requirement: the 747 had to be designed for cargo nose loading.

"Trippe told me he insisted on this," John Borger related, "because he believed in another ten years everyone would be flying around in supersonic transports and the 747 would be used mostly for air freight."

Trippe usually hedged his bets, and he did so with the 747. While Pan Am's engineers were discussing the 747's specifications with Boeing, Trippe was advised that Lockheed had won the C-5A contract. He promptly called Burbank suggesting that Lockheed might build a passenger version of the C-5A.

But Lockheed officials subsequently informed Trippe that a commercial C-5A was out of the question because their engineers were too busy with the military plane. Borger commented later:

"I'm glad we didn't get anywhere with that idea, because the 747 turned out to be a hell of a lot better airplane than the C-5A." Yet Trippe's perception of the 747 as potentially more of a freighter than a passenger plane had considerable influence on its design. It resulted in putting the cockpit above the cabin, and it determined the aircraft's width; Boeing studied more than 200 cross-sections of different shapes and sizes and finally settled on a width that would accommodate two-abreast cargo containers, each eight by eight feet, the dimensions that Pan Am preferred.

Trippe wasn't the only one who thought the 747 would be used primarily for cargo once the SST went into service. Many at Boeing felt the same way, as Joe Sutter himself testified. One Boeing official came to Sutter while Joe was in the middle of the initial design phase, and showed him the SST brochure Boeing was taking around to the airlines. It was predicting how profitable the supersonic transport would be, carrying 250 first-class passengers on lucrative intercontinental routes. (The projected operating costs, of course, were based on 100 percent load factors and jet fuel at 10 to 13 cents a gallon.)

"That's the airplane the airlines will want, Joe," he told Sutter. "Now here's your 747 flying around with a fifty-five percent load factor in an all-coach configuration—hell, you're not gonna survive. The SST will wipe out the 747."

At that stage, Sutter didn't feel qualified to argue this jaundiced view; all he knew was that people like John Borger and the rest of Pan Am were convinced that if the SST became a success, the 747 still would make a great air freighter.

"The first contract with Pan Am took this into account," Sutter said. "We agreed to design features into the 747 so it could easily be converted into an all-cargo plane. We didn't do everything Pan Am wanted, but we did most of it. In fact, the airplane initially was labeled the 747-PI, for Passenger Insurance. The takeoff and landing weight requirements of a cargo aircraft were built into the 747, which added weight, and that was one of the things that got us into early trouble."

Pan Am officially kicked off the 747 program by signing a contract for 25 planes at a cost of $550 million—up to then the largest single order in monetary terms ever placed by an airline. Naturally Boeing promised to give Pan Am delivery priority, but even then the canny Trippe hedged this, too. While the contracts called for Pan Am to receive most of the aircraft before any 747 was delivered to another carrier, Trippe gave Boeing permission to deliver a few to Japan Air Lines, Air France, and Alitalia if they ordered the giant plane. These airlines were Trippe's chief competitors on Pan Am's most lucrative routes, and he didn't want Japan, France, or Italy to ban his airline's 747s as too heavy and/or noisy.

But before Joe Sutter and his engineers could finalize the design, Malcolm Stamper and the rest of the 747 team had to create the factory.

It was carved out of a literal wilderness—more than 700 acres of woodland outside of Everett, Washington, about 40 miles north of Seattle.

The site was one of 50 considered by a site selection committee that actually placed the Everett location no higher than fifth on its preferred list. San Diego, Denver, Moses Lake, Cleveland, Livermore (Calif.), Marietta (Ga.), San Francisco, and Los Angeles were among the 50 candidates. Gil Jay, who was on the selection committee, said the initial intent was to go outside Washington state, and that California locations were rated higher than Everett. The company even had a temporary lease on land near San Francisco.

"It was apparent that wherever the plant was located, it was going to be manned by twenty to thirty thousand people," Jay said. "California ranked high for political reasons. Labor costs were another factor—in Colorado or Georgia, for example, labor would have been cheaper."

The early favorite, however, was in Washington state itself—a large chunk of land, consisting of about 20 individually owned parcels south of Tacoma and adjacent to Fort Lewis and McChord Air Force Base; the proximity of an airfield was a major factor in the consideration of any site, and McChord's presumed availability was tempting.

Elmer Sill, a partner in the Seattle real estate firm of Lambuth, Sill, and Sprague that handled Boeing's real estate acquisitions, took Bill Allen out to see the McChord area and Allen was impressed. But complications arose; several elderly people who owned homes on certain parcels balked at selling, and there also was some doubt whether the Pentagon would allow McChord, an active base, to be used partially for commercial purposes. It was obvious that some tough and lengthy negotiations were inevitable and with time running out, Allen knew the 747 would have to be built elsewhere.

Despite all the out-of-state locations being considered, Allen's heart really wasn't in such a move. He drove to Everett with Sill and John Yeasting to inspect available land in that area; unbeknown to the selection committee, which had Everett listed only as a possibility, Allen apparently made up his mind right then and there.

The site selection process had begun in October 1964, when Boeing knew it would need a new plant if it won the C-5A contract. The final choice wasn't made until the following April. When the committee presented its findings to Allen, its report downgraded Everett because there were no railroad facilities near the site. The closest line was five miles away.

Bayne Lamb, another committee member, recalled that Everett's lack of rail facilities was pointed out to Allen quite forcefully. There weren't any highways to speak of, either, and this was going to be an assembly plant receiving thousands of parts, many of them huge, from other Boeing plants and subcontractors throughout the country.

"We told him we had to have a railroad to move body parts and materials if we were to build at Everett," Lamb said, "and we couldn't see any way we were going to get a railroad there."

Everett probably would have ranked much lower than fifth except for one prime asset: it had an existing airport, Paine Field, but the committee didn't think this outweighed the rail transportation deficiency. Allen listened to the complete presentation and announced his decision:

"Well, fellows, I'll tell you what we're going to do. We're going to build this plant at Everett."

Boeing had to purchase some 2,000 acres owned by a developer, but the most difficult land negotiation involved a man who, with his wife, held title to a minuscule five acres. They were a crucial five acres, however, because they included the highest terrain in the area, and this was where the main plant was supposed to be built.

Smack in the middle of this five acres was his home, and Boeing sent a realtor to make him an offer. Gil Jay remembered that not only was the house run-down, the yard was filled with junked cars. The entire property was appraised at $4,700, including the wrecks. The agent was instructed to start at $5,000, but he made the mistake of driving up in a new Cadillac and his opening offer was $10,000.

"The owner," Jay sighed, "was smart enough to smell a rat—nobody in his right mind would give him more than twice what the place was worth, and he knew something was up."

Six weeks of haggling followed, before the owner settled for $50,000. Then a new problem arose—he was separated from his wife, she lived in Texas, and the husband didn't know exactly where in Texas.

"We tore down the house anyway," Jay said, "although it took another two months to find her and get her signature."

Building the pyramids couldn't have been much tougher than constructing the 747 plant at Everett. The Egyptians had to contend with heat and the quality of slave labor; Boeing put up with everything from windstorms and mud slides to seemingly unending rain—building Noah's Ark would have been more appropriate. There was so much mud around that the company had to keep tractors on alert to rescue stuck cars.

Bayne Lamb came into Stamper's office during the early days of construction and began firing off a list of demands to keep the project on schedule.

"I need more people," he announced, "or we won't get the railroad finished on schedule."

"You've got 'em," Stamper promised.

"And we're short some equipment, particularly bulldozers and a lot of other earth-moving stuff."

"Order what you want, Bayne."

In a voice that would have melted Scrooge himself, Lamb added, "And most of all we could use three weeks of clear weather."

"No problem," Stamper assured him. "The weather forecasts look good."

It rained for the next 67 consecutive days.

During the winter months, snowstorms harried the army of some 2,800 workers, most of them from the Austin Company. More than 250 contractors and subcontractors were involved, representing virtually every craft in the construction industry. Building a five-mile, $2 million rail spur was the first order of priority, for the line was needed to haul construction material to the site. It was a tough five miles; the railroad ended up as the second-steepest rail grade in the U.S., ascending to a height 500 feet above sea level by the time it reached the terrain on which the 747 plant was being erected.

The size of the airplane dictated the size of the factory—the world's largest airliner was built in what was then and still is, in terms of cubic volume, the world's largest industrial facility under one roof. The plant layout followed the space allocation rules first laid down for Renton: 50 percent for manufacturing, 25 percent for storage, 20 percent given to offices, and the remaining five percent allocated to miscellaneous use. Parking space was figured out to 150 cars per acre, an assignment based on the ratio of people per car sharing rides. The total acreage had a third allocated for buildings, another third for yard area, and the rest reserved for parking.

The enormous plant could hold 40 football fields, a 43-acre area under one continuous roof. To excavate the entire site, workers hauled away more dirt than was moved to build the Grand Coulee Dam. Not only did forests have to be cleared, the tops of hills were chopped off and ravines filled in to provide a flat area for the plant's construction. The usual new-plant procedure was to provide engineering office space first, but this wasn't possible at Everett; the 747 engineers worked at Renton temporarily and didn't get their offices until the assembly area was ready.

"They were virtually still building the factory around the airplane as we started up," Dale Graham of facilities remembered. "The walls of the mockup building weren't even finished when they began work on the first mockup. People were setting up the final assembly line wearing jackets and mackinaws during the winter, because there was no heat in the building yet."

Boeing spent $200 million to erect this 200 million-cubic-foot hatchery for the biggest bird of them all, an expenditure that put the 747 program in very deep hock at its very start and made the plane's success an absolute necessity. In almost every respect, it was a bigger gamble than Boeing and Bill Allen had taken with the Dash-80, for in its own way the 747 was just as revolutionary as the 707. Even its size represented a risk; the cynics, the doubters, and the scoffers raised questions about the safety of such a huge plane almost from the moment Boeing announced it would build it. They were fond of pointing out that a single 747 crash could result in more fatalities than the combined U.S. airline death toll over an entire year.

No one was more aware of this kind of talk and the overall risk involved than Allen. Shortly after the plant was completed and the first airplane almost ready for rollout, a representative from Defense Secretary McNamara's office came to see how the program was going. Bob Bateman and Russ Light took him to Everett for a first-hand look. Then he had lunch with Allen and said he was vastly impressed with what he had seen. But he added:

"You know, Mr. Allen, you have a lot riding on that plane. What would you do if the first airplane crashed on takeoff?"

There was a very long silence before Allen finally replied, "I'd rather talk about something pleasant—like a nuclear war."

And there were some pundits who questioned the need for a 400-passenger airliner, a point directed at the 71-year-old Juan Trippe's well-known obsession for Pan Am to operate almost every new type of airliner that came along. But that wasn't Trippe's main motive behind his half-billion-dollar commitment for the giant plane. In 1965, international air traffic was growing at the incredible annual rate of 15 percent, with domestic traffic not far behind; the jet revolution had taken hold.

By ordering the 747 ahead of everyone else, Trippe honestly believed he could cash in on the exploding international air travel market with an airplane carrying almost three times as many passengers as the 707, and offering the lowest operating cost per seat mile in history. To Juan Trippe, the 747 was a flying mint, a money-making machine with wings. The reason it became—at least for a few unhappy years—a flying white elephant was the unexpected 1970 recession that drastically eroded air traffic growth. The plane Trippe had ordered five years earlier had become, at least temporarily, an outstanding example of the airline industry's most dreaded fear: over-capacity.

More than anyone else, Trippe was insistent on the 747's size, going beyond what many of Boeing's own engineers first contemplated. Their elder statesman, Ed Wells, told an interviewer long after he retired that the airplane Boeing initially envisioned would have been the size of what eventually became the 747SP, a later long-range version 47 feet shorter than the original 747 and carrying 100 fewer passengers.

"Our negotiations with Pan Am began to escalate the size of the airplane," Wells said. And the more performance and payload Pan Am wanted, the more weight went up.

When Boeing's sales representatives began sounding out other airlines on the 747, they found interest but not in the size Pan Am was demanding. Both TWA and American suggested a somewhat smaller tri-jet, expressing concern over the operating costs of a four-engine plane that huge. The general feeling was the same expressed toward the SST: no one was really panting for a new giant, but everyone was scared to death a competitor might get it. That fear was most prevalent among foreign carriers—the prospect of Pan Am dominating international routes with a plane as dramatic as the 747 was a sobering thought.

The result was pleasant news to Boeing; the world's airlines began beating the proverbial path to Everett's door, as the 747 took shape in mockup form under the enormous roof of a still-uncompleted factory. Even carriers that had never bought a Boeing airplane before ordered the 747—and they included such Douglas loyalists as Delta, KLM, and SAS.

For Mal Stamper, the 747 program was traversing a gamut between exhilarating and exhausting. He ran it for four years and in that time took exactly one day off—a single Christmas. Many nights he slept in his office, on a conference table, his desk, or even on the floor. When he did make it home for dinner, he would eat a hurried meal, then drive back with his wife to the site and watch the night crews building the plant under spotlights.

During the 67-day deluge of rain, a mudslide caused an entire hill to engulf part of the construction area. It cost $5 million to clear away the mess and right in the middle of the cleanup efforts Bill Allen arrived, looking for Stamper, who was down in a muddy trench. Allen peeked over the edge at his bedraggled chief of the world's greatest airplane project.

"Getting enough challenge down there, Stamper?" he inquired.

Some 50,000 people were involved in the 747 program, including construction workers and subcontractors in virtually every state and

17 foreign countries bringing in 827,000 parts, some of them still under development while the airplane was being built. But no one was more important than the man heading the small army of engineers entrusted with the 747's design.

The greatest compliment Joe Sutter ever received came from T Wilson, who wanted all engineers to be "Sutter tough," as he phrased it.

"Once you've settled on a configuration, build it," T advised. "Don't screw around and worry about changing this and revising that, which is an engineer's delight. Get it built and if it can be improved later, do it—but build it first."

Which was exactly how this disciple of George Schairer and faithful adherent to the Ed Wells creed of engineering integrity tried to operate. Sutter came into the 747 project in August 1965. He began making rough sketches based on some rather vague concepts—all he had was the general idea that Boeing wanted an airplane at least twice the size of a 707. He formed his engineering team around a small nucleus of engineers he trusted, mindful of the fact that the company's heavy hitters were working on the SST and C-5A. Typical of the men he enlisted for the 747 was Row Brown, a shy, unassuming engineer whose quiet modesty was exceeded only by his devotion to Boeing.

"Row personified a lot of the guys who worked for me," Sutter philosophized with open admiration. "They were more interested in the job they had than in the money they got and their own careers. Row was a classic example. He once left Preliminary Design and went over to be a project engineer on the 707-320, designing the new wing, and he did a great job. It could have moved him up the promotion ladder, because by staying in PD, you don't get the broad experience you need to become a chief project engineer. But he wanted to go back to PD—that's what he was really interested in and where he made his greatest contributions, not to his own career but to Boeing."

Sutter forced him to make a few presentations on the 747, trying to overcome Brown's shyness.

"I wanted to develop him in the eyes of management," Joe explained, "and his presentations were excellent. But he spoke so quietly that I don't believe the executive types realized how good he was, and he never got the credit that was due him. He stayed in PD until he retired and I'll never forget how much help he gave me."

Sutter actually had begun working on a large commercial transport design before his official assignment to the 747 project. For several years Boeing had been trying unsuccessfully to figure out a way to stretch the 707. When not even engineers like Don Finley and Brown could solve the problem of that short landing gear, it became apparent that a totally new, much larger aircraft was the next logical step. Sutter was asked to look at the possibility of putting the high-ratio bypass engines being developed for the C-5A on a big airliner. He submitted three separate double-deck designs of varying sizes—a 250-seater, 300-

seater, and 350-seater; a brochure describing this trio was shown to the airlines, the general reaction being in favor of a 350-passenger plane but with some reservations—carriers like American and TWA, as previously noted, preferred a smaller airplane. The one real enthusiast for the biggest version was Juan Trippe. By the time Bruce Connelly and Clancy Wilde saw Trippe in New York months later, that "teaser" brochure already had Pan Am's chief hooked. Thus, contrary to one of the 747's many myths, it was Boeing that planted the concept of a true so-called "jumbo jet" in Trippe's mind, not the other way around. And Sutter, having done so much of the preliminary design work, was an obvious choice to be chief project engineer.

Given Pan Am's 400-passenger requirement, Trippe had assumed Boeing would build a double-deck airplane. Sutter and everyone else on his team began to hate the design for two principal reasons: putting half the passengers on the upper deck made emergency evacuation too difficult, and putting the rest of them on the main deck left very little room for cargo in the lower deck. The latter was vital; Sutter always had in mind a transport that could make money even if flying only half-full, provided there was plenty of cargo space in the belly.

Width, not height, was the answer to the question of how to accommodate 400 passengers. The engineers achieved this by going to a fuselage diameter capable of holding the two rows of eight-by-eight cargo containers, and at the same time provided the spaciousness of a twin-aisle cabin.

Because Trippe seemed to be sold on a double-decker, Sutter went to the trouble of building a rough mockup with that configuration, and Boeing invited Pan Am's top officials to inspect it. The temporary stairs leading to the upper deck were somewhat shaky, and a single upper-level escape slide had been installed. Allen escorted Trippe and the rest of the Pan Am party up the stairs; the scene from the second deck was enough to give a mountain climber vertigo, and things got worse when Sutter suggested that everyone try the escape chute.

Trippe flatly refused and so did everyone else, with one exception. Jim Fleming, a Pan Am senior captain, went down the slide, apparently figuring that someone should at least try it. His bravery didn't impress Trippe, however—that was the last time anyone mentioned a double-deck airplane, much to the relief of Ed Wells. He had kept asking Sutter if the double deck was really the right way to go.

The same day Trippe and the Pan Am delegation saw the double-deck mockup, Sutter also had a crude single-deck mockup ready, designed mostly by Ken Plewes. The interior was unfinished—Boeing's chief interior designer, Milt Heineman, and Frank Del Guidice of Walter Dorwin Teague Associates, hadn't completed their work yet—but enough had been done to give Trippe a good idea of what the airplane would look like.

The mockup included the hump on the top of the fuselage that became the 747's trademark and its most distinguishing feature. A lot of jokes were circulated about the hump, such as the story that Boeing designed it into the 747 so wealthy senior pilots wouldn't bump their heads on the cockpit ceiling while sitting on their wallets.

The hump began as merely a matter of aerodynamic streamlining; with the cockpit located above the cabin, it was necessary to gradually smooth out the area just behind the flight deck down into the top of the fuselage for a smooth airflow. Originally it was intended to hold air-conditioning ducts and other equipment. When Trippe saw the single-deck mockup, he came out of the cockpit and looked around at the empty space.

"What's this area going to be used for?" he asked Borger.

"It might make good crew rest quarters," Borger suggested. "Remember, if we fly more than twelve hours, we have to carry relief pilots and the first crew has to get some rest."

Trippe frowned. "This will be reserved for passengers," he decreed. He turned to Sutter. "Joe, do you suppose we could have a passenger lounge up here?"

Sutter liked the idea, but not another one Trippe proposed. He wanted to put a huge, wraparound window in the plane's nose so first-class passengers would get the same forward view as the pilots. Sutter found out that such a window, with its mandatory thick glass to withstand a bird strike, would weigh 800 pounds. He told an unhappy Trippe the additional weight was unacceptable.

Trippe wasn't the only one offering suggestions on how to utilize the 747's immense space. "A lot of people felt the plane was so big you could put almost anything in the cabin," Sutter said. "We got plenty of ideas—a fast-food restaurant, barber shop, ladies' hair salon, and a small movie theater. American and Continental actually put piano bars into their 747s for a time, until they decided they needed the space for more seats. One airline asked if it could have a gambling salon with slot machines, roulette wheels, and blackjack tables."

A fully equipped mockup was completed later under Heineman and Del Guidice's direction. Its real-life size stunned even supposedly blasé airline officials, and Trippe was no exception. Two months after signing the letter of intent, he had bet Allen $10 million—to be subtracted from or added to the contract price—that Boeing wouldn't go ahead with the plane. When he saw the massive, completely furnished and brilliantly lit mockup, he knew he had lost.

Harley Thorson gave Northwest's Don Nyrop a look at the Heineman–Del Guidice creation. Nyrop, a very religious man, was so overwhelmed that he went completely out of character. "Harley, you've got to call the plane 'the Savior' because all I can say is, 'Jesus Christ!'"

Pat Patterson of United had an identical reaction. Escorted by Allen, T, and Clancy Wilde to the mockup building, he took one look and also blurted, "Jesus Christ!"

(The size of the Everett plant awed airline people as much as the size of the plane. One South American visitor standing on the tour balcony overlooking the production area remarked, "It looks just like the 707 factory at Renton, except that the people are smaller.")

Two of the most critical groups from various carriers visiting the mockup were pilots and flight attendants. One portly captain complained about the spiral staircase leading to the upper deck.

"It's too narrow," he declared. "If we have more than one bag, we'll have to make two trips."

When a guide showed a group of flight attendants through the mockup, he noted with pride their awestruck stares and heard their incredulous gasps. After the tour, he asked if there were any comments and waited for the expected chorus of ecstatic, unqualified raves. Instead there was silence until one young woman spoke up.

"I think the coffee drains are too small," she announced. The guide should have known something like that was coming. No flight attendant who ever lived was completely satisfied with the galleys on a new airliner—Boeing's or anyone else's.

During the design phase, the input of the "safety committee" originated by Amos Wood during World War II became truly vital— uppermost in everyone's mind, from Joe Sutter on down, was the knowledge of what a fatal 747 crash blamed on faulty design would mean to Boeing's reputation and the future of the giant plane itself. The 747 was not really a radically new airplane; it was more of an enlarged 707, but with far more redundancy and with the most extensive attention to the "fail-safe" concept that had ever been bestowed on a commercial transport—the stakes were that high.

For the 747, a five-man safety engineering group used a new method of spotting potential hazards known as "fault tree analysis." The name was derived from the charts the committee drew up to determine the safety relationship of a system or component to the rest of the airplane. Each chart resembled the drawing of a tree, the trunk being the component or system in question and the branches the other components and systems. At a glance, for example, an engineer could tell what effect an autopilot failure would have on the control system, or whether the rupture of a control cable might spread to other cables by transferring too much load.

Fault tree analysis was first used on Boeing missiles, and the 747 became the first airplane to utilize its amazingly accurate forecasting of possible trouble. Into the tree was fed such computer data as the probability of failure of any one part—even the chances of a pilot pushing the wrong button and what the effects might be on *all* systems. Before approving the design of the 747's landing gear, the most complex ever created, the committee cranked into computers the details of every hydraulic gear malfunction that had occurred since the jet age began, and the most critical causes were engineered out of the 747 gear before the plane ever flew.

Every airline specification change, such as ordering a different kind of pilot seat or a new galley, was checked by the committee for the most minute possible effect on safety. Even coffee makers were subjected to fault tree analysis, to determine whether the coffee drain outlet was located far enough away from any wiring so no short circuit was possible.

One engineer came up with the idea for a system that would wash the plane's windows in flight. The safety group turned this down with three pages of technical objections, each one based on safety. Joe Sutter, who appreciated the engineer's ingenuity if not the device itself, explained the philosophy behind the fault tree system:

"As the state of the art got more sophisticated and complex, the job of the designer became more specialized. The result was that one designer will produce a system or individual component which looks great on paper but which could cause trouble when it's used in connection with other systems and components. We had to worry about these interactions, to make sure one engineer wasn't inadvertently fouling up the work of another."

Safety . . .

With the 747, it became not a slogan but a religion.

"The one thing I'm proudest of is that we really leaned over backwards to make it a safe airplane," Sutter said. "Safety had the highest priority—we were all so conscious of the fact that a jet crashing with four hundred people aboard could have more fatalities than five piston aircraft in five separate accidents. Upper management never once said, 'We'll compromise a little on safety.' My standing orders were: 'Make it as safe as you can.' "

One thing Sutter didn't have to worry about was the 747's strength. Its triple-spar wing was flexed upward 26 feet before it finally broke—at 116 percent of ultimate design load. But the static tests were one of the few early bright spots in a program plagued with the pains of giving birth to this 350-ton baby. Sutter's team had conceived it out of 50 possible configurations, but the 747 still needed an obstetrician—the production team that would bring it into the world.

What they were putting together was an airplane with 4.5 million parts, designed from some 75,000 engineering drawings, and so huge that just parking it at an airport took up an acre of ground. If you put the nose of the 747 on one goal line of a football field, the tail would be covering the opponent's 25-yard line—and that tail was equivalent to a six-story building in height.

It would carry enough fuel to drive the average automobile 10,000 miles a year for 70 years. With a full fuel load, the plane would weigh

170 tons more than the Pilgrims' *Mayflower*, and its cabin could hold 30 cars the size of a Cadillac or Lincoln. Lay the 747's wiring end to end with Seattle as the starting point, and it would fall only eight miles short of reaching Portland, Oregon, 143 miles away.

The man assigned to Stamper as the overseer of tooling up for and then building this monster was none other than the acerbic Chick Pitts, with Sof Torget as director of manufacturing. These were the days before Stamper became a health addict, and Torget remembered him as an overweight, heavy smoker who didn't mind taking a drink now and then. He also will be remembered for running the 747 program like a U.S. Marine Corps drill instructor.

There was some jealousy toward him within the company—Stamper was the naturalized immigrant from General Motors who was getting promoted over the heads of "Boeing natives." On one of his first ascensions up the management ladder, someone complained, "My God, we cut Stamper's head off and it rolled uphill." Stamper thought it was one of the funniest remarks he ever heard.

Torget came into the program as subordinate to Pitts, who had been vice president of operations (manufacturing) in Wichita and retained vice presidential status when Boeing sent him to Everett. It was like lighting matches around open gasoline cans putting him together again with Torget; Chick, who like so many hard-nosed bosses respected people who talked back to him, didn't give Sof any trouble but that wasn't true of his relations with Torget's people.

"We'd have coordination meetings with people from engineering, materiel and manufacturing," Torget recounted, "and here's Pitts—brand-new to the program—who didn't know any of them. He'd pick a victim and would virtually undress the guy in front of the whole room."

It was C. B. Gracey, a longtime admirer of Pitts, who had transferred him from Wichita to Everett. That it turned out to be a mistake was not entirely Chick's fault, although his personality didn't help matters. Everyone who knew him, especially the Wichita veterans like Ernie Ochel, Otis Smith and Fred Carroll, felt Pitts was a true genius at turning out military planes. But he had no experience with commercial transports and was simply in the wrong league with the 747. He was an old-fashioned manufacturing type who could walk through a shop and instinctively sense what was running well or badly, but the 747 was too sophisticated to be run on a gut feeling. When it came to tools, however, Chick was a true artist. He once built a cowling for a racing plane with his bare hands, and his curiously gentle hobby of raising rhododendrons seemed totally out of character.

Pitts occasionally revealed an unexpected sense of humor. When the 747 began to encounter serious overruns, Bill Allen, T Wilson, Hal Haynes and George Snyder came to Everett for a meeting on the various problems. Stamper conducted the frank session, explaining such difficulties as having 16 percent of the parts cancelled or replaced because of design changes. When he finished, Allen—who really liked Pitts—turned to him.

"Chick, do you have anything to add?"

"I guess I'd better tell you a story," Pitts began, "about this old Indian chief back in Oklahoma. He called his tribe together and said, 'I've got bad news and good news for you. The bad news is that there ain't no more buffalo, there ain't no more rabbits or any other wild game, the streams are all dried up so there ain't no more fishin', and so we're facing starvation. The good news is that we've got plenty of buffalo chips.' "

Everyone in the room roared, and no one was laughing harder than Stamper. When the meeting adjourned, Stamper wagged a finger at Jim Blue, who was then director of program management. "I want to see you in my office—and close the door behind you."

Blue complied, wondering what was coming. Stamper looked to make sure the door was shut, then asked, "Would you mind telling me what the hell is a buffalo chip?"

Eventually, Pitts was transferred to the Vertol division. By mid-1970, when 747 production was in full gear, the Everett "varsity" lineup included George Nible as Stamper's replacement, factory manager Don Whitford with Sterling Sessions as his assistant, and Wally Buckley who had been named director of operations in August 1968.

One of Buckley's greatest assets was his willingness to work with the 747 engineering staff. His door was always open to engineers, including the 747's two chief architects—Sutter and Everette Webb; they solved production/design problems together, instead of battling over what or who caused the problem in the first place.

Buckley's toughness and temper hid a heart softer than wet oatmeal. Wade Roberson had just returned from a tough mission to a supplier in an effort to expedite delivery of 747 window glass. He was in Buckley's office reporting the results, and Wally put his arm around Roberson's shoulder.

"You did one hell of a job, Wade," he enthused. "I know how hard it is to be away from your family and I really appreciate . . ."

Just then Buckley's staff arrived for a meeting. The arm came off the shoulder as if Wade's coat were on fire.

"Damn you, Roberson!" Buckley roared. "Either get those windows here in time or go find yourself another job!"

Both George Kau and John DePolo worked for Buckley in the early 747 days, and they attended a meeting at which DePolo was making a presentation that called for some kind of new organizational setup. The presentation included the usual Boeing flip charts and viewfoils, one of the latter displaying the suggested organization in the form of an umbrella.

DePolo was sticking his head into the lion's mouth, because Buckley already had told him he didn't like the umbrella idea. But John persisted in showing everyone else the viewfoil. Buckley grabbed it off the projector and tried to rip it apart with his bare hands. When he failed—he might as well have been Truman Capote trying to tear the Manhattan telephone directory in two—he threw it on the floor and stamped on it like a man trying to kill a snake.

"You could have heard a pin drop," Kau remembered.

"DePolo, get that damned chart out of my sight!" Wally yelled.

DePolo picked up the viewfoil and asked plaintively, "Buck, does that mean you don't like it?"

He was fiercely protective of the people who worked for him. Larry McKean had just started out in industrial relations and was at a meeting on labor problems in Joe Miles' office. Buckley was there sitting on a couch, when some Boeing official made a disparaging remark about the Everett work force.

"Buck shot off that couch like a cannon ball," McKean related, "and he kicked the guy's briefcase clear across the room. Joe Miles just sat there, smoking his pipe and smiling."

Like Boullioun and several others, Buckley was part of the Minuteman cadre that formed so much of T's varsity team when Wilson succeeded Allen as president during the 747's troubled days. Wally had almost as close a relationship with Tex as he did with Wes Maulden, but he wasn't averse to putting Boullioun down. Tex liked to play "mind games," reflecting the inherent desire of every ebullient extrovert to be genuinely liked. Buckley and several other officers were at a meeting in Boullioun's office when Tex brought up the subject of loyalty and true friendship.

"You can judge a man's real feelings about you when you're in deep trouble and need his help," Tex pontificated. "Say, for example, I was drowning a hundred yards offshore. Now if you just tolerated me, you might call the Coast Guard and have them send out a rowboat to rescue me. Of course, if you liked me, you wouldn't bother to wait for the Coast Guard—you'd get a boat yourself, row out and save me. But if you *really* loved me, you'd jump in the water, swim the hundred yards and pull me to safety."

He looked around the room at his silent Boeing brethren. "Okay, which would you guys do?"

Only Buckley answered.

"I'd throw you a friggin' rock," he drawled.

Buckley didn't get along too well with Mal Stamper—"I kept unexposed to him," was Wally's description of their relationship. But the miracle of Everett was forged by men who subordinated personal feelings to a common goal: to create the world's greatest airliner, stamped with the Boeing name.

Many in the work force drove to the Everett plant from as far away as Tacoma, commuting 140 miles every day. During the early days of the unfinished factory's construction, they had to wear hard hats on the assembly line and almost everywhere else; they might at times grouse, argue, complain, and curse the monster they were carving for the future—but they built it, and with pride.

Stamper suggested that the Everett army be called "the Incredibles." The name not only stuck but wound up on decals carrying the likeness of Paul Bunyan along with the slogan.

"They put that insignia on their hard hats, lunch pails, jackets, and everything else in sight," Stamper said proudly. "It was the most highly motivated work force I ever saw. They didn't need pep talks —their enthusiasm just welled up. Some guys would work two shifts voluntarily."

After Sterling Sessions succeeded Don Whitford as Everett factory manager, George Kau was his assistant superintendent. Sessions was known around the plant as "the Phantom"—his *modus operandi* was to show up unexpectedly at a different assembly station each morning and raise Cain with Kau if he found something wrong. One day he called George. "Kau, every day I come in, there's a guy standing around not doing anything. I want you to find him and put him to work."

"Sure," Kau agreed. "What's his name?"

"I don't know his name. How the hell would I know his name?"

Armed with this vague description of "a guy standing around not doing anything," Kau investigated but found no idlers in sight. He reported this to Sessions. "Apparently you can't do your job," Sessions scolded. "Meet me by my car tomorrow morning and I'll point him out."

Kau joined him the next day as instructed, and Sessions leveled an accusing finger in the direction of a man who, indeed, was just standing around doing nothing.

"That's him!" Sessions proclaimed triumphantly.

Kau sighed. "Sesh, that's the third-shift supervisor. He's standing there idle because his partner on the first shift is putting his crew to work, and this guy always stays there a few minutes until the first shift gets started. He's not goofing off."

Sessions was unconvinced. "Kau, he's standing there occupying company space. Can't you talk him into working while he's waiting?"

Stamper had his share of detractors when he ran the program, but he couldn't have cared less; he had tunnel vision when it came to getting the job done. But there also were some who thought at first he was the wrong man to run the 747 program and then changed their minds, among them George Nible. Jim Blue and Nible were as close friends as Buckley and Maulden, which is to say they were like brothers. When the program got under way, Blue was working for Bob Jewett on Minuteman modifications, and Stamper asked that he be transferred to the 747. Jewett didn't want him to leave and Blue asked Nible to intercede.

"You gotta help me, George," he pleaded. "Jewett won't release me and I want to work for Stamper."

Nible couldn't believe it. "You want to work for that ninety-day wonder? You're out of your mind."

"Have you seen the size of that airplane? I want to be part of it."

Blue's release was finally arranged, but after a few months of exposure to 24-hour workdays and the frustrations of constant design and production changes, he invaded Stamper's office.

"Stamper, you've caused us to change this master schedule about six times, and I'm getting damned tired of going back to manufacturing and asking them to change it again! This is ridiculous, so why the hell don't you get off our backs? We'll push this airplane out on time and you can put all those gold stars on your helmet."

Mal Stamper didn't get mad very easily, but this time he did. He looked Blue right in the eye and said coldly, "All right, Jim. I'll go home, and I'll be back on the day of rollout. Is that what you want me to do?"

Blue sighed. "Aw, what the hell—give me the changes."

If one could have a hundred dollars for each time that scene in Stamper's office was repeated—and not just with Blue—he could have bought his own 747. Stamper in those days would have made Captain Bligh and Simon Legree seem like doting grandfathers, but he worked as hard or harder than anyone else, and the work force—from managers to floor sweepers—caught his own fever. For Stamper himself had become infected with the Boeing can-do mystique, so exemplified and even magnified in the 747 ordeal.

He said to Blue once, "You know, Jim, you guys are totally wrapped around the company flag. In Detroit, there wasn't much company loyalty. You could go from Chrysler to Ford or General Motors in one day without missing a beat. This is the damnedest thing I ever saw."

It was a remark that impressed Blue. "Mal was right," he reminisced years later. "The thing that was great about all these characters, and nowhere was it more prevalent than when we were building the 747, was that every damned one of them was so completely dedicated to Boeing. We all had different ways of doing things. We all came from different backgrounds, but the one thing we had in common was Boeing. That hard-assed Wally Buckley told me once the proudest moment of his life was the day we rolled the first 747 out of the factory."

Bob Bateman was in charge of building the 747 functional mockup that laid out all the wiring and tubing, and those building the mockup acquired the name "Rainbow Team." Bateman wanted some kind of modest aural signal as notification that a mockup section had been completed, and the job was given to an engineer named Ed Teeporten.

At seven A.M. a few mornings later, the deafening shriek of the loudest siren anyone had ever heard went off, startling every worker

within a radius of five miles. Teeporten confessed that the only efficient aural signal he could find was the siren on a U.S. Navy destroyer
in drydock at Bremerton. He had borrowed it the night before and hung
it from the factory ceiling.

There also was a "Purple Team" whose main area of responsibility
was the breakneck schedule for the prototype—Airplane 001. Everett
was nothing more than a final assembly facility, collecting 800,000
parts and assemblies that had to be received on time and in proper
sequence, so 001 could be built in time for its scheduled flight tests.
This was crucial to the whole program, for the flight tests would
determine what further design changes might be required for the
production aircraft.

The goal of the Purple Team was to eliminate parts shortages and
establish some kind of system for tracking which parts were lacking
at each assembly position. It was decided to use the tunnels that had
been built under the factory as fire shelters as a means of tracking the
parts situation, instead of trying to set up separate rooms for the
individual assembly positions. So the Purple Team would meet every
morning, seven days a week, at a given assembly area, ascertain the
parts status, and post the results in the appropriate spot on the tunnel
walls.

The improvised system was overwhelmed when full 747 production
began, but it worked fine for getting 001 completed on schedule for
the rollout. There was one scary moment when *Life* photographers
showed up to take pictures of the new jet being assembled. It was
sitting on supporting jacks, with a huge air cushion underneath the
fuselage. Just as the cameras began clicking, one of the jacks gave way.
The cushion prevented any serious damage but it was not the photo
coverage Boeing needed.

Rollout day was September 30, 1968—less than three years after Pan
Am signed the letter of intent, an achievement that made the phrase
"the Incredibles" an understatement. Twenty-six stewardesses (the
airlines hadn't yet adopted the non-gender term "flight attendants")
were there, representing the 26 airlines that had ordered the plane.
Because many didn't speak much English, they missed the champagne-
smashing cues and instead of breaking the bottles in unison, the
christening sounded like the final scattered broadside of a sinking
frigate.

No matter—it still was one of the most dramatic moments in
Boeing's history. Three of the 747's smaller sisters—the 707, 727 and
737—flew by in a salute to N-7470, christened the *City of Everett*. It
was the first new Boeing transport that hadn't been painted in the
traditional prototype colors of brownish-copper and yellow. N-7470
was mostly white, with a red sash down the window line. The red
could have been symbolic; Stamper had spent about $1 million a day

before the rollout, and that didn't include the cost of the plant. The 747's total development costs were estimated to exceed $1 billion.

Stamper stayed in the program another year, long enough to witness the first flight on February 9, 1969, thus missing his target date of December 17, 1968, by slightly under two months (which T Wilson had predicted would happen), but subsequently meeting Allen's commitment to Trippe that the first production plane would be delivered by mid-December of 1969 in time for crew training.

One of Stamper's idiosyncrasies was the circuitous route he'd take to get a point across. It was a trait that drove most of his fellow executives bonkers. He called Nible in one day to discuss 747 production delays—not only were design changes slowing everything down, but too many subcontractors were delivering parts that were either late or failed to meet specifications.

Stamper launched into a lengthy discourse on the situation, Nible fidgeting and taking frequent glances at his watch. Stamper finally wound down, and Nible fumed at him, "You could have said that in two minutes instead of two hours, and I could have been out there doing my job."

It was, of course, a case of Stamper going through a thinking process out loud. "With Stamper," Dan Pinick remarked, "you'd sit there and let his random words flow over you, and eventually his thinking process would get him to where he wanted to go. You just had to understand the way he communicated."

Among those who did understand was Wes Maulden. One officer complained to Maulden that it was a waste of time listening to Stamper's rambling talks.

Maulden heard him out, then said coldly, "I have never found it a waste of *my* time to listen to Mal Stamper."

Stamper and Nible were aboard a 747 sent on a South American demonstration tour. The plane stopped in Mexico City, where government and airline officials hosted a dinner in the visitors' honor. Stamper concluded the evening by delivering a short thank-you speech in fluent Spanish, and at the hotel later Nible remarked, "I didn't know you spoke Spanish."

"I can't speak a word," Stamper admitted. "I had someone write it all out in Spanish and I memorized it."

He repeated this feat more than once, such as on an occasion when Boeing was delivering a new airplane to a Middle East carrier. Stamper thanked the customer in perfect Arabic, and later welcomed a visiting Soviet delegation in flawless Russian; he spoke neither language but had simply memorized what had been written down for him.

The 747 prototype that emerged from the gigantic Everett cavern could have used an aeronautical version of the Pritikin diet that Stamper later espoused—it was overweight, and there always has been some controversy as to who did most of the over-feeding. The most objective conclusion is that both Boeing and Pan Am were to blame, and that Juan Trippe had to share some responsibility personally.

His dreams for the plane were even more grandiose than Sutter's. Turning the hump into a passenger lounge, for example—which ultimately turned out to be a brilliant idea—still added unexpected weight. And Boeing's decision to install Pratt & Whitney JT-9D engines had repercussions—marrying the 747's bulk to the initial JT-9D was not a case of immediate conjugal bliss. Simply stated, the engine wasn't powerful enough for a 350-ton airplane. As Borger put it, "The engine was fine for a six-hundred-thousand-pound airplane, but not for a seven-hundred-and-ten-thousand-pound airplane."

Some of Boeing's top engineering talent tackled the imperative task of trimming weight off the 747—Maynard Pennell, George Martin, George Snyder, Ken Holtby, and Bob Brown among them. All ideas and suggestions were funneled to Charlie Brewster, working directly under Sutter as project engineer in charge of weight reduction.

One proposal was to eliminate the triple-slotted rear flaps that Sutter wanted to use, in combination with Krüger flaps on the leading edges to give the huge plane the same landing and approach speeds as a 707. Going to simpler trailing-edge double flaps would have saved 1,700 pounds, but when Sutter ran the suggestion by Borger, the answer was an absolute no.

"You can do what you damn well please with the flaps," he informed Sutter, "but we won't release you from the stall speed guarantee."

That meant staying with the triple-slotted flaps, which in the end turned out for the best. "When Borger told us to go stuff that flap change, it was a very fortunate thing," Sutter admitted. "The triple flaps, combined with the forward Krüger and a four-legged main landing gear, made the 747 the easiest airplane to land Boeing had ever built."

Just before the plane entered airline service in 1970, insurance underwriter actuaries were predicting there would be at least three fatal 747 crashes within the first 18 months. There were exactly five accidents involving fatalities in the *first 10 years*, and three of them were blamed on pilot error.

Borger, like Sutter, attributed the plane's superb safety record in part to its excellent stall characteristics; it lands no faster than much smaller jets. In fact, anyone who has seen a 747 approach and land would swear it's traveling about 40 miles an hour—almost floating to the ground, an illusion created by its great size.

The huge four-axle, 16-wheel main landing gear obviously created a lot of weight, and Boeing at first planned to use the same nose-wheel steering as on previous jetliners, supplementing this with the application of asymmetrical engine thrust to turn the plane on the ground. Sutter fought this arrangement, convinced that an aircraft this big needed steering help from the main gear. A steerable main gear was designed and installed on the prototype, over the objections of the engineers doing the weight/cost studies, and they were so vociferous that Stamper and other top officials refused to release it for production.

Came the first 747 taxi tests, with Jack Waddell in charge of the test program. The steerable gear had been disconnected and Waddell taxied the plane around, using nose-wheel steering and occasional asymmetrical thrust. He returned to the ramp and bluntly informed Sutter he'd better reconnect it. There also was some engineering opposition to a four-post gear, all for weight-saving reasons. The decision to stay with four was based on the fact that this configuration would spread the load more evenly and reduce the stress on runway pavement—not a minor point, because some critics were claiming that the 747 would tear up every runway it used.

The four-legged gear also was safer, for the 747 can land even with one leg ripped off—which actually happened when a 747 taking off from San Francisco hit some runway lights, tearing away almost half of the main gear.

"Some engineers felt we were overdoing the landing gear," Sutter recalled. "Yet you literally design an airplane around its landing gear. It doesn't seem that important, but it's so crucial to the structural architecture of the airplane that when you make your landing gear decision you determine a lot about the rest of the structure and how the airplane is going to fit together."

In the background, there was always quiet Ed Wells, ready to offer advice and help. He had one standard question for Sutter and the rest of the 747 engineering team: "Are you sure you've looked at all the ways of making this the best airplane possible?" And the number of times he asked made the plane that much better.

When it came to safety, seemingly minor items loomed large. Going to the heavier, more complex four-post gear allowed Boeing to use the same size wheels that were on the 707—and having 16 of them meant that you could blow out half the tires and still land safely.

Cognizant of how pilots might feel in a cockpit 29 feet off the ground—the equivalent of three stories—Waddell helped design a "taxi simulator." It was the shell of a 747 flight deck perched on stilts that were mounted on top of a truck. Waddell directed the truck driver via radio, and had airline pilots going through Boeing's 747 flight school ride with him in what was dubbed "Waddell's Wagon."

Subcontractors from 48 of the 50 states produced 747 components, Northrop being the largest supplier—it built most of the fuselage. But the nose section came from Wichita, and Everett relied heavily on the Auburn facility—a tooling and parts supermarket. Auburn's machine shop provided the precision tools and huge jigs—its work could be likened to the backstage crew that makes the scenery for a hit play. It didn't have Everett's glamor or drama, but the 747 couldn't have been created without the skills of Auburn's people. Auburn was conceived as a fabrication plant and fortunately was operative in time to participate in the 747 program.

Some Boeing engineers remembered working with British counterparts on the 747. England's aerospace industry was in a recession, and Boeing hired a number of UK engineers whose accents stood out like wearing brown shoes with a tuxedo. Maynard Wege had a British supervisor whose pep talk always ended, "Press on, chaps, press on!"

The United Kingdom contingent had as much trouble understanding the Americans as vice versa. One British engineer finally put a sign on his desk that read:

"English spoken here. American understood."

When the early 747 program began piling up overruns and production delays, Stamper wasn't averse to chopping heads. Sutter kept his engineering staff, which reached 4,500 at the program's peak, largely intact; some of his key people, like Al Weber, Milt Heineman, Ev Webb and Ed Pfaffman, stayed with him for the duration. But management turmoil and turnover in other areas were inevitable in a situation no American corporation had ever faced before. Boeing was building a new organization, a new factory, and a new airplane simultaneously. As Bruce Gissing observed: "You usually can do two of those things, but not all three at the same time. We tried to do them without the resources."

The real problem at Everett was the unrealistic timetable the 747 program was trying to meet. The plane was in product development from August 1965 to March 1966, only seven months in which engineering had to define the airplane and compute its weight and performance. It took just 34 months from program launch to delivery of the first certificated airplane; only four years elapsed between the 747's launch and its entrance into scheduled airline service. This is what the Incredibles achieved, but the cost was stiff and steep, and there was plenty of blame to spread around.

Boeing, for one, had been over-optimistic about the delivery schedule; to build an almost flawless, ready-for-service airplane of the 747's size and complexity in the time allotted was an impossible task to begin with. Pratt & Whitney had been equally over-optimistic about the JT-9D engine. Originally designed for the C-5A competition, it needed major modifications for commercial use and P&W had to rush its development to meet the Boeing–Pan Am timetable.

Many years after the 747 had become one of commercial aviation's greatest transports—and certainly the greatest of its time—Joe Sutter still had no regrets about its hasty design and production. He was asked if he wished his team could have had more time, and his reply was in direct contrast to the criticism a lot of other people have made of the rush job.

"If I could have had more time without losing the program altogether, the answer's yes, you bet. On the other hand, having more time could have meant that you can talk yourself out of continuing it, and I think that's what would have happened. The airplane got into weight problems, and the engines were a basket case. If we had taken a year to first find out what all these problems were, I believe any presentation to Boeing's board would have drawn a 'Hey, this thing won't make us money so let's ditch it.' "

Ken Holtby remembered that at one point Boeing and Pratt & Whitney seriously considered slowing down the 747 program for more research and development work on the engines. "We had a joint meeting on this," Holtby said. "Maynard Pennell favored a delay, but Bruce Connelly and other sales people were afraid that any significant slowdown would destroy the market. So P&W was simply told to get on with it and increase the thrust."

Engine inadequacies turned up early in the flight test program, although not as serious as the ones exposed when Pan Am and other initial 747 customers put the plane into service. The first flight itself was a success. Joe Sutter's wife, Nancy, broke into tears when Jack Waddell, Brien Wygle, and Jesse Wallick (Lew's younger brother) took off—friends had been telling her, in all seriousness, that it was too big to fly.

Waddell was a little uptight, too. He was just starting to board the plane when Allen stopped him.

"Jack," he said, "I hope you understand that the future of the Boeing Company rides with you guys this morning."

Waddell looked at him sadly. "Bill, up to now I haven't been feeling any pressure. I'm sure glad you let me know."

Fortunately for Allen's blood pressure, he didn't learn until the 45-minute flight was over that a flap malfunction forced Waddell to fly the entire time with the flaps down. But Waddell and Wygle praised the 747's handling qualities—the stick forces were as light as the 727's. And it was fast, so fast that the chase plane Boeing acquired for the program was a Canadian F-86 Sabre, the only subsonic fighter that could keep up with it. After more than two decades, the 747 still is the fastest of all subsonic jetliners.

It wasn't as fast as Juan Trippe expected it to be, nor did it fly as high as he hoped; it was 11,000 pounds over Sutter's weight target, and the engines were under-powered. Sutter and Borger had agreed that the 747 should have more range and speed than the 707 Intercontinental, and to achieve this goal Sutter's team had accepted Jack Steiner's original recommendation for a 37.5-degree sweep, adding a thick wing root and thin wings. The sweep was a compromise between the 35 degrees Boeing initially planned, and the 40 degrees Pan Am wanted in order to achieve Mach .90. In the wind tunnel tests, the overall wing configuration looked good at high Mach numbers, with excellent stability and no tuck-under or pitch-up.

The 747 was supposed to have a maximum altitude capability of

45,000 feet after fuel burnoff, but thanks to the excessive weight and the weak engines, the early models couldn't achieve that altitude. Weight was such a problem that Bruce Connelly wrote Borger a letter admitting that Boeing was probably in breach of contract by exceeding the two percent weight tolerance allowed by specifications. Gross weight had gone up to 710,000 pounds with no engine thrust increase, and the contract was heading for possible cancellation or major non-performance penalties until Pratt & Whitney agreed to boost thrust from less than 39,000 pounds to 43,500.

The flight tests disclosed flutter problems, resulting from the combination of heavy engines on thin wings—a development Sutter half-expected.

"To achieve high Mach capability," he explained, "we sensed we were going to have trouble, and some of the earliest test flights showed how much trouble we were in."

He turned the flutter difficulty over to the chief of the 747 technical staff, Everette Webb. He was another Row Brown type—an unsung engineering genius to whom Sutter freely gave much of the credit for the 747's design. Webb was one of the world's leading experts on flutter, and when the Lockheed Electra ran into catastrophic flutter problems in 1959, Webb had headed the delegation of Boeing engineers who went to Burbank and helped the rival company unearth the cause.

"Sort of a hard person to work with," Sutter said, "because he was very stubborn. Like Row, he never tried to promote his own career and he was just as brilliant."

Webb came up with a fairly quick and easy solution. He put weights on the front end of the outboard engines, like the lead weights on tire rims to keep the wheels balanced at high speed. When Boeing developed the 747-200, with a beefed-up wing and higher thrust engines, flutter was eliminated without the use of this "tuning" process.

Webb wrote several papers on the structural dynamics of large airplanes that were well-received in the U.S. and abroad. One of Ev's greatest fans, although they had never met, was Professor Ito of the University of Tokyo, also highly regarded in the aviation world. Most Boeing engineers got to know their counterparts in other countries, and language barriers meant little—in the engineering fraternity, there always was a way to communicate.

Webb was an exception—he didn't seek outside contacts very much. When Professor Ito visited Everett to see the 747, Sutter hosted a lunch in his honor. A Japanese associate approached Sutter before the luncheon. "Could you invite Mr. Webb?" he asked. "Professor Ito admires him greatly."

Sutter called Webb. "Ev, can you come to the luncheon I'm having for Professor Ito?"

"Aw, I'm pretty busy, Joe."

"Ev, do you know about him?"

"Sure. He's very influential in Japanese scientific circles."

"So break away and have lunch with us. He really wants to meet you."

Webb grudgingly promised to show up. The introduction took place in Sutter's office prior to the luncheon, and Webb arrived 15 minutes late—he had been working on some technical problem and obviously didn't have socializing on his mind.

"Everette," Sutter began, "this is Professor Ito. Professor, may I present Mr. Webb of the Boeing Company."

Ito, who spoke broken but clearly understandable English, bowed graciously. "Mr. Webb, this is one of the great moments of my life. I consider you to be the foremost expert on the structural dynamics of large airplanes. I have read everything you have ever written on the subject, and it is a great honor to meet you at last."

Webb, who hadn't been listening very hard, turned to Sutter. "Joe, you'd better tell him I don't understand Japanese."

When the 747 entered airline service January 21, 1970, the interlocking problems of excessive weight and weak engines hadn't been licked. Pan Am's inaugural flight on that date was a debacle. *Clipper Young America*, ready to take off for London with 336 passengers, was delayed several minutes because of a balky main door that wouldn't close properly. There was another 25-minute delay before the ground crew finally loaded 15 tons of cargo. The 747 then waddled to the end of the runway, poised for takeoff, and an engine began overheating. Back to the terminal, where mechanics tried in vain to correct the overheating. Pan Am gave up and substituted another 747, which took off seven hours late.

It was an ignominious beginning for an airplane that had attracted so much attention and excitement, an aerial Goliath whose gross weight equaled the combined poundage of 55 Boeing 247s—the first all-metal transport the company had built only 37 years ago. And it was to get somewhat worse before it got better. Carriers operating the early models reported one flight delay after another caused by engine troubles; on the bitterly competitive Los Angeles–Hawaii route, Western's 720-Bs began outdrawing Pan Am's and United's 747 flights because the latter two had so many delays and even cancellations. The Big Bird, once awesomely labeled "the Aluminum Overcast," was now being ridiculed as the "Dumbo Jet"—the world's largest flying white elephant.

Pan Am, which had more of the early 747s than the rest of the airlines combined, took as much public criticism as Boeing and Pratt & Whitney. Juan Trippe had called the plane "a great weapon for peace, competing with the intercontinental ballistic missile for man's destiny." When he retired in mid-1968, the forthcoming 747 was supposed to be his glorious swan song; it was more like a gigantic albatross draped around his company's neck.

At one time, Pan Am had five 747 "hangar queens" out of service simultaneously, all with sick engines. The FAA actually considered grounding the plane that had introduced "jumbo jet" into aviation's lexicon (Stamper hated the term). It would have been an ill-advised action, however; the engine situation was a major annoyance, not a safety matter.

Boeing had more than a few idle hangar queens on its hands. There was a whole fleet of engineless 747s parked at Everett early in 1970— some 30 completed airplanes that couldn't be delivered until P&W corrected the JT-9D's deficiencies. They sat in front of the factory for weeks, with cement blocks hanging from the wings instead of engines. Yet no one ever lost faith in the plane—it was basically sound, well-designed, and potentially viable. Mal Stamper came home one night and found someone had left a plaque at his front door. He looked at the inscription, a quote from Theodore Roosevelt:

"Far better to dare mighty things than to take rank with those who live in the gray twilight that knows not victory nor defeat."

He knew who had dropped the plaque on his doorstep. He had seen it hanging in Bill Allen's office.

T Wilson himself exemplified the universal pride in the 747. He showed up one Sunday afternoon at Everett, the day Waddell was scheduled to run the difficult V_{mu} (velocity minimum unstick) tests at Moses Lake. Wilson and Dix Loesch rode the jump seats over to the test site and were still in the cockpit after they landed and the plane had been refueled at the right weight for the V_{mu} test.

Waddell turned to the two flight deck passengers. "All right, both you guys get off. We're ready for the V_{mu}s."

Possible danger was all Waddell was thinking of when he ordered the company's new president and an off-duty test pilot to leave the airplane. "Those V_{mu}s from time to time can get kinda sporty," he said later, "and with this big machine we weren't sure just how sporty it was going to be."

But Waddell didn't realize that Wilson felt it was his responsibility to experience a V_{mu}. Loesch returned to the cockpit while Waddell and Jess Wallick were finishing the checklist. "Jack, T's really upset. He wanted to go with you on this one."

"On a flight like this?"

"He sure does."

Wilson went—through all three V_{mu}s conducted that day, and he loved to describe how Waddell's demeanor seemed to change from tense to nonchalant as they progressed from the first V_{mu} to the second, and then to the third, with a big oak tail skid preventing any damage during the abnormal rotation.

It was probably just as well T wasn't along on another test flight involving an RTO (refused takeoff) a few years later. This one occurred at Edwards Air Force Base with Paul Bennett flying the airplane. The gross weight was 825,000 pounds and when Bennett applied maximum braking at 176 knots, all 16 tires exploded. The engineers found that the brake energy buildup was so rapid, the fuse plugs didn't release the air in the tires fast enough.

N-7470 was one of five airplanes used in a test program that logged more than 1,400 hours and 1,013 separate flights; the other four 747s were production aircraft. FAA certification was awarded December 30, 1969, although the flight test program had raised doubts about the engines. During 15 months of flight tests, there were 55 engine changes; with the 737, only one had been needed.

Boeing was leery of the JT-9D from the very beginning. Before the engine was chosen for the 747, T had Ken Holtby conduct a study of the three power plants under consideration: P&W, Rolls, and GE. Holtby picked Bert Welliver as his assistant and they spent several months evaluating the three engines. Their conclusions: neither the Rolls nor the GE engine was far enough along in development to meet the 747's delivery schedule, and P&W's was the only one that would be available in time.

Welliver then began riding herd on P&W's progress and making sure it would be delivered on time. What he was seeing disturbed him, and his reports created concern in Seattle.

"I didn't like the design at all," Welliver admitted. "There was a groundswell at Boeing to abandon the JT-9D, but we finally concluded we had to stick with it because nothing else was on the shelf."

Once the decision was made, however, Wilson told Holtby and Welliver, "Okay, now you can go back to Hartford and give Pratt & Whitney the same pitch."

They did, spending half a day with P&W engineers discussing the JT-9D. Welliver did most of the talking and sensed the resentment—here was this young Boeing engineer, as Bert put it, "telling their whole engineering department that their design wasn't any good, and beyond that telling all this talent how to redesign the damned thing."

No one said a word during Welliver's presentation—they had agreed to let him finish without interruption, then spend the rest of the day digesting what he had told them. Holtby and Welliver were asked to return the next day and hear their comments. That subsequent session was something neither Holtby nor Welliver would ever forget.

It began with Dick Bassler, P&W's engineering chief, informing the two Boeing representatives, "Everything Welliver said was wrong." From there the meeting continued to go downhill, with Welliver refusing to retract one word of his criticism, which included his belief that a major redesign was necessary.

When they returned to Seattle, they reported to T, who already had heard from a top official of United Technologies, which is P&W's parent company. He had informed Wilson he didn't want some junior engineer coming in and telling Pratt & Whitney how to design an engine.

"Let me tell *you* something," T retorted. "If he's a young junior engineer who doesn't know anything about engines, by the time this program is over, your job is to make him the smartest young junior engineer or we're gonna fire your damned engine!"

Eventually, the JT-9D became a great engine. But as Welliver had predicted, it had to be drastically redesigned. Until the engine problems were licked, the Boeing–P&W–Pan Am relationship had all the tranquility of a dock workers' strike, and Joe Sutter's patience was stretched like a rubber band.

Sutter had a temper that occasionally went off like a nuclear explosion, yet even his targets liked and respected him. One of his disciples was Phil Condit, who worked for Joe as a lead engineer in the 747 program and replaced him as executive vice president of the commercial airplane division when Sutter retired in 1986.

"Working with him one on one was an absolute dream," Condit said. "You just went in with your data, sat down, explained it, and he understood. Get him in a crowd, however, and he could be quite volatile."

During the days of those sick engines, a General Electric representative came in to see Sutter, who proceeded to rip him apart. Sutter finally stopped for breath and the GE rep protested, "Wait a minute, Joe, we didn't build the 747's engines."

"I don't give a damn!" Sutter stormed. "You guys are all alike!"

Dean Thornton saw the typical Joseph Sutter in action during the subsequent 767 program.

"We were having problems with the flight management system made by Sperry," Thornton related. "A bunch of big wheels from Sperry came in to discuss the situation with him, and Joe starts off very calmly—'Now to fix this thing, we have to work together . . . the best minds in our two companies can solve what's causing the software to run behind schedule,' and so forth. Then Sutter starts leaning forward, his voice getting louder and louder, until he finally works himself into a lather and ends up screaming: 'You'd better fix this mess!'"

But Sutter's temper was no more legendary than his justified pride in an airplane that exemplified American aeronautical prowess. The fourth plane off the line, N-731PA, was the sensation of the 1969 Paris Air Show. It had flown non-stop from Seattle to Paris, a spectacular 5,160-mile demonstration of range that almost didn't happen. Because of the temperamental engines, there was some doubt at Boeing whether the Paris flight should even be attempted. Allen was among the doubters and he called Wilson to his office.

"Listen," he told T, "I'm going to the Paris Air Show and I've lost my objectivity. So you're in charge of deciding whether the airplane goes."

T started to leave and Allen stopped him. "Incidentally, T, if you have any doubts, come down on the conservative side."

"As if I needed to hear that from Allen," T remarked later to George Schairer.

Wilson conferred with Dix Loesch and asked him to write down "all the things we have to do if we decide whether to make the flight. If we meet them we'll go and if we don't, we won't go."

Loesch's list included one crucial item: N-731PA needed 20 hours of test flying prior to making the long trip to Paris. But because of weather and other problems, they didn't complete the required 20 hours and the time for departure neared. Loesch leveled with Wilson. "T, I believe we can go out and fly this airplane for twelve hours. We've got the engines going pretty well right now, and I think we'd be better off if we just take our chances and go."

Don Knudsen was assigned to the flight as chief pilot. Wilson took Knudsen aside before the takeoff. "Don, you're making all the decisions. If anything goes wrong, put the airplane down and don't worry about the air show." Then T had a sudden flashback to the Tex Johnston slow roll with the Dash-80.

"And by the way," Wilson added, "don't do anything foolish."

Knudsen, as conservative a pilot as Boeing ever had but like most of the company's airmen very informal even with high officials, had never called Wilson anything but T. He knew exactly what Wilson was talking about.

"Why, Mr. Wilson," he said, smiling, "you know I wouldn't do anything like that."

Bob Twiss of the *Seattle Times* was already at the Paris Air Show when the 747 arrived. It approached the Le Bourget airport, the same field where Lindbergh had landed 42 years earlier, through a thick overcast. Onlookers could hear the whine of the turbines before the giant snout suddenly poked through the clouds, and the 747 appeared out of the cloud cover like a stately galleon emerging from a fog bank.

"I don't mind telling you how I felt," Twiss reminisced two decades later. "When that proudest example of American technology came out of the overcast, it made me proud to be an American."

Some of the anti-SST sentiment spilled over to the 747 before it entered service. The SST's speed was the main target of its opponents; with the 747 it was sheer size that drew the unsubstantiated predictions of catastrophe. One critic claimed the 747 would be forced to fly in specially designated corridors completely free of storms, because its greater wingspan and weight decreased the plane's structural resistance to turbulence.

"Too much airplane for a mere human to handle"—the same fear once expressed toward the 707—was heard again about the 747. In-

cluded among the anti-747 attacks was the charge that its size created
so much turbulence in its wake, any plane following a 747 at normal
separation distance would be endangered—literally knocked out of
control. This one was taken so seriously that for a short time, the
French government banned Pan Am from flying its 747s into Paris,
while the FAA announced special separation rules to protect aircraft
flying behind the monster.

Boeing ran wake turbulence tests, flying the relatively tiny 737
behind a 747 at various separation distances, then put the 737 behind
a 707 to compare the difference. Surprisingly, the wake turbulence
generated by the two planes at normal separation distances, in both
strength and duration, was only slightly greater from the 747. In one
proximity test, however, Tom Edmonds was flying the 737 and got a
bit too close; the vortices swirling from the 747's wing tips kicked the
smaller plane around as if it were a Piper Cub. After he landed, some
of his fellow test pilots commented that from the ground, the buffeting
looked severe.

"The view from the cockpit," Edmonds said dryly, "was even more
dramatic."

There also were those who said the 747 would be impossible to
tame in a stiff crosswind. The test flights proved otherwise—Waddell
called its crosswind characteristics "better than any plane I've ever
flown." And as for the "too big and complex for mortal man" charge,
the finest accolade the 747 received came from true professionals,
namely the Air Line Pilot Association's 747 evaluation committee.

"We were pleased with the handling and characteristics of the
airplane, particularly in the low speed regime," its final report stated.
"High speed stability appears excellent. . . . Handling should not be as
difficult as we expected earlier."

Praise also came from a different kind of professional group—the
passengers who began traveling on the great new bird. There were some
complaints at first: not even 12 lavatories were always adequate on a
full plane during a long flight, retrieving luggage proved hectic until
some kinks were worked out, and the plane's enormous size was
intimidating to some people. One man boarded a 747 in San Francisco
for the first time, entered the enormous cabin, and remarked to his
wife, "Look honey, just like an ocean liner!"

"Yeah," she muttered. "The *Titanic*."

The basic 747 model Boeing offered the airlines had the galleys on
the main deck, but United and Qantas opted for installing them in the
lower lobe, preferring additional seats at the expense of cargo space.
Assembly-line workers thereupon dubbed the lower deck on UAL and
Qantas 747s as "deli-bellies."

The 747's spaciousness was hard to resist for several customers who
wanted some measure of customizing on their planes. Continental's
Bob Six was an outstanding example; he had his wife, television star

Audrey Meadows ("Alice" on "The Honeymooners") help Heineman and Del Guidice design Continental's 747's interiors.

Originally, Six had ordered his three 747s with pretty much the same interiors as everyone else's. But he rode on one already delivered to American (which had bought 20 lightweight Wurlitzers at $2,000 apiece), fell in love with the piano bar idea, and wanted a similar rear cocktail lounge for CAL's planes. Then he took Audrey to Everett for a look at the mockup and asked her for more ideas.

Six ordered his 747 interiors completely redesigned only three months before delivery and got his way mostly due to Tex Boullioun, who was one of the few officials at Boeing who could get along with him. He made Boullioun promise that no other airline executive would be allowed to get an advance peek at Continental's revised interior, which turned out to be one of the most beautiful ever put into any airplane. Of all the early airline-operated 747 interiors, only those on Japan Air Lines' 747s could equal it. Audrey added the finishing touches. She had always felt that lavatories were the most ignored areas in an airplane when it came to attractiveness and originality, so she had Boeing put small watercolor and oil reproductions of famous paintings in CAL's 747 blue rooms.

Audrey christened the first 747 delivered to Continental *Proud Bird of Seattle,* and no airline chief executive was ever prouder of an airplane than was Bob Six. Prior to the 747's inaugural flight from Los Angeles to Honolulu, he had signed a contract with Sears to fly all the company's air freight between Hawaii and the mainland, and as a gesture of gratitude he invited Sears' top officials and its board of directors to be his guests on the inaugural.

They landed in Honolulu and the news media was invited to inspect the *Proud Bird of Seattle* interior. Next on the agenda was a press conference at which a reporter asked the one question that should never have been asked.

"Mr. Six," he inquired, "what do you think of Pan Am's 747 interior?"

"Right out of a Sears Roebuck catalogue," he snorted.

It was the 747 that helped solidify Tex Boullioun's reputation as an airplane salesman with few peers. He had the knack of being able to deal with the most difficult customers, and Six ranked high in that category.

There was a great deal of Wellwood Beall in Tex Boullioun. Beall's forté was his relationship with military people, the Air Force in particular. He could drink all night and show up for a meeting the next morning bright-eyed and alert, chirping, "Okay, let's review yesterday's bidding. . . ."

"He was incredible," Dan Pinick remembered. "Every one of those generals he dealt with treated him like he could walk on water—the ultimate salesman and representative of the Boeing Company."

Pinick's description of Beall applied to Boullioun—he, too, could party all night and appear at a meeting the next morning looking as if he had just completed nine hours of innocent sleep. And he had the same reputation among the airlines that Beall had enjoyed with the military—they liked him, trusted him, and knew a Tex Boullioun handshake was as good as a signed contract.

As previously noted, he wanted to be liked—that was part of his personality. He once asked Tom Riedinger of public relations, "Tom, tell me what it takes to be a statesman."

"A statesman?"

"Sure. You know, this is the kind of job where I figure you have to be a statesman."

Riedinger composed an eight-page memo on what constituted a true statesman, the gist of it being that Boullioun should aspire to combine the qualities of Franklin Roosevelt, Winston Churchill, the Pope, and Albert Schweitzer. He left it with Tex and returned a few days later to check on the results.

"Did you read my memo?"

"Yeah," Tex sighed. "What's next best?"

Boullioun had other things in common with Beall—they both enjoyed hobnobbing with celebrities, they were well-known in some of the world's finest restaurants, and each could be outwardly cheerful even when Boeing was up to its corporate neck in hungry alligators.

There was a Saturday meeting convened at corporate headquarters to discuss some current problems. The board room was filled with officers and the meeting was just about to start when Jim Prince noticed a key figure was missing.

"Where's Tex?" he asked.

No one had seen Boullioun, and Prince shook his head in annoyance. "Well, he's either in his office at Renton or he must be sick."

At noon, they recessed and went across the street to Boeing Field for lunch. A television set was on, and all eyes swiveled to the screen.

There was Boullioun, playing golf in the Bob Hope Classic.

But Tex worked as hard as he played. It was Boullioun who broke the icejam at Delta after C. E. Woolman died—"If C. E. had lived," salesman Bob Perdue once commented, "Delta still wouldn't have a Boeing airplane." But Tex got along well with Woolman's successor, Dave Garrett, and laid the groundwork for Perdue to come in later as Boeing's sales rep at Delta.

Boullioun sold Garrett four 747s, the first Boeing airplanes Delta had ever operated. Many months later, Tex sat next to Garrett at an industry function and the Delta president confessed the planes were a disappointment.

"We didn't really need a plane that large for our routes," he told Boullioun. "We aren't making any money with them and we never should have bought them."

"Dave, I'll take 'em back whenever you want—tomorrow, as a matter of fact," Boullioun said. Garrett's eyes widened.

"You serious?"

"Dead serious. Just tell me when we can expect them back."

Delta did return the four planes eventually, but as of the end of 1990, the airline had ordered some 320 other Boeing jets.

"Garrett had found out what no one at Delta apparently had ever realized," Tex said. "Namely, that Boeing was sincere in wanting to make sure any deal it made had to work for the airline."

Another word for transactions like this, of course, was *integrity*. Boullioun had demonstrated it at a time when Boeing was hurting badly, and the whole airline industry was drowning in a sea of depressed traffic that had fallen miles short of projected growth, especially on domestic routes. U.S. carriers that had ordered 747s for those routes in the late 1960s found the plane simply too big, and during the fuel crisis of the mid-1970s a number of them were mothballed in the deserts of the Southwest.

By this time, it was painful to recall what Bill Allen had said the day of the 747 rollout. With excruciating accuracy, his proud remarks had included this cautious warning:

"The 747 will be a great enterprise for the Boeing Company, and for the aviation industry, unless it is introduced during an economic downturn."

It not only was introduced just as a recession was under way, but when the oil crisis was just around the corner. So the sneers, snide jibes and wisecracks about the flying white elephants were back in full force, and some industry analysts were saying Boeing had missed the boat—that it should have built a smaller widebody, like the McDonnell Douglas DC-10 and Lockheed L-1011, each carrying about 250 passengers.

Boeing did consider such a plane even while the 747 prototype was being built. A completely new 250-passenger airplane was proposed but quickly rejected in the spring of 1968, but then Don Nyrop let Bill Allen know Northwest was getting very interested in the upcoming DC-10 and L-1011—and Allen would have committed anything short of murder to keep Douglas or Lockheed planes out of Nyrop's hangars.

He asked Preliminary Design, under Lloyd Goodmanson's direction, to develop a three-engine, 250-passenger 747 to show to potential customers, including Pan Am. Lynn Johnson, one of the engineers who worked on this rush job, said three versions were prepared in only three weeks.

"Two had the rear S-shaped duct configuration like the 727," Johnson said, "and the third consisted of a bifurcated [twin-forked] inlet in the aft body with a T-tail."

Two of the three engines were hung from the wings, like those on the 737. Table models were built of the three versions and gave the impression the plane had been designed by engineers who got 737, 727, and 747 blueprints all mixed up. Each model carried the designation "747-300."

Despite this abortive effort, however, a 747 tri-jet was no flight-of-fancy airplane. Nyrop had told Clancy Wilde that Northwest wouldn't buy the DC-10 if Boeing built a three-engine 747, and some of Boeing's own engineers had felt at the very start of the 747 program that a three-engine plane would have meshed better with the JT-9D—a case of building the airframe to fit the most available engine. But other than Northwest, there was little airline interest in the design and it was Joe Sutter and Row Brown who a few years later came up with an even better idea: the 747SP (for Special Performance).

The main purpose of a shorter, lighter 747 was to increase range to almost 7,000 miles, accepting a reduction in passenger capacity to approximately 300. At the time, in 1973, Pan Am had begun serious talks with McDonnell Douglas on the DC-10, and the timing for the 747SP (originally called the SB for Short Body, a designation Wilson hated) was perfect. Borger remembered that his first reaction to the proposed design was an incredulous, "This can't be true."

Borger, accompanied by one of his engineers, saw the SB drawings on a trip to Seattle. His companion also laughed at its appearance, but by breakfast the following morning, he had changed his mind. Borger asked him, "What did you think of the SB?"

"You mean Sutter's balloon? To tell you the truth, John, I stayed awake until three A.M. thinking about it, and I still can't shoot it down."

A week later, Borger met with Pan Am's new president, Bill Sewell, and told him about the truncated 747. "The thing I like about it is that it fits into our fleet. If we buy something like the DC-10, it's an oddball airplane. This new Boeing ends up with the same engine and the same maintenance as the big 747."

It also ended up so identical to the standard 747 in flying characteristics, that Pan Am—which bought 10—needed no additional training for 747 pilots transitioning to the 747SP. "This was the most marvelous thing Boeing did with that airplane," Borger praised. "To completely duplicate the larger 747's handling qualities was a real feat, comparable to the way the little Mercedes-Benz 190 duplicated the larger Mercedes' driving characteristics."

Boeing guaranteed that the SP would fly nonstop from New York to Tokyo against a 25-knot headwind. To meet that kind of range requirement, Sutter knew he had to keep weight down. Adopting simpler, lighter flaps helped immensely, while simultaneously keeping the airframe as strong as the bigger 747's. Borger kept hounding him about the weight, but as the design progressed Joe felt more and more confident.

"I think we really know what the weight of this airplane will be," he told Borger, "and I think we've even got a good chance of beating it."

When Borger expressed skepticism, Sutter proposed a bet of 10 cents a pound—for every pound over the weight called for in the specifications, he would pay Borger a dime and for every pound under, Borger would have to cough up. When the plane was officially weighed, it was 1,800 pounds under, and Sutter gleefully phoned Borger.

"You'd better bring a hell of a lot of dimes next time you're out here," he chortled. Borger paid off and Joe found a good use for the 1,800 coins—over the next year, each time his little grandchildren would visit, Sutter would hand them a fistful of dimes.

World tours as part of the sales campaign for a new airplane had become a Boeing tradition, and the one staged for the SP was an outstanding success and routine except for one unpublicized incident.

"Everyone had bought oriental rugs on the tour," Dave Peterson related, "and we had so many of them that between the rugs and all the spare parts we were carrying, the cargo bins were full. But the second most popular item was sheepskin coats—we bought them for about twelve or fourteen dollars and the pilots especially went ape over them, getting as many as eight coats apiece. With all the cargo space filled, we piled them in the rear johns.

"The next morning, we smelled this terrible odor and we couldn't figure out the source. The mechanics even checked the lower bins for a stowaway skunk. By the next stop, the smell was even stronger. We used every kind of air freshener known to modern science and it didn't help. We finally discovered that the sheepskin coats had been cured in urine; as long as they were kept in a store where they got plenty of air, there was no odor.

"John Stuckey was crew chief in charge of the dozen or so mechanics on the plane—we had one for every major system—and he opened a back exit before the next takeoff, and threw every damned coat out. There must have been at least fifty of them. We had to scrub out the lavatories with disinfectant, but the smell didn't disappear until about three more stops."

Peterson always carried a supply of modest gifts for officials of a host country on a tour—lighters, tie clasps, airplane models, Boeing golf caps and neckties. They came into South Africa, where Peterson had planned to have a salmon steak barbecue; he even had brought barbecue chips with him. A customs inspector refused to admit either the salmon or the chips and when Dave protested, the inspector opened his luggage where he spotted a supply of golf caps.

"Take one," Peterson suggested.

"Well, we have twenty inspectors on duty here today."

"Take all of them," Peterson sighed. The salmon and chips cleared customs.

Occasionally, hosts would reciprocate with gifts of their own. One foreign ruler gave the entire Boeing party wristwatches carrying the royal crest. But when the recipients returned to Seattle, each man had to go before the ethics committee and get permission to keep his watch.

The SP, almost 50 feet shorter and grossing some 30,000 pounds less than its bigger sister, was the world's longest-legged transport until the 747-400 series was introduced early in 1989; the latter was another Boeing miracle—a 435-ton airplane with a range of more than 8,000 miles that could be flown easily by a two-man cockpit crew.

But the later 747s had something going for them that went beyond product improvement: choice of engines. It was one of T's major moves after he succeeded Allen, and it was typically T. It would cost Boeing about $75 million to recertificate the 747 with engines other than the JT-9D, because it meant different struts, weight, nacelle aerodynamics, bypass ratios, and inlets. Yet T proposed it at a time when Boeing was trying to climb out of its 1969–71 financial morass.

It wasn't really a new idea—Boeing had gone that route with BOAC when it sold 707s to the British flag carrier by agreeing to equip them with Rolls engines, and T resurrected it at a 747 marketing meeting. General Electric had developed the promising CF-6 for the new DC-10, and its availability attracted Wilson's interest. "I want you marketing guys to tell me how many more 747s we'd sell by giving customers an engine option," he ordered.

Clancy Wilde had his market research people survey the airlines, and Clancy took the results to T. "We'd sell three more airplanes," he reported.

"I don't believe it," Wilson snorted. "You guys flunked the course. Go back and take another look."

They did and returned with slightly improved numbers: maybe as many as five additional 747s if GE engines were offered, but no more than five. T still refused to accept the results. "Clancy, I don't think your market research people know what they're talking about."

Wilde shrugged. "Could be, T, but five's the maximum." Wilson leaned back in his chair. "Well, I'm probably going ahead anyway."

"Which he did," Wilde said. "Here was T, basically a technical man, making a marketing decision against the advice of marketing experts. He turned out to be right and they were one hundred percent wrong. We wound up giving GE at least a third of our business, maybe as high as forty percent."

The 747's hump, which had become an upper lounge mostly as an afterthought, also turned into one of the plane's most popular features and a definite sales tool. United bought additional 747s largely because Bob Wylie had sold UAL on adding more windows to an extended upper section. But adding windows also led to one of Boeing's most embarrassing moments.

Japan Air Lines had ordered a new 747 with 10 windows in the lounge area. When it arrived in Tokyo, however, JAL chief engineer Noda took one look and demanded, "Where are the windows?" There were only three on each side, the result of paperwork getting mixed up; Boeing had built the airplane with the wrong number of windows, and JAL's on-site inspector had missed the mistake. The company sent a special team over to add the extra windows.

To many foreign carriers the 747 was more than just another airplane—it was a symbol of national pride to operate the world's biggest airliner. JAL was no exception. For the delivery ceremony of its first airplane, the airline flew a native artist to Everett where he painted a huge sign in Japanese lettering on a long sheet of white parchment. JAL requested that it be hung over the 747 assembly line, and Bayne Lamb asked George Nible to authorize the $2,000 it would cost to put it in place.

"We don't have two thousand bucks," the harassed Nible replied.

Boeing's JAL sales rep pleaded with Nible in vain. Then JAL sent a vice president over to insist that the sign be hung, and Nible finally authorized the expenditure. After it was hung, however, there was much speculation over what message the sign was delivering. Nible's translation might have been the closest.

"I think it says, 'Get your butts back to work on our airplanes,' " he told his staff.

The window gaffe and sign incident aside, JAL's 747 order really marked the beginning of a long and friendly relationship between Boeing and the Japanese carrier, one that led to its becoming the biggest 747 operator in the world.

Tex Boullioun was in his glory selling the 747; he was the quintessential American—informal, friendly, and outgoing. Every Boeing salesman knew that if negotiations bogged down or reached total impasse, he could rely on Boullioun to catch the next flight to the trouble scene—and it didn't matter if the call for help came on Christmas Eve.

Typical was the way he dealt with Singapore Airlines, which was about to buy the DC-10 when Tex arrived to pitch the 747 instead.

"Your airline is going to grow," he predicted (with great accuracy). "You'll need the bigger airplane."

"We won't grow to the point of needing the 747," he was told.

"If you buy the 747," Boullioun promised, "and you don't carry enough passengers to reach the break-even load factor (about 60 percent), I'll write a contract in which Boeing will refund the difference. However, the number of passengers over the DC-10 that you get, you'll give that revenue to Boeing."

The airline seriously considered this offer, then informed Boullioun it would buy the 747 on a straight contract. "In a few more years," Tex noted, "they were very happy because they would have paid us a bundle under the deal I originally proposed."

Boullioun was especially adept at working out financial arrangements for airlines that might otherwise have shied away from the 747 because of its cost. King Hussein of Jordan had ordered a new 747, then found he couldn't make the final payment due on delivery. Boullioun brashly suggested that he borrow the money from well-heeled Saudi Arabia.

"That is an excellent idea," Hussein said, "but would you bring the airplane to Jordan and let us fly it to Saudi Arabia for the necessary meeting?"

Tex arranged this as requested, the meeting was successful, and Hussein returned to the airplane wearing a wide smile. He was a licensed pilot and was allowed to fly the 747 on the way back to Jordan. In gratitude, he had arranged to land at the coastal town of Aqaba, where he hosted a buffet luncheon and joined everyone on camel rides.

"He was the only man I ever knew who flew a 747, drove a Mercedes, and rode a camel on the same day," Tex commented later.

Hussein once visited Everett with an entourage of about 40 people, and after they landed the king's chief pilot approached Boeing's Dave Peterson. He handed him a $25,000 cashier's check and another $25,000 in travelers' checks. "His Majesty would like you to cash these for him."

It happened to be about four o'clock on a Saturday afternoon. Dave got Bill Allen to one side. "Mr. Allen, there aren't any banks open and I don't know where I can get this stuff cashed. Do you know any bank presidents?"

Allen made a few phone calls and discovered that the big downtown Seattle banks kept their vaults on time locks—not even a bank president could get into a vault until Monday. Peterson got the bad news and consulted with the one man he knew might have strings to pull: Boullioun. Sure enough, Tex called a neighbor who ran a small bank in suburban Richmond Beach. Boullioun and his wife drove to the bank, picked up $50,000 mostly in twenties and fifties, and brought them to Hussein's hotel suite in the largest box they could find—an orange crate.

His extrovertish nature and negotiating skills kept Tex in a constant spotlight, so much so that at times some in the aviation community seemed to regard *Boullioun* and *Boeing* as synonymous. This was unfair to Tex, but it also was unfair to other, less colorful officers in the commercial airplane division—executive vice president Dick Welch being the outstanding example.

Quiet and unassuming—the direct antithesis of Boullioun in personality—Welch was the division's "Mr. Inside" while Tex played "Mr. Outside"; in football terminology, he did the blocking while Tex scored the touchdowns. Frank Shrontz and Deane Cruze, making their own marks during the 747's early days, had identical judgments of the two men.

"Tex was the consummate salesman," Shrontz said. "He loved to get out on the road but he was fortunate to have people like Dick Welch to take up the slack at home and do so much of the hard work."

"A real gentleman, one of the company's unsung heroes," was Cruze's description of Welch. But Deane also mentioned a Boullioun quality that many either took for granted or never really noticed.

"No matter how far Tex rose in the company," Cruze observed, "he always remembered the little people who worked for him. Whenever there was a retirement party or some other special occasion, if Tex was in town he'd show up—unannounced and, for him, very unobtrusively. Sure, he was a high roller and wheeler-dealer, but I had great respect for him, and he did a lot for Boeing's image."

Eventual selection of the 747 as the replacement for the 707s that had served eight American presidents would be a kind of vindication for the plane once derided as unreliable, uneconomical, and even dangerous. It also turned out to be the plane the Air Force chose as a "flying command post"—a combined headquarters and haven for the nation's commander-in-chief in the event of a nuclear war. And it was a 747 that NASA purchased as the only plane capable of flying the space shuttles piggyback between Edwards Air Force Base and Cape Kennedy. Acquired from American Airlines, it was the 100th 747 to come off the Everett line and went into NASA's service still carrying American's red, white and blue fuselage stripes.

When Mal Stamper was running the 747 program, the most optimistic total sales forecast for the plane over its lifespan was 600 aircraft, a figure that many industry analysts thought ridiculously high. Stamper thought it was too low and predicted that by the time the 747 production line shut down for good, about 800 of them would have been sold.

By the end of 1991, total 747 orders stood well above 1,000—approximately 400 of them representing the 747-400 series priced at some $100 million more than the first 747 delivered to Pan Am.

Success admittedly came the hard way, over a long period of time. Director Weyerhaeuser remembered serving on the board's audit committee at a time when fewer than 200 planes had been sold, and the estimated break-even point was slightly over 400 aircraft.

"For a long time I thought the four hundred and first airplane was ten years off, and that perhaps we weren't even being conservative enough," Weyerhaeuser said. "We hung on to the four hundred and first target for maybe fifteen years, and then, boy, when we approached the one thousand figure, I told my wife, 'Well, I was wrong again.' Despite all its earlier troubles, the 747 put Boeing into a strong position for three decades."

Teddy Roosevelt had been right about the rewards of risk, although he couldn't have remotely imagined the enormity of the one Boeing took with the 747. It wasn't imagination but stark reality to T Wilson.

With Allen retaining his post as chairman, T had taken over the presidency and the duties of chief executive officer April 29, 1968. To the new head of Boeing, the as-yet-unborn 747 must have looked more like the world's largest hot potato. The dark clouds of a coming recession were on the horizon, making the timing for such a huge airplane abysmal, and Allen had placed in Wilson's hands the fate of a company heading for almost inevitable disaster.

EIGHTEEN

CRISIS AND COMEBACK

WHEN BOEING'S BOARD OF DIRECTORS ELECTED THORNTON
Arnold Wilson as the new president and Allen's eventual successor,
they got a man of simple tastes, strong opinions, and a low tolerance
for incompetence.

One could add several more adjectives to describe this product of a
typical middle class, Midwest American family with high values and
dedicated work ethics. Short-tempered, blunt, impatient, impulsive
and, above all else, decisive—the latter a quality inherent in every
natural leader whether in the military, industry, or politics.

Big T, Wilson's father, worked for the Missouri highway department.
For a time, his mother's skills as a seamstress supplemented the family
income but despite their modest finances, T's boyhood and teen years
were spent in a happy family environment—close-knit, affectionate,
and caring. "I grew up a happy little bastard who enjoyed life," Wilson
reminisced.

His father always wanted him to be an engineer, and T went to
junior college in his home town of Jefferson City, Missouri, primarily
because it was inexpensive. Two years later he transferred to Iowa State,
starting out in mechanical engineering and switching later to aeronautical engineering. His brother, Jasper Wilson, went in another direction—West Point—and during World War II served as a major on
General George S. Patton's staff. T was heading for the Army Air Corps
after graduation but broke his leg in a toboggan accident, an injury
that temporarily derailed his plans to enlist in the Air Corps.

So he wrote every airplane company on the West Coast and accepted
Boeing's offer of employment as a junior engineer. He obtained a
master's degree in aeronautical engineering from Cal Tech, and began
a steady climb up the management mountain.

There was no doubt he was the overwhelming choice as the new
president, both among the directors and by Allen himself. The only

other candidate in sight was John Yeasting, who once told Carl Dillon that he had Allen's support at first, but that the outside directors were concerned about his age—T was only 47 when he became president.

Allen obviously had great respect for both Yeasting and Wilson. He had endorsed Schairer's recommendation that Wilson study industrial management at MIT under a Sloan Fellowship for one year (1952), and Wells' recommendation to put him in charge of Minuteman. Allen finally brought T to corporate headquarters in 1964, first as vice president of operations and planning and then, in 1967, as executive vice president—an heir-apparent title that seemed to indicate Allen was grooming him for the presidency. Jim Prince, a great supporter of Wilson and a trusted advisor to Allen, undoubtedly had some influence.

T almost blew a shot at the presidency shortly after his transfer to corporate. He received a call from a headhunter in New York who represented a client with a controlling interest in a major West Coast aerospace company.

"Whenever you're in New York, we'd like to talk to you," the headhunter said.

T later admitted, "I was interested enough so I didn't turn him off, but when I went home that night I didn't feel too comfortable. The next morning I told Allen I had received an invitation from a headhunter and that I felt like a guy having his first affair. He didn't see any humor in that and told me to go ahead and have my interview, but not to make any commitment until I had talked with him again."

Two people did the interviewing, and before they suggested he might be offered a job, one asked bluntly, "Are you going for the brass ring at Boeing?"

Wilson, who knew what "brass ring" meant, replied, "Well, I don't know if that's the way I'd put it, but on the other hand nobody's counting me out."

"Hell, Mr. Wilson," the interviewer said, "you don't want this job."

So George Nible finally collected that $20 bet he had made four years earlier, and he wasn't the only one who sensed that T would be running Boeing some day. In 1954, when Wilson was working in preliminary design on a supersonic bomber concept, his brother came to Seattle and T asked B-52 project officer Guy Townsend to give him a jet airplane ride. Townsend took him up in a T-33, and after the flight he asked Guy, "By the way, what does T do around here?"

"He's working on a supersonic bomber concept."

"Okay, but what's his future with Boeing?"

"He's going to run this place one of these days."

Wilson's brother laughed. "Bull. Do you really believe that?"

"I do. The man has presence, he's a fine engineer, he has a country boy charm about him that's positively undeniable, he has the courage of his convictions, and he can make a decision."

George Martin had the same instinct about T's future with Boeing. Martin was in Allen's office one day and was asked what he thought of T. George praised him to the skies.

"You certainly seem to think highly of the young man," Allen observed.

Martin pointed to where Allen was sitting. "I think he could occupy that chair some day."

That these predictions all came true was no surprise to anyone who knew or had worked with Wilson. He did not suffer fools gladly, he had strong likes and dislikes, and his impatience was monumental, but he was undeniably a leader—the follow-me type who confronted every crisis and issue with the same philosophy: "If you don't like what I'm doing, just get the hell out of my way."

It was natural for a man with such strong convictions to have his share of feuds, and T never minced words when it came to voicing his opinion of individuals. He didn't get along too well with Carl Dillon and Bob Regan, among others, and his battles with Lysle Wood, Wilson's immediate superior for several years, were simply a case of mutual professional disrespect. They clashed heatedly once during the Minuteman program and Wood, normally a mild-mannered man, was steaming.

"Wilson," he finally shot out, "the trouble with you is that everyone is either black or white. You love 'em or hate 'em. And in my opinion, the guys you really like are the ones with the big mouths!"

But later T remarked to Stan Little, "You know, that was probably the most accurate thing he ever said to me."

Wood stayed on his back even after Wilson became a vice president. T's simple tastes extended to the cars he drove—invariably they were fairly dilapidated with more mileage on them than a DC-3. He was driving a beat-up 13-year-old Ford at the time he became a vice president, and Wood thought it was demeaning.

"Wilson, now that you're vice president, why don't you get yourself a decent car?" he remonstrated.

Even after he became president and then chief executive officer and chairman, T disdained the fancy automobiles usually associated with industrial chieftains. His first foreign car was a Datsun, and came the day when he was leaving Seattle's prestigious Rainier Club parking lot and a stuffy member drove up alongside him. "Wilson, why the hell aren't you driving an American car?" he yelled.

"Because the Japanese are the only ones who've bought an airplane from us in the past seventeen months!" T yelled back.

Long before he was first assigned to corporate, he bought a small house and was still living there 40 years later; he remodeled and added to it several times, doing some of the carpentry himself, considering it a perfectly adequate place in which he and his wife, Grace, could raise their family. When Jim Prince suggested discreetly that he should move to the affluent Highlands section, where Allen and several other top Boeing executives lived, Wilson politely refused—it just wasn't his style.

If human personalities could be compared to shoes, T was a pair of well-worn slippers—some people around Boeing even called him "the old shoe." He was seldom known to work in a suit jacket; in the winter he'd sit behind his desk in a sweater, and in summer he'd be in shirtsleeves.

After he became chief executive officer, he declined to move down the hall to Allen's larger and more prestigious office, and it is doubtful whether the chief executive officer of *any* major American corporation conducted business in more Spartan surroundings. The contrast between the dignified Allen and the freewheeling Wilson was the difference between winter and summer. Dean Thornton marveled at that difference, yet with one important exception:

"It is amazing that a company could transition so smoothly from someone like Allen to T. You called Bill Allen 'Mr. Allen' instinctively—the first time I called him Bill I got a dirty taste in my mouth. He was the picture of a dignified gentleman, usually in a very proper blue suit, and then there's Wilson, totally different, although they shared some very real fundamentals—their bottom line was integrity and intelligence.

"I remember seeing T come into the executive dining room for the first time after he became head honcho. We were used to seeing guys like Allen, Haynes, Mickelwait, Prince and Yeasting—all non-squirrels with pressed suits, white shirts, and well-combed hair. Take a picture of that group and you'd think it was the IBM board of directors or the Harvard Business School faculty. Then in ambles Wilson with a rumpled brown sports jacket and a crummy bow tie. Boy, you couldn't miss the contrast."

Wilson's secretary during most of the years he headed Boeing was a pixieish but tough woman named Jane Boyd, known to all around Boeing as "Attila the Hun." It was a nickname she claimed to abhor, but she even had a special license plate on her car inscribed *Attila*. She had worked for T before he became vice president, and was more than a secretary—she was a trusted confidante.

Her best friend at Boeing was Marge Blair, who was working for Allen as his staff assistant—a kind of combined office manager and executive secretary—when T was named president. She quickly discovered how much clout the spunky Boyd carried around corporate headquarters.

"She had the guts to tell T to go stuff it," Marge said. "If she liked you, fine. If she didn't, you were dead."

Wilson admired toughness in people and Boyd was both tough and loyal. She drank, swore like a Marine, and with her husband raced twin Porsche cars as a hobby. She ruled T's office in the same way a veteran master sergeant could control the environment around his commanding officer. If Blair wanted T to attend some function, it was Jane who'd make the decision whether he should go. It wasn't so much a case of her being arbitrary; she simply knew T's mind.

"Jane was always our calibration point," Bud Coffey recalled. "If you asked her if this was the day to talk to T about some subject, she'd either tell us, 'Yes, he's in the right mood,' or she'd say, 'No, this isn't the right time,' and then she'd let us know when the time was right."

It was standard Wilson that after he became president in 1968, it took several years before he finally consented to have his shabby office redecorated. Bob Craig of facilities made an appointment with Jane Boyd to inspect the premises—he had never been in T's office and was stunned at what he saw.

"The carpet leading to his office door was worn right down to the white nap," Craig related. "The paint above Jane's desk was flaking off, and I thought to myself, *Boy, this is one lousy corporate image.* I went into T's office and couldn't believe it. All he had was a desk, sofa, and a club chair, and at one end of the room was a small conference table that couldn't seat more than six people."

T saw him looking at the table and remarked, "I'd like to have a private conference room that could comfortably seat eight to ten people. And I'd like to have a little refrigerator someplace."

Craig knew what he really wanted was a complete kitchenette with a sink, dishes, and glasses; to ask for it in so many words was simply beyond him.

After Allen retired, Marge Blair became Wilson's office manager. In that post, she saw the mercurial Wilson at his best and at his worst.

During the 1974 World's Fair in Spokane, Marge had purchased Spokane–Seattle airline tickets for some of Boeing's guests who were attending the fair but had to return to Seattle the same evening. The weather turned bad and Marge, after consulting with several vice presidents, rented a helicopter for the return trip. About six months later, T was going over expenditures associated with the Fair and saw the outlay for the helicopter. He called Marge in and bawled her out.

She never said a word, although at least five Boeing officers had given her permission to rent the chopper, and she never told T that the expense had been authorized. Somehow he found out. Years later, on the occasion of her 30th anniversary with Boeing, he put a small model of a helicopter, encased in transparent plastic, on her desk.

"As far as I'm concerned," he said gruffly, "the helicopter incident is forgotten."

"Obviously it had bothered him all those years," Marge said, "but he didn't know how to admit it."

As he did with virtually everyone, including his fellow executives, T called Marge by her last name—"unless he was trying to be especially nice, or when he was introducing me to someone," she laughed.

Blair spent considerable time in his home because the Wilsons did a lot of official entertaining. It was probably just as well Marge and Grace did the planning for visiting VIPs, T's culinary tastes being on the plebeian side. Once, during a European trip, he was in Munich and the Boeing group was being wined and dined at very fancy gourmet restaurants. Someone commented on the excellent food and T grumbled, "I wonder if I could get a good sausage and sauerkraut meal somewhere."

He had a unique hobby—he raised bees for a number of years but gave it up, as he put it, "because I was out of town too much and they needed tender loving care." He preferred bridge and pool to poker, and for a long time professed a disdain for golf—which, however, he played with more frequency after he retired. He was playing one Sunday, with Ed Renouard as his partner, against two other Boeing officers. Renouard was using orange balls and sliced a drive about 90 degrees off course, into a clump of trees.

As they were walking down the fairway in the general direction of where the ball had landed, T asked Renouard, "Got any of those orange balls?"

"Sure."

"Gimme one."

Renouard handed him a ball and T dropped it on the edge of the rough where Ed's ball had disappeared. "Play that one," he ordered. They finished the 18 holes in record time as low net scorers, but it was confession time for Wilson. He pointed to Renouard and announced, "He cheated."

Wilson attacked a golf course with the hurry-up pace of football's two-minute drill, as if he were fighting the clock instead of a scorecard. "Compared to T," a fellow golfer commented, "Lee Trevino plays in slow motion." It was part of his impatient personality, a hatred of wasted time and effort.

Yet T could be curiously inconsistent; he hated to have anyone waste *his* time, but when things were going smoothly he got into a habit he shared with Bob Six—ambling around the executive offices like a big bear foraging for food. He'd drop in on some officer unexpectedly for a chat, which usually consisted of T's reminiscing about the past. If an officer was lucky, he might get a warning call—"T's on his way down"—but sometimes Wilson didn't tell his secretary where he was going.

It worked in reverse, too. He might summon someone to his own office, and it could be for one of his brief, incisive meetings or one of T's nostalgic trips. He loved to talk about his early years at Boeing, mostly incidents involving the B-52 and Minuteman programs that really had launched his career into the corporate stratosphere, and the "squirrels" who could make his life miserable but always interesting.

T's main problem was that he told the same stories over and over again, and it was engineer Ben Plymale—definitely a squirrel type himself—who finally had the courage to protest.

Plymale had been listening to Wilson deliver one of his reminiscences for about the 10th time. "T," he chided, "you either gotta get some new stories or some new friends."

Admittedly, these excursions took place during the later years of his regime, in periods when Boeing wasn't facing some crisis. At such times, T seemed to subconsciously assume the role of an elder statesman, a kind of corporate Socrates passing on wisdom to his younger disciples. No one saw this side of him more clearly than Doug Beighle, an attorney from Bill Allen's old law firm who joined Boeing's contracts office in 1980.

Beighle brought an updated resumé into T's office when he was interviewed for the contracts job, and Wilson didn't even look at it. He spent the next hour and a half telling Beighle what a great company Boeing was to work for. And from then on, Beighle added, "I never went into T's office knowing whether I'd be there for thirty seconds or an hour.

"If he called late in the afternoon and said he wanted to see me, I knew I'd never get out of his office before it was time to go home. Yet actually it was a learning process for me. Usually he'd bring up a problem I was having, it would trigger his memory banks, and he'd give me a twenty-year background on how this problem got to where it was. I finally realized he was a great teacher."

Wilson's temper was fearsome, his bluntness legendary, his informality refreshing, if startling, after exposure to Allen's demeanor. Allen may have had his Triscuits and two pairs of glasses, but T had a more ingratiating idiosyncrasy; he often conducted meetings with his shoes off and his stocking feet on his desk or conference table. And ingratiating he could be; when he was out of the office and away from stress, no one knew what remark he might come up with.

At a cocktail party one night, T was introducing Dorothy Sessions, Sterling's wife, to another guest. "This young lady," Wilson said, "is married to the most ornery son of a bitch in the whole company." Driving home that night, she said to Sessions, "Now I know why you're not getting anywhere at Boeing."

Beighle attended an executive council meeting, the chief topic being the pricing of jetliners. Doug, new to the company, asked a couple of questions obviously stemming from his unfamiliarity with the subject. After the meeting T said to him, "I want to talk to you in private." Beighle followed Wilson to his office, expecting a royal bawling out for his ignorance, plus an admonition to keep his mouth shut for at least a year.

"Sit there on my couch," T ordered, "and I'm going to explain to you how Hal Haynes keeps his books. He'll never tell you and no one else understands it." For the next hour, T diagrammed on a yellow legal pad exactly how Boeing priced its aircraft.

His temper and irascibility often generated fear and this, combined with the Draconian measures he took during the 1969–71 crisis, created the false impression that he was far more corporate-minded than people-oriented. Wilson actually had a blue-collar personality inside a white-collar mentality, with more understanding and sympathy for the hourly workers than most realized. During the long IAM strike of 1989–90, after T had retired, he was at a dinner party in Washington and someone made a disparaging remark about Boeing's "disloyal" work force.

"Let me tell you something," T said, bristling. "Boeing people will always be Boeing people. And those young people you've just called disloyal are *not* disloyal!"

For Thornton Arnold Wilson never forgot what he had to do when he took over the presidency of a company about to be flushed down the sewers of bankruptcy and oblivion.

The illness hadn't occurred overnight, nor was the cure achieved quickly. A major corporate crisis can be likened to an airplane accident. Both result from an accumulation of mistakes, circumstances, and situations that all seem to come together at the wrong time—in the case of the airplane, a crash; in the case of a company, a financial emergency that also could be fatal.

That certainly described the 1969–71 crisis. With such major programs as the 707, 727, 737, SST, and 747 in progress simultaneously, Boeing had increased its work force in the Puget Sound region to some 101,000. Between mid-1965 and 1968, the Seattle area payroll had more than doubled. Then the roof fell in.

Airline orders dried up, and so did military contracts, and on top of everything else was the cash-draining effect of the huge 747 commitment, with its overruns and massive development costs added to those of the 737's. Then came the SST cancellation in March of 1971, and it was like throwing a rock to a drowning swimmer. It followed the recession and downturn in airline traffic that had begun in 1969 and continued through the next year.

Wilson had seen trouble coming before it arrived like an unstoppable avalanche. As early as 1966, when he became executive vice president, he had called a meeting of all managers in the Seattle area and asked them to improve the company's cash flow by cutting unnecessary expenses.

"The response," Bob Bateman noted dryly, "was underwhelming. Too few of us felt our actions would have any effect on solving a problem we didn't really appreciate."

Only a few months after assuming the presidency, T called another management meeting and laid down the law in more specific terms. This time he got some results, but they were a Band-Aid applied to a severed artery. There were plenty of airplane deliveries between 1968 and 1970 but a drastic falloff in new orders. Starting in 1970 Boeing went 17 months without a single sale to any U.S. airline; only a few foreign sales kept the production lines going. The company actually had a negative cash flow during most of this time, steadily eroding its bank credit lines and threatening its ability to meet payrolls.

Hal Haynes, senior financial officer during Wilson's 17 years as CEO, in 1966 had put together a syndicate of banks that gave Boeing a credit line to finance the 747 program, and in anticipation of the supersonic transport project. Over time, the credit line was expanded to a level of about $1 billion, but by early 1970, the 747 program was one whose hemorrhaging cash flow was starkly symbolized by those 30 or so engineless planes parked in front of the Everett plant. Boeing's inventory investment had peaked at $3 billion, a figure including all those 747s producing not one penny of revenue.

Boeing fought the war against bankruptcy on two fronts. Externally, there were the lending institutions and creditors, the latter including suppliers; the company was about $1 billion in hock to these two sources. Internally, it was bite-the-bullet time—the need to turn negative cash flow into positive. There is unanimous agreement among those who fought the war that if one man deserved the title of hero on the external front it was quiet, taciturn Hal Haynes, whose dark hair actually turned completely white during the three-year battle to avoid insolvency.

It was no wonder. One of the most critical moments came in 1970 when Allen and Haynes went east to raise more capital. They talked to Boeing's lead commercial bank and insurance company, requesting that the company's bank credit line be increased, and that the insurance company lend additional funds. They were turned down.

"I was amazed at the reception we got," Haynes recalled. "We even offered to throw in an equity kicker but it was futile. Going to them had to be one of the most difficult experiences in Allen's career—he was a proud man."

Haynes believed the reluctance was based on the fact that Boeing already owed these lenders large sums, with less than sanguine prospects for the future—at that point in time, both the 737 and 747 programs looked sick. In desperation, Allen and Haynes turned to three major subcontractors: United Technologies, Northrop and Rohr. From them they obtained the equivalent of a $150 million loan—technically, it was an agreement to defer payments.

Haynes and two of his associates, Jack Pierce and Wayne Tavis, were in constant communication with the credit line banks. The credit line agreement had a "material adverse" clause that required annual renewal, and as cash requirements kept increasing and there were additional draws on the credit line, the degree of concern on the part of the banks escalated. It became absolutely essential that they stay in the credit line. There was considerable waffling on the part of some banks, but only one—a regional institution—pulled out.

One of the key factors in the syndicate staying intact was the reputation of Hal Haynes in financial circles, but preventing defection still couldn't prevent the steady drain from the $1 billion line of credit. As it dwindled, T had to swing the axe on the home front; payroll reductions began as a relative trickle in late 1969 and accelerated into a flood during 1970 and early '71, when Boeing found itself more than $1 billion in debt.

The company's problems involved more than expensive new airplane programs, recession, and a dearth of commercial and military orders. Boeing's chief weakness in the late sixties was a severe drop in productivity, which made it almost impossible to sell *any* airplane at a satisfactory profit. Even productivity in the established 707 and 727 programs had deteriorated; Boeing had expected their cash flow to compensate for a substantial part of the 737 and 747 overruns, but this didn't happen. "The 707 and 727 cash flow was only a fraction of what we had anticipated," Wilson recalled.

T added another pertinent reason for the crisis. "Everyone had thrown more manpower at problems, whether those problems were technical or operational. The best evidence of this is what happened when we stopped hiring and the payroll dropped about fifteen percent through voluntary terminations. Even though new orders weren't coming in, we had a good backlog at the time. Output increased, costs decreased, and productivity improved."

It hadn't improved sufficiently, however, to prevent further layoffs, because with the lack of new business the backlog shrank and the credit line drain continued. "We had to lay off many fine people," T recounted, "although when our fortunes improved most of them returned to Boeing."

No department escaped the carnage and at one point early in 1970, the company laid off 5,000 people in a single week. Not even engineering was exempt; the number of engineers and scientists on the payroll went from 15,000 to 8,000. Overall, office employees—administrative, clerical and semi-technical—numbered 24,000 at the start of the layoffs and ended up at 9,000. Hourly workers were hit hard, dropping from a peak of 45,000 to 15,000. And management was drastically affected, too; the management payroll, from first-line supervisors up through vice presidents, was slashed from 12,700 to 5,400. Eleven vice presidents were missing when it was all over, a third of those listed in the annual report of 1968.

Surviving officers took drastic paycuts, starting with Allen and T. The chairman cut his own salary by $50,000 a year, and Wilson voluntarily lopped $25,000 of his—a 25 percent reduction. Drops in the proverbial bucket yet symbolic in the sense that they got the point across—survivors had to make their own share of sacrifices. In fact, the most unusual aspect of the mass layoffs was the absence of the usual corporate practice: chopping off heads at the lowest levels and leaving the middle and upper levels intact.

This wasn't done during the 1969–71 crisis. Visualize the average corporate structure as a pyramid; in rough times, most companies cut off the bottom of the pyramid because that's the easiest and fastest way to reduce costs. Boeing sliced into the pyramid's side, so that each manpower cut might start with a vice president and then widen to include managers, supervisors, office staff, and production people.

As a matter of fact, proportionately fewer riveters and machinists were laid off than in any other category. Without them, Boeing couldn't build an airplane. In contrast, most of the white-collar workers, including technical writers, program planners and administrative assistants, were far more vulnerable.

The 737's inexperienced manpower was a prime example of what happened with an accelerated buildup of the work force. Quality was a victim and so was experience continuity. Turnover preceding the crisis years was abnormally high; in 1967, the company hired 37,000 new people but in the same period 25,000 left Boeing.

"Some people hired on just long enough to find the rest room, then left through the back door," was the way one officer described the turnover, and T added dryly: "Their net contribution at that time was probably less than zero."

There were enough individual tragedies and hardships to script a hundred soap operas. One young man from the hills of West Virginia had driven to Seattle with his wife and baby. He had no money or a place to stay, went to work on a Tuesday morning, and was laid off Wednesday night. He was rehired, but this was an exception.

The impact on Seattle's economy was crushing, and even an attempt to ease the pain through a little humor backfired. Two employees of a local real estate firm spent $160 to rent space on a billboard near the Sea-Tac Airport. This was in April of 1971, the SST had just been cancelled, and Boeing's payroll in the area had shrunk from its 1968 high of 101,000 to less than 38,000. And on the billboard was this message:

> # Will the *last person* leaving SEATTLE— *Turn out the lights*

For a couple of days, the perpetrators were hailed as men of great wit. Then public opinion did a 180 and the sign was criticized as a great example of sick humor. The billboard company removed the sign, its creators futilely explaining that it was only "a spoof on all the doom-and-gloom talk."

They did mean well, and sometimes humor is part of adversity's survival kit. It was prevalent even at Boeing during these dark months. Engineer Dave Carswell remembered a standard gag of the time: "A Boeing optimist was somebody who brought his lunch to work, and a pessimist was the guy who left his car engine running in the parking lot."

Impressed with all the imploring to cut costs, a certain manager at Plant Two decided the best way to achieve this was to eliminate all unnecessary phones. He ordered superintendent Cecil McNab to remove a specific number. McNab came within one telephone of his allotted quota and refused to go beyond it.

"You gotta give me that last one," his boss insisted. The next day the manager tried to call McNab to deliver further cost-cutting orders and discovered the last phone removed belonged to Cecil.

"Why did you take out your own phone?" he demanded.

"It was the one giving me the most trouble," McNab explained.

In the middle of the big downturn, a reporter from a major East Coast newspaper came to Seattle for interviews with Boeing officials. Jim Prince was on his list, and after asking several questions the reporter concluded, "I guess the trouble with the aerospace industry is that it's so cyclical."

Prince looked at him. "I sure as hell hope so," he grunted.

T was the irresistible force during the crunch, and there were no immovable objects; the friendship and respect he might have for individual officers meant nothing when it came to saving Boeing from extinction. Few were any closer to Wilson than Tex Boullioun, who had taken over the commercial airplane division in 1968. When T asked each division to submit drastically reduced budgets, Boullioun had come back with a request for an increase, and Wilson summoned him.

"Boullioun," he began, "last night I was lying in bed trying to figure out what our board is going to do. They're not smart enough to do it now, but in six months we'll be in such bad shape that they'll have to do something. And the only thing they can do is fire me. I just want you to know there's one guy going before I do."

He looked straight at Tex and continued, "And then what will they do? They'll go out and hire some ink-and-ice-water type to come in here and run the company. And he's gonna stop doing everything except where we have a commitment, and he'll probably stop doing a lot of things that shouldn't be stopped. So you and I can do what we should do—use the few dollars we have and spend it intelligently. You're gonna go over your operating plan and take a hundred million dollars out of it."

Tex got the message.

One of the minor economy measures involved a guard gate next to the administration building. Security chief Stan Leith would have manned every gate with a squad of Marines if the budget had allowed, but Wilson considered this particular post unnecessary.

"When we started pinching down, we closed that gate," T said. "Then we got back up to a hundred thousand people and the gate was still closed. We didn't need it then or twenty years later. That gate was kind of a bellwether for me."

T relied heavily on Wes Maulden's industrial engineering expertise when it came to cost-cutting, and Maulden's forté was productivity, or manpower efficiency. When Boullioun became head of the commercial division, T transferred Maulden from corporate to Renton as the division's executive vice president with one principal goal: to increase the ratio of people directly associated with actually building airplanes as opposed to indirect overhead.

In most industries, including Boeing, the accepted ratio was 75 percent devoted to overhead support—in other words, if you have 100 people employed in an industrial organization, 75 of them would be in sales, facilities, finance, accounting, etc., with only 25 manufacturing the product. Maulden never believed in those numbers and one of the first things he did at Renton, Sam Lowry remembered, was to summon all functional managers, who were told the support ratio at Boeing was going down to 65–35.

"It was unheard of," Lowry said, "but by God, we did it."

Maulden could be as tough as T, and there were other officers equally willing to play hardball: Boullioun, Stamper and Dan Pinick in the commercial division, and Ollie Boileau in aerospace. Pinick cited the case of one senior manager, a vice president, who got his notice to reduce manpower and flatly refused to comply.

"I'm not going to do it," he declared. Pinick glanced at Wes.

"You have to," Maulden said.

"I won't. The cut is wrong and I refuse to do it unless you make it an absolute order."

"But if we have to order you to do it," Maulden suggested with deceptive gentleness, "why do we need you at all?"

That particular vice president was gone within the month. Pinick, recalling the incident, said, "I realized later I had just watched a Boeing vice president get fired, and I learned that if you're not going to go along with a program, there's no reason to hang around."

One of the most perceptive appraisals of Maulden's value to the company came from Frank Shrontz. "His greatest contribution was the advice he gave people," Shrontz said. "His door was always open and he was always willing to listen. He had a tremendous ability to assess people, to take on the real issues and not sweat the little things. He was good for Wilson—he probably was one of the few senior executives who'd take T on and tell him he was off base when he was. It caused a stormy relationship between the two, but they had great respect for each other."

Among the intriguing anomalies within the Boeing hierarchy was the Wilson–Maulden–Stamper triangle, and Wes literally was a man in the middle. He was close to both T and Stamper, but his admiration for Mal wasn't always shared by Wilson. Yet T never let his attitude toward Stamper affect his relationship with Maulden, as a lesser man might have done. One of Wilson's greatest strengths and assets as a leader was his tolerance of the wide-ranging personalities existing in the Boeing family—the squirrels, the squares, the mavericks, and the off-beats. T didn't mind occasional feuding so long as no one lost sight of where one's final loyalty lay: Boeing.

And that tolerance, generating an all-for-one, one-for-all spirit, was badly needed in the three years the company tottered on the brink of disaster. Boeing was an army in retreat, and its morale at best could be described as grimly determined to survive. Dan Pinick, then a young executive in the middle of a bloody learning process, was an astute observer of the mood around corporate headquarters:

"In retrospect, it was Boeing's finest hour and management at its best, sizing itself down without losing it and literally going out of control. But on the human level, it was terribly difficult. I had to get rid of my own people, cutting hundreds. These were fellow managers, men with families and mortgages. Dean Thornton and I were heads of our respective finance departments, and we'd 'totem' the staff reductions. We'd take a section, listing everyone from top to bottom, and the bottom twenty-five went into the next increment down. Then you'd re-totem. Some guys would slide down two or three notches and eventually would hit bottom and get the pink slip.

"It was tough. You'd have all these senior managers making these personnel decisions, and then they'd have to do it again and then a third time. The people who went out first tended to be the most mediocre employees, but they soaked up all the available outside jobs in the area and later the better people had to go—and that was really tough, knowing there were no jobs left for them. Even those of us who were in the heart of the cutting process didn't understand at first how far we had to go. It was a rough way to mature, something no one who went through it will ever forget."

At every level, hourly and salaried, the layoff yardstick was job function. Some were combined with other functions, some were eliminated entirely, and all were subjected to streamlining—T wanted a "lean and mean" company. In one respect, salaried employees were subjected to closer scrutiny and tougher standards than the hourly people; their retention was based more on evaluated performance and capability than on length of service.

The totem pole technique cited by Pinick was especially rough on some veterans who found themselves in the lower 25 percent. Many were offered early retirement rather than face the stigma of demotion or outright dismissal. Downgrading, with salary reductions, was frequent during this painful process. Some employees who had come to Boeing from other states simply were sent home, which had little effect on Washington state's unemployment compensation fund—Seattle's unemployment rate reached a horrendous 17 percent at the height of the layoffs.

Boeing did everything possible to help people relocate. The personnel department was turned completely around; instead of hiring, it was assigned the task of aiding people to find other lines of work or continue their professions with other companies. As Stan Little described the effort:

"We helped people prepare resumés and mailed them to *Fortune* 500 corporations, we set up counseling programs to help people learn how to apply for a job, and we invited about a hundred companies to come in and interview laid-off Boeing employees, although the latter wasn't a great success because it was a bad time for all aerospace firms.

"When it was all over, we put together a team called 'Operation Homework,' which looked at the techniques we had used in hiring people and training them. There were a number of things we did wrong that we swore we'd never do again, but I'm afraid when the next boom hit, we made some of the same mistakes. The aerospace industry has a history of overmanning production lines, and Boeing is no exception. We hired too many and then cut—it's a terrible waste of manpower."

A lot of lessons were learned the hard way in those three years, the chief one being that it was possible to get along with fewer people than anyone realized, which still didn't make the discovery a matter of joy—there were too many familiar and friendly faces missing.

Streamlining was the magic word, and it took many forms. Consolidating facilities was one avenue, starting with the new Plant Two 737 facility and the 707–727 factory in Renton. Jack Steiner called in the six men who headed the respective engineering, manufacturing, and finance departments in these three airplane programs, and informed them they were to come back in two weeks with a plan for integrating the two facilities. "You'll also have to recommend the three men who'll head the combined division," Steiner added, "because three of you will be downgraded or even lose your jobs."

It was like telling a bombing squadron half the pilots on a mission were to fly as Kamikazes, but those six men returned within two weeks with the requested reorganization plan—including which of the six were to run engineering, manufacturing, and finance in the consolidated 707–727–737 division. The new 737 plant was shut down and temporarily put up for sale, with 737 production moving to the 707–727 factory at Renton.

Plant One was finally sold to the Seattle Port Authority, and the original Red Barn was later moved to the future Museum of Flight site next to Boeing Field. The government-owned Missile Production Center also was closed. By the end of 1972, Boeing had deactivated or disposed of about 10 million square feet of covered office, warehouse, and factory space, while selling more than $30 million worth of machine tools, office furniture, and test equipment.

All so-called "overhead activities" with some degree of commonality, such as transportation, mail, security, printing, and fire protection, were combined into a single organization: the Seattle Services division. Accompanying this consolidation was a new accounting system that required the separate operating divisions to buy their overhead service from Seattle Services.

The same reorganization plan was applied to computer operations. At the time, Boeing owned $100 million worth of computer equipment, almost entirely utilized to support company programs. As airplane orders shrank, unused computer capacity resembled Carlsbad Cavern, and Boeing Computer Services was established as a new subsidiary under Bob Tharrington. One by-product of this reshuffling was the assignment of 16 BCS specialists to the job of computerizing manufacturing control at Everett and Renton, a move that helped clean up an inventory jungle.

This was a reform close to Maulden's heart—he was something of a computer evangelist, preaching its virtues to the Boeing executive flock—including its most irreverent unbeliever. The infidel was Dean Thornton, who hated computers when they began appearing throughout the company and ordered the first one installed in his office removed. Maulden was shocked when he heard of the sacrilegious act and tried to convince Thornton how valuable and time-saving a computer could be.

He pointed to the one he was using. "Look, Dean, this one even stores a telephone directory."

"I can get a name out of a phone book faster than that thing can tell me," Thornton scoffed.

"That's impossible."

Thornton picked up a telephone directory. "Pick a name," he challenged.

Maulden did, but Dean found the same one faster. They raced a half-dozen more times and Thornton never lost, although this still didn't shake Maulden's faith in the computer chip.

The axiom "every little bit helps" applied to the crunch. At Everett, where 747 production had dropped from seven aircraft a month to one and a half, the lights and heat in a number of offices and rest rooms were turned off to save on utility bills and such areas were marked "Deactivated."

T's toughness had masqueraded the stress under which he constantly labored, stress of such magnitude that it almost cost the company its leader. Wilson was aboard a Northwest flight from Seattle to Washington, D.C., in January 1970—he was to attend the christening ceremony for Pan Am's first 747, with first lady Pat Nixon scheduled to swing the traditional champagne bottle. T was tired—he had been arguing with Lawrence Kuter, a Pan Am senior vice president, over delivery schedules and payments. He also was fed up with Pratt & Whitney's sick engines, and here, literally, was a heart attack on its way to happen.

Only a few minutes out of Sea-Tac, T began having severe chest pains. The plane landed in Spokane and Wilson was rushed to a hospital where he hovered between life and death for several days; at one point, he suffered a cardiac arrest and was pulled out of it just in time.

Assured that T was out of immediate danger, Bill Allen called Clancy Wilde.

"I imagine it cost Northwest quite a bit to make that emergency landing at Spokane," he said offhandedly.

Wilde wasn't sure why Allen had brought the subject up, but agreed. "They had a full fuel load and had to dump a lot of it," Clancy said. "Several thousand dollars' worth, anyway."

Allen promptly phoned Don Nyrop and offered to pay all costs for that landing. The surprised president of Northwest thanked him but declined. T laughed when he heard about it.

"The only thing more surprising than Allen making the offer," Wilson remarked, "was Nyrop's turning it down."

While he was incapacitated, Allen ran the company until T was ready to go back to work—ornery as ever and Boeing a long way from getting out of the woods.

The turnaround was due to a number of factors, T's achievement of his "lean, mean" goal being only one. A 1971 Air Force contract for a new Short Range Attack Missile (SRAM) was a relatively modest but welcome development. The moribund 737 production line was kept alive when the Air Force ordered 19 aircraft to be used as navigation trainers (T-43s). This came at a time when the demand for the baby Boeing was so skimpy that one Boeing engineer, Bruce Rayfield, came up with the idea of turning the 737 into a transport capable of taking off or landing on an aircraft carrier.

"Dumbest idea I ever heard of," Wally Buckley snorted, yet at that stage engineering was willing to try anything. To prove a carrier-based 737 was at least feasible, Boeing built a mock carrier deck 600 feet long on Whidbey Island and Lew Wallick landed one there safely, stopping 41 feet from the end. Not bad, considering the fact that the flight decks on the Navy's big fleet carriers were more than a thousand feet long.

Three more government contracts in this period helped the company's recovery. NASA picked Boeing to build the Mariner 10 spacecraft that eventually photographed Venus and Mercury, a project that not only proved brilliantly successful but one that put Boeing back into the space program on an ever-increasing scale. The second award involved integration of offensive avionics in the B-1 bomber, which proved to be a multi-billion-dollar program before its completion years later. The third was a contract for four 747 airborne command posts.

In the end, however, a single program stood above all the others as the one playing an immense role in the comeback from crisis. It was the rebirth of the 727, and the transformation of this supposedly obsolete, washed-up design into a modern airliner that literally created its own new market niche.

It was primarily Jack Steiner's idea to modernize the 727, and he fought for it at a time when many industry experts were predicting the demise of narrow-body transports the size of the 727—the public wouldn't accept them, they claimed, not with the advent of wide-body jetliners like the DC-10 and L-1011. A larger 727? No market, the analysts insisted, but Steiner thought they were wrong.

The 727-100 had been stretched late in 1965; under engineers Lynn Olason's and Bill Clay's direction, the fuselage had been lengthened to provide additional seats, and Boeing marketed the plane as the 727-200, with the same system, wing and engines. But the 200 didn't even have the 100's range; despite the 189-seat maximum capacity it offered, the initial 200 was not that attractive to the airlines.

When Olason discussed plans to stretch the 100 with Frank Kolk of American, Kolk was not only unimpressed but worried. "You're stretching it so much, you're gonna make it a dog," he warned.

Northeast and Northwest ordered the first 200 version, put into production after Boeing began getting airline input to the effect that the wide-body jets like the DC-10 and L-1011 were too big and uneconomical to operate on medium-haul routes, mostly between city pairs where traffic was too heavy for DC-9s and 737s, yet too small for the wide-bodies.

"Everybody was selling wide-bodies," Steiner recalled, "but the airlines suddenly found they needed smaller airplanes—it was a market niche nobody was filling, and by accident we hit the nail on the head."

Steiner originally had wanted Boeing to build the 727-300, putting a new wing and bigger, high-bypass engines on the 727-200. But he proposed the design when the company couldn't have financed anything that ambitious, and he was turned down. So Steiner compromised; he took advantage of an improved, higher thrust JT-8D to improve range, upgraded the 727's systems, and then added the real clincher—a completely modernized interior featuring large enclosed overhead storage bins, and cleverly designed sidewalls and lighting copied from the 747. It gave the cabin a "wide-body look" of spaciousness that was surprisingly effective, if mostly illusionary. He also reportedly bootlegged a new landing gear beam past T and Maulden that increased the plane's payload.

This was the Advanced 727-200, a bargain-basement rework that not even Boeing dreamed would achieve the success that it did. More than half of all 727s sold were Advanced 200s, and as late as 1990 an incredible 50 percent of all U.S. passenger traffic had flown on 727-200s since the advanced model was launched in 1971. For several years, it was this plane along with Minuteman II and other military programs that provided Boeing with its only positive cash flow, and almost singlehandedly wiped out the company's debt. By 1974, Renton was turning out 14 727s a month, at a record productivity figure of one manpower hour per pound of aircraft, an achievement that did not escape Wilson's attention.

T always felt Steiner had accepted too much credit for the original 727 program, and Wilson hoarded praise of executives anyway, but he recognized what the new 727 had done for Boeing. "Steiner," he remarked one day, "I don't know whether you designed the 727 or not, but I do know you helped pay off our billion-dollar debt."

There was general agreement on that assessment, including those who disliked working for Steiner.

"Jack saw the whole world through whatever he was working on," Dean Thornton said. "World War Three could start a block away and it would be incidental to him."

Thornton and Steiner were among the Boeing officers aboard the Dash-80 when it was flown to Washington for presentation to the Smithsonian in 1972. A number of airline guests also were on the flight, including Eddie Carlson, who had just been named United's new CEO. Carlson, a veteran executive with the Westin hotel chain, had no airline experience and any technical talk was pure Greek to him. During much of the flight, Steiner had him backed against a bulkhead, extolling the virtues of General Electric's new CFM-56 engine.

Danny Palmer of sales finally took pity on Carlson and stepped between them. But Jack couldn't resist one last shot.

"Eddie," he said earnestly, "the most important decision in your career will be the CFM-56."

"That well may be, Jack," Carlson said politely. He walked away and whispered to Palmer, "Danny, what the hell is a CFM-56?"

Maulden, who felt strongly that motion did not necessarily mean progress, wasn't the only officer who tried to cure Steiner of his workaholic habits. Mal Stamper and his wife invited the Steiners on a ski trip and Jim Morrison, who was working for Jack in Renton, got a call from the ski resort. It was Steiner, with instructions for Morrison to perform some important task, but his voice was muffled.

"Jack, I can hardly hear you," Morrison complained.

"Stamper doesn't want me to discuss business this weekend," Steiner explained, "so I'm calling from the closet."

Phil Condit reported to Steiner when the advanced 727-200 program was under consideration and was summoned to Jack's office.

"I just had a conversation with Tex Boullioun," Steiner confided, "and he informed me we were not going to work on any new derivative airplane." The rest of the conversation between Steiner and Condit consisted of a two-way conversation Jack had with himself.

"Now you might ask, Phil, why wouldn't we look at a new derivative? And I would say we always have to look at them, no matter what. You might say that Tex doesn't think we should do this right now. And I would say that if he really understood how the development process works, he'd want us to do it."

Added Condit: "For the next thirty minutes, so help me, Steiner acted out the two roles—himself debating with Boullioun. And by that time, he had convinced himself that what Tex really wanted him to do was to be working on derivative airplanes."

Delta's subsequent decision to keep Northeast's original 727-200s, combined with Boullioun's magnanimous offer to take back the airline's unwanted 747s, finally became Boeing's foot in Delta's door. The carrier ordered new Advanced 727-200s, although Boeing discovered that Delta's technical people could be just as tough as their counterparts at other major airlines. Its engineering chief was Don Hettermann, an ex-mechanic who rose to the post of vice president of technical operations and earned the respect of everyone at Boeing from T Wilson on down.

"When Delta bought the 727-200," Bob Perdue said, "Hettermann wrote down twenty-two items he thought needed to be fixed on the airplane. And he was right on twenty-one of them."

Perdue, who was Boeing's sales rep at Delta so long that he acquired a temporary Southern accent, was the one who clinched the sale. He was in Dave Garrett's office shortly after Delta asked the Civil Aeronautic Board for permission to acquire Northeast, and Garrett was lamenting the maintenance problems inherent in operating a fleet of mixed aircraft types; DC-8s and DC-9s constituted the bulk of Delta's equipment, but in addition to the 727s it would take over if the merger went through, Northeast also had six Convair 880s that would be added to the 10 Delta already owned. Delta had another maintenance "oddball"—some DC-8s it had purchased from Pan Am, a different model than the DC-8s it was flying.

This gave Perdue the opening he needed. "What would you think of us taking all your 880s and Pan Am DC-8s off your hands, and we'll sell you 727-200s as their replacements?" he suggested. "That would eliminate two types of airplanes from your fleet."

"It might make some sense," Garrett admitted.

This was in the fall of 1971. In October, Perdue arranged for a Lufthansa 727-200 to visit Atlanta. A number of Delta officials were invited on a demonstration flight, and several Delta pilots flew the plane. About a week later, Garrett informed Perdue he was ready to deal. Dick Welch, then head of airplane division finance and contracts, flew to Atlanta with Steiner to work with Perdue on contractual arrangements, the chief stumbling block being that all bets were off if the CAB rejected the Delta–Northeast merger. It finally approved the acquisition, but took so long doing so that Boeing feared the contract would be voided.

"Landing Delta at long last was really something," Perdue said. "It brought back a memory of my first day in Atlanta. I was reading a copy of *Delta Digest*, the employee magazine, and there was a letter in there asking the editor to settle a bet: had Delta ever owned a Boeing airplane? The tone of the answer was no, and we're damned proud of it!"

With the success of the 727-200 and Boeing's return to solvency came the real change in command: in 1972, Bill Allen decided on complete retirement, T replacing him as chairman. The official changing of the guard took place September 29, 1972, but a week before, the Bocing Management Association had staged a huge farewell bash for the beloved William McPherson Allen.

It was held in Building 14-01, the old Thompson site, and some 5,000 people showed up. Don Smith, then director of facilities, was chairman of the event, which featured Marni Nixon, the singer whose voice had been dubbed for Audrey Hepburn in *My Fair Lady*.

There were a number of displays keyed to the events, planes and missiles associated with Allen's 27-year career at Boeing, including a new 727-200. But the highlight was a B-47, symbolic of the sweptwing era that this aviation giant had helped create. Bill Allen had never admitted to great sentimentality, but the morning after the party he and Mef sneaked down to Building 14-01 and took pictures of all the displays.

Ed Wells also retired in 1972, but he stayed on as a consultant and was to play an important role in Boeing's next commercial jet venture. Allen, although he retained an office in the administration building, accepted the most tenuous link with the company for which he had done so much—he became chairman emeritus, a post he held until 1977 when the directors named him honorary chairman.

The legacy Allen bequeathed Boeing was expressed not so much in the airplanes on which he had risked the company's future—the 707 and 747 in particular—but in the unyielding, uncompromising integrity that he branded into the company's reputation. This was his hallmark, his greatest strength, his most impressive contribution.

His conservatism and dignified personality were the products of his legal background and upbringing. He once showed Marge Blair an old photograph taken at a family picnic. His father was wearing a black derby, vest, and stiff-collared shirt with one sleeve rolled slightly back. "I guess that was the extent of my father's being casual at a picnic," he remarked almost wistfully.

Allen had a reputation for coldness, but those who knew him intimately knew he was far from cold. "My chief regret," he told Marge after he retired, "was not having spent more time with my family." And on rare occasions, a sense of humor peeked out from under his reserve.

One day during the mid-fifties, Allen was touring Plant One in the company of Fred Lauden and Frank Terdina, the factory's general manager who had the voice of an itinerant hog caller—it was claimed that when Terdina issued an order, it could be heard in Plant Two. All three of the trio were as bald as a baby's rump, and under the plant's bright lights their scalps gleamed like three small searchlights. The lead man in quality control, Ken Queit, who had a voice even louder than Terdina's, was wrestling with some problem that he decided needed the general manager's immediate attention. He spotted Terdina marching through the factory with Allen and Lauden.

"Hey, Chrome Dome!" he bellowed.

The three men came to a halt. So did all work, and a dead silence descended upon Plant One as three bald heads swiveled in the direction of that booming voice. Queit's supervisor, Bob Bassett, held his breath.

Allen glanced quizzically at his two companions. "Okay," he asked, "which one of you is Chrome Dome?"

The laughter didn't die down for several minutes.

Allen's commitment to integrity infected every officer, even in the most dire times when it was tempting to cut a few corners just to get business. One salesman confided to Carl Dillon that he could sell a few 727s to a certain foreign country if Boeing would buy its president a Learjet.

"If you support the idea, Allen might go for it," the salesman suggested.

"There's no way Bill Allen would approve that deal," Dillon declared. "Or Yeasting, either. Forget it."

Allen tried to spread the company's travel business around, but he personally liked to fly Northwest. He stopped in Chicago one night on a 727 sales trip, accompanied by a team consisting of Steiner for technical matters and Bruce Connelly from the business side. On this particular trip, Allen also had invited Frank Shrontz, who was getting his feet wet in the mysteries of writing airplane contracts. They met for dinner with Pat Patterson, who inquired, "How was your United flight from Seattle?"

"We came on Northwest," Allen confessed.

Shrontz remembered, "There was a chill in the air for about thirty minutes before Patterson recovered."

Human nature being what it is, both Allen and Wilson had their favorites, and with the change in command some of Allen's saw their influence diminished, while some of T's found their futures brighter. Each had a policy of keeping executive salaries low, including their own. Both, however, would reward top talent with stock options and in the process made relatively wealthy men out of many officers of that era.

In 1974, Boeing stock was selling at less than $12 a share; it split six times in the next 16 years, stockholder equity soaring from a 1974 total of some $955 million to more than $8 billion. If one had purchased 25 shares on January 2, 1980, for $1,240.63, by December 1989 the stockholder would have owned 82 shares worth nearly $5,000, and would have received $707.58 in dividends.

Over the years, Allen's idiosyncrasies dimmed when compared to the lofty standing he achieved in the annals of aviation. "Inspirational" was the most perceptive adjective that could be applied to his career—he was a role model for corporate integrity at a time when corporate cynicism was a way of life.

The last years of his life were painful ones to those who loved him, and to Allen himself. He began to suffer memory lapses, attributed at first just to old age but later diagnosed as the dreaded Alzheimer's disease. Lowell Mickelwait saw the memory loss symptoms begin in 1980, five years before Allen died, and they grew progressively worse until he needed a male attendant by his side constantly. His brother Dudley had died of Alzheimer's and Allen believed his mother may have had the same affliction.

Allen died October 29, 1985, and flags were lowered to half-staff at every Boeing site across the nation. Memories of him are warm, golden, genuinely and deeply affectionate. For a long time, T could not talk about him without a catch in his voice. Even remembering Allen's tendency to be so starchly strait-laced can produce smiles instead of frowns. Typical was his adamant refusal to allow any alcoholic beverages to be served on company property, including the executive dining room, a rule that could prove embarrassing when Boeing was entertaining airline customers.

Ludwig Boelkow, head of a German aerospace company, ran afoul of the temperance edict during a Seattle visit. He was lunching in the executive dining room with several Boeing officers, including Allen, and the waitress unexpectedly asked, "Would anyone like a drink before you order?" Allen's face turned the color of freshly spilled blood, but Boelkow said innocently, "I'd love a cold beer."

"I'm sorry, but we don't serve alcohol here," Allen apologized, glaring at the waitress.

"The chef keeps a couple of cold bottles in the refrigerator," she chirped, and Boelkow got his beer—although no one else dared join him.

Much to some people's surprise, however, Allen went along willingly with a practical joke played on T right after he became president. Mal Stamper, Wes Maulden, Tom Riedinger and Ben Wheat were the instigators (although Wilson always thought Tex Boullioun also was responsible), and they laid out a plot the CIA would have admired. Their inspiration, or maybe motivation, was T's great pride in the first office he ever had with an adjoining bathroom that included a shower.

Step One of the scenario was to hire the shapeliest model in the Puget Sound area. The "committee's" choice was the reigning Miss Seattle Boat Show, a honey-haired beauty named Monica. Step Two was to figure out a way to get Wilson out of his office for a few minutes so they could smuggle in Monica. To achieve this, it was necessary to enlist Allen's aid—the plotters reasoned only a summons from Allen would get T out of the way, and Allen agreed to cooperate. He would call Wilson to his office, and after asking him some innocuous question he would mention that he'd like to see T's modest office.

The conspirators decided that the script called for both a Plan A and a Plan B in case Plan A didn't work. A was predicated on T's offering to show Allen his bathroom. If T didn't suggest this, Plan B called for Allen to request a look.

Riedinger was assigned the task of getting Monica to the administration building by five P.M., the established zero hour for Allen to phone Wilson.

Plan B was never needed; as soon as Wilson and Allen came in, T announced, "Hey, you gotta see my new john." He was all set to open the door when out popped Monica, clad only in a towel.

"T," she pouted, "you told me we'd be alone."

A company photographer, who was sneaked into the office seconds before, captured the stunned look on Wilson's face (T wisely kept the negatives). "You could see his whole career going by him in a minute," Stamper recalled. "We assumed she was wearing a bikini under the towel, but we weren't sure."

Allen, who was laughing as hard as anyone else, provided the crowning touch. Violating his own rule against drinking on company property, he opened a bottle of champagne and toasted T's promotion.

Wilson thought the gag was wonderful; he relished such moments of free-spirited comradeship and camaraderie, for the streak of nostalgic sentimentality within this granite-tough chieftain was a mile wide. "We had a lot of fun in those days," he often remarked wistfully to interviewers.

No group was more conscious of the differences in style between Allen and Wilson than Boeing's directors. George Weyerhaeuser, from the vantage point of observing both men for many years, offered a perceptive appraisal:

"Allen was both a father figure and a very strong, well-organized man whose board meetings were run more as a learning exercise for the directors. Bill gave us a chance to interact, but with him it was mostly a matter of listening to him and being informed, rather than debating or arguing. Occasionally, he'd even give me advice on how to run Weyerhaeuser.

"T was brutally frank, laying it all out in his unique and refreshing style. He called everything the way he saw it, and in colorful language. I suppose you could say that Allen's legal background made him more restrained and less emotional than T, but Wilson didn't discourage reaction or debate. He took bigger risks than Allen, although admittedly the 707 was quite a gamble. Bill was perfectly capable of doing what had to be done, but T was more wide-ranging, and risk didn't bother him."

And T listened to the board far more than Allen ever did. There was a directors' meeting during the worst time of the crisis, and Wilson announced at its conclusion, "There won't be a December meeting because of the holidays."

Weyerhaeuser frowned. "I think that with all the problems this company is having," he said sternly, "there *will* be a December meeting." And there was.

The directors were badly shaken when T had his second heart attack. Then, not many months after Wilson's recovery, another personal tragedy hit the company's executive ranks with the death of George Stoner. He had recently come to corporate as senior vice president of operations in 1970 and had been elected to the board of directors. Many considered him to be Wilson's possible successor in the years ahead, but his death put Mal Stamper in the running for the president's spot.

Wilson made the official announcement at a 1972 meeting of top officers and managers in the Plant Two theater.

"Malcolm Stamper will be Boeing's new president," he informed them. Then he added, as only Thornton Arnold Wilson could, "But if anyone wants to know who's boss, *I* am!"

It wasn't really fair to Stamper, but that was T—no matter which president the directors elected, there wasn't any doubt who was going to run Boeing, and he was going to run it for the next 15 years as one of the strongest, most dynamic and colorful leaders in the history of American industry.

NINETEEN

OF CUSTOMERS AND COMMANDOS

A FEW MONTHS AFTER THE 747 BEGAN FLYING THE WORLD'S airways, T Wilson got a firsthand look at a major problem that had been allowed to fester too long. While Allen was still chairman, T had accompanied George Nible, Tex Boullioun, and power plant specialist Art Smith of Pratt & Whitney on a trip to Europe where they planned to brief various airline customers on the 747's engine problems. Germany, France, and Italy were the three priority stops on their itinerary, and all three visits were unpleasant eye-openers.

At Lufthansa, Gerhard Hoeltje was joined by the airline's purchasing head, Walther Greitsch, a former tank commander in Rommel's Afrika Corps who had been a prisoner of war and liked almost everything about America except that part of Texas where his POW camp had been located. He spoke excellent English—too excellent for the trio of Boeing executives, who were lectured non-stop for an hour on how poorly the company was supporting its airplanes. "It used to be good," Greitsch declared, "but now it is at absolute bottom." Hoeltje nodded gravely.

After this shocker, they went to Paris where Paul Besson, a top Air France executive, launched into a lengthy dialogue covering all the Pratt & Whitney engine problems and poor engine support. He was so worked up that no one in the room got a chance to respond. There was a cocktail party planned for later that evening, but at the end of the meeting the party was cancelled at Air France's request; the Boeing and P&W people drank alone. Nible said later, "You know you've got one unhappy airline when T Wilson can't get a word in edgewise."

A meeting at Alitalia was an instant replay of the Air France engine and support complaints. The Boeing contingent flew home from Italy in full agreement, as Nible put it, that "we had to improve customer support or we weren't going to sell any more airplanes." After they returned, Boullioun discussed the situation with Mal Stamper and the two of them approached Jim Blue, who in 1970 was running pre-flight and delivery—a department that had been reduced to a skeleton staff. They asked him to take a look at whether customer support—the technical nomenclature was field services—needed an overhaul.

Blue subsequently reported back that field services as a separate organization didn't really exist; field service engineers reported to engineering, flight test reported to sales, maintenance reported to engineering, and so on—there was no integration of customer support activities.

"We have to pull all these groups into a single, autonomous new cadre of maintenance technicians to augment the field service engineers," Blue urged. Tex and Stamper picked Nible for the job and put Blue under him. They hated to pull Nible off the 747 program, which he then headed, but customer support needed top attention.

Before putting the new organization together, Nible and Blue headed for Europe where they had set up a meeting of some 40 airlines, all Boeing customers; Greitsch of Lufthansa chaired the no-holds-barred session that Blue ruefully described as "a wire-brushing."

"He tore George and me apart," Blue recounted. "He told us our customer support was terrible, yet here we were laying off thousands of people." But this didn't bother Nible when he briefed T on the meeting—because Wilson, despite the company's grim financial straits, said simply:

"Nible, when you set up a new support organization, I don't want to hear of any Boeing customer having a problem because you didn't have the resources to solve it."

It wasn't exactly a blank check, but it was enough for Nible and Blue to get the job done. They were a pair of new brooms sweeping clean, and they went into corners that hadn't been dusted for years. In Blue's own words:

"It wasn't that support didn't exist; it was just on a low burner. The previous support groups had acquired a Rodney Dangerfield complex— they were trying, but they weren't getting much respect from Boeing. Some of them wanted to do their jobs but were hamstrung by budgets. George and I went out and visited several airlines that hadn't seen anyone from Seattle for a long time.

"You have to earn respect and we worked our butts off. My wife told me that during the first three years I was on the job, I averaged a hundred and ninety-five days a year outside the United States.

"We brought in some excellent people, like Al Heitman and Willie Tattersall, but we also inherited some good people. The attitude we always tried to instill was simple: if a customer was having trouble with an airplane, we'll fix it first and then find out if Boeing or a supplier was at fault; that if an airline tells us it has a problem, it *has* one, and we don't try to convince it otherwise. I'll give you one good example: Qantas.

"George and I went to Sydney, were there a week, and came back with a book of handwritten action items. I fanned these out to our engineering people, we got all the answers, and had them back to Australia thirty days later. A lot of things Qantas was bringing up were painful because they were hard to solve that soon, but because of the input we built a better airplane. This was before delivery of the first Qantas 747; they had been checking out other 747 operators and were telling us, 'Look, we're ten thousand miles away from everywhere and our maintenance problems are unique.' "

Originally, Boeing's customer support operations had been spread around the various departments. The system worked in the early 707 days when Boeing was relatively small, but as its family of airplanes grew, as Nible phrased it, "customer support got away from everyone."

The reorganization took all support functions away from various departments and consolidated those functions into the new *independent* unit, with its own engineers, pilots, mechanics, and spares personnel. Every time Boeing delivered a new airplane, customer support put a team into the airline a month before the aircraft arrived. Depending on the carrier's technical capability, the team might consist of only a service engineer and maintenance technician, or as many as a dozen specialists—the size of the support group was dictated by the size of the airline's own engineering department.

It was a system not only admired but emulated by others. Mercedes-Benz once sent representatives to Seattle to study how it worked. Airbus looked at it, too; the European manufacturer, which became a strong challenger to Boeing's supremacy, actually requested—and received—Boeing's support manuals.

T's pride in Boeing's customer support was unlimited—he always felt it was one of the company's strongest assets. Wilson's own role was important, inasmuch as he had approved the choice of his two Minuteman alumni, Nible and Blue, as the customer support reformists. It didn't hurt that the pair were such close friends, a team that generated not only success but a collection of yarns that became a part of the Boeing legend.

Nible was not the world's greatest traveling companion, largely because flying was not his favorite pastime. Nor was he the typical tourist, anxious to sightsee. Once, however, Blue talked Nible into going swimming in the Red Sea. George traveled light and had only one pair of shoes with him, which he wore to the beach. While they were in the water, an Arab youngster came along and took off with his shoes.

"I met their flight in London," Al Heitman remembered. "Nible got off the plane wearing airline booties."

Dean Thornton accompanied Nible on a trip to Japan. "It was Thanksgiving," Thornton related, "and we had a terrible time finding a turkey in Tokyo. We finally located one, but approaching dinner time we couldn't find George. It turned out he was in the hotel kitchen. He had been telling the chef how to cook it."

His aversion to flying notwithstanding, Nible would go anywhere to solve a customer problem or complaint, and so would Blue. Like Boullioun, their word was as good as a 50-page contract drawn up by 10 lawyers, and the goodwill customer support people generated for Boeing, even in countries where Americans were not always welcome or trusted, was immeasurable. Clancy Wilde was another "ambassador from Boeing"; after he was instrumental in selling some planes to Thai Airways International, the Thai shipped an elephant to Seattle, which arrived already christened "Clancy."

The customer support people were often teachers who learned a few lessons from their "pupils"—the carriers who admired Boeing but weren't reluctant to point out shortcomings. The four "down under" carriers, Ansett, Trans-Australia, Air New Zealand, and Qantas, were typical of the airlines in that category. They were populated by some tough, demanding people who didn't think just the name Boeing automatically assured customer satisfaction.

One of them was Eric Kidd, who went to work for Qantas at age 13 and served the airline for 47 years before retiring as vice president of maintenance. When Heitman arrived in Sydney as Boeing's new customer service representative, he was ushered into Kidd's office and faced the 6'3" red-haired maintenance chief, who gruffly acknowledged the introduction, adding, "You'll be number seventeen."

"Seventeen what?" Heitman inquired.

"The seventeenth Yank bastard I've gotten rid of."

Heitman bristled. "Let me tell you something—I'll still be here when you leave."

Heitman was sitting next to him the night Qantas gave Kidd a retirement dinner. The airline's CEO was winding up a laudatory speech and Heitman tapped Kidd's knee.

"What's the matter, Yank?"

"You've got about ten minutes left, Kidd, and I'm still here."

There are enough stories about customer support to fill a book, let alone a chapter, and many provide evidence that the swift efficiency of the field service representatives occasionally surprised even the airlines. A few years ago, a British Airways 747 flew through a cloud of volcanic ash over Indonesia and all four engines flamed out. The flight was at 37,000 feet when the flameout occurred, and the plane dropped to 12,000 before the crew got the engines restarted.

The captain had radioed a "Mayday," and 44 minutes after sending the signal, he had made an emergency landing in Jakarta, where the first person he saw was Boeing's Jimmy Garber.

"Captain," Garber said, "I'm Boeing's field service rep here—I understand you had a problem, and is there any way I can help you?"

The pilot stared at him incredulously. He didn't realize the machinery that had been set in motion when he radioed "Mayday" and advised London he was putting down in Jakarta. Barry Gosnold of British Airways immediately called Seattle and informed Dave Cockrill of customer support what had happened. Cockrill called Jakarta and got Garber out of bed.

"Jimmy, you've got a problem with a British Airways 747 that'll be landing there within the hour."

"They don't land here on Thursdays," Garber pointed out.

"It's an emergency," Cockrill said, and went on to explain. Garber, a 747 specialist who knew every component and system in the plane (he had been a mechanic in 747 pre-flight and delivery at Everett), dressed hurriedly and was waiting for the flight when it landed.

Weeks later, the captain and copilot were visiting Seattle and Heitman took them to lunch. The main subject of conversation was the speed with which customer support had reacted, and Heitman told them how the call from Gosnold had ignited all the activity. The captain turned to his copilot.

"See, I told you what they were doing. They were watching us all the time—Boeing has a spy satellite!"

The Delivery and Flight Test Center at Boeing Field was a final checkpoint for catching such assembly line sins as a dented galley, and through the years it became tougher and tougher in its inspection procedures. The center was considered part of Boeing's commitment to customer support, and its responsibility did not end when an airplane was delivered to a customer.

During the first 30 days a new jet was in regular service, the center received daily reports on its performance, including pilot complaints and any mechanical problems. These "how's it doing" summaries were posted for the delivery staff to see and act on if necessary. John DePolo, who had worked on the delivery flight line for years and became the center's manager in the mid-eighties, liked to compare airplanes with people. "Some misbehave and some are almost perfect," he said. "The misbehavers we keep working on until they've reformed."

Al Heitman saw customer support's field service arm grow to an organization of more than 300 people stationed in 54 countries. Most are either carefully screened former airline mechanics or graduate engineers, licensed in both airframes and engines. There was some friction between the engineer and mechanic types at first, but the two categories gradually blended.

Heitman himself represented the mechanic-trained rep; Willie Tattersall, in charge of field services under Heitman, had an engineering background. But as Tattersall put it: "It's not important whether a rep has a college degree or not—what matters is how he performs."

Boeing adopted a policy of moving the reps to different stations every three to five years. Heitman explained:

"If you leave a guy at one location too long, he either becomes mayor of the city or his wife is so in love with the place she refuses to leave and you can't transfer him. Nor do you want to leave a man at one carrier forever—he starts working for the airline while Boeing sends him his check."

There was a third reason for the transfer policy, however, that was equally important. The reps were picking up useful maintenance tricks and tips from the airlines they worked with, and by transferring them to other carriers, these ideas for improvements went along with them.

The bottom line for customer support and field service is airline schedule reliability, which can become a problem when a carrier starts operating a new type of airliner that may have teething troubles, especially high-tech systems with minor bugs. When Boeing introduced the 747-400, field service reps met every flight to check on performance and correct any complaints. And there still is an unwritten law that the reps, whether they work for Boeing, McDonnell Douglas, Airbus, or anyone else, help each other. It isn't unusual for a Boeing field rep to see a DC-10, A-300, or L-1011 grounded because of a mechanical, and offer to help. Competitors' reps have reciprocated, too. "The important thing is to keep an airline's planes flying, no matter what company you work for," Heitman emphasized.

Human nature being what it is, however, Boeing's field reps like to cite instances where they performed above and beyond the call of duty when it came to solving problems on somebody else's airplane. Heitman came to Taiwan to check on how things were going at China Airlines and bumped into General Lee, the vice president of maintenance, who greeted him with extraordinary enthusiasm.

"I want you to meet the Airbus representative," he insisted. "He is the finest I have ever met—absolutely the best in the business."

Reluctantly, Heitman accompanied Lee to an office. Lee opened the door and pointed to the occupant. "There is the finest Airbus man in the Far East!"

Heitman was looking at Tom Tam, Boeing's field service rep in Taiwan.

It turned out the airline had an A-300 that lost a belly access door on takeoff, and all efforts to find the door failed. One of the local Airbus reps had asked his home office in Toulouse to ship a new door, but was told it would take several weeks to deliver one. Lee asked Tam for advice—without the access door, the plane couldn't be pressurized and would be out of service indefinitely.

"All you have to do is design a temporary patch," Tam told him.

"Would that work?"

"Sure. At least you can operate the plane until the new door gets here."

"Could you do it?"

"Yes, but it's not a Boeing airplane, General. Airbus has to do it."

Lee returned the next day. "Tom, Toulouse told their people here the patch won't work. You have to design it."

Tam did, the patch worked, and Heitman filed the incident in his memory as one more justification for the pride Boeing takes in its customer support organization.

Enhancing customer support is a small, highly specialized Boeing unit known as Aircraft on the Ground, or AOG, which performs miracles with damaged airplanes that even airlines have considered unrepairable. In its early days, AOG was known as "Regan's Raiders," after manufacturing chief Bob Regan who approved the initial organization.

Its first major job involved a 707 that had undershot the runway at Guadeloupe in the French West Indies in 1960, collapsing the main landing gear, wiping out the nose gear, and turning the belly skin into metallic spaghetti. No one was killed or seriously injured, although an elderly woman passenger suffered a fatal heart attack after she got out of the plane and saw the wreckage.

The pioneering 50-man AOG team that arrived on the scene included Floyd Nestegard as coordinator, Glenn Jones, and Al Heitman. Nestegard, who had joined Boeing out of a North Dakota teachers' college in 1941 and worked first in the Model 314 wire shop, became known as the "father" of the AOG program.

There was no hangar at the airport, so the crew worked through intermittent rain showers and under a broiling sun. The airline's local representatives thought the 707 should be written off as a total loss; Nestegard and Jones, whom Floyd named as team captain, believed otherwise and informed the carrier the plane would be repaired in 30 days; the job was finished in 29 but a minor hitch developed—a small oil leak was discovered in one engine. Pan Am had a spare oil cooler in San Juan, only a short hop away, so Boeing test pilot Sandy McMurray flew the 707 there early in the morning to pick up the part. As so often happens after an accident, the airline had painted over all identifying logos on the tail and fuselage before the AOG team had begun repairs.

Sandy had four people with him: his copilot and flight engineer, Glenn Jones, and an official from the airline. When they landed in San Juan, they were met by a U.S. Customs inspector who was extremely suspicious of five men who had arrived in an unmarked airplane. Only Jones had a passport with him, and the inspector wasn't impressed by the airline man's business card, the sole identification he had on him. Jones explained why the plane was unmarked, but the Customs official didn't believe him and summoned the local Pan Am station manager to examine the 707 and verify their story.

"Is this the plane that crashed at Guadeloupe?" the inspector asked.

"No way," the station manager said firmly. "I saw pictures of that wreck and it would have taken them six months to make it flyable."

The five men were arrested and jailed until Jones called Seattle and got someone at Boeing to convince Customs they were for real.

The AOG teams learned to work under horrendous conditions, from desert heat to icy winds. Nestegard once surveyed a 707 in Turkey where the temperature was 40 degrees below zero, and one group got caught in the middle of the revolution in Angola—Nestegard remembered being confined there for eight days in a hotel room, watching artillery shells bursting outside. He had a team in Cairo the day the 1973 Israeli-Arab war broke out. The Boeing group managed to finish repairing a 707 sufficiently so it could be flown out by a test crew, but without passengers. The rest of the team finally got out of Egypt on a bus normally only used within the airport confines—the trip to safety took 35 hours, and included 21 stops for military security checks.

One of the most demanding AOG assignments occurred after a freak thunderstorm over the Jan Smuts Airport in Johannesburg, South Africa, January 15, 1980. The storm lasted a half-hour, dropping hailstones up to the size of a man's fist and putting dents more than two inches deep into the wings and fuselages of parked planes. Among the damaged aircraft were four South African Airways 747s, a 727, four 737s, and a pair of 707s. The hailstone holocaust struck when most of the planes were out on the ramp, ready for departure, and even some in the hangars were damaged when the hail went through heavy plate-glass skylights.

It took the 747 survey team four days, working at least 12 hours a day, just to inspect the damage and compile a list of the parts and tools needed for repairs. The 707/727/737 team needed eight days, and a Flying Tigers 747 freighter had to be chartered to carry 63,000 pounds of replacement parts from Seattle to Johannesburg. Ailerons, elevators, flaps, spoilers, and huge skin sections were among the damaged components; not until mid-March were final repairs completed on the last of the 11 affected aircraft, although two of the 747s were back in service in a month.

In terms of time and manpower expended, Johannesburg topped the AOG list, but there were other missions equally or even more challenging. Typical, yet uniquely dramatic because of the circumstances, was an AOG assignment to Damascus, Syria, in 1969; hijackers had forced a TWA 707 to land there, then blew off the nose of the plane, including the entire cockpit. An advance AOG survey team rushed to the scene, advised TWA that the plane could be salvaged, and notified Seattle what was needed for repairs.

Boeing diverted a nearly completed 707 nose section from the Renton assembly line, and stuffed in the wiring, plumbing, and instrumentation that fitted the airline's specifications. Wiring and plumbing components were left extra long so they could be pruned later to the required length. The new cockpit was loaded on a whale-like "Guppy" transport—one of the converted C-97s—and flown to Damascus where a 58-man AOG crew was waiting.

They had a long wait—the Guppy took nine days to fly from Seattle to Syria, a harrowing trip delayed first by strong headwinds, and then a forced landing in Sicily because of engine trouble. But the Boeing team didn't sit around idle. Within minutes after arriving in Damascus, they had started preparing the fuselage for mating to the new section. There was a production break near the forward passenger entry door where the new nose would fit, so the first task was to clean up all the debris and torn metal from the area.

Then they jacked up the fuselage and cut away what was left of the old cockpit at the production break. When the nose finally arrived, the crew just wheeled it up on a dolly and began riveting. It took four days to connect all the instruments, wiring, and hydraulic plumbing.

The once-ravaged 707 was flown first to Rome, where TWA had good maintenance facilities, for a preliminary inspection and then to the airline's main maintenance base in Kansas City for final flight tests. It went back in service with a different serial number—for psychological reasons, TWA didn't want crews to know they were on the 707 "with the nose job." Vice president of flight operations Bill Meador then very quietly had the number changed again just in case anyone had caught on to the first switch. And one captain had.

He came into Meador's office and began teasing him about the secret switch. "You thought you were pretty smart, changing that number. I found out what the new tail number is just by checking the FAA records in Oklahoma City."

"That so? Have you seen it or flown it yet?"

"No, but I've been watching for it."

Meador smiled. He didn't have the heart to tell the captain he had just walked off the same airplane.

The Damascus job had followed the procedures Nestegard had established for AOG operations, one that still applies today. The survey team went in first and prepared a "flow chart" that outlined priority repair areas, those requiring more manpower and parts, plus the tools and other necessary equipment. TWA was given an estimate of the man-hours needed and the cost of repair.

More than one carrier has underestimated the speed at which these commandos can work. When Heitman was a field service rep in Australia, a tow tug ran under the nose of a brand-new Qantas 747 and tore off a large section of skin. An AOG team arrived and started the repairs at six A.M. Eric Kidd came into Heitman's office around nine.

"I want to go over and take a look at how those AOG people are doing," he announced. "We'll walk over there around noon on our way to lunch and find out if the structure was damaged."

"Eric," Heitman warned, "if you want to see that airplane, you'd better go right now."

"They won't have the skin off until this afternoon. Lunch time will be fine."

"I'm telling you, if you want to see the frame, noon's too late."

Kidd persisted and visited the AOG team on the way to lunch. The replacement skin was already on the airplane.

Heitman, however, fell victim to the truth of the ancient axiom: "Pride goeth before a fall." He headed an AOG team that went to Miami where a Northwest 707 had been damaged during refueling—a mechanic had overpressurized the outboard section of the right wing, which had swelled up like a balloon and popped all the ribs. It was one of Al's first assignments in charge of an AOG crew and after getting the initial survey report, he had convinced Northwest it would be cheaper to install a new wing than repair the old one.

Heitman arrived in Miami with his 12-man team at noon, checked them into a hotel, and by two P.M. they were at an Eastern hangar, where the Northwest 707 had been towed. He already had located a spare wing that had been shipped from New York, and by six P.M. they had the damaged wing off. A huge flatbed trailer rolled up to the hangar, carrying the crated new wing. Heitman thought, *Boy, you're really gonna make a name for yourself—they gave you ten days to do this job, we've already got the old wing off and the new one's here.*

They opened the mammoth crate and discovered New York had shipped a brand-new *left* wing. It took another six days before the right wing arrived; there were only two trucks in the United States capable of hauling a 707 wing—the one already in Miami and another in Philadelphia.

AOG team members learned to be self-sufficient, knowing they might have to work in remote areas far removed from civilized amenities. Carrying their own coffee and toilet paper became standard procedure; tools might range from the smallest wrench to jigs or airbags for raising a fuselage off the ground, but in AOG's early days the teams didn't always have access to portable jigs and big airbags. Heitman recalled a repair job in Lisbon that required the removal of a tail fin from a smashed-up 707; removing the four attaching bolts was easy, but they couldn't find anything capable of lifting the fin itself.

They finally located an old army wrecker, a World War II relic, but the fin was so heavy that when the cable lifted it, the front end of the truck rose two feet in the air. Nestegard had to hire several local residents to sit on the truck hood so the front wheels stayed on the ground.

Working for AOG definitely was not a nine-to-five job, and each team member kept a bag packed at all times. Nestegard once was ordered to fly to Las Vegas to survey a 707 whose nose had been blown off by a bomb. It looked like a fairly quick, easy trip, so he told his wife he'd be home that night. He caught a flight from Seattle to San Francisco where he was supposed to change planes for Las Vegas, but he was paged at the San Francisco airport and told to head for Johannesburg instead.

So he boarded a flight to Chicago, spent two hours shopping for clothes (he had only an extra pair of socks and shorts with him), and then flew to South Africa where he stayed a week surveying a damaged 707. On the way home, he stopped in London where Heitman met him.

"We've got a 727 down in Denmark," Heitman told him. "Seattle wants you to survey it."

When Nestegard returned home, his one-day trip had lasted three weeks. Such was life in AOG, but all the uncertainty and difficulties paled when measured against the pride Boeing takes in this elite group. Elite was no exaggeration; each man had to be certified in every aircraft category—electrical, structures, engines, flight controls, and hydraulics. They could call on specialists if necessary, but they themselves were real jacks of all trades.

Until AOG built up its own inventory of spare parts, for a long time the teams would take them off assembly line aircraft, or would cannibalize from older planes taken in trade-ins, which was faster than having to manufacture a new part. Speed was the determining factor, and meeting AOG's "ending date"—the day the airplane is ready to go back into service—became the greatest source of motivation.

In working with airlines of many nations, both AOG and customer support, not to mention Boeing's salesmen, came in contact with new cultures and mores that had to be respected, even though they could be frustrating simply because they were so unfamiliar to Western ways of conducting business.

This was particularly true in Japan, and even more so in the People's Republic of China—a market Boeing cracked in 1972, creating big headlines around the world. It may have been Richard Nixon who opened the door a crack when he flew there with Henry Kissinger in February of that year, the first American president to visit Red China. The Chinese subsequently bought 10 707s, and by late 1991 had purchased 112 Boeing jetliners including the 707, 737, 757, 767, and 747—the only model missing from their commercial fleet was the 727. And according to Boeing people who have worked with the Chinese, the initial 707 order stemmed partially from the great impression made by Air Force One.

That, for instance, was the opinion of O. M. "Rusty" Roetman, an ex-Navy pilot who joined Boeing in 1966 and was director of international sales at the time of the 707 sale.

"None of the routine aspects of a sales campaign occurred before that sale," Roetman said. "The main reason we got in there was because Kissinger and Nixon showed up in a 707."

Tex Boullioun had been trying for months to establish some kind of contact with Red China, mostly through their ambassador to Romania whom Tex had met while selling some 707s to the Romanian airline. But it was veteran Boeing salesman Byron Miller, like Roetman an ex-Navy pilot, who had taken over the China file Boeing had established in 1971 and actually opened the door wide enough for negotiations to begin.

There had been a spate of rumors even before Nixon's visit that the People's Republic of China might be ready to establish commercial ties with the West, jetliners being at the top of its reported shopping list. Nothing in the way of official overtures had come out of China, however, until Miller, early in March 1972, wrote to the China National Machinery Import and Export Corporation suggesting that Boeing was interested in selling some airplanes.

Three weeks later, Miller received a cable with two invitations, the first to the Canton Trade Fair and the second to a meeting in Peking for a technical discussion on jet transports. The cable sent Miller on a mission to China that began April 15 and lasted five months, a period in which he grew a mustache, made two trips back to the United States to prepare formal sales presentations and obtain a government export license, and learned the protocol for dealing with the Chinese. They were gracious hosts but tough bargainers, as both Miller and Boullioun—who eventually came into the negotiating process—discovered.

"The trickiest part was the financing," Tex related. "The Chinese didn't want to deal with American banks, and suggested that we work out some kind of arrangement with Canada—the airplane payments had to go through Canada. Very few Asian countries want long contracts, and that's true of the Japanese as well as the Chinese. They aren't like us, with platoons of lawyers dictating contract language.

"Yet the Chinese were difficult negotiators, because they wouldn't stay on one subject and deal with specifics. They'd nod and agree, but the next day they'd be arguing the same points again as if the previous agreement never existed. So you'd have to go over a particular clause, provision, or subject again and again, sometimes twenty or thirty times. They became easier to deal with, but even without lawyers, they can be tough negotiators."

CAAC (Civil Aviation Administration of China), the Chinese state airline, had been operating mostly Russian-made transports, all of them afflicted with what was then typical of Soviet commercial planes: they were overweight and engine unreliability was notorious. The latter was such a problem that when the Chinese ordered the 707, they also purchased a spare for every engine on the 10 planes, obviously expecting them to prove as troublesome as the ones on their Soviet-built aircraft. Al Heitman visited China some 17 years later and found 32 of the 40 spares still in their original crates.

Boeing's customer support organization took over from sales after the $125 million contract was signed, and that meant training Chinese pilots and mechanics to fly and maintain their new American jets.

About 200 air and ground crewmen made up the first contingent that arrived in Seattle to attend "University of Boeing" classes. Showing them hospitality was difficult at first; the group was under strict government orders to avoid fraternization with all Americans out of the classroom. They stayed in a sealed-off wing of Seattle's old Olympic Hotel, and even had their own cooks, all arranged by Dave Peterson's customer relations organization.

It so happened there was a group from the Taiwan state airline in the same training program; relations between the Taiwan government and the People's Republic of China being what they were, great care was taken to keep the two delegations apart. Even coffee breaks were scheduled at different times, so the Chinese mainland and Taiwan trainees wouldn't encounter each other in a hallway. Someone from the training department came into Nible's office one day and announced, "We really screwed it up—we put the two groups on the same bus this morning."

"How did they get along?" Nible inquired anxiously.

"How would I know? They were all speaking Chinese."

For that matter, the Chinese trainees wouldn't speak English in front of the friendly Boeing drivers at first, although they understood and spoke the language well enough to converse with instructors. At the suggestions of Matt Chen, longtime Boeing China salesman, the company established two technical schools in China itself, to supplement the maintenance training received in Seattle on Boeing equipment. The idea was to take youngsters fresh out of high school and teach them to become aircraft mechanics qualified to handle any type of plane the state airline operated.

Until they felt their own people were fully capable of servicing the 707, they contracted with Pan Am to handle maintenance. Once the schools were in operation, however, Chinese mechanics were used exclusively, and from all accounts they were good.

It took two years to build the schools and get them operational, including a curriculum aimed at qualifying them for U.S. airframe and powerplant (A & P) licenses. There were 28 youths in the first class, and the head of the Chinese government's transportation department was worried—the FAA's certification tests were in English, which none of them spoke or wrote.

All 28 graduated and came to San Francisco to take the FAA examinations. Twenty-six got both the airframe and engine licenses; two had problems with the airframe test but passed the engine exam. Boeing flew all 28 to Seattle for a graduation banquet where their top student delivered the class thank-you speech—in English.

Nible, as did so many Boeing people, became not only an admirer of both the Chinese and Japanese, but a good friend. He may have hated to travel, but the exception was the Orient where he built up a mutual admiration society that flourished long after he retired. Al Heitman could never visit China or Japan without having someone ask him, "And how is Mr. Nible—how is his health?"

Given modern tools, the Chinese could do a superb job; they even built a 707 clone. Eventually, they were awarded subcontracting work, manufacturing vertical fins for the 737. Nible was astounded at the product they turned out.

"In terms of quality control and workmanship, the fins were as good as anything built in Wichita," he said. "Their riveting is absolutely beautiful. You give 'em the right machinery and they'll turn out superior work."

When the People's Republic bought the 767, a very sophisticated airplane with a lot of digital cockpit instrumentation, Boeing sent a number of Chinese students through an electronics course. Their instructors found out that the youngsters were going downtown to buy used VCR sets, which they'd take back to their hotel, tear apart, and rebuild just for practice. Nible asked one instructor how the kids were doing.

"When a Chinese student graduates," he told Nible, "he could be an instructor himself. Believe me, they're sharp."

All of which meant a lot to Nible, who realized how far the Chinese themselves had come since that first 707 sale when maintenance had to be farmed out, and customer support was playing nursemaid to an airline totally inexperienced in Western operating practices. The fact that the Chinese, like everyone else, were flying the 767 with a two-man crew was an indication of their willingness to adopt modern standards. They used to operate their 707s with a five-man cockpit crew—captain, copilot, radio operator, navigator, and flight engineer plus—on many flights—a political commissar who actually made it a six-man crew.

"When they came out of the cockpit," Nible recalled, "we couldn't figure out where the hell they all sat."

The warm friendship Boeing customer support and sales people felt toward the Chinese also applied to Japan, and John Swihart was a good example. When Clancy Wilde reorganized the sales department around the time the SST was killed, he offered Swihart a chance to switch from engineering to sales; knowing he had worked with Lufthansa and Japan Air Lines during the SST program, he gave him a choice between Europe and the Far East, as director of international sales in either region.

Swihart picked the Far East, and in mid-1973 moved to Tokyo where T Wilson had beefed up Boeing's presence by opening a full-sized corporate office.

Boeing's relationship with Japanese civil aviation dated back to 1964 when it sold four 727s to All Nippon Airways. ANA's president had taken a demonstration ride during the prototype's world tour, and told

Byron Miller he would pick the 727 over the Trident if Boeing could match the British jet's earlier delivery schedule.

There was only one way to accomplish this; the fourth airplane off the line was slipped out of United's delivery slot and leased to All Nippon temporarily, nailing down the four-airplane order without affecting United's delivery commitments. But the ANA sale had even greater consequences—Japan's Civil Aeronautics Board refused to issue an import license unless Japan Air Lines also acquired 727s. So ANA offered to withhold announcement of its order for three weeks if JAL would join them in buying the Boeings.

Up to that time, Boeing salesmen hadn't been able to get JAL technical or management people to even talk to them, but under this government pressure JAL went along with the All Nippon proposal and not only became a 727 customer but, like ANA, a staunch Boeing supporter and friend.

Swihart decided to retain the JAL account for himself. His first assignment was to sell JAL the 747-SR (Short Range), the SR being a high-density airplane carrying some 500 passengers. He also was trying to convince JAL the airline should pick the 747-SP over the DC-10.

He had been in Tokyo less than three weeks when he decided it was time to contact JAL president Asada for an appointment. Swihart called Asada's male secretary on the phone—it was a Tuesday, Swihart remembered.

"I'd like to come over tomorrow afternoon and talk to Mr. Asada about the 747 and DC-10 competition."

"Oh, no, Swihart-san, you cannot see Mr. Asada until two weeks from Wednesday, and then only for ten minutes."

"I'll take the appointment and thank you," Swihart sighed.

Two floors up from Boeing's Tokyo office was the headquarters of Nissho-Iwai, one of Japan's top trading companies through which Boeing dealt with its Japanese customers, including JAL. A Mr. Kaifu was the trading firm's top officer, and Swihart—disappointed over the delayed appointment—went up to see him.

"Kaifu-san," he confided, "you know what we're trying to sell JAL, but I can't get an appointment with Mr. Asada until two weeks from tomorrow—and then only for ten minutes."

Kaifu pondered this dilemma. "Swihart-san, you play golf?"

Swihart confessed he had never swung a golf club in his life. Kaifu had five phones buried under a mountain of paper; he finally found one and dialed a number, speaking rapidly in Japanese. Swihart learned later he was talking to a Japanese pro golfer who ran a golfing school.

Kaifu arranged for three days of golf lessons, then set up a game with Asada and JAL executive vice president Takagi. This, plus dinner at the club, resulted in Swihart spending 15 pleasant social hours with these two important officials. When Kaifu dropped him off at his hotel

Saturday night, Swihart mentioned how productive and enjoyable the day had been. Kaifu nodded wisely.

"You see, Swihart-san," he smiled, "how important it is to play golf in Japan?"

By the time Swihart held his brief scheduled meeting with Asada, a politely formal affair in accordance with Japanese business customs, he already knew JAL was just about committed to the DC-10, and that while the airline considered the 747-SP a little too big for its needs, Boeing should keep trying with other airplanes.

The American sense of humor often was lost on foreign customers, language differences and unfamiliarity with American slang being two obstacles to understanding and appreciative laughter.

Jack Pierce, Boeing's treasurer for many years, was in Warsaw negotiating a financing arrangement with the Polish airline, LOT, for the 767-ER. Pierce was trying to make a point and used a familiar American expression. "It's like dealing with a deadbeat brother-in-law," he explained.

The remark drew blank stares from everyone in the room.

Pierce had a great inspiration. "How many of you are married?" he asked. "Raise your hands."

Almost everyone did.

"How many of your wives have brothers?"

Again, a large show of hands.

"Okay, how many of those brothers have borrowed money from you and never paid you back?"

Light dawned on about 20 faces and a roar of laughter swept the room. Pierce noticed several men writing down the word "deadbeat" on their notepads.

As the jet age matured from revolution to routine, Boeing encountered an increasing number of carriers whose governments wanted to share in the production of airplanes they were buying, China being just one example and Japan another. These subcontracting or supplier agreements were called "offset," because the production work partially offset the price of an airplane. These airlines, especially those that were government-owned, were motivated as much by political considerations as economic—they needed to tell their governments that by buying Boeing airplanes, they were providing domestic jobs. Australia became the first offset supplier in 1969, and Boeing's liaison engineer "down under" was Ron Woodard, who helped set up two production facilities to build 727 spar components, elevators and rudders, 747 escape chutes, and 707 thrust reversers.

Woodard had joined Boeing in 1966 literally by chance. He had just graduated from college and one day took rain shelter at the entrance to a Boeing recruiting office in Tacoma. He got to talking to the recruiter and was told the company had a program under way to convert bachelor of science graduates into aeronautical engineers. By the time the rain stopped, Woodard was a Boeing employee, went into structures training, and worked in the 727 and 707 programs before being assigned to Australia.

The recruiter had hired a perceptive young man whose job as liaison engineer consisted partially of trying to placate Australian resentment toward Boeing's then "do it our way because it's the only way" tendency. As a man in the middle, Woodard could understand Boeing's frustrations with Australian production methods, but also the Australians' irritation at what they considered interference. He flew back to Seattle and delivered a presentation to a management meeting on what was wrong with offset, the gist of it being that in Australia, at least, it was creating more enemies than friends. Frank Verginia heard the presentation and hired him as a program manager.

Generally speaking, offset worked well in many countries such as Japan, which became a major production partner starting with a contract to build 747-SP flaps. "It wasn't a competitive bid," Jack Steiner recalled. "We deliberately put something into Japan to test them—we wanted to find out how they operated, and they were quite good."

The whole sales organization went through a maturing process in the early 1970s under Clancy Wilde, who succeeded George Sanborn as vice president of sales in the commercial airplane division in 1969 after Sanborn left to join American Airlines. Wilde was a father-figure to virtually every salesman, a big lumbering man with the personality of a friendly St. Bernard puppy but possessing a rock-hard streak of toughness—his salesmen called him "Bigfoot."

Sales as a department had suffered from lack of organizational consistency before Wilde became its head honcho. A prior reorganization, one of many, had eliminated the international and domestic sales departments, splitting the former into three segments, each under a separate director—Europe, Far East, and a combination of Australia and Asia. In addition, there were separate sales groups for South America and Africa. Domestic sales as a separate department virtually disappeared.

In 1972, Wilde restored the old international and domestic sales departments, Ken Luplow assuming the newly created position of director of International Affairs. His duties were relatively undefined at first, but this changed when Tex Boullioun, whose sale of 707s to Romania was the first to an Iron Curtain country, was approached by a contact in the Soviet Union. The Soviets were not only interested in buying the 747, but suggested a package agreement under which Boeing would plan and manage construction of an Everett-type aircraft factory, and teach the Soviets certain commercial transport technology. They were backward in more ways than one; a Boeing official on an Aeroflot (the USSR's state airline) flight once saw a stewardess serving chilled wine out of an old Sears refrigerator.

Boullioun, Stamper and Luplow became heavily involved with the proposal, and over the next four years there were meetings between Boeing and Soviet officials in both Moscow and Seattle; the package deal came close enough to consummation for Boullioun to assign Bayne Lamb the task of working with the Russians on preliminary factory planning. But the whole project went down the drain late in 1975 when Congress prohibited the sharing of critical technology with the Soviets; aircraft technology, even when applicable to commercial aviation, was included in the ban.

Before everything fell apart, the Soviets had sent two separate technical groups to Seattle, mostly discussing wide-body transport design with Joe Sutter, who already had had some contact with Russian aeronautical engineers. Sutter and Bob Withington had met them at a previous Paris Air Show, a meeting set up with the approval of the U.S. State Department. The Soviet Union had asked State for permission to talk to Boeing about the 747, and in exchange agreed to discuss their own supersonic transport construction.

Held in a private room at a Paris restaurant, it turned out to be an interesting session. Engineers from both Tupolev and Ilyushin, Russia's two leading civil aircraft manufacturers, represented the USSR; Sutter had been instructed to discuss the 747 only if the Russians answered all of Withington's questions about the TU-144, which they did over the first hour. Boullioun was present, too, and after the three Americans agreed the Soviets had been open and extremely cooperative, Sutter began fielding their questions.

"The Ilyushin team started asking me why Boeing put engines under the wings," Joe recounted. "They were designing the IL-86, a wide-body almost as big as the 747, but it had four aft engines and it would have been a real clunker. I explained the engineering principles behind our design, drawing diagrams on the tablecloth because I hadn't brought any paper with me. When I finished, the Russians folded up the tablecloth and took it home with them."

When the first Soviet contingent came to Seattle later, they presented Sutter with a brass plaque that depicted an IL-86 flying over the Kremlin. All four engines were under the wings. "It looked like a fat 707," Joe remarked.

The Soviets originally wanted to buy 25 747s, but this was reduced to five and later to a single airplane; presumably they would have built copies of the big Boeing if the factory planning agreement hadn't been killed. Ironically, some of the sales Boeing made during the seventies were to countries the U.S. later blacklisted: Libya, Iran, and Iraq, which hadn't yet emerged as menaces.

Boeing enjoyed a special relationship with Iran when it was ruled by the Shah. Jim Blue, Vern Castle, Ron Woodard and Jim Morrison were among the many Boeing officials assigned there at various times prior to the Shah's overthrow, all of them expressing great affection for the

Iranian people. The same was true of Iraq, which between 1973 and 1975 bought every Boeing jet model from the 707 to the 747.

Boeing's salesmen compiled their own share of stories from their overseas assignments. Rusty Roetman remembered a bitter competition at Singapore Airlines between the 747 and DC-10. The airline went through three board meetings before reaching a decision but no immediate announcement was made. Roetman and his Douglas counterpart were still sweating out word when a Boeing public relations man happened to come across a new commemorative stamp ready for issuance. It carried a picture of a 747—and Roetman knew Boeing had won.

"One of the loneliest jobs in the sales department is when you lose," Roetman reflected. "A salesman is pretty reluctant to admit he didn't do his job, or that we didn't have the right product, or that the competition had a better airplane."

Yet those kinds of defeats were easier to take than the ones that involved Boeing's refusal to make payoffs in order to win a contract.

"Most foreign airlines are fine and their people very professional," Roetman said. "But with a few it can be a different matter. The hints, the innuendoes, the suggestions for payoffs are blatant. I had one foreign minister who told me to my face they had decided to buy Boeing jets and we haven't delivered one yet. The airline had picked us but that didn't count because we wouldn't pay up."

Restoring the old arrangement of putting all domestic sales under one roof and international under another was just one Wilde reform. He also refined and improved something George Sanborn had instituted: the system of combining sales with market analysis, to help guide an airline's decision on what kind of equipment it really needed and how it could be utilized most effectively on various routes.

"You had your salesman out front," Sam Lowry said, "but each one had a guy in the back room who was charged with the responsibility of understanding the customer's route system and its relation to equipment needs. Sanborn started this, but a savvy guy named Harry Carter actually devised Boeing's market analysis know-how. When Clancy took over from Sanborn, he turned this technique into a fine art and really emphasized this kind of approach."

Wilde also went back to a policy that had been allowed to slip somewhat—that of assigning salesmen to individual airlines on a long-term basis. He believed that "marrying" a salesman to a particular carrier established a close, trusting relationship valuable to Boeing and the customer alike. He was an excellent matchmaker, too, although some of his troops took on the colorings of the airline they worked with—like Bob Perdue acquiring a Southern accent when he worked Delta. Bob Wylie, after years with businesslike United, once remarked to his wife, "You know, I've been covering United so long, all I've got are blue suits."

What Wilde really sought for the salesmen was familiarity not merely with the officials who bought airplanes, but with those who flew, worked and maintained them. As Wylie phrased it:

"I called on the whole airline—fleet planning, scheduling, pilots, mechanics, flight attendants, public relations, finance, the whole works from top to bottom. This kind of method takes a lot of time and effort, but it makes all the difference in the world—that you know them and they know you. Clancy was smart enough to recognize this. Perdue did it at Delta and Northwest, although Clancy himself was point man at Northwest. Hal Crawford worked Eastern, Carl Munson lived with Pan Am, Danny Palmer was close to American, and so on. It worked in reverse, of course—if American had something go wrong with one of our airplanes, Danny would be the one who got bawled out, and if anything happened at United, I got taken to task. It all made for a healthy relationship between Boeing and the customer."

The international salesmen, with wider territories and often with several small airlines to cover instead of one or two large ones, didn't always have these really close relationships with every carrier. But they did their best to develop warm friendships, and these included the former Iron Curtain countries like Poland and Yugoslavia, where capitalism-vs-communism beliefs were subordinated to the excitement of delivering a brand-new Boeing jetliner—an excitement nurtured not only by the technological improvement over old equipment, but the attitude toward Boeing cultivated by its salesmen and customer support people.

On those occasions when Boeing delivered the first airplane of a multi-aircraft order to a foreign country, top Boeing executives usually were on board to make the delivery flight a special event. Allen set the precedent, and it's followed by senior officers to this day.

Boeing's customers came in all sizes and shapes, and included some colorful characters who headed the non-scheduled carriers. Edward J. Daly of World Airways, for example, a close friend of Clancy Wilde, once kept Boeing salesman Jim Chorlton waiting in a hotel room for five days before agreeing to see him. Then Daly took him out on a boat in San Francisco Bay for another two days but refused to discuss any business. Ten hours after they finally docked, Daly suddenly announced, "Okay, I'll buy three 747 convertibles and here's what I want on them. . . ."

Daly, whose airline already was operating five 707 freighters, couldn't resist the bigger plane's appeal. It was one more indication that the 707 was a has-been whose days inevitably were numbered—another 10 years, everyone figured, and Boeing's first jet transport was history.

Everyone was wrong. The 707 still had some history yet to write.

TWENTY

NEW VENTURES IN THE SKIES, NEW CHALLENGES ON THE GROUND

As MILITARY CONTRACTS GO, IT WAS RELATIVELY MODEST— $170 million for two modified 707s that would be used to test somebody else's product.

It was signed in July 1970, and not even the most optimistic soul at Boeing could have foreseen what was to evolve from those two airplanes. For the "somebody else's product" was a new type of powerful radar, the major component in the Air Force's Airborne Warning and Control System, otherwise known as AWACS.

Twenty years later, a number of these specially rigged 707s, designated the E-3A, were prowling over the Persian Gulf war zone— together with spy satellites, the most efficient "eyes in the skies" enemy target detection and identification system ever devised. They served not only the USAF but also NATO and individual forces of Saudi Arabia, Britain and France.

Boeing was the prime contractor in the AWACS program, assigned the task of building the airplane and radome that housed the enormously complex radar, communications, navigation, and data-processing equipment. In the airframe competition, Boeing won out over the McDonnell Douglas DC-8; although the basic AWACS airplane would be a 707, as the E-3A it was a military airplane and that put the program under Ollie Boileau's aerospace group.

Doug Graves was the first AWACS program manager, with Mark Miller as his deputy, and Marvin Eisenbach the chief engineer whose biggest problem was figuring out where to hang the huge radome—30 feet wide and six feet thick. Originally it was supposed to be mounted on the vertical stabilizer but Eisenbach, whom Miller described as "the chief brain behind AWACS," decided the best location was on top of the fuselage.

"They never flew it with the stabilizer configuration," Miller said.

"It was a crazy-looking thing and the engineers wanted it closer to the body."

The airframe was that of a 707-320 Intercontinental, a choice largely responsible for the Air Force selecting Boeing over McDonnell Douglas; the 707-320 was faster, longer-ranged, and structurally more compatible with the radome/fuselage mating than the DC-8.

Westinghouse and Hughes were the two companies competing for the internal radar system. The first two E-3A's were used as flying test beds, initially to determine whether an airborne radar-warning system was feasible, and then to test the capabilities of the two competing systems. Westinghouse won and the Westinghouse-707 integration went through almost five years of testing before Boeing put the E-3A into full production with an initial Air Force order for 34 aircraft. Visually, the AWACS radar looks like a giant Frisbee mounted on two huge pylons; the dome rotates at six revolutions per minute while scanning, but slows to ¼ RPM in a non-operation mode—the constant rotation is necessary to prevent congealing of the bearing lubricants.

But despite its rather unaesthetic appearance, AWACS' effectiveness is awesome. It has the ability to overcome the chief disadvantage of ground-based radar, which gets blocked by objects it cannot distinguish from potential targets—trees and hills, for example. This is why low-flying airplanes can come in under a radar screen without detection. They can't do this against AWACS, which looks down as well as forward, enabling it to separate "the innocent from the guilty," so to speak. AWACS became even more sophisticated and deadly with the development of a friend-or-foe identification system, an electronic fighter control that makes every AWACS plane literally a flying fighter command post.

AWACS was still in the testing phase when Boeing, late in 1972, started developing a remarkable military tactical transport—an airplane capable of lifting 27,000 pounds of cargo off a runway only 2,000 feet long, and then cruising at nearly 500 miles an hour.

The technical name was Advanced Medium Short Takeoff and Landing Transport (AMST). Boeing and McDonnell Douglas won a preliminary design competition, then were each awarded contracts to build a pair of prototypes with a full production contract going to the winner. The MCDD entry was called the YC-15; Boeing's was the YC-14 and, like its ill-fated C-5, must be listed in the company's history as another of the planes that "might have been" or, perhaps, "should have been."

Both YC-14s were built at the Developmental Center, their design the outgrowth of a small contract Boeing had with NASA. It was an experiment that put "wing blowers" on the wings of a conventional, straight-wing airplane to provide low-speed lift during takeoffs and landings. Boeing installed the blowers—a concept known as Upper Surface Blowing (USB)—on an old de Havilland that flew so slow, the chase plane was a helicopter. "You could fly that airplane at fifty miles an hour," Bob Withington recalled.

Boeing adapted the principle to the YC-14, utilizing the thrust from its two General Electric CF-6 turbofans to blow high-speed air over the upper surfaces of the wings and flaps, creating powered lift. The competing YC-15 also had powered lift, under a different name. The airplanes were almost identical in size, gross weight, and payload; the chief difference was that the YC-14 achieved the same overall performance with only two engines as the YC-15 did with four. Both were larger than Lockheed's reliable but aging C-130 propjet, which an AMST would have replaced as the Air Force's primary medium transport.

Bill Cook, Maynard Pennell, Jack Wimpress and Jim Copenhaver of the tech staff were among the veterans who worked on the YC-14, which George Schairer hated. He didn't think its design sound, and once told Guy Townsend, one of its staunchest supporters, "It's going to hurt somebody and we shouldn't be flying it."

Boeing and MCDD demonstrated their AMST prototypes at the 1977 Paris Air Show, and the YC-14 put on a spectacular performance. The test crew headed by Ray McPherson twice took off in just three airplane lengths, and twice landed in only two lengths—this in an airplane that weighed 85 tons.

But in 1978, after a year of successful flight testing, Secretary of Defense Harold Brown decided the Air Force needed a transport that could perform strategic and tactical missions alike and cancelled the entire AMST program, dooming both the YC-14 and YC-15 before there was any official flight test competition between the two airplanes.

The new military transport concept was called the CX, and Boeing entered a design competing against McDonnell Douglas and Lockheed for an airplane sized between the C-141 and C-5A; MCDD won this battle five years later with its C-17.

The two Boeing YC-14 prototypes remained in Tucson, Arizona, where they had been mothballed after the Pentagon cancelled the program. One is at the Davis-Monthan Air Force Base and the other on display at the nearby Pima Air Museum, where it sits next to another prototype—the YC-15 that had been its one-time rival.

Boeing tried in vain to sell Iran the YC-14; until the shah was toppled, Iran was one of Boeing's best Middle East customers. The Iranian Air Force operated KC-135s and a dozen 747s, the latter including the only three 747 tankers Boeing ever sold. (The Air Force picked the DC-10 over the 747 in a hotly contested heavy tanker competition.) Iran Air, the state airline, bought every Boeing jet from 707 to the 747, and the shah himself had two 707-320s with custom interiors. Iranian flight crews were trained by a Boeing support group, and at the time of the revolution the company had a special team in Iran under a contract to modernize all the country's major airports.

Vern Castle went there in the early 1970s in charge of a support group that trained pilots and mechanics on 707s and KC-135s, a 450-man force including 120 in flight operations.

"The main problem was technical language," Castle recalled. "It wasn't enough to have them speak English—they had to understand what we were teaching. Boeing ran its own technical language course that the pilots had to pass before they were allowed to begin ground school, and after ground school we didn't have one man who couldn't cut the mustard."

In maintenance, Boeing eventually trained nearly a thousand technicians in every field from wheels, tires, and brakes all the way up to avionics. Gradually, maintenance was turned over to Iranian graduates who, in turn, trained new students. By 1976, the Boeing team was able to turn over the first squadron of 12 KC-135 tankers to all-Iranian flight crews and all-Iranian mechanics.

During the unrest that preceded the shah's overthrow, the U.S. Embassy in Tehran and the CIA gave support group personnel instructions on how to avoid ambushes. They were warned to look out for anyone wearing military uniforms unless military visitors were expected. Drivers were put through a course on avoiding traps. Castle found himself being trailed once by a mysterious green car, and his wife, Barbara, was almost kidnapped while walking home from a hairdresser's—she had been warned never to walk alone in the streets. She just managed to break away, and finally got home safely; she didn't tell her husband what had happened for two weeks.

Jim Morrison was transferred to Iran in 1978, heading a team of about 40 architect-engineers who were helping the Royal Iranian Air Force upgrade its airfield facilities. He was another who liked the Iranian people. On the occasion of his birthday, his Iranian driver gave him a kilo of Caspian caviar. "I don't know where he got it," Morrison said, "but that was typical of an Iranian who liked you. He drove us to the airport on our last day and sobbed when we left."

When the shah's overthrow became inevitable, Blue called Wilson. "I think it's time we got all our people out of there," he suggested, and T agreed. Morrison was one of the last to leave and entered a mob scene at the Tehran airport, mostly panicked Iranians trying to flee the country. Morrison, his wife Noanie, and a group of other Americans were trying to reach the Pan Am ticket counter—Noanie was knocked down three times by people trying to break into line ahead of them. There were further delays because of constant security checks, including one aboard the plane that resulted in several Iranians being dragged off kicking and screaming—they didn't have permission to leave. A volunteer Pan Am crew flew the evacuation aircraft, a 747 whose passenger list included a hundred or so Boeing employees. They finally heard the most welcome PA ever delivered:

"Ladies and gentlemen, this is the captain. I have an announcement that will be of some interest to you. In ten seconds, we will be passing out of Iranian airspace and entering Turkey. Nine . . . eight . . . seven . . ."

At the sound of "one" the packed cabin burst into applause. Twelve years later, that scene was repeated when Boeing evacuated some of its employees and all their dependents from Saudi Arabia just before the Gulf War erupted. A 767-ER flew them from Riyadh to Wichita, and as the captain announced they had just crossed the Canadian-U.S. border, there were cheers and applause. Volunteers, including aircraft maintenance personnel, had stayed behind to help support the Saudi AWACS and KC-135 tanker fleet.

Nowhere was the wide scope of Boeing's military projects more apparent than in pre-revolution Iran; the airport modernization projects, for example, were conducted by a subsidiary unit called Logistics Support Corporation, one of several groups within the Boeing Aerospace Company that came into being late in 1972 when T Wilson put most military and space activities under one administrative roof, including the company's two latest missile programs.

The first was SRAM (Short Range Attack Missile), a program that dated back to 1966 when the Air Force sought development of a 14-foot-long guided missile that could be launched from B-52s or supersonic fighter-bombers like the F-111. There were 60 subcontractors involved in SRAM, but in 1971 Boeing won the contract for building the production model and ended up making 1,500 operational SRAMs.

Fred Maxwell headed the program at its start, Mark Miller worked in SRAM briefly, and Abe Goo remembered being in SRAM's Wichita laboratory facilities the day a delegation of high-ranking military people arrived on an inspection tour. Before they showed up, Bob Edelman told Goo there were electronic and computer problems.

"The equipment's on but nothing's moving," Edelman said. "The display screens are dead and the whole damn system's locked up. We'll try to get it operating before these guys come through, but I can't guarantee it."

He did try, but not in time. The military contingent came into the lab where Goo was waiting. They looked around, puzzled at the obvious inactivity.

"We're running a stability test," Goo informed them, his face bland and innocent. "You'll notice the system is rock-solid."

The first air launch of a SRAM from a B-52 was a cliffhanger. The test was done at the White Sands, New Mexico, missile range, and the biggest worry was the slim 10-foot space between the bomber's belly and the missile.

"We had to drop the missile away from the airplane before we ignited its rocket engine," Goo related. "So we did a trajectory analysis to figure out where the pieces would fly if the rocket engine blew up. We had problems controlling the rocket while it dropped because the parameters for firing the engine required the missile to be in level flight. We finally figured out a way to keep it level, and everyone agreed after the trajectory analysis that two thousand feet would be safe for ignition.

"When we launched the first one at White Sands, the length of time it took for it to drop two thousand feet seemed like an hour. But it worked perfectly. We had warned the people at Holoman Air Force Base that the SRAM would go out of their line of sight as it dipped over a hill, but not to worry. They panicked when the missile went out of radar sight behind the hill and the range safety officer blew it up, thinking it was off course. We found the pieces only forty feet from the prescribed line of flight."

Next came ALCM (Air Launch Cruise Missile); more than six feet longer than SRAM, it was designed to be carried either by the B-52 or B-1 supersonic bomber, and in 1980 Boeing won a heated competition with General Dynamics for a $1.6 billion production contract. Both companies had been developing their ALCM versions since 1977, when the Air Force asked them to build prototypes that would be tested against each other. It was a competition welcomed by Ray Utterstrom, who spearheaded the program.

Tested they were and brutally, over an unusually long eight-month period mostly at the Utah Test and Training Range near Dugway, Utah. Later test missiles were launched from B-52s over the Pacific and programmed to fly back to the Utah Range—Air Force F-4 Phantoms were used as chase planes, equipped with radio controls to take over the missiles if they strayed off course.

The tests simulated the kind of missions ALCM would have to fly against a real enemy—dropped or fired from a bomber, small wings would deploy from the missile fuselage, turning it into an unmanned subsonic aircraft; then its guidance system would take over and follow a programmed course to the target, no higher than 500 feet off the ground to avoid radar detection, while automatically veering around or over obstructing terrain. The Utah tests were conducted over a range 100 miles long and 30 miles wide, and each ALCM had to perform sudden maneuvers to clear obstacles between the missile and its target.

Boeing's ALCMs crashed four times, and so did the General Dynamics missiles. But Boeing's failures were judged less critical—two resulted from communication mistakes by the chase planes, a third went astray because of programming errors, and a fourth crash occurred when an engine failed after two and a half hours of violent maneuvering. Two of General Dynamics' missiles crashed for unknown reasons and a third flight failed when the wings refused to deploy. Air Force secretary Hans Mark praised both companies and admitted there wasn't much difference between the two designs, but said flatly:

"Boeing's system is better."

The supreme irony of Boeing's ALCM victory was that the man who headed the Boeing Aerospace Company during most of the seventies had become president of General Dynamics by the time the Pentagon made its decision. Oliver "Ollie" Boileau, associated with Boeing's space and missile projects for years, had resigned in January 1980 to accept the General Dynamics post. He had the grace to call T Wilson after the contract winner was announced and offer his congratulations.

Ed Renouard had been ALCM's proposal manager under Boileau while the missile was in the development stage. He got a good indication of T Wilson's interest in the program when Wilson insisted that regular status reports go directly to him, even though Renouard had several layers of organization between him and T.

Renouard's background was largely in production engineering, and Boileau sent him to T's office for a discussion on where ALCM would be produced if Boeing won the competition.

"Have you considered building a new factory?" T asked.

To a production man like Renouard, this was the equivalent of giving a child the key to a toy store—having a factory that fit the product, instead of grabbing whatever factory space was available.

"We haven't thought about a new facility, T," he replied, "but we'd like to."

"How much would a new factory cost?"

"I don't know. We haven't gotten to that point yet."

"I assume it would cost more than five million."

"Yes, sir."

"But it wouldn't be more than fifty million?"

"No, sir," Renouard answered.

It was built for $48 million at Boeing's space and science complex in Kent and was something of a showcase until it became a part of the company's classified "black world" facilities working on sensitive military projects. More than 1,700 ALCM missiles were built there, achieving a 65 percent improvement curve that Renouard said "was unheard of before or since—it was one hell of a product for the Air Force."

Ollie Boileau was only the latest of several major executives whose names were missing from the officers' roster as Boeing entered the decade of the eighties. Ed Wells had retired in 1972 as senior vice president-technical, although he stayed on as an active director and consultant for another five years. George Martin retired the same year as Wells, and three other engineering greats—Cook, Pennell, and Bob Jewett—retired in the mid-1970s, leaving a rich legacy for the younger engineers who had absorbed the traditions of innovation, excellence, and integrity these giants established—not merely for Boeing but for all aviation. The transition was completed in 1978 when George Schairer retired.

Don Schelp, who came to work for Boeing as a junior engineer in 1952, remembered above all else Ed Wells' modesty and the way he could make even the greenest engineer feel like his equal. While the 707 still was in final design stage, Schelp accompanied Wells on a business trip to Los Angeles and began talking about the rough mockup he had just seen. He had been particularly impressed with the 707's window treatment—Boeing had decided to use smaller windows, but place them only 20 inches apart instead of the customary 40 inches.

"I think this provides a much greater feeling of openness and gives passengers a better view," Schelp enthused.

"You really like it?"

"I sure do."

Wells smiled. "That was my idea," he said shyly.

Schelp also recalled going with Maynard Pennell to Germany in 1959 on a 720 sales trip. When the sales meetings were over they went on a walk together and finally reached one of the bridges crossing the Rhine. They were enjoying the view and watching the steady parade of boats below them—an idyllic scene about as far away from jetliners as anyone could get. Pennell suddenly turned away from the railing.

"Okay, Don," he said, "what's next? What kind of airplane should Boeing offer next?"

Remarked Schelp later, "I think Maynard relaxed by thinking about airplanes, always looking ahead to the next product."

So, for that matter, did the occasionally difficult but dedicated Schairer. One of his last ideas before retiring was to turn Minuteman into an airborne missile dropped from a 747; he didn't get anywhere with it, but a 747 as a Minuteman launching pad was typical of his always trying to develop something new, different, and even startling. Schairer and Pennell were Joe Sutter's role models—Schairer almost fired him once for a mistake someone else made, and Sutter's well-known temper at times seemed to emulate Schairer's. Sutter was always firing engineers. "If I didn't get fired two or three times a day," Schelp once remarked, "I thought something was wrong. I worked for him on the Dash-80 and ten years later I passed him in the hall. He turned around and barked, 'Are you still here? I thought I fired you years ago!' "

Pennell's quiet sense of humor was an endearing quality to those who worked with him and for him. During the SST's development period, Bob Wylie talked him into speaking about supersonic transports to the Houston Rotary Club, an audience of about 500 leading businessmen. A very tough audience, Wylie warned Pennell. Their last speaker had been Lee Iacocca, who had just introduced the Mustang automobile and was no act to follow.

Iacocca had concluded his remarks by announcing, "Gentlemen, there are five hundred of you in this room, and under one hundred of your seats there's a license number and a set of keys. I've got one hundred Mustangs parked outside, full of gas, and I want the lucky hundred guys to drive them for a week and tell me how you like 'em."

When Wylie and Pennell arrived at the next meeting, the Rotarians were still talking about Iacocca's speech and the pandemonium that followed. Maynard was introduced and proceeded to bring down the house.

"I'm here to tell you about our supersonic transport," he began, "but first I have to warn you—I don't have any samples parked outside."

Pennell's last official major project for Boeing was the YC-14, and that airplane also was Bill Cook's swan song. Both would remark years later that the SST was the most frustrating and disappointing experience of their illustrious careers. "Bill told me once that he was glad to get off the SST," Pennell said, "because on the 707 everything got easier as we went along, but with the SST everything got harder."

Pennell, who in his later years became badly crippled with Parkinson's disease, always expressed great admiration for his peers. "Cook was a very practical engineer who made both the 707 and 727 better airplanes," Maynard said. "Schairer went in the opposite direction— free-thinking and never wedded to the traditional. He came up with more oddball ideas than anyone else, yet many were good ideas."

But for Ed Wells, Pennell had the supreme compliment. "He influenced all our designs in a very constructive way, yet you always had the feeling that if he had been concentrating on your own program, he could have done a better job than you did."

For that matter, a lot of Boeing people thought Pennell had a lot in common with Wells; both were soft-spoken yet forceful when they had to be, both were self-effacing, and both had inherent dignity without ever letting dignity lap over into overbearing. They spoke to everybody on equal terms, and it didn't matter whether he was a floor-sweeper or a senior engineer. The chief difference between Pennell and Wells in personality was that Maynard was slightly more emotional; Wells seldom showed emotion.

And then there was George Martin, who retired with a reputation as one of the best structural engineers in the industry, as the airlines themselves would testify. One of his admirers was Dick Pearson, TWA's former vice president of maintenance and engineering.

"We had to take a 707 apart once and it was like dismantling a steel bridge," Pearson related. "Another time we had a 707 engine toss a turbine blade and the engine froze—so violently that it twisted in its mountings and ended up *facing the fuselage* without coming off. The pylon that held the engine to the wing was attached at five points; three would have been sufficient but Boeing wanted that little extra margin of strength. It was one hell of a demonstration of how they build airplanes."

It also demonstrated how George Martin wanted Boeing to build airplanes. T Wilson kept framed photographs of only five men in his office: Martin was one of them, and the others were Bill Allen, Wells, Schairer, and Jim Prince—those pictures were his ultimate mark of respect and gratitude.

The four senior engineers weren't the only legends to retire in the seventies—a machine did, too. Dash-80 left Seattle for what was assumed to be the last time in 1972, and flew to Washington in a reenactment of its first transcontinental flight back in the 1950s when it set a new coast-to-coast speed record; aboard were many of the passengers who had made the original trip.

Nostalgia also may have been an appropriate term to use in describing Boeing's gradually changing relationship with the military during the seventies and the eighties, and the flurry of high-tech defense contract competitions. Gone were those days when Air Force officers and their engineering and contractual counterparts at Boeing, Lockheed, and Douglas seemed to work together as teams forged out of mutual trust. Gone were the days when the word of a veteran contract negotiator like Howard Neffner was as good as his signature. Gone were the arguing, criticizing, and frank interchanges during working hours and the relaxing social contacts of the evening, contacts when trust was established and nurtured.

Some pretty good airplanes and missiles came out of the old relationships—the B-47, B-52, and Minuteman, to name just a few. Perhaps it all had to change, just as American society itself changed in so many ways. The seventies were the post-Vietnam years of cynicism and disillusion. The news media itself reflected the era's atmosphere, becoming critically adversarial and assuming more of a watchdog role rather than that of an impartial observer. Congress, too, adopted much the same attitude in its oversight of military-aerospace industry programs.

Jerry King spent almost his entire career at Boeing dealing with the military. Like everyone else from the fifties and sixties, he began to miss the close relationships and friendships that used to exist between Boeing's people and the military officers with whom they worked. "There was nothing wrong about those relationships, either; they were based on mutual respect and mutual goals," King said.

One very interested on-the-scene observer of the changing Pentagon–Boeing relationship was Frank Shrontz, and "on-the-scene" meant he was observing from Washington, not Seattle. In 1973, he left Boeing to become assistant secretary of the Air Force for installations and logistics, and three years later was named assistant secretary of defense. He served in that post until early in 1977 when he rejoined Boeing as corporate vice president in charge of contracts and planning.

During those three years and two months in the Pentagon, Shrontz saw the transforming military-industry atmosphere from a more impartial vantage point—he had served on the other side of the fence, giving him an objectivity that few either in the Defense Department or at Boeing could share.

"There isn't any doubt the relationship changed," he commented long after he had left Washington and had risen to the top at Boeing. "There isn't the feeling that 'Boeing can do no wrong,' because on occasions Boeing has been an embarrassment to the Defense Department. Yet it's also regrettable that the relationships aren't as personal as they used to be."

The Boeing that Shrontz came back to still bore the stamp of T Wilson's iron style of leadership, although by 1977 Mal Stamper had been president for five years—a period in which T concentrated on development of products, and Stamper devoted much of his time to employee motivation and welfare. Mal Stamper's total commitment to any project, campaign or crusade that nailed his interest applied to his own conversion to health addict, which had considerable visual and personal impact throughout the company—such as replacing candy bars in vending machines with apples. As a new disciple of exercise, he began running *up* the *down* escalator at corporate headquarters, drawing stares from startled employees.

But no one could find fault with what he did to improve the working environment. One of his first moves as president was to form a committee of company facilities directors and enlist them in a campaign to spruce up as many facilities as possible. The beautification program included creation of a tree-studded park and picnic area at Renton, and a number of recreation centers. Covered walkways were erected at Plant Two and other installations. Bare corridor floors in most office buildings were carpeted, and the walls lined with attractive prints and photographs from Boeing's past. One by one, cafeterias were remodeled.

Stamper partially "democratized" the ID badges, decreeing that they be the same regardless of position—the only exception was the one worn by hourly workers whose almost identical badge had a coded bar for recording in and out times. (A few years later, Frank Shrontz completed the one-badge-for-all policy by eliminating the bar.)

In the mid-1980s, Stamper began to implement a no-smoking policy for company offices, and this was long before most American firms jumped on the smoke-free bandwagon. More than anything else, he was the ultimate motivator and he shared with Wes Maulden a special concern for the health and welfare of every employee.

In 1971, Maulden had engineered the creation of the Seattle Services Division, a catch-all department reporting to Stamper that ran everything from food facilities to transportation. Bayne Lamb was SSD's first general manager and when Art Carter succeeded him, he discovered that Stamper's interest in employee welfare extended to the food they were being served on company property.

One of his first orders to Art was to "get the fat out of your hamburgers," an edict that Carter discovered was not only costly but downright unpopular.

After he proved this to Stamper, hamburger sales having fallen to a level that would have bankrupted McDonald's, Stamper told him to eliminate baconburgers from the executive dining room menu.

"I can't do it, Mal," Carter protested. "Baconburgers are my best seller and you can't make these guys eat peanut butter and jelly sandwiches." Stamper relented, but then insisted that yogurt be served at all cafeterias. For one Valentine's Day, Carter purchased about $6,000 worth of yogurt in special containers marked with tiny hearts and the message: "Be Kind to Your Heart." They were given away to anyone who asked, but most of the $6,000 supply ended up uneaten.

In addition to food service, always the biggest headache, Seattle Services also oversaw such departments as travel, transportation, and security. It was a multi-faceted domain—57 in all—with corresponding multi-faceted problems. One of the busiest units was the travel office, which was booking 84,000 trips a year. During the 1970s, there were only two major travel data bases—American's Sabre and United's Apollo—and each carrier was competing to get its system into Boeing's travel office. Boeing simultaneously was trying to sell the 767 to each airline, and Carter was trying to upgrade the travel department with some kind of data base in the middle of this Ping-Pong match.

Al Casey of American was lobbying Tex Boullioun in behalf of Sabre and United's Dick Ferris was plugging Apollo to T; Carter, meanwhile, had a travel office with such primitive reservations arrangements that booking a single trip required an average of eight phone calls. He never did get the data base system in place while he ran SSD, although Boeing installed one later.

Transportation also reported to Seattle Services, and this department included the drivers so widely praised by visiting customer officials, who considered them Boeing's *ex-officio* salesmen. "Guys like Mac McGuire and Jimmy Saylor would have a prospective customer sold before they got to the factory," Sam Lowry once remarked.

For years, the drivers were supervised by a well-liked old gentleman named Martin Cummings who ran a tight shop but got along with everybody. One of his best friends was Don Whitford, and their relationship went unchanged even when Whitford made vice president. In honor of Cummings' 25th anniversary with Boeing, Carter arranged for a luncheon at a fancy restaurant and rented a limousine for the occasion.

Whitford, invited to attend, saw the limo and frowned. "Carter, how the hell are you gonna explain that limo if someone like T looks out a window and sees it?"

"You're the vice president," Art said. "I'll let you explain it."

Boeing's relations with the Teamsters' union, the drivers' bargaining organization, were seldom acrimonious. One year a contract agreement was reached on a Tuesday, three days before the expiration of the old contract. This relatively fast accord presented a problem to the union negotiators. "We can't go out and announce that we've reached an agreement this soon," one of them said. "They'll think we've sold out, so we'll just have to stay here and play poker until the deadline Thursday night."

There were fewer than 300 people covered by the Teamsters' contract, a far less complicated situation than contract talks involving the thousands represented by IAM District Lodge 751. For more than a dozen years, the IAM's chief local negotiator was Al Schultz, the grand lodge master who was cast in the mold of the old-fashioned labor leader—profane, tough and also honest, totally aboveboard and understanding of the company's problems even though protecting his members was always his top priority.

He had a great sense of humor, loved jokes, and formed lasting friendships with both Stan Little and Jim Morrison. Little was vice president of industrial and public relations until his retirement in 1987, when industrial relations was split into two groups—human resources and labor relations—while public relations under Harold Carr achieved independent status, with all three units getting individual staff vice presidents.

Morrison came into industrial relations after returning from Iran in 1979—Little wanted him as his chief deputy and told Morrison, "That revolution in Iran was just the kind of training you need to take over labor relations."

Like Little, Morrison found it was easy to have good rapport with Schultz even when they were battling every three years over the IAM contract or current grievances. Schultz would show up at corporate headquarters at the start of negotiations, toss a copy of the IAM's new three-year proposal on Morrison's desk, and proclaim: "Jim, the only word I can use to describe this is magnificent!"

Morrison's first involvement in IAM contract talks was in 1979, during the Iran hostage crisis, and he kept telling horror stories about the Iranian revolution. Finally one union negotiator said, "Jim, I've got a great idea—if we don't reach an agreement, we won't go on strike. We'll just take *you* hostage."

This suggestion reached Little's ears via a company negotiator.

"Tell 'em they got a deal," Little said.

Management, particularly people like Little and Morrison, got along far better with Lodge 751's leaders than with the IAM's national officials; the district lodge, in fact, often was at odds with international headquarters in Washington. Little once talked Schultz out of quitting 751 because of this occasional friction. "I've just about had it and I'm resigning," Schultz told Little.

"You can't let your people down, Al," Little pleaded.

It took another 45 minutes before Little convinced him to stay. This was during an IAM strike in 1977 that shut Boeing down for more than 40 days, and Schultz thought it could have been settled sooner than it was.

The international president of the IAM at the time was William Winpisinger, whom everyone called "Winpy"; he was an old-style union man much like Schultz—a lot of tough talk and posturing for public and union consumption, but in private very likable and honest. He was very conscious of the IAM's image and one day called Little for a favor.

"*Sixty Minutes* wants to do a story on me, and I think it would be great if we could shoot some film in one of your plants."

"Winpy, if you think I'm gonna let that program into a Boeing plant alone, you're out of your mind," Little said. "And if you think I'm gonna let both you and *Sixty Minutes* in there, you're *really* out of your mind! You're always making speeches."

"Stan, I give you my solemn word I won't say anything controversial," Winpisinger promised.

Little finally gave in and Winpisinger kept his word. All he did was walk around one of Boeing's plants with a camera crew in tow, the theme being to portray a labor leader who kept in touch with the rank and file. The camera showed him introducing himself and shaking hands with assembly line workers. The entourage finally came to a woman worker, and Winpisinger stuck out his hand.

"Hi, there," he beamed. "I'm Bill Winpisinger, president of your union."

She didn't accept the handshake. "You're not president of my blankety-blank union," she snapped. "I don't belong to no [censored] union!"

Needless to say, that scene did not appear on *60 Minutes*.

Schultz finally retired after losing most of his clout within the union—he had made the mistake of taking sides in a Lodge 751 presidential election. Tom Baker was running against the current president, and Schultz thought it was more ethical to back an incumbent even though Baker was his protégé and a good friend.

"Al for some reason believed Winpisinger wanted the guy reelected," Morrison said, "and Schultz was a great one for maintaining the union party line. His mistake was overestimating the incumbent's popularity—right up to the last minute, Al thought he was going to win."

Baker was the new breed of labor leader—younger, intelligent, well-dressed, and articulate. But like Schultz he could be reasonable and cooperative if he thought a management position or policy was right. Baker and Morrison became personal friends, a relationship that survived many a labor-management skirmish.

The Boeing–IAM relationship, especially on the local level, has been a relatively friendly one, given the adversarial and union political factors inherent when management deals with a strong, organized work force. But that 1977 strike came at a time when Boeing was smack in the middle of another gamble.

It was about to commit itself to a pair of brand-new commercial transports and their almost simultaneous introduction.

TWENTY-ONE

THE TERRIFIC TWINS

*We are studying new airplane types employing advanced technology
that will make air transportation more efficient and more attractive. We
have established a design investigative effort, designated the 7X7, to
explore a possible new family of Boeing airplanes. Discussions of our
design concepts are under way with a number of major carriers.*

THAT QUOTE FROM T WILSON IN BOEING'S 1972 ANNUAL
report was the first public mention, albeit a vague one, of what were to
become the most ambitious new airliner introductory programs in
aviation history.

At a time when the company was struggling to extricate itself from
the financial vise of the early seventies, and new jets were mere gleams
in the eyes of the engineers, George Weyerhaeuser had remarked to T,
"You're never going to start a new airplane program with my approval
unless you have a plan that shows you're going to get a decent return
on investment."

T didn't argue that point. "At that time," he remarked later, "Boeing
had sold about twenty billion dollars' worth of commercial airplanes
and hadn't made any money, so I understood what Weyerhaeuser was
saying. I had never seen us come close to budget on any plane built
prior to the 757-767. We didn't on the 707, we didn't on the 727
although we came closer, we were an absolute basket case on the 737,
and we had great difficulties at the start on the 747 program, which
wasn't quite as bad as the 737."

T never thought Boeing took that much of a risk with the almost
simultaneous start of two new airliner ventures, and neither did Tex
Boullioun. "This was several years after Weyerhaeuser had made that
statement," Wilson pointed out. "In the meantime, we had cashed in
on the 727, we were still making money on the 707, starting to make

some on the 737, and the 747 was profitable. We had lots of money in the bank, and so when we started the two new programs, Weyerhaeuser didn't open his mouth—we laughed when we talked about it later."

The model numbers 757-767 were out of chronological sequence; the 767 predated its smaller sister in several ways—final design, first flight, and first to go into airline service, to name a few. But through their developmental years, the paths of the two programs merged into a simultaneous two-pronged invasion of the world airline market; their introduction into scheduled service, coming less than four months apart, was something no other airplane manufacturer had ever achieved. (Boeing rolled out the 747-400 and 737-400 on the same day in 1988, but both were derivatives; the 757 and 767 were new designs.)

The 767 began life as the 7X7, but originally 7X7 was the model number assigned to an entirely different airplane—a medium-size STOL transport Boeing was going to build in collaboration with the government-owned Italian company Aeritalia. Nothing came of this 1971 joint venture, but the design itself called for the same USB (Upper Surface Blowing) concept that was later adopted for the YC-14. When enthusiasm for a commercial STOL transport cooled, the 7X7 gradually evolved into a twin-aisle airplane with transcontinental range; it was aimed at the market niche for smaller wide-bodies Boeing had leap-frogged with the 747, but sized below the DC-10 and L-1011.

The 757 started out as the 7N7 and was intended to be simply the 727's logical replacement, really a derivative. But it turned out to be an entirely new and different airplane whose only similarity to the 727 was its single-aisle body width. Yet there was a surprising mixture of genealogical bloodlines in the 757-767 programs. The first rough 767 mockup was one originally built for what would have been a wide-body 727, and Jack Steiner's plan was to graft a 727 nose onto this wider fuselage. The 757, which wasn't supposed to have much in common with the 767 except the name Boeing, ended up with a flight deck identical to that of the larger plane.

Steiner insisted on calling the wide-body mockup a 727 derivative, a somewhat tenuous claim. "The only thing on it that came from the 727 was the windshield," Phil Condit remembered. But Steiner un-doubtedly figured a "derivative" label sounded less expensive. This was in 1973, long before the 757 program was approved and Condit named its chief engineer.

"Steiner had been told he couldn't work on new airplanes, only derivatives," Condit said. "But he was very creative and interestingly enough, that mockup was almost exactly the diameter that the 767 ended up."

Steiner had tried hard to sell the 727-300, stretched 20 feet longer than the 200 with 35 more seats, new engines, new leading edge flaps, and a revised landing gear. United had agreed to join Boeing in devel-oping specifications for the new derivative, and would have been the launch customer if it had gone into production. But after some $50 million had been spent on the program, United's enthusiasm waned and the agreement was cancelled by mutual consent.

But it was the 757 that really doomed Steiner's hopes of keeping the 727 series alive. And he was too good an engineer not to admit there was no comparison between the 727-300 and what the 757 was shaping up to be.

Bob Wylie, who was handling the United account while the 727-300 program still was very much alive, saw the 757's preliminary design drawings. Wylie turned to Steiner who was in the room. "This is one hell of an airplane, Jack. We've got to start showing this to somebody."

"Wylie, we can't," Steiner said. "It's so much better than the 'twenty-seven."

The salesman grinned. "What do you want to do—build something worse?"

Fuel efficiency was the name of the game when Boeing's salesmen began showing the proposed new airplanes to the airlines. The board didn't decide to proceed on the 7X7 and 7N7 programs until 1978, but the sales campaign already had hit high gear after the 1973–74 Arab oil embargo crisis sent jet fuel prices into the stratosphere. Aircraft noise had become a major environmental issue, too, and both airplanes promised to meet or surpass all new federal noise standards.

When the directors gave them a go-ahead in 1978, T's only real concern about introducing two new types in such close proximity was not financial but operational—he remembered the almost diastrous consequences of trying to add 737 production onto three other active commercial airplane programs. Yet the situation was different in 1978; the engineering and operations (manufacturing) team at the commercial airplane company was now performing efficiently—it was a smooth blend of well-tested veteran and fresh younger talent that had gone into the 757 and 767 programs. The youthful energy and innovative spirit of engineers like Phil Condit, for example, meshed with the experience of Ken Holtby and Joe Sutter, plus the counsel of Ed Wells and George Schairer who were extremely active in the 757's and 767's development.

For a man who ostensibly had retired, Wells' contribution to both airplanes went beyond what might have been expected for a consultant's input. He not only was the principal architect of the 767's landing gear (he obtained patents on the design), but was largely instrumental in the critical decision to make the 767 a twin-engine airplane instead of three.

Every engineer associated with the 767 program from its inception remembered the day in 1976 when Wells came into an engineering meeting during the design stage. At that point in time, the 767 was a trimotor, and the only reason a twin-engine configuration was even being considered at all was the forthcoming A-310 Airbus—it was a twin, and there were reports that it was going to be a very good airplane.

Wells had called the meeting, held in the conference room of Building 10-60 at Renton; Schairer was there and also Tex Boullioun and Steiner. Jack had brought in a pair of proposed 767 models—one with three engines, the other a twin.

"I know what's going on," Wells began in about as angry a tone as he could muster. "You're spending money on that three-engine project and paying lip service to a twin. You've got it backwards—you should be spending money on the twin and paying nothing more than lip service to a trimotor."

Wells made it clear that the 767's chances for success rested on fuel efficiency, and that no three-engine wide-body was going to have the operating economy of a twin. He also was well aware of the disastrous competition that had hurt the DC-10 and L-1011, two similarly sized trimotor wide-bodies battling head-to-head in a market that wasn't big enough for two almost identical planes. McDonnell Douglas and Lockheed had put them into service in 1971, and by 1976—when Boeing still was debating whether to put two or three engines on the 767— Wells considered the introduction of another trimotor, even a smaller one, pure folly. Yet as late as the spring of 1978 Boeing was not only still talking about a three-engine 767, but had distributed an artist's rendition of the plane showing a 727-type center engine arrangement, and the other two engines under the wings. Except for its T-tail, it looked remarkably like Lockheed's L-1011 TriStar. Much of the two-vs-three engine controversy centered around a difference of opinion between United and American; UAL wanted two and American preferred three. In February 1978, Boeing announced there would be two 767 versions: a twin-engine, double-aisle transport with one-stop transcontinental range carrying 180–200 passengers, and a trimotor that was basically the same airplane but with non-stop transcontinental range.

This was an obvious compromise, a replay of how the 727 ended up with three engines, but Ed Wells didn't think the 767 needed any compromise. The key to his confidence and his belief in the two-engine configuration was a new wing that had gone through more than 7,000 wind tunnel hours, and its potential was impressive. A combination of generous span and wing area, great thickness, and a decreased sweep promised markedly lower fuel consumption, with adequate range and speed. As the wind tunnel data continued to predict outstanding aerodynamic performance, the case for a trimotor weakened.

Wells and Schairer came in at least once a week to review the 767 program, and Schairer finally urged the establishment of another Red-vs-Blue team—the same kind of engineering study that had resulted in choosing underwing engines for the 737—to settle the 767's engine dispute. After these two separate design groups finished, the two-engine concept had emerged clearly as the better airplane and one that met the stiff requirements laid down by United: a twin-aisle, two-engine transport with the same fuel burn as a 727-200, and carrying 40 to 50 more passengers.

But the T-tail wasn't abandoned until the last possible minute. In fact, when United became the 767's launch customer in July 1978, the announcement was *Aviation Week*'s cover story, and the drawing on the cover itself depicted the new airliner with two engines and a horizontal T-tail.

"It had a T tail for a long time," Joe Sutter admitted. "We thought we had enough data to support that configuration, but Ed didn't think so, and some of the younger engineers resented this. They considered the T-tail design pretty well set and they wanted to get on with the job. We had a tense situation for a couple of days before Wells won the argument, but that airplane had a T-tail a lot longer than most people remember."

Initially, the 757 also had a T-tail, partly because it was considered at first to be just a revamped 727, and partly because so many engineers liked the lower drag of the T-tail. But Condit scrapped the T; he conceded its better drag factor, but preferred the superior stall recovery characteristics of the conventional fuselage-mounted tail. (Although the T-tail's bad habits had been engineered out of the 727, it may be significant that it was the last as well as the first T-tail commercial transport Boeing ever built.)

Condit was never averse to learning from either his peers or his elders. Schairer and Holtby were his mentors and role models, and what he learned from them he put into the 757.

"Ken was a lot like Schairer in laying down some inviolate rules," Condit said. "Rule number one was tameness—when a pilot loses an engine on any Boeing airplane, he must be able to control the aircraft with his feet on the floor, no rudder application should be necessary, and he can maintain stability with just the yoke. Rule number two involved stall recovery—no Boeing airplane should be put in a position in which elevator control is lost because the airflow to the tail is blocked out, and that is especially applicable to the T-tail. Schairer wrote the first rule, Holtby wrote the second, and they both wrote the third rule: every Boeing airplane must be able to recover from a vertical or near-vertical dive, a rule that has saved lives on three separate occasions." (Condit was referring to the 707 dive over the Atlantic in 1958, a 727 that went into a dive over Michigan in 1979 and dropped 34,000 feet at nearly the speed of sound before recovery, and a 747-SP on a Pacific flight that plunged 29,000 feet—it was pulling six g's when the pilot recovered.)

The 757 and 767 marked Ed Wells' final direct involvement with Boeing aircraft design. He went off the board in 1978, the same year the directors gave the projects their blessing, although he was awarded the status of director emeritus. He spent his remaining years in activities for which he had never before had time—painting, astronomy, travel, and refreshing his old interest in languages; he spoke five fluently.

Wells died of cancer in 1986, and of all the legacies bequeathed by Boeing's greats, his engineering integrity and vision are among the richest. He lived long enough to receive, in 1980, the prestigious Guggenheim Award, aviation's version of the Nobel Prize, an honor shared to date by six Boeing comrades—William Boeing, Eddie Allen, George Schairer, Bill Allen, T Wilson and Joe Sutter. Wells' citation read:

> *For his outstanding contributions to the management concepts for the development of complex aerospace systems, and for his significant personal accomplishments in the design and production of a long line of the world's most famous commercial and military aircraft.*

That tribute, however, could not adequately express the affection and respect he inspired for himself as a person. He probably is remembered best for his conviction that jet power represented the future for Boeing and all aviation. "All things being equal," Wells once remarked to an associate, "propellers are just too much trouble."

The one word always used to describe Wells was "gentleman." But T knew he was tougher than a lot of people thought. "Yes, he was a gentleman," Wilson said, "but he was deceptively firm. When he got mad it was more impressive because he did it so seldom, and you knew he was mad. He'd see through something and he'd clip you."

And it was that rare burst of anger that turned the 767 program away from the wrong road into a superb airplane. In a sense, the 767 became Edward Curtis Wells' most appropriate epitaph because it was one of the finest Boeing ever built, exceeding its overall performance promises and earning a place in aviation history as the first two-engine airliner certificated for intercontinental flight. It was designed and produced not by one or two key individuals, but a *team* of engineers and manufacturing people, those diverse personalities and characters who can blend together in a common cause. Such continued teamwork and company pride were to be extended to all future Boeing programs and services, in a reaffirmation of commitment to quality.

The 767 program's general manager in the initial design period was Ken Holtby, who was succeeded by Wally Buckley. Then the commercial airplane division went through a major reorganization in September 1978, a little over a month after United became the 767's launch customer. Buckley was promoted to another job and replaced by Dean Thornton, who was very conscious of his accounting background—he was neither a production expert like Buckley nor a brilliant engineer like Ken Holtby, to whom he had been reporting.

"There was some talk about letting a bean counter run the program," Thornton recalled, "and I had heard all the talk."

He called a staff meeting as soon as he was named, and his introductory remarks assured said staff it was getting a bean counter with a sense of humor.

"I'm trying to become a program manager," he confessed, "and I think I'm coming along pretty well. My hair is starting to get a little gray, and that gives me a look of dignity. I'm finally wearing glasses so now I've got something to fiddle with when somebody asks me a tough question. And I've got hemorrhoids, which give me an expression of concern."

The bean counter was accepted immediately.

While Thornton credited Holtby, Sutter, and Ev Webb as key figures in the 767's design, he also acknowledged the input of Wells and Schairer. "Ed was always writing memos to T with suggestions, criticism and advice, and things got short-tempered once in a while. It sure wasn't the Harvard Business School's way of designing an airplane but then, that was never Boeing's way."

The 767 emerged from a tremendous amount of wind tunnel work; it was what Thornton called a "clean paper" airplane—everything started from scratch. One of the design's chief virtues was the growth potential built into the airplane; the wing, huge for the plane's overall size, was structurally so powerful that the static destruction test failed to break it. The wing went far beyond the 100 percent of design load limit, and it was not the wing that failed but the aft fuselage near the area of a rear cargo door.

"We extrapolated from that test all the data we needed to assure us the airplane had tremendous growth potential," Ben Cosgrove remembered. "We never did find out how much it would take to break the wing—the static test ended when the rear fuselage broke, and we decided to use the wing for other test purposes."

The 767 was the first Boeing transport to have a truly "international" flavor. About 50 Japanese engineers were involved in the design process, for Boeing had agreed to let Japan play a major subcontracting role; such an arrangement had worked out well with the 747-SP. Mitsubishi had built the SP's inboard flaps, Kawasaki the outboard flaps, and Fuji the vertical rudder. Those three companies were given the job of manufacturing the entire 767 fuselage with the exception of Section 41—the cockpit; that assignment went to Wichita. (The term "Kansas cockpit" might be applied to all Boeing transports, for Wichita also makes 737, 747 and 757 nose sections and will do the same with the next airliner: the 777.)

The IAM naturally expressed concern over the cooperative arrangement with the Japanese, not to mention Italy where Aeritalia had been signed as a major subcontractor. Stan Little, Jim Morrison, and analyst Fred Kelley met with Bill Winpisinger and other union officials several times to explain the facts of life: 60 percent of Boeing's sales at the time were to overseas customers who, quite literally, wanted "a piece of the action." They pointed out the difficulties of competing against government-subsidized Airbus, with four European nations involved in its production (France, Britain, Germany, and Spain). The 767's direct and very formidable competition, they added, would come from the A-310, a truncated version of the A-300 that would be the same size as the new Boeing—its production go-ahead had been authorized about the same time as the 767. The Boeing officials emphasized that Japan would be building 10 percent of the total airplane, not an exorbitant share in terms of the jobs going overseas.

"I don't like it," Winpisinger concluded, "but if I was in Boeing's shoes I wouldn't do it any other way."

From its inception, the 767 was designed to be flown safely by a two-man crew, but the prototype and the first few production models were built with a flight engineer's station. This was at United's insistence; its pilots, having finally agreed to operate the 737 with two crew members, argued this time that a three-man crew was absolutely necessary in an airplane grossing over 300,000 pounds. Boeing's rebuttal was the 767's super-sophisticated flight deck, the first "glass cockpit" it had ever put into an airliner. There were some 40 computers performing various navigation and monitoring duties, and the outstanding feature was the utilization of color CRT (cathode ray tube) equipment—the entire flight management system was computerized this way.

For navigation purposes, the CRT's upper display shows a conventional horizon in blue and yellow, but the bottom display is a colorized map. The pilot sets up the planned flight path, entering necessary navigation data, and the course is laid out on the map—the pilot can even call up a display of the destination airport. If the plane has to get into a holding pattern in bad weather, the pilot merely pushes a button on the flight management system and the assigned holding pattern is drawn on the map.

The concept of the two-man glass cockpit was developed jointly by Sutter, Ron Brown, Holtby, and Webb. Their goal was to simplify and reduce pilot workload to such an extent that two people could safely fly even the largest aircraft. And Dick Taylor sold it to the regulatory authorities.

Despite its advantages, however, Boeing had planned to build all 767 cockpits with flight engineer stations, and the three initial customers—United, American, and Delta—expected to operate the plane with three-man crews. But while the 767 was going through certification tests, a presidential commission ruled that a two-man cockpit was safe; Boeing promptly modified the flight decks of already-completed production aircraft into a two-man configuration.

There may have been controversy over engines and T-tails, but there was engineering agreement on another decision: to make the 757 cockpit identical to that of the 767 in size, avionics, and computerization. Ev Webb, Holtby and Condit worked together in achieving the successful mating of the larger plane's nose section to the 757's narrower fuselage—it was like grafting the head of a German shepherd to the slim body of a greyhound. But Holtby said this wasn't nearly as difficult as assuring avionics reliability in the 767's digitalized cockpit.

"All those black boxes had to talk to each other," Holtby said. "We spent a lot of time in the lab trying to make all the units play together, and the problem was that there were about six different vendors involved—Sperry built the flight management computer, for example, and Collins made the instruments. Getting all the systems to function together was a major problem with the 767. By the time the 757 came along, we had the bugs ironed out."

Commonality of this sophisticated cockpit made it possible for carriers operating both the 767 and 757 to transition crews from one type to the other with little or no additional training. Of all the high-tech hardware on the 767, however, the most unique was a feature no other airplane ever had before: a sewer system.

Holtby got the idea from Gerald Lamb, KLM's chief engineer, while Ken was in the 747 program. They were discussing some technical matters relating to KLM's 747s, and Lamb unexpectedly suggested, "Why don't you put a sewer in the 747?"

"A sewer?"

"Yes, a central waste-disposal system. Then we could put the lavatories anywhere in the airplane."

Holtby settled for a noncommittal, "Gosh, I don't know—I'll have to think about it." And he did think about it, seriously enough to ask his 767 engineering staff if the idea was feasible for the new wide-body.

"They came back and said it was," Holtby recounted, "but they pointed out such a system would need suction to make it work. So we put it into the 767 and we had trouble with it at first; if the suction system goes down, you don't have any workable lavatories and we had a couple of flights where that happened. But we fixed the problem by installing an electrically driven pump to provide the suction."

Holtby took a lot of ribbing about all the effort that went into developing a "high-tech biffy," as he phrased it. But a similar system went into later models of the 747—the "sewer system" being the first major improvement in aircraft lavatories since the dawn of the jet age.

The gut feeling of confidence Boeing's engineers once had about the 727's potential even before it flew was repeated with the 767—from wind tunnel data and structural tests, they *knew* this was going to be a great airplane. Which, in turn, appealed to Tex Boullioun's gambling blood. He was trying to sell the 767 to TWA whose then-president, C. E. "Ed" Meyer, was all set to buy the new A-310 Airbus and made no bones about it.

"Airbus has assured me that the A-310's fuel efficiency will be better than the 767's," he told Boullioun. "Your airplane just can't hack it."

Neither plane had flown yet, and Boullioun held a meeting with Holtby's engineering staff. He asked for the 767's fuel consumption figures based on wind tunnel estimates; given these figures, he returned to New York for another meeting with Meyer and bet the pot.

"Ed, we'll guarantee that when those two airplanes are flying, the 767 will have better fuel efficiency. Boeing's will be this number and Airbus will be that number. If we don't make our fuel guarantee we'll pay TWA a penalty, but if we do make it, you'll pay us."

TWA signed for the 767, put the plane into service, and using its own fuel burn figures ended up paying Boeing.

Early in 1979, engineering had set September 30, 1981, as the target date for the 767's first flight. It took place four days ahead of schedule, on September 26, with Tommy Edmonds and Lew Wallick doing the piloting honors and John Brit in the soon-to-be-discarded flight engineer's seat. Edmonds remembered how optimistic everyone was, including himself.

"We had visions of making the greatest first flight ever—everything perfect and nothing going wrong," he said. "Then when we took off, we tried to retract the gear and lost the center hydraulic system—the gear wouldn't come up. All the photos taken by the chase plane that day showed the 767 with the gear extended."

The rest of the first flight went well, except for one incident involving the test plane's only functioning toilet. The crew had been drinking coffee all morning and Edmonds finally headed for the lavatory. But when he flushed the toilet . . .

KABOOM!

"It was just like a twelve-gauge shotgun going off in my ear," Edmonds related. "I thought the whole plane had blown up."

It turned out the noise came from a valve in the vacuum flushing system—a minor if temporarily terrifying flaw corrected quickly. The offending valve was henceforth known among the test pilots as the "Cosgrove valve" in tribute to Ben Cosgrove, who they claimed was responsible for its design.

Wallick also drew the copilot assignment on the 757's first flight four months and 25 days later, with John Armstrong in the left seat. In Wallick's honor, the ground crew had observed a tradition dating back to his 727 flight test days. The test pilots always conducted a thorough pre-flight check on a new airplane, a process consuming about a half-hour while the ground crew—which already had made an even stricter inspection—looked on impatiently. Wallick was no exception to that procedure, but when he came into the 727 program he decided a detailed pre-flight was a waste of time and an affront to the ground crews. He informed the crew chiefs that all he was going to do was kick the nose wheel, get on the airplane, and leave. So the crew chiefs had decals printed reading "KICK HERE" that they pasted on the nose wheel of every airplane Wallick tested. It was on the 757's when he and Armstrong walked to the flight line.

February 19, 1982, was cloudy and windy; the flight had been scheduled for the previous day but was scrubbed because of bad weather. After takeoff, Armstrong shut down one of the Rolls-Royce RB-211 engines in flight deliberately, intending to relight quickly. He couldn't get it relit for several minutes.

When the 757's maiden flight ended, Armstrong told a press conference everything had been routine. He said nothing about the problem of re-starting the engine because the shutdown had been deliberate. Several days later, one of the Seattle newspapers reported that the 757 had lost an engine on its first flight, accused Armstrong of hiding the truth from the press, and implied that the 757 might not be as great as Boeing claimed.

Actually, something *had* happened after the plane landed. They had taxied in, parked in front of the cheering crowd, and Wallick left the cockpit to open the main forward cabin door. It wouldn't open. Armstrong kept waving and smiling to the cameras until he ran out of both waves and smiles.

"Open the blankety-blank door!" he finally yelled to his laboring copilot.

It finally dawned on Wallick that the airplane was still pressurized— a relief valve in the pressurization system had malfunctioned. He returned to the cockpit, opened a side window to bleed out the air, and they were able to exit with proper dignity. *That* departure from routine didn't get into the newspapers.

The 757, too, lived up to and beyond all expectations, achieving a reputation as the most fuel-efficient transport Boeing or anyone else had ever built, better even than the 767, which was no slouch. Engineering had established two goals for the 757: 40 percent more seat miles per gallon than the 727-200, and a range of 2,500 statute miles. Boeing ended up producing an airplane whose most recent version had 76 percent greater fuel efficiency than the 727-200 in terms of seat miles per gallon, and a range of 4,000 miles.

In its early design phase, the 757 was supposed to have some of the 727-200's body sections, its nose, tail, and a modified wing. It evolved into an entirely different airliner; wings, tail, systems and structure were new, the latter incorporating new weight-saving aluminum alloys and composites. Boeing offered customers a choice of high-bypass-ratio engines—the proven Rolls RB-211 or either of two new Pratt & Whitney products: the PW-2037 and the higher-thrust PW-2040.

Airlines also had three engines available to them for the 767: Pratt & Whitney's PW-4000, General Electric's CF-6, and the RB-211. Enormously powerful and huge—the nacelle width of a PW-4000 or CF-6 is wider than a B-17's fuselage—these engines gave the 767 the muscle necessary to accommodate the airplane's tremendous growth potential, and provide safe two-engine operation on long-haul overseas flights.

British Airways and Eastern were the 757's launch customers, signing contracts in spring 1979. Not since the original 727-100 had Eastern helped launch a new Boeing transport, and its order for 21 757s came only five months after the airline had bought 23 A-300s from Airbus—the first invasion of the U.S. airline market by the European consortium that was to become Boeing's strongest competitor.

Eastern's CEO was former astronaut Frank Borman, who commanded the historic Apollo 8 mission that had orbited the moon in 1968. There was a lot of T Wilson in Frank Borman and vice versa; both were tough, decisive, demanding and impatient, and in Borman those qualities translated into a hard negotiator. He became interested in the 757 when it was just the 7N7 and existed only on paper. Boeing salesman Bob Norton showed him one of the proposed designs, a 160-passenger version.

"The economics aren't quite as good as they could be," Borman said, "not with that number of seats."

Norton then showed him a 7N7 design with 180 seats and Borman nodded. "That's more like it."

The 160-passenger plane was supposed to be the 757-100 but this model never was built, and what both Eastern and British Airways ordered was the 757-200. Tex Boullioun closed the deal with Borman after several days of fruitless discussion in Miami. They had reached an impasse and Tex finally decided further negotiations were useless.

"I'm sorry, but we're not getting anywhere," he told Borman. "I've got a plane to catch back to Seattle."

"Fine, I'll go with you to the airport," Borman offered.

Another Eastern official was driving the car, and Borman sat in the back seat with Boullioun. The car bounced over some railroad tracks and Tex suddenly blurted, "Okay, Frank, you've got a deal."

Borman remarked later, "It was almost as if the jolt had loosened his resolve."

Their agreement was based on what was known as Safe Harbor Leasing, a new tax bill that enabled companies heavily in debt—as Eastern was—to sell their tax write-offs to profitable firms. Borman planned to finance the 757s with cash raised from Safe Harbor income, but after the contract was signed the media began criticizing Safe Harbor as a refuge for inefficient companies. By 1981, the media campaign had convinced Congress to revise the law, and Eastern's $560 million order was in jeopardy—the revision had saved some of the planes Borman had bought, but not all of them, and he flew to Seattle for a meeting with Boeing's top officials. T Wilson was present and as Borman described the scene, "He was the only friend I had in that room.

"I was told later that his entire staff was in favor of cancelling our 757 contract," Borman related. "Apparently I had to impress only one man and that was Wilson."

Borman left Seattle with Boeing's promise to provide sufficient subordinate financing for the airplanes no longer covered under Safe Harbor. He subsequently was castigated for making the 757 deal in the first place, the IAM accusing him of plunging the airline further in debt by buying airplanes instead of giving pay increases, and causing Eastern to be sold eventually to Frank Lorenzo. It was an accusation Borman not only denied but bitterly resented.

"Actually, I wish we could have bought more 757s," he declared long after leaving Eastern, "because their capacity and operating economy saved us when air travel began booming in the era of discounted fares. I knew I might be hung out to dry for buying the 757 after going into deep hock with the A-300, but we had no choice. We had a fleet that was sixty percent obsolete and fuel-inefficient, and we were trying to compete with Delta, which was in the middle of a new equipment splurge."

Delta's fleet modernization program to which Borman referred included both the 757 and 767; one of the latter became a very special part of the airline's history—Delta's own employees purchased it with money raised through voluntary payroll deductions. Curiously, Delta's 757s differed from those delivered to Eastern and British Airways, those two carriers ordering the plane with four door exits and no overwing exits, while Delta eliminated one of the doors and opted for the overwing exits.

Borman had ordered the 757 with a conventional cockpit. Then he visited Renton to check on program progress, and Condit showed him the glass cockpit—an airman's heaven to this technically minded former astronaut and Air Force test pilot. He was hooked, and he never forgot what happened next.

"Boeing put the glass cockpit into all our 757s at no extra cost," he reminisced. "It wasn't in our contract but they did it anyway."

Condit did him another favor; folded life jackets, located under the seats, were disappearing from Eastern's planes in alarming numbers and Borman finally asked Condit for help.

"It seems women passengers are sliding the jackets out from under their seats, stuffing them into large purses, and walking off the airplane," he reported. "I think every damned boat in Miami must be equipped with our life jackets."

So Condit had his engineers design a new storage location in the overhead PSU (Passenger Service Unit), on the theory that people aren't as likely to steal something when they're in plain view of other passengers. This is why airplane reading lights are designed so passengers can't fiddle with them or steal them, and can be changed only by a mechanic. This explanation, however, failed to mollify Bob Crandall, American's CEO and a man never shy about voicing a beef, as Condit could testify.

Not too long ago, Crandall called him about a complaint American received from a first class passenger who had flown all the way from Dallas to Tokyo on a 747SP with the reading light above his seat burned out. The plane was full, there was no other seat available, and when American had an unhappy passenger, Boeing could have an unhappy Mr. Crandall.

"The guy had brought a whole bunch of work to do on the flight," Crandall said, "and we ended up refunding his first class fare. So would you mind telling me why it is that I can change the light bulb in a reading lamp in my home, but I can't change the reading light in your stupid airplane?"

The explanation may have been logical, but so was Crandall's question, and Condit decided to do something about it—with continued prodding from Crandall. "He's a delight," Condit said, "and he was bugging me with good reason. Every time I see him, he has another reading light story. A number of us great engineers have tried to explain to Bob the technical reasons, but he refused to listen. So we finally informed him that the reading lights on our next airplane, the 777, can be changed by a flight attendant."

Tex Boullioun regarded Crandall as one of the toughest airline CEOs he ever dealt with, but that same toughness won Boeing's respect. "I'm not interested in how much it costs you to build an airplane," he once told a Boeing executive. "All I'm interested in is the price American has to pay."

The two new twins sailed through FAA certification tests, but the 757 encountered a last-minute red tape snag that was almost a comedy. It was scheduled to receive its Type Certificate—literally a license to carry paying passengers—December 21, 1982, meeting a deadline date that had been set three years earlier when the airplane was still on the drawing boards.

A ceremonial noon luncheon in the executive dining room of building 10-60 in Renton was arranged for Boeing and FAA regional officials. Three hours before what was supposed to be a routine event, the FAA in Washington notified Condit that the 757's Type Certificate would not be issued because the airplane's "First Observer Seat" (one of the two cockpit jump seats) failed to comply with FAA regulations.

Condit protested in vain that the jump seat issue had been discussed just a week before with local FAA inspectors, who agreed that the seat's design and location was an operational matter, not a safety or technical item, and therefore wasn't covered by the Type Certificate process. No matter, Condit was told, this was Washington's decision and the unhappy regional office wasn't about to argue with Washington.

Condit conferred with Fred Zappert of Boeing's airworthiness department. Zappert, a German-born and British-raised engineer, urged him to stand firm.

"This was all decided a week ago," he reiterated. "The FAA here agreed that the seat issue should be settled separately because it had nothing to do with the Type Certificate."

More phone calls between Condit and the FAA. More discussions involving Condit, Tex Boullioun and Ernie Fenn, vice president and general manager of the 757 division. Shortly before noon, the FAA offered a compromise: it would grant the 757 a temporary six-month Type Certificate, pending resolution of the jump seat dispute. Condit turned it down and the luncheon, attended by some openly embarrassed FAA people who had always enjoyed a good working relationship with Boeing, began a half-hour late. There were flowers and a 757 model at each table, but the mood was not very festive.

Mal Stamper presided and after lunch was served, he rose to mention the excellent FAA cooperation on the 757 program and praised the team's work. Nothing was said about the Type Certificate and by 1:30 the dining room was deserted except for a glum Zappert and associate Paul Higgins. The flowers and models were still on the table.

Zappert and Higgins were about to leave when in walked Fenn and Condit. Fenn handed Zappert a piece of paper. "It's the Type Certificate," he said, "but we had to give in on the six-month restriction—it was the only way we could meet Eastern's delivery schedule."

Boeing had promised to deliver Eastern its first 757 by December 28, because the airline had to put the airplane into service before the first of the year in order to receive tax credits for calendar 1982, and those tax credits amounted to millions of dollars. Three months later, the 757 received full certification with minor changes to the offending jump seat, and Eastern had taken delivery of its first airplane on time. (Actually it was the fifth Eastern 757 off the line; the first four were used in the flight test program.)

Ernie Fenn was a well-liked Boeing industrial engineering veteran; he had come up from the Auburn fabrication division and was one of Bruce Gissing's mentors in the mysteries of managing airplane production. Gissing and a lot of other students learned their lessons well, because the 767 program came in five percent under its estimated development budget despite overruns in two areas—establishment of laboratories for avionics hardware and computer systems integration, plus changing the cockpits in the first 30 airplanes to a two-man crew configuration.

Gissing believed Boeing had profited immensely from the 747 experience. Before the 767 program began, Don Whitford gave him some advice:

"You can have a lot of bright ideas, Bruce, but if you think they're so damned great try them out first on an existing, mature organization. You can change, but don't change more than ten or fifteen percent."

To Gissing, that meant avoiding the frequent management changes so prevalent with the 747. "One of the concepts the 767 team had from the start," Gissing said, "was that the only way anyone was going to get out of the program was to get promoted. And that's exactly what happened.

"We took that baby right through the design, execution and cost stages with largely the same people, and management consistency stayed intact."

Sterling Sessions remembered another difference between the 767 and 747 programs, namely the absence of "shims" in the newer airplane—shims are used to smooth out poorly fitting joints when fuselage sections are mated. "The early 747s probably had a thousand pounds of shims," Sessions said, "but there are no shims on the 767."

Boeing was quite pleased with the foreign subcontractors who participated in the 767 program, particularly the high quality of the Japanese output, although that arrangement had gotten off to a somewhat rocky start. Dean Thornton was in Tokyo meeting with Mitsubishi officials to work out final contractual details and got in a dispute over some point with Mitsubishi president Tojo. Thornton finally lost patience.

"Dammit, no!" he barked. "We're not going to talk about it anymore!"

He slammed his fist on the table just as an earthquake tremor shook the building. Dead silence until Tojo said quietly, "Thornton-san, would you like to reconsider?"

The 767 got off to a brisk sales start with orders from United, Delta and American. Thornton was in on the first sales presentation to American, a meeting at which domestic sales director Carl Munson was extolling the plane's virtues to an audience consisting of chairman Al Casey and his two top officers, Bob Crandall and Donald Lloyd-Jones. "Munson was an extremely intense man," Thornton said. "Like George Martin, he'd get out of his chair and climb over the table to make a point."

In careful preparation for this important session, Munson had written out several statistical crib notes and put them on his lap for reference during the presentation. His head kept bobbing up and down as he talked until Casey, a master at one-liners, finally couldn't stand it anymore.

"Carl," he inquired, "do you keep notes on your fly?"

Early 757 sales were brisk, too, but orders for both airplanes then sagged, partly due to the 1980–81 recession but also because of an adverse factor no one had anticipated: deregulation of the airline industry, approved by Congress in 1978 and coinciding with Boeing's launch of the 757-767 programs. One of deregulation's major effects was the massive escalation of the "hub and spoke" concept, which Delta had pioneered at Atlanta. One by one, the nation's major carriers established hubs in various cities, feeding the majority of their flights into these traffic axles where passengers connected with other flights to their destinations.

There were distinct advantages to the hub system, such as greater schedule flexibility and an increase in flight frequency, but it also reduced sharply the number of point-to-point non-stop flights, many of them providing relatively long-haul service between major city pairs. There isn't much doubt this shift in airline operating strategy hurt the 767 and, albeit to a lesser extent, the 757 as well. But it also pumped new life into the 737 program, which prior to deregulation had been slowing down to a modest crawl, particularly in the domestic market. Although the 737-200 had benefited from gradual improvements—advanced engines and avionics modernization among them—basically it was the same airplane Boeing had introduced a decade earlier.

In 1980, while the two new twins were still to make their first flight tests, Frank Shrontz had taken over the 707-727-737 division and Boeing decided to build the 737-300. It was no mere face-lift. The fuselage of the 200 series was stretched by almost nine feet, and the latest high-bypass-ratio engines designed specifically for the airplane were fitted. The U.S./French engine consortium, CFMI, had made a daring decision to fund the development, even though such an engine had never before been applied to an airplane of this size.

Cockpit avionics were upgraded and included laser gyro technology as a base, allowing the use of advanced flight management computer techniques. The 737-300, Shrontz's first airplane program, literally was a transport designed for the era of deregulation and became a stunning sales success, although the McDonnell Douglas MD-80 was a powerful competitor.

The 737-300 incorporated much of the 757-767 technology, including the use of composites, and it was followed by two additional derivatives—the 400 and 500 series. Those three models were responsible for two-thirds of the nearly 3,000 737s Boeing had sold by the end of 1991, and it was the 300 that really turned the profit corner for the entire 737 program.

Southwest Airlines was the 737-300's launch customer, the first time in Boeing's history that a relatively small carrier had launched a new airplane program, and USAir followed with another order. But there were defeats, too—the MD-80 program had a three-year head start on the 737-300 and it was an excellent airplane; only three feet shorter than the original DC-8, it carried about 140 passengers in standard configuration, promised excellent fuel efficiency and was ideal for hub operations.

Boeing's sales strategy was the same Douglas had once employed against the 707: wait for the 737-300, prospective customers were advised, because it will be even better than the MD-80. That was the argument Boeing took into a meeting with Frank Hulse, the aging but hard-as-nails president of Southern Airways, which for years had been operating DC-9s. Ken Schneider made the pitch on behalf of a Boeing sales team and when he finished, Hulse stood up.

"You gentlemen from Boeing sure do impress me," he drawled. "You're coming in here telling me how good things will be if I wait for the 737-300. But you kinda remind me of that old pioneer sitting on the back of his covered wagon, with his rifle across his lap and the air full of arrows, and the poor guy is still trying to figure out which Indian to shoot first."

Needless to say, Southern picked the MD-80, but an even more disappointing loss was American's decision in favor of McDonnell Douglas. This was a case of Bob Crandall playing hardball. MCDD had offered to lease American 20 MD-80s for five years, with an option to return the airplanes at the end of the lease period if the airline wasn't satisfied with their performance. But for the 737-300, even more unproven than the MD-80 at that stage, Crandall insisted that American be allowed to turn back the airplanes after only three months in service. Boeing turned him down, much to Tex Boullioun's disappointment.

"The three months didn't bother me," Boullioun said, "because I figured once we got those airplanes in American's hands, Crandall never would have returned them. He did get a good deal from McDonnell Douglas and I'm convinced it saved their whole MD-80 program. It hadn't been selling well until the American contract."

Deregulation had the whole industry in a turmoil—especially large carriers saddled with high labor costs at a time when new low-cost airlines were invading the established carriers' markets with reduced fares that had to be matched. The hub concept became their major weapon against the newcomers, for it enabled them to dominate traffic at key cities. Before deregulation, United—which had turned down the 757—had been reducing its 737 fleet; after hubs became a way of life, UAL not only bought back some of the planes it had previously sold, but ordered the 737-300 in quantity.

Considering the adverse circumstances of deregulation, the 757 and 767 did better than many experts had predicted. The 757 was surprisingly successful, surprising in the sense that some industry analysts had criticized Boeing for having the temerity to introduce a new narrow-body jet at a time when wide-bodies were the rage. Yet the 757 achieved respectable success while bucking not only this trend, but three other obstacles: recession, deregulation, and the fact that the fuel crisis had eased considerably after the first round of sales.

The 767 might have had rough sailing except for its growth potential. Delta and American convinced Boeing to take advantage of that potential, both regarding the standard 767 as too short-ranged. And Boeing's own marketing people were urging engineering to stretch the 767's range, especially for the crowded West Coast–Hawaii route where traffic didn't justify operating 747s or even DC-10s.

The result was the development of two Extended Range (ER) versions, the 767-200ER and a 767-300ER that was 21 feet longer. They gave the airlines the best of three worlds: a wide-body with intercontinental range, generous cargo space (a traditional bonus in every Boeing transport), and twin-engine operating economy remarkable in an airplane carrying more than 200 passengers.

Some at Boeing worried that the long-range 767 would cut into 747 sales, but T didn't agree. He considered the ER ideal for overseas routes whose traffic didn't justify a 747. When the Extended Range model was first announced, he told an interviewer: "It's going to be almost as big as a DC-10, it'll have the same range, and it'll cost half as much to operate—it's just as natural as a goose going barefoot."

The ER's biggest hurdle was concern over safety: what if the 767 lost *both* engines on an overwater flight? Or, for that matter, could it stay airborne on only one engine long enough to reach a safe landing place? "Long enough" under FAA regulations meant that a twin-engine transport aircraft operating over water on one engine had to be able to reach an alternate airport within two hours. That rule alone prevented the airlines from using twins between West Coast cities and Honolulu, for there are no alternate airports on that route.

Then-FAA administrator Lynn Helms almost blew the proverbial gasket when Boeing's Dick Taylor first approached him in 1980 on the subject of modifying the twin-engine overwater requirement.

"It'll be a cold day in hell before I let twins fly long-haul, overwater routes," he told Taylor. But Dick kept plugging away at the recalcitrant FAA chief.

"Helms actually was more worried about systems failures than engine failures," Taylor recalled. "We finally won him over by providing additional sources of electrical power. We also installed a fire extinguishing system in the 767 cargo bays, alleviating another one of his concerns."

Three international carriers—Air Canada, El Al and TWA—began twin-engine flights over the Atlantic in the spring of 1984, operating modified 767s before the FAA issued formal approval. Qantas and Air New Zealand did likewise in the Pacific market, and American—fast expanding its international service—eventually became a major proving ground for twin-engine safety.

Boeing's Dick Welch appointed an overwater certification committee consisting of Taylor, John Swihart, Ev Webb and Brien Wygle. Their task was to convince the FAA once and for all that twins like the 767 could fly long-haul ocean routes safely. Even while several airlines were operating such routes under temporary authority, the committee was collecting a complete operational history of the engines offered on the ER, and compiled data on every failure and shutdown ever experienced. There were few instances, and where there had been a shutdown the manufacturers had determined the cause and taken corrective action. The record was so good that the certification committee's report to the FAA showed that the probability of both engines failing was once every 50,000 years. In fact, Boeing informed the FAA, the likelihood of 767 diversions to alternate airports statistically was less than that of a 747.

Boeing also had to prove that the 767's flight control system would remain operative in the event of engine or electrical failure—suppose, the FAA asked, an engine *and* a generator failed? Boeing answered this by installing an extra generator in the ER's wheelwell, running off either the remaining good engine or the APU (Auxiliary Power Unit).

The 767-ER not only met the government's two-hour rule for overwater, one-engine operation, but after three years of actual airline service the requirement was stretched to 180 minutes, which opened the Hawaii market to 767-ER flights. The most remarkable quality of the airplane was its awesome power reserve even on one engine. It could take off at maximum gross weight (407,000 pounds on the 767-300ER), lose an engine on rotation—the most critical moment—and still climb on the remaining engine. If an engine fails at a high cruising altitude, the 767 will lose altitude slowly for some 400 miles, and at about 26,000 feet can start a slow climb for the rest of the flight. And that is without using full rated power at any time.

Both the 757 and 767 completed their first eight years of airline service with a perfect safety record, and one of their most significant achievements was proving the reliability and enhanced safety of the glass cockpit. Boeing learned enough from 757-767 experience to make further improvements in the 747-400, the biggest of the 747 series, whose two-crew digital cockpit has 606 fewer lights, gauges and switches than the standard 747, 22 fewer than even the 757 or 767, and 100 fewer than the tiny 737.

As of December 31, 1991, Boeing had 770 orders for 757s and had delivered 412; for the 767, orders totaled 598 with 405 delivered. The sales totals hadn't reached the spectacular levels of the 737 and 747 but the twins have been profitable, justifying Tex Boullioun's dogged determination to introduce them within a few months of each other.

For a while, T had some doubts. Dick Albrecht, who came to Boeing in 1976 as the company's new general counsel and also succeeded Jim Prince as corporate secretary, was hired by T personally and occupied an office next to him. Wilson remarked one day, "You know, Albrecht, I think I'm overpaid."

"That's not true," Albrecht said. "You have a lot of responsibilities."

"Well, I don't have that much to do. Everyone's running his own thing." (Which was true: T's philosophy was that the divisions should run themselves without undue influence from corporate.)

But a few years later, when the 757 and 767 programs had been introduced amid recession and deregulation, Albrecht was in Wilson's office discussing various problems. T suddenly interrupted the conversation.

"Remember when I told you I was overpaid? I don't think so anymore."

Although Prince's duties included those of a legal advisor, Albrecht was the first to hold the title of general counsel. He had some large shoes to fill; when Prince retired in 1977, T lost a man he trusted, in whom he confided, and who wasn't afraid to take him on.

T was delivering a few choice remarks at a dinner one night and Prince was sitting there with his eyes closed. Wilson glared at him.

"Prince, are you awake?"

Prince opened his eyes. "Are you finished?"

"No."

"Then wake me up when you are."

Prince had a casual attitude toward health matters. A short man with an easy smile that went with his sense of humor, he put on weight in his later years and was a heavy smoker. T was giving a presentation at a staff meeting and Prince began coughing.

"Prince, quit that coughing," Wilson scolded.

"It's the only exercise I get," Prince said.

Such relaxed executive exchanges came as something of a culture shock to Albrecht, who had started out as a lawyer in Allen's old Seattle law firm and was with the Treasury Department when T offered him a job at Boeing. He had never worked for a large corporation before, came from the highly structured federal government, and discovered that Boeing was unlike any corporation or government agency.

"The thing that struck me about Boeing was that nobody paid much attention to organization charts or titles, which certainly was T's style. If you wanted something or needed to tell somebody something, you'd call the person who was most directly involved. No one worried about chains of command, which is healthy and one of the company's strengths, along with the fact that the senior officers have never come out of a single mold."

The latter happened to reflect one of T's outstanding strengths, too—his tolerance of the mavericks and squirrels who didn't fit any mold. Allen had tolerated them, too, but not to the extent Wilson did. Perhaps T's own outstanding achievement was branding Boeing with his personal style of leadership, yet retaining intact the legacy of technical and corporate integrity Allen had bequeathed.

But it was a legacy that would be tested during the decade of the eighties.

TWENTY-TWO

BLACK INK . . . AND BLACK EYES

THE COVER ON THE APRIL 7, 1980, ISSUE OF *TIME* FEATURED A picture of T Wilson, and inside the magazine's Economy and Business section were eight pages of glowing praise for Boeing.

The cover story, pegged to the company's winning the ALCM contract over General Dynamics, carried the lead headline "Masters of the Air."

"Since its founding . . . the Seattle planemaker has developed and nurtured a reputation for innovation, reliability and plain downright engineering excellence that is unmatched in the industry," *Time* declared. "Indeed, in an age when much of American business seems to have slipped into a search for quick profits and is marked by shoddy workmanship, the 104,000 engineers, designers, draftsmen, executives and salesmen of Boeing stand out as proof that, over the long haul, the only lasting standard of value in any market is quality itself."

What neither Boeing nor *Time* could anticipate, of course, were the recession of the early 1980s and the extent of deregulation's convulsive effects on the U.S. airline industry. Mal Stamper used a word for it: "Unk-unk"—the Unknown-unknown, events and situations that don't show up in anyone's crystal ball.

"The Unk-unks always get us," Stamper said. "And deregulation was a major Unk-unk. Delta, like United, was going to get rid of a bunch of 737s and all of a sudden it has competition coming from every direction, a hub concept to feed, and it's trading off three L-1011s for every new 737."

Yet Boeing had positioned itself to absorb the Unk-unks of the eighties far better than it ever had in the past—better than before the 1969–70 crunch, for example. Its ability to offer not merely new airliner types, but improved and different-sized versions of older models, surpassed that of other aircraft manufacturers. When 757 and 767 sales slowed in the early 1980s, it had the 737-300 waiting in the wings, plus the 747-300 series with upper-deck extension and additional windows—Big Bird literally became a two-deck airplane, the once intimate lounge area accommodating more passengers than the old Stratocruiser's main cabin.

In an industry so vulnerable to the cyclical nature of world economic conditions, airline revenues, and uncertainties of military funding, Boeing's versatility was something competitors had difficulty matching. Except for the DC-10, the brisk-selling MD-80 series was the only commercial transport venture for McDonnell Douglas until the late 1980s when MCDD launched the MD-11. Lockheed shut down the L-1011 line after selling fewer than 250 TriStars, ironically the best transport it had ever built, and abandoned the commercial arena. By the mid-eighties, Airbus had combined an excellent product line with heavy government underwriting of development costs to become Boeing's chief competitor. Yet the Toulouse-based consortium's market invasion initially was more at MCDD's expense than Boeing's.

Boeing almost added two more new types to its airline family during this decade. There was the 150-passenger 7J7, a radical new design that amounted to a hybrid. Its engines, called prop fans, were hitched to a revolutionary new type of propeller with counter-rotating blades, shaped in a way that increased their air "bite." In effect, the props were enlarged fanblades placed outside the engine nacelles, and wind tunnel tests pointed to fuel efficiency that made even the 757 seem like a guzzler by comparison.

Delta and British Airways were very interested, possibly becoming the 7J7's launch customers. But they were the only carriers showing much interest in a transport that had been conceived while the airline industry was reeling from the shock of the oil embargo crisis. Delta still wanted the plane after fuel prices eased, however, and wasn't happy when Boeing decided against a go-ahead. Equally disappointed were the Japanese, who had a 25 percent share in the program. But Frank Shrontz, Boeing's president when the 7J7 was put on indefinite hold, felt the decision was wise.

"I know Delta was clearly upset," Shrontz said, "but I think toward the end even their technical people had to agree that the risk involved in the engines and other things were too great for a go-ahead."

Boeing's other aborted transport project was the 7-Dash-7, a more conventional 150-passenger airplane. But again, except for Delta, it attracted little interest. The same was true of various proposals to modernize older 727-100s, one of them coming from Allen Paulsen who had originated the idea of converting C-97s into "Guppy" cargo planes. He suggested turning 100s into 200s simply by adding a fuselage plug, but after Dick Welch and Jack Steiner studied the possibilities, they told Paulsen Boeing wasn't interested.

Then someone at an American Airlines staff meeting came up with a more drastic 727-100 conversion plan: remove the center engine, restructure the top fuselage, replace the other two engines with larger, more modern fanjets, and if necessary put on a new wing. It was another idea spawned by the fuel crisis and Bob Crandall admitted he was "fascinated by its potential." Nothing came of this 727-100 surgical procedure because when fuel prices stabilized, American's enthusiasm cooled.

The suggested modernization of the 100 series was the 727's last hurrah; almost symbolically, the careers of both the airplane and the man whose name was so closely associated with its history came technically to an end within a year of each other. Steiner retired in 1983 and the 727 production line was shut down in 1984 with the delivery of the last of 15 new 727-200F freighters ordered by Federal Express.

In a historical sense, the 727 ranks with the DC-3 as a truly ageless airliner, and it has been called the DC-3 of the jet age. Designed with a projected life span of 20 years, its expected longevity was at least doubled by continuous modifications and improvement. The famed "three holer" earned industry respect and pilot affection from the first day it flew. Shortly after United began operating its new 727s, Pat Patterson phoned Bill Allen.

"I just want to tell you it's the first plane we ever bought that's better than what a manufacturer had promised," he declared. It was quite an admission; except for Delta's C. E. Woolman, there was no more loyal Douglas customer than Patterson.

When Alaska Airlines acquired a number of MD-80s, it planned to phase out its 727-200 fleet, then decided it couldn't afford to let them go. Alaska's then-president, Bruce Kennedy, said the airline realized that the 727's comparatively poor fuel efficiency was more than offset by the amount of cargo it could carry. And when the carrier announced plans to inaugurate the first scheduled passenger service between the West Coast and the Soviet Union—Anchorage to Magadan and Khabarovsk—727s were picked to fly the route.

The 727's most unique customer was an airline called Air America, which really wasn't an airline at all but a cover name for a clandestine fleet of aircraft operated by the Central Intelligence Agency. Its chief executive was George Brantzen Doole, Jr., an affable man of great bulk and wit who also happened to be a veteran CIA official. It was Doole who approached Boeing salesman Byron Miller one day with a question.

"How far could a 727 carry a ten-thousand-pound payload, drop to an altitude of five hundred feet, and dump some stuff out of the ventral stairs?" he inquired.

Miller got the figures from engineering and Doole bought three 727s whose presumed exploits are buried in the CIA files. The only publicized in-flight use of those rear stairs involved a skyjacker named

"D. B. Cooper" who parachuted out of a skyjacked Northwest 727 somewhere between Seattle and Reno in 1971, with $200,000 in ransom money; he was never seen again.

Boeing made a ceremonial occasion out of the 727's last production rollout—aircraft line number 1,832 on August 14, 1984. Bill Shineman, vice president and general manager of the Renton division, was master of ceremonies with Shrontz and Stamper as the speakers. The first 727 test flight crew—Lew Wallick, Dix Loesch, and Marv "Shuly" Shulenberger—was present along with 31 veteran 727 program employees honored with special recognition certificates.

Quite a few complimentary statistics were mentioned, such as the planes' 98.3 percent reliability record over the previous 10 years and the fact that since 1964 they had carried more than 2.3 *billion* passengers, the equivalent of half the world's population. The statistic most meaningful to Boeing, however, was the revenue those 1,800-plus airplanes had brought to Boeing: more than $15 billion.

It's doubtful whether anyone at the rollout ceremony would have dared predict that in a few years the once-troubled, occasionally maligned 737 would shatter the 727's record as the best-selling airliner in aviation history. Just as the 727-200 had helped keep Boeing afloat in the early 1970s, so did the 737 during the first three years of the eighties, a period in which the baby Boeing was the best-selling airliner in the world, garnering a record customer base of 115 airlines. Frank Shrontz once remarked that the 737's success finally vindicated one man's faith in the program—and that was Ben Wheat.

In those three years, the company's net profits had dropped from a healthy $600 million in 1980, to $473 million and $292 million in 1981 and 1982 respectively. The comeback began the following year, coinciding with the recession's end and a sharp upward swing in aircraft orders—over the next five years (1983–87), Boeing's new airplane sales totaled 1,417. The total for the previous five-year period was 1,502, but a third of those orders were placed in a single year—1978—before recession and deregulation hit.

To help sales, Boeing began accepting used airplane trade-ins, something the company had once frowned upon unless it was absolutely necessary. But the used airplane market had become glutted during the recession; by 1983, Boeing alone had 28 traded-in jetliners in storage around the country, with another 40 on the way. They were the responsibility of customer support, and the company decided to stick Jim Blue with the re-selling job.

Blue's biggest headache was invading a slow market with a 68-plane fleet that included 880s, 727s, 747s, L-1011s, DC-10s, A-300s, and even two brand-new A-310s that Boeing had acquired from Kuwait Airways in a 767 deal.

The latter were an eye-opener; they were the newest in Boeing's inventory and one had only 45 hours of logged air time. They were flown to Hanover, Germany, where a team of Boeing tech reps and engineers had been sent over to inspect them. They pushed one into a hangar, got out the A-310 maintenance manuals, jacked up the airplane, and for a week ran every possible test. They even took out all the instruments for bench tests, not just to see whether everything worked but to understand the airplane. The team went back and told everyone, "Hey, these guys build a good airplane, maybe not as good as ours in my opinion, but a very good product."

In the course of time, Boeing salesmen discovered this also was true of McDonnell Douglas and Lockheed aircraft. "We have never tolerated anyone at Boeing bad-mouthing our competition," one remarked, "but the trade-ins were really the first chance we got to look closely at what they were building and we found out, by God, they did have an excellent product. The TriStar was at the top of the list."

Boeing's incursion into the used airplane market carried firm marching orders: the company would support every aircraft it sold, regardless of whether it was a Boeing product. That rule was observed even though there were times when relatively inexperienced operators could drive customer support up the wall. Boeing had sold an L-1011 to a charter airline that flew the plane between Portland, Oregon, and Hawaii. Al Heitman once was informed that the airline had another TriStar with an inoperative entertainment system; mechanics had been trying to fix it for three days with no success, and the carrier wanted to know if Boeing had anyone who could help them.

Heitman immediately dispatched Dick Shaddell to Portland. The next morning, Heitman came into his office and found Shaddell there.

"Dammit, Dick, I told you to go to Portland and fix that L-1011," Heitman complained.

"I did," Shaddell said. "I got there by nine, had it fixed by nine-thirty, and was back home in bed by eleven. All they had was a blown fuse. Their maintenance chief pleaded with me not to tell his boss."

When Boeing announced it was establishing a separate used airplane department with a vice president in charge, Blue received considerable publicity in the aviation trade press. He was asked by one reporter how he planned to get rid of nearly 70 airplanes.

"We're gonna put all of 'em into Third World countries," he confidently predicted. He didn't sell a single airplane to a Third World nation; all 68 in the original inventory went to customers in the United States except for two sold to Virgin Atlantic, a British airline.

His first worry concerned the 28 airplanes scattered around various airports; they were parked in Tucson, Everett, Las Vegas, Yuma and at a field in Oregon, and Boeing was paying about $2 million a year in rental storage fees. He decided to ferry the whole fleet to Wichita where Boeing had a superb modification center.

Almost any deal was tempting; at that point the used airplane market looked so gloomy that Blue, only half-jokingly, suggested to an associate, "Why don't we take all of 'em to Arizona, dig a big hole, and cover 'em up?"

Recognizing his own lack of sales experience, he enlisted the aid of Ray Hogan, a former Boeing sales official who had gone with Pacific Southwest Airlines and had since retired. Hogan hadn't gotten his chair warm yet when Blue received a call from a company that wanted to acquire a 727-100 for use as a business jet.

"We'll give you twelve and a half million," the company official offered, and Blue almost fell out of *his* chair—used 727-100s were going for about $4.5 million at the time.

"I think we've got a bad connection," Blue muttered. "Let me get Ray Hogan in on this."

Hogan took over the conversation and finally hung up, shaking his head. "The guy doesn't want to pay cash," he reported. "His company makes men's underwear and he'll give Boeing twelve and a half million dollars' worth of underwear in exchange for the airplane."

Blue decided such a deal was beyond his authority and consulted T. "I can't figure out what the hell we could do with all that underwear," he told Wilson.

"If you can get assorted sizes, we might give 'em out as Christmas gifts," T suggested, not too helpfully.

Blue and Hogan spent another six months trying to work out a deal with the underwear manufacturer and finally gave up. Yet even the original offer bettered the one made by a prospective customer who wanted to trade $14 million worth of commercial television time for a 727-100.

"I thought it sounded pretty good," Blue admitted, "until I discovered the TV time he was offering was from two to four o'clock in the morning."

No matter what deal any Boeing salesman made, T—like Allen before him—insisted that everything had to be aboveboard. Doug Beighle became involved in some complex legal negotiations with a foreign government buying 747s, and Wilson told him, "I'd rather sacrifice the contract than cut corners."

And that's the way it was done, preserving Boeing's reputation for corporate integrity, and the legacy that dated back to its founding.

Which is what made several events occurring between the late 1970s and the mid-1980s bitter pills that Boeing had to swallow.

To put those events into proper perspective, it is essential to understand the time period in which they took place, an era of extremely intense competition within the aerospace industry that involved the overseas commercial airplane market and military contracts in the United States. Two factors were pivotal:

- It was a competitive atmosphere that invited trouble. Dealing with some foreign carriers through their governments was a road mined with different customs, different ways of doing business, and different standards. Dealing with the Pentagon, especially during the huge military buildup of the Reagan administration, had every aerospace company scrambling for its share, and it led to everything from unrealistic bidding with inevitable overruns, to frowned-upon means of obtaining advance information that might let one firm get a jump on another.
- By the mid-eighties, however, the aerospace industry found itself dealing with another kind of atmosphere: Congress, media, and the public had begun to question practices, methods and ethical standards that had once been considered acceptable, and under current laws perfectly legal; quite a few gray areas of right or wrong became definitely black.

Early in 1976, a Senate committee launched an investigation into alleged payoffs made by American manufacturers to foreign officials with influence over the awarding of contracts, including commercial airplanes. The probe spread to various federal agencies including the Securities and Exchange Commission (SEC), the Department of Justice, Internal Revenue Service, and Federal Trade Commission. The allegations also prompted Boeing's board of directors to form an internal auditing committee headed by David Packard, chairman of Hewlett-Packard, with an outside counsel to assure impartiality; Packard became a Boeing director in 1978 and was active on the audit committee for several years.

Out of all the interrogations of present and former Boeing employees, exhaustive examinations of tax returns, files, and documents involving the company's foreign sales and marketing practices, and the activities of the consultants Boeing frequently hired to aid it in negotiating airplane contracts with foreign governments, came these conclusions:

Boeing had never knowingly made a payoff to anybody in 162 separate agreements involving foreign sales over the 10-year period covered by the investigation. But some instances aroused suspicion that a payoff may have been made by a consultant; one case involved a consultant's check that had been endorsed by a foreign government official. And the company admitted it had erred in not always informing the Export-Import Bank, which requires detailed invoices on export transactions, that consultants had been used.

There were 40 such incomplete invoices and Boeing entered a guilty plea, paying a total fine of about $400,000 plus $50,000 in court costs. At least one invoice involved a technical violation—Boeing had paid a commission to a consultant for a sale to a foreign carrier, but the airline's government objected and Boeing told the consultant to keep the money as a termination of services fee. The end result of this massive government probe into industry practices in overseas sales was the Foreign Corrupt Practices Act, signed into law by President Carter, and giving overseas bribery the status of a felony punishable by heavy fines and/or prison terms.

Bob Bateman and Russ Light of Boeing's Washington office had lunch with Jim Prince one day to discuss what the company's representatives in the nation's capital could or couldn't do from an ethical standpoint. As usual, Prince sat through most of the conversation with his eyes closed. Light and Bateman had done almost all the talking and Bateman finally concluded, "Well, I guess we've covered everything."

Prince opened his eyes. "I will remind you gentlemen of one more thing. Corporations don't go to jail. People do."

Bud Coffey said the worst bawling out he ever got in his whole life came from T, and it involved a relatively minor incident that Wilson felt tainted Boeing's public image of corporate political impartiality. Coffey had given a young Boeing employee named Rod Scheyer permission to help Senator Jackson's staff when the senator came to Wisconsin on a 1972 presidential primary campaign trip; Scheyer was told he could assist Jackson only on his own time.

"But don't lie if somebody asks you who you are," Coffey cautioned.

Scheyer drew his first assignment from Jackson's staff, which asked him to pick up some reporters at the airport. On the way back into town, one newsman asked Rod what he did.

"I work for Boeing," Scheyer said with complete honesty.

"And you're helping Senator Jackson?"

"Yes."

That was all the media needed, especially those from Eastern papers. Boeing took an old-fashioned press battering and T summoned Coffey.

"I've had my butt chewed in this company a few times," Coffey said later, "but nothing approached what T gave me that day. Bateman, Light, Stan Little and I ended up personally paying for all costs connected with Scheyer's trip. Wilson could have fired me; he didn't but I got the message that one more screw-up and I was gone."

The company was understandably sensitive on the subject of political activities. In 1982, Boeing inadvertently billed the government for slightly over $81,000 it had contributed to various state and local political parties and candidates. The reimbursement request was in a list of overhead expenses associated with an Air Force contract. Overhead costs in a government contract are not supposed to include such normal corporation expenditures as contributions, public relations, advertising, and entertainment, which are not reimbursable. It was an honest mistake but another embarrassment that caused a brief media flap.

So did a 1986 Department of Justice (DOJ) civil suit filed against Boeing and five former employees who resigned or retired to accept high positions in the Department of Defense and Navy Department. Boeing was accused of giving them almost a half-million in questionable severance pay in 1981 and 1982, which DOJ said created a conflict of interest. Although Justice did not claim any of the five did anything to benefit Boeing during their government employment, the complaint said the severance pay was "completely discretionary" in that it was limited to employees leaving the company to accept "certain key government positions."

The inference was that Boeing was making sure they'd stay loyal to the company, but after litigation that dragged on for several years, the company was completely exonerated in a unanimous decision by the United States Supreme Court.

The federal systems group, a Vienna, Virginia, division of the parent Boeing Computer Services, earned some brief headlines in 1984 when the Interior Department suspended the unit from all government contracts for a year, the charge being that the group had cheated to win a $5.9 million contract for installing a computerized financial system for the National Parks Service.

The suspension didn't last long. Bob Dryden, then president of the computer division, launched a fast investigation that resulted in dismissal or disciplinary action against about a dozen of the unit's employees. The Interior Department reinstated the Vienna office three weeks after the suspension.

Another suspension involved the Washington office, which had earned a reputation for ethical conduct in the capital's highly political environment. A succession of capable and reputable men had headed the office through the years—Jim Murray, Bob Murphy, Bob Bateman, Dick Taylor, Russ Light and Boris Mishel.

Bateman and Dick Taylor had preceded Light in Washington, and when Russ took over he replaced the one man who hated the job—Taylor, the former engineer/test pilot, didn't like Washington, stayed there only two years, and couldn't wait to leave. Light learned from T that he had been named corporate vice president and when Russ began stammering his thanks, Wilson interrupted.

"Before you get a swelled head, Light," T growled, "just remember—it took twenty years before we finally found something you could do."

Light took over the Washington office in 1976 and served there for seven years. His successor was Boris Mishel, the only opera singer who ever became a Boeing vice president. Mishel, a trained baritone, actually sang opera in Europe after earning an engineering degree from the University of Southern California. He had been out of school for nine years and was singing in Munich, Germany, when a friend in Boeing flight test sent him a Christmas card and enclosed an employment application with it.

Mishel joined flight test in 1955, eventually went into sales, worked briefly in Marine Systems, and from there went to the Washington assignment. "The company took some risk," he said later, "because I was fairly naïve about Washington."

Mishel was still running the Washington office in 1985 when the Defense Intelligence Agency (DIA) found a number of classified budget documents in Boeing's Huntsville office, unauthorized papers relating to possible aerospace projects and estimating the amount of funding they might require. They were traced back to Richard Fowler, who had joined Boeing's Washington office in 1978 after many years of experience with the Defense Department's budget process.

Fowler admitted that after being hired, he had begun acquiring these documents from Pentagon sources he declined to name, and had continued to pass on hundreds of these documents until the continuing DIA investigation brought his activities to light.

Fowler was fired, subsequently found guilty of illegal trafficking in confidential government documents, jailed on contempt charges for refusing to name his Pentagon sources, and sentenced to a two-year prison term.

Boeing itself pleaded guilty to two felony counts of conveying the illegal documents, paid a $5.2 million fine, and chairman Frank Shrontz, who by then had succeeded Wilson, sent a letter to the court apologizing for the company's conduct.

The Washington office itself took its lumps on this matter in 1989 when the Air Force barred it, at least temporarily, from doing any business with the Pentagon. The Air Force also announced that Boeing's Washington employees were banned from conducting business with the Defense Department, whether they remained with the company or sought employment with any other government contract. The order demoralized the Washington staff.

"Seventy percent of the people there never knew Fowler," Mishel said. "They weren't in Washington when he worked for us. They couldn't do their job and they couldn't work for anyone else."

Boeing protested the Pentagon ban and eventually negotiated a settlement with government officials. The Air Force agreed to lift the ban, while Boeing agreed to provide assurance that it was committed to conducting itself ethically and legally. But the company's reputation at the Pentagon was badly damaged, and not just from this mess. There had been too many instances of overruns and program delays—"What's happened to the old Boeing?" an Air Force general asked a company official, almost plaintively.

In retrospect, the whole Fowler experience was an anomaly in Boeing's morally antiseptic world, but that didn't ease the company's humiliation. No sinning preacher ever fell from grace with a louder crash—the Seattle media had a merry time.

The calmest perspective—and from the standpoint of Fowler and those who accepted his documents the most compassionate—came from Shrontz:

"In the time period when Fowler got involved, there is little doubt in my mind that it was generally accepted practice for companies in the defense business to have access to such things as program planning documents, so they could perform the kind of competitive development they thought they needed to be ready for the next system under consideration. I suspect Fowler got caught up in this mentality.

"As time passed, ethics changed, legal requirements changed, and judged in light of today's standards it was clearly inappropriate behavior. We have put in place a lot of programs to prevent a recurrence. We're a big corporation and I don't have one hundred percent assurance there won't be another lapse, but I think we're far better off today than we were in the early eighties. I think the attitude of our executives is different, in terms of avoiding any appearance of questionable conduct."

But while Shrontz displayed a kind of charitable compassion in what he said to outsiders, inwardly he was angry at the way some of Boeing's people had let the company down. He told an associate shortly after he became CEO, "Before I leave this job, I'm going to turn over every rock in this company."

The press in the 1980s quite naturally jumped avidly on a revelation that the Air Force was paying Boeing $675 for a pair of pliers. The amount was correct; what wasn't usually printed was the reason behind the so-called "gouging." They were specially machined, oxide-coated pliers used on KC-135 engines. Boeing got them from the engine manufacturer who, in turn, had bought them from a supplier. The engine manufacturer charged Boeing $675 for the pliers and that was the price Boeing charged the Air Force. The story leaked, there were a number of red faces, and the unfavorable publicity washed into the lap of Lionel Alford, then senior vice president heading all defense and space activities. Abe Goo was reporting to him as vice president of military airplane programs in Wichita and Seattle.

"What do you think we should do?" Alford asked Goo.

"Give 'em back their money," Goo suggested.

So Alford wrote the Air Force a letter advising of the refund, and adding that any spare part the Air Force had in its inventory whose price was considered excessive could be returned for a full refund—provided the part hadn't been in inventory for more than a year.

"The Air Force returned some they had been storing for as long as three years," Goo related, "but we didn't hold them to the one-year limit and gave refunds on these, too."

The fuss over the pliers hadn't died down when Goo was notified that an Air Force base had sent in a new order. He called the general commanding the base.

"General, have you seen all the stories about the six hundred and seventy-five dollar pair of pliers?"

"Yeah," the general chuckled. "You guys are sure getting a lot of bad press."

"Well, I want you to know your outfit just ordered ten more of the damned things. And unless you do something to stop it, there's gonna be another horror story."

For a reason no one was able to determine, someone decided Boeing itself should manufacture plastic tips that went on the stool legs of the navigator's seat in AWACS planes to protect aircraft carpeting. About 1,500 tips were turned out, but through the years the Air Force kept losing or misplacing them until eventually the supply ran out and Boeing received a replacement order for exactly three tips. By this time, the original cap mold had been destroyed and tooling had to machine three new caps, a process that cost Boeing $1,100 per tip. It then charged the Air Force $907 for each replacement. When the case of the $907 stool caps hit the newspapers, Boeing took them back and bought three plastic tips from Sears, which the equally embarrassed Air Force accepted.

Mal Stamper became heavily involved in the hubbub over the expensive pliers and stool caps, and ended up performing a minor miracle—he turned the unfavorable publicity into nationwide praise for Boeing.

Those incidents had led to Congress, the Pentagon, and media applying a catch phrase to industry pricing practices: "Fraud, Waste, and Abuse." The Aerospace Industry Association (AIA) wanted to put up some defense against the stigma, such as explaining that when the Pentagon orders a half-dozen units of an item that has to be manufactured from scratch in accordance with complicated military specifications, it is no wonder that a pair of special pliers can cost almost $700 and a stool cap more than $900.

But Stamper's advice to AIA went in the other direction. He believed the situation had progressed to the point where perception, not truth, was the real issue—if the public, press and Congress perceived industry as a bunch of gougers, the best strategy was not to deny the charges but change the image through positive corrective action.

As far as Boeing was concerned, Stamper was ready to put the company's reputation on the line. He spread the word that employee suggestions for cutting costs would not only be welcomed, but regarded as a patriotic gesture that warranted public attention. If a congressman appeared on television denouncing industry for some alleged sin, he would quickly receive a letter signed by Stamper thanking him.

"I saw your statement on the news," the letter would say. "I certainly share your concern and here's what we at Boeing are doing about this situation . . ."

What began as a rather informal effort led to establishment of a corporate office to encourage, process and implement employee cost-saving ideas. It was called Operation Eagle; Bob Bateman was its first chairman, with Ed Renouard as his deputy and Bob Jorgensen as head of program management and communication. In the two years Operation Eagle existed—1986 and 1987—more than 90,000 cost-saving suggestions were submitted, and those that were adopted (about 19,000 just in the first year) were called to the attention of key lawmakers and Pentagon officials in a series of regular reports on Eagle's progress.

Boeing had announced the Alford/Goo "money-back guarantee" on any military part priced under $100,000: if the part was unsatisfactory for any reason, it could be returned and Boeing would pay a full refund. This offer, combined with Operation Eagle, generated compliments in Congress and the Pentagon; Secretary of Defense Caspar Weinberger even held a news conference at which he pointed to Boeing as setting an example for the rest of the industry.

As the "gouging problem" faded from the front pages and evening newscasts, so did Operation Eagle's importance. It acquired the image of a temporary campaign rather than a permanent one, and gradually lost both steam and effectiveness. Yet in some ways it was really the forerunner of Continuous Quality Improvement, a strategy that in the late 1980s was to form the cornerstone of Frank Shrontz's plans for Boeing's future.

Headlines about alleged scandals and overcharges weren't the only shock Boeing received during the turbulent eighties. On August 12, 1985, a Japan Air Lines 747SR lost most of its vertical fin when a rear pressure bulkhead failed and caused catastrophic explosive decompression; only four people of the 524 aboard survived in the worst single airplane crash in commercial aviation history.

That it could have happened to a 747, protected by so much redundancy, was almost unbelievable. What was even harder to absorb was the investigation's finding that a faulty repair job by a Boeing AOG team seven years earlier had contributed to the disaster.

JAL had been the launch customer for the SR, a 747 variant first conceived by Will Hughes of Boeing's analytical group, who had suggested configuring the 747 for higher-density seating on short-haul routes. With fuel load reduced and certain structures beefed up, the SR was a money-maker in densely populated Japan.

To this day, no one on the AOG team involved in the bulkhead repair job knows for sure what went wrong. Ben Cosgrove spent months talking to them, trying to ascertain specific mistakes, and so did Boeing's own investigative team headed by Bob Siems.

"The accident affected the structures organization deeply," Cosgrove said. "It made no difference that a structure hadn't been installed properly—it still was a structural part that failed, and that's not supposed to happen on Boeing airplanes."

Boeing instituted changes in 747 manufacturing and quality control procedures that Cosgrove was convinced would prevent any similar situation from ever happening again. And the company, through its top executives, expressed its contrition and sympathy to the affected families.

As Boeing's top structures man, Cosgrove found himself heavily embroiled in a later incident that brought the problem of aging aircraft to the surface in dramatic fashion. On April 28, 1988, almost a third of the top fuselage skin blew off a 20-year-old Aloha Airlines 737, touching off worldwide concern that older jets might be unsafe.

Ben was driving on Interstate 5 to have dinner with Joe Sutter when he heard a news bulletin on his car radio—there had been a near-crash and a miraculous landing in Hawaii. "The airplane is a 737 with a big hole in it," the announcer said. Cosgrove headed for the nearest phone to call a Boeing engineer who, it turned out, had been watching television coverage.

"Ben, this thing has a hole in the fuselage you wouldn't believe."

"How big? Twenty inches? Thirty inches?"

"The whole top of the front fuselage is gone. You can see people sitting in their seats."

Cosgrove made a few more calls, trying to confirm the extent of damage. "I had to see it myself before I believed it," he admitted. "I often looked at that picture to remind me how good the people were who flew it, and how good the airplane was."

The Aloha 737 was an early model, but age had nothing to do with the skin rupturing; corrosion, built up from years of exposure to salt water air particles, was responsible. But a few weeks later, an Eastern 727 lost pressurization during a flight and when the plane landed safely, a 12-inch crack was found in the fuselage skin. Coming after the scary pictures of the Aloha jet—and if one had five dollars for every time it was shown on TV or appeared in print he'd be rich—the Eastern incident touched off media hysteria questioning the safety of older jets. Actually, long before Aloha happened, Boeing had started inspecting aircraft in the field, in different operating environments. It was gathering data on fatigue and corrosion, cognizant that aircraft were being flown beyond their expected lifespan.

"The media made a crisis out of a problem," Cosgrove said, and it was Ben who became a major spokesman for the industry in quelling the fears of both public and press. Under the auspices of the Air Transport Association (ATA) and the FAA, a joint industry-government committee of technical experts drew up new aircraft inspection and maintenance procedures designed to spot or prevent potentially serious corrosion or fatigue problems. Cosgrove and some of his colleagues from McDonnell Douglas and Lockheed attended numerous seminars, briefings, and news conferences at which they calmly explained the facts about aging aircraft.

Corrosion problems didn't surprise anyone at Boeing, and exposure to corrosive salt elements wasn't even the principal concern. One of the points Cosgrove kept making to the press was that a lot of the damage inflicted on an airplane has nothing to do with fatigue.

"It's people dropping things on an airplane," he said. "It's leakage from hazardous cargo, like hydrochloric acid. You can't believe what shippers try to put in airplane bellies—they're not supposed to, but they do."

Cosgrove cited one case in which Boeing inspected the belly of a jet and found advanced corrosion. It was in an area just below the galley, and the engineers discovered the corrosion had come from the little salt packages the airlines put on meal trays; a bunch of them had fallen into the belly and the paper gradually disintegrated, releasing the corrosive salt.

AOG teams reported a number of unsuspected corrosion problems. Floyd Nestegard remembered one in particular. "I pushed a pencil against metal in a pressurized area, and the pencil went clean through."

When it became apparent that aging aircraft posed a problem but not a full-blown safety crisis, and that the entire industry was doing something about it, the furor died down. But it took time; one of the first news conferences after the Aloha incident was held at ATA's office in Washington, and Clyde Kizer of the Association's technical staff was briefing a room packed with skeptical reporters.

"Our belief is that the system works, that the interaction among the FAA, airlines and manufacturers really works," he said earnestly. "It just so happens that in the case of Aloha, there was a little hole in the system."

That night the networks re-ran shots of the Aloha 737 with that gaping hole, and timed the visual to coincide with Kizer's "a little hole in the system" remark, with more than one commentator adding: "This is what the industry considers a little hole."

One of Cosgrove's media briefings on aging aircraft took place in Hawaii. He attended a luncheon at which he was seated next to an attractive young woman. Ben thought she was an Aloha flight attendant, then learned she was Mimi Thompkins, copilot on the crippled 737. Ben complimented her on the way she and the captain had handled the emergency. When the top of the fuselage blew off, they slowed down, found the airplane unstable below 170 knots, and kept experimenting with the throttles until they found the most stable speed. They landed with very little flaps left and no green light indicating the nose wheel was down and locked—as Cosgrove said later, "They had to learn to fly that airplane in five minutes."

Cosgrove was more than the company's point man during the aging aircraft hubbub; he also spoke for the airlines and other aerospace firms, and with the authoritative voice of a senior vice president who had 11,000 employees from engineering, customer support and flight test under him. His was another of Boeing's Horatio Alger stories;

Cosgrove started out as a $265-a-month engineer designing small parts for a bomber tail, absorbing knowledge from veterans like Paul Sandoz and Al Larsen. Ben never forgot the advice he got from Larsen, a tough-minded structures man.

"Cosgrove, you want to get ahead in this company?" Larsen asked him one day.

"Sure."

"Well, if they ask you to sweep the floor, go sweep it."

As the Cosgroves, Condits, Pinicks, Cruzes, Thorntons and Wellivers moved higher in the executive ranks, they were filling the shoes of some well-known figures in Boeing's history; over the four-year period of 1983–86, many of Wilson's old Minuteman cadre went into retirement, led by Tex Boullioun.

And there was T himself, by the mid-1980s approaching retirement and wrestling with the choice of his successor.

TWENTY-THREE

PROSPERITY'S PROBLEMS

MALCOLM STAMPER SERVED AS BOEING'S PRESIDENT FOR 12 years. When the directors named Frank Shrontz president in 1984, Stamper became vice chairman—a title new to Boeing with mostly undefined duties.

But Stamper found a new niche at Boeing, an area of active responsibility that belied his vague title. He became fascinated with "alternative dispute resolution"—the settling of major lawsuits between companies by getting senior executives together in a kind of mock trial, and solving the dispute without having to go to court. Doug Beighle began referring him cases in which Boeing had filed suit or had claims against suppliers, and vice versa.

"He was one of the best negotiators I ever saw," Beighle said admiringly. "He'd make a study of the people involved on the other side and map out a psychological warfare path. We had some major problems heading for litigation and he settled all of them to everyone's satisfaction."

One dispute concerned two Boeing suppliers making cockpit windshields; one of them had taken Boeing's blueprints and tooling and began producing its own windshields for non-Boeing customers. After efforts to settle out of court failed, Boeing won a big judgment, then ran into a bitter quarrel with the other windshield manufacturer, which had been honoring its commitments.

"They got upset with what their competitor was doing," Beighle explained, "so they filed for permission to sell windshields using Boeing's drawings. We sued, and they counter-sued charging anti-trust violations. I felt it was wrong to take it to court—they were a reliable supplier and no one needed expensive litigation. So I set up an alternative dispute resolution hearing and asked Stamper to represent us. He was magnificent; he really studied the other side, met with them socially, got to know them and understand them. In the negotiations, he got more than we could have through a lawsuit, yet the opposition was happy—they were restored as valuable suppliers, all animosity ceased, and their chief counsel even called thanking me for taking the course we did."

Dick Albrecht, too, thought Stamper performed brilliantly as a negotiator. "He did a hell of a job for us in several cases. It was the sort of thing he was good at, because he'd focus on one issue, he refused to get distracted, and he had great loyalty for the company."

There was a bit of squirrel in Mal Stamper. Boeing's film files contain a brief movie Stamper made with Jim Blue and other executives to plug minority small businesses; titled *Boeing Brass*, the clip shows Stamper playing drums and Blue strumming away on a guitar. It was one of those personal touches that endeared Stamper to subordinates, even those like Dave Peterson whom Stamper would wake up at six A.M. and insist that they go jogging.

Stamper and Hal Haynes retired together early in 1990, and at their joint retirement party they were greeted by life-size cardboard cutouts of themselves. A retirement party for T Wilson on the occasion of his relinquishing the CEO post achieved the same height of irreverence as the Haynes–Stamper event. This one had a number of top executives wearing Wilson's trademarks: a white cap, polka-dot red bow tie, and a long false nose. When T entered the room they all had their feet on the conference table. And laughing as hard as anyone was the man who had succeeded him as chairman and CEO—a low-key, easily met, people-oriented lawyer from Idaho who had never practiced law.

Wilson had begun the successor selection process as far back as 1976 when director William Batten suggested, "Why don't you draw up an executive organizational chart for the next ten years?"

What he actually was proposing was a chart projecting what jobs top Boeing officers were likely to have in the future—a forecast of their promotions, assignments and responsibilities, all with the end view of establishing a small list of possible candidates for the company's next leader.

"I thought it was the most juvenile suggestion I had ever heard," Wilson commented later, "but I had so much respect for Batten that I decided to try it. Then I found out it wasn't so damned easy."

He enlisted Stan Little's aid in drawing up a plan that they submitted to Batten as chairman of the board's organization committee. David Packard took over after Batten retired. The group began by creating a chart for the next four years, then revised it every two years until the 10-year projection had been completed.

"It was very evident early on," T related, "that what we were trying to establish was who would be Boeing's CEO ten years down the line, and what kinds of jobs he should have in the interim. We had about a half-dozen people as potential CEOs; from time to time we'd add someone to the list and take one or two off, and there were some arguments—one of our executives thought we should go for a younger, hot-rod type. So we had a period of musical chairs with names going on and off. A lot of our customers had their own favorites, and they'd complain if their Boeing salesman hadn't been made vice president when somebody else's was."

Wilson asked a number of his top officers what they thought of this gradual selection process, and there was general agreement it was about as fair and efficient a method as could be devised. As the end of the 10-year performance scrutiny drew to a close, two names stood out among the six submitted to Boeing's board as T's possible successor: Dean Thornton and Frank Shrontz, coincidentally both natives of Idaho and graduates of the University of Idaho. Wilson had made sure each had been given a chance to perform in relatively unfamiliar areas—Thornton, who had been running the 767 program, was pulled into corporate headquarters on a planning assignment, and Shrontz went from corporate planning to run the 707-727-737 division, where one of his finest achievements was the successful 737-300 program, followed by his taking over the head sales job of the commercial airplane division.

"I wanted to see how each did," T explained. "I don't think anyone agreed with me on this—they considered Thornton as the ideal guy to run commercial and Shrontz as ideal at corporate. But that wasn't what I was trying to find out—I wanted just the opposite. And neither made it easy because they both did a good job. Some of our airline friends, like Delta, wondered what the hell we were doing."

But Wilson knew exactly what he was doing, although flipping a coin would have resulted in an excellent choice no matter which side landed up. An engineer himself, he had no problem with the fact that Thornton was a self-admitted bean counter in a company heavily influenced by engineering commitments. Nor did Shrontz's legal background bother T. "I know managing engineers is tough," Wilson conceded, "but I'd say that the percentage of lawyers who are capable of managing engineers is about the same as the percentage of engineers who can manage other engineers."

Boeing's board had to make the final decision, but as T dryly put it, "There's no question my recommendation constituted the majority of the input." Yet he did consult others before making that recommendation, among them Wes Maulden, who advised him to pick Shrontz. When T asked him why, Maulden replied:

"Because Thornton would be another Wilson, and I think the company deserves a change."

As chairman of the nominating committee, David Packard made a point of phoning Governor Clements of Texas, for whom Shrontz had worked while both were in the Defense Department. That government experience weighed in Shrontz's favor among many Boeing directors, yet the feeling around Boeing was that Thornton would be picked.

Privately, Frank Shrontz thought so, too. For a long time, he had assumed Mal Stamper, as Boeing's president, would eventually succeed Wilson, but during the year Shrontz spent in corporate planning, he had a chance to watch what was happening between the two men.

"I know T had great expectations for Mal that were never satisfied in terms of Stamper taking hold and moving into the president's job in an aggressive way," Shrontz said. "But Mal's approach was so different from T's, I don't think Wilson could have ever been satisfied in that regard."

The question of who would succeed Stamper as president was the key to who eventually would succeed Wilson. It was answered in January 1985. At the time Shrontz was serving as president of the commercial airplane division (he had taken over from Dick Welch), while Thornton was on assignment at corporate headquarters.

All the action took place at the board's January meeting, although no official announcement was made until the directors met a month later. In the press release that came out of Harold Carr's public relations office announcing that Shrontz had been elected president of The Boeing Company, Wilson referred to the promotion as part of an "orderly transition" leading to his own retirement. The same release disclosed that Thornton had been named president of the commercial airplane division, and it left no doubt who was going to be Boeing's next chief executive. Wilson stepped down as CEO in 1986, turning over the board chairmanship to Shrontz January 1, 1988, when T retired and became chairman emeritus.

But that January board meeting was nail-biting time for both Shrontz and Thornton. As far as Frank was concerned, all signs pointed to his old schoolmate from Idaho as the winner. The directors were gathering at corporate headquarters when T sent word he wanted to see Shrontz in his office after the board adjourned. Wilson wasn't expected to make his succession recommendation until the board's February meeting, but as the directors began gathering outside the board room, Shrontz noticed that Thornton had come in with several members of the organization and nominating committee, which had just met.

"I figured T must have gone to the committee meeting, told them he had decided to pick Dean, who then must have been invited to talk to them, and that it was all over," Shrontz recalled. "So I went into T's office convinced Dean was his choice, and that Wilson was simply informing me of his decision as a courtesy. When he told me I had been picked, I was surprised—not because I wasn't a serious contender, but because I thought Dean was the odds-on favorite."

There was not one iota of resentment on Thornton's part. "Actually—and this is going to sound like b.s.—I won because I think I've got a better job running the commercial airplane division," Thornton said with great feeling. "I really mean it—I don't have all Frank's headaches. Like the way this government procurement thing has gone with an adversary relationship, where you have to worry about auditors, inspector generals, defense contract cancellations, and whether it's illegal to buy somebody a cup of coffee—I don't need that."

Shrontz believed him. "Dean was enough of a competitor that he wanted to win, but aside from that he really preferred to run the commercial airplane division. I think we have a good relationship, and I know I could have worked for him if T's choice had gone the other way."

The man who made that choice continued to be relatively active in the company's affairs after retiring—a totally inactive T Wilson was as unthinkable as the earth pausing in orbit. Yet while he maintained an office at corporate headquarters, he was determined not to look over Shrontz's shoulder and interfere with the new command. He did, in fact, tell his successor to be his own man.

"He told me that sometimes I should change things for the sake of change, to do things differently just because it would give me a stamp of independence a CEO doesn't always have," Shrontz recounted. "It boiled down to advising me I should make changes just to show there's a different way of doing things."

T was autocratic, even dictatorial at times, yet unlike most strong executives of that ilk he had a self-deprecating sense of humor that softened the image. No one knew Wilson better than he knew himself; what made him special was his willingness to admit flaws, acknowledge mistakes, and concede that his penchant for total honesty occasionally got him into hot water. Above all else, he had a unique kind of ego—he had one and it was large, but T could make fun of it.

Shortly after Shrontz became president, he walked into Wilson's office to ask him a question about some business matter. T leaned back in his chair.

"Well, Shrontz," he drawled, "I really don't want to get involved, but I think it would be a shame to deprive you of the benefit of my counsel."

An Austrian manufacturer of sunglasses asked Boeing for permission to market a new line named after the company and offered to pay a royalty on every pair sold. The product was excellent, and despite the $200-plus retail price they sold relatively well—many to airline pilots flying Boeings. They also made great customer gifts and were regarded as a good way to promote Boeing products worldwide.

After the sunglasses were introduced with a big advertising splash, Doug Beighle suspected some stockholders might bring up the Boeing sunglasses deal at the annual shareholders meeting. So he cautioned T, "If someone asks a question about those sunglasses, just let Shrontz answer and keep quiet."

Sure enough, a stockholder rose and asked T what he thought of the sunglasses arrangement.

"I don't know who did it," Wilson replied, "but it's the dumbest thing we ever did."

Shrontz immediately rose and explained calmly why Boeing had made the deal. After *Fortune* printed Wilson's reply as one of the most interesting business quotes of the month, T told Beighle, "Well, I probably should have kept my mouth shut."

"If T decided to say something," Beighle sighed, "there was no way to head him off."

By his own admission, T was the company's worst negotiator, an opinion shared by most of Boeing's executives. His impatient, impulsive bluntness and refusal to play games stood him well in most instances, but not when it came to the mating dances that are a natural part of bargaining. Boeing once got involved in a plan to sell energy control systems, a computer program designed to run a big utility company. It was tried at Con Edison of New York, but contract problems developed so Beighle asked T to meet with the utility's CEO and negotiate a way out of the contract.

"The reasonable dollar amount you can offer is twenty million," Beighle advised, "and the most you can give is twenty-seven million."

"You know what I'll say," T admitted. "I'll tell the guy our bottom offer is twenty, our top offer is twenty-seven, and he'll take the twenty-seven."

Which is exactly what happened.

Dick Albrecht, who became close to Wilson, said he was great to work for. "You knew what was expected of you, and all he expected was an honest response—and if he didn't like your answer, he'd let you know that, too."

The first executive meeting Albrecht attended when he joined Boeing involved a proposal to move corporate headquarters to some other site in the Puget Sound area. This was before the old administration building was remodeled, and the company had hired a consultant to advise on potential new locations. Sites at Boeing Field, Kent Valley, Renton and Sea-Tac Airport were still on the list being considered at the meeting, but it was quickly made obvious that Wilson was enamored with the idea of establishing headquarters at a major airport. Curiously, no one was supporting downtown Seattle at the meeting, and Albrecht couldn't understand why—downtown was where most of the movers and shakers in the Seattle area worked.

"Well," T finally said, "we have to make a decision at our next meeting, so if anyone has any strong opinions, write me a one-page memo."

Albrecht sent him one. It pointed out that having headquarters at an airport just because Boeing made airplanes made no more sense than Weycrhaeuser having its main corporate offices in the middle of a forest—which it does. He couldn't understand why the consultant or anyone else hadn't shown more interest in downtown Seattle, where establishing headquarters would be logical and practical.

About two weeks later, T accosted the new boy on the block. "By the way, Albrecht, I read your memo. I don't agree with you."

End of discussion. Boeing actually went ahead planning a new headquarters building at Sea-Tac until environmentalist groups filed a lawsuit against the proposed construction. When the airport location was eliminated, Albrecht's only ally for downtown was Dean Thornton; it was decided to remodel the old administration building—one of the few battles T ever lost.

T was a tough act for anyone to follow, of which his successor was well aware. The day he stepped into Wilson's shoes, not only did news stories give more space to T's accomplishments than to Shrontz's own impressive track record and qualifications, but the following day Boeing stock actually fell. It was unfair to the new CEO but, typically, he laughed it off. When an interviewer reminded him he was taking over a company made prosperous by his colorful predecessor's leadership, Shrontz just smiled.

"I guess I'd just like them to say one day that I didn't screw up," he said wryly.

Shrontz held the obligatory news conference after he became Boeing's new chief and, as expected, one of the first questions asked was how he felt about succeeding a legend.

"It was a tough one to answer," he admitted later. "I'm still being asked if I feel intimidated, and what are the real differences between me and Wilson. It's only with the passage of time that I've gained some perspective. First of all, T's objectives for Boeing and mine are not dissimilar—they're pretty much oriented to keeping the company's concentration on its main line of business, building airplanes. I think we're both inclined to take prudent risks, and not go out into left field. I think our judgments of people are the same on the whole, although he reached his judgments quite differently.

"What is different is how I run the company. I'm more anxious to have a more participatory form of management—up to a point. I don't believe that's a substitute for decisiveness when a decision has to be made, but T was instinctively oriented. So it was tough to succeed him in that sense. Yet he made it very, very easy for me. In no way did he try to step in and second-guess my decisions, to undercut me or get involved when it was inappropriate. It was difficult for him not to speak his mind, but that's Wilson. I thank my lucky stars we were able to have the smooth transition we did."

Smooth transition it was, but not without some bumps. T may have handed over the reins to a company soaring to new heights of prosperity, but he also bequeathed Shrontz a few large problems, just as Wilson had inherited some headaches from Allen. Hal Haynes once remarked that no brand-new CEO of a major corporation ever went through the totality of different crises that Shrontz had to face in his first four years at the helm.

First there was the Fowler case and defense budget cuts that bathed Boeing's military side in red ink. The new 747-400 program was in trouble, not only behind schedule and way over cost but plagued by customer complaints of poor workmanship. Quality control, so much a part of Boeing's heritage, had slipped for the same reason the 737 program had gotten off to a bad start: too many inexperienced workers. By 1989, approximately half the company's work force had been with Boeing only five years or less.

On the up side were the unbelievable number of orders Boeing booked during Shrontz's first years at the helm: 300-plus in both 1986 and 1987, 632 in 1988, and 883 in 1989. Dick Albrecht's sales staff could hardly keep up as old records for sales, orders and backlog were smashed. As backlog neared $100 billion, Dean Thornton shook his head whenever he heard the number. "The backlog dollar figure is so high, it's incomprehensible," he marveled.

Yet morale did not necessarily walk hand-in-hand with prosperity. The huge backlog meant higher production rates for the 737, 757, and 767. Then there was the 747-400, which had received a go-ahead in the fall of 1985, but was headed for major problems when production began. The situation at Everett wasn't as bad as it had been during the big plane's birth in the late sixties, but resentment toward mandatory overtime began festering.

This was a new breed of worker, too—relatively young and not as receptive to conventional motivation efforts, nor as pliable to supervisory authority. "Culture change" was the term used by industrial sociologists, and it applied not merely to assembly line people but to many younger engineers.

Culture change was just one problem Shrontz had to cope with, a different kind of challenge than any of his predecessors ever faced— undefined, elusive, and somewhat difficult to grasp because it was more a state of mind than anything else. Another was the matter of a controversial acquisition Boeing made early in 1986: the de Havilland Aircraft Company of Canada.

What Boeing purchased was a beautifully designed commuter airplane—the twin engine Dash-8—and a company in absolute shambles. Not until Boeing actually began operating de Havilland did anyone realize it also had acquired an abysmal labor situation, a demoralized work force, a rundown factory, a totally unrealistic production schedule that couldn't meet delivery commitments, and top management people who regarded anyone from Boeing as an unwelcome meddler.

There was great logic behind the de Havilland deal. The major airlines were aligning themselves with commuter carriers, exchanging traffic at their hubs and integrating connection schedules; in many cases, the commuters even painted their airplanes with the same color scheme as the partner trunk carriers, and adopted similar names— American Eagle and United Express, for example.

"The commuters were coming under the umbrellas of the big guys where Boeing was very strong," Shrontz explained, "and the feeling was that because of our relations with the large carriers we could penetrate the commuter airplane market significantly because they were having a major say in what the commuters could buy. Only de Havilland could give us an immediate entry into this different market segment that Boeing lacked. We also felt that we could bring the commuters into the Boeing family of airplanes by getting them started on de Havilland products."

Those products included the Dash-7, a four-engine propjet that Boeing engineers had helped design—a good airplane but handicapped by the higher operating cost of its four engines. The Dash-8, smaller but more fuel-efficient than the Dash-7, was de Havilland's best seller and the Canadian company's most attractive asset. The company itself had been government-owned for many years; when the Conservative Party came into power in the mid-eighties, it called for privatization of Canadian industry and that included de Havilland, which went up for bids.

Boeing's executive ranks were deeply divided on the wisdom of acquiring a company with known poor labor relations—there had been numerous strikes at de Havilland—and that had five other companies competing against it for the commuter airplane market. Boeing previously had rejected overtures from Cessna and Gates Learjet—both wanted the Boeing name in the general aviation market, and they weren't the only ones. "We had offers from virtually every airplane company to come into Boeing," Wilson recalled.

But with all its obvious drawbacks, de Havilland apparently was a different proposition with that tempting link between the commuters and trunk airlines. In general, Boeing's manufacturing officials lined up solidly against the purchase. The commercial airplane marketing side was strongly in favor. Engineering was mostly neutral except for Ken Holtby's opposition to the purchase. More important, marketing finally won Shrontz over and that was the major deciding factor.

The asking price was around $200 million, which, considering the state of affairs at the Toronto-based company, was no bargain. Shrontz told an executive staff meeting that de Havilland was going to have to cut the asking price in half before Boeing would seriously consider the acquisition. The Canadians did this, and Boeing bought de Havilland for about $100 million, which in Shrontz's view might have been deceptively low.

"We got overly enamored with the reasonably attractive price," he admitted. "What we overlooked were the subsequent costs you have to bear when you buy into a problem."

"We didn't do our homework," Dean Thornton acknowledged candidly. "We did a superficial job of investigating the company before we bought it. One of Boeing's strong points is our 'we can do anything' attitude, but it's also one of our weaknesses. This has resulted in some miracles and also in some disasters, and de Havilland was a disaster. We looked at it and told ourselves, 'Yeah, the factory's all screwed up but we can fix it. Their labor relations are lousy but we can fix that, too.' That's where Wes Maulden was so smart—he knew more about de Havilland's labor problems than all the bright wizards who went to Canada and analyzed the situation. And he was against the deal."

Maulden, in fact, refused to attend the executive council meeting at which the final decision was made. He told another officer, "I won't come because there isn't anybody dumb enough to buy that company."

The president of de Havilland, Bill Boggs, stayed on as president but Boeing decided it needed one of its own production experts on the scene to straighten matters out.

The man chosen was Norm Kingsmore, a native Canadian who was born in Toronto and graduated from the University of Toronto with a degree in mechanical engineering. Added to these diplomatically appropriate credentials was a good track record in aircraft production—Kingsmore had worked for Avro of Canada before joining Boeing in 1957, and had been involved in the B-52, 707, KC-135 and 757 programs among others.

He visited de Havilland off and on for a couple of months after the formal acquisition papers were signed, and in March 1986 Boeing named him vice president of operations for the Canadian subsidiary. He might as well have been named de Havilland's head janitor from the greeting he received—Boggs considered him an interloper, and the rest of de Havilland's management followed the president's example.

Kingsmore had to find his own office space in the factory; company management worked in an office building next to the plant, a structure in a lot better shape than the factory. Out of their sight, Kingsmore went to work and discovered de Havilland had quite a few Dash-8 orders but no production schedule to build them on time.

The factory was working only on the Dash-8; production of venerable Twin Otters and Dash-7s had been halted so de Havilland could concentrate on the 75 Dash-8s that management had promised to deliver by the end of 1986. Kingsmore called Boggs and several officers to his factory office one night and informed them he was cutting 12 airplanes off the total production goals.

"You can't build seventy-five airplanes by the end of the year," Norm said bluntly.

The de Havilland vice president of operations, who despite Kingsmore's appointment was still on the premises, disagreed and so did the company's sales director. So Kingsmore insisted that Boggs accompany him to Seattle for a meeting with Boeing's manufacturing brass, a session held in Maulden's office, which as usual was illuminated by a single table lamp, with all blinds drawn.

"I actually felt sorry for poor Boggs," Kingsmore said. "It was like walking into a dark cage filled with hungry tigers."

Maulden was joined by Deane Cruze and Wally Buckley, the latter present because he had seen the Toronto facilities firsthand. Kingsmore explained why he had cut the year's Dash-8 production to 63 airplanes, and emphasized the need for a more realistic production schedule in 1987 and beyond.

After the meeting, Boggs knew his time at de Havilland was up. Boeing decided to put in its own man as head of its third and largest Canadian facility—it already had a factory in Winnipeg that manufactured parts for the commercial airplane division, and another in Arnprior that renovated Canadian government helicopters. He was Ron Woodard, the lanky, unflappable ex-chemist who had first attracted attention at Boeing by criticizing the way the company had handled its Australian subcontracting relations.

Woodard was form-fitted for the de Havilland assignment—he thrived on controversy and confrontation, as he once demonstrated during a program to put an automatic flight control system into the 737-300 for Lufthansa and British Airways. Woodard was director of the program management office. Operations was feuding with engineering over production delays, so Woodard held a program review meeting at which both sides could hash out their differences.

The meeting was a verbal version of a street brawl. During a lull in the mutual cursing, Ron leaned back in his chair, a beatific smile on his face.

"God, I love this place!" he declared happily.

It took some time before he could apply any word of endearment to de Havilland of Canada, and the Canadian work force that had become so alienated toward management during the plant's more than 12 years under government ownership. The Canadian Auto Workers (CAW) represented de Havilland's hourly and technical employees, a union with a reputation for stubbornness.

Yet Woodard felt empathy for the rank and file at de Havilland, if not for its union.

"Yes, labor relations was a problem," he conceded, "but it had become a problem because this was a work force that had been abused for years. I found they were good people, that they responded, and that if we could make them feel we were consistent and that we cared, they could do amazing things."

With Kingsmore as the *only* vice president of operations, Woodard set about to turn things around. Like Kingsmore, Woodard found it hard to believe the factory itself was in such sorry shape. Roof leaks and unworkable toilets weren't the only items that plagued the people trying to build airplanes; plant power failed at least once a week, and when that occurred the factory simply shut down and everyone went home. Every transformer on the premises had to be replaced, and the toilet problem was fixed by installing new sewer lines.

There were two high-bay areas that were supposed to be utilized as assembly line space, but only a skeleton framework had been erected; under the framework was nothing but dirt. These two areas were cleaned up and finished, existing production bays were rearranged, and what had been a million square feet of assembly line space was now 1.4 million square feet under a new lighting system.

Gradually relations with the union improved, although not to the point where either Woodard or Kingsmore felt they were completely out of the labor relations woods. Most of the problems were with the local leadership. Bob White, national president of the Canadian Auto Workers, had never visited the de Havilland plant since the Boeing takeover, and he was invited to Toronto to see what two years of reform had accomplished.

White came, saw and supported all the changes that had been made. But while he appreciated the fact that Boeing had invested a small fortune in de Havilland to make it a better facility, the union itself claimed credit for the improvements.

"They said they had forced Boeing to clean the place up and make all the health and safety reforms," Kingsmore noted, "but this didn't bother us. It was just posturing and we said fine—our assignment was to get the airplanes built and never mind who received the credit."

Under the new leadership, de Havilland met its revised goal of 63 airplanes pushed out of the revamped plant by the end of 1986. "That sixty-third Dash-8," Kingsmore recalled, "was finished at midnight on December thirty-first—it was one hell of a struggle."

Subsequently, a more realistic production rate was established: one Dash-8 completed every four days for an average of five a month, taking into consideration non-working weekends and holidays. A new contract negotiated with the CAW in 1990 was the first agreement in 22 years that hadn't been preceded by a strike.

In 1990, after four consecutive unprofitable years, Boeing began negotiating for de Havilland's sale—strongly opposed, incidentally, by the CAW, which asked Boeing to stay. By the end of 1991, Boeing's last full year of ownership, the de Havilland division had delivered 331 airplanes, and was working on a backlog of 80 aircraft. Early in 1992, Boeing completed the sale to Montreal-based Bombardier, a worldwide transportation conglomerate, and the province of Ontario.

For such a huge company wielding enormous influence and financial muscle, Boeing possessed at times an unusual willingness to "give"—

as it demonstrated when it bent its giant corporate knee before an elderly lady named Frances Shields.

Mrs. Shields owned a little frame house located only 1,500 feet from the corporate headquarters building. She inherited the property, bought originally by her grandparents at the turn of the century, and had been living there for more than three decades. In the mid-eighties, Boeing purchased land in the area to provide additional employee parking space. A number of commercial establishments gladly sold their land to Boeing, but Mrs. Shields didn't want to—she had lived in that tiny house when she was a little girl, and came back to it years later.

Andy Gay, vice president of facilities, entered into some friendly negotiations with Mrs. Shields, but she wouldn't budge. She also pointed out very politely to Gay that she owned a few Boeing shares and did he really want to dislodge a stockholder?

"I've settled down here, I have a lot of memories associated with this place, and I don't want to move," she said firmly.

So the land that Boeing acquired to relieve parking congestion ended up fencing the Shields home on three sides; the company declined to inflict further pressure or—as so many large corporations might have done—institute legal proceedings aimed at condemnation of a property zoned for commercial use. No one, from T Wilson on down, had the heart to even try to dislodge her—Frances Shields was a very special stockholder.

The Shields home is an oasis with trees, bushes and flowers nestled incongruously in the middle of a parking lot. The house actually was closer to the former 2-01 Building than the regular Boeing parking facility, so Mrs. Shields provided about 35 parking stalls, which she rented out on a monthly basis.

And that's the story of the love affair between the world's largest aerospace company and a tiny, gray-haired lady stockholder named Frances Shields—proving, it seems, that love means you don't have to throw your weight around. But it's also a story in uncomfortable contrast to one that began unfolding in the Auburn fabrication plant in the summer of 1987.

Boeing during the eighties became increasingly involved in the use of composite materials for aircraft structures. The advantages were obvious: composites saved weight without sacrificing strength, and they were more corrosion- and fatigue-resistant than aluminum. What wasn't so obvious were the potential health hazards for workers dealing with these exotic materials.

The composite materials being used at Auburn consisted of fiberglass, graphite, and other synthetic fibers, impregnated with epoxy or phenol-formaldehyde resin to form rigid aircraft components. In the summer of 1987, several workers began complaining of nausea, headaches, shortness of breath, coughing, chest pains and skin rashes. The number of Auburn employees reporting such symptoms multiplied until there were more than 100 such cases by mid-1988.

A local allergist who had examined several workers diagnosed the problem as formaldehyde poisoning. Boeing asked the National Institute for Occupational Safety and Health to test the air quality at the fabrication plant, and when the Institute found exposure to chemical effects well below the standards it had set for a safe working environment, the company tended to discount the sickness reports.

But the complaints continued, and several affected employees went to the IAM for help. They were sent to the same allergist who had first made the diagnosis of formaldehyde poisoning. This time he not only confirmed his initial diagnosis, but told his patients that formaldehyde poisoning could cause permanent organic brain damage. He even coined a name for what he informed the media was a new disease: "Aerospace Syndrome."

The media naturally ran with this revelation. Inevitably the allergist's announcement had a corresponding effect on the Auburn work force; now employees were reporting not only previous symptoms but indications of mental problems, such as loss of memory. The panic was on, spreading to the Developmental Center where Boeing was doing subcontracting work on the all-composite B-2 Stealth bomber.

Boeing's chief medical officer, Dr. Manuel "Manny" Cooper, had never heard of formaldehyde exposure causing a brain disorder, permanent or temporary, and neither had any of the other medical authorities he consulted. A cardiologist himself, he had affected workers examined by independent specialists. They did find some patients with legitimate symptoms, but others either with previous histories of respiratory illness, or victimized by psychosomatic panic—and the latter could bring on visible symptoms.

By now the two camps had polarized—the IAM insisted there was something seriously wrong at Auburn, and management was at least halfway convinced it was dealing with a case of mass hysteria. Fortunately for both sides, each had a man of reason and objectivity to deal with the situation: Deane Cruze, senior vice president of operations, and Tom Baker, president of the IAM District Lodge.

Cruze took immediate action. The majority of affected workers were women handling fabrics and other materials used in aircraft interiors; these were made of a new vinyl formaldehyde compound developed by Boeing's engineers to meet FAA's new fire-resistant requirements. Cruze ordered the use of this formaldehyde-based compound discontinued, and a different fire-resistant material substituted. The case histories of the Auburn "epidemic" were turned over to a panel of six distinguished medical experts in occupational health, psychiatry and allergy illnesses. Baker agreed to work with Larry McKean, who had been named Boeing's new vice president of labor relations in 1987 when Morrison retired.

Both agreed on the necessity of calming everyone down before the situation developed into a more serious labor-management dispute than it already had become. And Cruze sent a special committee on a fact-finding mission to leading U.S. companies experienced in dealing with worker exposure to chemical poisoning, an itinerary that included the superb laboratory facilities at Massachusetts Institute of Technology.

The group consisted of Jim Morrison, called out of retirement for the assignment; Don Smith, Boeing's director of health, safety and environmental affairs; and Dr. Cooper. Baker himself accompanied the committee on part of the tour, highlighted by visits to Mobil and Du Pont, which had made impressive strides in industrial safety.

"We were told that what happened at Auburn was low-level toxic poisoning," Morrison said, "and when that happens immediate action is required—protective clothing and more discipline in training people to handle toxic materials. We found out we needed to educate first-line supervisors on how to deal with the problem. Boeing had a long tradition of providing a clean working environment with spotless floors and bright, cheerful lighting, but we had our eyes opened on the tour and from subsequent inquiries at Boeing itself—the company could do even more."

The committee also was impressed with the advice they received at virtually every facility visited: achieving industrial safety is no overnight job, but rather a long-term commitment that mostly requires lengthy training and worker indoctrination.

"Don't be impatient," a General Motors official cautioned. "If you see things looking better in another four years, count your blessings."

Actually, Boeing achieved significant improvements with relative swiftness; the Auburn incidents diminished almost immediately after the use of a particular formaldehyde compound in vulnerable areas was banned. The medical panel Boeing had commissioned to study the poisoning incidents came back with a report confirming what Dr. Cooper had thought: there was no such new disease as "Aerospace Syndrome," and exposure to formaldehyde didn't cause brain damage. The panel also confirmed that quite a few people had really become ill, but that there was a fairly high percentage of "psychosocial factors" involved in the reported symptoms—in other words, some people were affected more by all the publicity and scare stories than by actual toxic poisoning.

Morrison and Larry McKean alike praised Baker and his local IAM union for approaching the Auburn situation with responsibility and impartiality.

"When we began working on the formaldehyde fiasco," Morrison said, "Baker was completely supportive. This was something in which both Boeing and the IAM could do the right thing and not be adversarial, something on which we could get together."

McKean believed the company learned from the experience:

"I feel that having unions involved in an industry of this size and complexity is an important element in keeping us on our toes. When I look back over the last two or three years, I can cite several instances where if it hadn't been for the IAM, Boeing would have gone its own merry way and management wouldn't have done anything about certain problems. The formaldehyde business was a case in point. If the union hadn't pushed us to do something about it, we'd still be working with the stuff.

"It's a system of checks and balances, almost like having an auditor come into a bank. You don't like it, but that auditor helps keep you honest. There has to be some representation of the employees because no matter how much we in management want to think we're representing them, we don't think the way they do, and we don't understand a lot of the issues that they consider important. And sometimes we don't get down in the bowels of this organization and find out what the real issues are. Nor do we listen a lot of the time. Just as we didn't listen to the overtime issue at Everett."

. . . the overtime issue at Everett.

More than anything else, it provided the emotional impetus for a 48-day IAM strike that reduced aircraft production to a walk at a time when Boeing was trying to cope with a backlog of airplane orders fast approaching the $90 billion mark.

It had been 12 years since the last IAM walkout, and at first there was a feeling on both sides that a strike could be averted—nobody in the local union leadership or in management wanted one.

Boeing has 34 labor contracts, all on a three-year cycle, but the one with the IAM is vital—the union in 1989 had 57,000 members in the Seattle, Portland (Oregon), and Wichita areas, and most of them built airplanes. When negotiations began early that year, the machinists were asking for a hefty wage increase and elimination of mandatory overtime at Everett. The wage demands were expected, and a compromise might have been reached without a strike. But overtime was an emotional issue, and emotions can cause more strikes than money issues.

Yet this was an emotional issue for Boeing, too. The negotiations were played against the backdrop of the troubled 747-400 program. Because of production problems and some technical headaches with the new state-of-the-art jet, Boeing had missed promised delivery dates for the first time in two decades, and it had some very unhappy customers. Japan Air Lines and British Airways had complained about quality defects in their new $125 million planes; Lufthansa and KLM weren't getting their 400s on time, and added to Boeing's difficulties were several instances of miswiring in brand-new aircraft.

Assembly line workers at Everett weren't any happier than the customers; the company was requiring excessive hours of individual overtime per quarter to catch up with the backlog and meet delivery schedules. Overtime wasn't the only major issue on the bargaining table, however; almost as explosive was the IAM's demand for a double-digit wage increase, and doing away with the annual lump sum payments that had been the pattern since 1983. In addition to such payments, the existing IAM contract allowed for COLA (Cost of Living Adjustment) increases; the union insisted on improvements in these, too.

While Larry McKean hoped the strike could be avoided, he had no illusions—there were a lot of odds against it.

"We went into the 1989 negotiations with images of Frank [Shrontz] shaking hands with a customer who had just bought another billion dollars' worth of airplanes," McKean said, "and at least half of the hourly workers had never gone through contract negotiations—they hadn't been with Boeing three years. They saw all the hype in the newspapers about the huge backlog, and on top of this, overtime was the big emotional issue to be addressed. It was a very unfavorable climate in which to head off a strike."

McKean brought IAM international officials to Seattle for a "look at the books" briefing. He explained why the huge commercial airplane backlog was misleading because so many of the company's other divisions were either in the red or only marginally profitable; on $17 billion in total sales during 1988, Boeing's profit was a relatively modest $614 million. He emphasized some of the non-monetary advantages of working for Boeing, such as upgraded facilities, the company's excellent health and pension plans, and a long-term employment base. He pointed out the enormous spending requirements of research and development, because a high-tech company lives or dies on the quality of its research efforts. He showed how liquid assets evaporate quickly when a new airplane is introduced, and in 1989 Boeing was marketing not one but three: the 747-400, 737-400, and 737-500—the latter a derivative only 10 inches longer than the original 200 model, with better range and 25 percent less fuel burn.

The entire corporate effort, McKean told the IAM delegation, was geared toward long-range stable employment. He concluded with a description of what Boeing was planning for its next commercial transport project and what its impact would be on employees' future, along with the importance of pricing the airplane competitively.

"They couldn't have cared less," McKean remarked later. "All they talked about was a double-digit general wage increase."

Justin Ostrow, vice president of the IAM's western region, was a hardliner whose influence on the union's negotiating team was exceptionally strong; while he had no vote, he had plenty of clout. Ultimately, Boeing's offer included 10 percent in general wage increases spread over the three-year life of the contract, plus a 10.5 percent hike in lump sum payments, a reduction in mandatory overtime, but no improved COLA formula.

The union, whose dues scale was hinged to the average hourly rate, held out for a higher general increase. At one minute after midnight October 4, 1989, Boeing's machinists struck. When they went back to work 48 days later, it was generally for the same pre-strike wage the company had offered originally, but with significant modifications to the overtime limits. Mandatory overtime was reduced from 200 hours to 144 hours.

What was equally and perhaps even more important were agreements reached on two significant non-economic issues. Boeing promised to establish a jointly administered "Quality Through Training" program, funded by the company, which accomplished two purposes: to provide training for employees whose jobs might be endangered by technological innovations, and training to improve skills or obtain new skills. The other called for a joint IAM/Boeing Health and Safety Institute—a byproduct of the Auburn experience.

Both sides lost heavily from the long strike, Boeing in terms of delayed delivery schedules involving millions of dollars in interrupted cash flow. The real tragedy was the strike's duration, amid evidence that the workers themselves were ready to go back long before the union and company finally settled. During the strike, McKean set up a hotline to answer employee questions. Quite a few involved the cost of health insurance, which came as a surprise to many. "You mean Boeing pays for that?" one worker asked. "I thought the union did."

"For the first three weeks we didn't hear much from the work force," McKean recalled. "Then we began getting calls demanding to know what was going on."

Pressure from Lodge 70 in Wichita and Lodge 751 in Seattle, combined with the initiative of federal mediator Doug Hammond, sent the negotiators back to the bargaining table to reach an eventual agreement.

Despite the bitterness of the 1989 IAM strike, Boeing actually had less of an adversarial relationship with its unions than most aerospace companies, one of which had a backlog of about 5,000 grievances in the spring of 1990 and was averaging 300 arbitration cases a year.

"If we have four arbitrations a year at Boeing, it's a lot," McKean said. "I don't believe you can get a job done in an adversarial situation. You have to sit down and talk out a grievance. Somebody's wrong and you have to face up to that."

The strike, in fact, had a cathartic effect on company and union alike, a mutual realization of past mistakes by both sides that had an adverse impact on what should have been common goals. Both had to change their attitudes, and perhaps management had to change more drastically than the union. The new Boeing worker required a different kind of motivation to win loyalty toward the company. Employees didn't take kindly to what was considered petty tyranny on the part of management. They sought more respect, more assurance that performance meant something in career opportunities. They wanted better training to open up these opportunities and no matter what the workers' jobs, they needed to feel they carried dignity and importance.

The strike was a crossroads for Frank Shrontz, a chance to stamp his own image on Boeing and its future paths. He recognized the partial roots of that 48-day shutdown long before it occurred. Boeing had been built by *people*, the men and women who breathed a human quality into an inanimate corporation and created an American industrial institution. Too many companies forget they are made up of individuals; Boeing didn't forget it, but under the pressures of breakneck technological challenges and intense competition, the human element gradually had been subordinated—given a lower priority than in the past, and by a management actually far more people-oriented than most American corporations. Bill Allen was a people person and T even more so, but Shrontz was the one who didn't need a strike to convince him of the need for fresh priorities.

"If you look back on the history of that strike," he said later, "you realize it never should have happened. Nobody gained, and nobody was destined to gain. I certainly blame the duration on the fact that there were often two conflicting objectives—that of the IAM international and that of the local. I wish the international didn't have as much clout in negotiations, because the local issues could have been resolved much more quickly if we didn't have to deal with the tug of war within the union's own ranks."

The entire company mourned the death of Wes Maulden from a heart attack May 16, 1989, and it was impossible to forget this pudgy man with an impish smile and the idiosyncrasies that seem to go with genius.

Maulden died as he had lived through most of his Boeing career; he was alone when the fatal coronary struck. He had plenty of hobbies to occupy his retirement years—a wood shop that would have done justice to a master carpenter, the clocks he loved to build or repair, the gold jewelry he crafted. He made his own wine and built at least one violin.

Doug Beighle inherited Maulden's office; he didn't realize it had a window or how large it was until he opened the blinds and let in some light. To Beighle, Wes had been a kind of father confessor, as he was to a lot of people—the ultimate purveyor of advice and counsel.

During Stamper's presidency, Maulden was the conduit through which Mal effected many of his health and environmental programs.

T was more likely to accept what Maulden supported or recommended than if it had come straight from Stamper; the fact that Wes enjoyed the trust of both these conflicting personalities helped them co-exist.

Maulden refused any consulting deal when he retired, and Beighle tried to change his mind.

"Wes, I've got to have such an agreement because I want to keep your security clearances intact and I can't do it unless you're a consultant. Second, you have to be indemnified against anything you do as a consultant."

"I don't need the money," Maulden grumbled.

"We'll draw up an agreement that pays you a dollar a year," Beighle offered, and Maulden accepted. A few weeks later, he phoned.

"Doug, where's my dollar?"

"I'll send you four quarters," Beighle promised.

"I don't want four quarters. I want a check from the Boeing Company for one dollar."

"Wes, it costs us about twenty dollars to draw up a check. Look, I'll send you the buck out of my own pocket and we'll call it even."

"That won't do. The check has to be from Boeing."

He received not only a check but a phony IRS form that reminded Maulden he would have to pay income and social security taxes on the dollar. For weeks, Maulden thought the form was for real.

Wesley M. Maulden had been a key part of the team that T built, a superb team that had overcome adversity capable of destroying many companies. An era seemed to die with him, but a new one already was taking shape.

TWENTY-FOUR

A NEW BOEING . . . AND A NEW AIRPLANE

"IF YOU LOOK BACK ON BOEING'S HISTORY AND THE SIX chief executives it has had, you'll find that in each case the right man was chosen at the right time."

This observation was made by a veteran officer who witnessed more than half that history over four decades, served under three of the company's CEO's, and saw it from a vantage point ranging from the shops to senior executive.

It is the same conclusion an impartial historian can draw, one that starts with William Boeing, the company's founder. Then there was Phil Johnson, followed by Claire Egtvedt, Boeing's first real aeronautical engineers at a time when flying an airplane was more of a stunt than a means of transportation. Johnson returned to guide Boeing through the war years. Next came Bill Allen, who took Boeing into the jet age and launched its climb to the top of the aerospace industry . . . T Wilson, who solidified that position while saving the company from bankruptcy . . . and Frank Shrontz—inheritor of his predecessors' legends and legacies. Just at a time when both legend and legacy seemed frayed, he recognized that improving the ways management motivates and communicates with the work force, to achieve superior productivity, had become Boeing's top priority.

Everett and the 747-400 program were examples of a problem that had many facets: a too rapidly expanded work force, inexperienced, unmotivated, and in some cases directed by supervisors and managers who themselves were not trained to manage. This applied to the engineering corps, too; Boeing discovered that being a good engineer does not necessarily make one a good boss. It also learned that tradition, however noble and inspiring, is an inadequate means of coping with the challenges of a subtly changing society.

It would be hard to find any American company that has subjected itself to the kind of introspection and soul-searching Boeing's top management has gone through during the last half of the eighties; the 1989–90 strike merely served to re-emphasize the need for change. The process actually began *before* that walkout; the settlement itself, incorporating such measures as Quality Through Training and the joint Boeing–IAM health and safety institute, reflected a new management attitude that already had started to surface.

Significant was the 1987 hiring of an expert on industrial culture change, Gary Jusela, a move that only someone like Shrontz would have countenanced—an outsider invited to look at Boeing's management methods as they applied to the changing work culture.

Jusela had done this at Ford, where he operated under the somewhat ostentatious title of "internal organizational development consultant." The job nomenclature was a lot fancier than the quiet, young, personable man himself; Jusela graduated from the University of Michigan with a degree in psychology, then earned a master's degree and doctorate in organizational psychology at Yale. Ford hired him to advise on how to improve worker morale, break down barriers between groups, and move from an old-line authoritarian bureaucracy to a more participative system.

His father had been an electronics technician at Boeing during the sixties, so Gary expected to find the kind of informal, unstructured company he had always heard about, the kind of loose managerial environment that had made it so attractive to the veterans of years past. A former vice president once remarked, "Boeing has two organizational systems—the one on paper and the one used to run the company."

But that wasn't quite what Jusela encountered when he delved deeply into management's methods and means. The company may have seemed unstructured to men like Stamper and Bob Dryden, who came to Boeing from the rigid corporate structures of General Motors and IBM respectively, but not to someone with the fresh perspective of a new-generation specialist in industrial psychology.

"I found Boeing to be a company of paradoxes," Jusela said. "In some ways, it was the most loosely structured and informal system you'd ever want to see. But in other ways, it was very rigid, formalized, and bureaucratic. And I think both held true simultaneously.

"One of the things that surprised me was that despite the senior officers having been here a long time, and well-entrenched in their management ways, they showed an openness to looking for new ways, new patterns, and new opportunities. I didn't expect this, and it's another of those funny paradoxes. They weren't blaming any of Boeing's shortcomings on the work force, the union, or anyone else. They were asking what management processes did *they* create that weren't useful anymore.

"It wasn't uniform and still isn't. Not everyone was looking for ways to throw out old practices and adopt new ones. But there was enough dissatisfaction among the senior ranks about performance in some basic areas, especially in terms of profitability, that the majority was looking for new directions."

Specifically, one situation Jusela discovered at Boeing was the same thing that had existed at Ford: what he called "turfism"—the establishment of individual turfdoms within individual departments and divisions, a kind of invisible boundary over which no one from another department or division was supposed to step. At Boeing they were called "rice bowls," and they prevented effective interdepartmental cooperation—they were barriers that separated one organization from another.

The rice bowl attitude existed among various Seattle organizations, and Seattle itself had become one huge rice bowl in terms of geography, with facilities like Wichita, Philadelphia, Huntsville, New Orleans, etc., feeling left out. To Jusela, this was a classic example of Boeing not being as unstructured as both history and many individuals had assumed.

"It demonstrated the existence of a very formal system," Jusela said, "a formal boundary drawn between Seattle and the off-site divisions. One of the consequences is that we can have some fantastic innovation take place in, say, Wichita, and it might stay limited to Wichita. I've heard stories about innovations introduced at one division or another that were never transferred to the others because every rice bowl had the old 'not invented here' syndrome."

Wichita, in truth, has been innovative. When Bob Dryden came from Boeing Computer Services in 1987 to take over the Wichita division, Jack Potter was the facility's vice president of operations. Potter was an old-fashioned kind of boss, a man who had come up from the ranks himself and had learned his trade from tough supervisors like Bud Hurst and Chick Pitts. When he first arrived in Wichita he told his secretary he wanted to have a staff meeting for all supervisors at 7:30 the next morning.

"Mr. Potter, they don't come in until eight."

"Not anymore," he growled.

Yet while Potter was tough as a corncob, he knew from experience what it was like to work in the shops; he spoke the language of the assembly line and understood its people. He began the practice of meeting frequently with hourly workers, getting a small group together and listening to their gripes and suggestions.

"Okay, there aren't any supervisors around," he'd say, "so tell me what your problems are. I'm not gonna quote you and I won't use your name—just get whatever's bothering you off your chest."

Gradually, he let everyone know he was one of them. It took time to win their confidence; when he announced he was going to refurbish and redecorate the cafeteria, he got word back that nobody believed it. They started to believe when the cafeteria *was* remodeled.

Dryden and Potter formed an interesting and effective combination of the old and the new style of management—Potter rough and outspoken; Dryden just as decisive but in a quieter, smoother manner. Wichita was 10 years behind Seattle in providing decent working conditions, and together they did something about it, the new cafeteria being just the start.

Covered bus stops were built. Cooling trucks were brought in to provide air conditioning for the high-bay areas, where summer temperatures reached upward of 115 degrees. A plant-wide television system was installed for more effective employee communications. More space was allocated to relieve parking congestion, although Dryden got some flak on this reform. He had invited employees to write him whenever they had complaints. After he began reorganizing parking assignments, he got 150 letters of protest in one day.

"Why did you move my space?" was a typical reaction. "I've been parking there for twenty-five years."

The Wichita reforms reached into the ranks of management, an effort aimed at a problem that had been developing in both operations and engineering throughout Boeing during the company's rapid expansion to meet higher airplane production demands. As the work force swelled, so did the supervisory cadre; the trouble was that many people being promoted to managerial jobs hadn't been trained to manage, and this was as much a problem in engineering as it was on the assembly lines.

"One of the things engineers don't learn in college is how to communicate," Dryden noted. "They know how to use slide rules and play with computers, but they don't talk to anybody."

This was a low- and middle-management–level Achilles heel that had attracted Jusela's attention, too. Dryden, with a far smaller work force to deal with than Seattle, already had tried a communication technique called "skip level" interviewing—letting an employee be interviewed by his supervisor's boss, a session at which the worker could freely answer such questions as, "What's on your mind . . . what's happening in your department . . . what problems do you want to talk about . . . ?"

Dryden emphasized that skip level interviewing was not a case of having someone go behind a supervisor's back to voice petty grievances. "It's a kind of amnesty arrangement," Dryden explained. "Every manager is responsible for documenting these one-hour interviews and feeding them every four months up through the organization, letting us know what the trends are, what people are thinking and saying, so we can act on problems."

Potter noticed something from his own informal let-your-hair-down sessions. "They didn't have a lot of specific problems," Jack commented. "Minor stuff, mostly, like gripes about parking. But they did want to know what's going on in the company, what's Wichita's role in Boeing's future, and where did they fit in?"

Frank Shrontz, on visits to Boeing facilities around the country, began meeting with random groups of employees—hourly, engineering, office and middle management. The groups were small enough to keep them wieldy and informal, but large enough for him to get a feel for overall mood. After numerous meetings, he summed up the experience with cautious optimism:

"I found out we've got a lot of work to do if we're to convince the people on the shop floors and elsewhere that we're going to make this culture change happen. I don't think they question our credibility in that intent, but they feel we have to match words with actions to make it happen. And some of them are concerned that we may not stay the course long enough for it to happen. There's a feeling that we have to get a significant number of managers more in tune with what we're trying to do, more adaptable to taking employee suggestions, and better able to communicate.

"There were many complaints that some of our first-line supervisors didn't understand what it takes to be receptive to ideas flowing up from the bottom. There was some feeling that their supervision was too preoccupied with other things to give this kind of attention, and that some supervisors weren't people-oriented. I didn't get anyone saying outright that's why workers have to rely on their union for representation. But I think they might as well have said it—that when management leaves a leadership vacuum, the union obviously is going to step in and fill it."

No one from management was allowed to attend these meetings, but in Philadelphia JoAnne Carroll of the public relations staff was there to take notes so Shrontz could refer to them later. Her observations:

"The hourly workers who were invited to breakfast were picked at random, from drawn numbers. Some of them at first thought it was a joke—they didn't believe that the top boss himself was willing to sit down and listen to them.

"The workers didn't have solutions; they merely voiced their concerns. Worry over the morale situation in the shops. A general recognition that the company was really trying to improve relations and was willing to listen, but that progress was awfully slow. And the feeling still existed that the helicopter division wasn't really considered part of the Boeing family, that we're really not important to Boeing.

"Shrontz did a lot of listening and asked most of the questions. He asked everyone to put his concerns down in writing, sign his name, gave them his mail stop number, and promised to read all signed letters, and address each complaint."

The "left out" feeling impressed Shrontz as much as anything else, fortifying his determination to make every person and every department in the company, from a one-person office in Boston to the more than 100,000 in the Puget Sound area, feel that Boeing is one family, not an uncoordinated collection of individual rice bowls playing second fiddle to the big rice bowl in Seattle—namely the lack of organizational unity that Jusela found so harmful.

When Shrontz began these employee meetings, he and his senior officials already were aware of the need to change some of the old management attitudes and methods, not because they hadn't worked—Boeing's much-envied reputation certainly hadn't been built by poor management—but because the challenges were new and different. In 1972, Mal Stamper had inaugurated the practice of having the two dozen or so top executives gather at an off-site location every spring and fall, away from all distractions, to discuss the company's future directions.

These bi-annual meetings were really an early form of the intense self-examination process that Boeing launched as the decade of the eighties drew to a close. They became far more introspective when Gary Jusela and Bob Clos, vice president of planning, drastically changed the format.

"The old style of such meetings was organized around a kind of show-and-tell format," Jusela said. "People would sit around a huge U-shaped table and deliver a series of presentations, usually with viewfoils. One person would get up and talk on some topic, followed by a critique or a question-and-answer period. A few of the more voluble, extrovertish officers would dominate or monopolize the discussion."

With Shrontz's approval, Jusela and Clos scrapped the clichéd meeting formula for something entirely new, and introduced it at the bi-annual meeting held in Scottsdale, Arizona, May 1990. There were 28 executives present and by pre-arrangement they were distributed among four tables, seven to a table. Each table was a kind of microcosm of the whole company, occupied by officers from different divisions and/or departments—seven people sharing their views, and giving everyone a voice instead of having two or three officers dominate the show.

Before anyone arrived in Scottsdale, an article describing how the world's most successful companies plan their future strategies was distributed for reading. It cited Honda as the classic example of a company that in the 1960s was building small motor bikes without anyone realizing its long-term strategy: to become a giant in the internal combustion engine field, including the auto industry.

The article provided the theme for the Scottsdale meeting, and a kickoff report by Bruce Gissing was the pivot around which the agenda revolved. Gissing had just returned from a fact-finding trip to Japan, where he studied some of the most successful Japanese companies. He gave his fellow officers a sobering analysis of what he had seen and how impressed he had been with the Japanese quest for continuous improvement in their manufacturing process.

Having been given that report, each seven-officer group was given a difficult assignment. They were told to analyze Boeing's strengths and weaknesses. To look at their company not only through their own eyes, but through the eyes of competitors, as if they had been handed the job of trying to unseat Boeing from its position of aerospace dominance—how might this be achieved, what kind of products would be offered, what kind of markets might be invaded, and what Boeing should do to prevent this from happening.

The responses were detailed, and in many cases brutally frank; these were men willing to look at their company's shortcomings as well as its successes. Next, the meeting was broken down into different groups, each assigned topics directly relating to their individual areas of management responsibility.

What came out of that three-day strategy session was a series of specific action items the executives agreed needed to be worked on as a group if Boeing was to move forward as a total, unified company. But the emphasis was on a single priority that could be summed up in a single word: people.

People. How to train them better, supervisors and the work force alike. How to communicate with them, motivate them, make them feel they are important and not mere faceless payroll numbers. How to assure employees that the company is willing to listen to their ideas for doing their work better and more efficiently.

No executive, especially Frank Shrontz, believed all this could be accomplished quickly. And there were some who cautioned against too rapid change, because there are times when an enthusiastic reform pendulum swings too far. Shrontz himself once warned that in adjusting to the culture change, Boeing must make sure it doesn't "throw out the baby with the dirty bath water, because what we've done so far is not all bad."

It was a remark that made an impression on George Kau, one of Boeing's numerous "mustangs" who rose from a beginning mechanic to vice president of operations in the helicopter division.

"I'm aware of the cultural change being wrought at Boeing and the realization that what worked for us ten or twenty years ago isn't going to necessarily work today," he remarked. "But I don't want to see anyone forget the management cadre that was selected for one reason or another and progressed through the years. I see some degradation in the trust they need, some downplaying of their importance, some accusations of incompetence backed up only by opinion.

"The main thrust has been for the very high levels to listen to the very low levels, and that's the right thing to do. But I think we should listen to the middle level, too. I agree there have been some very bad promotions, but on the whole the fifteen thousand managers in this company are the cream of the crop from the standpoint of loyalty, dedication, intelligence and hard work. I'm talking about the first-, second-, and third-level supervisory guys who aren't executives. It's nice to be a vice president but you sure as hell better not forget how you got there."

Part of Boeing's supervisor problems, however, did not involve the veterans Kau was talking about—it often was the inexperienced, younger manager who was drawing complaints, the supervisor who had won promotion into management before he was ready to manage. This was a situation inadvertently caused by the mass layoffs during the 1969–71 crunch. Hundreds of younger people who had the potential to go into future supervisory positions left the company and never returned, thus creating a 10-year gap in what should have been an adequate supply of promotable personnel. Contributing to this situation was the huge employment jump during the last half of the 1980s, a period in which Boeing added 10,000 people to the payroll annually for five years. By the mid-eighties, when an inordinate number of veteran managers began reaching retirement age, Boeing lacked enough experienced people to replace them; the necessary promotions often went to those who, through no fault of their own, weren't ready to manage.

Upper management began taking corrective action in this area, too. In Wichita, for example, Dryden put 2,500 managers through a communications course. In Philadelphia, Kau started teaching a 20-hour course on Continuous Quality Improvement; his first class consisted of his own staff, and this group passed the lessons on down the line—in effect, he created a management teaching cadre. In Seattle, the number of managers going to "management school" grew to the point where Deane Cruze finally blew a soft whistle and cut down the scholastic hours for operations managers.

"You can't keep management in school all the time," he declared, "when they should be out there doing their work."

Veteran John DePolo, manager of the delivery and flight test center, exemplified what the new culture is all about. He took over the delivery center at Boeing Field at a time when Boeing had started getting complaints from several carriers about aircraft paint. In some cases, deliveries had been delayed because inspectors had spotted paint imperfections on new airplanes that had to be repainted. Some airlines, especially an unhappy United, reported they were having to repaint their jets every three years instead of the usual five because the paint wasn't holding up.

DePolo didn't rant and rave at his painting crews; he sat down and talked to them—more important, he listened to them. He found that the chief problem wasn't with their work, but with *where* they worked—over the years, the old paint hangar had become contaminated from overspraying. DePolo got the money to clean up the facility, acquired a better quality of paint, and to assure that the improvements would stay in place he instituted a policy of meeting with the line-crew hourly workers at least every six months.

At one meeting, a young painter spoke up after DePolo had finished discussing various paint shop matters.

"I heard you mention the word *quality* at least four times in your presentation," he observed.

"That's right, I did."

"Well, *you're* the reason I can't do a quality job."

"Me?"

"Yeah. It's the way you schedule the shifts. I work the second shift and when I come on, either the airplane isn't dry yet from being washed, or the paint isn't cured [air-dried]. I have to wait for everything to dry, which means then I have to rush my own work to finish on time. Now if you bring me in two hours later, I'd have time to do quality work."

"What about your tie-in with the first shift?"

"Mr. DePolo, we haven't talked to those guys for seven years."

DePolo stared at him. "What about your tie-in with your supervisor?"

The painter stared right back. "He works for you. You can bring him in any time you want."

DePolo checked food service and the guard gate on the practicality of having the second shift report two hours later. He put the new schedule into effect at both Boeing Field and Renton, and remarked later, "We improved the painting process so much that United came out and did a video on our procedures."

The painting incident was typical of the changing attitude among veteran managers like DePolo, and their willingness to accept new ideas and methods. And even if there had been serious opposition, it would have collided with the resolve of the man most committed to creation of the new Boeing: Shrontz.

There had been unhappiness among the younger engineers as well as the hourly workers. The engineers had their own union, the Seattle Professional Engineering Employees Association (SPEEA), with 15,000 members—many of them reflecting the same culture change so apparent on the assembly lines.

"Consciously or unconsciously," a senior executive said, "we sent them a message that they're not as important as they thought they were, or not as important as the factory workers." Contract negotiations began with SPEEA after the IAM strike in 1989, and Boeing hung tough—which may have been natural in the wake of the 48-day shutdown, but which still alienated a lot of engineers. The early negotiating atmosphere was sufficiently acrimonious to give them the idea that this engineering-oriented company was downplaying their importance.

For the engineers, too, were a new breed. Such senior engineering executives as Phil Condit and Bert Welliver recognized this, and were convinced that lack of communication was at the root of their morale problem. As Welliver put it:

"The company grew so fast during the eighties that the whole management lost its ability to communicate. The popular perception is that the younger engineers have a 'what's in it for me?' attitude instead of 'what can I do for Boeing?' There is some of that, but it's not the message I got from talking to them. I found fear very prevalent, a fear that Boeing's management might not be aggressive enough. They perceived us as resting on our laurels, of just trying to concentrate on derivatives and not developing a clear winner over the competition.

"They're really worried about their future. They saw what happened to Detroit, where the American automobile industry was king of the heap, and all of a sudden the Japanese took it away from us with frightening speed. I don't think anything bothers a young engineer more than to see examples of bad management, and that's not anything that came with the culture change. When I was a twenty-two-year-old at Curtiss-Wright and saw how obviously the company was misman-aged, I knew it was no place to spend a long-term career. When an engineer sees things that need fixing and aren't getting fixed, his confidence in his own future is shaken."

So executives like Condit and Welliver began to firm up the lines of communication within engineering. Welliver on one occasion talked to a group of about 60 young engineers in which he tried to demolish their impression that Boeing was resting fat, dumb, and happy on past achievements. He pointed out that in 1989 alone the company spent more money on research and development than the entire NASA aeronautical budget combined with the total Wright Field laboratory budget.

"So tell me again that we're lagging," Welliver added. "We've just built the world's largest indoor radar range, and that's because in order to be number one in that field we must have the best equipment."

That was communicating. Welliver received a number of letters thanking him for confiding in them. Condit, meanwhile, began ad-dressing another problem area: communicating at the supervisory level. He was only too conscious of those cases where engineers inexperienced in managing people had been moved into managerial positions. He started talking to management training classes, and to each beginning class he delivered this speech:

"We have this really neat system. When you get promoted, we call you in, congratulate you, and shake hands. But we fail to tell you that you just changed careers. All the stuff you've learned is no longer your job. An awful lot of our first-level supervisors have gone on just being engineers; they spend their time trying to do their engineering jobs, and they don't tell others how to do it. So when we tell them to communicate with the people under them, they don't have that skill."

Condit, who learned how to communicate from role models like Wells, Sutter, and Holtby, found himself in the position of being a role model to his own young engineers. He once remarked to a University of Southern California professor, "You know, I've got an undergraduate degree in mechanical engineering, a graduate degree in aeronautical engineering, a graduate degree in business administration, and now I find myself being a practicing psychologist because what I do ninety percent of the time is deal with people."

So Condit understood what happens in engineering when relatively new engineers become first-line supervisors. "If you're lucky, he survives," Condit commented. "If you're unlucky, you've lost a good engineer because you picked him and didn't get a good manager."

Awareness of this on the part of management may have meant more in the long run to the engineering corps than the more immediate resolutions of their contract dispute. The timing for action on the engineering morale problem couldn't have been more opportune. SPEEA and the company reached agreement on a new contract in January 1990; on October 15, Boeing ended months of rumors, speculation and guessing when it announced it was going ahead with the 777—the world's largest twin-engine airliner, and a dramatic answer to those who claimed Boeing was still parked smugly and complacently in its glorious past.

The Triple-Seven began life as the 767-X, perhaps to give competitors the impression that Boeing was planning to stretch the 767 further, but also because it really did start out as a 767 derivative.

Marketing strategy was the initial impetus: an airplane that would replace aging DC-10s and L-1011s, its size between those wide-bodies and the 747. Stretching the 767 again was first proposed in late 1986 as the fastest and least expensive way to go, and this plan went through several evolutionary stages for the next three years. It also was a period during which the company's involvement with the 747-400 program was so great that some officials questioned whether Boeing could make a serious commitment to anything beyond a derivative.

Phil Condit, as executive vice president of the commercial airplane division, wasn't happy with any purely derivative designs; he wanted a brand-new airplane, and desire became conviction when McDonnell Douglas and Airbus began signing up customers for their own high-tech, long-range transports aimed at the inviting market niche: an aircraft not quite as large as the 747, but bigger than the 767-300, DC-10 or L-1011.

McDonnell Douglas was far ahead of the pack with its 323-passenger MD-11, actually a completely modernized DC-10 with new fuel-efficient engines. Boeing's old competitor was holding out a juicy plum to the airlines—first deliveries starting in 1990.

Slightly behind the MD-11 was Airbus, offering two new designs: the four-engine A-340, a 300-passenger airplane with a promised 1992 delivery date, and the A-330, a big twin carrying 35 more passengers than the A-340 but with less range, and deliveries starting a year later.

American and Delta already had ordered the MD-11 when Boeing, three days before Christmas 1988, finally decided to offer customers a far cry from a mere 767 derivative. The 767-X would be an all-new airplane that, if successfully launched, would become the 777. It would have the awesome task of catching up to the competition's lead, which in MCDD's case was a whopping five years. In fact, as of October 15, 1990—the day Boeing announced a firm 777 go-ahead with United as the launch customer—32 airlines already had ordered 173 MD-11s, and 25 carriers had signed up for 217 Airbus A-340s and A-330s. Boeing was trailing by almost 400 airplanes, with a design still on the drawing board.

Yet perhaps not quite so far behind as its competitors would have preferred. In a way, it was the 737 story all over again; Boeing launched that program at a time when the DC-9 and BAC-111 had more than 300 orders between them, and to play catch-up represented the same brand of engineering and marketing challenge the 777 was to face. In the case of the 737, Boeing combined a basically solid design with growth potential and the enticement of a wider cabin. Condit planned to repeat this strategy with the 777, but he took it a step further—he invited eight U.S. and foreign carriers to help Boeing design the airplane.

Dubbed the "Gang of Eight," the group included United, American, Delta, British Airways, Japan Air Lines, All-Nippon Airways, Qantas, and Cathay Pacific. For almost a year, technical representatives from these carriers met with Condit's engineering staff in a series of three-day "tell us what you want in this airplane" sessions. What they wanted, of course, varied among the eight customers, but there was consensus on one salient point: fuselage width should be greater than either the MD-11 or the two Airbus models. Boeing finally decided on an interior cross-section girth five inches wider than the MD-11 and about 25 inches wider than the A-330. And the old "dirty pool" mockup display was revived—a mockup with the 777's fuselage compared to those of the MD-11 and A-330, dramatically emphasizing what that five-to-25-inch width differential meant in terms of seating capacity and flexibility: at least 30 more seats than the MD-11 and 31 more than the A-330.

Better overhead bins for carry-on baggage was another demand voiced unanimously by the Gang of Eight. They fell in love with a Boeing-designed bin that pivoted down and then back, increasing cabin headroom by a considerable amount; the airline advisors insisted on this feature even though some Boeing engineers argued that the pivoting bins were harder to manufacture and also added weight.

An optional feature was something American proposed: that the 777's wingtips fold up, so the plane could utilize the same airport gates as American's DC-10s and 767s. The 777 would have a 199-foot wingspan, only 12 feet shorter than the 747-400's, and 44 feet greater than the DC-10's; to meet American's parking space criteria, Boeing had to design a means of folding 22 feet of each wing, leaving a parked 777 with roughly the same wingspan as the DC-10, L-1011 and 767.

In both scope and intent, the Gang of Eight's input into the 777's design was unprecedented. Phil Condit's favorite fantasy, as he expressed it, was "to have a customer come in and find we already had thought of everything—but I just don't expect that will ever happen." In the Gang of Eight, however, he had the next best thing: a representative cross-section of the world's finest carriers telling an aircraft manufacturer what *they* considered essential in the design of a new commercial transport, and doing this long before a single production blueprint had been drawn, or any final design decision made. Boeing, like all manufacturers, had welcomed airline input before, but never to this extent.

What the Gang really contributed through its various requests and suggestions was reinforcement of Condit's belief that no 767 derivative was the answer; the preference for a wider interior alone made a derivative impossible. British Airways, in fact, had pointed out that a stretched 767-300 parked at a gate would protrude out too far. And once the general specifications and configurations were laid out, Alan Mulally, the 777's new vice president of engineering, made a few critical decisions of his own.

First, he abandoned the old practice of having a single chief project engineer, as Steiner had been with the 727 and Sutter with the 747. Instead, Mulally assigned several chief project engineers to the 777, each with a specific area of responsibility, and each with access to the input from their airline counterparts; this kept lines of communication open on a much broader front.

Ronald Ostrowski was named chief project engineer for overall configuration development and design while Walt Gillette—who shared Mal Stamper's mountain-climbing hobby—became chief project engineer for performance. John Roundhill's primary task in the early stages was handling liaison with airline customers. His nine-year-old son Daniel, impressed with his father's unending preoccupation with the Triple-Seven, drew his own perception of what the plane would look like; it was transferred to a slide and became part of the 777's sales presentation, drawing appreciative chuckles every time it was shown—a little boy's version of his father's dream, effectively humanizing the entire process.

The 777 team worked in tandem with Bert Welliver, senior vice president of engineering and technology, who embarked on something of a personal crusade with this airplane; he had become almost obsessed with the fact that a company grossing billions was counting its profits in mere millions. Both he and Condit agreed that the 777 had to be the most profitable airplane Boeing had ever built simply by reducing the cost of building it. They knew Airbus and McDonnell Douglas had a price advantage; Airbus could sell an airplane for less because its development costs were government subsidized, and McDonnell Douglas was pricing aggressively to stay alive in the commercial transport business. The traditional Boeing strategy was to offer customers a product whose superiority justified a higher price, but Condit and Welliver were willing to try an additional strategy.

In 1988, Welliver appeared before Shrontz and the rest of Boeing's senior management to reveal the results of something he had been studying for several months. He had zeroed in on the company's financial performance during the previous year, a period in which Boeing had grossed $15.5 billion and netted $480 million. Welliver said at least $2.5 billion had been spent on non-value added costs. That should have been $2.5 billion in additional profits.

"Non-value added costs" include what a manufacturer must spend when engineers make design changes, expensive revisions that lead to further cost-incurring changes in a production process already geared to what engineering initially had turned over to manufacturing. Non-value added costs had plagued the original 737 and 747 programs; the sermon Welliver began preaching, with Condit right behind him singing the chorus, was that Boeing couldn't afford this kind of luxury with its next airplane—especially one still in the starting gate while Airbus was rounding the first turn, and McDonnell Douglas was heading into the backstretch.

So the 767-X became, in effect, a huge experiment—an entirely new method of designing, developing and building a new commercial transport, and in another sense one more element of the culture change under Shrontz's direction. The Gang of Eight's participation was just the first phase; what lay ahead was an even more radical departure from the conventional. When one of Welliver's old bosses expressed skepticism, Bert's reply echoed his impassioned belief that it was going to work because it *had* to work.

"If we can pull off what we're trying to do with this new airplane," he told the retired veteran, "I could put the damned wings on upside down and still make money!"

The basic goal was simple: turn over to manufacturing a 777 design as near perfect as possible, to drastically reduce non-value added costs. And the way the 777 team planned to achieve this was to design an airplane, for the first time in aviation history, entirely by computer. In Welliver's words:

"We're digitizing the entire airplane, using three-dimensional, solid models for the parts instead of the usual three-view drawings. Then we have computerized pre-assemblies; before we give the operations people a single drawing, we put the whole airplane together on computers and make sure everything fits. And if it doesn't fit, it's redesigned until it does. We look at all the pre-assemblies before we ever build parts, so we can see where simpler is better, making it less complex, which, in turn, means we're taking costs out of the manufacturing process whether the parts are being made by a Boeing facility or a supplier.

"The 767 was a well-designed airplane, but the 777 will be even better, with at least ten percent fewer design changes—and that alone represents a ten percent reduction in non-value added costs. We're doing it right the first time, and that's how we're getting manufacturing into the design process instead of tossing the design over the wall and telling operations to build it. Operations can say, 'Yes, we can build this, we know how to manufacture it and how much it's going to cost.' "

Computerizing the design process was extended even to the functional mockups. The conventional method is to build a mockup and then install all the wiring, tubing, ducts, and so forth—an expensive, laborious, and sometimes hit-and-miss way to determine where everything is supposed to go, and whether it fits. Not with the 777, whose functional mockups are all computerized.

"It's simply a new era," Welliver said. "In my view, it's as big an experiment as the original 747 was, because we're trying to redesign the Boeing Company even as we design this airplane. Some friends of mine have told me Boeing may be going too far and too fast, that the process is ten years ahead of where Boeing should be. My answer is that we can't sit around for ten years doing nothing. Yes, it's a gamble, but I think we can do it. If there's one thing current management can leave as a legacy to future management, it's to fix our system of designing and building airplanes and get rid of all non-value added costs."

Condit refused to make one break with the past—he utilized the advice and counsel of his old mentors, Sutter and Holtby, just as those two had once relied on Wells, Schairer, and Martin. Condit used them in different ways, because their engineering philosophies differed. "I needed Joe for his practical experience," Condit said. "He had a feeling for when you needed to make a decision—to realize your gut was telling you whether something was good or bad. Ken had a broader, more philosophical view. He was much less prone to drive you toward a decision, much more analytical than Sutter. Given his druthers, Holtby liked to study it one more time."

Both had the grace—and the courage—to acknowledge they were merely consultants whose once powerful authority no longer existed. After one 777 meeting, Sutter remarked to Condit, "You know, Phil, there comes a time when you gotta tell us old fogies to get the hell out of the way and make your own decisions."

Condit was determined not to repeat the mistakes that were made with the 747-400 and got that high-tech program into hot water. "Fundamentally, to use our own vernacular, we let the work statement get out of control," he admitted. "You always have to know how you're doing, how big your job is, but as the program went along it got bigger and bigger. There were more orders than anyone anticipated and the flight deck became more advanced.

"Originally, the 400 cockpit was intended to be much like the 767's. Then the airlines told us they wanted even more sophistication, like side-by-side displays instead of up-and-down, and then they'd tell us, 'While you're changing the displays, you could add this feature or that feature.' Any single modification would have been a piece of cake by itself, but integrating all of them wasn't that easy. The 400's central computer touches every major electronics box in the airplane, and when you start connecting all these different computers so they can talk to each other, the integration job becomes immense.

"With the 747-400, we just got behind the curve on how big the job was, and we didn't get it done on schedule. It was a classic case of the straw that broke the camel's back. Each change was a little straw at a time, not very big, but they added up. We had three different engines and eighteen different customers in the first year, and the mountain got too high for an inexperienced work force. In the 777 program, we're making sure what the work statement is, and if it changes we'll know exactly what it will take to accomplish it and in how much time."

Because the 767-X started down the derivative path, its cockpit at first was supposed to duplicate the 767's. But the flight deck modifications going into the 747-400, troublesome though they were, proved so successful that Condit was tempted to use the 400's even more sophisticated high-tech cockpit. Welliver suggested putting the choice up to the Gang of Eight's vote, but Condit was dubious.

"We'll wind up with a four-four split," he predicted.

The vote was 8–0 in favor of the 747-400 cockpit.

Some engineers talked about making the 777 a truly radical transport by building it entirely out of composites. In 1988, Boeing designed, built and flew the Condor, an all-composite robot airplane with a 200-foot wingspan, and guided by on-board computers. In 1989 it set a world's altitude record for piston engine airplanes by climbing to 67,000 feet. The Condor was strictly an experimental aircraft, of course, but while the 767-X project was under consideration there was some industry speculation that Boeing might really stun the competition with an all-composite airliner. In that sense, the announced plans for the 777's design came as somewhat of a disappointment to those who expected something radically different.

In fact, there was talk that Boeing hadn't gone far enough with the

777, that it was actually just a "me too" airplane differing from its competitors only in size, and maybe a few gimmicks; that Boeing was going to get its tail kicked saleswise by offering an airplane that not only wasn't really new but was being marketed too late. This criticism and gloomy prediction Condit had heard before.

"There's one thing about Boeing you have to remember," he said. "We haven't been first very often, but very frequently we've been best. The first jet transport was the British Comet. The first trijet was the Trident; only about a hundred were built, while we sold more than eighteen hundred 727s. The first twin jet was the Caravelle, the second was the BAC-111, the third was the DC-9, and we were fourth with the 737, which outsold them all. People worry about Boeing being late, but being late has given us a chance to really gauge what the customer wants, and make sure we're meeting it."

An amen to that came from Welliver. While he admitted that the 777 does not constitute a huge technological jump in operating performance over its competitors, he insisted it still will be a better airplane. "There comes a time in subsonic airplanes where the improvements get smaller and smaller," Welliver pointed out. "The technology on the 767 isn't really any better than what Airbus has, but the 767 is a better airplane because we know how to integrate all that technology to *make* it a better airplane. And that will be the 777's margin of superiority over the competition."

Welliver once had a long conversation with T Wilson about the changes underway in Boeing's fresh approach to new aircraft development. T nodded and said thoughtfully, "You know, five years ago we should have been where we are today."

Should have been perhaps, but not *could* have been—not until the final decade of the 20th century dawned was the need for a new Boeing really perceived. Up to that time prosperity had covered up mistakes; success had concealed certain weaknesses; tradition and past reputation had become security blankets against the realities of present and future.

That was why Continuous Quality Improvement, or CQI, was being implemented as a way of life, not as just another slogan; in fact, Bruce Gissing was given the job of concentrating on its implementation throughout the commercial company, so CQI would become a permanent part of the Boeing mystique instead of a temporary reform. That was why nearly 100 top Boeing executives went to Japan in 1990 and 1991 on fact-finding missions—to understand and learn from the Japanese their techniques in production and work force motivation.

That was why the 777 achieved a status far more significant than that of just another new commercial transport venture. It also symbolized the new Boeing and the company's willingness to adapt, change, and reform for the future. Even the initial launch customer involved a certain historical symbolism. In 1932, United had been the launch customer for the 247, with a $4 million order for 60 planes. Fifty-eight years later, the same airline signed for $11 billion worth of airplanes—34 777s plus options for an additional 34, and 30 747-400s. That $4 million 247 order wouldn't have paid for the flight control system on a single 777.

There was some symbolism in the 777's second launch customer, too. All-Nippon Airways ordered 15 of the new twin jets, a $2.6 billion commitment, and took options on another 10. ANA also bought the Airbus A-340, signing for five with options for another five; one possible key to the larger 777 contract was Boeing's agreement to have Japan's three leading aircraft manufacturers—Mitsubishi, Kawasaki, and Fuji Heavy Industries—assume 20 percent of the plane's structural production work.

Boeing was between the devil and the deep blue sea on this one, fearing negative congressional reaction to such a deal. But it did try to forestall union criticism of that 20 percent subcontracting agreement; five months after giving the 777 project its green light, Boeing announced it would build a $1.5 billion addition to the Everett plant, providing a brand-new production facility for the twin jet. The need for factory expansion was critical: Everett's 747-400 backlog alone totaled orders for almost 300 airplanes.

All airplane programs benefited from reorganization of the materiel procurement system, and its relations with Boeing's 3,500 suppliers around the world. A consolidated materiel division was created in 1984 and put into operation by Bruce Gissing as its first vice president, with Jim Blue succeeding him three years later. It brought supplier parts procurement under centralized control; the old procurement system had allowed each airplane division to handle its own procurement needs, and the result often was a chaos of delays that not even consolidation could solve immediately; it took several years before the new system became effective.

Under the old system Boeing had cases in which one division was cancelling a supplier contract for failure to deliver, while another division was handing the same supplier an award for superior performance.

Boeing organized supplier seminars, with the emphasis on improving quality. The message was simple: if they could promise a new commitment to delivering quality products on time, Boeing was willing to commit itself to longer-term contracts.

Suppliers were enlisted in the new Continuous Quality Improvement (CQI) program, but Boeing went beyond this approach. It brought 18 major suppliers directly into the 777 program long before it was officially launched, by having them consult with the project engineers and potential customers. The aim of this direct involvement with the design process was to reduce the unexpected changes and special requests that are headaches to Boeing and supplier alike.

The new relationship established with suppliers gave some of them a welcome chance to expand, for the long-term contractual policy provided long-term security. Weber Aircraft, which makes airplane seats and galleys, used such a contract to finance the hiring of 300 additional workers and a $7 million plant modernization program. Similar capacity expansion took place at Germany's Buderus Sell, which manufactures airplane galleys, and Japan's Jamco, which builds lavatories and galleys.

But not even a new Boeing could guarantee Utopia for all suppliers. Someone in Boeing's accounting department was approving a supplier's bill and in acknowledging the amount due, a decimal point was misplaced. The supplier had billed Boeing for $50,000 but was notified he would be getting a check for $5 million. The supplier, whom Diogenes would have embraced fervently, called the person in accounting who had signed the letter.

"I think you've made a mistake there," he said pleasantly. "We billed Boeing fifty thousand dollars and you've got it down as five million."

"That's impossible," he was told. "Our billing system is foolproof."

Twice more the supplier insisted the billing was wrong. Twice more accounting insisted there was no mistake. But the billing system finally caught the error, and the supplier received a check for $50,000. Whereupon he sued for the full $5 million.

He lost, but Boeing general counsel Ted Collins confessed a certain amount of sympathy for that particular supplier—and a certain amount of disdain for that foolproof billing system.

Collins had succeeded Doug Beighle as the company's top legal officer in 1986, when Beighle moved up to the post of senior vice president. This was one of several upper-echelon changes brought on by retirements of some senior executives, and as Shrontz formed his own management team. The new Boeing he envisioned was more streamlined than lean, the subtle difference between making a huge company more efficient rather than merely downsizing it.

Procurement consolidation was a streamlining move made just before his administration began. In January 1990, Shrontz took another major reorganization step—acting on Dan Pinick's recommendation, he combined the six separate divisions dealing with defense and space activities into a new Boeing Defense & Space Group. Pinick, who had been heading aerospace and electronics, became the overall commander of military airplanes, missiles, electronics, space projects, scientific research, and helicopters, and it was the military side that gave him his greatest concern.

Boeing had lost $95 million on its defense business in 1988. The following year, the company grossed nearly $4 billion on various military transportation products and related systems, and took a $559 million bath. In 1990, the new Defense & Space Group had revenues of almost $6 billion and wound up with a net loss of $418 million—a deficit attributed almost entirely to unprofitable military contracts. What had once been a Boeing strength had turned into a major weakness, yet Pinick—fully aware that some officers thought Boeing should get out of a profit-draining business and concentrate on building airliners—refused to get discouraged.

"We've had a long history of success in doing business with the government," he insisted, "and I see no reason why we can't return to that. If I thought for one minute that we couldn't, I'd say 'Let's get out of here.' We're not going to do that because we can't. We *have* screwed up. We grew too fast. We did over-commit. We spread our resources too thin. But we're trying to recover and I think we will. It took us several years to get into this mess and it'll take us several years to get out of it. Growth got in the way of performance. Growth became a solution rather than a goal."

The light helicopter and tactical fighter contracts awarded in the spring of 1991, after years of developmental effort, gave Boeing's defense business a double shot in the arm, even though those victories had to be shared with bidding partners. And Boeing's tradition of building the world's best bombers still lived in the B-2 Stealth; as Northrop's major subcontractor in that program, Boeing throughout the 1980s played an important role in the design and production of the Stealth's outboard and aft center sections, the fuel system, and the weapons delivery system. Its work on the B-2 in the "Black World" facilities at the Developmental Center was so secret that one Boeing official who needed security clearance had to wait eight months for it to come through—by which time the reason for clearance no longer applied.

As of January 1, 1992, some 42,000 people were directly involved in Boeing military projects worth $5 billion a year in revenue to the company. The military actually had as many engineers as the commercial airplane division. And Pinick looked just as hard at the defense and space group's broad customer base—Air Force, Navy, Army and NASA—as he did at the occasional stumbles.

Admittedly, the end of the Cold War combined with the federal budget crunch shrank those markets. Yet the Defense & Space Group ended 1991 with a small profit in the fourth quarter, a dramatic turnaround from the deficits of the previous three years, and an encouraging indication that the reorganization was paying off.

Mal Stamper, in an interview shortly before he retired, said much of Boeing's future lay in the nation's space program, a belief Pinick shared. "Space is a growth market," Pinick remarked, "and NASA's budget should rise. But when you come right down to it, space isn't a market. It's a place."

The most visible space project, of course, was the future NASA space station for which Boeing was designing the living, laboratory, and support modules. Less dramatic but eminently successful was the Boeing-built Inertial Upper Stage (IUS) booster rocket, with a spectacular record of successful performances for NASA, the Air Force and the European Space Agency—including the Ulysses mission, a probe to study the sun's poles. The IUS takes shuttle payloads into space beyond a shuttle's reach.

Boeing began working on a space station concept as far back as 1978, at a time when the Saturn project was just a memory of a proud achievement, and staffing at Huntsville was fast dwindling to a small cadre of engineers. As late as 1980, Huntsville's entire payroll numbered not more than a handful out of the 5,000 who had worked there during the Apollo missions. As Bob Hager, vice president and general manager of the Huntsville division, remembered: "We had a small office with a contract manager and an office manager—that's all that was left out of five thousand. The office reported to me in Seattle when I was vice president of engineering, and it was doing mostly work on a radio frequency simulation laboratory for the Army Missile Command."

But in 1984, Boeing entered the preliminary design competition for the space station's living and working quarters, winning out over Martin Marietta three years later as NASA's choice to design and construct the habitation modules. By 1990, Huntsville's aerospace division was up to 3,700 employees and Boeing was back in the space business—to stay, Bob Hager was convinced, although NASA's budget fluctuations caused more trouble than the technical aspects of the station.

"We haven't had any major crisis in the program except for funding," Hager said. "The budget was cut the first year in about half, then another third the next year. When you go through several years of cuts, you begin to either reduce the size of the station or slide the dates— you don't have much option."

Hager was another Boeing officer who believed the company had a great future in space, even though the market itself is unpredictable because the program funding is so erratic, with a timetable almost totally dependent on the funding. Yet he was convinced there will be a manned mission to Mars 15 to 20 years into the 21st century, and perhaps an inhabited scientific colony established on the moon sooner than that.

"If you look at where we are today in space," he philosophized, "we're like we were in the airplane business in 1930. We knew we could fly but we weren't quite sure where the aviation business was going. Were we going to carry mail? People? We couldn't even imagine an airplane like the 747 then, yet it was only forty years away. Sixty years from now we'll be in the year 2051, and where do you think the space program will be by then?

"And what role will Boeing play? Well, we're in the transportation business. We haul people in a closed habitat, and the space station is important because it's an extension of what we do so well. Only this time I'm not talking about people flying for five to fifteen hours. I'm talking about people living in space for something like fourteen years, in a moon colony, for example. When that happens, there will be roads built and we'll need transportation, like the lunar rovers we built years ago—we understand such things. We don't understand installing sewer lines or power plants; that's a role for other people. But providing a safe environment for people and their transportation are logical roles for Boeing."

According to Hager, a moon colony actually might be a mining colony. The moon, with no magnetic field or atmosphere, has been collecting helium for four billion years, and within its helium deposits is a material called Helium 3, or UM-3. Regular helium used in a thermal fusion process can create energy, but Helium 3 creates the same energy with 1/10,000ths of the radiation associated with nuclear fusion.

"If we brought back the Helium 3 that's trapped in the upper levels of the lunar soil," Hager predicted, "we could provide all the power the entire world is consuming at today's levels for the next two thousand years! Now that's a pretty good reason for going to the moon and there's another reason. Helium 3 is one of the best propulsion systems you can think of, because it has the highest energy potential of any system. If we're thinking about going to Mars, we're going to have that kind of propulsion."

Hager joined Boeing in 1955 as a specialist in nuclear weapons testing, with a civil engineering master's degree, and worked for T Wilson during the early phases of Minuteman. He eventually became the program's seventh manager before his assignment to the space program, where he seemed to have absorbed George Stoner's visions of things to come. When he lectured to grade school children on the space station as the first step toward moon colonization and beyond, he liked to show a picture of a little girl sitting at a computer. Under the picture was this caption:

"The first person to walk on Mars is alive on Earth today."

And, Hager would add, "I hope that little girl is from the United States."

Frank Shrontz looked to the future, too, with an avowed goal to make people and technology allies rather than adversaries.

He sat in his comfortable but decidedly unpretentious office one day and explained what that goal means to every Boeing employee:

"One of management's biggest challenges is to properly understand, motivate, and manage the people resources of the company. But it would be a mistake to interpret our history as not being people-oriented. The two predecessors I have known—Bill Allen and T Wilson—were people-oriented but in different ways. We did have, however, a very hierarchical kind of management structure that was somewhat aggravated by our being in the defense business.

"I'm trying to change the culture to the extent of getting the workers more involved in improving the process, rather than just simply doing their job. We have built up over the years an enviable record of handling large, complex systems in an effective way, and I think our systems management capability is one of Boeing's greatest strengths. But along with that growth have come some built-in bureaucratic practices that work, but are very expensive to operate. There are some substantial improvements to be made by going back and looking at those practices, in light of today's technology, and seeing if we can't simplify them.

"I'm convinced we aren't going to get there with just a top-down look. We have to get people involved, to participate, to take ownership of that improvement and have a broad enough view across the corporation to be able to zero in on where improvements can be made. I want middle management as well as senior management imbued with trying to get the workers at whatever level involved in the change.

"In that sense, I'm trying to change the culture, but not because I think this hasn't been a people-oriented company. Past management was dealing with different eras and change is a slow process—you just don't go from one approach to another overnight."

"Different eras," yes, but eras never forgotten or unappreciated. Boeing is a company with a rich, almost devout sense of historical significance that acknowledges the challenges of present and future without losing pride in the past.

Early in March 1991, Air New Zealand announced it was buying four 767-300ERs and its third 747-400, adding these five aircraft to its all-Boeing fleet. It was a contract signed 73 years after that carrier's government bought the first two airplanes Boeing ever built. History at Boeing has a way of coming full circle, just as it did May 19, 1990—the day Dash-80 came home.

She was a 36-year-old airplane that looked her age after 18 years at a sun-baked Arizona airfield. Dash-80's resurrection had begun three years before when Dave Knowlen, director of technical affairs under Bert Welliver, heard an engineer idly ask one day, "Whatever happened to the Dash-80?"

Knowlen knew where the plane was: Davis-Monthan Air Force Base in Tucson, where supposedly it would sit until the National Air and Space Museum opened its auxiliary museum near Dulles International Airport. But he also knew that project was on hold with no funding in sight, and he began sounding out various Boeing officials on the prospects of bringing the old plane home.

His chief ally was Del Hoffman, formerly of customer relations in the commercial airplane group, and their mutual resolve was stiffened when they saw a photograph of the Dash-80 that Tom Craig of commercial airplane marketing showed them. The 707 prototype was parked forlornly amid a cluster of retired B-52s, obviously decrepit and decaying.

"If that plane stays there much longer," Knowlen remarked to Hoffman, "it'll never leave Tucson."

He called the National Air and Space Museum, to whom Boeing had transferred the airplane's title, asking if the museum would be interested in returning it to Seattle for restoration. The answer was a flat no, but Knowlen refused to get discouraged.

He made the rounds of top Boeing officials and won their support. Then he accompanied an AOG team to Tucson to inspect the plane. "We found that if the airplane was left there for another three or four years, it would never fly again," he recounted. "There was enough corrosion and general airframe deterioration to make us realize it had to be restored relatively soon or not at all."

There were meetings with NASM officials in Washington where Knowlen pleaded his case and tried to resolve some haggling over where Dash-80 would go after restoration. NASM at first wanted to release the plane only for the few months it would take to restore it, and insisted it then would have to be flown to Dulles. Knowlen pointed out that the airplane couldn't be stored out of doors in Washington, D.C., and an eventual compromise was reached: Dash-80 would be loaned to the Seattle Museum of Flight.

The next step was actual restoration, for which Boeing had budgeted $325,000. Dash-80 was under the care of the Aerospace Maintenance and Regeneration Center (AMARC), the Air Force unit responsible for the thousands of mothballed aircraft parked at Davis-Monthan. Initially, the AOG team that began the rejuvenation job expected little or no help from AMARC; in fact, when they first arrived, the Boeing people were informed they'd have to move the airplane off Air Force property over to an adjacent field owned by a fixed base operator.

But it was never moved. Jerry Fugere, head of AMARC, started off with a grudging, "We'll wash the airplane for you but that's all." From there Fugere progressed to offering more and more help as he and his men began absorbing the AOG team's enthusiasm. Then it became full-scale participation—"You guys have a lot of things to do," Fugere would say, "so let us help you with some of the work on the hoses."

AMARC had done a good job of sealing up (mothballing) the airplane. The biggest problem was deterioration of every component made of rubber or plastic; the hot Arizona sun either had virtually destroyed them or made them so brittle that new parts were needed. Despite the sealing, water had leaked into hydraulic acuators and corroded them. The 20-man AOG team, headed by Gary Horton, ended up replacing all rubber tubing, tires and brakes. All control cables were removed, cleaned, and oiled before reassembly. The interior was in remarkably good shape and needed only cleaning. Installation of new igniters was the only major work needed on the engines; when they were started up for the first time in 18 years, they were noisy and smoked a little, but no extensive overhaul was necessary.

On May 7, 1990, Dash-80 flew from Tucson to Moses Lake for some additional work and inspection. Pilot Paul Bennett made the entire trip with the gear down; to rejuvenate all the gear hydraulics would have been too costly and lengthy a task, but except for a few oil leaks that had to be fixed, Dash-80 was ready to come home.

Early on the morning of May 19, a company plane flew Joe Sutter, Wally Buckley, Tex Johnston, and Bob Bateman to Moses Lake; these retirees would be N-70700's symbolic passengers from the past. None had seen the Dash-80 for years and the ravages of its long Arizona exile were only too apparent. The yellow paint on the top of the fuselage was flaked, and the old coppery brown lower paint was badly faded. The engine cowlings seemed to be carrying a few hundred pounds of rust, but this turned out to be more faded paint. Over the large cargo door on the forward left fuselage was a word that stood out like Braille: *Experimental.*

There was a patch on the rear fuselage where Boeing had once hung a 727 engine. No one could identify a small top hump left over from some previous test flight chore, and the general impression at first sight was that of an ancient relic that somehow had been transported to Moses Lake by a time machine. The time-warp feeling was enhanced by a couple of JAL 747 training flights making touch-and-go landings at the field, giants of the present dwarfing the old pioneer from the past.

Tex Johnston, wearing his inevitable snakeskin cowboy boots and 10-gallon hat, looked disappointed. "I thought they were gonna paint it," he remarked upon first seeing the Dash-80.

Joe Sutter sighed, "It looks like it's been running drugs for the last ten years."

And boarding Dash-80 really *was* like boarding a time machine. The interior was spruced up and its 60 seats spotless. "All we had to do was vacuum," flight test superintendent Darrell Smith reported. Actually, the cabin looked exactly as it did when the prototype was demonstrating jet flight to airline customers. A framed sign that had been placed on a forward bulkhead in 1957 was still there:

> This airplane is the Boeing 707 prototype, America's first jet transport, forerunner of the 707 Stratoliner and 707 Intercontinental that will enter scheduled airline service beginning in 1959 (sic). Boeing jet transports have been ordered by the following airlines: PAA, AAL, CAL, Braniff, Air France, Sabena, TWA, Lufthansa, Air India, Qantas, BOAC.

The sign, covering almost the entire bulkhead, listed the speed records Dash-80 had set, noted that the KC-135 tanker version already was "in quantity production," and reminded prospective airline customers that "a full scale simulated interior demonstrating the possibilities of Boeing 707 passenger cabins and employing the latest transport ideas has been constructed for airline inspection in New York City."

It was nostalgia time for the present-day passengers. Sutter remembered taking a demonstration flight with a doubtful, somewhat cynical delegation from Sabena. "We took off light from Boeing Field and climbed like a fighter, almost at a forty-five-degree angle," he recalled. "The Sabena chairman blurted, 'This is the future.' It reminded me of what Ed Wells used to tell us engineers: 'Life's too short to work on propellers.' "

The brief flight to Seattle was cold; Bennett flew at 12,000 feet doing about 250 knots—like the gear, the pressurization system was inactive and so was the cabin heater. The cabin was drafty and Sutter murmured, "She leaks a little."

There were only 10 windows in the main cabin, seven starboard and three portside—another reminder that Dash-80 was an experimental prototype, and a very tired old one at that. But when Bennett came over the Seattle area, he circled the city several times at a low altitude, banking so sharply at times that one got the feeling Dash-80 had been fueled from the Fountain of Youth. Sutter chuckled.

"Bennett will probably get off the airplane and deliver the classic test pilot report on every first flight," he said. "I can just hear him: 'Best airplane I ever flew. It exceeded all expectations and we'll sell a thousand of them.' Then he'll go into debriefing and tell the engineers, 'This damned thing flies like it has four battleship anchors hanging from each wing!' "

A crowd of some 500 welcomed Dash-80 when it landed at Boeing Field. She waddled her way to the Museum of Flight at the end of the field where a reviewing stand had been erected, and a recording was playing the theme music from *Star Trek*. T Wilson spoke for everyone.

"She may need a new coat of paint," he declared, "but she looks damned good to us!"

The media descended on Tex Johnston for interviews, and he was in his glory talking about the day he rolled the prototype. And while he reminisced, Dash-80 basked peacefully under the warm spring sun, home at last.

Another legend that had become a legacy.

EPILOGUE

SEVENTY-FIVE YEARS IS BUT A MERE HEARTBEAT IN HISTORY, not much more than an average person's lifespan.

In terms of a company's longevity, however, Boeing's 75 years deserve the label of a corporate Methuselah; most of the top American companies that were flourishing in 1916 no longer exist, or have gone into oblivion through absorption by other firms. And Boeing did more than survive and prosper—it became a symbol of American technological excellence, establishing standards by which others are judged, and turning the simple sentence "I work for Boeing" into a declaration of pride.

This has been the story of Boeing's first three-quarters of a century, a story written by the people who dreamed and labored through those 75 years. A German named Otto von Bismarck-Schoenhausen said it best:

> History is simply a piece of paper
> covered with print; the main thing is
> still to make history, not to write it.

INDEX